Labor Relations
Development, Structure, Process

Labor Relations
Development, Structure, Process

John A. Fossum
Industrial Relations Center
University of Minnesota

1989 Fourth Edition

Homewood, IL 60430
Boston, MA 02116

To all my parents

PETER, ALMEDA, HERB, and JANE

Executive editor: Gary L. Nelson
Project editor: Gladys True
Production manager: Bette Ittersagen
Compositor: Better Graphics, Inc.
Typeface: 10/12 Trump
Printer: R. R. Donnelley & Sons Company

LIBRARY OF CONGRESS
Library of Congress Cataloging-in-Publication Data
Fossum, John A.
    Labor relations : development, structure, process / John A.
  Fossum.—4th ed.
        p.   cm.
    Includes bibliographies and indexes.
    ISBN 0-256-05823-7
    1. Industrial relations—United States.   2. Collective bargaining-
  -United States.   3. Trade-unions—United States.   I. Title.
  HD8072.5.F67 1989
  331′.0973—dc19   88–25837
                                                             CIP

Printed in the United States of America

2 3 4 5 6 7 8 9 0 DO 5 4 3 2 1 0 9

PREFACE

The fourth edition of *Labor Relations: Development, Structure, Process* follows the publication of the first edition by one decade. During this decade, the practice of labor relations has changed radically. Membership in labor unions has declined markedly. Unions, for the first time since the 1930s, have agreed to major economic concessions. Pattern bargaining has eroded substantially. At the same time, public sector unions have gained members and held their own in economic settlements.

During the 1980s, labor unions and collective bargaining have become a topic of increasing research interest. Major efforts have yielded increasing amounts of information about the influence of unions on economic outcomes of employees and organizations. These are perhaps best represented in Richard Freeman and James Medoff's *What Do Unions Do?* Additional work has been done to explore the adaptation of organizations and unions to the changing economic environment of the 1980s, culminating in the publication of *The Transformation of American Industrial Relations* by Thomas Kochan, Harry Katz, and Robert McKersie. This edition, like the last, benefits substantially by the burgeoning research in labor relations.

Major changes in this edition include an examination of the role of political action committees of unions, additional evidence on the increasingly contentious area of union organizing, the effects of unions on the economic performance of organizations and employee outcomes, new models and evidence related to union-management cooperation, and models and evidence related to grievance processing and contract administration. Additionally, evolutionary changes and increased inclusion of evidence related to the effects of labor relations have been added.

I hope that you will see this book as presenting a balanced perspective—balanced from a labor or management viewpoint, and balanced from a behavioral, institutional, and economic perspective. In the development of this approach, I am indebted to many institutions and individuals—my graduate school professors at the University of Minnesota and Michigan State University, my colleagues over time at the University of Wyoming, University of Michigan, UCLA, and now in the Industrial Relations Center at the University of Minnesota.

Specific acknowledgments are also necessary to credit those who have assisted me with the preparation of this book. The thorough reviews and helpful comments of Hoyt Wheeler of the University of South Carolina and I. B. Helburn of the University of Texas significantly assisted the preparation of the first edition. The second edition was aided by suggestions and comments from Jim Chelius of Rutgers University, Sahab Dayal of Central Michigan University, and George Munchus of the University of Alabama at Birmingham. The third edition was aided by the reviews of George Bohlander of Arizona State University, Richard Miller of the University of Wisconsin, Edmond Seifreid of Lafayette College, and Bobby Vaught of Southwest Missouri State University. This edition has benefited from the reviews of Edward Reinier of the University of Southern Colorado and Jack E. Steen of Florida State University.

Reference materials are particularly important in preparing a text, and reference librarians are thus helpful in pointing out new information and locating it. I have been assisted by several in preparing this text. For the first two editions, JoAnn Sokkar, Mabel Webb, and Phyllis Hutchings of the Industrial Relations Reference Room at the University of Michigan provided this assistance. For editions three and four, Georgianna Herman and Mariann Nelson of the Industrial Relations Center Reference Room at the University of Minnesota have found obscure sources and provided quick turnaround. Library services are very important in preparing a text and also important for students in making the maximum use of the exercises in this book. It's likely that many graduates of the Master of Arts in Industrial Relations program at the University of Minnesota are indebted to Georgie Herman for information she found for them that enabled them to complete papers required by their degree programs. Research assistants are also an important resource that substantially facilitates text preparation. I was particularly fortunate to have two energetic, persevering, and analytic assistants who helped me locate material for this text; Kelli Watson, now with Pfizer; and Molly Casserly, who is completing her degree during the quarter in which this book is published. My thanks to all of these people who assisted me. Any errors or omissions in this text should not be attributed to them. I have occasionally ignored advice which was probably beneficial and may have overlooked information provided to me.

Finally, I owe a permanent debt to all of the parents of my family who provided me with the examples and support to undertake an academic career; to my wife, Alta, who has made the personal sacrifices of moving several times, has subordinated her interests during times when I was writing, and has offered the wisest counsel; and to my children, Andy and Jean, who had to explain to their friends that their father was not "terminally weird" for spending many consecutive weekends in front of a microcomputer display after being harassed for failing to meet deadlines. And yes, Jean, you can sneak a copy of this edition into the junior high library, just like you did with the last edition in the grade school library, but don't expect your classmates to move it to the top of the "most borrowed" list.

John A. Fossum

CONTENTS

CHAPTER 8   Wage and Benefit Issues in Bargaining   *176*

CHAPTER 9   Nonwage Issues in Bargaining   *204*

CHAPTER 10   Contract Negotiations   *229*

CHAPTER 1

Introduction

Most readers of this book are or have been employed, but most have probably not been union members, and most do not expect to be union members in the future. But readers have likely formed attitudes toward labor unions and collective bargaining. These opinions have been formed largely through information provided by the news media. Media attention is usually focused on unusual events. In labor relations, this usually means a major negotiation, strike, lockout, or an unlawful practice charge. The media shouldn't be faulted for this—excitement does draw viewers and sell newspapers, but it does not reflect day-to-day labor relations in the United States. Overt disagreement, reflected in strikes, lockouts, and unlawful practices, occurs relatively infrequently.

Labor relations and employment have undergone major changes during the 1980s.[1] The proportion of employees represented by unions has declined substantially; unionized employees in many industries have agreed to economic concessions; and employers have become more successful in resisting union-organizing campaigns. Many commentators marked the 1981 air traffic controllers' strike and their subsequent discharge as a major event in the recent decline in union power. However, future commentators may note the organization of the National Air Traffic Controllers Union and its certification in 1987 as the bargaining representative to negotiate with the Federal Aviation Agency as the beginning of a renewed vitality in the union movement.

---

[1] For a comprehensive examination, see Thomas A. Kochan, Harry C. Katz, and Robert B. McKersie, *The Transformation of American Industrial Relations* (New York: Basic Books, 1986).

PLAN OF THE BOOK

The title, *Labor Relations: Development, Structure, Process,* was not chosen haphazardly. The first part of the title indicates a focus on the employment relationship in unionized settings. The words following the colon establish the topical flow of the book.

Development

The present state of the labor movement and collective bargaining is the result of a variety of economic and social situations in which strategic choices were made by labor leaders and managers. In examining the *development* of the labor movement, the conditions related to the initial formation of unions must be understood. Public opinion influenced the response of public officials toward both the subsequent formation of unions and their operation.

Other areas of interest concern the reactions of employers to unions. Where did unionization begin? In what industrial sectors have unions been most prevalent? How have the parties adapted to each other over the long run? What are the present stances of employers toward unions, and where are the greatest changes taking place?

Chapters 2, 3, and 4 address development issues, tracing the historical evolution and present public policy environment in which American labor operates. Although union activity has occurred throughout the history of the country, effective labor organizations are just over 100 years old. These chapters indicate that labor law and its enforcement have played an important role in the development of collective bargaining. The development chapters trace societal and economic changes and detail the statutes that have contributed to the development and particular shape of collective bargaining in the United States. In particular, legislation passed in the 1930s to protect employees in forming unions and engaging in collective bargaining contributed to union growth.

Structure

The examination of union *structure* focuses on the offices and institutions that either make up the labor movement or have major impacts on it. In this regard, the last part of Chapter 4 details the federal institutions involved in regulating collective bargaining. Chapter 5 examines the various organizational levels in the labor movement and identifies the location of the power centers within the movement. Chapter 5 also discusses the organizational structure of several national unions, the roles played by union officers, and the causes and consequences of the recent increase in union mergers. The various structures within which negotiations between labor and management take place are detailed in Chapter 7.

Process

The greatest emphasis in this text is on *process*. This section concerns methods used to organize employees into unions, identifies issues of importance in bargaining, explains the organization and processes involved in negotiations, and details how labor and management deal with differences that occur during bargaining and after a contract has been signed. These areas are covered in Chapters 6 through 14.

Special Chapters

The last three chapters of the book involve special issues that cut across *development, structure,* and *process* areas. The first of the three, Chapter 15, covers collective bargaining in the public sector and issues unique to it. The second, Chapter 16, examines the recent increase among private-sector employers in implementing formal policies and programs for nonunion employment relations. Chapter 17 examines the immediate future of the labor movement in light of recent trends, the professed goals of labor and management, and recent changes in individual collective bargaining relationships.

WHY WORKERS UNIONIZE

Less than 20 percent of the U.S. labor force belongs to unions. But the proportions of employees organized across occupations and industries greatly differ. Further, the points in American history at which occupations and industries began to organize vary substantially.

The creation of unions and the tenacious struggle some employee groups made to secure collective bargaining are examined in Chapters 2 and 3. In Chapter 6, the conduct of union-organizing campaigns is studied. Chapters 8 and 9 consider the specific demands unions and managements make in collective bargaining. All of these issues help explain why workers attempt to unionize. In this section, we are concerned with a general explanation of why workers join unions and of what they expect unions will accomplish for them that they have been unable to achieve individually.

Employees become union members through one of three different processes. First, a group of nonunion employees may decide it would be better off with representation and thus organize a union to bargain collectively for it. Second, an employee who works in a unit covered by a collective bargaining agreement may decide to become a union member. Third, a newly hired employee may become a union member as a condition of continued employment if the collective bargaining agreement requires it.

The Catalyst for Organization

Specific situations probably have specific events that trigger organizing activity. General evidence across elections suggests that employee dissatisfaction is significantly related to both union activity and actual voting for union representation when elections are held.[2] Not only do employees vote for unions more often as their dissatisfaction increases, but they are also more likely to be employed in units in which significant organizing activity takes place, even if that activity does not ultimately result in an election. Available evidence also clearly indicates that individuals are influenced to vote for unions more by employment conditions than by job task characteristics. Dissatisfaction with job security, economics, and supervisory practices were most predictive of a prounion vote across a set of studied elections.[3] These findings are summarized in Table 1-1. Attitudes predicting the pres-

TABLE 1-1

Correlation between Job Satisfaction and Voting for Union Representation

Issue	Correlation with vote for union
Are you satisfied with the job security at this company?	−.42
Are you satisfied with your wages?	−.40
Taking everything into consideration, are you satisfied with this company as a place to work?	−.36
Do supervisors in this company treat all employees alike?	−.34
Are you satisfied with your fringe benefits?	−.31
Do your supervisors show appreciation when you do a good job?	−.30
Do you think there is a good chance for you to get promoted in this company?	−.30
Are you satisfied with the type of work you are doing?	−.14

Source: Adapted from Jeanne M. Brett, "Why Employees Want Unions." Reprinted, by permission of the publisher, from *Organizational Dynamics,* Spring 1980, p. 51. Copyright © 1980 by AMACOM, a division of American Management Associations. All rights reserved.

---

[2] Julius G. Getman, Stephen B. Goldberg, and Jeanne B. Herman, *Union Representation Elections: Law and Reality* (New York: Russell Sage Foundation, 1976); W. Clay Hamner and Frank J. Smith, "Work Attitudes as Predictors of Unionization Activity," *Journal of Applied Psychology,* August 1978, pp. 415–21; and Chester A. Schreisheim, "Job Satisfaction, Attitudes toward Unions, and Voting in a Union Representation Election," *Journal of Applied Psychology,* October 1978, pp. 548–52.

[3] Jeanne M. Brett, "Why Employees Want Unions," *Organizational Dynamics,* Spring 1980, pp. 47–59.

ence and level of organizing activity in units of one large, multiloca-
tion company centered around supervision, co-worker friction,
amount of work required, career progression, feelings about the company, physical surroundings, and the kind of work done.

Dissatisfaction alone does not automatically mean that a union-
organizing campaign will result or that an election will be won by the
union. Two conditions have to exist to predict organizing attempts and
a union win. First, individuals have to be dissatisfied and perceive that
they are unable to influence a change in the conditions causing dissatisfaction. Second, a large enough coalition of employees would have to
believe that it can improve conditions through collective action and
that the benefits of this action outweigh the costs.[4]

Individuals and Union Organizing

In an election campaign, people must decide whether unionization is
in their best interest. To make this decision, individuals assess what
the likely outcomes of unionization will be, whether each outcome is
positive or negative, and the likelihood that their working for or voting
for a union will lead to the positive or negative outcomes. An individual might first examine the present job situation and assess the possibility of receiving positive or negative outcomes as a result of holding
that job. Where a job presently has some negative outcomes, individuals may weigh such actions as convincing supervisors or management
to behave differently, doing nothing, or organizing to change the situation. A person's experience with the efficacy of a particular action
determines whether that action will be pursued or abandoned. Figure
1-1 outlines a motivational model that follows this approach.[5]

Figure 1-2 depicts a hypothetical belief system for two employees
in a situation where organizing is being considered. The figure suggests
that each employee evaluates the likely outcomes from organization.
The same set of outcomes and valuations is specified for both employees in the example, but the outcomes are not required to be the same,
especially if the employees have major individual differences. If the
outcomes and their valuations are examined, differences between the
two individuals are seen. Individual A positively values a union leadership position, while B apparently attaches no positive or negative
value to it. Other differences also exist, such as preferences for individual treatment.

---

[4] Ibid., pp. 48–49.

[5] This is a variant on the expectancy model of motivation. For further information,
see Victor H. Vroom, *Work and Motivation* (New York: John Wiley & Sons, 1964);
Lyman W. Porter and Edward E. Lawler III, *Managerial Attitudes and Performance*
(Homewood, Ill.: Richard D. Irwin, 1968); and Edward E. Lawler III, *Motivation in Work
Organizations* (Monterey, Calif.: Brooks/Cole Publishing, 1973).

FIGURE 1-1

A Motivation Model

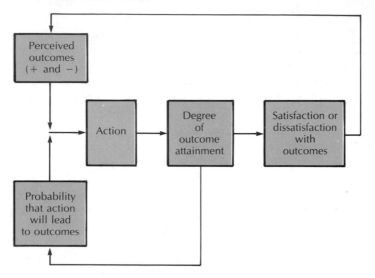

The next explanatory component links the outcomes with the result of an action—in this case, success or failure in organizing. For individual A, success in organizing is associated with six positive and two negative outcomes. Failure to organize leads to one positive, one negative, and two neutral items. If individual A believes taking action will increase the likelihood of unionization, efforts to do so would be expected since the greater net balance of positive outcomes results from a union. Individual B, on the other hand, expects four positives and three negatives from a union and four positives and one neutral from no union. B would be predicted to oppose the union.

Some consequences or outcomes could follow directly from the action taken rather than the result of the action. For example, if individual A thinks neither working for nor against the union will affect the organizing campaign outcome, then no effort would be expected. Why? It is easier. On the other hand, effort would be predicted from individual A if A thinks an effort is necessary for organization and believes his or her effort will contribute to winning the election.

Some might argue that this model makes predicting what people in a group will do very difficult. This is the case if they have extremely diverse backgrounds or widely differing beliefs as to what actions will lead to results or what outcomes will follow from results. However, a number of things might reduce this diversity.

People often see avenues other than union membership to attain valued outcomes from employment. For example, if promotions and interesting work are highly valued but seen as unattainable on the jobs

FIGURE 1-2

Beliefs about Organizing

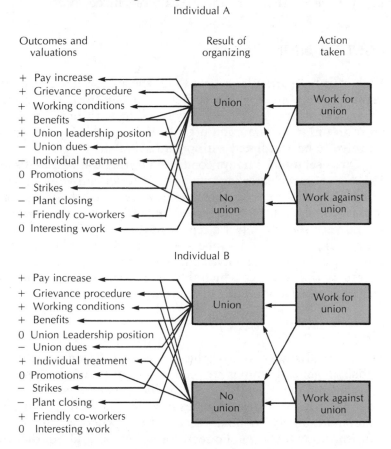

considered for unionization, then many of the employees desiring them would probably leave. Achievable, positive, past job outcomes also become increasingly important to employees. Thus, unionizing attempts may begin because management withholds rewards or changes the system so that rewards differ from what people in the jobs value.

The degree to which unionization is seen as leading to the attainment of positive outcomes and the avoidance of negative outcomes may also be changed through campaign attempts. Both labor and management attempt to direct employees toward a stronger belief that unionization will have positive and negative consequences, respectively.

One thing that should become clear by examining the perceptions and choices individuals make regarding unions is that, before unionization is possible, employees must hold a common belief that a union will benefit them. This means a large heterogeneous unit would probably be difficult to organize, whereas a smaller, more stable employment situation should be more easily organized.

BELIEFS ABOUT UNIONS

Each of us has particular beliefs about the appropriateness of organized labor's role in society. These beliefs result from our family backgrounds and experiences, our involvement with union members, our work in union or nonunion organizations, and the gains or costs we perceive to be associated with organized labor.

Cross-sectional surveys conducted during the late 1970s and early 1980s give us a clearer idea about how American workers view labor unions.[6] In the surveys, respondents were asked their opinions about unions in general. Nonunion respondents were asked whether they would vote for a union if a representation election were held where they work, and union members were asked what they believed their unions ought to be involved in, what the unions were actually involved in, the degree to which they were participating in union affairs, and their satisfaction with the union.

Beliefs of Employees in General

Survey results suggest that the public sees unions as powerful and selfish. In general, unions are seen as out for themselves, more powerful than employers, and able to strongly influence the course of legislation. As might be expected, older persons and white-collar employees were more likely to hold these beliefs, whereas union members, women, nonwhites, public-sector employees, and Southerners were less likely. Overall, however, a majority of *both* unionized and nonunionized employees shared these beliefs.

However, the survey also found that respondents believed unions were effective in protecting workers from unfair treatment and in improving wages and job security. More positive attitudes were held by union members, more highly educated individuals, and southern residents. Table 1–2 details the respondents' beliefs.

---

[6] Thomas A. Kochan, "How American Workers View Labor Unions," *Monthly Labor Review,* April 1979, pp. 23–31; and a 1984 Harris poll conducted for the AFL–CIO Evolution of Work Committee.

TABLE 1-2

American Workers' Beliefs about Trade Unions (in percent)*

Beliefs	Strongly agree	Agree	Neither agree nor disagree	Disagree	Strongly disagree
Big-labor-image beliefs:					
Influence who gets elected to public office	37.5%	46.0%	1.8%	12.7%	1.1%
Influence laws passed	24.0	56.6	3.8	14.4	1.2
Are more powerful than employers	24.8	41.6	6.2	25.4	2.0
Influence how the country is run	18.1	53.4	4.8	21.7	1.9
Require members to go along with decisions	18.5	56.0	3.9	20.1	1.6
Have leaders who do what's best for themselves	22.8	44.7	6.4	24.0	2.1
Instrumental beliefs:					
Protect workers against unfair practice	20.5	63.0	3.4	11.2	2.0
Improve job security	19.2	61.0	2.8	14.5	2.5
Improve wages	18.9	67.6	3.2	8.7	1.7
Give members their money's (dues') worth	6.9	38.5	6.3	36.9	11.3

* In the survey, 1,515 workers were polled.

Source: Thomas A. Kochan, "How American Workers View Labor Unions," *Monthly Labor Review*, April 1979, p. 24.

Nonunion Respondents

Among individuals whose occupations were eligible for unionization, almost one third said they would vote for a union in a representation election. For blue-collar workers, attitudes and characteristics most strongly associated with a propensity to vote for a union included difficulty in exerting influence, severity of job dangers, inadequate income, member of a racial minority, and beliefs that unions are effective in gaining important outcomes. Factors leading to negative feelings about voting for a union were residence in the north central United States and government employment. White-collar workers expressing dissatisfaction with bread-and-butter issues and the nature of their work showed a willingness to vote for the union. Other important issues that influenced the direction of white-collar workers' votes were desired on-the-job influence, inadequate fringe benefits, inequitable pay, being a racial minority group member, beliefs about labor's ability to gain important ends (all positive), and residence in the north central region (negative).

Persons who would vote against a union generally felt their jobs were presently satisfactory, and/or they preferred to deal with their employer on an individual rather than collective basis.

Union Members

Although we will cover the preferences of union members for bargaining outcomes in much greater detail in Chapters 8 and 9, we note here that union members place the highest priorities on the following issues: their union's handling of grievances, getting feedback from their unions, additional fringe benefits, having a say in the union, better wages, and job security. Generally, union members are satisfied with the performance of their unions, particularly on economic issues. Ironically, the satisfaction rate (about 73 percent) is about the same as the historic job satisfaction rate in the United States. Among union members, confidence in union leaders rose during the 1970s.[7]

Among a sample of public-sector union members who could choose to join or not join the union that represented them, satisfaction with their union's performance was related to beliefs in the goals of the union movement and endorsement of the union's preferred positions on promotions and job security. Less favorable attitudes were found among those who joined for social reasons or who felt pressured to join.[8]

AREAS OF FRUSTRATION

Very few employers find themselves targeted with an organizing campaign shortly after they open their doors and hire employees. A union-organizing campaign begins when something in the employment relationship causes employees to determine that their expectations are not being met or that they are being treated unfairly or inequitably in relation to others.

General preferences for job outcomes vary across organizations.[9]

[7] Thomas J. Chacko and Charles R. Greer, "Perceptions of Union Power, Service, and Confidence in Labor Leaders: A Study of Member and Nonmember Differences," *Journal of Labor Research*, Spring 1982, pp. 211–21.

[8] Michael E. Gordon and Larry N. Long, "Demographic and Attitudinal Correlates of Union Joining," *Industrial Relations*, Fall 1981, pp. 306–11.

[9] Lloyd H. Lofquist and Rene V. Dawis, *Adjustment to Work* (New York: Appleton-Century-Crofts, 1970).

But several classes of outcomes may be of considerable importance to large groups of employees. These might include compensation policies and practices, advancements and transfers, rules and discipline, and supervisory practices and decisions.

Employees may find they are earning less than comparable employees in other organizations. They may also find their employer is making considerably higher profits than in the past and has a greater ability to pay. Promotions may be awarded on the basis of favoritism or other criteria that seem irrelevant or unfair to those interested in advancement. Employees may believe seniority norms should govern entitlement to advancements and transfers. Supervisors may be seen as imposing discipline or offering rewards capriciously. Differences between shifts and units in terms of supervisory behavior may be noted. All of these factors may stimulate the desire for union organization if they are perceived by a large enough group of employees.

COLLECTIVE BEHAVIOR

Group formation occurs for a variety of reasons. Some groups evolve because of mutual interests or similarities, and we have suggested that these common interests might be necessary for union formation. Another reason groups form is to react to perceived danger or threat. An employer who exercises a fear campaign in supervision may lead to this type of collective behavior. "Wagon-circling" behavior seems to be a pervasive phenomenon. Studies of inexperienced combat troops in World War II found that they tended to group when under fire, even though spreading out reduced their vulnerability to attack. Other studies indicate that assisting or affiliating behavior requires that the danger be applicable to a majority of individuals in an area before group activities occur.[10]

When individuals are dissatisfied with their present employment, one might ask why they don't simply leave. These employees may feel they have invested parts of their lives with their employers or alternative employment will be hard to find. One theory suggests that people can dissent in two ways—either by leaving an organization (exit option) or by actively trying to change conditions within it (voice option).[11] Forming a union enables use of a collective voice in influencing change at work.

---

[10] See, for example, Stanley Schachter, *The Psychology of Affiliation: Experimental Studies of the Sources of Gregariousness* (Stanford, Calif.: Stanford University Press, 1959).

[11] A. O. Hirschman, *Exit, Voice, and Loyalty* (Cambridge, Mass.: Harvard University Press, 1970).

Group Cohesiveness

A group is labeled *cohesive* when a generally lower variance in behavior of the group's members is observed. Many studies show that the productivity of some work groups remains relatively constant over time and varies little among members. This indicates that group members are adhering to a collectively adopted output norm.

What are the underlying reasons for cohesiveness? First, the members of the group are likely to hold the same basic values and to agree on the methods used for their attainment. Second, age, seniority, and other background characteristics are probably quite similar. Third, the group has probably informally chosen a group leader. This member often has values closest to the overall values of the group. Finally, cohesiveness may be a function of external threat.

If external threat increases cohesiveness, how does it do so, and is the relationship linear or at least monotonic? To answer the first part of this question, we might go back to expectancy theory. If someone perceives that negative outcomes will occur for one who must act alone but not for one acting within a group, then acting as a group is perceived to have positive consequences. If a united front is perceived to be strong, then cohesiveness will be high. If an employer is unwilling to grant a wage increase to a single employee and dares the employee to quit, the same employer might not be willing to risk denying a collectively demanded raise if the alternative is a strike.

How far would we expect group members to go in individually sacrificing for the good of the group? When the benefits perceived from remaining a group member are outweighed by the costs of membership, then cohesiveness will break down. As Figure 1–3 shows, the

FIGURE 1–3

Hypothesized Relationship between Threat and Cohesiveness

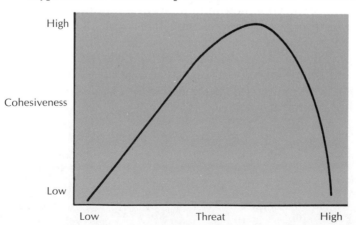

hypothetical relationship between threat and cohesiveness is an inverted *U*.

Unions cannot ensure background similarities among their members because management makes the hiring decisions and unions are obligated to admit all employees who desire membership. Thus, only one avenue is available to the union to maintain cohesiveness: perceived threats from management. To maintain cohesiveness through threat, an adversarial relationship is necessary. Thus, management acting against individuals or the group may be to the union's *benefit*, since management action can then be rebuffed, modified, or rescinded through what members perceive as *group action.*

SUMMARY AND PREVIEW

Our study of labor relations will examine the historical development of the labor movement, the structure of union organizations and federal agencies involved in labor relations, and the processes of collective bargaining, including the identification of bargaining issues, negotiations, and contract administration.

Evidence suggests that employee dissatisfaction leads to interest in organizing. For the most part, the general population sees unions and their leaders as out for their own interests but effective in achieving their goals. A significant minority of unorganized employees say they would vote for union representation if an election were held in their work unit. Feelings about unions have remained quite stable recently.

Cohesiveness appears to be a necessary property for successful organization. Similarities among group members and external threats have a positive influence on cohesiveness. The adversary role that unions take is likely to enhance the cohesiveness of their memberships.

Preview

In this text, each chapter begins by introducing the subject and highlighting some major issues. These highlights primarily suggest major areas of concern and point out issues that should be explored to gain an understanding of the development, structure, or process of labor–management relations.

Most chapters end with a set of discussion questions. These either relate to relatively broad issues raised in the chapter or ask that a position be formulated for labor or for management on one of these issues. Many chapters also conclude with case material. Most of these cases relate to a simulated organization, General Materials & Fabrication Corporation (GMFC), a heavy-equipment manufacturer. The first case involving GMFC—a mock negotiation exercise—follows Chapter

10. Later, contract administration cases and cases discussing arbitration issues arising from the contract are presented. These cases should help you gain a greater appreciation of the process involved in the collective bargaining relationship.

Point of View

In this text I have tried to include information that will increase your ability to understand labor relations as it is practiced in the United States. This understanding must be based on the evolution and development of the labor movement to its present form, the subject matter and jurisdiction of labor law, and the practices of the two major parties in the process—management and labor.

The subject should be interesting. In teaching courses in organizational behavior, personnel/human resource management, and labor relations, I have always found that most students are more intrinsically interested in labor relations than in the other two. Perhaps this is because we are likely to have strong attitudes about what we think are the proper roles each party should take in the process and notions about which side should be blamed for the problems surrounding labor relations. I do not expect your basic posture toward labor relations to change as a result of either this book or the course you are in, but I expect you to gain a far greater understanding of why the parties act as they do. I also expect you to become more willing to agree that, in most instances, both parties do a good job of representing their constituents and arriving at a means for settling conflicts, thereby minimizing disruptions in their organizations and, as a result, minimizing disruptions to the public at large.

CHAPTER 2

The Evolution of American Labor: I

Labor relations in the United States has a history as old as the nation. Understanding the present operation and goals of the American labor movement requires an understanding of the events, personalities, and philosophies that shaped it. Among the questions that need to be asked are the following: What are the concerns of the labor movement, and how do concerns in the United States differ from those in other countries? How has the movement grown, and in what occupational and industrial sectors is its strength currently growing or waning? What place has organized labor been accorded by public opinion and the development of public policy over time? The next three chapters examine the history of the American labor movement and trace the evolution, growth, and demise of major labor organizations. The American labor movement has been predominantly results, rather than ideologically, oriented. Surviving labor organizations have adapted to change and been responsive to member needs.

This chapter concentrates on the path the labor movement traveled from the nation's founding to the end of the 1920s. Particular questions you should ask include:

1. What was the legal, public policy, and public opinion climate surrounding early American labor relations? Consider the influence of legislators, judges, and the news media on early labor relations.
2. What form did the American labor movement develop? Be aware of the properties that appear necessary for success in the United States. Ask whether the ingredients change over time.
3. What types of events contributed to and detracted from union growth? Do these still operate in the same manner?
4. How have the personalities of the major actors within the labor movement contributed to union growth?

EARLY UNIONS AND THE CONSPIRACY DOCTRINE

The genesis of the American labor movement parallels the birth of the nation. In 1778 the first successful collective action to win a wage increase was implemented by the New York journeyman printers.[1] However, union growth in the United States did not keep pace with the growth of the nation during most of the following 200 years. Substantial impediments were raised by legal decisions, the predominantly rural nature of 19th-century America, and the substantial number of relatively unskilled immigrants who competed for jobs at relatively low wages. In fact, most collective actions taken through the 19th century were aimed at resisting wage cuts rather than attempting to gain increases.

Philadelphia Cordwainers

The Federal Society of Journeyman Cordwainers (shoemakers) was organized in Philadelphia in 1794.[2] Its formation resulted from some substantial changes in the manner in which shoes were marketed. Until about 1790, journeymen had been almost exclusively involved in the manufacture of "bespoke" (custom) work. Master shoemakers took orders and supplied material for the journeymen, who produced a pair of shoes or boots for an agreed wage. This arrangement required that the customer be willing to wait for completion of the work. Since this was inconvenient, and expensive as well, three other market classes were developed by the masters—"shop," "order," and "market" work. Shop work was for the master's stock, order work was for wholesalers, and market work was to sell in the public market. Each commanded a lower price than its predecessor, and the master attempted to differentiate wage rates depending on the type of market being supplied. The journeymen cordwainers responded by attempting to fix wages for shoemaking at the rate paid for bespoke work. This attempt was a forerunner of the union demand of equal pay for equal work.

The refusal of the cordwainers to work at rates that varied depending on the ultimate market for their output was seen by the employers as a criminal act. The courts found that the collective actions of the cordwainers in pursuit of their personal interests contravened the interests of citizens in general and was, hence, a criminal conspiracy. Each member of the union was fined $8 on conviction (see Exhibit

---

[1] U.S. Department of Labor, Bureau of Labor Statistics, *A Brief History of the American Labor Movement*, Bulletin 1000, rev. (Washington, D.C.: U.S. Government Printing Office, 1970), p. 99.

[2] For a thorough analysis of this group, see John R. Commons, *Labor and Administration* (New York: Macmillan, 1973), pp. 210-64.

EXHIBIT 2-1

Charge to the Jury in the *Philadelphia Cordwainers* Case

"What is the case before us? . . . A combination of workmen to raise their wages may be considered in a twofold point of view: one is to benefit themselves . . . the other is to injure those who do not join their society. The rule of law condemns both. . . . [T]he rule in this case is pregnant with sound sense and all the authorities are clear on the subject. Hawkins, the greatest authority on criminal law, has laid it down, that a combination to maintain one another, carrying a particular object, whether true or false, is criminal."

Source: Condensed from 3 Commons and Gilmore 228-33, which was partially reprinted in Jerre S. Williams, *Labor Relations and the Law*, 3rd ed. (Boston: Little, Brown, 1965), p. 20.

2-1).[3] This decision established the *conspiracy doctrine,* under which a union could be punished if either its *means* or its *ends* were deemed illegal by the courts.

Commonwealth v. *Hunt*

In 1842, the conspiracy doctrine was softened substantially by the Massachusetts Supreme Court's decision in *Commonwealth* v. *Hunt.*[4] This decision set aside the conviction of members of the Boston Journeymen Bootmakers' Society for refusing to work in shops where nonmembers worked for less than the negotiated rate. The court held that the society's action was primarily to convince nonmembers to join the organization rather than to secure criminal ends. The court refused to enjoin organizing activities, but it did not say that injunctions aginst other collective activities would be stopped (see Exhibit 2-2).[5]

Pre-Civil War Unions

During the first half of the 19th century, unions were faced with a number of problems, including employers who did not see them as legitimate organizations, courts that enjoined and punished collective activity, and competition from a growing supply of immigrant labor. Despite these impediments, collective activity still took place. Most

---

[3] Jerre S. Williams, *Labor Relations and the Law*, 3rd ed. (Boston: Little, Brown, 1965), p. 18.

[4] 4 Metcalf 111 (1842).

[5] Williams, *Labor Relations and the Law*, p. 22.

EXHIBIT 2-2

Interpretation of Conspiracy Doctrine under *Commonwealth* v. *Hunt*

"The manifest intention of the association is to induce all those engaged in the same occupation to become members of it. Such a purpose is not unlawful. It would give them a power which might be exerted for useful and honorable purposes, or for dangerous and pernicious ones. If the latter were the real and actual object and susceptible of proof, it should have been specially charged. . . . In this state of things, we cannot perceive that it is criminal for men to agree to exercise their acknowledged rights in such a manner as best to subserve their own interests."

Source: 4 Metcalf 129, as contained in Jerre S. Williams, *Labor Relations and the Law*, 3rd ed. (Boston: Little, Brown, 1965), p. 22.

was among skilled artisans, such as the cordwainers, but even unskilled textile workers in Massachusetts became involved.

Workingmen's parties were organized, and they contributed to the election of President Andrew Jackson.[6] Following Jackson, Martin Van Buren promulgated an executive order decreasing the length of the workday for federal employees to 10 hours. Unions in major U.S. cities successfully used strikes to secure wage increases. Union membership swelled in the early 1830s; however, poor economic conditions soon tipped the scales in favor of employers, and union activity waned where membership threatened workers' continued employment.

THE BIRTH OF NATIONAL UNIONS

Beginning in the 1850s, a number of national trade unions were formed. Of those formed at this early stage, all have either disappeared or merged into other surviving unions. Until the end of the Civil War, the organized unions were representative only of certain trades or industries. This pattern ultimately prevailed in American unions, with workers joining unions representing their skills or industries. After the Civil War, however, the first major movements were organized on a national scope, without craft or industry distinctions.

---

6 See Foster Rhea Dulles, *Labor in America: A History*, 3rd ed. (New York: Crowell, 1966), pp. 35-52.

The National Labor Union

The National Labor Union (NLU) was founded at a convention in Baltimore in 1866. Its goals were largely political and reformist rather than economic or immediate. Its leader, William Sylvis, had been instrumental in organizing the National Molders' Union in 1859. Goals of the NLU included introduction of the eight-hour day, establishment of consumer and producer cooperatives, reform of currency and banking laws, limitation on immigration, and establishment of a federal department of labor.

The NLU was open not only to skilled trades workers but also to other interested and sympathetic individuals. Suffragists, particularly prominent at its national meetings, attempted to get the NLU to endorse their efforts to gain voting rights for women.

Sylvis was the backbone of the NLU; but, with his death in 1869 and the NLU's subsequent alliance with the Greenback party in 1872, the movement failed. The lack of leadership and inattention to immediate problems contributed most to the NLU's demise.[7] However, the first attempts to coordinate labor organizations nationally had begun— and would ultimately be successful.

The Knights of Labor

The Knights of Labor was organized in Philadelphia in 1869. Its goals and membership differed from those ultimately embodied in the U.S. labor movement, but it more closely approximated the final pattern than did the NLU. It was part labor organization and part fraternal lodge. Workers were organized on a city-by-city basis across crafts rather than primarily along craft lines. When assemblies (the Knights' local units) had a group of members from a particular craft large enough to be self-sustaining, then another assembly was spun off within the same city. A basic position of the Knights of Labor held that all workers had common interests that blurred craft distinctions.

From a philosophical standpoint, the Knights of Labor was more willing to recognize the short-term legitimacy of capitalism than was the NLU. The leaders of the Knights—first Uriah Stephens, then Terence Powderly—were essentially idealists who advocated such tactics as favoring arbitration over strikes. Employers used these prestated positions to their advantage. But in confrontation situations, the rank and file were more militant than the leadership in their use of strikes to counter employer initiatives.

The Knights of Labor grew slowly. It took three years to gain

---

[7] Ibid., 110–113.

enough members to establish a second assembly in Philadelphia. In 1873, the first district assembly (a collection of five assemblies) was created; and, by 1875, district assemblies had headquarters in Reading and Pittsburgh, Pennsylvania, as well. Because it was a secret society, the Knights of Labor was involved in conflict with the Roman Catholic Church. Clergy believed members of the Knights might be required to take secret oaths that could possibly commit them to beliefs inconsistent with Roman Catholic dogma. Ultimately, negotiations between Terence Powderly and James Cardinal Gibbons led to a ruling that Roman Catholics could belong to the Knights.[8]

As often occurred during the 19th century, the country entered a depression in the beginning of the 1880s. These periods had usually taken their toll on labor organizations in the past, but this time the strength of the Knights of Labor grew. In a number of railroad strikes in 1882 and 1883, the Knights successfully organized workers and won their demands—a sharp contrast to the crushing defeat railroad strikers had suffered in 1877. When railroad financier Jay Gould attempted to break the union by laying off its members in 1885, the union's strike on the Wabash Railroad and its refusal to handle Wabash rolling stock on other lines forced him to cease discriminating against Knights of Labor members. The nationally publicized negotiations surrounding this dispute gave added impetus to organization so that by the middle of 1886, membership in the Knights of Labor reached 700,000.[9]

There was a degree of irony in the Knights' success against Jay Gould.[10] A large influx of new members entered the ranks to gain the same types of concessions from their employers that Gould had given. But Powderly and the other leaders took a much more long-run–oriented position than just the satisfaction of day-to-day grievances. They did not espouse a collective bargaining approach that would lead to an ultimate goal on a piecemeal basis. They also firmly opposed using the strike as a weapon for pressuring employers. The long-run perspective of the leadership and its belief in "rational" processes for achieving ultimate objectives is typified by these quotes from Powderly and Knights of Labor publications: "You must submit to injustice at the hands of the employer in patience for a while longer"; and "Do not strike, but study not only your own condition but that of your employer. Find out how much you are justly entitled to, and the tribunal of arbitration will settle the rest."[11]

---

[8] Philip Taft, *Organized Labor in American History* (New York: Harper & Row, 1964), pp. 84–89.

[9] Dulles, *Labor in America*, pp. 139–41.

[10] Neil W. Chamberlain and Donald E. Cullen, *The Labor Sector*, 2nd ed. (New York: McGraw-Hill, 1971), pp. 97–98.

[11] Ibid., p. 98.

EXHIBIT 2-3

The Ascetic Terence Powderly on Labor Picnics

"I will talk at no picnics. When I speak on the labor question, I want the individual attention of my hearers, and I want that attention for at least two hours, and in that two hours I can only epitomize. At a picnic where the girls as well as the boys swill beer I cannot talk at all. . . . If it comes to my ears that I am advertised to speak at picnics. . . . I will prefer charges against the offenders for holding the executive head of the Order up to ridicule."

Source: Foster Rhea Dulles, *Labor in America: A History*, 3rd ed. (New York: Crowell, 1966), p. 136.

The reformist and long-run objectives were inconsistent with the immediate results sought by the new membership. To some extent the differences between the ascetic Powderly (see Exhibit 2-3) and the interests of the burgeoning rank and file hastened the decline of the Knights. Besides the leadership-membership cleavages, an antagonistic press increasingly linked anarchy and radical action with the Knights of Labor. Public pressure, internal power vested in individuals with reformist sentiments, and an inability to get employers to arbitrate all contributed to the decline of the Knights' membership to 75,000 by 1893. But the withering of the Knights of Labor did not bring an end to national organizations. At the height of the Knights of Labor's success, the first enduring national federation was formed.

The American Federation of Labor

The American Federation of Labor (AFL) was created in a meeting of national unions in Columbus, Ohio, in 1886.[12] It was born out of the frustration craft unionists felt about the mixing of skilled and unskilled workers in Knights of Labor assemblies and the Knights' increasingly reformist orientation.[13] The Knights of Labor also tended toward centralization of authority, which diminished the autonomous power of individual craft unions.

Twenty-five national labor groups representing about 150,000 members initially formed the federation. The individual unions maintained autonomy and control over aspects related to their trades while ceding authority to the AFL to settle disputes among them.[14] The AFL

---

[12] Dulles, *Labor in America*, p. 161.

[13] *Craft* is used to mean a particular skilled trade that normally requires an apprenticeship period to learn the skill (for example, carpentry, typography, tailoring).

[14] Dulles, *Labor in America*, p. 161.

was formed by unions of skilled employees. During most of its history, it maintained a skilled-worker, or craft, orientation and an antipathy toward involving unskilled workers in its unions.

The AFL concentrated on winning tangible gains for its members by entering into collective agreements with employers. It aimed at rationalizing the workplace by contracting conditions of employment.

Much of the early direction of the AFL was influenced by the philosophies of its first president, Samuel Gompers. As a member of the New York local of the Cigarmakers, he had seen radical action punished by civil authorities and experienced the Knights of Labor's advocacy of unskilled demands within the Cigarmakers. As a labor leader, these experiences led Gompers to pay close attention to the workers he *presently* represented, not necessarily the interests of all laborers. Experience also led him to take a pragmatic approach, seeking gains at the bargaining table rather than through legislation. His long incumbency (1886–1924, except for one year) is in large part responsible for the "business" orientation of U.S. unions.

Gompers and other early leaders, such as Adolph Strasser, cemented the base on which the American trade union movement stood. Their approach accepted the system as it existed and worked within it. They were primarily concerned with improving the lot of the members they represented. This approach is basically retained in the present agency role taken by unions in representation (see Exhibit 2–4).

Taking this pragmatic, business-oriented viewpoint necessarily limited the AFL in sponsoring major social reform initiatives. The AFL approach advocated legislation only in situations in which it could not bargain successfully for its objectives. Perhaps the immediacy and absence of an underlying ideology is best typified in the answer, attributed to Gompers, to a question asking what labor's goals were: "More, more, more."

Another aspect of the pragmatic genius of the AFL's founders was

EXHIBIT 2–4

Testimony of Adolph Strasser, President of the International Cigarmakers' Union, before the Senate Committee on Education and Labor, 1885

Q: You are seeking to improve home matters first?

Strasser: Yes, sir, I look first to the trade I represent . . . the interests of the men who employ me to represent their interests.

Q: I was only asking you in regard to your ultimate ends.

Strasser: We have no ultimate ends. We are going on from day to day. We fight only for immediate objects—objects that can be realized in a few years.

their structural design for the federation. Its early structure, broadly maintained to the present time, preserves the autonomy of the international unions and makes their locals subsidiary to them. This approach serves two purposes: first, the leaders' focus is toward the job problems unique to the trade they represent; second, discipline is maintained over the activites of the locals, and thus a more united and rational front is presented when initiating actions or responding to management.

LABOR UNREST

The last three decades of the 19th century and the first decade of the 20th saw some of the bitterest labor struggles the United States has ever experienced. This period was characterized by frequent financial panics resulting in depressions, continuing adamancy by owners refusing to recognize or negotiate with labor unions, and intervention by the government on the side of employers. Some of the unrest was localized and grew out of either radical political action or the nationalistic solidarity of immigrant groups, but much of it was of a general nature within an area or industry.

In one of the first outbursts, coal miners in Pennsylvania struck when mine operators unilaterally cut wages below an agreed minimum. As the strike lengthened, some miners returned to work, but a few diehards formed a secret organization (which became known as the Molly Maguires) to continue resisting the mine owners. This group sabotaged the mines, threatened owners and supervisors, and conducted other terrorist activities until it was infiltrated by James McParlan, a Pinkerton detective hired by the owners. In 1875, as a result of his testimony, 10 of the Molly Maguires were hanged, and another 14 were jailed, ending the mine warfare.[15]

In the summer of 1877, the railroads cut wages while maintaining high dividends to their stockholders. Eastern rail employees struck and, in some instances, seized railway property. In Pittsburgh, federal troops were called in to retake the property but not before 25 people had been killed. Widespread rioting broke out. Railroad property was burned, and local business establishments were looted.[16]

In 1886, violence broke out between strikers and strikebreakers at the McCormick Harvester plant in Chicago. The police intervened, and four persons were killed. To protest the use of police, a meeting was held in Haymarket Square. As the peaceful meeting was dispersing, the police arrived and ordered everyone to leave. Just then a bomb

---

[15] Ibid., pp. 117–18.
[16] Ibid., pp. 119–20.

exploded among the police, killing one of them. Before the battle was over, seven more police and four workers were killed, and more than 100 persons were injured. The riot was blamed on anarchists. Eight were rounded up and charged with murder; seven were ordered to be hanged, and the eighth was imprisoned. All were pardoned six years later, and those still alive were released.[17]

Two major strikes in the 1890s helped shape the constituency of the labor movement while casting doubt on the power of industrial employees to win their demands. These were the Homestead strike in the Carnegie Steel Company in 1892 and the Pullman Company strike in 1894.

Homestead workers refused to accept a company-ordered wage cut and were then locked out by Henry Frick, Carnegie's general manager. The workers correctly assumed Frick would attempt to reopen the plant by hiring strikebreakers. To accomplish this, Frick barged 300 armed Pinkerton detectives up the Monongahela River behind the plant. As they neared the works, the entrenched workers opened fire on them. The battle raged all day. Workers attempted to sink the barges with a small cannon and poured oil onto the river and set it on fire. The Pinkertons surrendered.

The workers' victory was short lived; the governor called out the militia, which took over the plant. Frick staffed the reopened plant with strikebreakers. The union was crushed to the extent that serious attempts to organize the steel industry were not made again until the 1930s.[18]

The Pullman strike of 1894 began as a local issue, but it took on nationwide proportions before being crushed by the combined use of federal troops and court injunctions. The Pullman Company produced railroad cars. Pullman workers lived in company-owned houses and paid rent for their occupancy. They had no other choice of living accommodations; the company required them to use company-owned housing. In 1893, the company laid off half of its employees and cut the wages of those remaining up to 40 percent. There was no corresponding reduction in rents, and the company continued to pay dividends to stockholders.

Pullman employees attempted to get the owners to adjust their economic grievances, but the company refused and discharged several of the employee leaders. The Pullman locals of the American Railway Union (ARU) reacted by striking. The company refused the union's offer to have the differences arbitrated; and, as a result, ARU leader Eugene Debs ordered ARU members not to handle Pullman rolling stock.

[17] Ibid., pp. 123–25.
[18] Ibid., pp. 166–69.

Railroad employees throughout the country stopped trains and uncoupled cars manufactured by Pullman. The railroads retaliated by discharging employees found cutting out Pullman cars. But whole train crews quit and abandoned their trains if one of their members was fired.

One management strategy led to the end of the strike. When trains were assembled, Pullman cars were connected to U.S. mail cars so that if the Pullman cars were later uncoupled, the mail car might also be cut out. This action would thus lead to interference with the mail—a federal offense. When this occurred, the federal government intervened, supplying federal troops and permanently enjoining interference with mail delivery and the movement of goods in interstate commerce. Debs was sent to jail for conspiracy to obstruct the mails, and the strike was broken.[19]

The failure of these early industrial actions convinced members of one faction of the labor movement that the capitalistic system must be replaced by socialism if worker goals are to be achieved. Revolutionary unions were spawned in the West in mining and timbering and in textiles in the East.

The IWW and the Western Federation of Miners

The inability of the Knights of Labor to win important settlements and the antipathy of the AFL toward industrial organization led to more radical approaches. Just as Eugene Debs's jail term convinced him that revolutionary unionism and the abolition of capitalism were necessary, so too did the results of numerous mine strikes and wars convince "Big Bill" Haywood that miner solidarity and resistance were the answer to employer intransigence.

Haywood played an active role in organizing the Western Federation of Miners (WFM), which had withdrawn from the AFL in 1897. After the long-smoldering Cripple Creek, Colorado, strike was crushed in 1904, the WFM realized it needed national support. Thus, in 1905, Haywood, Debs, and other leading socialists banded their unions together to form the Industrial Workers of the World (IWW) (see Exhibit 2–5).[20]

Immediately embroiled in internal political struggle, the IWW was decimated by the withdrawal of the WFM in 1906, but Big Bill Haywood stayed with the IWW. No doubt its rhetoric was radical, but whether its demands were is another question. When involved in collective action, the IWW's usual demands related to wages and hours

[19] Ibid., pp. 171–79.
[20] Ibid., pp. 208–11.

EXHIBIT 2-5

Preamble to the IWW Constitution

The working class and the employing class have nothing in common. There can be no peace so long as hunger and want are found among millions of working people and the few who make up the employing class have all the good things of life.

Between these two classes a struggle must go on until the workers of the world organize as a class, take possession of the earth and the machinery of production, and abolish the wage system.

We find that the centering of management of the industries into fewer and fewer hands makes the trade unions unable to cope with the ever-growing power of the employing class. The trade unions foster a state of affairs which allows one set of workers to be pitted against another set of workers in the same industry, thereby helping defeat one another in wage wars. Moreover, the trade unions aid the employing class to mislead the workers into the belief that the working class have interests in common with their employers.

These conditions can be changed and the interest of the working class upheld only by an organization formed in such a way that all its members in any one industry, or in all industries if necessary, cease work whenever a strike or lockout is on in any department thereof, thus making an injury to one an injury to all.

Instead of the conservative motto, "A fair day's wage for a fair day's work," we must inscribe on our banner the revolutionary watchword, "Abolition of the wage system."

It is the historic mission of the working class to do away with capitalism. The army of production must be organized, not only for the everyday struggle with capitalists, but also to carry on production when capitalism shall have been overthrown. By organizing industrially we are forming the structure of the new society within the shell of the old.

---

rather than usurpation of the management function.[21] And although violence related to strikes occasionally broke out, these incidents were often sparked by management action similar to that facing the 19th-century industrial labor movement. It is important to note, however, that the *purpose* of the IWW was not to achieve better wages and working conditions—instead, it was to abolish the wage system. This may be why it encountered such resistance from employers and why it had little success in building permanent organizations.

Perhaps the most successful IWW strike occurred in Lawrence, Massachusetts, in 1912 after textile workers there had suffered a wage cut. Although most of the workers were unorganized, 20,000 walked

---

[21] Joseph G. Rayback, *A History of American Labor* (New York: Free Press, 1966), p. 248.

out, and IWW organizers took over the direction of the strike. After two months, during which several violent incidents occurred (some perpetrated by the owners and local authorities, others resulting from clashes with strikebreakers), worker demands were met, and the mills reopened.[22]

Despite this union victory, the IWW lost a subsequent textile strike in 1913 in Paterson, New Jersey. This loss, coupled with the advent of World War I, during which the IWW took the position that its members would fight for neither side since only the capitalists would benefit, led to the IWW's demise. Big Bill Haywood and other leaders were tried and convicted of sedition for allegedly obstructing the war effort. The IWW was effectively finished.[23]

The Boycott Cases

The strike was not the only weapon used against employers by labor organizations prior to World War I. While local employees struck, national unions urged other union members and the general public to boycott struck or "unfair" products. Two major national boycotts to support strikes led to sharp legal reverses—the *Danbury Hatters* and *Bucks Stove* cases—for labor organizations.

In the *Danbury Hatters* case, the employer, D. E. Loewe and Company, retaliated by filing charges against the union for conspiring to restrain trade, a violation of the Sherman Antitrust Act. Under provisions of the Sherman Act, if a restraint was found, actual damages could be punitively trebled. The union lost, and for a time it appeared that Loewe employees would have to pay damages, but the AFL and the United Hatters national organization "passed the hat" and paid the fines.[24] In the *Bucks Stove* case, a federal district court enjoined the boycott and held Samuel Gompers in contempt of court. The old spectre of the conspiracy doctrine reappeared in the application of court injunctions to halt union actions. Strikes, union organizing, and other union activities were increasingly interpreted by federal district courts as leading to a restraint on interstate commerce and, hence, as enjoinable and punishable.[25]

Early Legislation

The early attempts by unions to engage in collective action on an industrial scale had been generally met by a two-pronged attack: adamant resistance by employers and injunctive relief to employers by the courts. In an effort to balance the power between the conflicting

---

[22] Dulles, *Labor in America*, pp. 215–19.
[23] Ibid., pp. 219–22.
[24] Ibid., p. 197.
[25] Rayback, *History of American Labor*, pp. 224–26.

parties and to substitute statutory law for court-made common law, Congress began to consider labor legislation toward the end of the 1890s. The Erdman Act, passed in 1898, was the first federal labor statute guaranteeing that railroad employees could not be discriminated against for union membership. However, it was held unconstitutional in 1908 as an abridgment of personal liberty and the rights of property.[26]

The rulings of the federal courts in the *Danbury Hatters* and *Bucks Stove* cases applied the Sherman Antitrust Act to union activity. Union leaders felt this application hamstrung collective activity. With the election of President Woodrow Wilson and a Democratic Congress, labor expected legislative relief to be forthcoming. In 1914, their hopes were realized with passage of the Clayton Act, hailed by Samuel Gompers as the "industrial Magna Carta upon which the working people will rear their structure of individual freedom."[27]

Sections 6 and 20 of the Clayton Act, which removed labor from the jurisdiction of the Sherman Act and limited the use of federal injunctions, contributed to Gompers' euphoria. However, enthusiasm was short lived since the ambiguity of the act's wording ultimately led to judicial interpretations that disappointed labor.[28] In fact, the Supreme Court held in *Duplex Printing* v. *Deering* that although the antitrust laws could not be construed as rendering trade unions illegal per se, the unions' actions might still be construed as restraining trade.[29] The Court also held that a strike terminated the normal employer–employee relationship, thereby removing the protection against injunctions for lawful employee activities.[30] Thus, the Clayton Act lost whatever teeth labor believed it had gained.

TRADE UNION SUCCESS AND APATHY

World War I

Although World War I spelled the end of the IWW, AFL unions made solid gains. During 1917, a large number of strikes, many fomented by the IWW, protested static wages during a period of steadily advancing prices. To reduce the incidence of strikes, the National War Labor Board was established in 1918 and included five representatives each

---

[26] *Adair* v. *United States*, 208 U.S. 161 (1908).

[27] Samuel Gompers, "The Charter of Industrial Freedom," *American Federationist*, November 1914, pp. 971–72.

[28] S. I. Kutler, "Labor, the Clayton Act, and the Supreme Court," *Labor History*, 1962, pp. 19–38.

[29] 254 U.S. 445 (1921).

[30] Dallas L. Jones, The Enigma of the Clayton Act," *Industrial and Labor Relations Review*, 1957, pp. 201–21.

from labor and management, with two members as cochairpersons to represent the public interest. Labor's right to organize and bargain collectively was recognized by President Wilson's administration. By the end of the war, average earnings of even semiskilled union members exceeded $1,000 annually, and the AFL had added more than a million members, thus exceeding 4 million in 1919.[31]

The American Plan

A variety of factors combined to erode labor's growth after World War I. The 1920s was a decade of relative prosperity and freedom from economic panics. The declining flow of immigrants reduced the competition for jobs among unskilled workers. Management identified labor as politically extremist, and several leaders of the IWW were prosecuted for sedition. Although they did not represent large portions of the labor movement, they became symbols of its danger in the public's eye. At the same time, the Bolsheviks gained power in Russia, and warnings were made that this pattern could occur in the United States as well if trade unions became too strong.

Against this backdrop the "American Plan" was implemented. Employers subtly began to associate the union movement with foreign subversives. They questioned whether it was appropriate for workers to be represented by union officials who may have had no close employment ties with their plant. Employers also championed the open shop, which was ostensibly aimed at preserving the freedom of employees to refrain from joining unions. But the freedom to join was not zealously protected and, in fact, was discouraged through the use of yellow-dog contracts, which applicants and employees were required to sign, indicating they were not, nor would become, union members.

Local communities organized open-shop committees to protect local citizens from outside labor organizers. Reinforcing the local-control–local-concern idea, many employers improved wages and working conditions in unorganized plants. Where employees began to organize, employers encouraged them to establish a company union, autonomous from a national union but not necessarily autonomous from the employer (see Exhibit 2–6).[32]

The End of an Era

The 1920s, a decade of transition for the United States in many ways, saw organized labor touched by the changes that occurred. The country was shifting from an agricultural to an industrial society. Henry Ford introduced the assembly line. Job skill demands declined in many

---

[31] Dulles, *Labor in America*, pp. 226–28.

[32] See Chamberlain and Cullen, *Labor Sector*, pp. 109–10; and Taft, *Organized Labor*, chap. 27.

EXHIBIT 2–6

Charles M. Schwab, Chairman of the Board of Bethlehem Steel, in a Speech to a Chamber of Commerce Audience, 1918

"I believe that labor should organize in individual plants or amongst themselves for the better negotiation of labor and the protection of their own rights; but the organization and control of labor in individual plants and manufactories, to my mind, ought to be made representative of the people in those plants who know the conditions; that they ought not to be controlled by somebody from Kamchatka who knows nothing about what their conditions are."

Source: Charles M. Schwab, "Capital and Labor: A Reconstruction Policy," *Annals of the American Academy of Political and Social Science,* January 1919, p. 158.

---

areas, creating an industrial rather than a craft orientation. Immigration to the United States was limited by quotas so that the influx of impoverished potential employees dwindled to a trickle. And, while the AFL took a stand-pat approach to industrial organization, some of its newer leaders began to see the importance of organizing unskilled workers.

Before the 1920s, public policy had generally left the development and interpretation of labor law to the courts. The rulings of the courts were predominantly in favor of business, severely restricting the lawful boundaries of union action. The World War I experience and a more sympathetic Congress showed that the conduct of labor–management relations needed some explicit ground rules. The 1920s spawned the first permanent labor legislation and laid the groundwork for later legislation.

American labor by the end of the 1920s cannot be adequately described in terms of a stage of development. Looking at the surface of the AFL, one might describe it as a withering, elderly, senile recluse, attending only to its own interests and conserving a shrinking base. In examining the changing role of industry, it might be described as a sleeping giant awaiting the dawn. Its internal politics might be seen as a festering mass of irreconcilable factions. But, regardless of the factionalism, American labor did have a mainstream and a distinctive flavor that was vital and unique to its movement.

Union Philosophies and Types in the United States

Since the beginning of the union movement, certain ideas fueled its creation and direction. Their intensity has varied at different points in time and in different labor organizations, but they underlie the actions of all. The ideas can be summarized as follows: society contains a productive class that ultimately creates the tangible products or services people demand. Labor is thus the ultimate creator of wealth and is entitled to its returns. Society generally includes a moneyed aristocracy, in which society's wealth is excessively unequally distributed. Without major efforts to avoid it, education is unequal and undemocratically provided. Class distinctions exist, and the goals of workers differ from those of employers. Thus, trade unions are necessary to protect workers' rights.[33]

In 1921, Robert Hoxie established a still-useful classification of unions in terms of their goals.[34] Hoxie recognized four categories of unions: uplift, revolutionary, business, and predatory. Uplift unionism, concerned with social issues, is aimed at the general betterment of educational and monetary outcomes and labor–management systems for workers. The National Labor Union is an example of this type. Revolutionary unions are primarily oriented toward changing the fabric of society, overthrowing the capitalistic system, and replacing it with worker ownership of industry. The IWW serves as the prime American example of this type. Business unionism relates to the representation of employees' immediate employment interests. It is primarily concerned with regulating wages, hours, and terms and conditions of employment as represented by the AFL unions. This philosophy was typified by Adolph Strasser (one of the AFL's founders) in 1883, when he testified in Congress, "We have no ultimate ends. We are going on from day to day. We are fighting only for immediate objects—objects that can be realized in a few years." Predatory unionism occurs when the union's prime goal is to enhance itself at the expense of the workers it represents.

No U.S. union exists in one of these absolutely pure forms, but most appear to duplicate the characteristics of business unionism—concerned with immediate goals, accepting the system as it is, and working for union goals within that system. This approach has contributed to the durability of the labor movement, but it has also led to missed chances to contribute to meaningful changes involving the mainstream of American society.

SUMMARY AND PROLOGUE

The following major points should be apparent to students examining the early U.S. labor movement:

1. Labor organizations have been an integral part of the nation's growth at all stages.

---

[33] Maurice F. Neufeld, "The Persistence of Ideas in the American Labor Movement: The Heritage of the 1830s," *Industrial and Labor Relations Review*, January 1982, pp. 207–20.

[34] Robert F. Hoxie, *Trade Unionism in the United States* (New York: Appleton-Century-Crofts, 1921).

2. Prior to the end of the 1920s, labor was faced with a hostile national environment.
3. Most of labor's activities could be—and were—enjoined by the courts when they were effective.
4. Most successful labor leaders were concerned about labor's role in representing their members' immediate concerns and refrained from advocating ideological positions.

In summary, labor passed over several hurdles in its early organization: the conspiracy doctrine, initial uplift union movements, the link with radicals, and injunctions aimed at union activites. Personalities who shaped the early American labor movement included Terence Powderly and Uriah Stephens, Samuel Gompers and Adolph Strasser, Eugene Debs and Big Bill Haywood.

The 1920s was a decade of retrenchment. Underneath the surface was a growing interest in industrial union organization, particularly by John L. Lewis, president of the United Mine Workers.

Interest in labor legislation was growing. Then, in late 1929, the Depression began. The following decade—the 1930s—saw most present labor legislation shaped and many present-day industrial unions formed. It was a decade of turbulence, formation, and definition and an adolescence necessary for America's labor–management relations to endure to reach adulthood and relative maturity.

DISCUSSION QUESTIONS

1. Trace the evolution of the legal status of American unions. What activities were restricted by laws and courts? Did constraints increase or decline with time?
2. What were the major contributing causes to the failure of uplift unionism?
3. What were the advantages and disadvantages of taking a "business union" approach as opposed to advocating a labor political party?
4. Who were the leading personalities in 19th-century labor relations? Which ones contributed to the definition of labor relations in the United States?

CHAPTER 3

The Evolution of American Labor: II

To say the Great Depression of the 1930s caused a reorientation of many American social institutions would be an understatement. Increased regulation of private business activities resulted. The economic security of wage earners was protected. The federal government assumed the role of employing out-of-work persons. Government fiscal policy was expressly tailored to affect the economy. And American labor emerged with legislation guaranteeing its legitimacy and protecting many of its activities.

Immediately after the Depression and its labor surpluses came World War II and its labor shortages. The growth of union power resulting from legislation and employer demands for labor made itself felt on the consuming economy after the war ended. The growing power of labor led to legislation restricting union activities and encouraging labor and management to bargain collectively without outside interference as long as the public's well-being was not seriously threatened.

This chapter examines the development of industrial unions, their split with the AFL and subsequent reunification, the effect of federal labor law, the new administrative procedures occasioned by the laws and World War II, and the thrust of unionization into the public sector of employment. This chapter emphasizes several major themes or issues that affected the evolution of our labor relations system. Among these are:

1. The continuing opposition of the AFL to industrial organization.
2. The shift in public sentiment toward unions in the 1930s and away from them in the late 1940s and the influence of this shift on union success.

3. The conflict between revolutionary and business union factions in the newly founded industrial unions.
4. The role of legislation in creating an atmosphere for collective bargaining, seeking to balance the power of the contending parties and introducing rules constraining the behavior of both (toward each other and toward individual employees or members).
5. The recent size reductions of the organized component of the work force and the effects of concessions on the labor movement's direction.

INDUSTRIAL UNIONS

Until the 1930s, attempts to organize industrial unions were generally unsuccessful. This lack of organizing success was due to a number of factors, including the continuing supply of unskilled workers provided by immigration, the relative disinterest in industrial unions shown by the AFL, and the tendency of industrially oriented unions to adopt revolutionary goals. By the mid-1930s, a new set of circumstances created an atmosphere more favorable for industrial organizing. The Depression and legislative initiatives in labor–management relations helped. Established union leaders with a business-union orientation took up the industrial organizing crusade. Elected officials became more tolerant of, or actively in favor of, union activity.

The Industrial Union Leadership

The early leadership of Eugene Debs and Big Bill Haywood had lapsed for more than a decade when industrial organizing efforts resumed. This time the leadership came from within the AFL. John L. Lewis and other officials of the United Mine Workers (UMW), an AFL union, spearheaded the drive over the objections of the craft unions.

Lewis was an established leader within the AFL, but his UMW was faced with membership problems in a declining industry. In the 1930s, Lewis—a realist—decided the time had come to make a push for industrial organizing. He was not prepared for the adamant opposition to industrial unionism that he met within the AFL. In an acrimonious debate at the 1935 AFL convention, Lewis and "Big Bill" Hutcheson, president of the Carpenters' Union, actually came to blows (see Exhibit 3–1). The convention voted 18,000 to 11,000 to uphold craft unionism and not embark on industrial organization. After the convention, leaders of the UMW (Lewis and Philip Murray); the Amalgamated Clothing Workers (Sidney Hillman); the International Ladies' Garment Workers (David Dubinsky); the Typographical Union (Charles Howard); the Textile Workers (Thomas McMahon); the cap and millinery department of the United Hatters (Max Zaritsky); the Oil Field, Gas Well,

EXHIBIT 3–1

Lewis and Hutcheson at the 1935 AFL Convention

The industrial union report was defeated, but the question kept recurring. Delegates from rubber, radio, mine, and mill kept urging a new policy. Their way was blocked, though, not least by the towering figure of Big Bill Hutcheson, powerful head of the Carpenters' Union. Hutcheson and Lewis had always held similar views and frequently worked together. Like Lewis, Hutcheson was a big man, six feet tall and 220 pounds. When a delegate raised the question of industrial unions in the rubber plants, Hutcheson raised a point of order. The question had already been settled, he contended. Lewis objected; the delegate should be heard on a problem facing his own union. "This thing of raising points of order," he added, "is rather small potatoes."

"I was raised on small potatoes," Hutcheson replied.

As Lewis returned to his seat, he paused to tell Hutcheson that the opposition was pretty small stuff. "We could have made you small," was the reply. "We could have kept you off the executive council, you crazy bastard."

Lewis swung a wild haymaker. It caught Hutcheson on the jaw; the two men grappled, crashed against a table, and fell awkwardly to the floor. President Green wildly hammered his gavel as delegates tried to separate the two heavyweights.

Source: David F. Selvin, *The Thundering Voice of John L. Lewis* (New York: Lathrop, Lee, & Shepard, 1969), pp. 103–4.

---

and Refining Workers (Harvey Flemming); and the Mine, Mill, and Smelter Workers (Thomas Brown) met to form the Committee for Industrial Organization (CIO).[1]

Organizing the Industrial Work Force

Major efforts began to organize workers in basic industries: steel, textiles, rubber, and auto. Philip Murray headed the Steel Workers Organizing Committee (SWOC), which succeeded in establishing 150 locals totaling over 100,000 members by the end of 1936. In early 1937, through the secret efforts of John L. Lewis and Myron Taylor (head of U.S. Steel), SWOC was recognized as the U.S. Steel employees' bargaining agent. The 8-hour day and 40-hour week were granted, and a wage increase was won. The other steel firms were not so readily organized. During an attempt to organize Republic Steel, violence

[1] Joseph G. Rayback, *A History of American Labor* (New York: Free Press, 1966), pp. 348–50.

broke out at a parade, and 10 strikers were killed by Chicago police on Memorial Day, 1937.[2]

The auto workers were next. Despite the relatively high wages pioneered by Henry Ford, the jobs were tedious and fatiguing, and the owners had established private police forces to keep the workers in line.[3] Initial organizing began in 1936. By the end of the year the United Automobile Workers (UAW), under President Homer Martin, sought recognition from and bargaining with General Motors. GM refused, but worker sentiments were so strong that "quickie" strikes against the company resulted.[4]

Then, in late 1936, the UAW embarked on a strategy that succeeded in forcing GM recognition and negotiations—the "sit-down" strike. Auto workers at GM's Fisher body plants in Flint, Michigan, refused to leave their workplaces and took over the plants. GM viewed this as criminal trespass, but the workers asserted that job rights were superior to property rights. Injunctions obtained to oust the workers were ignored (see Exhibit 3–2). Attempts to persuade Michigan governor Frank Murphy to mobilize the militia to enforce the injunction failed. Realizing that the workers could hold out, GM capitulated in February 1937, agreeing to recognize the UAW and promising not to discriminate against union members.[5]

A short time later this tactic was used successfully to organize

EXHIBIT 3–2

Telegram from Sit-Down Strikers to Governor Murphy

"Governor, we have decided to stay in the plant. We have no illusions about the sacrifices which the decision will entail. We fully expect that if a violent effort is made to oust us many of us will be killed and we take this means of making it known to our wives, to our children, to the people of the state of Michigan and of the country that if this result follows from the attempt to eject us you are the one who must be held responsible for our deaths."

Source: Sidney Fine, *Sit-Down: The General Motors Strike of 1936–1937* (Ann Arbor: University of Michigan Press, 1969), p. 278.

---

[2] Foster Rhea Dulles, *Labor in America: A History*, 3rd ed. (New York: Crowell, 1966), pp. 299–302.

[3] Martin J. Gannon, "Entrepreneurship and Labor Relations at the Ford Motor Company," *Marquette Business Review*, Summer 1972, pp. 63–75.

[4] Rayback, *History of American Labor*, p. 353.

[5] Sidney Fine, *Sit-Down: The General Motors Strike of 1936–1937* (Ann Arbor: University of Michigan Press, 1969).

Chrysler workers as well as the glass, rubber, and textile industries. Industrial unionization had been achieved. In fact, by the end of 1937, the CIO unions' membership of 3,700,000 exceeded membership in the older AFL by 300,000.[6]

LEGISLATION

Organized labor did not achieve overnight success in its efforts to unionize workers. But, by the 1930s, public policy toward unions had shifted radically from the previous two decades. Prior to the Railway Labor Act in 1926, no legislation facilitated organization or bargaining. Courts had consistently enjoined unions from striking, organizing, picketing, and other activities, even if they were peacefully conducted. State laws regulating injunctive powers of state courts were likewise struck down by the Supreme Court in *Truax* v. *Corrigan*, a case testing an Arizona statute.[7]

Norris-LaGuardia Act (1932)

By the time the Norris-LaGuardia Act was passed in 1932, Congress had recognized the legitimacy of collective bargaining. In view of earlier judicial decisions, it pointed out that capital had been collectivizable through incorporation, while labor had not been allowed to collectivize. Up to that time, acceptance of a collective bargaining relationship had to devolve from a voluntary employer action.[8]

To grant organized labor relief from federal court injunctions against collective activity, the act guaranteed the rights to strike for any purpose, to pay strike benefits, to picket, to ask other employees to strike, to financially aid persons involved in court actions over labor disputes, to meet on strike strategy, and to organize using non-employees. The act safeguarded these rights by severely restricting the power of federal courts to issue injunctions in labor disputes. The act also forbade federal courts from enforcing the yellow-dog contract, which required employees or job applicants to agree, as a condition of employment, not to join a labor union. Previously, if a worker joined a union after signing such an agreement and was discharged as a result, federal courts could and did uphold the discharge.[9]

While the Norris-LaGuardia Act protected numerous previously enjoinable activities, it was neutral policy—it did not open any right to

---

[6] Rayback, *History of American Labor*, pp. 354–55.

[7] 257 U.S. 312 (1921).

[8] Benjamin Taylor and Fred Witney, *Labor Relations Law*, 2nd ed. (Englewood Cliffs, N.J.: Prentice-Hall, 1975), pp. 144–46.

[9] *Hitchman Coal Co.* v. *Mitchell*, 245 U.S. 229 (1917).

demand employer recognition. Other than the removal of the yellow-dog contract, explicit federal ground rules for employer conduct in labor–management relations still did not exist. This would be changed following the inauguration of President Franklin D. Roosevelt.

National Industrial Recovery Act (1933)

The National Industrial Recovery Act (NIRA), adopted in 1933, was not principally labor legislation. Its major focus was to encourage employers to band together and set prices and production quotas through industrial codes. To complete an industrial code, however, employers were required to include a provision enabling employees to bargain through representatives of their own choosing, free from employer interference.

NIRA survived for only two years before being found unconstitutional.[10] Labor is perhaps fortunate that the law did not survive, since it included no enforcement mechanism to guarantee rights to organize. It did, however, sow the seeds for the first piece of comprehensive labor legislation enacted in the United States.[11]

Wagner Act (National Labor Relations Act, 1935)

NIRA was bogging down even before it was ruled unconstitutional. Big business objected to the requirement that the legitimacy of union activities be recognized in their codes, and smaller businesses objected to the monopoly powers inherent in the codes. Unions lost their safeguards when NIRA was wiped out, although the 1935 amendments to the Railway Labor Act secured them for some transportation employees. The Wagner Act was rolled into place to resecure organizational rights as well as to specify activities that would be illegal if practiced by employers.[12]

Section 7, the heart of the act, specifies the rights of employees to engage in union activities: "Employees shall have the right to self-organization, to form, join, or assist labor organizations, to bargain collectively through representatives of their own choosing, and to engage in concerted activities, for the purpose of collective bargaining or other mutual aid or protection." To specify the types of actions presumed to interfere with Section 7 rights, Congress created Section 8. Section 8 broadly forbade interference with employees' rights to be represented, to bargain, to have their labor organizations free from

---

[10] *Schechter Poultry Corp.* v. *United States*, 295 U.S. 495 (1935).

[11] Taylor and Witney, *Labor Relations Law*, pp. 147–48.

[12] Dulles, *Labor in America*, pp. 273–75.

employer dominance, to be protected from employment discrimination for union activity, and to be free from retaliation for accusing the employer of an unlawful (unfair) labor practice.

To investigate violations of Section 8 and to determine whether employees desired representation, the Wagner Act established the National Labor Relations Board (NLRB), whose major duties were to determine which, if any, union was the employees' choice to represent them collectively and to hear and rule on alleged unfair labor practices.

The Wagner Act also statutorily established the agency relationship between the union and the employees. Where a union was certified as the choice of the majority of employees, all employees in that unit, regardless of union membership, would be represented by the union in issues of wages, hours, and terms and conditions of employment.

The Wagner Act did not apply to all employers and employees, although a major portion of the private sector was covered. Specifically exempted were the following employers: federal, state, and local governments; those subject to the Railway Labor Act; and labor organizations (except in a case when its members were acting as another's employees). Employee groups specifically exempted were supervisors and managers, agricultural workers, domestic employees, and family workers.

However, passage of the Wagner Act did not immediately presage a shift in U.S. labor relations. With NIRA recently having been declared void by the Supreme Court and with Section 7 of the Wagner Act closely duplicating the NIRA section, some employers expected the courts to rule against Congress on a constitutional challenge.

EMPLOYER INTRANSIGENCE

Congressional investigators disclosed that between 1933 and 1937, companies had systematically spied on union activities, infiltrated union governments, and spent almost $10 million for spying, strikebreaking, and munitions. In strike preparations, Youngstown Sheet and Tube amassed eight machine guns, 369 rifles, 190 shotguns, 450 revolvers, 109 gas guns, 3,000 rounds of gas, and almost 10,000 rounds of shotgun shells and bullets. Republic Steel purchased almost $80,000 worth of repellent gases and allegedly possessed the largest private arsenal in the United States.[13]

Another device employers used was a strategy called the *Mohawk Valley formula*, aimed at linking unions with agitators and commu-

---

[13] Ibid., pp. 277-78.

nists. Proponents of this strategy organized back-to-work drives during strikes, got local police to break up strikes, and aligned local interests against the focus of union activities.[14]

While employers doubted the constitutionality of the Wagner Act and remained adamant in opposing union activity, workers viewed the congressional action as a legitimization of their position. The act had created a mechanism for determining whether unions would represent units of employees. That almost half of the strikes between 1935 and 1937 were not over bargaining issues but rather to obtain recognition reflects the adamancy of employers as well as the new militancy of unions. Both sides had reasons to believe their positions were valid. Management had seen a long line of Supreme Court decisions adverse to labor, not the least of these being the striking down of NIRA, which was partially similar to the Wagner Act. Labor had seen sympathy for its position grow throughout the country and, with President Roosevelt consolidating his position through the overwhelming electoral endorsement of the New Deal in 1936, felt the Court would find it difficult to invalidate the law.[15]

The answer came on April 12, 1937, with the Supreme Court's decision in the *Jones & Laughlin* case.[16] The NLRB had previously determined that Jones & Laughlin had violated the Wagner Act by coercing employees and discriminating against union members. It had ordered 10 employees reinstated with back pay and told the firm to cease its unfair labor practices. The appeals court had held that the board's action was beyond the range of federal power, but the Supreme Court agreed to review the case.

In a 5–4 decision, the Supreme Court sided with the board and upheld the validity of the act. The Court held first that Congress may regulate employer activities under the Constitution's commerce clause. Second, it reaffirmed the right of employees to organize and recognized Congress' authority to restrict employer activities likely to disrupt organization. Third, the Court ruled that manufacturing, even if conducted locally, was a process involving interstate commerce. Fourth, it was reasonable for Congress to set rules and procedures governing employees' rights to organize. Finally, the Court found that the board's conduct at the hearing and its orders were regular, within the meaning of the act, and protected.

Thus, the Wagner Act passed the Supreme Court's test and opened an era of rapid industrial organization.

---

[14] Ibid., p. 278.

[15] Taylor and Witney, *Labor Relations Law*, pp. 161–64.

[16] *NLRB* v. *Jones & Laughlin Steel Corp.*, 301 U.S. 1 (1937).

LABOR POWER

Pre–World War II

The momentum gained by the CIO in its split from the AFL continued for the remainder of the 1930s. Both federations engaged in raids of each others members, and employers were helplessly caught in the midst of these disputes. These jurisdictional disputes created public hostility and led to some state legislation outlawing certain union activities.[17]

Although labor had been instrumental in getting its friends elected since the Depression began, its ranks split in 1940 when John L. Lewis abandoned President Roosevelt and announced his support for Wendell Wilkie. The split began in 1937 when Lewis had obviously expected the Democratic administration to repay labor for its campaign assistance by providing help during the GM sit-down strike. During the strike, Lewis said, "For six months the economic royalists represented by General Motors contributed their money and used their energy to drive this administration [Roosevelt's] out of power. The administration asked labor for help, and labor gave it. The same economic royalists now have their fangs in labor. The workers of this country expect the administration to help the workers in every legal way and to support the workers in General Motors plants."[18]

President Roosevelt did nothing except urge meetings between the UAW and the company. During the strike, some of Lewis's other pronouncements were equally dramatic (see Exhibit 3–3).

Later, during the "Little Steel" campaign, Roosevelt again incurred Lewis's wrath by criticizing labor and management jointly: "A plague on both your houses." Lewis responded by chastising Roosevelt: "It ill behooves one who has supped at labor's table and who has been sheltered in labor's house to curse with equal fervor and fine impartiality both labor and its adversaries when they become locked in deadly embrace."[19]

During the prewar period, it became apparent that an increasingly large number of industrial union staff positions were held by communists. They did not join in President Roosevelt's support for the Allies after Germany and Russia signed their nonaggression pact in 1939.

---

[17] A jurisdictional dispute occurs when two or more unions claim to (1) simultaneously represent or attempt to bargain for the same employee group or (2) simultaneously assert that their members are entitled by contract to perform a certain class of work.

[18] Rayback, *History of American Labor*, p. 368.

[19] Ibid.

EXHIBIT 3-3

The Rhetoric of John L. Lewis

[The mid 1930s were] a time of virtual class warfare. The National Guard was called out more than a dozen times a year; strikes were broken not only by "goons and ginks and company finks," in the words of the old labor song, but by tear gas and machine guns. And when a particularly disdainful Chrysler president asked for Lewis's comment in the midst of a negotiation inspired by a spontaneous sit-down at Chrysler, the six-foot-two Lewis stood up and said, "I am 99 percent of a mind to come around the table right now and wipe that damn sneer off your face." Lee Pressman, of the new CIO, later observed, "Lewis's voice at that moment was in every sense the voice of millions of unorganized workers who were being exploited by gigantic corporations. He was expressing at that instant their resentment, hostility, and their passionate desire to strike back."

When F.D.R. lumped labor with management, declaring his famous "plague on both your houses," . . . Lewis intoned: "Labor, like Israel, has many sorrows. Its women weep for their fallen, and they lament for the future of the children of the race. It ill behooves one who has supped at labor's table and who has been sheltered in labor's house to curse with equal fervor and fine impartiality both labor and its adversaries when they become locked in deadly embrace."

The "sup" to which he had made reference was a $500,000 UMW contribution to F.D.R.'s 1936 campaign. Lewis was unabashed about demanding his money's worth. "Everybody says I want my pound of flesh, that I gave Roosevelt $500,000 for his 1936 campaign, and I want quid pro quo. The UMW and the CIO have paid cash on the barrel for every piece of legislation gotten. . . . Is anyone fool enough to believe for one instant that we gave this money to Roosevelt because we are spellbound by his voice?"

Although Lewis was rarely photographed smiling ("That scowl is worth a million dollars," he once confided to a friend), one can see the demon gleam in his eye as he scratched out his answer [to Roosevelt's plea for a wartime no-strike pledge]. "If you want to use the power of the state to restrain me, as an agent of labor, then, sir, I submit that you should use the same power to restrain my adversary in this issue, who is an agent of capital. My adversary is a rich man named Morgan, who lives in New York," Signed, in letters which ran two and a half inches tall, "Yours humbly."

Source: Victor Navasky, "John L. Lewis, Union General," *Esquire*, December 1983, pp. 264–66.

1941 was a year of crisis for labor–management relations. The ambivalent stand of some industrial union leaders toward the war caused employers to brand them nonpatriotic. While this stand shifted when Philip Murray became president of the CIO in 1940, the label was not entirely removed. Employers refused to recognize unions, although union organization of Ford and Little Steel was finally successful. Perhaps for the first time labor's goal of "more, more, more now" was becoming intolerable to the general public. More than 4,300 strikes broke out in 1941, involving more than 8 percent of the work force. This widespread industrial disruption would probably have been moderated by congressional action had not the attack on Pearl Harbor involved the United States in World War II.[20]

World War II

At the outbreak of World War II, the AFL, the CIO, and management representatives pledged to produce together to meet the war effort. Labor pledged not to strike if a board were established to handle unresolved grievances. Management did not entirely concede, and, as a result, President Roosevelt established the National War Labor Board (NWLB). As the war got under way, prices rose more rapidly than in the previous several years. Labor's demands for wage increases grew, but the NWLB attempted to maintain a policy whereby wage increases (unless not recently attained) would equal changes in the cost of living. Labor objected to the dual check of collective bargaining and NWLB policy on wages, but the policy was not changed.[21]

Although no-strike pledges had been given, in 1945 4,750 strikes involved 3,470,000 workers, and 38 million worker-days were lost. This exceeded the pre-war high of 28,400,000 days in 1937. Major sporadic strikes in the coal industry, led by John L. Lewis, were particularly evident to the public. At one point the coal mines were seized and run by Secretary of the Interior Harold Ickes (see Exhibit 3–4).[22]

The strike activity led to congressional action with the passage of the War Labor Disputes Act over President Roosevelt's veto. This act authorized the seizure of plants involved in labor disputes, made strikes and lockouts in defense industries a criminal offense, required 30 days' notice to the NWLB of a pending dispute, and required the NLRB to monitor strike votes.[23]

While this overview of World War II has not reflected accommodation and innovation, the evidence reveals they were there. In only 46 of 17,650 dispute cases going before the NWLB did the parties fail to reach or accept agreements. The war experience also led to a widespread acceptance of fringe benefits in lieu of wage increases. Holidays, vacations, sick leaves, and shift differentials began to be approved by the NWLB as part of labor contracts. For the first time, labor shortages led to policies advocating equal employment opportunities for minorities and equal pay for men and women in the same jobs.[24]

---

[20] Ibid., pp. 370–73.

[21] Philip Taft, *Organized Labor in American History* (New York: Harper & Row, 1964), pp. 546–52.

[22] Ibid., pp. 553–56.

[23] Ibid., p. 557.

[24] Ibid., pp. 559–62.

EXHIBIT 3-4

Comments by President Roosevelt on Coal Strikes during 1943

On June 23, the president issued a statement in which he said that "the action of the leaders of the United Mine Workers coal miners has been intolerable—and has rightly stirred up the anger and disapproval of the overwhelming mass of the American people."

He declared that the mines would be operated by the government under the terms of the board's directive order of June 18.

He stated that "the government had taken steps to set up the machinery for inducting into the armed services all miners subject to the Selective Service Act who absented themselves, without just cause, from work in the mines under government operation." Since the "Selective Service Act does not authorize induction of men above 45 years into the armed services, I intend to request the Congress to raise the age limit for noncombat service to 65 years. I shall make that request of the Congress so that if at any time in the future there should be a threat of interruption of work in plants, mines, or establishments owned by the government, or taken possession of by the government, the machinery will be available for prompt action."

Source: Arthur Suffern, "The National War Labor Board and Coal," in *The Termination Report of the National War Labor Board, vol. 1: Industrial Disputes and Wage Stabilization in Wartime* (Washington, D.C.: U.S. Government Printing Office, 1948), p. 1009.

Reconversion

As the war ended, consumers anticipated the return of goods unavailable during the war. Labor looked forward to wage increases to offset the cost-of-living increases that had taken place during the war. The inevitable clash of labor and management led to the greatest single-year period of labor conflict in U.S. history. Between August 1945 and August 1946, 4,630 strikes involved 4,900,000 workers and the loss of 119,800,000 worker-days (or 1.62 percent of total days available). Most major industries were affected, with major strikes occurring in coal, rails, autos, and steel. These were settled with wage increases averaging about 18.5 cents per hour; and some, especially in steel, resulted in price increases as well.[25]

The end of the war, the strikes, and the election of a more conservative Congress led to legislation that balanced the power between unions and managements.

---

[25] Ibid., pp. 563–78.

RESTORING THE BALANCE

The Wagner Act was passed during a period in which industrial organizing was just beginning and employers had an overwhelming array of weapons with which to battle labor. The act was to have struck a balance between the contenders. Over the 10 years since its passage, however, the challenger had become the champion. The strikes of 1941, the coal problems during World War II, and the labor difficulties encountered in 1946 all stimulated legislation to expand and clarify rules applying to the practice of U.S. labor relations.

The Wagner Act addressed only employer unfair labor practices, but critics of the labor movement argued that unions could also engage in tactics that might coerce individual employees and constitute a refusal to bargain collectively. The balancing legislation was enacted in amendments and additions to the Wagner Act entitled the Labor–Management Relations Act of 1947, better known as Taft-Hartley.

Taft-Hartley Act

Employee rights were expanded in Section 7 to include not only the right to join but also the right to refrain from union activities unless a contract between an employer and a union required union activity. This right to refrain allowed collective bargaining agreements to require, at most, joining a union or paying dues. But Congress went further by adding Section 14(b), which enabled states to pass more-restrictive legislation regarding employees' rights to refrain from union activities. In these states, right-to-work laws make illegal any contract provision requiring union membership as a condition of continued employment. Most of the states passing right-to-work laws are either in the South and West or in predominantly agricultural states where union strength has never been high.[26] Efforts at passage in Ohio and California failed in 1958, and Indiana voters repealed a state statute in 1965. Right-to-work laws are highly emotional issues to both their proponents and their opponents. Organized labor refers to them as "right-to-wreck" laws, enabling nonmembers to act as free riders by using union gains applicable to an entire bargaining unit without contributing money or effort to the cause. Proponents see the laws as essential to freedom of association and protective of the right to join or

---

[26] Alabama, Arizona, Arkansas, Florida, Georgia, Iowa, Kansas, Louisiana, Mississippi, Nebraska, Nevada, North Carolina, North Dakota, South Carolina, South Dakota, Tennessee, Texas, Utah, Virginia, and Wyoming.

not join organizations. The heat of the rhetoric from both sides is probably greater than the impact of the statutes, as we will note in Chapters 5, 6, and 7.

Section 8 was amended to restrict a union's treatment of its members, recognizing the agency role the union plays for all bargaining unit members. Unions were required to bargain in good faith with employers and were forbidden to strike to gain recognition or to put pressure on uninvolved second parties to get at a primary employer.

Title II was an entirely new addition to U.S. labor legislation. First, it established the Federal Mediation and Conciliation Service (FMCS) to aid settlement of unresolved contractual disputes. These acts of assistance could be requested by the parties or offered directly by the FMCS. Second, provision was made for intervention in strikes likely to create a national emergency. A president who determined that a current or pending labor dispute imperiled the nation could convene a board of inquiry to determine the issues and positions of the parties. If the president then believed it was a national emergency, the attorney general could seek to have the strike or lockout enjoined for 80 days. During the first 60 days of the injunction, the parties would continue negotiations. At the end of this period, if agreement had not been reached, the board of inquiry would report the last position of both parties. The NLRB would then hold an election in which union members would vote to accept or reject management's last offer. The results of the election would be certified by the end of the 80 days. If the membership voted to accept, the contract would be ratified; if to reject, they would be free to strike, although the president was directed to submit a report to Congress so that it could consider taking action.

Title III dealt with suits by and against labor organizations. Suits seeking damages from either employers or unions for violating labor contracts were permitted. Recovery of damages was restricted to the assets of the organization, not the individual members. Union officials were forbidden to accept money from employers, and employers could not offer inducements to them. This title further provided that boycotts to force an employer to cease doing business with others (i.e., a struck or nonunion firm) were illegal. Corporations and labor unions were forbidden to make political contributions. Finally, federal employees were forbidden to strike.

The overall thrust of the legislation balanced the relative power of the contenders and provided mechanisms (the FMCS and national emergency dispute procedures) to reduce the likelihood of a recurrence of labor strife of the magnitude seen in 1946. Since the bill represented a retreat from the initiatives labor had previously enjoyed, it was, to say the least, not greeted with enthusiasm in that quarter. But the bill satisfied business, Congress, and the public. The bill passed by wide margins in both houses, was vetoed by President Truman, and repassed over his veto.

RETRENCHMENT AND MERGER

The AFL and CIO both regarded the Taft-Hartley Act as a "slave-labor" bill. They foresaw the possibility that labor disputes would be again subject to injunctions through the national emergency procedures.

In one major case where the emergency procedures might arguably have been employed, President Truman seized the nation's steel mills in 1952 rather than invoke the national emergency steps. When the Supreme Court declared his action unconstitutional, he was forced to return operations to management, and a strike ensued. We will examine the mechanisms and uses of Taft-Hartley injunctions in greater detail in Chapter 11.

Organized labor realized two things following Taft-Hartley. First, it would have to exert more influence in legislative activity and adopt a more publicly advocative stance on issues concerning labor. Second, the strength of management and labor had been equalized by the Taft-Hartley Act. The time had come to direct labor's energies toward unity rather than division. The old guard present at the sundering of the AFL was disappearing. Green and Murray both died in 1952. Their deaths resulted in the election of a new president of the AFL, George Meany, and of the CIO, Walter Reuther. John L. Lewis's UMW was unaffiliated, thus greatly reducing the historic friction.[27]

Merger

The first step toward rapprochement was the ratification of a no-raid agreement by AFL and CIO conventions in 1954. A Joint Unity Committee was also established to explore ways to devise a merger. On February 9, 1955, a merger formed the combined AFL–CIO. George Meany became president of the merged federations.[28]

Meany expounded the merged federation's goals in 1955. He reendorsed Gompers' concept of "more" as it applied to a person's standard and quality of living. He reaffirmed labor's commitment to collective bargaining. He was unwilling to involve labor in management but demanded that management's stewardship be high (see Exhibit 3–5).[29] Essentially, his essay reiterated the goals and past behavior of the union movement: careful, member-oriented activity, yet with a degree of social concern, recognizing that advances for its members may lead to advances for society.

The merged AFL–CIO did not become a more powerful movement than the single federations had been in the past. In fact, union membership as a proportion of the labor force reached its peak in 1956 at

---

[27] Dulles, *Labor in America*, pp. 360–72.

[28] Ibid., pp. 372–74.

[29] George Meany, "What Labor Means by 'More'," *Fortune*, March 1955, pp. 92–93.

EXHIBIT 3–5

George Meany on Labor's Role

Plain realism dictates, therefore, that our thinking about the America of the quarter century ahead must be limited to goals rather than to predictions. Yet long-range goals, if they are meaningful, originate in the world of today and are shaped by one's tradition and one's philosophy. In a single man's lifetime, 25 years is a long time, perhaps half the span of his mature, vigorous life. Institutions, and the men who reflect them, have a longer perspective than individuals alone, and in the A.F. of L. our traditions and our philosophy have emerged from an experience of 75 years. Our goals can be understood only in terms of that experience. Moreover, the goals of a future but a quarter of a century away will not appear so unreal when measured against a philosophy hammered out by millions of Americans over the course of three quarters of a century.

Our goals as trade unionists are modest, for we do not seek to recast American society in any particular doctrinaire or ideological image. We seek an ever-rising standard of living. Sam Gompers once put the matter succinctly. When asked what the labor movement wanted, he answered, "More." If by a better standard of living we mean not only more money but more leisure and a richer cultural life, the answer remains "More."

But how do we get "more"? Imperfect in many details as our system may be, this country has adopted a flexible method for increasing the standard of living while maintaining freedom. It is the method of voluntary collective bargaining, of free decision making outside the coercions of government, in the solution of economic disagreement. And it is through the give-and-take of collective bargaining that we seek to achieve our goals.

Source: George Meany, "What Labor Means by 'More'," *Fortune,* March 1955, p. 92.

---

about one third. By 1964, this proportion had fallen to 30 percent, and an absolute decline of 700,000 members had been recorded. Part of the decline was due to less-aggressive organizing, some to better nonunion employee relations, and a portion to the reduced relative proportion of blue-collar manufacturing workers in the labor force. Whatever the reasons, the 1956–65 decade was one of malaise and retreat for the labor movement.[30] Unions did not gain stature in the public eye either, but they did gain some unwanted notoriety as congressional investigators uncovered gross malfeasance by some major national union officers.

---

[30] Dulles, *Labor in America,* pp. 377–81.

Corruption

In 1957, the Senate Select Committee on Improper Activities in the Labor–Management Field convened its investigations under Chairman John L. McClellan. For the next two and a half years, the American public was exposed to televised hearings in which a parade of labor officials invoked the Fifth Amendment to avoid self-incrimination.

The Teamsters Union drew the lion's share of the spotlight as witnesses disclosed that its president, Dave Beck, had converted union funds to his own use, borrowed money from employers, and received kickbacks from labor "consultants." James R. Hoffa was accused of breaking Teamster strikes and of covertly running his own trucking operation. "Sweetheart" contracts, offering substandard benefits and guaranteeing labor peace, were uncovered in the New York area in unions chartered by the Teamsters and operated by racketeers.

Other unions, such as the Bakery and Confectionery Workers, Operating Engineers, Carpenters, and United Textile Workers, were also involved. Management contributed to the corruption by providing payoffs for sweetheart contracts, which prevented other unions from organizing but paid substandard rates.[31]

The publicity associated with the hearings cast a pall over the entire labor movement. By inference, all labor was corrupt. The AFL–CIO investigated internally and considered charges against the Allied Industrial Workers, Bakers, Distillers, Laundry Workers, Textile Workers, and Teamsters. The Textile Workers, Distillers, and Allied Industrial Workers agreed to mandated changes. The Bakers, Laundry Workers, and Teamsters did not and were expelled from the AFL–CIO in 1957.[32] Meanwhile, the congressional investigations led to legislation to reduce the likelihood of corrupt practices and also to amend the Taft-Hartley Act.

Landrum-Griffin Act

As a result of congressional investigations, considerable legislative interest in monitoring internal union affairs was expressed. In 1959, Congress passed legislation giving the U.S. Department of Labor greater power to audit union financial and political affairs. The Landrum-Griffin Act, formally titled the Labor–Management Reporting and Disclosure Act of 1959, also amended portions of the Taft-Hartley Act.

The Landrum-Griffin Act contained seven major titles. Title I

---

[31] Taft, *Organized Labor*, pp. 698–704.
[32] Ibid., p. 704.

established rights of individual union members to freedom of speech, equal voting rights, control of dues increases, copies of labor agreements under which they worked, and retained the right to sue. Title II required labor organizations to file periodic reports of official and financial activities and financial holdings of union officers and employees and required employers to report financial transactions with unions. Title III required reporting of trusteeships (in which the national union takes over a local union's operations) and specified conditions under which trusteeship would be allowed. Title IV dealt with internal union elections. Title V required bonding of officers, restricted loans, and prohibited recently convicted felons from holding office. Title VI contained miscellaneous provisions, including the prohibition of extortionate picketing.

Title VII amended the Taft-Hartley Act. Major changes strengthened the prohibitions against secondary boycotts (pressuring uninvolved employers to cease doing business with a struck or nonunion firm), restricted the use of picketing of unorganized employers to force recognition, made "hot-cargo" clauses (wherein employers agree not to use nonunion goods) illegal, reestablished the legality of what amounted to a closed shop[33] in building and construction, and established minimum levels of economic activity necessary before the NLRB would assert its jurisdiction in representation and unfair labor practice cases.

RECENT LEGISLATIVE ATTEMPTS

The 1970s saw several legislative initiatives to modify and expand Taft-Hartley. One was successful: in 1974, coverage of the Taft-Hartley Act was extended to employees of private nonprofit hospitals. Additional rules governing collective bargaining in private health care facilities were also fashioned.

A construction industry bargaining bill passed in late 1974 would have allowed a union in dispute with one of the contractors on a site to picket the whole site rather than only its reserved gate. This so-called common situs picketing would have established more pressure for settlement since all workers would likely refuse to cross picket lines established to cover all entrance gates. As an inducement to gain the support of a majority of Congress, a comprehensive construction bargaining mechanism aimed at establishing regional and national control of settlements was included. All parties predicted the bill would become law since President Ford had indicated he would sign if the comprehensive bargaining title were included. But in January 1976 he

---

[33] A closed shop requires a worker to be a union member as a condition of obtaining employment.

vetoed it. The bill was reintroduced without the bargaining titles after President Carter's inauguration, but it failed to pass.

In 1977, a bill amending Taft-Hartley to make organizing and representation easier for unions was introduced. The amendments would have imposed punitive damages on employers who intentionally interfered with employees' Section 7 rights. A great deal of acrimony surrounded this bill, and both labor and management exaggerated its supposed equity and punitive aspects. The labor reform bill passed the House but failed, by one vote, to survive a Senate filibuster during the summer of 1978.

Finally, attempts were made in the mid-1970s to introduce and pass a law similar to the Wagner Act for employees of federal, state, and local governments. The prime movers behind this were the National Education Association, the American Federation of Teachers, and the American Federation of State, County, and Municipal Employees. Labor's initial optimism about the law's chances of debate and passage vanished in the dust clouds surrounding the virtual financial collapse of New York City. Critics argued that public employee unions were already too powerful, as evidenced by high pay rates and heavy future pension liabilities cities and states had incurred through bargaining.

PUBLIC–SECTOR UNION GROWTH

As private-sector organizing activity sank into the doldrums of the late 1950s and early 1960s, public employees became increasingly interested in unionization. In the federal service, the Taft-Hartley Act had forbidden strikes. Most state statutes forbade strikes by public employees, generally made strikers ineligible for any gains won by striking, and included summary discharge as a penalty. Concomitantly, most federal and state statutes had no mechanism for the recognition of bargaining representatives.

Federal Executive Orders

In 1962, President Kennedy issued Executive Order 10988, a breakthrough for federal employee unions. This order enabled a majority union to bargain collectively with a government agency. Negotiations open to the union were restricted to terms and conditions of employment, not wage levels. Unions could not represent employees if they advocated strikes or the right to strike. While a grievance procedure was outlined, final determination was to be made by the federal government, not an impartial arbitrator.[34]

---

[34] Taylor and Witney, *Labor Relations Law*, pp. 545–49.

Executive Order 11491, effective January 1, 1970, amended 10988. It required secret-ballot elections for recognition, established procedures for determining appropriate bargaining units, required Landrum-Griffin–type reporting by unions, and granted arbitration as a final settlement procedure for grievances. The order specified unfair labor practices and created procedures for redressing them. Finally, a Federal Impasse Panel was created to render binding decisions when collective negotiations reach an impasse. This provision ameliorated the statutory no-strike provisions facing federal government employees.[35]

Executive Order 11616, implemented in August 1971, allowed professionals in an agency to decide whether to join a bargaining unit, allowed individuals to pursue unfair labor practice charges through grievance channels or through the assistant secretary of labor for labor–management relations, required a grievance procedure in exclusively represented units (but also narrowed the range of issues allowed arbitration), and allowed some negotiating on government time.[36]

Executive Order 11491 required the Federal Labor Relations Council(FLRC) to review the status of labor relations at the federal level and report to the president. As a result of its recommendations, President Ford issued Executive Order 11838 in 1974. This order provided for the consolidation of some bargaining units, increased the area covered in negotiations, and dealt with structural aspects of the FLRC.[37]

Civil Service Reform Act

Title VII of the Civil Service Reform Act of 1976 regulates labor–management relations in the federal service. The act codifies the provisions written into the executive orders. It also establishes the Federal Labor Relations Authority, which acts as the federal service equivalent of the NLRB. Requirements and mechanisms for alleviating bargaining impasses and unresolved grievances under the contract are also spelled out.[38]

State and Local Governments

Since no federal law asserts jurisdiction over state and local employees, the laws for and development of these employee unions differ substantially. For most areas, the development is a relatively recent phe-

35 Ibid., pp. 550–53.

36 Ibid., pp. 553–55.

37 Murray A. Nesbitt, *Labor Relations in the Federal Government Service* (Washington, D.C.: Bureau of National Affairs, 1976), p. 133.

38 Henry B. Frazier III, "Labor–Management Relations in the Federal Government," *Labor Law Journal*, March 1979, pp. 131–38.

nomenon, with police and firefighters more likely to have specific laws enabling organization and specifying bargaining. Employees occasionally acquired unionization when previously private employers, such as local transit companies, were taken over by public authorities. Chapter 15 details the development and growth of labor unions in public employment.

PASSING THE TORCH

The year 1982 was the 100th year since the founding of the American Federation of Labor. In that time, with the exception of a one-year period, the AFL and its successor, the AFL–CIO, have had only four presidents: Samuel Gompers, William Green, George Meany, and Lane Kirkland. George Meany retired from the presidency in November 1979 at the age of 85. He died January 10, 1980. Meany's service to the labor movement was great, but his passing, like the earlier passings of Green and Murray, created opportunities for rapprochement and change. Since Lane Kirkland took office, the United Auto Workers have reaffiliated with the AFL–CIO, and the Teamsters have been invited to consider rejoining.

But while organized labor changes, it maintains its ties to the past and its interest in outcomes important to its members. Exhibit 3–6 contains excerpts from George Meany's farewell address, delivered just two months before his death.

SUMMARY

The 1930s provided the environment necessary for successful industrial unions. Both the Norris-LaGuardia and Wagner acts were passed, eliminating injunctions against most union activities and establishing collective bargaining as the preferred mode for resolving employment disputes.

The CIO was formed by dissident AFL leaders. It concentrated its early organizing efforts in primary industries, such as auto, steel, and rubber. Employers strongly resisted, but sit-down strikes and changes in public policy toward unions strengthened the CIO's efforts. By 1937, membership in the CIO was moving toward 4 million and had surpassed the AFL.

Industrial strife increased until the outbreak of World War II. The National War Labor Board was established to cope with employment problems during the wartime mobilization and to resolve disputes. Arbitration of grievances was introduced and later incorporated into collective bargaining agreements.

Following the war, strikes reached unprecedented levels. In 1947,

EXHIBIT 3-6

Excerpts from George Meany's Farewell Address, November 1979

Today is the last time I will have the honor of opening a convention of the AFL–CIO. By coincidence it is also an historic anniversary for the American trade union movement.

Ninety-eight years ago on this day—in Pittsburgh, Pennsylvania—107 trade unionists established the first, continuing national trade union center. The AFL–CIO is its direct descendant.

On November 15, 1881, the Federation of Organized Trades and Labor Unions was born for one simple reason—the unions of that day knew—as we know—that in unity there is strength.

Of course, there were many trade unions, assemblies and councils in many cities, even national and international labor unions in 1881. They had already made many important gains. But the founders of this great movement knew that much more could be accomplished through a combination of all those organizations.

So they organized and adopted a charter to "promote the general welfare of the industrial classes and secure that justice which isolated and separated trade and labor unions can never fully command."

Each succeeding generation of trade unions has given that charter life and breath. It has been a torch handed down from generation to generation— sometimes flickering, but never dimmed. It is now our responsibility—individually and collectively—to preserve that charter, to give it life and meaning in our time, and to pass it, intact and shining, to those who follow us; to carry that torch high, with pride, with honor.

Despite what some of my friends in the media may believe, I did not attend that convention in 1881. But I have read the proceedings and I believe Gompers, Foster, Leffingwell and all the courageous founders of our movement would look with favor upon the stewardship of their successors. . . .

* * * * *

I am confident that the labor movement is about to embark on another period of significant growth and expansion. The growth in unionization among public workers is continuing at a strong pace—and there are significant organizing breakthroughs by unions in the service trades. White-collar and professional workers are seeking organization. Farm workers are proving their strength against the most oppressive tactics used by any employers anywhere in the nation. . . .

* * * * *

Today the American trade union movement is vital, dynamic, growing. It is strong and unified.

But it needs to continue to grow, to consolidate its strength. And, I predict with certainty, it will.

the Taft-Hartley Act passed over President Truman's veto, provided for national emergency dispute procedures, established the Federal Mediation and Conciliation Service, and designated several union unfair labor practices. In 1959, the Landrum-Griffin Act limited the possibility of corruption in union–management relations.

The AFL and the CIO merged in 1955; but, shortly after, the union movement reached its maximum growth as a share of the labor force. With the exception of the public sector, union membership has recently been on the decline. Later chapters identify the causes of these changes and their consequences for the labor movement.

DISCUSSION QUESTIONS

1. Why was the AFL reluctant to organize industrial workers during the early 1930s?

2. What were the major reasons for the rapid increase in labor's power during the 1930s and 1940s?

3. Why didn't the industrial unions embrace uplift or revolutionary unionism instead of business unionism?

4. Who were the most effective union leaders during the 1930s and 1940s? What are your criteria for effectiveness? Would these same leaders be effective now?

5. What impact did the 1988 presidential and congressional elections have on the growth and practices of the labor movement?

CHAPTER 4

Labor Law and Federal Agencies

This chapter covers federal law related to collective bargaining. The relevant laws include the Railway Labor Act, the Norris-LaGuardia Act, the Wagner Act (as amended by Taft-Hartley and later legislation), the Landrum-Griffin Act, and the Civil Service Reform Act.

These laws established several government agencies. Other agencies also influence labor relations directly. This chapter gives an overview of the statutes, major government agencies, and their organizational structures as of 1986.

In studying this chapter, keep the following questions in mind:

1. What specific types of activites are regulated?
2. In what areas have regulations been extended or retracted?
3. What employee groups are excluded or exempted from various aspects of the regulations?
4. How do administrative agencies interact with employers and unions in implementing laws and regulations?

OVERVIEW

As noted in Chapters 2 and 3, statutory labor law is relatively recent in the United States. Current laws governing organizing and collective bargaining date back to 1926, when the Railway Labor Act was enacted. Since then, five other significant pieces of legislation have followed: Norris-LaGuardia (1932), Wagner (1935), Taft-Hartley (1947), Landrum-Griffin (1959), and the Civil Service Reform Act, Title VII (1978). Each was enacted to clarify and/or constrain the roles of management and labor. While six acts may not seem a significant number, it is important to remember that labor relations is generally more legislated in the United States than in most western European countries.

This chapter presents a broad overview of the laws in tabular form and then discusses the legislation in detail. Following the laws, federal agencies are identified and discussed. Table 4–1 lists each piece of major legislation and the areas of labor relations to which they apply.

TABLE 4–1

Federal Labor Law

Law	Coverage	Major provisions	Federal agencies
Railway Labor Act	Nonmanagerial rail and airline employees and employers in the private sector.	Employees may choose bargaining representatives for collective bargaining; no yellow-dog contracts; dispute settlement procedures include mediation, arbitration, and emergency boards.	National Mediation Board; National Board of Adjustment.
Norris-LaGuardia Act	All private-sector employers and labor organizations.	Outlaws injunctions for nonviolent union activities; outlaws yellow-dog contracts.	
Labor–Management Relations Act (originally passed as Wagner Act, amended by Taft-Hartley and Landrum-Griffin acts).	Nonmanagerial employees in nonagricultural private sector not covered by Railway Labor Act; postal workers.	Employees may choose bargaining representatives for collective bargaining; both labor and management must bargain in good faith; unfair labor practices include discrimination for union activities, secondary boycotts, and refusal to bargain; national emergency dispute procedures are established.	National Labor Relations Board; Federal Mediation and Conciliation Service.
Landrum-Griffin Act	All private-sector employers and labor organizations.	Specifies and guarantees individual rights of union members; prohibits certain management and union conduct; requires union financial disclosures.	U.S. Department of Labor.
Civil Service Reform Act, Title VII	All nonuniformed, nonmanagerial federal service employees and agencies.	Employees may choose representatives for collective bargaining; bargaining rights established for non-economic and nonstaffing issues; requires arbitration of unresolved grievances.	Federal Labor Relations Authority.

RAILWAY LABOR ACT

The Railway Labor Act applies to rail and air carriers and their employees. To be covered by the act, an employee must not be a supervisor or manager. The act claims to have five general purposes:

1. Avoiding service interruptions.
2. Eliminating any restrictions on joining a union.
3. Guaranteeing the freedom of employees in any matter of self-organization.
4. Providing for prompt dispute settlement.
5. Enabling prompt grievance settlement.

Section 2 prescribes a number of general duties: (1) the carriers and employees are called on to maintain agreements relating to pay, rules, and working conditions and to settle disputes about these to avoid the interruption of services; (2) the disputes are to be settled by representatives of the carriers and the employees; (3) the parties cannot influence the choice of the other's representative, and the chosen representative need not be an employee of the carrier; (4) employees are free to choose a representative by majority vote, and this representative shall be free from any dominance or financial relationship to the carrier; (5) no one can be forced to refrain from union membership or activities as a condition of employment; (6) a procedure for settling grievances must be established and be consistent with the provisions of the act; (7) no aspect of pay, rules, or working conditions can be unilaterally changed by the employer if covered in a contract; (8) carriers must notify employees of their intention to comply with the act; (9) the National Mediation Board (established by the Railway Labor Act) will determine majority status of a union where questioned; (10) criminal penalties for violations of the act are established; and (11) if unions are shown to be nondiscriminatory in fees and dues, union-shop clauses may be negotiated with the carriers.[1]

Section 3 established the National Railroad Board of Adjustment. The board consists of an equal number of union and management members and is empowered to settle grievances of both parties. If the board is deadlocked on a grievance, it must obtain a referee to hear the case and make an award. Awards are binding on the parties, and prevailing parties may sue in federal district courts for orders to enforce the awards.

Section 4 established the National Mediation Board, composed of three members appointed by the president. Section 5 detailed the functions of the board. First, the board's services may be offered or

---

[1] A union-shop clause requires an employee to join a union as a condition of continued employment.

requested to mediate a bargaining dispute. If agreement is not reached through mediation, the board is to urge the parties to arbitrate. Second, the board may be called on to interpret mediated contract agreements. Third, if the parties cannot agree on an arbitrator, the board is empowered to appoint one.

Section 6 requires 30-day notice of an intent to renegotiate a contract. Sections 7, 8, and 9 deal with arbitration, selection of arbitrators, procedures, and enforcement of awards.

Section 10 states that when the National Mediation Board determines a dispute will deprive a section of the country of transportation, the president is empowered to establish an emergency board of neutrals. The emergency board has a fact-finding duty in the dispute, and no party involved in the dispute may change employment conditions within 30 days of the board's filing of conclusions.

Sections 11 through 13 extend coverage of the act to air carriers.

Overview

In comparison with later acts, the Railway Labor Act is excessively detailed concerning dispute handling. Subsequent bills generally left this up to the parties. Another problem in the Railway Labor Act is the requirement that employees be organized by craft (or occupational area). This forces the employer to bargain with several unions, some of which may have conflicting goals.

One should temper criticism of the act, however, by observing that the technological changes railroads faced would have engendered a great deal of controversy. The advent of diesel locomotives rendered firemen obsolete. Rather than facing slow attrition, as would occur in most industrial unions, a single craft was faced with rapid extinction. A further assessment of the Railway Labor Act's relative effectiveness is covered in a section of Chapter 11 analyzing impasse procedures.

NORRIS–LaGUARDIA ACT (1932)

The Norris-LaGuardia Act was the first piece of legislation drafted to protect the rights of unions and workers to engage in union activity. It is comprehensive in its application to workers and firms and absolute in its prescriptions. The federal court system has been extremely reluctant to allow any enforcement loopholes to develop.

The Norris-LaGuardia Act has two major purposes. First, it forbids federal courts to issue injunctions against a variety of specifically described union activities. Second, it forbids employers to require employees to sign yellow-dog contracts (in which they agree that continued employment is dependent on abstention from union membership or activities). These contracts had been upheld by the Supreme Court.[2]

The act recognizes that freedom to associate for collective bargaining purposes may be seen as the corollary of the collectivization of capital through incorporation. Injunctions and yellow-dog contracts interfere with freedom of association.

Besides the absolute prohibition of yellow-dog contracts, a number of activities are specified as outside the scope of injunctive relief. These specifications apply regardless of whether the act is done by an individual, a group, or a union. The following cannot be enjoined:

1. Stopping or refusing to work.
2. Union membership.
3. Paying or withholding strike benefits, unemployment benefits, and the like to people participating in labor disputes.
4. Aid or assistance for persons suing or being sued.
5. Publicizing a labor dispute in a nonviolent, nonfraudulent manner.
6. Assembly to organize.
7. Notifying anyone that any of these acts are to be performed.
8. Agreeing to engage or not engage in any of these acts.
9. Advising others to do any of these acts.

The Norris-LaGuardia Act also finally and completely laid to rest the 18th-century conspiracy doctrine. Section 5 prohibits injunctions against any of the above activities if pursued in a nonviolent manner. The effects of the *Danbury Hatters*[3] decision (which required union members to pay boycott damages) were substantially diminished by Section 6. That section mandates that an individual or labor organization may not be held accountable for unlawful acts of its leadership unless those acts were directed or ratified by the membership.

Section 7 ensures the act may not be used as a cover for violent and destructive actions. This section states that an injunction may be issued under the following circumstances:

1. Substantial or irreparable injury to property will occur.
2. Greater injury will be inflicted on the party requesting the injunction than the injunction would cause on the adversary.
3. No adequate legal remedy exists.
4. Authorities are either unable or unwilling to give protection.

Before an injunction can be granted, the union must be given the opportunity for rebuttal. If an immediate restraining order is sought and there is insufficient time for an adversary proceeding, the em-

---

[2] *Hitchman Coal & Coke Co.* v. *Mitchell*, 245 U.S. 229 (1917).
[3] *Loewe* v. *Lawlor*, 208 U.S. 274 (1908).

ployer must deposit a bond to compensate the union for possible injuries done to it by the injunction. Section 7 also requires surgical rather than broadbrush injunctions; that is, the injunction is to be issued against only those persons or associations actually causing the problems.

Section 8 further restricts injunction-granting powers by requiring the requester to try to settle the dispute before asking for the injunction. Section 9 states that the injunction cannot be issued against all union activities in the case, only those leading to the injury. For example, mass picketing might be enjoined if it is violent; but the strike, payments of strike benefits, and so on could not be enjoined.

While the Norris-LaGuardia Act did not require an employer to recognize a union or bargain with it, it provided labor some leverage in organizing and bargaining activity. Labor could, henceforth, bring pressure on the employer through strikes, boycotts, and the like, without worrying about federal court injunctions.

WAGNER AND TAFT–HARTLEY ACTS (AS AMENDED)

The Wagner and Taft-Hartley acts were enacted 12 years apart, but Taft-Hartley was, to a large extent, an amendment of and extension to the Wagner Act. In 1959, the Landrum-Griffin Act extended the amending process. Finally, the Taft-Hartley act was amended in 1974 to apply to private nonprofit health care organizations and modified some provisions for these organizations only. All of these laws aimed to make clear the public policy preference for collective bargaining as the desired mode for resolving differences in the employment relationship and for roughly balancing the power of labor and management. As such, the Wagner Act, passed during a period of relative weakness for organized labor, only spoke to employer practices. As the pendulum swung in the other direction, the Taft-Hartley amendments added union practices to the proscribed list. Finally, Landrum-Griffin attempted to "fine-tune" the statutes consistent with day-to-day realities. We now examine the major substantive provisions of these laws.

Section 2, Taft-Hartley

Section 2 defines the terms used in the act. From our standpoint, the most important definitions are related to the terms *employer, employee, supervisor,* and *professional employee.*

Employer. An employer is an organization or a manager acting on behalf of the organization. However, certain types of organizations are specifically excluded from the act's jurisdiction. These are federal, state, and local governments or any organizations wholly owned by these agencies (except the U.S. Postal Service); persons subject to the Railway Labor Act; and union representatives when acting as bargaining agents.

Employee.   An employee does not necessarily have to be a member of an organization against which a labor dispute is directed. For example, if firm A is being struck and employees of firm B refuse to cross the picket lines, even though no dispute exists with B, B's workers are considered employees for labor–management relations purposes under the act. An individual also is considered to remain an employee if on strike for a contract or if on strike or being discharged as the result of an employer's unfair labor practice. Employees are considered to remain within this definition, even if employers do not consider them employees, until they take new employment at or above a level equivalent to their previous jobs. Domestic workers, agricultural workers, independent contractors,[4] individuals employed by a spouse or parent,[5] or persons covered by the Railway Labor Act are excluded.

Supervisor.   A supervisor is someone with the authority to make personnel decisions and to administer a labor agreement through the use of independent judgment. Examples of personnel decisions include hiring, firing, adjusting grievances, making work assignments, and deciding pay increases.

Professional employee.   A professional is an employee whose work is intellectual in character, requiring independent judgment or discretion; whose performance cannot readily be measured on a standardized basis; and whose skills are learned through a prolonged, specialized program of instruction.

Section 3

This section establishes the National Labor Relations Board. The board consists of five members appointed by the president and confirmed by the Senate. Members serve five-year terms and may be reappointed. One member, designated by the president, chairs the board.

The board may delegate its duties to any group of three or more members. It can also delegate authority to determine representation and election questions to its regional directors. The board has a general counsel responsible for investigating charges and issuing complaints.

Sections 4 through 6 relate to salaries, locations, and administrative procedures used by the board.

---

[4] *P.Q. Beef Processors, Inc.,* 231 NLRB 179 (1977).
[5] *Viele & Sons, Inc.,* 227 NLRB 284 (1977).

Section 7

This section, the heart of the original Wagner Act, still embodies public policy toward the individual worker and collective bargaining. As amended, Section 7 reads:

> Employees shall have the right to self-organization, to form, join, or assist labor organizations, to bargain collectively through representatives of their own choosing, and to engage in other concerted activities for the purpose of collective bargaining or other mutual aid or protection, and shall also have the right to refrain from any or all of such activities except to the extent that such right may be affected by an agreement requiring membership in a labor organization as a condition of employment as authorized in Section 8 (a) (3).

Section 8

Section 8 specifies employer actions constituting a violation of an employee's Section 7 rights and includes union violations of Section 7 and refusals to bargain with an employer. Part (a) deals with employer practices, part (b) with those of unions.

Employer unfair labor practices. An employer may not interfere with an employee engaging in any activity protected by Section 7. The employer may not assist or dominate any labor organization. For example, if two unions are vying to organize a group of workers, an employer may neither recognize one to avoid dealing with the other nor express a preference for one over the other.

An employer may not discriminate in hiring, assignment, or other terms of employment on the basis of union membership. However, employers and unions may negotiate contract clauses requiring union membership as a condition of continued employment (a union-shop agreement). But if such a clause is negotiated, the employer cannot discriminate against nonmembership if the union discriminatorily refuses to admit an employee to membership.

Employees may not be penalized or discriminated against for charging an employer with a violation of the act.

Finally, employers may not refuse to bargain with a union over issues of pay, hours, or other terms and conditions of employment.

Union unfair labor practices. Unions may not coerce employees in the exercise of Section 7 rights, but this does not limit union internal rule making, discipline, fines, and so forth. Unions cannot demand or require an employer to discriminate against an employee for any reason except failure to pay union dues.

Unions are also forbidden to engage in—or encourage individuals to engage in—strikes or refusals to handle some type of product or work if the object is to accomplish any of the following ends:

1. Forcing an employer or self-employed person to join an employer or labor organization or to cease handling nonunion products (except in certain cases, detailed later).
2. Forcing an employer to bargain with an uncertified labor organization; that is, one whose majority status has not been established.
3. Forcing an employer to cease bargaining with a certified representative.
4. Forcing an employer to assign work to employees in a particular labor organization unless ordered to do so or previously bargained to do so.
5. Requiring excessive initiation fees for union membership.
6. Forcing an employer to pay for services not rendered.
7. Picketing an employer to force recognition of the picketing union if:

   a. The picketing group has not been certified as the employees' representative; and

   b. Either no union election has taken place within the past 12 months or the picketing union requests a representation election within 30 days after picketing begins; but

   c. Nothing can prohibit a union's picketing to advise the public that an employer's employees are not unionized, provided the picketing does not interfere with pickups and deliveries.

Protected concerted activity. Where no evidence of threat, reprisal, or promise of benefit exists, the parties involved in collective bargaining activities are free to express views in any form.

Duty to bargain. Unions and employers have a mutual duty to bargain in good faith about wages, hours, and terms and conditions of employment. Each must also be willing to meet at the request of the other to negotiate an agreement, to reduce it to writing, and to interpret its meaning when a disagreement arises. Neither party is required to concede any issue to demonstrate good faith. Notification of the Federal Mediation and Conciliation Service (FMCS) is required as a condition for contract modification. Specific and more stringent requirements are laid out for health care organizations.

Prohibited contract clauses. Except in the construction and apparel industries, employees and unions cannot negotiate contracts providing that particular products of certain employers will not be used. This is the so-called hot-cargo issue. For example, a trucking union could not negotiate a contract prohibiting hauling goods manufactured by a nonunion employer. But a construction union could refuse to install nonunion goods if a contract clause had been negotiated.

Construction employment. Contractors can make collective bargaining agreements with construction unions, even without a demonstration of majority status. The agreements may also require union membership within seven days of employment and that the union be given an opportunity to refer members for existing job openings. These exceptions recognize the relatively short-run nature of many construction jobs. Labor agreements may also provide for apprenticeship training requirements and may give preference in job openings to workers with greater past experience.

Health care picketing.   A union anticipating a strike or picketing at a health care facility must notify the FMCS 10 days before commencing the activity.

Section 9

Section 9 deals with representatives and elections. The act provides that if a majority of employees in a particular unit desire representation, all employees (whether union members or not) will be represented by the union regarding wages, hours, and terms and conditions of employment. Individuals can present their own grievances for adjustment if the adjustment is not inconsistent with the contract.

The NLRB determines what group of employees constitutes an appropriate unit for a representation election and subsequent bargaining. Its discretion has some limitations, however. First, it cannot include professional and nonprofessional employees in the same unit unless a majority of the professionals desire inclusion. Second, it cannot deny separate representation to a craft solely on the basis that it was part of a larger unit determined appropriate by the board. Third, it cannot include plant guards and other types of employees in diverse units. Also remember that supervisors are not employees as defined by the act; so, for example, a unit of production supervisors would be an inappropriate group for representation.

In cases of questionable union majority status, the board is authorized to hold elections (subject to certain constraints, detailed in Chapter 6). The board may also conduct elections to determine whether an existing union maintains a continuing majority status.

Sections 10, 11, and 12

These sections deal with (1) the prevention of unfair labor practices and (2) procedures used by the NLRB in investigating and remedying them. If the board finds an unfair labor practice has occurred, it can issue cease-and-desist orders, require back pay to make wronged persons whole, and petition a court of appeals for enforcement of its orders.

Section 11 deals with the procedures the NLRB has available to obtain evidence, such as subpoena powers. Section 12 provides for criminal penalties for persons interfering with board activities.

Sections 13 through 19

These sections limit the applicability of other sections. Section 13 indicates that nothing in the act limits the right to strike. Section 14(a) holds that supervisors cannot be prohibited from belonging to a union, but an employer need not recognize membership for bargaining purposes. Section 14(b), one of the most controversial in the act, permits passage by the states of so-called right-to-work laws. In states with these laws, employees represented by unions cannot be compelled to join a union or pay dues as a condition of continued employment. Section 14(c) allows the NLRB to decline jurisdiction in cases where the impact on commerce is judged insignificant, but state agencies can assert jurisdiction if the board declines. Section 15 deals with bankruptcies (a subject covered in more detail in Chapter 11). Sections 16 through 18 cover nonsubstantive issues. Finally, Section 19 provides that employees of health care organizations whose religious beliefs preclude union membership may donate a sum equal to union dues to a nonreligious charity in lieu of membership in a union or agency shop.

Title II

This title begins the major additions made by the Taft-Hartley Act to the original Wagner Act. Obviously, some of those previously mentioned, such as union unfair labor practices, were important; but Title II broke new ground in public policy toward collective bargaining.

Title II, Section 201, indicates that it is in the public interest to maintain stable labor relations. If problems between the parties interfere with this stability, the government should be able and willing to offer assistance. Thus, Section 202 created the FMCS, whose duties (defined in Section 203) are to offer its mediation services whenever a dispute threatens to interrupt commerce or involves a health care organization. The FMCS is directed to emphasize services in contract negotiations, not grievance settlements.

A second major feature of Title II is the national emergency sections. If, in the opinion of the president, a labor dispute will imperil the nation, a board of inquiry may be appointed to look into the issues surrounding the dispute. After the board of inquiry submits its report, the attorney general may be directed to ask a district court to enjoin a strike or lockout. If the court agrees the dispute involves a substantial area and if national security is threatened, an injunction against the strike or lockout may be issued. If an injunction is ordered, the board of inquiry is reconvened and charged with the duty of monitoring the settlement process. If an agreement is not reached after 60 days, the board reports the positions of labor and management and includes management's last offer. Over the next 15 days, the NLRB holds an election among the employees to determine whether a majority favors accepting management's last offer. Five more days are taken to certify the results. At this time (or earlier, if a settlement was reached), the injunction will be discharged. If a settlement was not reached, the president forwards the report of the board, the election results, and recommendations to Congress for action.

Title III

This title speaks to suits by and against labor organizations. The title enables a union to sue on behalf of its members and to be sued and found liable for damages against its organizational (but not members') assets.

The title also forbids financial dealings between an organization and the representative of its employees. Union agents are forbidden to demand payment for performing contractual duties. Certain regulations relating to the establishment of trust funds are also included.

Unions and corporations are forbidden to make political contributions in any elections involving the choice of federal officeholders.

Summary

The important aspects of the Labor–Management Relations Act (LMRA) relate to the establishment, function, and powers of the NLRB; the delineation of employer and union unfair labor practices; the promulgation of rules governing representation and certification; the creation and functions of the FMCS; and the national emergency injunction procedures. These aspects aim at balancing the power of labor and management and interjecting the public's interest in stabilizing industrial relations.

LANDRUM–GRIFFIN ACT (1959)

The Landrum-Griffin Act resulted from congressional hearings into corrupt practices in labor-management relations. This act, formally named the Labor–Management Reporting and Disclosure Act of 1959 (LMRDA), regulates internal activities of both labor and management. The Landrum-Griffin Act regulates internal activities of employers and unions covered by both the Taft-Hartley and Railway Labor acts.

Title I—Bill of Rights for Union Members

Section 101 provides union members with equal rights and privileges in nominating, voting, and participating in referenda, meetings, and the like. Each member is afforded an opportunity to be heard and to oppose the directions of the leadership insofar as this opposition does not interfere with the union's legal obligations. Dues, initiation fees, and assessments cannot be increased unless the majority of members vote to approve the increase. Members' rights to sue their labor organizations are guaranteed as long as they have exhausted internal union procedures and are not aided by an employer or an employer association. Finally, members of labor organizations cannot be expelled unless due process consistent with this section is followed.

Section 104 provides that copies of the labor agreement between the employer and the union be available to every member.

Title II—Reports Required of Unions and Employers

Section 201 provides that all labor organizations have constitutions and bylaws deposited with the secretary of labor. Unions must file annual reports detailing assets and liabilities, receipts, salaries and allowances of officers, loans made to officers, loans made to businesses, and other expenditures prescribed by the secretary of labor. The report must also be made available to the membership.

Section 202 requires *every* officer and employee of a labor organization (except clerical and custodial employees) to submit an annual report to the secretary of labor detailing the following: any family income or transaction in stocks, securities, or other payments (except wages) made by a firm in which the labor organization represents employees; income or other payments to a business that had substantial dealings with these firms; or any payments made by a labor consultant to such a firm.

Section 203 requires employer reports on payments made to union officials (even if only to reimburse expenses); payments made to employees to convince other employees to exercise or not exercise their rights to organize and bargain collectively; payments made to obtain information about labor organizations or individuals involved in disputes with the employer; and agreements with or payments to a labor relations consultant whose purpose is to influence workers in their choices under Section 7 of the Taft-Hartley Act.

Title III—Trusteeships

A union may take over one of its subsidiaries for breaching the national's constitution or bylaws. To reduce the possibility of imposing trusteeship to stifle dissent, Title III requires imposing the trusteeship only to restore democratic procedures, correct corruption or financial malfeasance, assure performance of collective bargaining agreements, or other legitimate union functions. If a union imposes trusteeship on one of its subsidiaries, it must file a report with the secretary of labor detailing the reasons for the takeover. It must also disclose the subsidiary's financial situation. A labor organization exercising a trustee relationship cannot move assets from the organization it took over or

EXHIBIT 4-1

P-9 Trusteeship Gets Judge's Approval; Local Leadership Out

A federal judge ruled Monday that the United Food and Commercial Workers (UFCW) union can take control of striking Local P-9 of Austin, Minn.

The ruling clears the way for the international union to negotiate a labor contract with Geo. A. Hormel & Co., according to the international and Hormel.

It also enforces the suspensions of P-9 officers. They contended in their fight with the international that they were elected by the membership and could not be replaced as the sole bargainers for the striking meatpackers.

Joe Hansen, an international vice president, district director of the UFCW and the international's trustee, said late yesterday that Hormel has agreed to meet later this week to resume contract negotiations in the nearly 10-month-old labor dispute.

"The trustee is the bargaining agent for Local P-9," said Hansen. "Jim Guyette (P-9's president) and all of the officers of P-9 have been suspended and all business of the local will be conducted with me or with the (two) deputy trustees."

U.S. District Judge Edward Devitt [said] . . . "Since Local P-9 did not comply with the international's directive to cease its strike against Hormel (in March) or to cease its roving picket line activities, the international acted within its authority in appointing the trustee to manage P-9's affairs."

Source: Neal St. Anthony, "P-9 Trusteeship Gets Judge's Approval; Local Leadership Out," *Minneapolis Star and Tribune*, June 3, 1986, 1A, 9A.

---

appoint delegates to conventions from it (unless they were elected by secret ballot of the membership). Recently, the United Food and Commercial Workers (UFCW) placed its local P-9, which represented employees of Hormel's Austin, Minnesota, plant, under trusteeship for refusing to end a strike. Exhibit 4-1 contains some background information on the controversy surrounding the trusteeship.

FEDERAL DEPARTMENTS AND AGENCIES

All three branches of government—legislative, executive, and judicial—are involved in labor relations. The legislative branch writes and amends the law; the executive agencies implement and regulate within the law; and the judicial branch examines the actions of the other two in light of the Constitution, the statutes, and common law. This section examines the departments and agencies concerned with labor relations functions.

Department of Labor

The Department of Labor, created as a cabinet department in 1913, has a broad charter.

> The purpose of the Department of Labor is to foster, promote, and develop the welfare of the wage earners of the United States, to improve their working conditions, and to advance their opportunities for profitable employment. In carrying out this mission, the department administers more than 130 federal labor laws, guaranteeing workers' rights to safe and healthful working conditions, a minimum hourly wage and overtime pay, freedom from employment discrimination, unemployment insurance, and workers' compensation. The department also protects workers' pension rights, sponsors job training programs, helps workers find jobs; works to strengthen free collective bargaining; and keeps track of changes in employment, prices, and other national economic measurements. As the department seeks to assist all Americans who need and want to work, special efforts are made to meet the unique job market problems of older workers, youths, minority group members, women, the handicapped, and other groups.[6]

The organization of the Department of Labor is shown in Figure 4-1.

Labor–Management Services Administration (LMSA). The LMSA is responsible for collecting reports from employers and unions as required by the Employee Retirement Income Security Act of 1974 (ERISA) and the Landrum-Griffin Act. The LMSA also provides research assistance in collective bargaining for long-range changes (for example, automation) and immediate negotiations. The LMSA administers the legislation pertaining to federal employee labor relations by determining appropriate bargaining units, supervising representation elections, ruling on unfair labor practices, and deciding whether grievances are subject to arbitration.

Occupational Safety and Health Administration (OSHA). OSHA is responsible for the interpretation and enforcement of the Occupational Safety and Health Act of 1970. It investigates violations and assesses penalties through hearings held by Department of Labor administrative law judges.

Employment and Training Administration (ETA). The Bureau of Apprenticeship and Training in the ETA assists employers and unions in establishing high-quality training programs in the skilled trades to ensure consistent standards across jurisdictions.

Bureau of Labor Statistics (BLS). The BLS collects, maintains, and publishes data used by interested persons to assess the current

---

[6] Office of the Federal Register, National Archives and Record Service, General Services Administration, *U.S. Government Manual, 1986–1987* (Washington, D.C.: U.S. Government Printing Office, 1986), p. 399.

FIGURE 4-1

Department of Labor

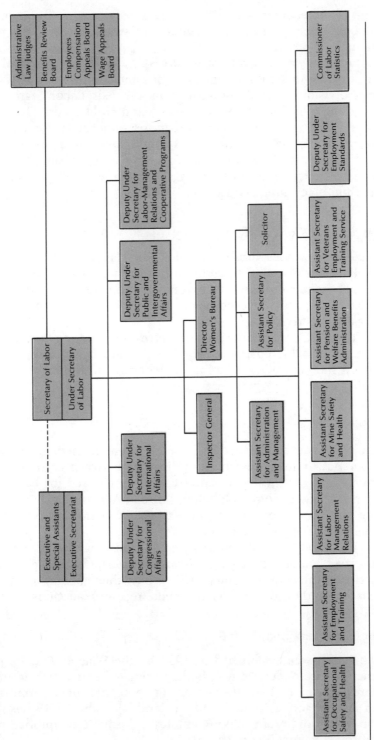

Source: U.S. Government Manual, 1987–1988, Federal Register Office (Washington, D.C.: U.S. Government Printing Office) p. 401.

state of the economy—nationally, regionally, or locally. It publishes the consumer price index, conducts area wage surveys, and provides unemployment data.

Employment Standards Administration (ESA). Several offices within the ESA are important to unions and employers. The wage-and-hour division enforces provisions of the Fair Labor Standards Act governing overtime, minimum wage, and child labor. The Office of Federal Contract Compliance Programs monitors federal contractor actions in affirmatively hiring and employing women, minorities, and the handicapped. The Office of Workers' Compensation Programs administers federal programs for longshore workers and for miners suffering from black lung diseases.

Federal Mediation and Conciliation Service (FMCS)

The FMCS was established by the Taft-Hartley Act to help parties resolve labor disputes. In contract negotiation, it may mediate either through invitation or on its own motion. Mediators assist the parties in bargaining but have no power to impose settlements or regulate bargaining activity.

The FMCS maintains lists of arbitrators and, on request, provides names from which parties may choose an arbitrator to settle disputes within the contract. In listing or delisting an arbitrator, the FMCS applies established qualification rules.

National Mediation Board (NMB)

The NMB was established in 1934 by an amendment to the Railway Labor Act. It mediates contract disputes between carriers and their unions and certifies representatives of employees for bargaining. It refers grievances to the National Railroad Adjustment Board (NRAB). The NMB may appoint a referee to assist in making NRAB awards when the panel is deadlocked.

The NMB is also responsible for notifying the president if an unsettled, mediated dispute threatens to cripple transport in some section of the country. The president may then appoint an emergency board to study the situation and make recommendations.

National Labor Relations Board (NLRB)

The NLRB was established in 1935 by the Wagner Act. Its primary functions are to determine whether groups of employees desire union representation and whether unions or companies have committed unfair labor practices as defined by federal law. The NLRB has jurisdiction over most profit-making employers, private nonprofit hospitals, and the U.S. Postal Service.

Figure 4–2 shows the board's organizational structure. NLRB

FIGURE 4-2

National Labor Relations Board

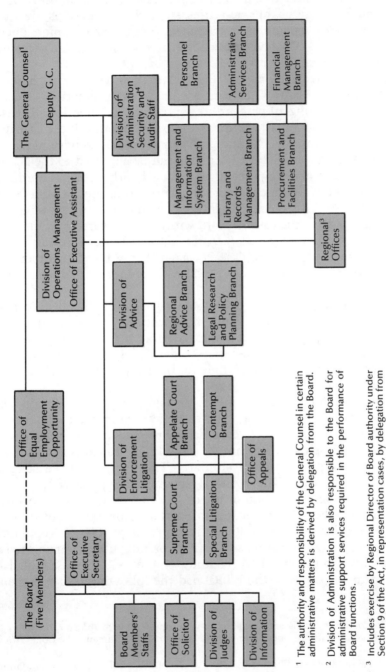

[1] The authority and responsibility of the General Counsel in certain administrative matters is derived by delegation from the Board.

[2] Division of Administration is also responsible to the Board for administrative support services required in the performance of Board functions.

[3] Includes exercise by Regional Director of Board authority under Section 9 of the Act, in representation cases, by delegation from the Board.

[4] The Auditor is authorized to bring findings directly to the Board or G.C. as appropriate.

Source: "NLRB Organizations and Functions," Rules and Regulations and Statements of Procedure (Washington, D.C.: U.S. Government Printing Office, 1987), p. 281.

members are appointed by the president for five-year terms, and the Senate must confirm the appointments. The general counsel coordinates much of the board's activities since determinations are made there on whether to proceed against an employer or union once a complaint is filed. The board does not initiate action but only responds to complaints from the involved parties.[7]

The board receives about 50,000 cases per year through its 33 regional offices. About 80 percent are unfair labor practice (C) cases, while the remaining 20 percent are representation election (R) cases. When a C case is filed, the regional office investigates. If the case does not appear meritorious, the charging party is asked to withdraw it, or charges are dismissed. These decisions can be appealed to the general counsel but only about 4 percent are reversed. If the case has merit, the regional director attempts to get the parties to fashion a remedy and settle the case. This tactic presently succeeds in about 94 percent of cases. Failing that, the case is heard within one to three months by an administrative law judge (ALJ). After the ALJ issues a ruling, exceptions can be filed, and the case is assigned to a board member. The board must then study the case, and a three-member panel issues a ruling.[8]

If one of the parties does not comply with an NLRB decision, the board may petition a U.S. court of appeals for enforcement. Board orders must be publicized to employees and/or union members. The board may issue "cease-and-desist" orders, "bargaining orders," and decisions making employees whole for illegal personnel actions, such as termination for union activity.

Since the NLRB makes initial decisions regarding unfair labor practices in the absence of judicial review, employers and unions might regard the decisions as establishing precedents. To have value as a precedent, employers and unions would have to expect subsequent boards to interpret practices similarly. However, evidence suggests this is not the case. The political appointment process appears to influence the determination of unfair labor practice charges. A board member could be a Democrat appointed by a Democrat president (DD), a Democrat appointed by a Republican president (DR), a Republican appointed by a Democrat president (RD), or a Republican appointed by a Republican president (RR). A study of the 1977 cases decided by three-member panels of the NLRB had the following results: when a

---

[7] For complete details, see Kenneth C. McGuinness, *How to Take a Case before the National Labor Relations Board*, 4th ed. (Washington, D.C.: Bureau of National Affairs, 1976).

[8] Donald L. Dotson, "Processing Cases at the NLRB," *Labor Law Journal*, January 1984, pp. 3–9.

majority were DD members, rulings favored unions 12 percent *more* often than when the majority were RD or DR; and when the majority were RR members, unions received favorable rulings 20 percent *less* often than if RD or DR panels decided the cases. The general counsel's political orientation may also strongly influence outcomes since that office decides what cases should be referred to the board members for decisions.[9]

NLRB decisions may alter the bargaining power between labor and management if a previously used practice is prohibited. Filing rates appear influenced by the level of economic activity, and filing rates increase for *both* unions and managements when it appears board composition will lead to more favorable decisions for management. Employers may increase their filings because they believe pro-management decisions may deter union tactics.[10] A good deal of controversy surrounds recent board decisions, with union leaders suggesting they might be better off without labor legislation.[11]

SUMMARY

U.S. labor law consists primarily of the Railway Labor, Norris-LaGuardia, Wagner, Taft-Hartley, and Landrum-Griffin acts. These enable collective bargaining, regulate labor and management activities, and limit intervention by the federal courts in lawful union activities.

The legislative branch of government enacts the laws; the executive department carries them out; and the court system tests their validity and rules on conduct within their purview.

As a cabinet department, the Department of Labor is primarily responsible for the implementation of human resource programs and monitoring activities. It has little direct influence on collective bargaining.

Rule-making, interpretive, and assistance agencies have major influences on employers, through either direct intervention or regulation. The FMCS and NLRB probably have the greatest impact on collective bargaining.

---

[9] William N. Cooke and Frederick H. Gautschi III, "Political Bias in NLRB Unfair Labor Practice Decisions," *Industrial and Labor Relations Review*, July 1982, pp. 539–49.

[10] Myron Roomkin, "A Quantitative Study of Unfair Labor Practice Cases," *Industrial and Labor Relations Review*, January 1981, pp. 245–56.

[11] See, for example, *NLRB at 50: Labor Board at the Crossroads* (Washington, D.C.: Bureau of National Affairs, 1985).

DISCUSSION QUESTIONS

1. In the absence of federal labor laws, what do you think the scope and nature of labor relations would presently be in the United States?

2. Should workers now under the Railway Labor Act be brought within the jurisdiction of the Labor–Management Relations Act?

3. Are current laws strong enough to preserve individual rights in collective bargaining?

4. To what extent should the federal government have power to intervene in collective bargaining activities?

5. Should such administrative agencies as the NLRB be allowed to render administrative law decisions that can be enforced by the courts, or should an agency be required to go directly to court?

CHAPTER 5

Union Structure and Government

Labor unions and employing organizations are governed differently. Employees are hired to perform tasks to accomplish certain objectives, and most employees have little voice in what the objectives will be. The objectives are determined by high-level managers and are monitored by owners or boards of directors elected by shareholders or, in the case of public agencies, by their elected or appointed boards. A corporation's legal members are the shareholders. A labor union's members are the workers it represents. The goals of unions reflect member interests, since the elected leadership must generally be responsive to member desires if they are to remain in office.

This chapter examines the organizational components of the labor movement. The functions and government of unions and how these relate to and involve the membership are described. Some union activities in influencing public policy are also explored. This chapter addresses the following major questions:

1. What are the major organizational levels within the labor movement?
2. What roles do the local union, the international, and the AFL–CIO play?
3. How do international union organizational structures and politics differ?
4. To what extent are unions autocratically or democratically governed?
5. How does organized labor become involved in the political process?

The U.S. labor movement is composed of three major hierarchical structures: the local union, the national union, and the labor federation. These are all discussed in the following sections.

THE LOCAL UNION

The local union is the institution through which the individual deals with the employer on a day-to-day basis. A local union is not strictly defined in terms of size, geographic jurisdiction, or numbers of employers with which it deals. Local unions exercise jurisdiction along four major dimensions: (1) the specific duties workers perform or the industrial classification in which they are employed (craft and industrial jurisdictions), (2) a specified geographic area, (3) the specific purpose of the jurisdiction (organizing, bargaining, and so on), and (4) the level of union government applying the jurisdiction.[1] The exact definition of a local's constituency can vary within these parameters. As examples, Local 12 of the United Auto Workers in Toledo, Ohio (an amalgamated local), represents employees of several employers in different industries; Local 65 of the Retail, Wholesale, and Department Store Union in New York City represents employees in over 2,000 different establishments; Local 3 of the Operating Engineers covers portions of four western states; and Local 459 of the International Union of Electrical Workers (IUE), based in New York, bargains with employers in Milwaukee, New Orleans, and Chicago.[2] These are exceptions, however. Many local unions operate in a specific municipality, representing workers in a single industry or job classification and frequently bargaining with a single employer.

A local union's jurisdiction affects its size, constitution, officers, and organizational structure.[3] A president, vice president, recording secretary, financial secretary, treasurer, sergeant-at-arms, and trustees are generally elected. Unless the local is large, these posts are part time and usually unpaid. Locals interested in expanding to, or currently dealing with, multiple employers will often create a "business agent" position. The business agent's job is to ensure that contractual rights of members are not being violated and to refer union members to available employment. Business agents are most necessary in industries in which union members often move from employer to employer as work is finished on one project and becomes available on another.

Two major committees operate within most locals: the executive committee (made up of the local's officers) and the grievance or negotiation committee. The executive committee establishes local policy; the negotiation committee reviews members' grievances and negotiates over grievances and contractual changes with management. Other

---

[1] Jack Barbash, *American Unions: Structure, Government, and Politics* (New York: Random House), 1967.

[2] Ibid., pp. 12–14, 43.

[3] Leonard R. Sayles and George Strauss, *The Local Union*, rev. ed. (New York: Harcourt Brace Jovanovich, 1967), pp. 2–5.

committees deal with organizing and membership, welfare, recreation, and political action.

At the work-unit level, the union elects or appoints stewards. Stewards are responsible for ensuring that first-line supervisors comply with the contract. When grievances are presented, the steward acts as a spokesperson. Stewards also collect dues and solicit participation in union activities. Many collective bargaining contracts recognize the vulnerability of the steward's advocative position by according it superseniority. As long as one remains a steward, he or she is, by definition, the most senior member of the unit. Exhibit 5–1 gives an example of how one steward views his work.

The steward situation—as a full-time company employee and also the unit employees' representative when they have grievances against the employer—is paradoxical. To whom is the steward committed, the union or the employer or both? A recent study among approximately 200 stewards in one employer found that about 80 percent were committed to the union, 36 percent were committed to the employer, and 12 percent were committed to neither. Almost 30 percent were committed to the union and the employer simultaneously. Dual commitment was related to stewards' positive beliefs about the employer's supervisors, promotional opportunities, and the union's influence on the employer; positive beliefs about the union's decision-making process; beliefs about low opportunities with other employers; and beliefs that the grievance procedure is not a tool to punish supervisors.[4]

Local Union Democracy and Participation

Local union political activity resembles municipal politics. Union elections usually generate only moderate interest, and incumbents are usually reelected unless the rank-and-file members believe a critical issue has been mishandled. The local typically holds regular business meetings, which are open to all members.

Two aspects of local union government and politics bear examination: (1) the type of business conducted by unions in their meetings and (2) the degree to which the local union is democratically operated. Local union business meetings are fairly mundane unless contract negotiations are approaching. Most meetings deal with reporting disbursements, communications, and pending grievances. Attendance is generally low, with one study reporting attendance rates between 1 and 33 percent of membership. Higher rates were found more often in smaller locals or locals with more highly skilled workers.[5] The meet-

---

[4] James E. Martin, John M. Magenau, and Mark F. Peterson, "Variables Related to Patterns of Union Stewards' Commitment," *Journal of Labor Research* 8 (1986), pp. 323–36.

[5] Ibid., p. 97.

EXHIBIT 5-1

Example of the Role of a Shop Steward

East Chicago, Ind.—Alan Moseley, still sweating from his workday in the steel mill, lumbers into the office of United Steelworkers Local 1010 and slams his briefcase down in frustration.

Mr. Moseley is a union "griever" (or shop steward, as he would be called in some unions), handling union members' complaints against his employer, Inland Steel Industries, Inc. His frustration at the time results from a year of sometimes rancorous talks with Inland over whether eight new jobs in its plant should go to union or salaried workers.

Yanking the complaint from his bulging briefcase, he grouses that a tentative agreement is meeting resistance from his own members. "It's total unrest out there," Mr. Moseley says, gesturing toward Inland's sprawling mill down the street. "It's a daily battle over jobs."

Mr. Moseley's recent struggle over the eight new jobs at Inland reflects the deep tension. As his negotiations with the company dragged on, workers grew angry at the delay. Last summer, they circulated a cartoon depicting Mr. Moseley as a fat hog with a hoof in the company's till. Enraged, Mr. Moseley telephoned dozens of members but failed to find out who distributed the cartoon.

"You've got to have a leather hide in this business, but that hurt me," the 41-year-old Mr. Moseley says.

After more than a year of effort, Mr. Moseley in February finally worked out a compromise with the company: Inland promised to let union members take four of the eight jobs in a new automated steel-testing laboratory.

But despite all the frustrations and despite a high defeat rate among grievers who seek reelection, Mr. Moseley has continued to run every three years. Shunning the hard-hat decals many candidates pass out, Mr. Moseley laboriously handwrites a letter to each member, asking for his vote.

He continues at this often-thankless job, he says, "because of the injustices out there." He recalls handing out food last Christmas to a long line of laid-off workers: "It made me want to hold on to the jobs I have." Besides, he adds, "I enjoy defending people. If I had my life to do over, I'd probably be a lawyer."

ing's agenda also affects attendance. In a newly organized local of utility workers, the highest attendance—for the contract ratification— was 42 percent. It exceeded 15 percent in only 3 of the other 16 meetings (18 percent for a discussion of contract demands, 20 percent for an election of temporary officers, and 18 percent for a report on the completed contract).[6] That so few members attend local union meetings raises questions about breadth of support and union democracy. Ironically, member involvement seems low at the local level, although this is where most of the members' interests in collective bargaining are centered.

Local union democracy is manifested by the combination of factions into coalitions around certain issues. It is also demonstrated by the fact that two or more candidates may run for an office and that elections for major offices are occasionally close. Members of a Canadian public employee union's locals found members more willing to participate in union activities and less opposed to internal political positions if they believed they had strong relationships with their leaders. Centralization of authority reduced democracy. Participation in local activities declined with increases in the size and organizational complexity of the union, the amount of its formal communications to members, its age, and internal factionalism. Participation increased as the ratio of leaders to members in the local structure increased. Closeness of elections seemed to depend on size, specialization of the union, its formal communication process, lack of an incumbent in the race, and absence of hostility from management.[7]

Evidence related to participation in union activities and satisfaction with the union is mixed. Among a group of professional employees, willingness to represent the union was associated with the level of financial responsibilities of the member, beliefs about the union's legitimacy, involvement in the employing organization, and the importance of having influence and being involved in decision making.[8] Another study found that members who attended union meetings were more likely to be committee activists, voters, campaigners, and union newspaper readers. Participation was not greater among those filing grievances; individual grievances are normally independent of internal union participation activities.[9] In a cross-sectional sample of U.S. union members, participation was higher among members who expressed dissatisfaction with their unions; but participation was higher when members indicated their unions were effective in gaining member goals and were interested in both the intrinsic and extrinsic goals of

---

6 Ibid., p. 98.

7 John C. Anderson, "A Comparative Analysis of Local Union Democracy," *Industrial Relations,* October 1978, pp. 278–95.

8 William Glick, Philip Mirvis, and Diane Harder, "Union Satisfaction and Participation," *Industrial Relations,* May 1977, pp. 145–51.

9 John C. Anderson, "Local Union Participation: A Re-Examination," *Industrial Relations,* Winter 1979, pp. 18–31.

members.[10] Race differences do not appear to be associated with participation.[11]

Participation in unions may involve administrative activities; attending meetings; and voting in elections, strike authorizations, and contract ratifications. Participation in administration is predicted primarily by interest in union business, educational level, seniority, beliefs in the value of unions, and low job involvement.[12] Participation varies according to the environment in which the union operates. Democracy appears greater where unions are not faced with a hostile environment. Political processes may be more active in larger unions, but rank-and-file participation declines for many activities. The reduction in participation in larger unions may not be contrary to member desires, since participation and satisfaction do not appear linked.[13]

Unions are relatively democratic. Pressures by the membership to handle grievances and improve conditions require responses by union officers. But if management is intransigent, the pressure to maintain a united front may lead to suppression of dissent.[14]

With these findings in mind, are local unions run democratically? If democracy requires two or more relatively permanent factions, the answer must generally be no. But if democracy demands only that leaders respond to individuals and groups, the answer is generally yes. Democracy is a constitutional requirement within the local through the specification of electoral proceedings and terms of office. Also, the Landrum-Griffin Act requires locals to conduct elections at least once every three years. Further, under exclusive representation requirements, the union must apply the terms of the contract equally to all bargaining unit employees.

Democratic operation requires individual commitment to union activity. While most members believe their union works to their benefit, many were not involved in its founding and may view the union simply as their agent in employment matters. In return for dues, many members expect the union to relieve them of the effort and detailed work involved in regulating the employment relationship. What the members may want is representation in return for their dues, not participation and involvement in the union.

---

[10] Thomas I. Chacko, "Member Participation in Union Activities: Perceptions of Union Priorities, Performance, and Satisfaction," *Journal of Labor Research* 6 (1985), pp. 363–73.

[11] Michele M. Hoyman and Lamont Stallworth, "Participation in Local Unions: A Comparison of Black and White Members," *Industrial and Labor Relations Review* 40 (1987), pp. 323–35.

[12] Steven L. McShane, "The Multidimensionality of Union Participation," *Journal of Occupational Psychology* 59 (1986), pp. 177–87.

[13] Ibid.

[14] Sayles and Strauss, *Local Union*, pp. 135–47.

Functional Democracy

In a unionized employer, an individual is simultaneously an employee and a union member. The parties in the "functional democracy" of employment are the employer and the union. Thus, democracy in unionized settings does not require two or more factions to exist and be tolerated within the union.[15]

Union members are entitled to due process under at least two sets of rules: one is contained in the local union's constitution, the other in the collective bargaining agreement. Each is administered by separate sets of officials. For the local's day-to-day operation, a president, secretary-treasurer, executive board, and other officials as necessary are elected. The agreement is administered by the negotiating committee and stewards. Thus, an internal check-and-balance system helps ensure that the contract is administered fairly for all bargaining unit members and that the contract is not contrary to union standards.[16]

Figure 5-1 pictures the idea of dual governance. Assume a local includes three bargaining units in an open-shop industry. Three separate contracts are administered by the local through three separate negotiating committees. Each bargaining unit's union members are eligible to vote for the officers of the local. Each bargaining unit's employees are eligible to vote on the contract. The shaded area represents workers who are both union and bargaining unit members, while those outside the local circle are bargaining unit members only.

The question of whether local unions are democratic boils down to asking *how democratic*. They are probably less democratic electorally than governmental units are. But this may not be a problem since union members generally are interested in similar types of outcomes, view the union as their agent, and evaluate it on the outcomes it produces rather than on the ideological stand of a faction.[17] Union members do not generally feel a need to be "protected" from their union; on the contrary, it's management they are worried about. Besides, if union members are concerned about a lack of democracy in the union, they can attempt to have it decertified. Legal safeguards are sufficient to require responsiveness, if not democracy, and that appears to be enough for most members.

The local union is not an autonomous, freestanding organization. It most often owes its existence to—and almost certainly must comply with—the directives of a parent international.

---

[15] Neil W. Chamberlain and Donald E. Cullen, *The Labor Sector*, rev. ed. (New York: McGraw-Hill, 1971), pp. 194–96.

[16] Alice H. Cook, "Dual Governance in Unions: A Tool for Analysis," *Industrial and Labor Relations Review*, April 1962, pp. 323–49.

[17] Sayles and Strauss, *Local Union*, p. 141.

FIGURE 5-1

Dual Governance in Unions

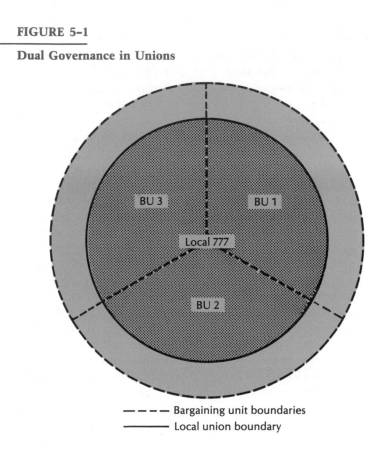

- - - - Bargaining unit boundaries
———— Local union boundary

INTERNATIONAL UNIONS

International unions originally established jurisdictions over workers in specific crafts, industries, or other job territories. They are called *internationals* because many have members in Canada as well as in the United States. As noted in Chapters 2 and 3, the (inter)national union is the unit in which authority is vested within the union movement. Most local unions are chartered by a parent national, and many local activities are constrained or must be approved by the national body.

In its most recent directory, the Bureau of National Affairs lists more than 150 national unions, of which 96 are affiliated with the AFL–CIO, about 68 percent of the total U.S. union membership of 19.4 million belongs to unions affiliated with the AFL–CIO.[18] In 1985, 41

---

[18] *Directory of National Unions and Employee Associations, 1985–1986* (Washington, D.C.: Bureau of National Affairs, 1985), p. 4.

unions and associations had more than 100,000 members each. Over half of all union members belong to the 10 largest national unions and associations. Table 5-1 lists national unions and associations with 100,000 or more members in 1985. The modal national union has fewer than 10 affiliated locals, while the median size is about 150 affiliates.

TABLE 5-1

Labor Organizations Reporting 100,000 Members or More, 1985

Teamsters	1,900,000
National Education Association (Ind.)	1,700,000
State, County, and Municipal Employees	997,000
Food and Commercial Workers	989,000
United Automobile, Aerospace, and Agricultural Implement Workers	974,000
Electrical Workers	791,000
Service Employees	688,000
Carpenters and Joiners	609,000
Steelworkers	572,000
Communications Workers	524,000
Machinists and Aerospace Workers	520,000
Teachers	470,000
Laborers	383,000
Operating Engineers	330,000
Hotel and Restaurant Employees and Bartenders	327,000
Paper Workers	232,000
Postal Workers	232,000
Amalgamated Clothing and Textile Workers	228,000
Plumbing and Pipe Fitting	226,000
Ladies' Garment Workers	210,000
Mine Workers (Ind.) (estimated)	200,000
Government Employees	199,000
Electronic, Electrical, Technical, Salaried, and Machine Workers	198,000
Letter Carriers	186,000
Government (NAGE) (Ind.) (estimated)	180,000
Nurses (Ind.) (estimated)	180,000
Police (Ind.) (estimated)	150,000
Electrical (IUE) (Ind.) (estimated)	146,000
Fire Fighters	142,000
Graphic Arts	141,000
Bridge and Structural Iron Workers	140,000
Painters and Allied Trades	133,000
Bakery, Confectionery, and Tobacco Workers	115,000
Boiler Makers, Iron Ship Builders, Blacksmiths, Forgers, and Helpers	110,000
Oil, Chemical, and Atomic Workers	108,000
Sheet Metal Workers	108,000
Retail, Wholesales, and Department Store	106,000
Rubber, Cork, Linoleum, and Plastic Workers	106,000
California State Employees (Ind.) (estimated)	105,000
Railway, Airline, and Steamship Clerks, et. al.	102,000
Associated Actors and Artistes of America	100,000

Source: *Directory of National Unions and Employee Associations, 1985-1986* (Washington, D.C.: Bureau of National Affairs, 1985).

National unions are full-time operations. Officers are full-time unionists. Departments, with appointed and hired specialists, are established. Most national unions elect officials at their union conventions, required by law to meet at least every five years. Delegates to the convention are designated by each local and sent on a per capita basis or are national union officials and field representatives. The union convention is similar to a political convention. If the national leadership can appoint many delegates, its chances of staying in office are greatly enhanced.

NATIONAL UNION GOALS

All organizations in an economy depend on each other to a degree. Companies that own mines sell their ore to smelters. Smelters sell the finished metal to manufacturers. Manufacturers convert the metal into parts and assemble them into products. Retailers sell these products to consumers (who frequently earn the money to buy the goods by working for one of these companies). Few organizations are as directly dependent on another organization as labor unions are. Labor unions in the United States exist only in the presence of employment. Their dependence on employment directly determines their major goals.

As noted in Chapter 1, individuals form or join unions when they believe a union would improve their employment outcomes. Chapter 2 noted that unionists have traditionally believed that the inequality in income distribution in the United States is excessive.[19] Chapters 3 and 4 examined the legal environment in which labor relations take place and recognized that U.S. labor law limits the union movement in representing employees. The exclusive agency relationship created in collective bargaining stimulates a competitive environment for employee relations services that influences how both unions and managements operate.

National unions have two major goals: organizing an increasing number and share of the labor force and providing representation services that enhance the well-being of their members. The two goals are obviously interrelated. To an extent, organizing success depends on the success the union has had in representing employees in a manner visible to potential new members. Successful representation depends on organizing a group of employees through which bargaining power can be exerted on the employer.

---

[19] Maurice F. Neufeld, "The Persistence of Ideas in the American Labor Movement: The Heritage of the 1830s," *Industrial and Labor Relations Review*, January 1982, pp. 207–20.

National unions were formed for economic reasons. As U.S. industry became more national through the development of transportation facilities, the bargaining power of local unions declined. National unions were established to exert greater pressure on employers and to assist local unions during difficult periods in which they might not have survived on their own. Support and control thus became lodged in national unions.

The organizational form of the union movement adapts to reflect the form of industrial organization among employers whose employees it represents. As this form changes, union organization changes with it.

The national unions and associations in the United States have their own goals. But do any common elements help predict what each might do? Unions are generally composed of members who anticipate services and permanent employees who supply them. The members evaluate whether they want continued representation by comparing the level of contract outcomes and services received from their union with those available from alternative sources (other unions or nonunion personnel departments). Leaders desire growth to enhance their power and stability. Elected leaders and appointed full-time union employees desire membership approval to enable reelection.[20] Thus, leaders might be expected to promote organizing, while the rank and file would probably prefer services for present members first. Unions in highly organized industries spend a smaller proportion of their resources for organizing than do those in jurisdictions with lower union penetration.[21]

The union movement is also beginning to look at alternative forms of representation that do not involve exclusive agency. Many employees now work in part-time situations and/or for small employers who do not have personnel or other employee relations functions. The union could act as a vehicle for counseling about workplace problems; providing information on job opportunities elsewhere; purchasing group medical, dental, and other insurance benefits; and other activities. In return, "associate" (or nonrepresented) members would pay a service fee or dues to the union.[22] Exhibit 5-2 is an excerpt from the labor movement's statement recognizing the need for changing patterns of representation.

---

[20] Richard N. Block, "Union Organizing and the Allocation of Union Resources," *Industrial and Labor Relations Review*, October 1980, pp. 101-13.

[21] Ibid.

[22] See Thomas A. Kochan, Harry C. Katz, and Robert B. McKersie, *The Transformation of American Industrial Relations* (New York: Basic Books, 1986), pp. 221-23.

EXHIBIT 5-2

New Methods of Advancing the Interests of Workers

. . . First, unions must develop and put into effect multiple models for representing workers tailored to the needs and concerns of different groups. For example, in some bargaining units workers may not desire to establish a comprehensive set of hard and fast terms and conditions of employment, but may nonetheless desire a representative to negotiate minimum guarantees that will serve as a floor for individual bargaining, to provide advocacy for individuals, or to seek redress for particular difficulties as they arise. In other units, a bargaining approach based on solving problems through arbitration or mediation rather than through ultimate recourse to economic weapons may be most effective.

Second, . . . unions must continually seek out and address new issues of concern to workers. For example, the issue of pay inequity has become a proper concern of women workers; collective action provides the surest way of redressing such inequities. There is a strong concern among workers about health and safety issues and a high degree of impatience with the inadequacy of government programs in this area. Again, collective action through labor unions can develop constructive steps to meet these concerns . . .

. . . Approximately . . . 27 million workers . . . are former union members; most . . . left their union only because they left their unionized jobs. There are hundreds of thousands more nonunion workers who voted for a union in an unsuccessful organizing campaign . . . These individuals might well be willing to affiliate with a union with which they have had contact or with which they have had some logical relationship provided that the cost were not prohibitive; this would be especially true to the extent unions offered services or benefits outside of the collective bargaining context . . . New categories of membership should be created by individual unions or on a Federation-wide basis to accommodate individuals who are not part of organized bargaining units, and affiliates should consider dropping any existing barriers to an individual's retaining his membership after leaving an organized unit.

Source: *The Changing Situation of Workers and Their Unions,* Report of the AFL–CIO Evolution of Work Committee, February 1985, pp. 18-19.

National Union Jurisdictions

National unions have traditionally operated as either craft or industrial unions. Generally, the craft unions formed the AFL, and the industrial unions formed the CIO. Craft and industrial jurisdictional boundaries blurred as AFL and CIO unions competed for members before their merger and as craft and industrial employment patterns changed.

National unions often concentrate on certain jurisdictions, and many define their jurisdictions in their constitutions. For example, the jurisdiction of the Carpenters' Union is asserted as follows:

The trade autonomy of the United Brotherhood of Carpenters and Joiners of America consists of the milling, fashioning, joining, assembling, erection, fastening or dismantling of all materials of wood, plastic, metal, fiber, cork and composition, and all other substitute materials. The handling, cleaning, erecting, installing and dismantling of machinery, equipment and all materials used by members of the United Brotherhood.

Our claim of jurisdiction, therefore, extends over the following divisions and subdivisions of the trade: Carpenters and Joiners, Millwrights, Pile Drivers, Bridge, Dock, Wharf Carpenters, Divers, Underpinners, Timbermen and Core Drillers, Shipwrights, Boat Builders, Ship Carpenters, Joiners and Caulkers; Cabinet Makers, Bench Hands, Stair Builders, Millmen; Wood and Resilient Floor Layers, and Finishers; Carpet Layers; Shinglers, Siders; Insulators; Acoustic and Dry Wall Applicators; Shorers and House Movers; Loggers, Lumber, and Sawmill Workers; Furniture Workers; Reed and Rattan Workers; Shingle Weavers; Casket and Coffin Makers; Box Makers, Railroad Carpenters and Car Builders, regardless of material used; and all those engaged in the operation of woodworking or other machinery required in the fashioning, milling or manufacturing of products used in the trade, or engaged as helpers to any of the above divisions or subdivisions, and the handling, erecting and installing material on any of the above divisions or subdivisions; burning, welding, rigging and the use of any instrument or tool for layout work, incidental to the trade. When the term "carpenter(s)" or "carpenter(s) and joiner(s)" are used, it shall mean all the divisions and subdivisions of the trade.[23]

The largest U.S. nationals tend to be unions with broad jurisdictions. In 1985, these were the Teamsters; the National Education Association (NEA); the State, County, and Municipal Employees (AFSCME); the Food and Commercial Workers (UFCW); the Auto Workers (UAW); the Electrical Workers (IBEW); and the Service Employees (SEIU). The Teamsters originally organized transportation and warehouse employees employed outside the railroad industry. Presently, about half of all Teamster union members work in occupations and industries with no primary relationship to transportation. The NEA represents both public and private school teachers at primary, secondary, and post-secondary educational institutions. The UAW has expanded its organizing to nonteaching employees in colleges and universities. AFSCME organizes employees in many occupations across a broad spectrum of nonfederal public and private nonprofit employers. The IBEW began as a craft union but has successfully organized electrical workers in electrical equipment manufacturing. Where employment in traditional jurisdictions is declining, union leaders would be expected to push for expanding jurisdictions.

---

[23] *Constitution and Laws of the United Brotherhood of Carpenters and Joiners of America,* as amended (Washington, D.C.: United Brotherhood of Carpenters and Joiners, 1975), sect. 7, pp. 6–7.

National Structure

The organizational structure of national unions results from the interaction of two factors: first, the union will be structured so as to provide the types of services members demand; second, it will be structured to interact more closely with the organizations in which it represents employees. To demonstrate these relationships and the differences between national unions, the structural properties of the UAW, Teamsters, Carpenters, and AFSCME will be examined.

Organizational structure in the UAW. The UAW has traditionally organized workers in industries that fabricate and assemble surface and air transportation, construction, and agricultural equipment. It has also organized companies supplying parts to these industries. The assembly industries are highly concentrated (that is, relatively few manufacturers account for most of the production). For example, prior to the 1980s, virtually all domestic automobiles were assembled by four manufacturers: American Motors, Chrysler, Ford, and General Motors. Recently, Honda, Mazda, and Nissan have opened U.S. assembly plants, and Chrysler has acquired American Motors. To best service employees in a consistent manner across operations of these major manufacturers, the UAW has established *national departments*. Since the domestic automakers' production facilities were virtually 100 percent unionized, the national departments concentrated on representation rather than organizing. A major recent activity of the UAW has been an attempt to reduce job erosion in auto manufacturing. Exhibit 5–3 is an example of lobbying material to support the passage of domestic content legislation in automobile manufacturing. Figure 5–2 shows an organizational chart of the UAW at the national level.

National departments are the line portion of the organization. This is where national–local interfaces occur. Each national department has a council consisting of delegates from that department's locals. In turn, the councils form subcommittees based on common interests of the members, such as seniority and work rules. Subcommittees designate members to take part in the national negotiation council from that department.

Staff departments provide information for the national departments and also assist locals through the UAW's international representatives. Besides having a "product-line" orientation in its national departments, the UAW is geographically broken into regions based on the concentration of UAW members in a given area. The regional staffs' primary responsibilities are conducting organizing drives and assisting remote locals or those not closely affiliated with national departments in negotiation, administration, and grievance handling. Regional staffs may also have experts in such areas as health and safety or industrial engineering.

EXHIBIT 5-3

Congress Hears from the UAW

[The] fear of lost jobs was underscored April 12, 1983, when UAW President Douglas Fraser told a congressional subcommittee that even with an upturn in sales, auto-industry employment "will continue to nosedive unless the U.S. government adopts a policy to assure substantial local production for the domestic market."

Fraser told the House Subcommittee on Commerce, Transportation, and Tourism that since 1979, 1.1 million jobs have been lost due to the decline in the U.S. auto industry.

"By the end of the decade, in the absence of the [domestic] content law, U.S. automotive production as a share of the market can be expected to fall to about one half of U.S. auto sales," he said. The present domestic value share is about 75 percent.

The impact on jobs would be catastrophic, Fraser added. "A fall from three fourths to one half of the auto market would eliminate the jobs of more than 200,000 auto workers—and 5½ times that many outside the auto industry," he testified.

Source: *Solidarity*, April 1983, p. 10.

The organizational makeup of the UAW is largely a function of employer concentration and the level at which economic bargaining occurs. Thus, it has tended to be quite centralized. However, the trend will probably decrease because automakers are finding that the differing efficiency levels among plants require more careful scrutiny regarding whether certain facilities should be shut down. This situation necessitates more concern by the UAW for local bargaining issues.

The Carpenters' Union structure. The Carpenters' Union differs from the typical industrial union in that it represents a narrower occupational group and generally deals with smaller employers. The construction industry tends to be locally or regionally based, with several employers in a given area. Construction employers also tend to concentrate on certain types of construction (for example, business and government contracts for large buildings or residential construction).

The Carpenters' Union usually bargains at the local or regional level. The national union has responsibility to review actions of local unions against its members, to authorize strikes, and to adjudicate jurisdictional disputes between its locals or between the Carpenters and other unions. The national also administers its members' pension plan. This arrangement is common in the trade unions since tradespersons may work for many employers during their careers and the union

FIGURE 5-2

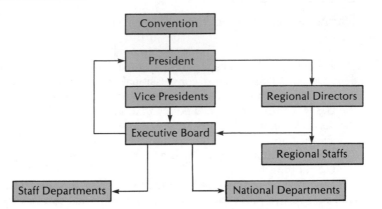

Staff Departments	National Departments
Accounting	Aerospace
Arbitration Service	Agricultural Implement
Auditing	American Motors
Circulation	Bendix
Community Action Program (CAP)	Champion Spark Plug
Community Services	Chrysler
Competitive Shop	Dana
Conservation and Natural Resources	Eltra
Consumer Affairs	Ford
Education	Foundry
Fair Practices and Anti-Discrimination	General Motors
Family Education Center	Independent Parts and Suppliers
International Affairs	Mack Truck
Job Development & Training	Technical, Office and Professional
Legal	(TOP)
Organizing	
Public Relations and Publications	
Recreation and Leisure Time Activities	
Research	
Retired Workers	
Skilled Trades	
Social Security—Health and Safety	
Social-Technical-Educational Programs (STEP)	
Strike Insurance	
Time Study and Engineering	
Veterans	
Washington Office	
Women's and Women's Auxiliary	

Source: Abstracted from *You and Your Membership in the UAW*, publication 383 (Detroit: United Auto Workers, 1978).

is the only employment-related organization with which they have long-run relationships.

The organizational structure of the Teamsters. The Teamsters' Union is the closest to a general union in the United States. After its expulsion from the AFL–CIO in 1960, it broadened its jurisdiction from trucking and warehousing to cover all workers without limitation. The mergers of several smaller national unions, such as the Brewery Workers, with the Teamsters have made the Teamsters the dominant union force in industry. The Teamsters reaffiliated with the AFL–CIO in 1987.

Given the early background of the Teamsters and the local or regional nature of much of the trucking industry, the union's organization is somewhat decentralized, particularly regarding representation and organizing in the transportation industry. The executive board of the Teamsters consists of the general president, the general secretary-treasurer, and 15 vice presidents. Several vice presidents are also international directors of the five area Teamster conferences. Ten trade divisions address the bargaining issues associated with the industries in which Teamster members are employed: airline; automotive, petroleum, and allied trades; building material and construction; freight; food processing; laundry; warehouse; household goods, moving, and storage; trade show and movie making; and public employees. Four trade conferences (Bakery, Communications, Brewery and Soft Drink Workers, and Dairy) coordinate activities in these industries.

The Teamsters' Union has established 44 local area joint councils. These semiautonomous bodies administer activities among affiliated locals. Each local is required to belong to a joint council and must get council permission to sign a contract or to strike. Each joint council is indirectly controlled by the executive branch. Thus, much of the organizing and representation activity involving the individual member is initiated or controlled at the joint council level.

AFSCME's organization. AFSCME is an industrial-type union with jurisdiction over nonelected public employees outside of the federal government and employees in private, nonprofit public-service organizations. Its organizational structure reflects the fact that its members are employed in a variety of governmental jurisdictions and bargain under many different laws. Unlike most industrial unions, AFSCME does not require the national's approval of local contract settlements. The decision to strike is also handled at the local level. All locals are expected to affiliate with one of the regional AFSCME councils, which are operated within jurisdictions relating to the bargaining laws associated with the occupations represented.

The national executive staff provides support for the regional councils and locals. An international executive board that includes regional representatives advises the executive board.[24] AFSCME's federal nature recognizes that its affiliated locals bargain with employers who operate under a myriad of collective bargaining laws and that different laws may apply to different employee groups it represents within the same jurisdiction.

National–Local Union Relationship

National unions charter the locals, offer services, and generally require that locals refrain from striking or ratifying contracts without the national's permission. This requirement reduces the possibility of competition between locals and increases the discipline of locals when it becomes necessary to pressure a large national employer.

Service to local unions, particularly from industrial unions, is provided by international representatives, usually recruited from local union officer positions or activists interested in a union career. They usually obtain their jobs through appointment by the present national union officers. The Supreme Court has ruled that incoming union officers may discharge permanent staff employees as long as it doesn't interfere with their roles as union members.[25]

International representatives, unlike many local union officers, are full-time union employees. Their major responsibilities are to organize nonunion employees in industries or occupations in which the national union has an interest, to provide assistance to employees interested in starting an organizing campaign, and to assist in representing union members, particularly in negotiating contracts and processing grievances. International representatives are typically assigned to regional staffs and may be responsible for a certain number of local unions. National unions employ international representatives when they want consistent policies established across employers, where locals are relatively small, where local officers lack sophistication, and where the area is thinly organized.

Where local unions have a great deal of autonomy, particularly where they operate in a local labor market and where employment with a given employer is likely to be transient, the business agent is the primary contact local union members have for solving problems. Business agents have many of the same responsibilities as the international representatives and are concerned with employers' compliance with the contract. Since established negotiating committees or a steward structure may not exist in transient employment, the business agent must monitor the employment relationship.

---

[24] *AFSCME Officers Manual* (Washington, D.C.: AFSCME, no date), pp. 31–43; and *Constitution of the American Federation of State, County, and Municipal Employees, AFL–CIO* (Washington, D.C.: AFSCME, 1980).

[25] *Finnegan* v. *Leu*, No. 80–2150, U.S. Supreme Court, 1982.

National Union Politics

National unions are ultimately governed by their periodic constitutional conventions, which establish broad policies for the union, may amend its constitution, and frequently elect officers. Membership participation in union activities depends to an extent on how union officers are elected and how delegates to conventions are chosen. Although national unions are required by law to hold constitutional conventions and elect officers at least every five years, they differ greatly in the degree to which member involvement is sought and the degree to which democratic ideals are applied to their operation.

National union democracy can be measured by identifying the degree of control union members have in the major decision-making areas unions face: contract negotiations, contract administration, service to members, union administration, and external political and community activities. Members' control in each area could range from complete autocracy to consultation, veto power, or full decisional control and participation.[26] Desire for democracy may be inferred through the level of union member participation in decisions open to them and their satisfaction levels in relation to opportunities for, or actual participation in, union decision-making activities.

Most national unions do not have two-party systems, but a union's constitutional organization has an impact on the degree to which dissent may lead to a change in the union's direction. Unions electing officers on an "at-large" basis among all the eligible voters (either as delegates or through a general referendum) are much less likely to be responsive to factional viewpoints than are unions electing executive board members on a geographic basis.[27] In the Mineworkers and the Steelworkers (both of which have seen national general president changes as the result of internal dissent), regionally elected executive boards have served as springboards to national campaigns. However, in national referendum elections, unions may prevent candidates from obtaining financial assistance from outside the union to forward their campaigns.[28] If officers are elected by convention and if the composition of delegates to the international convention includes not only those selected at a local level but also officials appointed by the incumbent, then the chance of mounting a successful drive to oust the incumbent is virtually nonexistent.[29]

---

[26] Arthur Hochner, Karen Koziara, and Stuart Schmidt, "Thinking about Democracy and Participation in Unions," *Proceedings of the Industrial Relations Research Association*, 1979, pp. 16–17.

[27] Sara Gamm, "The Election Base of National Union Executive Boards," *Industrial and Labor Relations Review*, April 1979, pp. 295–311.

[28] *United Steelworkers of America, AFL–CIO–CLC* v. *Sadlowski*, No. 81–395, U.S. Supreme Court, 1982.

[29] Arthur L. Fox II and John C. Sikorski, *Teamster Democracy and Financial Responsibility* (Washington, D.C.: Professional Drivers Council for Safety and Health), 1976.

National Unions and Public Policy

Representation is aimed at enhancing union members' employment outcomes through collective bargaining. Unions also serve the needs of their members through attempts to influence public policy. Some are aimed at membership interests in particular industries, while others are aimed at improving the lot of the membership as a whole or of an identifiable subgroup across industries.

Examples of public policy initiatives that cut across industries include labor's support of occupational safety and health legislation, opposition to lower minimum wages for younger workers, and reduction of pay inequality between men and women. Exhibit 5-4 is an example of a union position on the pay inequality issue.

As competition changes within industries, unions may engage in political activity to restrict the employment-cutting options of employers. For example, the deregulation of airlines and trucking has created incentives for employer efficiency and allowed the entry of new employers. Since these new employers have neither senior employees nor labor unions, competition between union and nonunion employees is thus injected. Where domestic markets have opened to

EXHIBIT 5-4

AFSCME Position on Pay Equity

On September 16, 1983, AFSCME won a landmark pay equity lawsuit against the state of Washington. Federal District Judge Jack Tanner ruled that the evidence is "overwhelming" that the state has been practicing sex discrimination in violation of Title VII of the Civil Rights Act. Judge Tanner said the discrimination is "pervasive, intentional and in violation of the law." [This decision has since been overturned by a Court of Appeals whose decision was sustained by the Supreme Court.]

AFSCME and its affiliate, the Washington Federation of State Employees, brought suit against the state of Washington charging that the state practices sex-based wage discrimination by artificially—and illegally—segregating its workforce by sex and holding down salaries for people in female-dominated jobs, even when the jobs are of comparable value to higher paying jobs dominated by men.

A 1974 study showed that, overall, women workers in the state received about 20 percent less pay than men doing work requiring comparable skill, knowledge, mental demands, accountability and working conditions. For almost 10 years the state refused to begin adjusting the salaries in the female-dominated jobs. That's why AFSCME took the state to court.

Source: "Winning the Fight for Pay Equity," (Washington, D.C.: American Federation of State, County and Municipal Employees, AFL-CIO, 1984), p. 3.

foreign competition (for example, autos and steel), lower wage costs among foreign competitors may reduce the demand for domestic unionized employees, and thus unions may push for protective legislation in the form of tariffs, domestic content laws, or reregulation.

Chapter 4 noted that National Labor Relations Board decisions are related to its political composition, with Republican members appointed by Republican presidents particularly likely to rule against labor. Given that a Republican president held office from 1981 through 1988 and that the Republicans held a majority in the Senate from 1981 through 1986, labor would seem vulnerable from a public policy standpoint. An examination of the first four years of this period shows, however, that no existing labor laws were reversed, and while no improvements occurred, labor organizations won approval for several measures they supported. Education organizations, such as the American Federation of Teachers and the National Education Association, were particularly successful.[30]

Political activities of national unions increased markedly in the 1980s. Activity is greatest among unions involved with public employers and those in which executive boards are democratically chosen.[31] Political action committees (PACs) have been important vehicles for providing financial support to election campaigns of individuals thought to be friendly to PAC viewpoints. Evidence suggests that the receipt of PAC contributions by a candidate who subsequently becomes or remains an incumbent is directly related to roll-call voting records and indirectly related to the number of candidates elected.[32] PACs do not, however, give contributions to all who support their causes. Contributions to candidates appear to depend on the willingness of the organization to give, the compatibility of the candidate's ideology with that of the contributing PAC, the probability of the candidate's winning (with more given when the race is close), and the magnitude of the vote margin the candidate had in the last election (if an incumbent).[33] Contributions also appear related to the closeness of an incumbent's committee assignment to interests of labor, voting record, and electoral security.[34]

---

[30] Marick F. Masters and John Thomas Delaney, "Union Legislative Records during President Reagan's First Term," *Journal of Labor Research* 8 (1987), pp. 1–18.

[31] Marick F. Masters and John Thomas Delaney, "The Causes of Union Political Involvement," *Journal of Labor Research* 6 (1985), pp. 341–62.

[32] Gregory M. Saltzman, "Congressional Voting on Labor Issues: The Role of PACs," *Industrial and Labor Relations Review* 40 (1987), pp. 163–79.

[33] Allen Wilhite and John Theilmann, "Unions, Corporations, and Political Campaign Contributions: The 1982 House Elections," *Journal of Labor Research* 7 (1986), pp. 175–86.

[34] Kevin B. Grier and Michael C. Munger, "The Impact of Legislator Attributes on Interest-Group Campaign Contributions," *Journal of Labor Research* 7 (1986), pp. 349–59.

While unions (and corporations) are heavily involved in PAC activities, the attitudes of their members toward issues do not appear to be monolithic and, in most cases, seem less liberal than the positions espoused by their unions' PACs. Further, PACs appear to be more successful in influencing legislative outcomes peripheral to labor's interest, such as education, rather than outcomes directly affecting its environment, such as labor law reform.[35]

When national unions attempt to speak as one voice on public policy, they use the AFL-CIO.

The AFL–CIO

The AFL–CIO is a federation of national unions banded together to provide some overall direction to the labor movement and technical assistance to individual nationals. It also contains a number of directly affiliated independent local unions. To maintain membership in the AFL–CIO, a national union must comply with the federation's Ethical Practices Code, avoid dominance by nondemocratic ideologists, and agree to submit interunion disputes for mediation and adjudication by the AFL–CIO.[36] Just as changes in the structure of the labor movement after the deaths of William Green and Philip Murray helped end the conflict between the AFL and the CIO and facilitated their merger, the retirement and death of George Meany, coupled with leadership changes over time in the UAW and Teamsters, resulted in their recent reaffiliation with the AFL–CIO.

The organization of the AFL–CIO is complex due to its federal nature and its simultaneous role as coordinator of national union interests and director of state and city central body activities. Figure 5–3 gives the general organization of the AFL–CIO. At the top is the biennial national convention. Delegates are apportioned to the convention on the basis of size and are elected or appointed according to individual national union policy. Other delegates are sent by directly affiliated locals, state and city central bodies, and national industrial and trade departments. The AFL–CIO convention amends the constitution, elects officers, and expresses official positions of the federation. The general board consists of the executive council, presidents of each affiliated national, and representatives from each constitutionally described department within the federation.

The ongoing business of the AFL–CIO is handled by the top executives, their staffs, and the constitutional departments. One set of con-

---

[35] Marick F. Masters and John Thomas Delaney, "Union Political Activities: A Review of the Empirical Literature," *Industrial and Labor Relations Review* 40 (1987), pp. 336–53.

[36] *Directory of National Unions and Employee Associations, 1982–1983* (Washington, D.C.: Bureau of National Affairs, 1982), pp. 7–10.

FIGURE 5-3

Structural Organization of the American Federation of Labor and Congress of Industrial Organizations

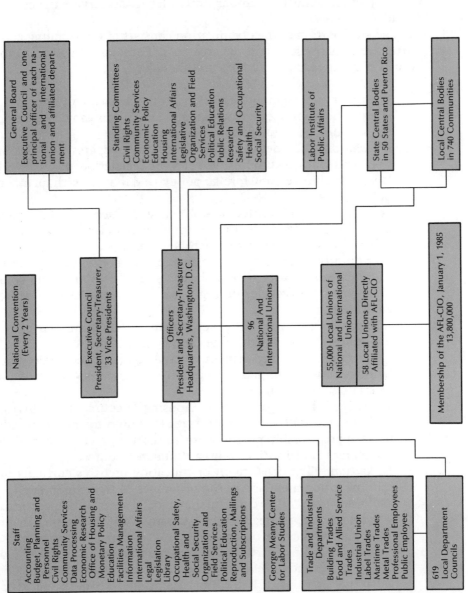

stitutional departments—the seven trade and industrial departments—relates to jurisdictional interests of the national members: building and construction trades, maritime trades, metal trades, railway employees, industrial unions, union label and service trades, and public employees.

The staff portion of the organization consists of the standing committees and their equivalent departments. These are involved in the normal ongoing federal activities and include:

1. *Organizing.* Field representatives of the department of organizing and field services encourage and assist unorganized workers or local unions in unionization campaigns.
2. *Legislation.* The department of legislation prepares official positions; provides testimony on relevant legislation dealing with labor, social issues, and foreign policy; and lobbies with members of Congress.
3. *Politics.* The committee on political education evaluates legislative records of federal, state, and local candidates and provides political information to the membership.
4. *Community services.* The department of community services coordinates activities with and assists local charitable and community service agencies during fund drives, local crises, and regional disasters.
5. *International affairs.* The department of international affairs maintains a liaison with trade unions in the free world.
6. *Civil rights.* The department of civil rights polices union violations of civil rights and pursues liaison activities with state and federal civil rights agencies.
7. *Housing.* The department of housing encourages the investment of pension funds in mortgages for union members, coordinates apprenticeship programs for minorities, and works toward the increased utilization of urban human resources.
8. *Education.* The department of education prepares curricula for training union members in the principles of trade unionism.
9. *Social security.* The department of social security advises affiliates on matters related to social security, unemployment insurance, and workers' compensation.
10. *Research.* The department of economic research analyzes economic trends and the effects of legislative and economic policy on collective bargaining. It also maintains specialists in industrial engineering, consumer affairs, and natural resource problems.
11. *Public affairs.* The department of information maintains liaison with the media and communicates the official position of the federation on current issues. It also serves as the major link between the federation and the individual member through publication of the weekly *AFL-CIO News* and the monthly *AFL-CIO Federationist.*

12. *Economic policy.*   The committee on economic policy formulates AFL–CIO positions on the development of public policy regarding wages and employment.
13. *Occupational safety and health.*   This department works closely with government agencies administering health and safety legislation. It also provides technical support to unions and education programs on job safety to union members.

In addition to these departments, the AFL–CIO has a direct relationship with almost 800 state and local central bodies. These bodies reflect the composition of the parent AFL–CIO and the particular industrial mix of their geographic areas. The state and local centrals are directly responsible to the AFL–CIO, not to the internationals.

Political activity and lobbying are major AFL–CIO activities. Many issues before Congress have potential direct and indirect effects on the labor movement. Exhibit 5–5 describes some of the activities of Robert M. McGlotten, the AFL–CIO's chief lobbyist.

EXHIBIT 5–5

Labor Lobbying Activities

It is evening in the Capitol, and Robert M. McGlotten, chief lobbyist for the AFL–CIO, emerges briskly from a closed meeting with Representative Dan Rostenkowski, the Ways and Means Committee chairman.

The lobbyist jabs a finger into the air to make a point with a colleague, pauses to trade jokes with two members of Congress, then forms a tight corridor huddle with his fellow labor lobbyists to plot the next move on a trade bill.

"I've been running around like a chicken without a head," Mr. McGlotten declared, describing the quickened pace of life four months into his job of representing the interests of the AFL–CIO.

Mr. McGlotten faces . . . hurdles. While most lobbyists are expected to master and become influential on a certain topic, he is expected to be persuasive on dozens of issues that concern big labor, from unemployment to taxes to trade to health and, of late, the budget.

Much of Mr. McGlotten's work these days is devoted to defeating the Reagan administration's proposed budget cuts. To that end, as an experienced corridor pacer, one who knows by first name a dizzying array of people involved in the day-to-day operations of Congress, Mr. McGlotten sometimes seems to be everywhere at once, working the labyrinthine halls of the Capitol, trading gossip and vital information, breathing the air, feeling the pulse.

"From day to day, from hour to hour, nothing is the same on the Hill," he said. "You have to be there, one on one. If you're not there, you're missing something."

Source: Kenneth B. Noble, "Labor Lobbyist's Task: Be Everywhere at Once," *New York Times*, May 25, 1986, p. 18Y.

STATE AND LOCAL CENTRAL BODIES

State and local central bodies are primarily involved in political and lobbying activities. However, activities in national elections must be consistent with the position taken by the AFL–CIO.[37] Major stress is given to endorsements of state and local candidates and testimony and lobbying on local and state legislative matters. The major difference between the parent AFL–CIO and the state and local central bodies is that the AFL–CIO consists predominantly of affiliated internationals, while state and local centrals draw on affiliation with local unions. Figure 5–4 shows the relationship of state and local central bodies to other labor organizations.

OVERVIEW OF THE UNION HIERARCHY

The major locus of power in the labor movement clearly resides in the nationals, and locals and the federation derive their power from the nationals. Local unions are structured to handle the day-to-day activities of the membership. Much of their effort involves policing the contract and handling grievances.

The national union could be compared with the corporate staff division of a large company, where policies are developed, actions are

FIGURE 5–4

The Relationship of the AFL–CIO
to State and Local Central Bodies

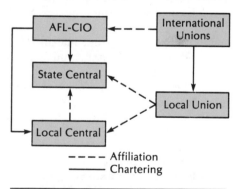

———— Affiliation
———— Chartering

Source: Adapted from Joan G. Kilpatrick and Miles C. Stanley, *Handbook on Central Labor Bodies: Functions and Activities.* West Virginia University Bulletin, series 64, no. 4–6, October 1963, p. 5.

---

[37] *Rules Governing AFL–CIO State Central Bodies,* Publication No. 12 (Washington, D.C.: AFL–CIO, 1973), p. 21.

audited to ensure conformity to policy, and advice is given to generalists in the plants (or locals) on specific issues. Although the convention ultimately governs the national, many presidents have broad powers to take interim actions and also to markedly influence the delegate composition of future conventions.

The AFL–CIO serves the same function as a trade association, a chamber of commerce, or a national association of manufacturers. It coordinates activities among the nationals and amplifies their voices. The federation's prime functions are information, integration, and advocacy. Its greatest areas of autonomy relate to legislative and political processes.

NATIONAL UNION MERGERS

Several national unions have recently been involved in mergers. Mergers appear to take two forms: *absorption,* in which a small or rapidly declining union becomes a part of a larger national[38] (for example, the 450-member Window Glass Cutters League's 1975 merger into the 80,000-member Glass Bottle Blowers); and *amalgamation,* in which two unions of roughly equal size merge to form a new union (for example, the 1979 merger of the 500,000-member Amalgamated Meat Cutters and Butcher Workers with the 700,000-member Retail Clerks to form the United Food and Commercial Workers.[39]

Three different reasons have been suggested for a merger: (1) a *symbiotic* merger, in which two unions represent workers whose outputs are interdependent; (2) a *commensalistic* merger, in which two unions have competed for the organization of the same employees; and (3) a *scale* merger, wherein a large union seeks to increase its efficiency or power. Evidence suggests that symbiotic mergers prevail when unions are expanding membership and commensalistic mergers are more common during contraction. Recessions are associated with greater merger activity.[40]

Population ecology models of organization can help us understand some of the environmental changes leading to union mergers.[41] First, unions cannot exist in the absence of employers (obviously, the reverse is possible). Second, differences in jurisdictions claimed by unions are not accidental. Jurisdictions developed because the particular needs of

[38] Charles J. Janus, "Union Mergers in the 1970s: A Look at the Reasons and Results," *Monthly Labor Review,* October 1978, pp. 13–23.

[39] Gary N. Chaison, "Union Growth and Union Mergers," *Industrial Relations,* Winter 1981, pp. 98–108.

[40] John Freeman and Jack Brittain, "Union Merger Process and the Industrial Environment," *Industrial Relations,* May 1977, pp. 173–85.

[41] See, for example, Michael T. Hannan and John Freeman, "The Population Ecology of Organizations," *American Journal of Sociology,* 1977, pp. 929–64.

employees in certain occupations or industries were better met by specialization, and these needs created niches for the formation of new unions. Specialization, however, carries a risk. If the occupation or industry served declines, the union may not survive if it remains specialized. But, general unions cannot be expected to have the expertise of a specialist union in serving the representational needs of particular subgroups. As an example, District 1199 (a health care industry subsidiary) has tried for some time to separate from the Retail Workers in order to join the Service Employees. It was finally able to separate, but not to merge, when the AFL–CIO chartered the National Union of Hospital and Health Care Employees. Further symbiotic and commensalistic mergers will likely take place. However, the emphasis will probably remain toward commensal mergers as the labor movement continues a period of contraction.

One consideration in merger decisions involves how the duplication of national union officers and services will be eliminated. Another consideration is related to the potential redundancy of more than one local union in a given area. Symbiotic mergers are probably the easiest since the needs of the merged membership may have little overlap. Commensalistic mergers require agreements on the role of present union officers and the fate of local unions following the merger. Mergers are eased when few integration issues exist, as where craft identities are preserved, the regional penetration of one union is great, important historical traditions are preserved, leadership duplication problems are accommodated, and merged structures are based on strong individual union identities.[42]

UNION FINANCES

Union finances are generally related to two different functions. The first involves the day-to-day operations of the union, and the second is associated with the fiduciary obligation of officers in some unions in the collection, trusteeship, and disbursement of pension and welfare benefits to members. The latter is usually found in craft unions or unions in which employers are too small or marginal to administer their own pension programs.

Organization Receipts and Disbursements

Three major sources of revenue are available to unions: dues from members; fees, fines, and assessments from members; and investment

---

[42] Gary N. Chaison, "Union Mergers and the Integration of Union Governing Structures," *Journal of Labor Research* 3 (1982), pp. 139–51.

income. Dues and fees are collected at the local level. The only entities dependent on the dues themselves are the locals. The nationals and the AFL–CIO levy a per capita tax on the local. The current AFL–CIO per capita tax is 13 cents monthly; many nationals require locals to remit about 50 percent of dues for their operations.[43] Dues vary widely among unions; some require a flat fee, while others scale fees to earning levels. The dues usually have minimum and maximum levels set by the parent national, with the local given flexibility to adjust within those limits. Occasionally, an assessment is added to replenish or maintain strike funds.

About 85 percent of local unions require an initiation fee. Most new members pay $40 or less to become members. Dues vary among locals, but a common rule of thumb is to make them equal to two hours' wages per month.[44]

According to the U.S. Department of Labor, local unions received 72 percent of their income from dues; 9 percent from fees, fines, and assessments; and 19 percent from other sources. Of the funds they disbursed, 30 percent went for per capita taxes, 26 percent for officer and employee salaries, 8 percent for office and administrative expenses, 7 percent for member benefits, and 29 percent for other items. National unions received 29 percent of their income from per capita taxes; 1 percent from fees, fines, assessments, and work permits; and 70 percent from investments and other sources. Investments in securities, real estate, and other ventures reflect the business orientation of U.S. unions. National unions spent about 7 percent of their funds for affiliation payments, 8 percent for salaries, 3 percent for office and administrative expenses, less than 1 percent for loans, 11 percent for benefits, and the other 71 percent for other payments.[45]

Union Officer Compensation

The compensation of national union officers is relatively modest in comparison with executives of large private-sector corporations. During the most recent survey year, the average compensation for a national union president in one of the large national unions or associations was $118,619. Highest paid was Jackie Presser, general president of the Teamsters, with total pay from his three union jobs of $571,960.[46] Variables that appear most strongly related to national

---

[43] *This Is the AFL–CIO*, pamphlet no. 20 (Washington, D.C.: AFL–CIO, 1980), p. 5.

[44] Charles W. Hickman, "Labor Organizations' Fees and Dues," *Monthly Labor Review*, May 1977, pp. 19–24.

[45] U.S. Department of Labor, *Union Financial Statistics, 1976* (Washington, D.C.: U.S. Government Printing Office, 1978).

[46] Jonathan Tasini and Jane B. Todaro, "How Much Top Labor Leaders Made in 1986," *Business Week*, May 4, 1987, p. 96.

officer compensation include total expenditures of the national union, dues levels, total assets owned by the union, and number of locals.[47] Industrial unions may pay less, given the sizes of their memberships, than craft unions.[48]

Pension Administration

Pension plans are frequently administered by craft unions and other unions where the number of employers is small. Craft union dues are greater than those in industrial unions, with a portion set aside for benefits. Other unions require employers to make a per capita payment, as in the Central States Carriers and Teamsters agreement (1985), which called for $69 per employee per week in pension and welfare payments. A royalty on coal tonnage is negotiated in the coal industry, and this income is used to pay retirement benefits.

The administration of pension programs has become an increasingly important issue for both union administrators and members. The Employee Retirement Income Security Act of 1974 requires pension administrators to follow practices to safeguard the contributions made toward retirement. Certain investment practices, such as risky or low-interest loans, are illegal. Investments in one's own organization are also largely precluded.

SUMMARY

Organized labor has essentially a three-tiered structure (local, national, and AFL–CIO), with power concentrated at the second level. At the local level, the most typical structure is the single bargaining unit. Multiemployer units are perhaps most common in the construction industry. National unions are of two major types; craft, representing workers in a specific occupation; and industrial, representing occupations in a specific industry. The AFL–CIO is the only major U.S. labor federation, with over three quarters of all union and association members affiliated since the Teamsters rejoined.

Although the local is the workers' direct representative, members' interests in internal affairs are generally low. They appear to view the union as their employment agent and allow a cadre of activists to control its internal politics.

---

[47] Marcus H. Sandver and Herbert G. Heneman III, "Analysis and Prediction of Top National Union Officers' Total Compensation," *Academy of Management Journal*, 1980, pp. 534–43.

[48] Philip Taft, "Understanding Union Administration," *Harvard Business Review*, 1950, pp. 245–57.

National union structures, particularly the industrials, adapt to both the breadth of their constituencies and the concentration within their industries. For example, the UAW has a "General Motors Department," and the USW has a "basic steel" component in its industry conference.

Whether unions operate *democratically* depends on the definition of the term. Most do not have two-party systems, and many equate dissent with attempts to undermine union goals. On the other hand, local officers are directly elected, and international officials are chosen in a manner similar to a presidential nominating convention. Unions introduce democracy into the work setting by requiring a bargaining contract. Within a union, the checks and balances initiated through its constitution and contracts serve to increase democracy and safeguards for members.

DISCUSSION QUESTIONS

1. If you were recommending an organizational structure for a national union, what factors would you advise it to take into account (industrial concentration, occupations it represents, and so on)?

2. Should unions be permitted to endorse political candidates and engage in political action?

3. How could a union local increase the involvement of its membership?

4. Defend or attack the usual method of electing an international president (through local delegates and international staff members at the convention).

CHAPTER 6

Union Organizing and Employer Response

Chapter 1 examined some of the reasons workers desire representation. This chapter examines the flow of organizing campaigns, involvement of the National Labor Relations Board, (NLRB), effects of union avoidance programs, strategies and tactics used by employers and unions during election campaigns, and recent results in NLRB-monitored representation elections.

In studying this chapter, consider the following questions:

1. At what points and in what ways is the NLRB involved in representation elections?
2. What effects have recent employer union avoidance programs had on the incidence of union organizing?
3. What new initiatives in representation have unions taken recently?
4. What common strategies and tactics are used by employers and unions during organizing campaigns?

HOW ORGANIZING BEGINS

Attempts to organize unrepresented workers begin at either the local or national union level. National union-organizing campaigns send full-time organizers to a specific set of locations to encourage or assist local employees in establishing a union. An organizing campaign initiated by a national union often occurs when a unionized firm establishes a new plant not covered by an existing contract. The national union representing the employees in the firm's other plants campaigns to organize the new plant's employees to bring the firm's practices at the new plant into line with those in the rest of the organization. Other national organizing attempts target a nonunion firm in a predominantly unionized industry. Most organizing attempts begin at the local level when some portion of the employees decide that they would be better off if they could bargain collectively with the employer.

The Framework for Organizing

In our examination of organizing, campaign activities, typical patterns and exceptions, and the legal basis for present NLRB policy toward organizing will be covered. Figure 6-1 presents a generalized sequence of organizing events.

FIGURE 6-1

Sequence of Organizing Events

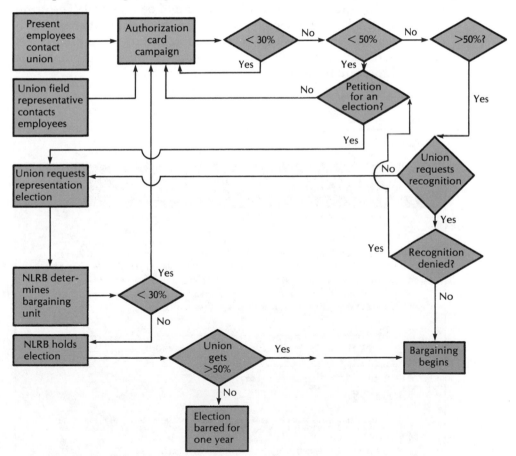

Union organizing begins with an authorization card campaign. By signing authorization cards, employees empower the union to act as their agent in negotiating wages, hours, and terms and conditions of employment. Figure 6–2 is an example of an authorization card.

The authorization card campaign tries to enroll as many employees as possible in the work unit the union desires to represent. If a majority of employees join, the union can directly request recognition from the employer as the employees' bargaining agent. In most cases, this request will be refused. The union will then petition the NLRB for a representation election and include evidence of support in the form of the signed authorization cards. The NLRB cross-checks the signed cards against a roster of employees in the work unit. If fewer than 30 percent have signed, the NLRB will dismiss the petition for lack of sufficient interest. If more than 30 percent have signed, the NLRB will schedule an election, unless the unit is not legally within its jurisdiction or the employer contests the appropriateness of the proposed unit. The makeup of an appropriate bargaining unit is frequently contested, thus requiring the NLRB to decide who should be included. The criteria used by the board for deciding whether a proposed unit is appropriate is discussed in detail later in this chapter. For the present, it is sufficient to say that bargaining units usually consist of employees with common interests, as determined by the board.

FIGURE 6–2

Authorization Card

YES, I WANT THE IAM

I, the undersigned employee of

(Company)

authorize the International Association of Machinists and Aerospace Workers (IAM) to act as my collective bargaining agent for wages, hours and working conditions. I agree that this card may be used either to support a demand for recognition or an NLRB election, at the discretion of the union.

NAME (print)_____ DATE_____
HOME ADDRESS_____ PHONE_____
CITY_____ STATE_____ ZIP_____
JOB TITLE_____ DEPT._____ SHIFT_____

SIGN HERE X

NOTE: This authorization to be SIGNED and DATED in Employee's own handwriting. YOUR RIGHT TO SIGN THIS CARD IS PROTECTED BY FEDERAL LAW.

RECEIVED BY (Initial)_____

When an appropriate bargaining unit is defined, if at least 30 percent of the employees have signed authorization cards, the NLRB will order an election unless the union withdraws its petition. If the union wins a majority of the eligible votes cast in the election, the board certifies it as the employees' bargaining agent and negotiations on a contract can begin. If the union loses, the board certifies the results, and no other representation election may be conducted in that unit for a one-year period.

Representation Elections

Figure 6–3 shows that if interest in repesentation (or decertification) is sufficient, the union (or the employer, in the absence of a demand for recognition) can petition the NLRB to hold an election to determine the desires of the employees. This section traces the basic steps involved.

FIGURE 6–3

Avenues to Election Petitions

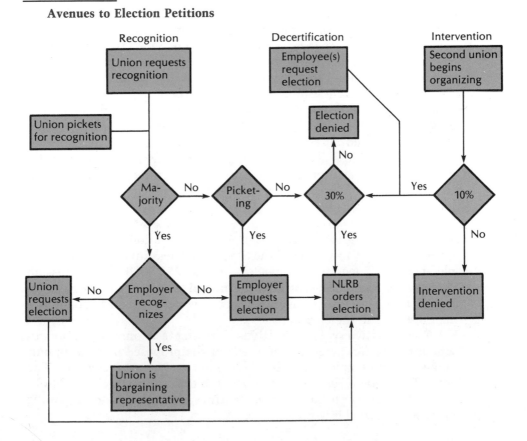

Recognition requests. An election initially takes place to determine whether employees desire representation. If doubt later arises whether the union continues to retain its majority status, a *decertification election* will be held.

A union will not usually make a recognition request unless a substantial majority of employees has signed authorization cards. The union prefers a margin since the employer will likely question the eligibility of some workers to be represented or vote in the election. An employer faced with a recognition request usually claims the union's majority status is doubtful. The union may offer to have a neutral third party match the authorization card signatures with a list of employees to establish that a majority actually exists. If a majority has signed and the employer is satisfied with the appropriateness of the proposed bargaining unit, recognition can be granted voluntarily.

A union may picket an unorganized employer for up to 30 days, demanding that it be recognized as the employees' bargaining representative. If this occurs, the employer can petition the NLRB to hold an election among the employees the union seeks to represent. If the union loses, further recognitional picketing would be an unfair labor practice.

Election petitions. An election petition may be filed with the board by a labor organization, an employer, or an individual. In certain types of elections, however, employers are precluded from filing petitions since early petitions might find inadequate union support to pursue the election. Proof of interest must be shown in its petition or within 48 hours. The union must specify the group of employees it desires to represent. If an employer has had a recognition demand from a union (for example, recognitional picketing), it can directly petition the board to hold an election. A union or an employee (but not an employer) can file a decertification petition alleging that the present union is no longer supported by a majority of employees and that its removal as bargaining agent is desired. The 30 percent interest requirement exists here as well.

Preelection board involvement. The NLRB first determines whether it has jurisdiction in the proposed election. Jurisdiction requirements vary according to the type of business involved. For example, nonretail operations must do at least $50,000 of business in interstate commerce per year to be included. When the board takes jurisdiction a number of avenues open. Figure 6–4 details board procedures prior to the election.

There are two types of elections. The first is a *consent* election, in which the parties agree on the scope of the proposed bargaining unit and on which employees will be eligible to vote in an election. The second is a *board-directed* (or *petition*) election, in which the NLRB regional director determines, after hearings, the appropriate bargaining unit and the eligible voters.

FIGURE 6–4

NLRB Involvement: Petition to Election

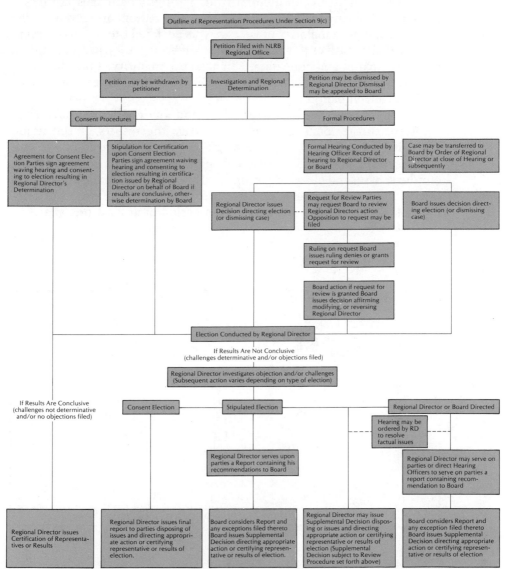

If the board directs an election, the employer is required to provide, within seven days, a so-called Excelsior list containing the names and addresses of employees in the proposed bargaining unit.[1] Then, after 10 days but not more than 30 days, the election will normally be held.

[1] *Excelsior Underwear, Inc.*, 156 NLRB 1236 (1966).

The election. The NLRB supervises the secret ballot election. Both company and union observers may challenge voter eligibility but may not prohibit any individual from voting. Challenges are determined subsequent to the election. After the ballots are counted, the choice receiving a majority of *votes cast* is declared the winner. If more than two alternatives (for example, two different unions and no union) are on the ballot and none obtain an absolute majority, a runoff will be held among the two highest choices. Figure 6-5 is an example of an NLRB election ballot.

After the election has taken place and any challenges have been resolved, the regional director will certify the results. If the union wins, it becomes the exclusive bargaining representative of the employees in the unit and is entitled to begin negotiating a contract. If the employer wins, no election petition will be honored by the NLRB for a one-year period. In effect, certification guarantees the union or non-union status of a bargaining unit for a period of at least one year.[2]

FIGURE 6-5

Specimen NLRB Ballot

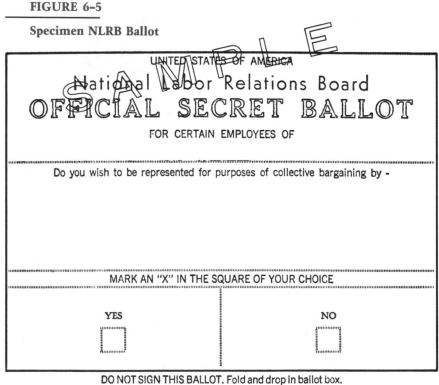

UNITED STATES OF AMERICA

National Labor Relations Board

OFFICIAL SECRET BALLOT

FOR CERTAIN EMPLOYEES OF

Do you wish to be represented for purposes of collective bargaining by -

MARK AN "X" IN THE SQUARE OF YOUR CHOICE

YES	NO
☐	☐

DO NOT SIGN THIS BALLOT. Fold and drop in ballot box.
If you spoil this ballot return it to the Board Agent for a new one.

[2] *Brooks* v. *NLRB*, 348 U.S. 96 (1954).

BARGAINING UNIT DETERMINATION

The NLRB determines bargaining units by considering a variety of factors, including (1) legal constraints, (2) the constitutional jurisdiction of the organizing union, (3) the union's likely success in organizing and bargaining, (4) the employers' desires in resisting organization or promoting stability in the bargaining relationship, and (5) its own philosophy in unit determination.

Bargaining units may differ depending on whether we are referring to organizing and representation or to contract negotiations. For example, several retail stores in a given chain may constitute an appropriate bargaining unit for representation election purposes; while for bargaining purposes, several retail stores owned by different companies may associate in multiemployer bargaining. The discussion of bargaining unit determination in this chapter is concerned only with representation activities, and bargaining units for negotiations are discussed in Chapter 7.

Certain legal constraints limit the potential scope of a bargaining unit, but within these constraints the contending parties—labor and management—are free to jointly determine an appropriate unit. If they do, a consent election results. If they don't the NLRB has the responsibility for determining unit appropriateness.

Legal Constraints

Section 9(b) of the Taft-Hartley Act details the constraints placed on unit determination. First, no unit can be composed of both professional and nonprofessional employees without the express approval of a majority of the professionals. Second, a separate craft unit within an employer's operation may not be precluded from forming simply because the board had earlier included it in a broader group; however, this subsection has been broadly intepreted by the NLRB in continuing the inclusion of craft groups in larger units. Third, no bargaining unit may jointly consist of guards hired by employers to enforce the company's rules and of other employees. Fourth, supervisors and managers are precluded from inclusion in a unit and/or bargaining collectively since their roles as agents of the employer place them outside the employee defintion in Section 2. Other than those proscriptions, the board is free to develop its own rules for bargaining unit determination.

While this chapter does not detail organizing in employers covered by the Railway Labor Act, it should be noted that the National Mediation Board handles elections in those units. The major difference between the two jurisdictions is that the Railway Labor Board requires bargaining units to be formed on a craft basis.

Jurisdiction of the Organizing Union

Some unions concentrate on organizing certain occupations or industries. Many other unions organize in areas other than their traditional jurisdictions because of a shrinking employment base.

If an AFL–CIO union is attempting to organize where another AFL–CIO union already represents employees, the NLRB will notify the AFL–CIO when a petition is filed to allow the federation to adjudicate the problem internally according to its constitution. This process almost always resolves the jurisdictional problem, since one condition of AFL–CIO affiliation is agreeing to let the federation resolve internal disputes.

The Union's Desired Unit

The union is faced with several problems in deciding what bargaining unit configuration it desires. It must balance the optimal configuration of a unit for purposes of winning an election against its objectives in later contract negotiations. A craft union would likely seek a bargaining unit that includes only workers of relatively similar skills. Industrial unions would tend to be inclusive, seeking recognition for most employees (coverable under the law) within a given plant or company.

A union must gain recognition before it can bargain. Therefore, it might suggest a unit in which an authorization card majority already exists or one it believes will be easiest to organize. On the other hand, organizing a unit that would have little impact on the company's business if the union were to strike would be futile. For example, gaining a majority in a unit of custodial employees in a manufacturing plant may be relatively easy, but negotiating a favorable contract might be more difficult since the employer could readily subcontract the work for little incremental cost during the strike.

The goals of the union, then, are twofold: (1) the establishment of a "winnable" unit and (2) the definition of a unit that will have some bargaining power with the employer.

The Employer's Desired Unit

The employer's desired unit is often different than—but not necessarily diametrically opposite of—the union's desired unit. It may prefer a unit in which the union is unlikely to win an election. If a craft union is organizing, the employer will generally favor a plant-wide unit. In some circumstances, the employer will seek to narrow the unit so that groups strongly in favor of the union will not lead to a majority among a variety of groups that marginally support management. Figure 6–6 details a situation in which management might argue for a smaller unit than the organizing union desires.

The firm also would like the unit configured so as to minimize the

FIGURE 6-6

Conflicting Unit Desires

	ST	P and M	S and R	OC	Total
Percent pro-u	40	76	45	30	60
Percent pro-m	60	24	55	70	40
Number pro-u	20	760	90	120	990
Number pro-m	30	240	110	280	660

union's bargaining power if it obtained recognition. Thus, management might desire functionally independent units, which would allow continued operations if a strike occurred. On the other hand, it would like to avoid fragmented units, which might require continuous bargaining due to different contract expiration dates and might result in conceding to excessive demands of single units to avoid a siege of rotating strikes among the unions.

NLRB Policy

NLRB policy determines bargaining unit appropriateness where disputes exist. Although the board has not exercised completely consistent decision making in unit determination, it has applied the following criteria.[3]

1. *Community of interests.* The mutuality of interests among employees in bargaining for wages, hours, and working conditions is frequently applied.[4] However, this criterion is difficult to interpret because no benchmark is used to define the degree of similarity necessary among employee groups.

---

[3] John E. Abodeely, Randi C. Hammer, and Andrew L. Sandler, *The NLRB and the Appropriate Bargaining Unit*, rev. ed., Labor Relations and Public Policy Series, report no. 3 (Philadelphia: Industrial Research Unit, Department of Industry, Wharton School of Finance and Commerce, University of Pennsylvania, 1981).

[4] *Continental Baking Co.*, 99 NLRB 777 (1952).

2. *Geographic and physical proximity.* The more separated in distance two or more locations are, the more difficult it is for a single union to represent employees. This factor may be given considerable weight when the employer's policies differ substantially across locations.

3. *Employer's administrative or territorial divisions.* If labor relations or personnel management within a firm were uniform over a given territory (for example, 46 grocery stores located in five counties of southeastern Michigan and managed as a territorial subdivision of a multistate chain), then this unit rather than a single store or subset may be appropriate.

4. *Functional integration.* This factor relates to the degree to which all potentially includable employees are required to maintain the company's major production processes. For example, in its decision in *Borden Co.*, the board recognized that although 20 different facilities were involved in the seemingly independent processes of manufacturing (3 plants) and distributing (17 plants) ice cream and had varying personnel policies, an appropriate unit would contain all 20 plants due to the interrelationships between facilities necessary to market the final product.[5]

5. *Interchange of employees.* If employees are frequently transferred across plants or offices, their community of interest may be similar, thus leading the board to designate a multiplant unit.

6. *Bargaining history.* In applying this factor, the board may take into account the past practices of the union and the employer (if it were a decertification or unit clarification election) or typical industry practices in bargaining. For example, if an employer had a company-wide unit that had served the mutual bargaining interests of both the employer and the union, the board would probably leave it undisturbed.

7. *Employee desires.* Early in the board's history, the *Globe Doctrine* was developed.[6] Where a bargaining history involving several units exists, the board may allow employees to vote for or against their inclusion in a more comprehensive unit.

8. *Extent of organization.* The board may consider, after the foregoing factors are analyzed, the degree to which organization has taken place in a proposed unit, although this is not considered the prime factor.[7] The Supreme Court has ruled that the board could consider it because Section 9(c) (5) of the Taft-Hartley Act requires

---

[5] *Borden Co., Hutchinson Ice Cream Div.*, 89 NLRB 227 (1950).
[6] Abodeely et al., *NLRB and the Appropriate Bargaining Unit*, pp. 66–68.
[7] *NLRB v. Metropolitan Life Insurance Co.*, 380 U.S. 438 (1965).

consideration of allowing employees the fullest freedom in exercising their rights.

Many of these factors are interrelated. For example, employee interchange is more likely to occur within a defined administrative unit, and, in turn, an interchange should establish a broader community of interests. Thus the board's determination frequently rests on several factors. Although these factors are generally utilized, there have been exceptions to each.[8]

Craft severance. The term *craft severance* means that a group of employees with a substantially different community of interests within the proposed unit is allowed to establish itself as a separate unit. Craft severance can occur during initial unit determination or as the result of a group of presently represented employees voting to leave their bargaining unit.

The current board's opinion on craft severance is enunciated in the *Mallinckrodt Doctrine.*[9] In *Mallinckrodt*, a group of instrument mechanics sought severance from a larger unit of production and maintenance employees. The petition was denied by the NLRB, which reasoned that the instrument mechanics were integrally involved in the production process and that the interests of the employer and the union representing the unit had to be considered in deciding the severance request. The board enumerated the following hurdles necessary to gain severance: (1) a high degree of skill or a functional differentiation and a tradition of separate representation; (2) a short history of bargaining in the present unit and a low degree of disruption likely if severance were granted; (3) a high degree of distinct separateness in the established unit among members of the proposed unit; (4) a different collective bargaining history of the industry; (5) a low degree of integration in production; and (6) a high degree of experience of the union desiring severance as a representative for that craft.[10]

Severance or establishment of separate units is easier during initial organization. Craft severance has been allowed in cases of a recognizable difference in the communities of interest and when no prior contrary bargaining history exists.[11] The degree of functional integration in the production processes for the firms involved in these cases was not substantially different than in *Mallinckrodt*.

---

[8] Abodeely et al, *NLRB and the Appropriate Bargaining Unit*, pp. 11–86.

[9] *Mallinckrodt Chemical Works*, 162 NLRB 387 (1966).

[10] Ibid., p. 397.

[11] *E. I. du Pont de Nemours & Co.*, 162 NLRB 413 (1966) and *Anheuser-Busch, Inc.*, 170 NLRB No. 5 (1968).

What factors are used? For severance, the overriding factor appears to be bargaining history, buttressed by the functional integration in an employer's operation. For representation, community of interest and functional integration are important. The workers' community of interest is affected to a great extent by the production process, employee interchange policies, geographic proximity, and administrative decision making. However, no hard-and-fast rules apply, and the board determines bargaining unit appropriateness on a case-by-case basis.

Judicial precedents are few, since the NLRB bagaining unit determinations are not "final orders" and are, therefore, unappealable. If an employer is dissatisfied with the board's determination, its only recourse is to refuse to bargain after losing an election and to have the courts determine the appropriateness of the board's determination.[12] In most cases, the courts will leave it undisturbed.

Other Issues in Unit Determination

The structures of organizations change over time. What was initially an appropriate unit may not be presently. Major factors involved in the continuing definition of a unit include company growth and acquisitions, reorganization, reclassification of jobs, or puchase by another firm.

Accretion. Accretion occurs when a new facility is included in the bargaining unit or when an existing union in an organization gains representation rights for employees previously represented by another union. The NLRB generally applies the same standards to accretion as it does to initial unit determination. However, the board tends to give extra weight to the desires of employees in the unit subject to accretion.

Reorganization and reclassification. An employer will occasionally reclassify jobs or reorganize administrative units. These changes might make a previously defined bargaining unit inappropriate, and the parties may redefine the unit by consent. Failing this, the employer would have to refuse to bargain, and the union would have to file an unfair labor practice charge in order for the board to reexamine appropriateness.

Successor organizations. Generally speaking, a firm taking over another company or merging with another assumes the contractual bargaining obligations accrued up to the time of the merger.[13] An employer who assumes another's operations where the employees simply change employers is obligated to recognize the union but need

---

[12] Abodeely et al., *NLRB and the Appropriate Bargaining Unit*, pp. 28–29.
[13] *John Wiley & Sons, Inc.,* v. *Livingston,* 376 U.S. 543 (1964).

not honor the predecessor's contract with the union.[14] But a substantial and apparent continuity in operations does not create an obligation if the union lacks majority status, even if the absence of a majority is due to layoffs and new hires by the successor.[15]

THE ORGANIZING CAMPAIGN

The organizing campaign begins with attempts by the union to gain signed authorization cards. During the early part of the campaign, organizing may be done surreptitiously until the viability of the drive can be assessed. While employers may not know immediately that an organizing drive is taking place, many have installed preventive measures to make organizing difficult, particularly for nonemployees.

No Distribution or Solicitation Rules

Most employers prohibit solicitations by an organization on company property or on company time. These rules prohibit labor organizers from gaining easy access to employees since labor organizers cannot be treated differently than representatives of other organizations. An organizing campaign is much more difficult if workers must be contacted off the job, especially if the organizer does not know where they live.

But no-solicitation rules do not apply to employees. A line of Supreme Court decisions differentiates the rights of employee and nonemployee organizers. These rulings allow employees to solicit fellow workers on company premises (during nonworking time) unless a clear showing can be made that the solicitation interferes with production.[16] On the other hand, nonemployee organizers (for example, international union field representatives) can, in most instances, be prohibited from soliciting on company property.[17] As a result of these decisions, very early support in the plant is required for the drive to be successful.

In special cases, a union organizer may solicit on the company's property. These cases occur where no other reasonable access to the

---

[14] *NLRB* v. *Burns International Security Services,* 406 U.S. 272 (1972).

[15] *Howard Johnson Co., Inc.* v. *Detroit Local Joint Executive Board, Hotel and Restaurant Employees & Bartenders International Union, AFL–CIO,* 417 U.S. 249 (1974).

[16] *Republic Aviation Corp.* v. *NLRB;* and *NLRB* v. *LeTourneau Co.,* 324 U.S. 793 (1945).

[17] *NLRB* v. *Babcock & Wilcox Co.; NLRB* v. *Seamprufe, Inc.;* and *Ranco, Inc.* v. *NLRB,* 351 U.S. 105 (1956).

employees can be had, as in remote operations (logging) or where workers live in a company town.[18] On the other hand, organizers are forbidden to take advantage of the quasi-public nature of some of the company's property, such as retail store parking lots or shopping center malls, to solicit workers.[19]

Employers can lessen the chance of solicitation by requiring employees to leave working areas and plants immediately after their shifts end.

Union Strategy and Tactics

Once the campaign begins, both parties enter a period during which their actions are scrutinized. Labor law provides that individuals cannot be coerced or restrained in their rights to engage in or avoid concerted activity and to be represented by their own chosen agents. This means neither party may legally interfere with an employee's right to join or not to join a union.

The union is faced with a delicate early strategy problem. It must publicize its activities enough to induce others to join, but it wants to conceal the activities from the employer to avoid triggering a reaction. If a union suspects that an employer will retaliate against employee union organizers, it may deliberately inform the company of the activists' names so the company cannot later plead that any disciplinary actions taken against them were not based on antiunion feelings.[20]

If they want to avoid unfair labor practice findings, employers must take care to not treat employees differently as a result of their union activity. Once an organizing campaign begins, the employer must take particular pains to carry out personnel practices consistent with past practices and equally across workers. Exhibit 6–1 illustrates this point in a decision involving an extreme case of a personnel practice reversal toward an individual.

The union may encounter difficulties if employees do not want to sign cards authorizing the union to act as their bargaining representative. If signers do not authorize an agency relationship, the cards cannot be used to gain a representation election.[21] Employees may also be concerned that their employer will find out they are personally interested in unionization.

Chapter 1 stressed that an individual might see benefits in a union if membership were seen as leading to more certain attainment of

---

[18] *Marsh* v. *Alabama*, 326 U.S. 501 (1946).

[19] *Central Hardware Co.* v. *NLRB*, 407 U.S. 539 (1972); and *Hudgens* v. *NLRB*, 91 LRRM 2489 (U.S. Supreme Court, 1976).

[20] Stephen I. Schlossberg and Frederick E. Sherman, *Organizing and the Law*, rev. ed. (Washington, D.C.: Bureau of National Affairs, 1971).

[21] Ibid., p. 51.

EXHIBIT 6-1

Edward G. Budd Manufacturing Co. v. NLRB

U.S. Court of Appeals, Third Circuit, 1943, 138 F. 2d 86, Biggs, Circuit Judge. . . .

The complaint alleges that the petitioner, in September 1933, created and foisted a labor organization known as the Budd Employee Representation Association upon its employees and thereafter contributed financial support to the association and dominated its activities. The amended complaint also alleges that in July 1941 the petitioner discharged an employee, Walter Weigand, because of his activities on behalf of the union.

The case of Walter Weigand is extraordinary. If ever a workman deserved summary discharge it was he. He was under the influence of liquor while on duty. He came to work when he chose, and he left the plant and his shift as he pleased. In fact, a foreman on one occasion was agreeably surprised to find Weigand at work and commented upon it. Weigand amiably stated that he was enjoying it. He brought a woman (apparently generally known as the "Duchess") to the rear of the plant yard and introduced some of the employees to her. He took another employee to visit her, and when this man got too drunk to be able to go home, punched his time card for him, and put him on the table in the representatives' meeting room in the plant in order to sleep off his intoxication. Weigand's immediate superiors demanded again and again that he be discharged, but each time higher officials intervened on Weigand's behalf because as was naively stated he was "a representative" (of the association, found to be a dominated union). In return for not working at the job for which he was hired, the petitioner gave him full pay and on five separate occasions raised his wages. One of these raises was general; that is to say, Weigand profited by a general wage increase throughout the plant, but the other four raises were given Weigand at times when other employees in the plant did not receive wage increases.

The petitioner contends that Weigand was discharged because of cumulative grievances against him. But about the time of the discharge it was suspected by some of the representatives that Weigand had joined the complaining CIO union. One of the representatives taxed him with this fact, and Weigand offered to bet a hundred dollars that it could not be proved. On July 22, 1941, Weigand did disclose his union membership to the vice chairman (Rattigan) of the association and to another representative (Mullen) and apparently tried to persuade them to support the union. Weigand asserts that the next day he, with Rattigan and Mullen, were seen talking to CIO organizer Reichwein on a street corner. The following day, according to Weigand's testimony, Mullen came to Weigand at the plant and stated that he, Mullen, had just had an interview with Personnel Director McIlvain and Plant Manager Mahan. According to Weigand, Mullen said to him, "Maybe you didn't get me in a jam." And, "We were seen down there." The following day Weigand was discharged.

As this court [has] stated . . . an employer may discharge an employee for a good reason, a poor reason, or no reason at all so long as the provisions of the

124

EXHIBIT 6–1 *(concluded)*

National Labor Relations Act are not violated. It is, of course, a violation to discharge an employee because he has engaged in activities on behalf of a union. Conversely an employer may retain an employee for a good reason, a bad reason, or no reason at all, and the reason is not a concern of the board. But it is certainly too great a strain on our credulity to assert, as does the petitioner, that Weigand was discharged for an accumulation of offenses. We think that he was discharged because his work on behalf of the CIO had become known to the plant manager. That ended his sinecure at the Budd plant. The board found that he was discharged because of his activities on behalf of the union. The record shows that the board's finding was based on sufficient evidence.

important outcomes. Therefore, a successful union campaign should stress issues important to employees and should show them how a union would enable them to achieve these ends.[22]

What issues do unions stress? A study of 33 representation elections showed that 15 issues were raised by the union at least half the time.[23] Table 6–1 displays union campaign issues and the percent of elections in which each was raised. The issues call attention to inequitable or threatening treatment by the employer and create a strong impression that the union's agency role will yield important gains to the employee, countering expected employer positions and establishing the legitimacy of the union and its activities.

After a recognition request or election petition is made, the union's tactics become more open for three reasons. First, the strongest proponents have already signed up, and thus each additional prounion vote will require increasingly concentrated collective pressure. Second, since the employer is now definitely aware of the campaign, secrecy is not needed. And third, publicity eliminates any possibility of an employer claiming ignorance of union activity as a defense when taking action against employees.

During the preelection period, the union may show its strength by asking adherents to wear campaign buttons or union T-shirts. The union can hold meetings during nonwork time and utilize the *Excelsior* list to make personal contacts at workers' homes. Leaflets and cartoons may be distributed. Figure 6–7 is an example of a suggested late campaign leaflet.

The union will frequently stress how target wages, hours, and working conditions differ from those in unionized organizations.

[22] For a detailed plan for organizing, see Ken Gagala, *Union Organizing and Staying Organized* (Reston, Va.: Reston Publishing, 1983), pp. 95–195.

[23] Julius Getman, Stephen Goldberg, and Jeanne B. Herman, *Union Representation Elections: Law and Reality* (New York: Russell Sage Foundation, 1976), pp. 80–81.

TABLE 6-1

Prevalent Union Campaign Issues

Issue	Percent of campaigns
Union will prevent unfairness, set up grievance procedure/seniority system	82
Union will improve unsatisfactory wages	79
Union strength will provide employees with voice in wages, working conditions	79
Union, not outsider, bargains for what employees want	73
Union has obtained gains elsewhere	70
Union will improve unsatisfactory sick leave/insurance	64
Dues/initiation fees are reasonable	64
Union will improve unsatisfactory vacations/holidays	61
Union will improve unsatisfactory pensions	61
Employer promises/good treatment may not be continued without union	61
Employees choose union leaders	55
Employer will seek to persuade/frighten employees to vote against union	55
No strike without vote	55
Union will improve unsatisfactory working conditions	52
Employees have legal right to engage in union activity	52

Source: Adapted from Table 4-3 in *Union Representation Elections: Law and Reality*, by Julius G. Getman, Stephen B. Goldberg, and Jeanne B. Herman. Copyright © 1976 by Russell Sage Foundation, New York.

Unions have the advantage over management since they can speculate on changes likely to occur after organization, but the employer must not communicate benefits that might result if organization fails.

These strategies and tactics describe a general model of a simple local organizing campaign. But unions also conduct area-wide, total company, or industrial campaigns. They may also encounter substantial employer resistance, which they seek to overcome with other methods. Four new strategies have been suggested: (1) corporate campaigns involving financial and product market pressures and confrontations with top-level management who are not closely involved in the organizing attempt, (2) employer neutrality pledges and accretion agreements for new plants, (3) identifying the union with significant community interests, and (4) coordinating or pooling resources of several unions.[24]

Management Strategy and Tactics

Management strategy and tactics may be determined at two major levels: the highest levels of the organization and the level at which

---

[24] James A. Craft and Marian M. Extejt, "New Strategies in Union Organizing," *Journal of Labor Research*, Winter 1983, pp. 19-32.

FIGURE 6–7

Specimen Union Communication

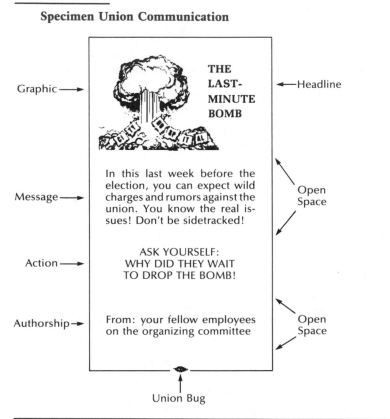

Source: Ken Gagala, *Union Organizing and Staying Organized* (Reston, Va.: Reston Publishing, 1983), p. 173.

organizing activities occur. At the organizing level, management generally opposes the union. At the corporate level, a variety of responses are possible. If substantial portions of the organization are already unionized, top management may make one of three general responses. First, it might take a more-or-less neutral approach, allowing any opposing activity to be implemented at the local level. Second, it might vigorously combat union organizing by sending out advisors at the first sign of union activity. Third, it might take a militantly antiunion stance, fighting organizing and seeking to rid itself of presently unionized situations. Many major firms have specific goals for repelling or containing union-organizing activities.[25]

---

[25] Audrey Freedman, *Managing Labor Relations* (New York: Conference Board, 1979), p. 33; and *The New Look in Wage Policy and Employee Relations* (New York: Conference Board, 1985), pp. 5–6.

Managements in many organizations periodically sample the attitudes of employees and ask supervisors to inform them of potential organizing activities. When organizing takes place, consultants may be hired to assist management in conducting an antiunion campaign. Evidence suggests uncovering union activity in a covert manner, retricting solicitations, waging an intense campaign, and opposing a consent election influence the election outcome in management's favor.[26]

If the union seeks an election, management must decide whether it wants to contest the makeup of the proposed bargaining unit. The trend is toward contesting. Research conducted by the AFL–CIO suggests the time delay required by petition elections works to management's advantage. On the average, the union's authorization card position erodes by 2.5 percent for each month the election is delayed.[27] Delays contribute to both reduced participation in elections and proportions of prounion votes.[28]

Management must also decide whether it will actively oppose the union or assume a neutral stance. The greater the differential between union wages in an industry and the employer's wage, the greater management resistance will be. Employer resistance appears to increase more rapidly with differentials than with desires for unionization by the employees.[29] Evidence suggests that an active union avoidance strategy for new facilities decreased the likelihood of organizing from about 15 percent to 1 percent.[30] Neutrality likely leads toward representation.[31]

---

[26] Kent F. Murrmann and Andrew A. Porter, "Employer Campaign Tactics and NLRB Election Outcomes: Some Preliminary Evidence," *Proceedings of the Industrial Relations Research Association*, 1982, pp. 67–72.

[27] Richard Prosten, "The Longest Season: Union Organizing in the Last Decade, a/k/a How Come One Team Has to Play with Its Shoelaces Tied Together?" *Proceedings of the Industrial Relations Research Association*, 1978, pp. 240–49. Delays, however, do not appear to have increased over time; see Richard N. Block and Benjamin W. Wolkinson, "Delay in Union Election Campaigns Revisited: A Theoretical and Empirical Analysis," *Advances in Industrial and Labor Relations* 3 (1986), pp. 43–81.

[28] Gary Florkowski and Michael Schuster, "Predicting the Decisions to Vote and Support Unions in Certification Elections: An Integrated Perspective," *Journal of Labor Research* 8 (1987), pp. 191–207.

[29] Richard B. Freeman, "The Effect of the Union Wage Differential on Management Opposition and Union Organizing Success," *American Economic Review* 76 (1986), pp. 92–96.

[30] Thomas A. Kochan, Robert B. McKersie, and John Chalykoff, "The Effects of Corporate Strategy and Workplace Innovations on Union Representation," *Industrial and Labor Relations Review* 39 (1986), pp. 487–501; see also John J. Lawler and Robin West, "Impact of Union-Avoidance Strategy in Representation Elections," *Industrial Relations*, 1985, pp. 406–20.

[31] See Jeanne M. Brett, "Why Employees Want Unions," *Organizational Dynamics*, Spring 1980, p. 54; and A. H. Raskin, "Management Comes out Swinging," *Proceedings of the Industrial Relations Research Association*, 1978, pp. 223–32.

Management campaigns emphasize that unions may be run by outsiders less concerned than the employer with employee welfare; that conditions may not improve after unionization; and that employees will be unable to deal individually with their employer on wages, hours, and working conditions. Table 6–2 displays the issues emphasized most often by management in the same campaigns from which union issues were portrayed in Table 6–1. Management typically communicates personally with employees to urge them to oppose the union. Figure 6–8 is an example of management material urging employees to vote against the union.

Consultants or campaign advisors suggest employers direct large-scale communications efforts toward employees, including mass meetings, small-group discussions with management representatives, and individual interviews to give information on *present* (not anticipated) company personnel programs.[32] Supervisors, a key management group in communicating with rank-and-file employees, need extensive briefings on the company's position and on the avoidance of unfair labor practices.[33]

Tactics that gain early warnings of union activity and that combine outside consultants, strong inside involvement, the use of delay-

TABLE 6–2

Prevalent Management Campaign Issues

Issues	Percent of campaigns
Improvements not dependent on unionization	85
Wages good, equal to/better than under union contract	82
Financial costs of union dues outweigh gains	79
Union is outsider	79
Get facts before deciding, employer will provide facts and accept employee decision	76
If union wins, strike may follow	70
Loss of benefits may follow union win	67
Strikers will lose wages, lose more than gain	67
Unions not concerned with employee welfare	67
Strike may lead to loss of jobs	64
Employer has treated employees fairly/well	60
Employees should be certain to vote	54

Source: Adapted from Table 4-2 in *Union Representation Elections: Law and Reality*, by Julius G. Getman, Stephen B. Goldberg, and Jeanne B. Herman. Copyright © 1976 by Russell Sage Foundation, New York.

[32] For an overview and incidents involving consultants for both sides, see *Labor Relations Consultants: Issue, Trends, and Controversies* (Washington, D.C.: Bureau of National Affairs, 1985).

[33] Louis Jackson and Robert Lewis, *Winning NLRB Elections* (New York: Practising Law Institute, 1972).

FIGURE 6–8

Specimen Employer Communication

Home mailing

Wednesday

Dear Fellow Employee:

At our plant gate yesterday, the union distributed a leaflet in which it discussed how it will back up its demands at our company.

In other words, the union is stating that it can fulfill its promise by the use of force. This is absolutely untrue. While the union can make promises and threaten to force us to do things, it is the company which pays your wages and provides you with benefits.

I think you should know some facts about what the union <u>cannot do</u> to your company, and some of the things they <u>can do</u> to you.

First, let's look at what it <u>cannot</u> force your company to do:

1. It cannot force the company to agree to any proposal that the company is unwilling or unable to meet.
2. It cannot increase any wages or benefits unless the company feels it is in its best interest to do so.
3. It cannot guarantee job security or furnish you a day's work or a day's pay.

Now let's work at what it <u>can</u> "force" employees to do.

1. It can force the employees to pay dues each and every month where there is a union-shop clause in the contract.
2. It can force members to stand trial and pay fines for violation of any of the provisions of the "book of rules" (constitution).
3. It can force members to pay assessments whenever the union treasury requires more money.

Consider the many advantages and benefits you now enjoy. These have been provided without a union. Consider the many disadvantages of union membership. When you do, I am sure you will vote "no."

Sincerely,

General Manager

Source: Louis Jackson and Robert Lewis, *Winning NLRB Elections.* (New York: Practising Law Institute, © 1972), p. 134.

ing tactics, and a strong campaign characterize a vigorous and successful management campaign.[34] Unfortunately, some managements may also purposely commit unfair labor practices to blunt an

---

[34] Murrmann and Porter, "Employer Campaign Tactics;" John Lawler, "Labor-Management Consultants in Union-Organizing Campaigns: Do They Make a Difference?" *Proceedings of the Industrial Relations Research Association,* 1981, pp. 374–80; and John J. Lawler, "Union Growth and Decline: The Impact of Employer and Union Tactics," *Journal of Occupational Psychology* 59 (1986), pp. 217–30.

organizing drive. One analysis has pointed out that the cost to employers of restoring discriminatorily fired union activists to their jobs with
back pay is far outweighed by the potential costs of wage increases in a
union contract if they were to be organized.[35] Employers may learn
that the consequences for unlawful discrimination are slight since
these practices appear most prevalent where unionization is pervasive
and among employers who had previously violated the labor acts.[36]
Further evidence suggests discrimination by employers against employees for engaging in union activities decreases the probability of a
union victory by an average 17 percent.[37]

THE ROLE OF THE NLRB

The NLRB's responsibility is to conduct the election and certify the
results. If charges of unfair campaign practices are brought, the board
must decide before certifying the results whether the practices occurred and whether they interfered with the employees' Section 7
rights to freely choose to be represented or not. The prevailing position
of the NLRB has been that an election should "provide a laboratory in
which an experiment may be conducted, under conditions as nearly
ideal as possible, to determine the uninhibited desires of the employees."[38]

The board may examine employer conduct in interrogating employees, scheduling meetings, the content of communications, and
campaigning during the day prior to the election. The board may also
assess the "totality of conduct" of the union or the employer in an
election.

Interrogation

Interrogation would probably be legal if used only to test a union's
claim to majority status.[39] Interrogation would likely be unfair in the
following circumstances: (1) a history of employer hostility toward
unions, (2) the information is likely to be used to take action against a
particular individual, (3) the questioner is a high-level manager, (4) the

---

[35] Charles R. Greer and Stanley A. Martin, "Calculative Strategy Decisions during
Union-Organizing Campaigns," *Sloan Management Review*, Winter 1978, pp. 61–74.

[36] Morris M. Kleiner, "Unionism and Employer Discrimination: Analysis of 8(a)(3)
Violations," *Industrial Relations* 23 (1984), pp. 234–43.

[37] William N. Cooke, "The Rising Toll of Discrimination against Union Activists,"
Industrial Relations, 1985, pp. 421–42.

[38] *General Shoe Corp.*, 77 NLRB 127 (1948).

[39] *Blue Flash Express Co.*, 109 NLRB 591 (1954).

interrogating takes place in an intimidating atmosphere, or (5) the responses to the questions indicate fear on the part of the respondent.[40]

Communications

The employer may generally require employees to attend meetings on company premises during working hours to hear management representatives speak in opposition to the union.[41] However, if the employer bars solicitation during nonworking time (as in a retail establishment), the employer may be required to give equal access to the union.[42]

The content of communications in both employer and union campaigns has long been considered by the board. Employers are forbidden to promise employees new benefits if they vote against the union but are not forbidden to point out that if the union is certified, all present levels of wages and benefits will be subject to negotiation.

The subject of untruthful campaign communications has been one of great controversy. Since 1977, the NLRB has changed its position three times on whether campaign distortions constitute an unfair campaign practice that would require a remedy. Prior to 1977, the board operated under the *General Shoe* laboratory condition rule requiring truthfulness.[43] However, its present stance is that it will no longer look into the truth or falsity of communications in union representation elections, reasoning that voters were experienced in political campaigns and many had voted in union representation elections. Thus, voters were able to personally evaluate the campaign information and were not naive subjects who would be swayed by rhetoric and falsehoods. Evidence suggests voters make their decisions in representation elections relatively early in the campaign; thus, truth or falsity may have little effect during the waning days.[44]

The 24-Hour Rule

Because it would be almost impossible for a union or an employer to rebut a last-minute campaign statement, the NLRB's *Peerless Plywood*

---

[40] *Bourne,* v. *NLRB,* 322 F. 2d 47 (1964).

[41] *Livingston Shirt Corp.,* 33 LRRM 1156 (1953).

[42] *May Department Stores Co.,* 136 NLRB 797 (1962).

[43] Beginning with *Hollywood Ceramics Co.,* 140 NLRB 221 (1962), which required truthfulness; adopting *Shopping Karet Food Markets, Inc.,* 229 NLRB 190 (1977), which did not; shifting to *General Knit of California, Inc.,* 239 NLRB 101 (1978), which did; and concluding with *Midland National Life,* 263 NLRB No. 24 (1982), which did not.

[44] J. Malcolm Walker and John J. Lawler, "Union Campaign Activities and Voter Preferences," *Journal of Labor Research* 7 (1986), 19–40.

rule prohibits employers or unions from holding a captive-audience presentation within the 24-hour period directly preceding the election.[45]

EMPLOYEE RESPONSES TO CAMPAIGNS

A study examining attitudes and behavior in 33 different union representation election campaigns found that employees do not appear to respond to many of the campaign issues raised. The campaign research began subsequent to the filing of a petition with the board, so prepetition activity was not examined.

Attendance at either union- or management-sponsored gatherings was significantly related to a familiarity with issues but had little effect on voting unless the meeting was union sponsored. Persons who remembered the issues generally voted for the side expressing those issues. For example, three of the four most familiar management issues were given as reasons for voting against the union, and the three most familiar union issues had the most influence on prounion votes.[46]

Unions seldom gained support during the campaign. They tended to win elections only in units where they held clear authorization card majorities prior to the filing of a petition. Between the petition and the election, average erosion of union support was about 4 percent. The only activity through which unions gained support was the attendance of noncommitted employees at union-sponsored meetings. The evidence generally suggests undecided employees tend to vote for the company rather than for the union.[47] Whatever the reason, unless an employee makes an effort to gain exposure to the union's position, he or she will clearly have heard much more management information before the vote is taken.

Employees are also influenced by co-worker attitudes. Recent studies find that positive attitudes toward unionization by co-workers influence the intention of employees to vote for the union.[48]

---

[45] 107 NLRB 427 (1953).

[46] Getman et al., *Union Representation Elections*, pp. 95, 98–99.

[47] Ibid., pp. 100–108.

[48] Ruth Montgomery, "The Determinants of Voting Intentions and Votes in a Union Certification Election," *Industrial and Labor Relations Review*, in press; and Joseph G. Rosse, Timothy A. Keaveny, and John A. Fossum, "Predicting Union Election Outcomes: The Role of Job Attitudes, Union Attitudes, and Co-Worker Preferences," unpublished manuscript, College of Business Administration, University of Colorado, Boulder, 1986.

The Effects of Unfair Practices

The evidence suggests the vigor of management's campaign is related to its likelihood of winning the election. Unfair labor practices during a vigorous campaign might influence voters away from the union and may not involve large costs to the employer, even if the employer is penalized. One study used the *Union Representation Elections* data and simulated the relative effects of various employer practices on the outcomes of representation elections.[49]

As part of the *Union Representation Elections* study, an NLRB administrative law judge was asked to review the campaigns to determine whether an unfair labor practice was committed by either party during the campaign. Actual charges were filed in some of the elections, and the NLRB issued rulings on them. In 31 campaigns that had elections, 9 resulted in the board issuing a "bargaining order" (discussed below), and 13 resulted in other remedies (such as election reruns for 12 of the campaigns). Thus, the sample showed both fair and unfair conduct.

Data analysis indicates that several campaign practices influence election outcomes. Among the most important were one legal practice (early letters to employees) and one unfair practice (threats and actions against union supporters). Table 6-3 shows the effects of individual, election background, and campaign measures on voting behavior. In the actual campaigns, unions won 36 percent of the elections. Table 6-4 shows the effects of various campaign levels on simulated election outcomes. If the company fails to campaign against the union, the union's probability of winning increases by about 31 percent over the average campaign. In an intense legal campaign, companies win 14 percent more frequently; and an intense campaign using both legal and illegal approaches reduces union victories by about 32 percent to only 4 percent (or 1 in 25 elections). Thus, the evidence suggests employees may not pay much attention to issues raised by both parties, but they do respond to early employer campaign efforts and illegal tactics.

ELECTION CERTIFICATIONS

After the election, the ballots are counted to determine which alternative, if any, received a majority of the votes cast. If no objections question a majority and no unfair campaign tactic charges are filed, the

---

[49] William T. Dickens, "The Effect of Company Campaigns on Certification Elections: *Law and Reality* Once Again," *Industrial and Labor Relations Review*, July 1983, pp. 560-75.

TABLE 6-3

Estimates of the Reduced-Form Voting Model*

	Specification	
Independent variable	Specific violations—average percent impact	NLRB remedy—average percent impact
Individual background		
1. Tenure < year	.008%	.010%
2. Part-time worker	−.064	.066
3. Age code	.047†	.044
4. Age code squared	−.011	−.010
5. Married	−.047†	−.051†
6. No. of dependents	.008	.008
7. Education code	−.018	−.021†
8. White	−.000	−.001
9. Relative a union member	.057‡	.065§
10. Initial disposition	.430§	.427§
11. Not asked to sign card	−.158§	−.159§
12. Potential wage change	.127§	.130§
Election background		
13. U.A.W.	−.213§	−.180§
14. Teamsters	−.150§	−.115§
15. Steelworkers	.173§	.226§
16. Retail clerks	−.320‡	−.316‡
17. Machinists	−.416§	−.339§
18. Percent for union	.006§	.006§
19. Average education	.264§	.354§
20. No. of workers	.003§	.003§
Campaign measure		
21. Illegal speech	−.022	—
22. Illegal actions	−.024	—
23. Threats and actions vs. union supporters	−.155‡	—
24. Early letters	.010‡	.021§
25. Late letters	−.037§	−.035§
26. Early meetings	−.052‡	−.068§
27. Late meetings	−.025	.004§
28. Percent talked to by supervisor	.001	−.001
29. Remedy is bargain	—	−.073
30. Other remedy	—	−.051†

* Dependent variable equals one if the worker voted union and zero if otherwise.
† Significant at the .10 level in a one-tailed test.
‡ Significant at the .05 level in a one-tailed test.
§ Significant at the .01 level in a one-tailed test.
Source: William T. Dickens, "The Effect of Company Campaigns on Certification Elections: Law and Reality Once Again," Industrial and Labor Relations Review, July 1983, p. 568.

NLRB certifies the results. If a union wins, it becomes the exclusive representative of the employees in the election unit and can begin bargaining with the employer. If the union loses and no challenges are successful, then no election can be conducted in that unit for a one-year period.

TABLE 6-4

Simulated Effects of Campaigns on Election Outcomes, in Percentages of 3,100 Simulated Elections Won by the Union

Specification	Actual campaign	All violations committed in every case	No violations committed in any case	No company campaign in any case	Intense company campaign in every case	Intense legal campaign in every case	Light legal campaign in every case
				Type of campaign			
NLRB remedy	36%	25%	44%	66%	5%	9%	58%
Specific violations	36	17	47	67	4	22	63

Source: William T. Dickens, "The Effect of Company Campaigns on Certification Elections: *Law and Reality Once Again*," *Industrial and Labor Relations Review,* July 1983, p. 572.

Even if a winning union were to lose its majority status within the year, the board would not order a new election. The Supreme Court and the board reason that certification is the equivalent of a term in office for an elected official, even if the official's constituency no longer supports him or her.[50] If the union loses, it cannot call for another election until one year elapses, even if it subsequently attains majority status. Thus, an election precludes another union from requesting one during the year.

If the union fails to win the election, the employer cannot legally take action against its supporters. Even though they are not represented by the union, the supporters are legally protected from discrimination.

Setting Aside Elections

If challenges to elections are filed and the board finds the alleged activity occurred and interfered with the employees' ability to make a reasoned choice, the election will be set aside and rerun. If the violations are trivial, the board proceeds to issue a certification of the results.

Bargaining orders. In some cases, the board considers a party's improper actions to be so coercive that the inherent strength of the opposition is eroded. For example, assume a majority of employees sign authorization cards and attend union-organizing meetings. Also assume that the employer threatens cutbacks in the operation, possible plant closings, or strikes over bargaining issues if the union wins, and that it interrogates employees. Then, when the election is held, the union loses and charges that the employer's inflammatory and threatening statements undermined an actual union majority. The board may remedy the situation through a bargaining order, requiring the employer to recognize and negotiate with the union. The reasoning behind this remedial approach is that the union would have won if not for the employer's illegal conduct.[51]

The Impact of Board Remedies

In addition to election reruns or bargaining orders, the NLRB can issue cease-and-desist orders to companies committing unfair labor practices during organizing drives. If individuals have been discriminated against on the basis of union activity (e.g., leading an authorization card campaign) and have suffered as a result (e.g., being discharged), the

---

[50] *Brooks* v. *NLRB*, 348 U.S. 96 (1954).

[51] *NLRB* v. *Gissel Packing Co.*, 395 U.S. 575 (1969); for a case in which the NLRB issued a bargaining order where a majority had not been demonstrated but where the employer's behavior was seen as preventing a majority from being established, see George R. Salem, "Nonmajority Bargaining Orders: A Prospective View in Light of *United Dairy Farmers*," *Labor Law Journal*, March 1981, pp. 145–57.

board will order their reinstatement with back pay and interest to cover the differences between wages they would have earned and what they actually earned during the period of their discrimination. Balancing the employer's possible savings by avoiding unionization against the costs of being found guilty of discriminatory discharges frequently indicates an employer would gain a financial advantage by flagrantly violating the law.[52] Exhibit 6-2 chronicles the events in the famous *Darlington Mills* plant-closing case, which involved employer unfair practices during and following a representation election.

Evidence also indicates unions do not win rerun elections as frequently as elections in general. Unions were certified in less than 30 percent of rerun elections in fiscal 1982, compared to 41 percent in all elections.[53] And in many elections, unfair labor practices could arguably be found, but employees and unions do not file charges.

Election Outcomes

In 1983, more than 213,000 persons were eligible to vote in NLRB-conducted representation elections. In all, 4,481 elections resulting in certifications were held. Of these, 3,241 were requested by unions or employees to obtain initial representation (RC cases), 242 were filed by employers (RM cases), 922 were filed by employees seeking decertification (RD cases), and 76 were filed by employees requesting deauthorization of union-shop clauses (UD cases). Table 6-5 gives data on election frequency and numbers of employers involved.

Table 6-6 shows the size of bargaining units, numbers of employees eligible to vote, total elections, and percent won by a union in initial certifications. Over half of all elections were conducted in units of less than 30 employees. Representation rights were won in about 47 percent of all elections. Contrary to recent experience, win rates in larger units were only slightly lower than in small units.

Unions involved in elections are likely to be those organizing in industries where the proportion of organized employees is not extremely large. Where organizing has been successful in the past, the international union is more likely to concentrate on representation activities.[54] Evidence also suggests the economic returns from union representation to employees in most industries is substantially greater than the union's costs of organizing.[55] Thus, the union may recoup its investment through the receipt of union dues, and the employee re-

---

[52] Greer and Martin, "Calculative Strategy Decisions," pp. 61–74.

[53] *Forty-Seventh Annual Report of the National Labor Relations Board* (Washington, D.C.: U.S. Government Printing Office, 1982), pp. 202, 204.

[54] Richard N. Block, "Union Organizing and Allocation of Union Resources," *Industrial and Labor Relations Review*, October 1980, pp. 110–13.

[55] Paula B. Voos, "Union Organizing: Costs and Benefits," *Industrial and Labor Relations Review*, July 1983, pp. 576–91.

EXHIBIT 6-2

Darlington Mills Chronology

March 1956—Textile Workers Union of America, AFL–CIO (now the Amalgamated Clothing and Textile Workers Union, AFL–CIO), began an organizational campaign at the Darlington Manufacturing Company mill in Darlington, South Carolina.

September 6, 1956—Darlington employees selected the Textile Workers as
their collective bargaining representative in an NLRB-conducted election, by
vote of 256 for the union, 248 against it.

　　The bulk of Darlington's employees were discharged in October 1956,
and the plant ended operations on November 24, 1956. Plant machinery and
other assets were sold, beginning in December 1956.

October 16, 1956—Unfair labor practice charges were filed with the NLRB by
the Textile Workers against Darlington, Roger Milliken as its president, and
Deering Milliken, Inc.

　　Four hearings into various aspects of the case were conducted by Lloyd
Buchanan, NLRB trial examiner, with reports on his findings issued on April
30, 1957; April 30, 1959; December 31, 1959; and March 23, 1962.

October 18, 1962—The five-member National Labor Relations Board issued
its decision, finding that the mill had been unlawfully closed to avoid
dealing with the Textile Workers as bargaining agent for the Darlington
employees. The board held that the discharged employees were entitled to be
made whole for lost earnings. The board ruled that Darlington and Deering
Milliken and the latter's affiliated corporations constituted a single employer, and the parent corporation and its mills must share backpay and
other obligations to the discharged workers.

November 15, 1963—The U.S. Court of Appeals for the Fourth Circuit, in
Richmond, Virginia, denied enforcement of the board's decision and order.
The court held that a company has the right to close out a part or all of its
business regardless of antiunion motives.

March 29, 1965—The Supreme Court vacated the judgment of the Court of
Appeals and directed that the case be remanded to the NLRB for further
findings on the "chill unionism" issue.

　　The Supreme Court said that while an employer has the absolute right
to terminate his entire business for any reason, the partial closing of a
business is a violation of the National Labor Relations Act "if motivated by a
purpose to chill unionism in any of the remaining plants of the single
employer, and if the employer may reasonably have foreseen that such
closing will likely have that effect."

August 10, 1966—Trial Examiner (now Administrative Law Judge) Buchanan's
supplemental decision was issued. He found insufficient evidence that the
Darlington mill closing was undertaken to "chill" unionization at other
Deering Milliken plants.

July 27, 1967—The board, in a supplemental decision, reversed the trial examiner. It held that Deering Milliken violated the act when it closed the
Darlington plant almost immediately after the workers chose union repre-

EXHIBIT 6–2 *(concluded)*

sentation and discharged the more than 500 Darlington employees with a purpose, at least in part, to discourage union organization in Deering Milliken's 26 other textile plants. The board said the shutdown gave the employer an opportunity to create "a graphic example of the hazards of unionism."

June 3, 1968—The U.S. Court of Appeals for the Fourth Circuit upheld the supplemental decision of the board. The court conceded that the Darlington mill had run into financial difficulites but asserted that the close timing of the union victory and the plant shutdown that quickly followed had shown a deliberate effort to frighten textile workers away from the union in other Deering Milliken plants.

January 13, 1969—The Supreme Court denied the company's request to review the decision of the Court of Appeals. The denial was in a brief order, without comment.

November 29, 1974—The NLRB Regional Office in Winston-Salem, North Carolina, issued backpay specifications, a 4,000-page document. The determination came after a monumental task of locating and interviewing 553 former Darlington employees who were potential claimants. Many had moved to distant locations. The interview of each discriminatee had to cover his or her entire employment history since the Darlington mill closed, as well as such items as possible valid insurance claims and expenses in seeking subsequent employment. Voluminous company records had to be reviewed to establish equitable backpay standards.

January 21, 1975—The initial pretrial conference occurred in the compliance case arising from the employer's disagreement with the backpay specifications.

May 28, 1975, to January 21, 1978—The hearing before Administrative Law Judge Lowell M. Goerlich was conducted in the backpay compliance case.

September 26, 1978; February 2, 1979; and June 27, 1979—Installments of briefs were filed with the administrative law judge.

October 2–3, 1979—Oral arguments was conducted by the administrative law judge. In all, there were 400 days of trial in the compliance case. The record reached 37,000 pages.

December 3, 1980—Proposal for $5 million backpay settlement made to employer and union by General Counsel William A. Lubbers.

Source: *Daily Labor Report*, no. 234 (December 3, 1980), pp. A13–A14.

---

ceives at least a one-time boost in wage levels compared to nonunion employees. Evidence on win rates suggests few differences exist between industries, unions, and geographic locations except those due to the size of the proposed unit (wins less likely) and degree of union effort in the campaign (wins more likely).[56]

---

[56] William T. Dickens, Douglas R. Wholey, and James C. Robinson, "Correlates of Union Support in NLRB Elections," *Industrial Relations* 26 (1987), pp. 240–52.

TABLE 6–5

Types of Elections Resulting in Certification in Cases Closed, Fiscal Year 1984

Type of election

Type of case	Total	Consent	Stipulated	Board-directed	Regional director-directed	Expedited elections under 8(b)(7)(C)
All types, total:						
Elections	4,512	144	3,668	24	676	0
Eligible voters	254,305	3,614	204,780	3,260	42,651	0
Valid votes	224,934	3,041	182,563	2,866	36,464	0
RC cases:						
Elections	3,336	77	2,769	19	471	0
Eligible voters	205,717	1,905	168,616	1,881	33,315	0
Valid votes	182,444	1,583	150,713	1,668	28,480	0
RM cases:						
Elections	225	12	165	1	47	0
Eligible voters	5,979	174	4,677	237	891	0
Valid votes	5,225	156	4,124	222	723	0
RD cases:						
Elections	875	49	696	4	126	0
Eligible voters	37,816	1,319	29,242	1,142	6,113	0
Valid votes	33,354	1,134	25,915	976	5,329	0
UD cases:						
Elections	76	6	38	0	32	—
Eligible voters	4,793	216	2,245	0	2,332	—
Valid votes	3,911	168	1,811	0	1,932	—

Source: *Forty-ninth Annual Report of the NLRB* (Washington, D.C.: U.S. Government Printing Office, 1988), p. 199.

Decertifications

Besides organizing and representing employees, unions are at risk in maintaining their right to represent. If a majority of workers vote for the ouster of their representative after the one-year certification period has elapsed and during a period in which no contract is in effect, the union is decertified from its right to represent bargaining unit employees. Decertification elections tend to be more successful in small units having a lack of local leadership, low member involvement in union activities, a changing composition of represented employees, and affiliation with a large national union.[57] Economy-wide variables associ-

---

[57] See John C. Anderson, Gloria Busman, and Charles A. O'Reilly III, "What Factors Influence the Outcome of Union Decertification Elections?" *Monthly Labor Review*, November 1979, pp. 32–36; "Union Decertification in the United States: 1947-1977," *Industrial Relations*, Winter 1980, pp. 100–107; "The Decertification Process: Evidence from California," *Industrial Relations*, Spring 1982, pp. 178–96; I. Chafetz and C. R. P. Fraser, "Union Decertification: An Exploratory Analysis," *Industrial Relations*, Winter 1979, pp. 59–69; and James B. Dworkin and Marian M. Extejt, "Why Workers Decertify Their Unions: A Preliminary Investigation," *Proceedings of the Academy of Management*, 1979, pp. 241–46.

TABLE 6-6

Election Results by Unit Size

Size of unit	Number eligible	Total elections	Percent won by union
under 10	4,641	836	54.5%
10–19	11,087	801	49.9
20–29	10,738	448	49.1
30–39	10,109	295	44.1
40–49	8,432	191	38.2
50–69	16,969	291	43.6
70–99	18,046	219	38.4
100–149	22,433	185	47.0
150–199	13,436	79	30.4
200–299	17,756	74	35.1
300–399	8,957	26	46.2
400–499	6,257	14	42.9
500–999	9,982	16	50.0
1,000–1,999	10,012	7	57.1
2,000–2,999	2,693	1	100.0

Source: Adapted from *48th Annual Report of the NLRB* (Washington, D.C.: U.S. Government Printing Office, 1987), p. 215.

ated with decertification elections include inflation, low union density in the industry, frequency of strikes, and small bargaining units.[58] Evironmental variables associated with decertification, include employee turnover in the unit and lowered industrial production (as in a recession).[59] Currently, unions are removed in more than 75 percent of decertification elections.[60]

Contextual Characteristics Influencing Elections

Characteristics associated with representation election outcomes have recently been examined. These characteristics include whether the bargaining unit is contested, the size of the bargaining unit, the region of the country in which the election is conducted, the union seeking to organize the unit, economic factors, and the like. Evidence from these studies suggests the probability of the union winning a representation election is negatively related to the size of the unit, in cases where the Teamsters are the organizing union, in southern right-to-work–law states, and delays between the petition and the election. The following

---

[58] Dennis A. Ahlburg and James B. Dworkin, "The Influence of Macroeconomic Variables on the Probability of Union Decertification," *Journal of Labor Research* 5 (1984), pp. 13–28.

[59] Ralph D. Elliott and Benjamin M. Hawkins, "Do Union Organizing Activities Affect Decertification?" *Journal of Labor Research* 3 (1982), pp. 153–61.

[60] Marcus H. Sandver and Herbert G. Heneman III, "Union Growth through the Election Process," *Industrial Relations*, Winter 1981, pp. 109–16.

factors are associated with union wins: high unemployment rates during the previous years, consent rather than petition elections, and degree of unionization in the industry being organized.[61] Unions win more elections if they are larger and more democratic. Benefits directly provided to members and relatively lower dues enhance organizing success for white-collar employees but make no difference for blue-collar workers.[62] Some evidence shows that size and petition-versus-consent-election differences account for North-South differences,[63] but lower organizing success in the South may result from a lower proportion of petitions filed.

Research in hospital organizing finds that previous union activity, the presence of other unions, and the opportunity to organize influence union victories; nonmedical occupational units and nonprofit or religious hospitals are associated with union losses. Size is generally negatively related to organizing across all hospitals, although positively related to larger cities.[64]

Organizing and Membership Trends

Recent information on union membership rates, as given in Chapter 5, clearly indicates both the absolute and relative numbers of employees who are union members have fallen recently. Membership has been falling absolutely since 1979.[65] Whether this trend will continue is open to speculation. Election results reveal many more certification than decertification elections. Although unions do not win a majority of representation elections, many more individuals are initially included in new bargaining units each year than are lost through decertification. However, countervailing explanations help resolve this apparent paradox. First, much of the change is due to declining employment in heavily unionized industries.[66] Second, the median size of

[61] William N. Cooke, "Determinations of the Outcomes of Union Certification Elections," *Industrial and Labor Relations Review*, April 1983, pp. 402–14.

[62] Cheryl L. Maranto and Jack Fiorito, "The Effect of Union Characteristics on the Outcome of NLRB Certification Elections," *Industrial and Labor Relations Review* 40 (1987), pp. 225–39.

[63] Marcus H. Sandver, "South–Nonsouth Differentials in National Labor Relations Board Certification Election Outcomes," *Journal of Labor Research*, Winter 1982, pp. 13–30.

[64] Brian E. Becker and Richard U. Miller, "Patterns and Determinants of Union Growth in the Hospital Industry," *Journal of Labor Research*, Fall 1981, pp. 307–28; and John T. Delaney, "Union Success in Hospital Representation Elections," *Industrial Relations*, Spring 1981, pp. 149–61.

[65] Edward C. Kokkelenberg and Donna R. Sockell, "Union Membership in the United States, 1973–1981," *Industrial and Labor Relations Review* 38 (1985), pp. 497–543.

[66] William T. Dickens and Jonathan S. Leonard, "Accounting for the Decline in Union Membership, 1950–1980," *Industrial and Labor Relations Review* 38 (1985), pp. 323–34. For a more detailed look at the employment changes of unionized and nonunion workers, see Larry T. Adams, "Changing Employment Patterns of Organized Workers," *Monthly Labor Review*, February 1985, pp. 25–31.

bargaining units in which elections are held is declining over time. Third, if unionized firms existing in the same industry as nonunion firms have higher wage costs, they are either more vulnerable to closure or require productivity increases to balance increasing wage costs. Frequently, the reaction to increased wages is to substitute capital for labor in the long run.

SUMMARY

Organizing is an extremely complex issue involving unions, employers, and the NLRB. The union's goal is to organize a majority of employees; the employer seeks to avoid unionization. The NLRB's role is to preserve the free choice of employees to be represented or to remain unorganized.

Crucial aspects of organization include the authorization card campaign, bargaining unit determination, the post-petition campaign, and certification. The NLRB's decisions on bargaining units and unfair campaign charges have important bearings on many election outcomes.

Recent investigations show that most union victories occur in smaller election units where employees may be more homogeneous or closer geographically. Recent behavioral research suggests pre-petition management activity is more influential on election outcomes than post-petition activity and unfair practices do influence employee voting decisions.

DISCUSSION QUESTIONS

1. To what extent should the NLRB get involved in determining bargaining units? Shouldn't the vote be in the unit preferred by the employees?
2. Should union organizers have greater or less access to employees in organizing campaigns than they have now?
3. What do you think explains the relatively poor recent record for unions in attempting to organize large bargaining units?
4. Do employers have an unfair tactical advantage in union-organizing situations?

CASE

Doug Kellogg just graduated from Midwestern University with a business administration bachelor's degree. He expected to return in the fall to begin work on his master's in industrial relations. He believed he would have a good head start on his program since he had landed a summer internship in the personnel and industrial relations department of General Computer Corporation (GCC). He was assigned as an administrative assistant to Ed Wheeler, director of industrial relations. Wheeler reported in turn to Dick Snyder, vice president of personnel and industrial relations.

With the exception of one recently acquired small subsidiary, none of GCC's 10,000 production and maintenance employees were unionized. The company had taken pains to provide wages, benefits, and working conditions at levels equal to or above its unionized competitors. All of its local plants had been built within the past 10 years, were air conditioned, and had ample parking and cafeteria facilities. Its wage-and-benefit packages were purposely structured to match prevailing labor contracts for comparable employers. These efforts were not altogether altruistic, since the company expected to have substantially more freedom to make decisions about its operation if it remained nonunion.

The first assignment Ed had given Doug was to update the salary survey information the department had gathered the previous December. Doug decided he would call other employers in the area to find out what they were paying workers in comparable jobs and grade levels. (Companies frequently cooperate in these types of surveys.) Since pay at GCC had not changed since December (usually done just after survey data were taken), he was not surprised to find the pay at GCC slightly lower than that of its competitors. Exhibit 1 shows GCC's pay as a percentage of local area pay for comparable grades as of the previous December.

Shortly after Doug completed the survey, an urgent call came in for Mr. Wheeler from Frank Page, personnel manager at the firm's largest manufacturing facility, Mainframe Operations. Since Mr. Wheeler was out of town for the day, Doug took the call. Mr. Page said he had heard a reliable rumor that 20 of the 25 truck drivers at the plant had signed authorization cards with the Teamsters and that they were dissatisfied with their pay and were going to demand recognition for the Teamsters as their bargaining agent at the beginning of the following week. After Doug hung up, he decided he should get as much data together as possible to brief Mr. Wheeler when he came in the next day.

First, Doug obtained the job description for the truck driver position. (See Exhibit 2.) Then he again phoned the firms he had just

EXHIBIT 1

GCC Pay Comparison (Central City plants)*

Grade level	Production workers			Maintenance and other nontechnical workers		
	Number of employees	December	June	Number of employees	December	June
1	602	102	98	151	99	94
2	219	100	97	147	101	97
3	84	103	99	136	98	96
4	36	100	96	79	100	100
5	13	99	94	34	102	98
6	6	101	98	27	100	96
7	4	103	98	25	99	93
8	2	100	96	10	102	99

Note: Pay in each grade is about 10 percent greater than immediately lower grade; for example, pay in Grade 2 is 110 percent of Grade 1.

* All figures are calculated as follows:

$$\frac{\text{GCC pay in grade}}{\text{All surveyed firms' pay in grade}}$$

Revised: December and June annually.

EXHIBIT 2

General Computer Corporation Job Description

Intraplant Truck Driver

Grade: 3
Position code: 047
Job family: Maintenance

Duties

Under the supervision of the plant transportation department supervisor, job holder loads and unloads manufactured goods and components into and from assigned vehicle. Drives vehicles between plants in same city. Operates vans, straight trucks, and short trailer semis. Checks trucks for safety equipment, reports and records equipment malfunctions. When not driving or loading, performs duties in loading or production area as assigned.

Specifications

Chauffeur's license
No disabling health problems
Vision correctable to 20/20
Ability to lift and move up to 100 lbs.
Insurance on company motor vehicle policy

contacted in his salary survey to find out what they paid their intracity truck drivers. GCC apparently had "dropped the ball," because wages at competitive firms averaged 50 percent higher. The problem began to look more and more serious, since almost half of the central city employees were located at Mainframe Operations, and any labor trouble there would have an extremely disruptive influence on the total organization.

Once he had gathered the pay and job description data, Doug decided to formulate a strategy to recommend to Mr. Wheeler when he returned.

If you were Doug Kellogg, what would you recommend? What actions should Mr. Wheeler take in this situation? What consequences do you see? What risks are involved in the action you recommend? Would your recommendations be the same if a strike were to be avoided at all costs?

CHAPTER 7

The Environment for Bargaining

Organizing campaigns focus on the individual employer and the union trying to organize a bargaining unit. While the organizing campaign is in progress, both parties concentrate on the issue at hand—whether the employees desire representation. If employees decide to be represented, then the employer and the union must bargain within the realities of the environment in which they operate. Some environmental aspects that influence bargaining are the degree of competition in the product market in which the employer participates, the financial condition of the employer, the capital–labor mix used by the employer, the bargaining issue interests of the organized employees, the effects of unionization on the employer's relationship with the labor market, and any public policy issues relating to the industry in which the employer operates or the fact that it is now unionized.

This chapter explores three major areas: the economic environment in which collective bargaining occurs, the influence of the economic environment and the bargaining structure on bargaining power, and bargaining structures that unions and managements design. The chapter serves as the basis of a four-chapter section on bargaining issues and negotiations. Chapter 8 concentrates on wage and benefit issues and evidence related to the effects of unions in these areas. Chapter 9 concentrates on nonwage issues and union members' perceptions of their unions' effectiveness. Chapter 10 covers the organizational structures in which employers and unions negotiate, types of negotiation issues given organization and union goals, the negotiation process, and the identification and quantification of contract issue costs.

In studying this chapter, consider the following questions:

1. How does the degree of competition within the product market influence the bargaining behavior of the parties?

2. What effect does unionization have on the wage and employment decisions of employers?
3. What influence does regulation or deregulation have on collective bargaining?
4. What joint decisions do employers and unions make in their bargaining relationship to attempt to insulate themselves from market conditions?
5. How do economic conditions, product market concentration, and bargaining structure influence bargaining power?

THE PRODUCT AND SERVICE MARKET

Organizations in both the private and public sectors create products and services. Some of these products and services result from responses to consumer demands, while others result from the organizations' new discoveries and developments, which consumers will demand in the future. Obviously, the degree to which consumers need (demand) certain products or services, the level of competition among suppliers of the products and services, and the availability of acceptable substitutes will all influence how employers relate to the market.

To create products and services, employers must combine raw materials, capital, and labor. To create steel, iron ore, limestone, scrap iron, coke, and other ingredients are combined (raw materials) in a blast furnace within a steel mill (capital) operated by steelworkers and their supervisors (labor). This combination of production factors is not as obvious where services, such as education, are provided. In a university, students (raw materials) use libraries, classrooms, computers, and audiovisual equipment (examples of capital), with the assistance of faculty, librarians, clericals, food-service and residence workers, and maintenance employees (examples of labor) to obtain a degree.

The economy is a dynamic process in which the supplies of raw materials, capital, and labor interact with the demand for the products and services that organizations supply. At various stages in the process, raw materials, capital, and labor may be demanded or supplied, depending on who the vendor and who the purchaser are. But the use of raw materials, capital, and labor is ultimately a result of the final consumers' demand for products and services that organizations produce. The producer's demand for each factor of production is said to be *derived* from the final demand by consumers. Therefore, the demand for each is proportionately related to the good or service produced. Other things being equal, we would expect the quantity of any product or service demanded to decrease with the price charged in the market by the producing organizations.

How consumers react to price changes determines the elasticity of demand. Demand is inelastic if price changes (up or down) have rela-

FIGURE 7-1

Examples of Elastic and Inelastic Demand

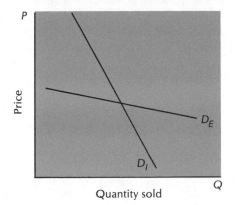

tively little effect on the amount of a product or service sold, while an elastic demand schedule is highly sensitive to price changes. Figure 7-1 shows examples of relatively elastic (D_E) and inelastic (D_I) demand schedules where Q is the quantity sold and P is the price.

Levels of demand may vary over time. Some changes in demand are *cyclical* (the demand for types of clothing is related to seasons), while others are *secular* (long-term changes related to shifts in demand or the introduction of substitutes, such as fewer women's hats or increased use of artificial fibers). Short-run (or cyclical) demand changes mean that employers will change their derived demands for inputs to make the products or offer the services. In most instances, however, the use of capital cannot be changed rapidly. For example, when the demand for automobiles declined during the late 1970s and early 1980s, auto producers did not immediately sell plants or assembly lines to accommodate the reduction. Instead, they reduced purchases of steel, fiberglass, aluminum, tires, parts, and other auto components and laid off workers at various levels (production employees first) to accommodate the reduction in overall demand for motor vehicles. Some plants were shut down in the long run, but substantial reductions in raw material and labor purchases occurred first.

If there are several suppliers of relatively similar products and services, the consumer can pick and choose among them based on price. Where the amount of capital investment necessary to become a competitor is relatively small, more competition should result. It's no accident that software suppliers for microcomputers outnumber manufactureres of equipment, because the capital outlay required to produce software is far less than required to produce hardware. The more producers there are, the more elastic is the demand for the products of each individual producer (an area we will examine shortly).

The willingness of consumers to substitute one product for another or the degree to which the demand for one product is influenced by the demand for another is also important to the employer. Consider fast food, for example. As menus become more complete, consumers have more price-quality-taste decisions to make. If the price of hamburgers goes up and consumers therefore switch to chicken or fish sandwiches, they are *substituting* chicken or fish for hamburgers. Thus, the quantity of beef demanded decreases, resulting in a decreased demand for packinghouse workers, cattle, and beef-processing plants. On the other hand, fishing and fishery workers, chicken processors and their employees, and chicken producers will be positively influenced by the change. Complementary relationships between products also exist. If the demand for fish sandwiches goes up, so too will the demand for tartar sauce.

If the relative prices of production factors change, employers will change the ratios in which they use each one. For example, when the price of silver increased substantially in 1980, printing establishments began installing devices to recapture silver from photographic plates. Here capital was substituted for raw materials. Automakers who install robots to update assembly lines are substituting capital for labor. When homeowners install insulation to reduce heating costs, labor and capital (insulating materials) are substituted for raw materials (gas, oil, or electricity).

Public policy constraints on markets have also been enacted. Some retard the changes that would occur rapidly as the result of major market shifts (e.g., rationing or allocations during fuel shortages), while others prohibit the formation or operation of monopolies.

PUBLIC POLICY AND INDUSTRIAL ORGANIZATION

Since the passage of the Sherman Antitrust Act in 1890, public policy has limited industrial concentration and collusive activities between producers in a single industry. Excessive industrial concentration is not defined in the statute, by the courts, or by the Federal Trade Commission. On the other hand, price fixing and other collusive activities have been vigorously prosecuted when discovered, and persons or organizations who have been harmed by these activities have been entitled to recover damages.

A general pattern seems to develop in the growth and maturation of most industries. During their infancy, the production process is labor intensive. Products and their capabilities are relatively diverse. As consumer preferences become known, some producers go out of business because their products do not meet consumers' needs. As production methods become standardized, capital and cheaper labor may be substituted for skilled craft work, and more-efficient producers lower prices, thus driving less-efficient producers from the industry. Over time, an industry becomes dominated by relatively few producers, and the less dominant either mimic the leader or occupy particular niches in which the leader chooses not to produce. The U.S. auto industry involved several hundred firms in the 1900–10 decade; but by the late 1940s, only Chrysler, Ford, General Motors, Hudson, Nash, Packard, and Studebaker remained. By the 1970s, Hudson and Nash had combined to form American Motors, and the merged Packard and Studebaker had dropped out of motor vehicle production. In 1987, American Motors merged into Chrysler. In the presently developing microcomputer industry, several entrants have dropped out or scaled back, including Texas Instruments, Atari, and AT&T. Survivors have tended to concentrate on a certain market niche (Japanese manufacturers in laptop computers; Apple and Compaq in technological leadership) or to mimic the expected market leader, IBM (Zenith, Leading Edge, Epson, etc.).

In competitive markets, producers' pricing decisions may have a relatively major effect on the quantities they sell; thus, they may face a very elastic product demand curve. For example, at colleges and universities that have several bookstores, prices for textbooks are lower than where there is a college monopoly. If the bookstores are within a reasonable distance from campus, students' loyalties appear highly price related. Thus, a price-cutting textbook supplier will find its market share increasing rapidly. As noted later, the elasticity of demand for the individual firm has major effects on its demand for labor. However, competition will probably not increase the overall demand for textbooks in the college market. A student will only purchase one copy of each required text.

In highly concentrated markets (only one dominant producer or a few major producers), the effect of pricing decisions on the quantity demanded from a single supplier is much more dependent on the demand in the overall market. For the monopolist, the effect of a price cut on total revenue is exactly equivalent to the elasticity of demand in the total market. As corporations tend toward monopolies, their reasons for cutting prices are reduced because the product demand curve is less elastic than in the competitive market situation.

Concentration is a likely natural consequence in most industries, particularly when the overall demand for goods or services is inelastic. Some companies whose costs are high as a result of inefficiency, poor management, or other factors will be forced out of business as competitors drop their prices to increase market share. This process will take longer when the product market is growing (which would lead to a more elastic demand for each), but ultimately we would expect concentration to result.

Regulation and Deregulation

Regulation of certain industries was a tradition in the United States for almost a century. The Interstate Commerce Act was passed in 1887 to regulate interstate rail freight rates. Congress intended to reduce or eliminate price discrimination between small and large shippers and to maintain an incentive for transportation companies to provide service to rural areas. Other industries have also been the focus of regulations regarding services and charges, including communications, banking, petroleum products and natural gas, electrical utilities, interstate trucking, and airlines. But over the past several years, federal regulation in many of these areas has been reduced or eliminated. The initial result has been the elimination of monopolies and the restoration of price competition.

Deregulation enabled new companies to enter these markets and created competition in wages between union and nonunion sectors of the industries. To this point, labor has been most affected by deregulation in trucking and air carriers in the areas of wages and employment. Exhibit 7-1 is an example of the Teamsters' reaction to deregulation in trucking. Other unionized organizations have also found their positions eroded by deregulation and have taken steps to counter the problems.

FOREIGN COMPETITION

Many manufacturers encounter substantial foreign competition. Steel is an example. Because it is essentially a commodity, the differences in the costs of production and shipping cannot be passed to consumers. Fixed costs are also associated with plants and equipment. Producers may benefit by selling steel at a loss for a short time rather than shutting down a plant. Where excess capacity exists in the short run, the possibility always exists that foreign firms may "dump" steel in the United States at prices below their costs. They may also be able to operate more efficiently at all production levels, which enables them to underprice domestic producers.

In the auto industry, competition developed through interaction of the change in fuel prices and the lower costs of foreign producers. Relative costs may increase or decrease depending on the relationship between the dollar and foreign currencies. When fuel economy was not a consumer concern, the large-size auto market was filled by domestic producers and a few high-priced European producers (e.g., Mercedes, Rolls-Royce). Japanese producers were concentrated in the economy and low-priced sports car market. As fuel economy became a concern, the bulk of the demand for automobiles moved to smaller cars.

When these types of changes occur, the elasticity of demand for a

EXHIBIT 7-1

Testimony of Jackie Presser, General President of the Teamsters, before the Senate Committee on Commerce, Science, and Transportation, September 21, 1983

We are here today to tell you that while deregulation is touted as a major success by the Interstate Commerce Commission . . . the opposite has been true for the [Teamsters] and its affected members in this vital industry.

Deregulation has . . . had disastrous consequences for our members in the regulated sector of the trucking industry. And it has brought incredibly bad times to a number of formerly stable motor carriers who face, instead of once-profitable operations, bankruptcy and the prospect of continuing bad times.

We must note . . . that continuing actions by the Interstate Commerce Commission do more damage every day to the trucking industry—through such policies as wide-open entry, overbroad grants of jurisdiction, by ignoring the common carrier obligation in the law to service the needs of small communities and small shippers, by ignoring its mandate to minimize disruptions to the industry and by engaging in policies that clearly don't enable carriers to earn adequate profits to maintain a competitive stance or provide for fair working conditions and wages, again as provided by the [Motor Carrier] Act.

[Our Layoff Survey] shows that unemployment among our regulated trucking industry membership has increased to 32.5 percent of that membership on layoff status this year, up for the third year in a row since deregulation!

We learned that few of our laid-off members have found other employment within the jurisdictions of their local unions and that it is unlikely laid-off workers covered by this survey obtained other employment at all in establishments covered by our local unions' collective bargaining agreements.

These people are professional truck drivers, not doctors. Truck driving is likely their principal occupation, one not easily exchanged for another job.

We're not talking about people looking for a free ride either, but about workers committed to the work ethic; about people who've spent a lifetime providing the nation with goods and services in the fastest, most efficient, most economical way possible, who've always been self-sustaining and independent, and whose jobs now have been legislated out of existence.

People who've spent a lifetime working to own a home now find themselves scraping to pay mortgage payments, car loan notes, bills for the kids' educations, and worrying about how to put food on the table. There's damn little left over, believe me.

---

particular producer's products increases substantially since the industry is no longer concentrated. Wage increases cannot be as easily passed through. The concessions that occurred in the 1980s were partly due to labor costs (combined with other costs) that would not permit U.S. manufacturers to operate at a profit. After short-run reductions in wages (labor) and parts suppliers' prices (raw materials), some obsolete plants (capital) were also shut down to reduce the cost content of new vehicles.

The advent of foreign competition in basic industries had drastic short-run effects on the employment of unionized workers. Tariffs and domestic content legislation (requiring a certain percentage of the parts or labor for products sold domestically to come from domestic producers) would reduce the impact in the short run. The overall effect of these requirements on employment is difficult to determine. They clearly preserve the jobs of persons in the affected industries, but they also reduce employment in domestic importers.

EMPLOYER INTERESTS

As noted in Chapter 5, private-sector organizations' legal members are their shareholders. Labor is hired to accomplish organizational objectives. The major objective of investors is an acceptable return, which means the organization's original purpose may no longer be the one by which the investors can best realize their objectives. Organizations might be expected to leave previous markets and enter new ones as the environment changes the rates of return for various industries.

To meet these investment objectives, management is interested in achieving certain profit levels in its present operations and in being able to move its investments from areas with declining returns to those in which anticipated returns will improve. To achieve goals, management desires the greatest amount of flexibility possible.

Labor as a Derived Demand

Labor is necessary to produce and sell products. The quantities of the products sold depend on the aggregate purchases made by consumers. Thus the employment of labor is a derived demand influenced by the elasticity of demand for the employer's products.

However, in a number of situations the derived demand for labor tends to be inelastic, such as: (1) the more essential the given type of labor is in the production of the final product, (2) the more inelastic the demand is for the final products, (3) the smaller the fraction of total cost accounted for by the item in question, and (4) the more inelastic is the supply of competing production factors.[1] The situations indicate skilled trades in relatively small bargaining units where substitutes are not readily obtainable and where price has little influence over sales

---

[1] Alfred Marshall, *Principles of Economics*, 8th ed. (New York: Macmillan, 1920).

would be least likely to concern the employer when wage rates are established.

When an employer is a relatively small factor in a labor market and/or when there is substantial unemployment, the supply of labor will likely be very elastic, and hiring more employees will have little effect on the wage rate. But if several employers hire the same type of employees simultaneously and/or unemployment is low, a wage increase will be necessary to obtain a larger supply of labor. Employers are likely to be able to pass on the cost of a wage increase if they are in a noncompetitive product market, since a price increase will not greatly reduce quantities sold when demand is inelastic.

Employers generally prefer to view labor from a short-run perspective. When more employees are needed, they can be hired; when less are needed, they can be laid off. The amount of labor hired would be determined by the firm's productivity, given the capital equipment and the product market in which the employer operated. Economic theory suggests an employer will hire additional workers until the wage rate equals the value of the additional product that the last hired worker adds. This value (the amount of the product times the price) is called the *marginal revenue product.* If the demand curve shifted or changed its elasticity, the employer would need more or fewer workers and would like to react quickly and accordingly.

In the short run, the marginal product of additional labor declines because the employer is using a fixed amount of capital. For example, a university contains a fixed number of classrooms in the short run. At some point, hiring additional faculty would not allow the admission of more students since there would be no place to teach them. The declining marginal product of labor means the demand for labor is somewhat inelastic (downward sloping), even though the demand for the company's product might be completely elastic. In concentrated industries, the demand for the firm's product is never completely elastic since the firm is such a large proportion of the industry. Therefore, the demand curve for labor is less elastic than in the competitive situation since the marginal revenue at the point where market demand intersects the labor supply price would be less than the price of labor. Figure 7-2 gives examples of the employment changes that might take place in both competitive and concentrated situations.

Labor–Capital Substitution

A combination of labor and capital is required to produce products and services. Besides being interested in leaving and entering product and service markets quickly, employers would like to change capital–labor mixes when one or the other becomes more productive. For example, the ordering and checkout processes in a supermarket might be han-

FIGURE 7-2

Effects of Product Market Concentration on Employment When Demand Changes

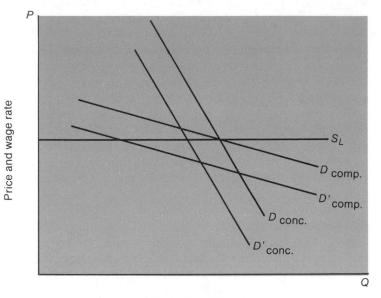

Quantity sold and
quantity of labor purchased

dled in two separate ways. In one, the checker would total prices using a conventional tape-printing cash register. Stock clerks would keep track of shelf and backroom inventory and then tell the store manager when to order certain items. In the other, the checker would use an optical scanner that reads universal product codes, retrieves prices from a computer, prints them on the register tape, and simultaneously subtracts the purchased item from the stock in the store's inventory. When sufficient purchases have been made, the item would be automatically added to a reorder list.

Assume in the first situation that one stock clerk is required for every eight checkers. Assume also that each employee is paid $25,000 in wages and benefits annually. If a store had 16 checkers, its checking and stock clerk payroll costs would be $450,000 annually. Assume that with optical-scanning equipment, the checkers are slightly less productive (scanning takes slightly longer than checking), so an additional checker is needed for the same volume. But stock clerks are no longer needed. Assume also that the costs of the scanning equipment are $2,000 per checker per year. But the scanners' quicker feedback and greater precision in ordering reduces stockouts, excessive inventories, and outdated goods are reduced, so the store makes an identifiable additional profit of $15,000 per year. The cost of checkers using the old capital goods was $450,000 per year. Under the new system, payroll costs would be $425,000 (17 checkers and no stock clerks), equipment costs would increase by $34,000 (17 checkstands), and profits related to better inventory management would increase by $15,000. The net savings of the new system would be $6,000 per year. As a result, we would expect the store to reduce its staff by one (add one checker and eliminate two stock clerks) while expanding its use of capital.

Employers would like to make adjustments whenever a different combination of factors would improve returns. Changes in the use of capital are generally based on relatively long-run payoffs. Labor contracts change labor decisions to long-run decisions and may change long-run labor–capital cost relationships, leaving the employer with what it believes is a suboptimal combination.

Labor Markets

Employers are generally assumed to be in competition with all other employers for labor. In some situations, this is not the case. Where an employer is a significant factor in a particular labor market (e.g., in public schools, as an employer of elementary school teachers in a given geographic area), the wage rates may be affected. Such an employer, called a *monopsonist* (single purchaser of labor), may exist for certain occupations (e.g., schoolteachers but not janitors) or for all occupations in a given location (e.g., a remote mining operation). Where a monopsony exists, the employer's relevant wage rate is the marginal supply curve, since it would take an overall wage increase to hire additional workers because the employer would have to increase wages to retain those hired at lower wages. In this case, the wage rate will be below a market equilibrium level, and the employer will be free to select among those who apply. Figure 7–3 is an example of the monopsony situation.

EMPLOYEE INTERESTS

Employee labor interests differ from those of employers because employee interests are realized in the long run. Employees invest in training and forgo other opportunities to receive the higher benefits they associate with long-term employment. When employees receive firm-specific training, employers seek to tie them to the organization by making some benefits contingent on length of service.

A variety of job outcomes are important to employees. Issues

FIGURE 7–3

Effects of Monopsony on Wage Rates and Employment

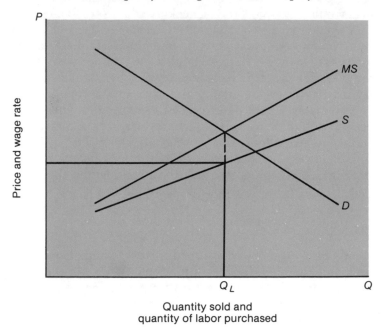

Quantity sold and
quantity of labor purchased

initially involved in the growth of the trade union movement remain important to members. Analysis of a survey of members' attitudes toward unions found that grievance handling, fringe benefits, wages, and job security were the most important issues.[2] The relative importance of each probably varies with the economic and employer environment. For example, when layoffs are rising, job security becomes more important than wage and fringe benefit improvements.

Employees' interests can often be met in their employment; but when they are not and when the employees do not have other opportunities, forming a union can often create bargaining power by changing the economic relationship between the employer and its employees.

UNION INTERESTS

Employees organize for collective bargaining in an attempt to obtain outcomes they believe are unavailable to them as individuals. Member

[2] Thomas A. Kochan, "How American Workers View Labor Unions," *Monthly Labor Review*, April 1979, pp. 23–31.

desires have a major impact on the bargaining goals of labor organizations. The organizational structure and voting differences within unions influence the degree to which member preferences are reflected in bargaining demands. In many situations, local union officers are elected by a single bargaining unit. Their bargaining success directly influences the ability of local officers to be reelected. Similarly, labor agreements are customarily ratified by the membership. This means the contract must gain the approval of at least a majority of the membership to go into effect.

It has been suggested that contract demands reflect the preferences of the "median voter" in a unit.[3] When local unions service several bargaining units and when ratification must be affirmatively rejected by the membership (e.g., the Master Freight Agreement negotiated by the Teamsters must be rejected by two thirds of the membership for it to fail to be ratified), local officers might be less concerned about the contents of individual contracts.

As an institution, the union desires recognition as the legitimate employee representative and some assurance of its place through union security agreements. Unions demonstrate their effectiveness by attracting new members and by organizing additional units. Effectiveness is also frequently measured by economic gains won by the union, which, in turn, have long-run effects on union membership.

Economists have suggested the two major goals of labor organizations are higher wages and increased membership.[4] Labor is presumed to prefer both, but in its dealings with management, the union must usually make trade-offs between these goals. If wages increase relative to those of other firms, an employer might be forced to reduce employment (membership) to remain competitive. To expand employment, wages must rise less rapidly than productivity. On occasion, unions may believe they can simultaneously increase wages and membership through bargaining, but this is only possible when additional capital would be less productive than additional labor.

Generally, unions would be predicted to seek wage gains for present members before pursuing expanded employment. Figure 7–4 shows the presumed direction of preferred union trade-offs. The theoretical preference path is not straight because union members may not equally value employment changes and wages. For example, members may prefer wage increases over additional membership. When facing a cutback, senior members (the median voter) may prefer employment reductions to wage cuts. Evidence suggests widespread job

---

[3] Michael D. White, "The Intra-Unit Wage Structure and Unions: A Median Voter Model," *Industrial and Labor Relations Review*, July 1982, pp. 565–77.

[4] Allan M. Cartter, *Theory of Wages and Employment* (Homewood, Ill.: Richard D. Irwin, 1959), pp. 88–94.

FIGURE 7-4

Wage–Employment Preference Path

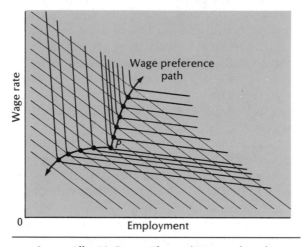

Source: Allan M. Cartter, *Theory of Wages and Employment* (Homewood, Ill.: Richard D. Irwin, 1959), p. 91. Copyright © 1959 by Richard D. Irwin, Inc.

insecurity occurred in 90 percent of the cases in which concessions were granted by unions during the first half of 1982. Concessions were tied into job security guarantees in 96 percent of these agreements.[5]

LEGAL REQUIREMENTS

Public policy establishes the ground rules for the issues the parties will discuss and the way negotiations will be conducted. Section 8(d) of the Labor–Management Relations Act of 1947 sets forth in one sentence the essence of collective bargaining in the United States.

> For the purposes of this section, to bargain collectively is the performance of the mutual obligation of the employer and representative of the employees to meet at reasonable times and confer in good faith with respect to wages, hours, and other terms and conditions of employment, or the negotiation of an agreement, or any question arising thereunder, and the execution of a written contract incorporating any agreement reached if requested by either party, but such obligation does not compel either party to agree to a proposal or require the making of a concession.

[5] Peter Cappelli, "Concession Bargaining and the National Economy," *Proceedings of the Industrial Relations Research Association,* 1982, pp. 362-71.

This broad definition of collective bargaining has had impacts on both the process and the issues. For example, in terms of process, what does "good faith" mean? On issues, what do "wages, hours, and other terms and condition of employment" signify? Unions, employers, the NLRB, and the courts have all grappled with these questions. Novel demands and bargaining tactics have been challenged to determine whether they conform to the statute. Chapters 10, 11, 13, and 14 examine the definition of *good faith* and its impact on process. Chapters 8 and 9 examine the meaning of "wages, hours, and other terms and conditions of employment" to identify bargaining issues.

Bargaining issues can be divided into three legal categories: mandatory, permissive, and prohibited. *Mandatory* issues fall within the definition of wages, hours, and other terms and conditions of employment. The first two classifications are fairly apparent, dealing with economics and work schedules. "Terms and conditions of employment" is a more amorphous concept. A reasonable test of whether an issue is within this area asks if the practice would have a direct and immediate effect on union members' jobs. An example is a plant closing or a reassignment of work between job groups. *Permissive* issues are raised but need not be responded to since they have no provable direct impact on jobs. A demand by a union to have a say in the establishment of company product prices would be permissive. *Prohibited* issues are statutorily outlawed, such as demands that employers use only union-produced goods. Another distinction between mandatory and permissive issues is that neither party may go to impasse (refuse to agree on a contract) over a permissive issue. Table 7–1 lists issues considered mandatory by the NLRB and the courts. The inclusion of an issue in this table does not mean a union will demand it or it will ultimately be included in a contract.

BARGAINING POWER

Bargaining power does not necessarily reside in the degree to which the employer controls its product or service market. Bargaining power is better conceptualized as "my cost of disagreeing on your terms relative to my cost of agreeing on your terms."[6] For example, a gasoline service station owner (in a highly competitive market) may find that agreeing to a wage demand will push the cost of the gasoline sold higher than sales receipts. Thus the owner would object to a union wage proposal in this area. The employees would likely pressure the union to lower

---

6 Neil W. Chamberlain and Donald E. Cullen, *The Labor Sector*, 2nd ed. (New York: McGraw-Hill, 1971), p. 227.

TABLE 7-1

Items Mandatory for Bargaining

Wages
Hours
Discharge
Arbitration
Holidays—paid
Vacations—paid
Duration of agreement
Grievance procedure
Layoff plan
Reinstatement of economic
  strikers
Change of payment from hourly
  base to salary base
Union security and checkoff
Work rules
Merit wage increase
Work schedule
Lunch periods
Rest periods
Pension plan
Retirement age
Bonus payments
Price of meals provided by
  company
Group insurance—health,
  accident, life
Promotions
Seniority
Layoffs
Transfers
Work assignments and transfers
No-strike clause
Piece rates
Stock purchase plan
Work loads
Change of employee status to
  independent contractors
Motor carrier—union
  agreement providing that
  carriers use own equipment
  before leasing outside
  equipment
Overtime pay
Agency shop
Sick leave
Employers insistence on clause
  giving arbitrator right to
  enforce award
Management rights clause

Cancellation of seniority on
  relocation of plant
Discounts on company products
Shift differentials
Contract clause providing for
  supervisors keeping seniority
  in unit
Procedures for income tax
  withholding
Severance pay
Nondiscriminatory hiring hall
Plant rules
Safety
Prohibition against supervisor
  doing unit work
Superseniority for union
  stewards
Checkoff
Partial plant closing
Hunting on employer forest
  reserve where previously
  granted
Plant closedown and relocation
Change in operations resulting
  in reclassifying workers from
  incentive to straight time, or
  cut work force, or installation
  of cost-saving machine
Plant closing
Job-posting procedures
Plant reopening
Employee physical examination
Union security
Bargaining over "bar list"
Truck rentals—minimum rental
  to be paid by carriers to
  employee-owned vehicles
Musician price lists
Arrangement for negotiation
Change in insurance carrier and
  benefits
Profit-sharing plan
Company houses
Subcontracting
Discriminatory racial policies
Production ceiling imposed by
  union
Most favored nation clause
Vended food products

Source: Reed Richardson, "Positive Collective Bargaining," in *ASPA Handbook of Personnel and Industrial Relations*, ed. Dale Yoder and H. G. Heneman, Jr. (Washington, D.C.: Bureau of National Affairs, 1979), pp. 7-120 through 7-121.

its demands unless strike benefits were equivalent to present wages or unless alternative employment was available. On the other hand, an employer who sells products in a less-than-competitive market may accept a relatively large wage demand that it might otherwise resist to forgo the risk of consumers switching to substitute products.

The elasticity of demand for products and labor has a major impact on the bargaining power of the parties. Power is enhanced by obtaining a monopoly in the product or service market. For example, customers would be at the mercy of the only food store within miles. As prices increased, they might buy less of each commodity, but total revenues would continue to rise with lower volume since the community needs to eat. This is an extreme example, and sooner or later news about the amazing profits made by the remote food store would leak out, and some new operator would build a store to get a share of those profits. Competition would ensue, and prices would fall.

Unionization reduces the elasticity of the supply of labor, and some bargaining relationships can create characteristics of a product market monopoly. When unions can organize an employer in a purely competitive industry, negotiating a wage increase (other things being equal) will necessarily lead to a reduction in employment as the employer will be forced to replace labor with capital or to cut back on employment in the short run to remain in the black. Thus, it is to the union's benefit to cooperate in creating a more inelastic demand curve in the employer's product market.

A grocery clerks' union in the remote food store example should be able to gain a large wage increase since the cost could be passed through to the food store's customers. But how might the union gain a wage increase in a large city with hundreds of food stores? By bargaining in a unit that includes all stores, each store will pay the same wage increase and will attempt to pass the increase through to consumers. No competitive advantage would accrue to any store having the same capital–labor mix. Less motivation would exist for any single store to resist a wage increase because all stores would encounter the same wage outcomes, leading to relatively little impact on the volume of sales if the market demand curve is relatively inelastic. This rationale, the establishment of multiemployer bargaining units, is discussed later in this chapter.

Ability to Continue Operations (or Take a Strike)

In addition to the demand and supply characteristics of the product market in which a firm operates, employer bargaining power is enhanced substantially by its ability to take a strike. A variety of conditions influences this ability, including timing, perishability of the product, technology, the availability of replacement employees, and competition.

Timing. An employer will resist a strike to a greater extent if it comes during off-peak periods. Facetiously, a strike of Santa Clauses on December 26 would have little impact on an employer. If timing cannot be controlled, it can frequently be neutralized by the company by having large inventories or accelerating deliveries to customers for their inventories.

Perishability. A food processor would be at a relative disadvantage if a strike occurred just when the fruits or vegetables it was going to pack were ripening. There might be a momentary "window" during which the produce must be processed or it would spoil. Similarly, striking transportation carriers would lose quasi-perishable goods, like business travel, permanently because the opportunity to take them will not recur for the customer.

Technology. If the firm is highly capital intensive, it can frequently continue to operate by using supervisors in production roles. For example, if a telephone operating company were struck tomorrow, operations would unlikely be interrupted. Exhibit 7–2 describes briefly how supervisors were involved in a telephone strike.

Availability of replacements. Strike replacements might come from either of two sources. First, and most possible in capital-intensive firms, supervisors may be able to perform enough of the duties of strikers to maintain operations. Second, the looser the labor market and the lower jobs' skill level, the easier it will be for an employer to hire and utilize replacements effectively. In several recent instances, hiring replacements or the threat of hiring them has influenced negotiations.

Multiple locations and staggered contracts. If an employer has several plants producing the same product and different contract expiration dates, production can be shifted to the nonstruck plants and a large fraction of normal output can be continued. This is the primary reason Hormel could withstand the United Food and Commercial Workers Local P–9 strike of 1985–86.

Integrated facilities. When output from one plant is necessary for production in several others, strikes in the supplier plant convey more bargaining power than usual for the union. This situation frequently occurs in the auto industry at supplier plants producing, for example, electrical equipment or radiators for all vehicles in a manufacturer's line. Problems associated with strikes in supplier facilities have become more critical as manufacturers have moved toward "just-in-time" parts deliveries.

Lack of substitutes. The ability to take a strike increases if no adequate substitutes for the organization's goods or services are available. Revenues are then not irretrievably lost, but only postponed until

EXHIBIT 7-2

AT&T's Managers Weather Strike, despite Long Hours, Tedious Work

The nation-wide telephone strike is starting to take its toll on Linda Watson. The telephone-company supervisor says working 12-hour days as an operator is tiring and disrupts her personal life. But despite the pressures, she is determined to help keep the system functioning.

Mrs. Watson normally works a 40-hour week as an assistant manager in an engineering office of the Chesapeake and Potomac Telephone Co. When three unions struck . . . on August 7, she and about 11,000 other managers and nonunion employees of C&P Telephone began doing some of the jobs of the company's 31,900 union members who walked out. Along with about 40 other workers here, Mrs. Watson is assisting those callers who dial "operator."

About 97 percent of all telephone calls are dialed directly and handled automatically by computers, according to the telephone company. Still, the striking unions insist that over time, both the company's equipment and its people will falter and the strike will more seriously affect service. To the unions, then, Mrs. Watson and her co-workers are Ma Bell's weak point—the one that will give first in the confrontation.

Despite the long hours and the tedious work, morale appears to be good. William Callahan, who normally works in marketing, says the most interesting [calls] come from the city jail, where all calls must be made collect.

"The prisoners use a lot of strange names," he says. "I had a call the other day from a guy called 'The Pig' who wanted to make a collect call to his mother. I called and said 'Ma'am, will you accept a collect call from 'The Pig'? She said, 'Of course,'" He grins and adds: "It provides a little entertainment."

Although emergency repair work and installation work is being done, routine repair work and installation work is beginning to pile up. The company is using some employees with technical backgrounds for this work, but a spokesman says that only about half of the approximately 8,000 repair and maintenance jobs have been filled by nonstrikers.

---

the firm is back in production. Public education is an example of this type of product or service.

Union Bargaining Power

Just as employer bargaining power is enhanced by its ability to take a strike, union bargaining power is increased by its ability to impose costs with a strike. General evidence suggests union wage gains in bargaining are higher in cases of significant barriers to entry for new employers, relatively few present employers in the industry, and low foreign competition. Within the industry, high union coverage by a dominant union also facilitates bargaining power.[7]

Studies of the airline industry following deregulation demonstrate that the bargaining power of unions—as measured by their ability to resist concessions—is highest among unions representing occupations employable in other industries (mechanics, as compared to pilots and cabin attendants), where the wage cut associated with changing employers is smaller (cabin attendants, as compared to pilots), and where the national union exerts strong control over the approval of collective bargaining agreements (International Association of Machinists).[8]

BARGAINING STRUCTURES

Chapter 6 noted the election unit is not necessarily the unit in which bargaining takes place. The parties may decide a larger (but not smaller) negotiating unit would be to their mutual interest. This section explores the types of and reasons for variations in bargaining unit structures presently used for negotiating contracts.

Bargaining structures for negotiation purposes have often aggregated employer units, either collecting numbers of small employers who operate in the same industry in a given region or lumping together various plants or geographically separated units of a single employer. Less often, unions representing employees within a single employer have gotten together to coordinate bargaining. Bargaining structures larger than election-unit size occasionally bargain over wage issues only and leave nonwage issues for local determination.

Aggregations of employer units will be explored first, followed by the union side, including public policy issues influencing the structure of the negotiating relationship.[9]

Multiemployer Bargaining

Many industries comprise large numbers of relatively small employers, many in a single geographic region. Examples include contract

---

[7] L. Mishel, "The Structural Determinants of Union Bargaining Power," *Industrial and Labor Relations Review* 40 (1986), pp. 90–104.

[8] Peter Cappelli and Timothy H. Harris, "Airline Industrial Relations in Transition," *Proceedings of the Industrial Relations Research Association*, 37, 1984, pp. 437–46.

[9] For a retrospective look at some of these issues, see Arnold R. Weber, ed., *The Structure of Collective Bargaining: Problems and Perspectives* (New York, Free Press, 1961).

construction, garments, and retail and wholesale trade. Within the industries, the issues leading to unionization will likely be relatively common across employers, and one union is often the bargaining agent for employees in many employer units.

In the local product market, these employers compete for sales. Since all employers in the local industries (e.g., grocers) offer essentially similar goods and services, the demand for each employer's products is highly elastic (price sensitive). Therefore, a wage increase would be difficult to pass through to customers. To remain competitive, the employer must cut back on its use of labor and also produce less. As a consequence, many jobs might be lost. Figure 7-5 shows why this result occurs.

From the union's standpoint, besides the political risks associated with job loss, differences in the willingness of each employer to grant wage increases will lead to a varied pattern of wages throughout the area, and union members in units where wage increases are lower than those in other units may become dissatisfied with their representation. Employers will also be more motivated to compete on the basis of labor cost differences.

To reduce these problems and to gain the monopolist's advantage in passing wage increases on to consumers, employers and unions have

FIGURE 7-5

Effect of a Wage Increase for a Single Employer in a Competitive Product Market

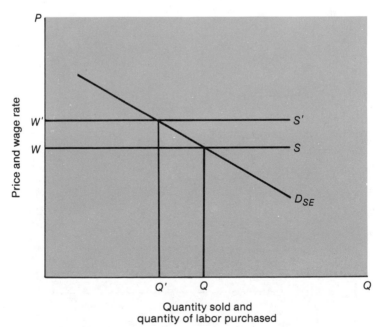

Quantity sold and
quantity of labor purchased

freguently formed multiemployer bargaining units. In a multiemployer unit, a single set of negotiators speaks for all employers, and the negotiated wage provisions apply to all members of the bargaining association. The contract expires at the same time for all, so everyone faces the same economic risks of strikes. Each employer, as a member of the unit, faces a product and service demand curve essentially equivalent to the market demand curve, since wage-related costs will likely be passed through by all members simultaneously. Figure 7–6 shows the effects of a wage increase in a multiemployer bargaining unit. If the market demand for the employers' goods and services is quite inelastic, most of the wage increases can be passed through with relatively minimal effects on employment.

The most successful multiemployer bargaining occurs when employers have roughly comparable nonlabor costs, all employers have been unionized, and new firms have a relatively high cost of entry. If so, an employer member of the bargaining unit would probably not be differentially affected by a wage increase, nor would the union have to compete against nonunion labor.

Industry-Wide Bargaining

While most multiemployer bargaining is done within a relatively small geographic area, it also occurs on an industry-wide basis when

FIGURE 7–6

Effects of a Wage Increase in a Multiemployer Bargaining Unit

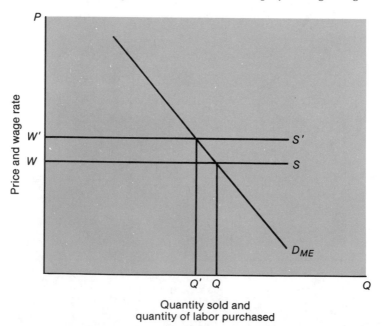

Quantity sold and
quantity of labor purchased

products or services are essentially commodities or are undistinguishable among suppliers. The two most prominent examples have been among the eastern coal-mining companies and organized interstate trucking companies.

The bargaining relationship between the Bituminous Coal Operators Association and the United Mine Workers involves bargaining between a team representing most employers in the eastern belowground coal-mining industry and the United Mine Workers. In the trucking industry, negotiations occur between the major interstate truckers and the Teamsters Union, resulting in the National Master Freight Agreement.

Maintaining an industry-wide bargaining structure is a perilous proposition. As more employers are included, the sizes of each and their respective abilities to take strikes become dissimilar. In the coal industry, mining operators that also operate in other energy-producing areas may be more able to withstand a strike than bargaining unit members who concentrate on coal. In both coal and trucking, employers face significant competition from nonunion sources (in mining, from western coal; and in trucking, from owner-operators).

Political considerations within the union also affect bargaining structures. As unions become involved in industry-wide bargaining, the power and autonomy of local or regional officials decrease. Some commentators have suggested the Master Freight Agreement is vulnerable to regional factionalism within the Teamsters Union.

National/Local Bargaining Issues

In some corporations, bargaining takes place on an organization-wide basis for wage and benefit issues and on a local basis for terms and condition of employment. In most cases, the local management and union negotiate work rules and other items after the national economic agreement has been reached. Work rule agreements are occasionally negotiated simultaneously, but usually the local may not strike over local issues until the national economic settlement has been reached. Where the local represents employees in a critical plant (e.g., a parts supplier necessary for all final assembly products), the local may have considerable bargaining power.

Since plant efficiency levels vary given the equipment available, wage increases may have different effects in different plants. In one plant, a wage increase may push the costs over the limit that can be recouped in sales, thus leading to the plant closing. The employees represented by local unions might then lose their jobs as the result of the national-level increase. Recently, more economic settlements have been negotiated at the plant level, particularly those involving concessions. However, this occurred more frequently in cases of wide differences in the difficulties experienced among plants. When both management and labor believe contract difficulties are related to local

EXHIBIT 7-3

Plant-Level Talks Rise Quickly in Importance

It is nothing new for work rules to come up in local talks, but the importance of these discussions is rising rapidly. "Almost every plant involved in the basic steel industry has made some form of accommodations in crew size and job combinations that lend to more efficient operations," says Sam Camens, a United Steelworkers official. Moreover, 12 of GM's 22 assembly plants now have "competitive" agreements, in most cases because the local unions agreed to reopen local contracts before their September 1987 expiration. The contract changes usually consist of reducing classifications (increasing the variety of jobs that one worker can do) and limiting the times workers can switch jobs.

But not only are the companies benefiting from the changes. For industrial workers, job security has become the top issue. While union leaders are struggling to make some headway in that area at the national table, the companies are making it clear that a "competitive" local contract is the best thing a union can do to keep a plant open or to retain work in-house.

GM was scheduled to close its Fairfax, Kansas, plant by the end of this year; but, in 1985, it said it would replace it with a new plant that it might put near the antiquated facility. Two months after the union local signed a letter of intent saying it would consider drastic changes, the company agreed to build the new plant there. Local 31 believes its cooperation was "damn important" to preserving the 4,900 hourly jobs, says Charles Knott, the local's president. "Had we taken a hard line and said we weren't willing to look at anything, chances are we wouldn't have a $1.05 billion plant along the Missouri River."

However, unions are increasingly afraid that the emphasis on local talks is threatening their power. Workers at Mack Truck plants in Hagerstown, Maryland and Allentown, Pennsylvania, recently approved concessionary local contracts providing various wage cuts and a no-strike clause in return for job guarantees. But the UAW International vetoed the agreements, saying they would "compel accommodations by our members . . . at present and future Mack facilities.

problems or when the union expects to get trade-offs in response to concessions, organization-wide bargaining appears more prevalent.[10] Exhibit 7-3 reports some effects for management and labor of plant-level bargaining.

[10] Cappelli, "Concession Bargaining."

Wide-Area and Multicraft Bargaining

The construction industry has bargained at local levels in the past. The extreme decentralization of bargaining has led to many strikes and many bargaining attempts to keep up with or exceed what some other unit has won. In most instances, each craft has bargained on its own instead of banding together. However, some construction employers and unions bargain on a wide-area and multicraft basis. These configurations may involve all unions of a particular set of crafts in a given geographic regional market. Where unions have strong national leaders, this arrangement will likely be successful because it solidifies their positions through use of regional staff assistance in bargaining and the appointment power of the nationals. On the other hand, internal politics at the local level become more difficult, because the rank and file may still place a great deal of pressure on local leaders to match other settlements instead of concentrating on smoothing the bargaining process.[11]

Pattern Bargaining

In several major industries, the dominant union has chosen one of the dominant employers as a bargaining target. Negotiations are concentrated with this target firm, and it is struck if agreement is not reached. When an agreement is reached, the union moves on to the remaining firms in turn and usually quickly concludes an agreement along the lines of the initial bargain. Pattern bargaining has occurred frequently in the auto and rubber industries.[12]

Pattern bargaining has broken down recently due to major differences between efficiency levels among plants of single employers and between employers and the location (particularly in the rubber industry) of new plants in areas with lower levels of unionization.

Conglomerates and Multinationals

A conglomerate is a business organization operating in a variety of distinct industries. For example, a firm may operate a chain of fast-food franchises, market data processing time and services, manufacture and sell agricultural chemicals, and produce household appliances. This

---

11 Paul T. Hartmann and Walter H. Franke, "The Changing Bargaining Structure in Construction: Wide-Area and Multicraft Bargaining," *Industrial and Labor Relations Review,* January 1980, pp. 170–84.

12 For detailed examinations of current and historical bargaining structures in these (and other) industries, see Harry C. Katz, "Automobiles," and Mark D. Karper, "Tires," in *Collective Bargaining in American Industry,* ed. David B. Lipsky and Clifford B. Donn (Lexington, Mass.: Lexington Books, 1987), pp. 13–54, 79–102.

firm bargains differently than a firm specializing in a given product line, such as autos or steel. Conglomerates often bargain with several unions because they operate in several distinct industries likely to have been organized by different unions. By its nature, a conglomerate has high bargaining power—no single part of its business is very large relative to others, and its distinct parts probably do not depend on each other for components or processes. Thus, the company could take a very long strike at almost any subsidiary.[13]

Multinational organizations are not necessarily organized conglomerates in terms of product-line diversity, but their bargaining power is also great due to the differing jurisdictions within which they operate. Because the union that represents U.S. employees does not represent offshore employees of a U.S. multinational, the firm can (just as a conglomerate can) withstand strikes by shifting production or simply forgoing small proportions of its revenues.

Public Policy and Court Decisions

Legislation has had an impact on bargaining structure. For example, transportation firms covered by the Railway Labor Act do not bargain with industrial-type unions, because the act requires bargaining on a craft or class basis. Hence, an airline may have reservationists represented by the Brotherhood of Railway and Airline Clerks, pilots represented by the Air Line Pilots Association, and mechanics represented by the Machinists. Craft bargaining and the perishable nature of air travel (passages to certain destinations at certain times) enhances each union's bargaining power because a strike by any might shut a line down.[14]

In the past, airlines insulated themselves from the perishability problem by providing strike insurance to struck members through a mutual aid pact.[15] The legislation that deregulated the airline industry eliminated this tactic, but the deregulation itself reduced union bargaining power by allowing new carriers that used nonunion labor to enter the market more easily.

Coordinated and coalition bargaining has been permitted by the NLRB.[16] The NLRB required General Electric to bargain with a negotiating committee comprising representatives from several unions so long as each union represented GE employees. Outside representatives could not vote on any offers but could observe and comment. Unions

---

[13] Charles Craypo, "Collective Bargaining in the Conglomerate, Multinational Firm," *Industrial and Labor Relations Review*, October 1975, pp. 3–25.

[14] Wallace Hendricks, Peter Feuille, and Carol Szerszen, "Regulation, Deregulation, and Collective Bargaining in Airlines," *Industrial and Labor Relations Review*, October 1980, pp. 67–81.

[15] S. Herbert Unterberger and Edward C. Koziara, "The Demise of Airline Strike Insurance," *Industrial and Labor Relations Review*, October 1980, pp. 82–89.

[16] *General Electric Co.*,173 NLRB 46 (1968).

have also been permitted to demand common contract expiration dates among employers in a single industry.[17]

At its most elemental level, a bargaining unit is what labor and management say it is. This is a seeming tautology, but Chapter 6 noted that the NLRB ordered consent elections in companies where labor and management *did not dispute* the makeup of the bargaining unit for representation purposes and no prohibited employees were included. But once past the representation stage, the parties are free to make the bargaining unit more (but not less) inclusive in negotiations, which may lead to novel bargaining structures to accommodate peculiarities of the unions, firms, or industries involved.

The expansion of a bargaining unit results only from the voluntary agreement of the parties. In a case where a union charged a company with refusing to bargain when it would not consider a company-wide fringe benefit program, the NLRB held that only the local units are certified and any expanded unit would have to be by mutual agreement.[18]

Where employers and unions have negotiated a multiemployer unit, the NLRB and the courts have generally held that employers cannot unilaterally withdraw from the unit during negotiations without the consent of the union, even if a bargaining impasse has been reached. The Supreme Court did not see impasses as unusual in bargaining or sufficiently destructive of group bargaining to allow the withdrawal of unit members.[19]

Figure 7–7 represents a flow chart predicting the type of bargaining structures that could evolve in the special situations discussed.

Influence of Bargaining Power and Structure

Bargaining structure can influence bargaining power, and the relative effects for both unions and managements can be altered by the structures to which they agree. The next two chapters examine a variety of bargaining issues. Just as the inelasticity of demand for labor influences the degree to which management will grant wage increases, the inelasticity of demand related to any of the separate demands of labor will influence the outcome of the bargaining relationship. The employer is much more likely to grant in total a demand expected to have relatively little effect on overall costs than to grant a demand that will broadly affect outcomes. This is one reason pension benefits and health care have grown from small-cost to large-cost items in the labor contract.

---

[17] *AFL–CIO Joint Negotiating Committee for Phelps-Dodge* v. *NLRB* (3rd Circuit Court of Appeals, No. 19199, 1972), 313.

[18] *Oil, Chemical, and Atomic Workers* v. *NLRB*, 84 LRRM 2581 (2nd Circuit Court of Appeals, 1973).

[19] *Bonanno Linen Service* v. *NLRB*, 109 LRRM 2557 (U.S. Supreme Court, 1982).

FIGURE 7–7

Bargaining Patterns

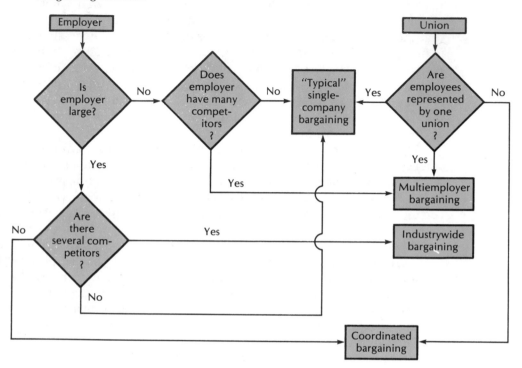

SUMMARY

Labor, capital, and raw materials combine to produce products or services. Employers generally adjust labor and raw material inputs in the short run and capital in the long run. Labor is a derived demand depending on the level of consumers' demands for the firm's goods and services. The elasticity of this demand influences wages and employment. In the United States, legislation prohibits employers from creating product or service market monopolies; thus, employers compete regarding the costs of their products and attempts to reduce labor costs. Deregulation and foreign competition have recently increased the elasticity of consumer demand for products and have allowed competition by lower-cost forms of labor: nonunion and foreign. This situation has led to concessions by unionized employees in industries affected by these changes.

Employers generally create strategies allowing them to concentrate in product and service markets with the greatest returns on investment. Where necessary, they want to be able to substitute capital for labor (because its efficiency is higher). Employees, concerned about gaining a return on their investment in training and employment, require job security and wages commensurate with their investment.

Bargaining power is determined by assessing whether one's costs of agreeing are greater or less than costs of disagreeing. Bargaining power relationships are sometimes purposely altered to create more power in the product or service market vis-à-vis consumers. Multiemployer bargaining is an example of this strategy.

Several bargaining structures exist. The election unit may be expanded as the result of mutual agreements between the employer and the union. Small employers often form multiemployer bargaining units to deal with a single union. Occasionally, nationally based employers form industry-wide units to bargain with a national union. Pattern bargaining, in which one company's settlements serve as a basis for negotiating in the rest of the industry, is declining. Conglomerates and multinationals generally have a great deal of bargaining power due to their fragmented business and bargaining relationships.

DISCUSSION QUESTIONS

1. What effect does a lower elasticity of demand have on the wage and employment outcomes for the employer and the union?

2. How is bargaining power influenced by deregulation and foreign competition? Who is most affected by these changes—labor or management?

3. Why are employers less likely to approve coalition bargaining than unions to approve multiemployer bargaining?

4. Why does the current public policy for bargaining that applies to the Railway Labor Act sector create more bargaining impasses?

CHAPTER 8

Wage and Benefit Issues in Bargaining

Since the beginning of union activity in the United States, wages have been a central issue in bargaining. Economic improvement has always been one of the most important union goals. Managements are also concerned with wage and benefit issues in bargaining because their ability to compete depends to some extent on their labor costs. Organizations producing equivalent output but with lower labor costs will have higher profits and be more able to operate during downturns.

Both labor and management are concerned about a variety of pay aspects. Each is concerned with the overall level of pay, but both are also concerned about how pay rates for different jobs in the organization and pay increases are determined and about what form of wages and benefits are paid to employees.

This chapter examines the components of wage demands made by unions; specific aspects of wage and benefit issues from level, structure, form, and systems standpoints; the effects unions have on wage levels in both union and nonunion organizations; and the present level of inclusion of wage and benefit issues in labor agreements.

In studying this chapter, consider the following issues and questions:

1. What are the strongest current arguments unions and/or managements can raise in the proposal or defense of future or present wage and benefit levels?
2. What effect do wage and benefit levels have on the economic performance of the employer and on nonunion employment of the same or other employers?
3. How does the form of wage costs influence employer and employee outcomes?

4. How does the system for allocating salary increases differ in union and nonunion organizations?
5. How does the usual structuring of union wage and benefit demands alter the structure of wage differentials in an organization over time?

COMPONENTS OF WAGE DEMANDS

In framing its justification for wage demands, the union relies on three major criteria: equity within and across employers, the company's ability to pay, and the standard of living. These criteria suggest the union must make a number of comparisons in formulating wage demands.

Equity

From an equity standpoint, unions desire the wages for jobs they represent to exceed—or at least be consistent with—those of equivalent nonunion jobs in the firm. They also expect fringe benefit package equivalence across jobs, particularly in insurance benefits because personal risks are generally equal regardless of job or salary level. Unions pay attention to bargains forged in other industries; but, due to increased foreign competition and deregulation (as discussed in Chapter 7), pattern bargaining has been substantially reduced. Unions also attempt to introduce uniformity in wage rates for the same jobs in different locations of the same company. For example, an auto assembly worker at Ford's Twin Cities (Minnesota) assembly plant earns the same rate as another on a similar job in Wixom, Michigan. These patterns within a single employer are eroding, however, as plant-level negotiations often lead to concessions in older, less efficient plants to avoid shutdowns and the resulting loss of jobs.

Ability to Pay

While ability to pay takes two forms, the major argument relates to the profitability of the firm. When employers' profits are increasing, unions expect to receive pay increases. They have been reluctant to accept reduced pay when profits decline, but they have recently done so when employers have incurred substantial losses and job loss would be the alternative to not conceding.

The ability-to-pay issue is also associated with the proportion of labor costs in a company's total costs. Generally speaking, the lower a firm's labor intensity (lower share of costs going to labor), the greater unions consider its ability to pay. This assumption is based on the relatively lower elasticity of the derived demand for labor in the cap-

TABLE 8-1

Cost Comparisons for Labor- and Capital-Intensive Firms

	Labor- intensive firm	Capital- intensive firm
Material cost	$ 500,000	$ 500,000
Capital cost	100,000	400,000
Labor cost	400,000	100,000
Total cost	$1,000,000	$1,000,000
Cost of 10 percent wage increase	40,000	10,000
New total cost	$1,040,000	$1,010,000

ital-intensive firm. Table 8-1 shows an example of the effects of wage increases on the costs of labor- and capital-intensive firms.

Standard of Living

This component also takes on two meanings. One relates to the purchasing power of employees' pay (real wage). If prices increase by 10 percent for the things the average worker buys, but wages rise only 6 percent over the same period, real wages have been eroded by 4 percent. Cost-of-living adjustments (COLA) are aimed at maintaining parity between wages and prices over time. With lower inflation rates and more employer interest in knowing future wage rates, COLA is now less often included in contracts than it was in the past.

Standard-of-living issues also arise with unions' beliefs that their members' purchasing power needs improvement to enable them to enjoy higher qualities of goods and services; for example, home-owning rather than renting. We can see some comparison or equity aspects included here, but the comparison is with society in general, not with a specific work group.

Figure 8-1 represents the components of wage demands just discussed. The equity issue relates to both internal and external comparisons, ability to pay relates to profits and labor intensity, and standard of living relates to real wages and absolute improvement. Although we discussed equity issues first here, none of these pay issues are, a priori, more important than another. Both sides will emphasize issues they feel will enhance their bargaining power.

PAY PROGRAMS

Collective bargaining seeks to alter the status quo in pay administration by substituting a collective agreement for management's unilaterally determined practices. One useful way to examine pay

FIGURE 8-1

Wage Demand Components

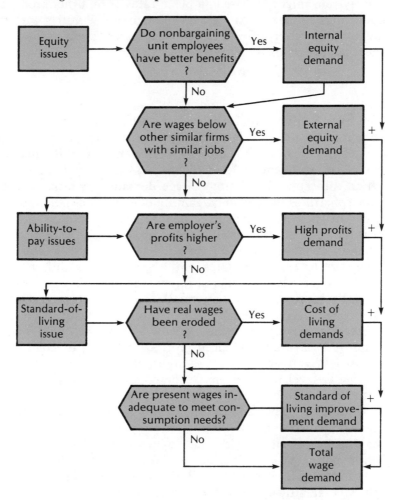

programs and categorize demands divides them into four major components: pay level, pay structure, pay form, and pay system.[1] *Pay level*
refers to the average pay rates for a given job or for the organization as a
whole. It is used to compare rates between organizations. *Pay structure*
consists of the sets of wages applied to different jobs in the organization. *Pay form* is the method by which compensation is received and
may include such components as money, insurance payments, deferred income, preferential discounts, payments in kind, and recrea-

---

[1]Herbert G. Heneman III and Donald P. Schwab, "Work and Rewards Theory," in
ASPA Handbook of Personnel and Industrial Relations, ed. Dale Yoder and Herbert G.
Heneman, Jr. (Washington, D.C.: Bureau of National Affairs, 1979), pp. 6-1-6-2.

tional and entertainment programs. *Pay system* refers to the methods used to determine how much each *individual* will earn within a job. The system might be based on piece rates or on other productivity or performance indexes, skill level, time worked, seniority with the organization, or other factors. Union and management goals relating to these pay program components are examined in the following sections.

Pay Level

The basic components associated with pay-level changes were those shown in Figure 8–1: ability to pay, equity, and standard of living.

Ability to Pay. A variety of considerations influence ability to pay. First, the general level of business activity influences profits. When the economy is strong, wage demands increase, and the incidence of strikes to support bargaining demands rises. Second, in industries with fewer competing companies, employers are more able to pass the costs of wage increases along to consumers, particularly if all firms in the industry negotiate with the same union and have relatively similar expiration dates for their contracts. Third, those employers who have relatively capital-intensive production processes or who bargain with several relatively small units do not have the incentive to avoid large wage increases that labor-intensive organizations have. The ability-to-pay issue has usually been raised by the union, but recently employers have cited reduced profits (or losses) or changes in their industries' competitive level as arguments for demanding pay reductions. Pay-level comparisons become more difficult to make as pay form becomes more complex.

Employers have become increasingly interested in reducing the fixed proportion of pay. Employees may also have some interest in making pay flexible if it leads to lower employment fluctuations. Profit sharing has been increasingly negotiated into contracts, particularly in return for concessions. Both General Motors and Ford employees have significant opportunities for profit sharing if their organizations do well. If profits are down, or losses are turned, the lower base-pay level enables the employer to make a profit at lower levels of output or to cut losses.

Another new type of payment depends on the union ratifying an agreement. In an attempt to reduce the size of employees' base wage levels, companies have been offering relatively large lump-sum bonuses for agreeing on a contract. For example, assume the union is seeking a 4 percent pay increase for employees earning about $20,000 annually. If the employer pays a $1,000 bonus instead of the 4 percent, it may be saving money because the base for future pay increases remains at $20,000 and no benefits are paid on the $1,000. If the proportion of wage-tied fringes is greater than 20 percent, the employer benefits in the first year.

Equity. Equity involves comparisons with other unions, with the same jobs in other organizations, and between regions. One method of comparing searches for "wage contours" in which groups of employees receive relatively similar wages.[2] For example, a contour may consist of electricians in a given geographic area or workers in several occupations within a specific industry, such as steel production. However, a wage contour must have some underlying logical connection among jobs. Finding equivalence in pay between garbage collectors in Great Falls, Montana, and quality control inspectors in Quincy, Illinois, is not enough to establish a wage contour.

Some have argued that major national unions are responsive to the bargaining success of their counterparts. Trade union leaders presumably expect their members to demand settlements equivalent to or better than others recently wrung from management. Succeeding rounds of bargaining follow what has been called "orbits of coercive comparison."[3] Major settlements are presumed to be key-comparison or pattern-setting agreements; however, wage imitation is likely to be decreased by (1) differences between industries in which employers operate, (2) differences in ability to pay within these industries, and (3) the time between the pattern setting and later settlements.[4] As competition has grown in many industries recently, management bargainers have increasingly emphasized company productivity trends and profit levels and deemphasized industry patterns and settlements in other industries.[5] Table 8–2 indicates a relatively wide range in recent settlements across manufacturers whose employees are represented by the United Auto Workers.

Standard of living. Inflation increases the importance unions place on maintaining a standard of living. The negotiation of COLA clauses increased rapidly during the 1970s when inflation was high. However, the escalation of wages in response to inflation seldom equals the level of the measured inflation rates.[6] During the 1980s, firms increasingly made the deferral of COLA adjustments or the modification or elimination of COLA clauses from contracts a major bargaining objective, particularly in concession situations.[7]

Where COLA clauses exist, pay levels are tied to changes in the consumer price index (CPI). Contracts usually provide for quarterly

---

[2] See John T. Dunlop, "The Task of Contemporary Wage Theory," in *New Concepts in Wage Determination,* ed. George W. Taylor and Frank C. Pierson (New York: McGraw-Hill, 1957), pp. 117–39.

[3] Arthur M. Ross, *Trade Union Wage Policy* (Berkeley: Institute of Industrial Relations, University of California, 1948), p. 53.

[4] Daniel J. B. Mitchell, *Unions, Wages, and Inflation* (Washington, D.C.: Brookings Institution, 1980), p. 50.

[5] Audrey Freedman, *The New Look in Wage Policy and Employee Relations* (New York: Conference Board, 1985), pp. 7–12.

[6] Mitchell, *Unions, Wages, and Inflation,* pp. 48–50.

[7] Freedman, *New Look in Wage Policy,* pp. 10–12.

TABLE 8–2

Recent UAW Contract Settlements (Early 1987)

Colt Industries, Chandler Evans Div., Hartford, Conn.
  3 years, with pay increases of 4% in each of the 2nd and 3rd years.
Kelsey-Hayes, Detroit and Romulus, Mich.
  3 years, with pay increase of $.15 and 2.25% bonus in third year. COLA of $.01
    for each .026 increase in CPI.
Motor Wheel, Lansing, Mich.
  3 years, with pay increases of 3% in 2nd and 3rd years.
Trico Products, Buffalo, N.Y.
  Reopener and 2 yr. extension to 1990 with $1.75 pay increase plus $.50 for addi-
    tional team skills and $.50 for team leader skills.
Dana Corporation, multistate
  3 years, with 3% in 2nd year and $500 bonus beginning of 3rd year. COLA of
    $.01 for each .03 increase in CPI.
Whirlpool Corp., LaPorte, Ind.
  3 years, with 1% in 2nd and 3rd years. COLA of $.01 for each .04 increase in CPI
    with $.12 semiannual cap.
Robbins and Myers, Inc., Fluids Handling Div., Springfield, Ohio
  3 years, with increases of $.05, $.10, and $.15, $.65 COLA roll-in. COLA of $.01
    for each .034 increase in CPI.
Webster Electric, Racine, Wis.
  3 years, no increase, COLA with $.20 annual maximum.
Tenneco, Inc., Case IH Division, multistate
  39 months, no increase, COLA of $.01 for each, .026 increase.

Source: Abstracted from *Collective Bargaining Negotiations and Contracts* (Washington, D.C.:
Bureau of National Affairs, 1987).

payments based on the difference between the CPI at the time the
contract became effective and the index level at the end of the current
quarter. As an example, assume a contract effective January 1, 1989,
provided for a base wage of $8 per hour and a COLA of 1 cent for each
.3-point increase in the CPI. If the CPI increased 6 points by December
31, 1989, then employees would receive a lump-sum payment of 20
cents for each hour worked during the preceding quarter.

An important consideration with COLA clauses is whether the
increases become part of the base wage rate. Unions prefer to include
them in the base before the current contract expires because an extremely large increase would not be needed to bring the base up to a
real income standard equivalent to that earned at the end of the
expiring contract.

A variety of factors seems associated with the inclusion of COLA
in labor agreements. It is far more prevalent in multiyear contracts and
more prevalent in less-competitive product markets (such as concentrated industries), larger bargaining units, and heavily unionized industries.[8] While COLA clauses provide some protection for employees in

---

[8] Wallace E. Hendricks and Lawrence M. Kahn, "Cost-Of-Living Clauses in Union
Contracts: Determinants and Effects," *Industrial and Labor Relations Review*, 36 1983,
pp. 447–60.

inflationary periods, the evidence suggests their effect on total wage changes has not been large.[9]

Pay Structure

Pay structure refers to the pattern of wage rates for jobs within the organization. Within the bargaining unit, the union has the right to negotiate these rates with management. The union is also concerned with rate comparisons between bargaining unit jobs and the unorganized jobs in the employer's work force. However, management's adjustment of unorganized rates usually follows negotiations. It is not unusual for unorganized employees to hope the union receives a large settlement, which might obligate management to do the same for its nonbargaining unit employees.

Differentials between jobs may be negotiated on a job-by-job basis or may result from the use of a negotiated job evaluation system. Job-by-job negotiations often create difficulties over time because the original job structure established a hierarchy of jobs separated by specific price differences. Over time, bargaining tends to negotiate across-the-board pay increases of equal magnitude for all bargaining unit jobs. While the absolute wage differentials are maintained, the relative difference shrinks, causing wage compression. For example, two jobs with original pay rates of $4 and $6 per hour have a 50 percent differential. Over time, across-the-board accruals of increases of $4 per hour shrink the relative differential to 25 percent. Establishing rates for new jobs during the course of the contract and determining wage rates for jobs where no external comparisons are readily available are also problems. Methods have been devised to deal with both problems and are included in job evaluation systems.

Job evaluation. Job evaluation determines the relative position of jobs within an organization.[10] The procedure has several steps and requires judgment processes that must be negotiated. In general, job evaluation includes the following steps: (1) the jobs to be evaluated must be specified (usually the jobs covered by the contract); (2) jobs must be analyzed to determine the behaviors required to be performed and/or the traits or skills necessary to perform the job; (3) of the behaviors or traits identified, those that vary across jobs and are agreed to be of value to the employer are grouped into compensable factors; (4)

---

[9] Wayne Vroman, "Cost-Of-Living Escalators and Price–Wage Linkages in the U.S. Economy," *Industrial and Labor Relations Review* 38 (1985), pp. 225–35; and R. T. Kaufman and G. Woglom, "The Degree of Indexation in Major U.S. Union Contracts," *Industrial and Labor Relations Review* 39 (1986), pp. 439–48.

[10] For more information on job evaluation techniques, see George T. Milkovich and Jerry M. Newman, *Compensation*, 2nd ed. (Plano, Tex.: Business Publications, 1987), pp. 99–172.

for evaluation purposes, each factor is clearly defined, and different levels of involvement for each factor are determined (degrees); (5) point values are assigned to factors and degrees within a factor; (6) job evaluation manuals used to apply the method are written; (7) all jobs are rated. Table 8–3 is an example of identified factors, point assignments, and degree levels within factors. Figure 8–2 is a specimen of the types of definitions assigned to factors and degrees within a factor.

Job evaluation normally requires either (1) joint cooperation between union and management through formation of a bilateral committee that determines compensable factors and their relative inclusion in bargaining unit jobs or (2) negotiating the point–pay relationship to apply to evaluations completed by management.

Advantages associated with a well-designed and -administered job evaluation system include (1) the reduction of compression in wage differentials if increases are given as a percentage of the total points assigned to the job and (2) the ease with which new jobs can be slotted into an existing pay structure. The primary disadvantage is the requirement for initial agreement between union and management on the identification, definition, and point assignments associated with compensable factors.

Skill-based pay. Most pay programs in unionized settings structure pay differences on the grade and job classification of employees. Skill-based pay (SBP) is a relatively recent innovation that ties pay to the skills possessed by the employee. An employee is hired at a base rate, usually lower than the average starting wage in the area. As the employee demonstrates learning of prescribed skills, pay is increased. Relatively few job classifications exist, and employees can be moved within the organization based on the employer's present needs. This pay plan combines structural (job or task relationships) and system (pay changes based on individual behavior or skills) aspects. The practice is usually related to team-based production, which sharply blurs job boundaries, and thus is not found in many unionized plants. Where it does exist in unionized settings, it was usually implemented before representation.[11]

Two-tier pay plans. Two-tier pay plans are an effort by employers to lower their wage costs by decreasing the starting rate offered to newly hired employees. Two types of two-tier plans exist. The first starts employees at a lower rate and requires a longer time to reach top rates than for present employees. The second creates a permanent differential with newly hired employees never expected to earn the top rate of present employees. Managements benefit most when turnover is high or when the company plans to expand. The rate of change is most rapid when retirement rates are also increasing. Both the em-

---

[11] Thomas A. Kochan, Harry C. Katz, and Robert B. McKersie, *The Transformation of American Industrial Relations* (New York: Basic Books, 1986), p. 158.

TABLE 8-3

Points Assigned to Factors and Degrees

	Percent	Degrees and points						Weight in percent
		1st degree	2d degree	3d degree	4th degree	5th degree	6th degree	
Skill	50%							
1. Education and job knowledge		12 points	24 points	36 points	48 points	60 points	72 points	12%
2. Experience and training		24	48	72	96	120	144	24
3. Initiative and ingenuity		14	28	42	56	70	84	14
Effort	15							
4. Physical demand		10	20	30	40	50	60	10
5. Mental and/or visual demand		5	10	15	20	25	30	5
Responsibility	20							
6. Equipment or tools		6	12	18	24	30	36	6
7. Material or product		7	14	21	28	35	42	7
8. Safety of others		3	6	9	12	15	18	3
9. Work of others		4	8	12	16	20	24	4
Job conditions	15							
10. Working conditions		10	20	30	40	50	60	10
11. Unavoidable hazards		5	10	15	20	25	30	5
Total	100%	100%	100%	100%	100%	100%	100%	100%

Source: Herbert Zollitsch and Adolph Langsner, *Wage and Salary Administration*, 2nd ed. (Cincinnati: South-Western Publishing, 1970), p. 186.

FIGURE 8-2

Definition of Job Evaluation Factor and Degree Assignments—Factor 4: Physical Effort

Definition: The degree and continuity of physical exertion necessary to meet the demands of the job.

Explanation: This factor gives credit for the strength and stamina required to perform the duties of the job. Consider the work position, the weight of the materials handled, and the continuity of effort.*

Degree	Physical effort and weight of materials handled	Continuity of effort		
		Occasional	Frequent	Continual
A	Negligible (5 lbs. or less)	10	20	32
B	Light work (6–25 lbs.)	20	32 Welder A	44 Department helper Sheet metal operators A & B
C	Medium work (26–60 lbs.)	32 Storekeeper B	44 Machine operator B or C	56 Laborer
D	Heavy work (61–100 lbs.)	44 Welder B	56	68
E	Strenuous work (over 100 lbs.)	56	68	80

* If the work is performed in a cramped area or from a difficult work position, multiply each of the values by 1.25.

Source: Thomas H. Patten, Jr., *Pay: Employee Compensation and Incentive Plans* (New York: Free Press, 1977), p. 228. Copyright © 1977 by the Free Press, a Division of Macmillan Publishing Co., Inc.

ployer and the union might expect problems when the lower-tier employment levels begin to exceed half of the total. Successful implementation of these plans requires careful employee communications and assurances that job security will be enhanced.[12]

Two-tier pay plans are more prevalent in union than nonunion organizations and have usually been negotiated without significant concessions from management.[13] Unless substantial numbers of new

---

[12] Thomas A. Kochan, Harry C. Katz, and Robert B. McKersie, *The Transformation of American Industrial Relations* (New York: Basic Books, 1986), pp. 132, 170.

[13] Sanford M. Jacoby and Daniel J. B. Mitchell, "Management Attitudes toward Two-Tier Pay Plans," *Journal of Labor Research* 7 (1986), pp. 221–37.

employees are hired, the union should not run into severe political problems from new members for some time. Management may be faced with a problem, however, in that employees doing equal work will receive unequal pay.

Comparable worth. Pervasive evidence shows women earn substantially lower wages than men, even when employed in similar occupations.[14] A variety of explanations have been proposed, including differences in the way women and men are distributed in occupations, industries, and union–nonunion employment. One reason could be employer discrimination in favor of men.[15]

Occupations predominantly populated by women are generally paid less than those in which men predominate. Several plausible reasons account for this situation, including: (1) occupational choices for women may be narrower than those for men, thereby crowding their supply of labor, (2) women may be willing to accept lower pay than men; thus, jobs offering low pay will be accepted more often by women, and (3) employers purposely pay less to jobs in which women predominate, regardless of the jobs' worth to the organization.

Some unions, particularly AFSCME, have begun to demand employers pay employees their "comparable worth." Under this approach, all occupations in an organization should be compared with each other to determine their relative importance or contribution, regardless of the relationships found in the external market. Wages for each occupation would be established on these internal comparisons, and a base level would be negotiated. The comparable worth negotiation receiving the widest publicity was the 1984 negotiation involving clerical and technical workers at Yale University, in which the union struck to gain adjustments for occupations predominantly occupied by women. Exhibit 8-1 contains a brief summary of the results of that strike.

Unions representing units with large numbers of women or interested in organizing units with large proportions of women would be most likely to advocate comparable worth in negotiations.

Pay Form

Economic components not received in cash are received as either insurance or deferred compensation. Insurance typically applies to hospital and medical needs, life, disability, and dental benefits. Deferred compensation usually takes the form of pension benefits. Non-

---

[14] See, for example, Nancy F. Rytina, "Earnings of Men and Women: A Look at Specific Occupations," *Monthly Labor Review*, April 1982, pp. 25–31.

[15] For an overview of possible determinants of male–female wage differentials, see George T. Milkovich, "The Emerging Debate," in *Comparable Worth: Issues and Alternatives*, ed. Robert Livernash (Washington, D.C.: Equal Employment Advisory Council, 1980), pp. 23–47.

EXHIBIT 8-1

Labor Unrest in the Ivy League

. . . On September 25, [1984], Local 34, a newly formed union representing Yale's clerical and technical workers, went out on strike. Over the next ten weeks, . . . Yale made the headlines and TV news spots around the nation, not as a center of enlightenment, but as an embattled employer faced with a striking union of librarians, secretaries, and lab workers, most of them women, claiming that they were being discriminated against for their sex.

. . . [F]or higher education, the struggle by Yale's clerical and technical workers may be only the first chapter in a resurgence of the union movement on college campuses around the nation . . .

The [clerical and technical] workforce was 85 percent female; its members were also, on the average, well educated. Yet their average salary was substantially less than that of Local 35 [food service worker] members, this indicated discrimination--if not overt discrimination, then at least an acceptance of the standards of the society as a whole, standards that consistently undervalued the worth of women's work. [The organizer] took these feelings of frustration and found a label for them; the label was comparable worth.

Source: Excerpted from Crocker Coulson, "Labor Unrest in the Ivy League," *Arbitration Journal*, September 1985, pp. 53–54.

---

monetary wage forms have advantages and disadvantages. For the employee, the benefit of the form depends partly on usage. Unmarried persons need life and family health care less than those who are married. On the other hand, the value of many of the benefits is untaxed income. When the company directly purchases medical insurance, the value is not reported as income to the recipient. A wage earner purchasing an equivalent amount may have already been taxed on the money paid for the individual benefit. Some benefits, such as holiday or vacation pay, are paid in cash.

Employers have been much more concerned recently about the form of pay. In the past, the form of the economic package was generally considered the union's province. An employer willing to give an equivalent of 50 cents per hour in wages (as shown in Figure 8-3) did not care how it was apportioned. As benefits became more complex and as medical, dental, and other health care costs began to escalate more rapidly than the cost of other goods, employer interests in the allocation of pay increased. Table 8-4 details what might happen to costs over the course of a contract. Given employers' desires for certainty or predictability in the contract's effects, their resistance to benefit packages with unknown future costs would be expected, since these packages generally specify coverages, not costs. The example in

FIGURE 8-3

Wage Forms

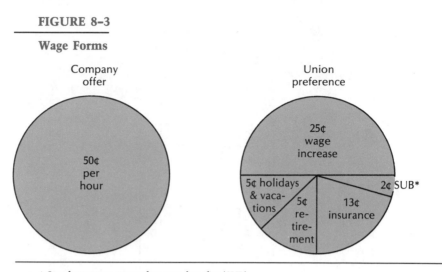

* Supplementary unemployment benefits (SUB).

Table 8-4 shows that a health insurance program costing 60 cents per hour at contract time becomes 90 cents per hour if the carrier increases rates by 50 percent. The second example reflects the fact that fringes are not as easy to control as wages. In this example, the employer effects a one-third cutback in hours worked. Because wages are not paid for unworked hours, costs are reduced when hours are reduced. But because health insurance is paid for each person employed, costs of this fringe benefit still increase by 50 percent, even though only two thirds as many hours are worked. Health care cost containment has increased in importance for both parties. Managements have sought to negotiate contribution limits rather than to pay for coverage, or at least to require deductibles or co-payments.[16] Unions have pressured health care providers to be more efficient so coverage costs do not escalate so rapidly.

Pensions have plagued both unions and managements. For management, before sound financial funding was required by the Employee Retirement Income Security Act of 1974 (ERISA), an aging labor force could easily have resulted in staggering yearly costs for employers who paid their pensions from current earnings. Unions had the same problem. For example, increases in the number of retired coal miners in the 1950s and 1960s, coupled with a reduction in coal production, caused the United Mine Workers to continually demand higher tonnage royalties on coal to support the pension plan. The higher royalties led to higher coal costs, which led customers to convert to alternative fuels or to conserve, thus exacerbating the effect on retirees. Contract nego-

---

[16] See, for example, George Ruben, "Labor and Management Continue to Combat Mutual Problems in 1985," *Monthly Labor Review*, January 1986, pp. 3-15.

TABLE 8-4

Cost per Employee for Wage and Fringe Increases*

	Present rate	Total cost/year	Increase offered	Anticipated cost	Possible cost†
Health insurance rate increase					
Wage cost	$7/hr.	$14,560	40¢/hr.	$15,392	$15,392
Health insurance	$100/mo.	1,200	30¢/hr.	1,824	2,736
Total cost		$15,760‡	($52 more/mo. in insurance)	$17,216§	$18,128#
Reduction in hours worked					
Wage cost	$7 hr.	$14,560	40¢/hr.	$ 9,707	$ 9,707
Health insurance	$100/mo.	1,200	($52 more/mo. in insurance)	1,824	2,736
Total cost		$15,760		$11,531‖	$12,443**

* Assumes standard work year of 2,080 hours.
† Assumes 50 percent increase in premiums for similar coverage by carrier.
‡ Cost per hour is $7.58.
§ Cost per hour is $8.28.
‖ Cost per hour is $8.32.
Cost per hour is $8.72.
** Cost per hour is $8.97.

tiations resulting in pension increases for already retired employees create an immediate cost to mangement as it will not have had time to set aside funds for the increases.

Two major types of pension plan arrangements are defined benefit and defined contribution plans. A defined benefit plan specifies, in advance, the rules used to determine the amount of a pension benefit (for example, 2 percent of hourly pay at the time of retirement times the number of years of service). A defined contribution plan specifies what the employer will set aside for the employee's retirement (for example, 3 percent of total pay per hour). The defined benefit plan makes the amount of contributions uncertain for employers because investment experience may vary over time. On the other hand, employees may prefer to avoid a defined contribution plan because the investment risk is shifted to them.

Because federal wage and hour laws (for example, the Fair Labor Standards Act) require employees to receive a 50 percent bonus for time worked in excess of 40 hours per week, an employer might be expected to hire new employees when more work is needed. However, if person-tied fringes exceed 50 percent of base pay, an employer would prefer overtime in the absence of a higher premium in the contract. Arguments have been raised that fringe benefits are a barrier to employment expansion.[17] Evidence indicates fringes now equal about 39 percent of salaries on the average.[18] If the trend continues, labor's position favoring fringes may not only restrict new entries but may also reduce opportunities for its present membership. If fringes are below 50 percent and if costs incidental to hiring and fringes exceed that of the overtime premium, new hiring will be resisted.[19]

Pay System

The pay system refers to the methods used to decide the pay for each employee. All of the methods for bargaining unit employees will be specified under the collective bargaining agreement. In this section, we identify many of the negotiated arrangements for individual employee pay changes.

Membership.   Many contracts have provisions guaranteeing compensation simply for membership in the organization. These items are not related to length of service but are distributed equally among bargaining unit members or designated subgroups. Many employee-tied fringe benefits (such as health, life, and disability insurance) are based on membership. They are usually unrelated to the numbers of

---

[17] Joseph Garbarino, "Fringe Benefits as Barriers to Expanding Employment," *Industrial and Labor Relations Review*, April 1964, pp. 426–42.

[18] U.S. Chamber of Commerce, *Employee Benefits, 1986* (Washington, D.C.: 1987).

[19] John A. Fossum, "Hire or Schedule Overtime? A Formula for Minimizing Labor Costs," *Compensation Review*, Spring 1969, pp. 14–22.

hours worked in a given month, as long as the employee was active at some time during a designated period

Tenure.   Several pay system features are related to seniority. *Benefit status seniority* refers to the entitlements an individual accrues as a result of continued membership. Many pay systems provide for step pay increases based on length of service within a job or grade level. These increases usually have a cap because a certain range is assigned to a given job.

Entitlements to participate in pension plans also may be based on service. ERISA requires employees over age 21 to participate in an employer's noncontributory retirement plan. In a noncontributory plan, the employee makes no contributions toward future retirement benefits. However, contributions do not become vested (owned) until the employee has met certain statutorial minimum service requirements.

Frequently, entitlements to longer vacations are based on length of service. Low-service employees frequently earn only one or two weeks' vacation, and long-service employees may accrue five or more weeks.

Tenure also entitles employees to use such accrued benefits as retirement. Some contracts contain provisions entitling employees to retirement benefits after a defined length of service (for example, 30 years) rather than at a specific age. Auto workers pioneered these benefits in the private sector; in the public sector, they are most prevalent in the uniformed services.

Time worked.   Most contracts base pay to a large extent on the amount of time worked and when it is worked. Wages are calculated on an hourly basis in these cases. In addition, the level of wages frequently depends on the amount of time worked during a given period (overtime) and the time of day during which the work is accomplished (shift differentials).

Productive efficiency.   Slightly more than 33 percent of contracts base wages of some bargaining unit employees on output levels.[20] These incentive plans have a bargained base output level, above which employees receive extra compensation. Depending on the plan, these additions are on a straight-line, increasing, or decreasing basis as production increases.

Negotiating an appropriate base is often difficult, and grievances frequently occur when employees are transferred into jobs where they lack sufficient experience to exceed the standard. Circumstances beyond the employees' control often intrude, eliminating their chances to achieve high output (for example, poorly fitting components on an assembly job).

Group incentive plans have often been of greater interest to unions

---

[20] *Collective Bargaining Negotiations and Contracts* (Washington, D.C.: Bureau of National Affairs, 1984), Tab Section 93.

EXHIBIT 8-2

Excerpts from the GM–UAW Profit Sharing Agreement

2.08 "Minimum Annual Return". . .means 10 percent of the Net Worth of U.S. Operations plus 5 percent of the excess of Total Assets of U.S. Operations over the Net Worth of U.S. Operations.

2.15 "Profits" . . .means income earned by U.S. Operations before income taxes and "extraordinary" items (with "extraordinary" defined as under generally accepted accounting principles). Profits are before any profit sharing and bonus plan charges are deducted. . .

2.19 "Total Profit Share". . .means an obligation by the Corporation for any Plan Year in an amount equal to 10% of the excess of Profits over the Minimum Annual Return less one-tenth of one percent of the excess of Total Assets. . .

In any Plan Year in which a Total Profit Share is achieved, the minimum Total Profit Share will be $50 multiplied by the total number of participants eligible for distribution. . .

4.02 Allocation of Profit Sharing Amount to Participants

The portion of the Total Profit Share for the Plan Year. . .will be allocated to each Participant entitled to a distribution. . .in the proportion that (a) the Participant's Compensated Hours for the Plan Year bears to (b) the total Compensated Hours of all Participants in this Plan entitled to a distribution for the Plan Year.

Source: *Collective Bargaining Negotiations and Contracts* (Washington, D.C.: Bureau of National Affairs, 1985), pp. 93:994–93:995.

because they avoid competition between employees. Implementing the plans frequently requires significant management–union cooperation. These plans are covered in detail in Chapter 12.

Profit sharing. In another effort to make labor costs more flexible, employers have proposed and implemented profit-sharing plans when workers agree to forgo increases in their base wages. The employee's total pay is based on both job level and employer profitability. Profit sharing has perhaps been most visible among U.S. auto producers. The size of an employee's bonus depends on his/her proportion of total pay in the unit, the size of the employer's profit, and the agreed formula for determining the size of the pool to share. Exhibit 8-2 contains the UAW–GM formula for profit sharing.

Time not worked. Employees are paid when not at work in a variety of situations. Many contracts include provisions for paid holidays, vacations, sick leave, jury duty, and so forth. Supplementary unemployment benefits (SUB) are paid during layoffs under some contracts. SUB add income from a trust fund to required state unemployment insurance benefits. Typically, the addition enables a worker to maintain income close to regular straight-time wages. If layoffs are pervasive and of long duration, total benefit payments may exceed the funds available to pay them, and SUB ends until the funds are restored.

UNION EFFECTS ON PAY

Unionization reduces the elasticity of the labor supply, and the bargaining structures established by labor and management frequently decrease competition among employers. This section examines unions' influence on wages and some specific environmental characteristics involving unions that are related to wage differences.

Union Effects on Pay Levels

A great deal of debate surrounds the issue of whether unions increase wages over and above what employees would receive without them. The answer depends on the definition of *wage increase*. If the definition is an increase in the share of costs apportioned to labor rather than to capital by the organization, then economic theory argues that labor's share would not increase in the long run. The reason is that the employer could increase its return on investment by purchasing capital goods to substitute for labor. For example, if arc welders can make 200 welds in an hour on a given product and are paid $10 per hour, welds would cost 5 cents each in labor costs. If an industrial robot could produce 200 welds per hour and had a useful life of three years (ignoring interest and depreciation advantages of tax laws) and if the price of that unit were less than $60,000, the employer should prefer the robot over arc welders (assuming a one-shift operation). If the arc-welding units cost $70,000, then the firm would begin replacing welders with robots whenever the welders' pay exceeded $11.66 per hour without an increase in their productivity.

In terms of labor's relative share of the national income, data suggest it has slowly increased during this century. However, the share increases in the unionized sectors have been virtually nil over the past 50 years, while shares have risen substantially for nonunion employees.[21]

An exhaustive analysis of evidence on the role of unions in influencing wages finds consistent, significant positive effects for unions on employees' wages.[22] The effects of wage gains are substantially greater for increased unionization within an industry than for increased

---

[21] F. Ray Marshall, Allan G. King, and Vernon M. Briggs, Jr., *Labor Economics: Wages, Employment, and Trade Unionism* (Homewood, Ill.: Richard D. Irwin, 1980), pp. 375–82.

[22] Richard B. Freeman and James L. Medoff, *What do Unions Do?* (New York: Basic Books, 1984), pp. 43–60.

unionization within an occupation. The size of industrial effects are inversely related to the level of competition in the industry, while occupation effects are most pronounced through increased union representation at the local labor market level.[23] A variety of differential effects of unions on wages across definable groups occur; Figure 8–4 shows that individuals who have less education, are nonwhite, younger or older, male, short tenure, transport operatives, or laborers, are more highly advantaged.[24] Evidence also finds that, across worker subgroups, becoming unionized, remaining unionized, or becoming employed in unionized organizations is associated with higher wages.[25] It should be recognized that unionization may have occurred because of dissatisfaction with low wages as compared to other employers or to others in one's community. Thus, unions can also raise wages from a below-average position to one of equivalence with others.[26] A study of wage levels in firms facing an organizing drive found pay levels in the year subsequent to the drive were higher than for a control group facing no union activity. The study also found firms in which organizing activity took place had pay levels lower than comparisons before the drive began. The premium following unionization activity was nowhere near the level found between union and nonunion firms, in general, with initial contract demands focusing more heavily on workplace democracy issues.[27]

Wage level difference effects over time.   The last 70 years have seen wide swings in the degree to which unionized workers are paid a premium. Premiums have ranged from a high of 46 percent in the early 1930s to a low of 2 percent in the late 1940s.[28] Premiums were greater during recessions and narrowed during inflation, perhaps due to the rigidity of rates in long-term contracts.[29] Improved productivity and reduced labor intensity are both associated with larger wage increases. Profits and wage increases are negatively related. This may mean wage increases have been granted independently of profitability and, as a result, future profits have suffered. Employers were most willing to

---

[23] William J. Moore, Robert J. Newman, and James Cunningham, "The Effect of the Extent of Unionism on Union and Nonunion Wages," *Journal of Labor Research* 6 (1985), pp. 21–44.

[24] Freeman and Medoff, *What Do Unions Do?*, p. 49.

[25] Ibid., pp. 46–47.

[26] See Orley Ashenfelter and George E. Johnson, "Unionism, Relative Wages, and Labor Quality in U.S. Manufacturing Industries," *International Economic Review*, October 1972, pp. 488–507.

[27] Richard B. Freeman and Morris M. Kleiner, "The Impact of New Unionization on Wages and Working Conditions: A Longitudinal Study of Establishments under NLRB Elections," *Journal of Labor Economics*, in press.

[28] George Johnson, "Changes over Time in the Union/Nonunion Wage Differential in the United States," unpublished paper, University of Michigan, February 1981, Table 2.

[29] Mitchell, *Unions, Wages, and Inflation*, pp. 80–83.

FIGURE 8-4

The Union Wage Advantage by Demographic Group, for Blue-Collar Workers, 20-65, 1979

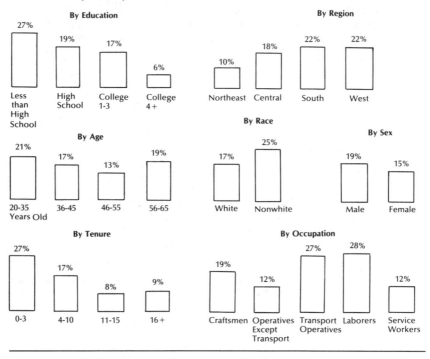

Source: Richard B. Freeman and James L. Medoff, *What Do Unions Do?* (New York: Free Press), 1984, p. 49.

grant concessions in less concentrated industries with improving productivity. Bargaining power in these industries is reduced because competitive products are easy substitutes.[30]

During the 1967-77 decade, union workers received a 24 percent premium, other things equal. Particularly high returns to unionization were experienced by nonwhites, Southerners, and low-educated persons. Evidence also suggests real wages for both the union and the nonunion sectors increased in tandem during this period.[31]

Although unions have obtained wage premiums, the share of total employment covered by unions has declined substantially as a re-

[30] Davinder Singh, C. Glyn Williams, and Ronald P. Wilder, "Wage Determination in U.S. Manufacturing, 1958-1976: A Collective Bargaining Approach," *Journal of Labor Research*, Spring 1982, pp. 223-37.

[31] William J. Moore and John Raisian, "The Level and Growth of Union/Nonunion Relative Wage Effects, 1967-1977," *Journal of Labor Research*, Winter 1983, pp. 65-79.

sult.[32] Employers in unionized settings apparently substituted capital for labor or moved employment from old unionized to new nonunion establishments. Adjustments to changed conditions involve employment changes first, and wage changes second.[33]

Structural and legal factors. An analysis of a cross-sectional sample of employees surveyed in 1977 found unions raised wages for their employers about 18.3 percent over those who were not represented, other things equal. Other factors positively influencing wage levels were plant size (about 5.3 percent per 1,000 employees) and industrial concentration (about 7.4 percent when the largest four firms produce 50 percent rather than 30 percent of the total product of the industry).[34]

In states with right-to-work laws, individuals in bargaining units cannot be required to join unions as a condition of continued employment. For union members, right-to-work laws or strong campaign activity for them are associated with lower wages.[35]

Union spillovers. Wages might increase first in either union or nonunion sectors. But what direction is most prevalent? Do wage changes in nonunion situations affect union wage levels, or is only the reverse the case? Recent evidence shows union wage increases lead to nonunion increases, while the reverse is not the case. High unemployment rates tend to dampen the union increase rate, while upward changes in the cost of living increase them. Union-union spillovers are also found, suggesting that, where it exists, pattern bargaining has influenced union settlements. Nonunion wage changes do not appear to have any subsequent effect on union wage levels.[36]

Union Effects on Pay Structures

When unionized organizations are compared with nonunion firms in the same industries, variances in wage rates are more often lower in unionized firms. In a national sample of employees, individuals who moved from nonunion to union employment had lower wage dispersions, while those who made opposite moves had increased disper-

---

[32] P. Linneman and Michael L. Wachter, "Rising Union Premiums and the Declining Boundaries among Non-Competing Groups," *American Economic Review* 76 (1986), pp. 103–8.

[33] R. Edwards and P. Swaim, "Union–Nonunion Earnings Differentials and the Decline of Private-Sector Unionism," *American Economic Review* 76 (1986), pp. 97–102.

[34] John E. Kwoka, Jr., "Monopoly, Plant, and Union Effects of Worker Wages," *Industrial and Labor Relations Review,* January 1983, pp. 251–57.

[35] Walter J. Wessels, "Economic Effects of Right-To-Work Laws," *Journal of Labor Research,* Spring 1981, pp. 55–75.

[36] Susan Vroman, "The Direction of Wage Spillovers in Manufacturing," *Industrial and Labor Relations Review,* October 1982, pp. 102–12.

sions. Compression in wages is increased by across-the-board wage increases. The average decrease in dispersions attributed to unionization is about 22 percent.[37] The results are consistent with negotiating contracts that focus on the desires of the median voters and put together coalitions best served by settlements reducing variance in wage increases. They are also consistent with the ideal that unions foster an ideology favoring a reduction in the inequality of wages.

Union Effects on Pay Form

Union members prefer larger proportions of their pay to be in the form of fringe benefits. Managements prefer a lower proportion. In terms of costs, unions have the greatest impact on small or low-wage employers; and they most greatly influence costs of insurance, followed by vacations and holidays, overtime premiums, and pensions. When compared to nonunion situations, unions have the greatest relative influence on pensions—possibly reflecting the returns to seniority included in most contracts—followed by insurance and vacations and holidays. Unions have a negative effect on the use of overtime (but not premium rates), sick leave, and bonuses. Evidence suggests the union impact is 17 percent greater for fringes than it is for straight-time pay.[38]

Pension wealth for employees covered by collective bargaining agreements is substantially greater than for comparable nonunion employees. Differences in plans appear greatest for collectively bargained plans having higher initial benefits, earlier retirement opportunities, and larger post-retirement increases in benefits.[39]

Union Effects on Pay Systems

Relatively few data showing how unions influence pay systems are available, and existing data are based at the industry level. Unionized employees are much more likely to have pay increases determined by easily identifiable criteria and by automatic progressions and are less likely to have merit reviews or other forms of individual determinations. Across-the-board increases related to membership are frequent, causing compression in the pay structure.[40] A summary of the effects of unions on various aspects of pay is given in Table 8-5.

---

[37] Richard B. Freeman, "Union Wage Practices and Wage Dispersion within Establishments," *Industrial and Labor Relations Review*, October 1982, pp. 3-21.

[38] Richard B. Freeman, "The Effect of Unionism on Fringe Benefits," *Industrial and Labor Relations Review*, July 1981, pp. 489-509.

[39] Steven G. Allen and Robert L. Clark, "Unions, Pension Wealth, and Age-Compensation Profiles," *Industrial and Labor Relations Review* 39 (1986), pp. 502-17.

[40] Freeman, "Union Wage Practices."

TABLE 8-5

**Recent Evidence on Union/Nonunion Differences Based on
Cross-Sectional Data**

Variable	*Finding*
Compensation	
Wage rates	All else (measurable) the same, union/nonunion hourly wage differential is between 10% and 20%.
Fringes	All else the same, union/nonunion hourly fringe differential is between 20% and 30%. The fringe share of compensation is higher at a given level of compensation.
Wage dispersion	Wage inequality is much lower among union members than among comparable nonmembers and total wage dispersion appears to be lowered by unionism.
Wage structure	Wage differentials between workers who are different in terms of race, age, service, skill level, and education appear to be lower under collective bargaining.
Cyclical responsiveness of wage rates	Union wages are less responsive to labor market conditions than nonunion wages.
Determinants of compensation differential	Other things equal, the union compensation advantage is higher the greater the percent of a market's workers who are organized. The effects of market concentration on wage differentials is unclear. The differentials appear to be very large in some regulated markets. They appear to decline as firm size increases.

Source: Richard B. Freeman and James L. Medoff, "The Impact of Collective Bargaining: Illusion or Reality?" In *U.S. Industrial Relations 1950–1980: A Critical Assessment*, ed. Jack Stieber, Robert B. McKersie, and D. Quinn Mills (Madison, Wis.: Industrial Relations Research Association, 1981), p. 50.

UNION EFFECTS ON ORGANIZATIONAL EFFECTIVENESS

Unionizations and the usually resulting seniority rules change employees' orientations toward long-run employment and the benefits accruing with seniority. The effect of unionization on mobility and turnover is explored in the next chapter, but it should recognized that unionized employees are older and more experienced, other things equal, than their nonunion counterparts. Estimates indicate human capital per worker (knowledge, skills, and abilities related to the job) is about 6 percent higher in unionized settings.[41]

Productivity

Because the evidence suggests a unionized work force increases wage costs as compared with unorganized firms in the same industries, a

---

[41] Richard B. Freeman and James L. Medoff, "The Impact of Collective Bargaining: Illusion or Reality?" in *U.S. Industrial Relations, 1950-1980: A Critical Assessment*, ed. Jack Stieber, Robert B. McKersie, and D. Quinn Mills (Madison: Industrial Relations Research Association, 1981), pp. 47–98.

unionized firm should be at a competitive disadvantage, other things equal. But these other things are not equal. Recent industry-level studies have found unionized establishments to be 24 percent more productive on average than nonunion establishments. If the extent of unionization in the industry is considered, the productivity effect increases to 30 percent. Unionization also apparently has an impact on worker quality within the establishment as measured by experience, training, schooling, and the like. The effects indicate the production worker quality in union establishments is 11 percent higher, while nonproduction worker quality is lower by 8 percent.[42]

Within industries, unionization appears to have differential effects. Research on construction industry productivity found unionized workers on private-sector projects up to 30 percent more productive than their nonunion counterparts. The differentials decreased markedly in public-sector construction projects, however.[43] In education, student achievement is negatively affected by unionization among public-school teachers through increased use of administrators and reductions in instruction time; but student achievement is positively influenced through increased preparation time, teacher experience, and smaller student/teacher ratios.[44] In hospitals and nursing homes, productivity was higher among unionized establishments in the private sector, but little difference was noted in the public sector.[45] A study in the auto parts industry found little difference in productivity levels between organized and unorganized establishments, and failure to account for firms that have gone out of business may upwardly bias the union effects on productivity that have been found.[46]

Possible explanations for productivity differentials include higher turnover in nonunion organizations (examined in Chapter 9). If experience is related to skill levels, unionized firms will have higher skill levels, leading to greater productivity. Because union contracts reduce the dispersion of wages within jobs in firms, employees may believe nonperformance-based compensation systems eliminate competition between workers for a wage pool and enable them to willingly share job information and train new employees.

While recent evidence shows labor productivity in the United States has grown more slowly than in other industrialized countries (United Kingdom, France, Japan, and Germany), the U.S. employment

[42] Ibid.

[43] Steven G. Allen, "Unionism and Productivity in Office Building and School Construction," *Industrial and Labor Relations Review* 39 (1986), pp. 187–201.

[44] R. W. Eberts, "Union Effects on Teacher Productivity," *Industrial and Labor Relations Review* 37 (1984), pp. 346–58.

[45] Steven G. Allen, "The Effect of Unionism on Productivity in Privately and Publicly Owned Hospitals and Nursing Homes, *Journal of Labor Research* 7 (1986), pp. 59–68.

[46] Robert S. Kaufman and Robert T. Kaufman, "Union Effects on Productivity, Personnel Practices, and Survival in the Automotive Parts Industry," *Journal of Labor Research* 8 (1987), pp. 333–50.

level in manufacturing was the only one to have increased across countries during the middle 1970s.[47] This would suggest that the cost of labor relative to the cost of capital is lower in the United States than in other industrialized countries and that capital is substituted for labor at a much lower rate here. Where negative productivity rates exist, it is likely that low capacity utilization occurs and relatively large proportions of machinery and plants are unused.

Profitability and Returns to Shareholders

A substantial body of research finds unionized firms less profitable than their nonunion counterparts and less profitable subsequent to unionization.[48] Additional evidence points to lower shareholder returns as a result of unionization. Passage of the Wagner Act substantially facilitated organizing by unions. A study tracking organizing success in the 1930s found that organized firms had about a 20 percent lower rate of return to shareholders than firms that remained nonunion.[49] Firms recently involved in organizing drives and whose securities are publicly traded have experienced about a 4 percent reduction in equity value following a successful campaign—and a 1.3 percent loss even if they won the campaign.[50] The latter probably occurs because firms facing union activity have been found to increase wages more than those who don't, win or lose.[51] If unionization leads to lower rates of shareholder returns (and the evidence supports this premise), other things equal, as the agents of shareholders, top managers could be expected to embark on strategies to reduce unionization within their firms.[52]

WAGE ISSUES IN CURRENT CONTRACTS

Contracts differ in the degree to which they contain particular types of wage and benefit clauses. Table 8-6 displays major types of wage and benefit clauses and the proportions in which they appear in recent U.S. collective bargaining agreements.

---

[47] D. Quinn Mills, "Management Performance," in *U.S. Industrial Relations, 1950-1980: A Critical Assessment,* ed. Jack Stieber, Robert B. McKersie, and D. Quinn Mills (Madison: Industrial Relations Research Association, 1981), pp. 99–128.

[48] Freeman and Medoff, *What Do Unions Do?* pp. 181–90.

[49] Craig A. Olson and Brian E. Becker, "Does the NLRA Matter? Evidence from the 1930s," unpublished manuscript, 1986. State University of New York at Buffalo.

[50] Richard S. Ruback and Martin B. Zimmerman, "Unionization and Profitability: Evidence from the Capital Market," *Journal of Political Economy* 92 (1984), pp. 1134–57.

[51] Freeman and Kleiner, "Impact of New Unionization."

[52] This and other issues are discussed and analyzed in Brian E. Becker and Craig A. Olson, "Labor Relations and Firm Performance," in *Human Resources and the Performance of the Firm,* ed. Morris M. Kleiner, Richard N. Block, Myron Roomkin, and Sidney W. Salsburg (Madison: Industrial Relations Research Association, 1987), pp. 43–86.

202

TABLE 8–6

Basic Wage Clauses in Contracts (1986)

Clause	Percent containing clause
Insurance	
Accidental death and dismemberment	74
Dental care	79
Doctor's visits	54
Hospitalization	79
Life	96
Long-term disability	21
Major medical	74
Maternity benefits	54
Miscellaneous medical expenses	61
Optical care	40
Prescription drugs	35
Sickness and accident	83
Surgical	77
Pensions	
Early retirement	98
Noncontributory plans	95
Some provision	99
Income maintenance	
Severance pay	41
Some provision	52
Supplemental unemployment benefits	16
Wages	
Deferred increases	80
Cost-of-living adjustments	38
Wage reopeners	10
Shift differentials	86
Incentive plans	33
Job classification procedures	57
Hiring rates	15
Wage progression	42
Two-tier structure	17

Source: *Collective Bargaining Negotiation and Contracts,* 1986 data.

Between 1979 and 1987, some changes have occurred in the pervasiveness of certain types of contract clauses. Dental insurance has increased; but hospitalization has decreased, and other forms of medical insurance have stayed about the same or have slightly increased. Income maintenance has remained at about the same level, while cost-of-living allowances have declined. Concessionary situations have often been accompanied by improvements in job security clauses.

SUMMARY

Wage demands are a central part of every contract negotiation. In forming their bargaining positions, unions are often concerned with equity between employee groups, the ability of the company to pay an increase, and the change in the standard of living of its members since the last negotiation.

Pay programs, whether negotiated in contracts or formulated by the employer, address issues related to the level of pay in relation to the market, the structure of pay rates for jobs within the organization, the form in which pay is received as wages or benefits, and the system used to determine individual entitlements to varied pay treatments. A variety of concerns are subject to negotiation, with unions stressing equity and ability-to-pay issues and management favoring pay programs that positively influence employee behavior. Managements have also been increasingly interested in lowering base pay levels and in making a larger proportion of pay flexible and responsive to changes in economic conditions.

Recent evidence suggests unionization is associated with significantly higher pay levels. Pay structures tend to be somewhat flatter than in nonunion organizations, with a larger proportion of pay given in benefits. Collective bargaining agreements generally contain fewer contingencies surrounding pay increases and have a larger proportion of pay in the form of deferred compensation and insurance.

Evidence suggests organized companies are about 20 percent more productive than unorganized ones. However, they are also about 20 percent less profitable. Productivity differences in favor of unionized organizations appear confined to blue-collar occupations and the private sector.

DISCUSSION QUESTIONS

1. What are the costs and benefits for management in allowing the union to decide how the economic package should be divided?

2. What demands would be most likely advocated by union leaders interested in obtaining a ratification for the contract?

3. What information would you use to make predictions as to the economic demands and probable settlement for a particular union–management negotiation?

4. What are the economic benefits of union membership to employees, and to what extent can these benefits be increased before employers face problems?

5. What are the trade-offs between increased wages for unions, productivity effects, and profitability effects on organizations?

CHAPTER 9

Nonwage Issues in Bargaining

Wage and nonwage issues are not completely separable. For example, contract provisions relating to hours of work frequently specify when entitlements to overtime premiums begin. This chapter first considers issues primarily associated with hours and terms and conditions of employment and then examines the effects of unions on nonwage outcomes for individuals and organizations.

Nonwage issues are important to both union members and management. For management, the length of the contract and the scope of management rights clauses are important. For the union member, job security provisions (particularly those related to promotions and layoffs), grievance procedures, and work schedules are important. As an institution, the union is concerned with the security level it is provided through contractual requirements for employee membership in the union. How promotions and layoffs are handled influences outcomes important to each party.

In studying this chapter, attention should be paid to the following questions:

1. What impacts do federal regulations and contract provisions have on management decision making in employment as it relates to hours of work?
2. How do discipline and discharge procedures operate, and what procedures are available for redress of improper discipline by management?
3. What do the terms *benefit status* and *competitive status* seniority mean, and how do they affect the employment relationship? How are equal employment opportunity issues tied into seniority?
4. What effect do seniority clauses have on employee behavior?
5. What impact does collective bargaining appear to have on the job satisfaction of represented employees?

NONWAGE PROVISIONS OF CURRENT CONTRACTS

Just as trends and patterns exist for wage issues, certain types of contract clauses appear in a relatively large proportion of collective bargaining agreements. Table 9-1 displays the prevalence of nonwage contract terms in a sample of recent contracts.

Contract clauses relating to issues included in Table 9-1 have become more prevalent during the last four years. For example, recognition of seniority as a criterion for employment decision making and clauses related to entitlement to, restrictions on, and acceptance of overtime have increased. However, union security provisions have not increased recently.

UNION AND MANAGEMENT GOALS FOR NONWAGE ISSUES

Chapter 8 suggested that unions (1) are concerned with equity, ability to pay, and standards of living in formulating wage demands and (2) have simultaneous economic and membership goals. Managements are expected to resist demands that would interfere with their abilities to be flexible, to be certain of the types of cost they are likely to encounter, and to respond to changes in their operating environments through the introduction of new production technologies.

Many nonwage issues relate directly to the union's membership goals. To the degree that the employer is penalized through overtime rates, hiring more employees is seen as a possible alternative to scheduling overtime, thus boosting union membership. Contract provisions can be negotiated to ration job opportunities during recessions or as employers introduce labor-saving equipment. Many nonwage issues relate to management's ability to anticipate outcomes if environments change and to direct and deploy its work force in ways most likely to achieve important objectives. To accomplish these ends, contracts frequently contain clauses recognizing the legitimacy of both parties and spelling out the rights and responsibilities of each in their day-to-day relationships.

DESIGN OF WORK

The design of work has important cost and flexibility implications for management and job security consequences for union members. Ironically, the job security aspects tied to work design in the past may now exacerbate layoffs, while changes toward more flexible jobs along with more flexible compensation may improve job security in the long run and employment levels in the short run.

Part of work design involves specifying the tasks, duties, and responsibilities assigned to particular jobs. Jobs have been narrowly

TABLE 9-1

Basic Nonwage Clauses in Contracts (1986)

Clause	Percent containing clause	Clause	Percent containing clause
Contract term		Leaves of absence (cont.)	
1 year	3	Funeral	84
2 years	13	Civic	82
3 years	79	Paid sick	28
4 or more years	5	Unpaid sick	52
Contract reopeners	14	Military	72
Automatic renewal	86	Management and union rights	
Discipline and discharge		Management rights statement	100
General grounds for discharge	94	Restrictions on management	89
Specific grounds for discharge	74	Subcontracting	54
Grievance and arbitration		Supervisory work	59
Steps specified	99	Technological change	25
Arbitration as final step	99	Plant shutdown or relocation	26
Hours and overtime		In-plant union representation	55
Daily work schedules	83	Union access to plant	56
Weekly work schedules	60	Union bulletin boards	69
Overtime premiums	96	Union right to information	71
Daily overtime	93	Union activity on company time	36
Sixth day premiums	24	Union-management	
Seventh day premiums	26	cooperation	45
Pyramiding of overtime		Seniority	
prohibited	64	Probationary periods at hire	82
Distribution of overtime work	68	Loss of seniority	80
Acceptance of overtime	25	Seniority lists	69
Restrictions on overtime	38	As factor in promotions	73
Weekend premiums	70	As factor in transfers	53
Lunch, rest, and cleanup	60	Status of supervisors	31
Waiting time entails	20	Strikes and lockouts	
Standby time	5	Unconditional pledges (strikes)	59
Travel time	23	Unconditional pledges	
Voting time	7	(lockouts)	66
Holidays		Limitation of union liability	39
None specified	1	Penalties for strikers	40
Less than 7	2	Picket line observance	28
7, 7½	6	Union security	
8, 8½	8	Union shop	60
9, 9½	9	Modified union shop	14
10, 10½	23	Agency shop	10
11, 11½	18	Maintenance of membership	4
12 or more	33	Hiring provisions	23
Eligibility for holiday pay	86	Checkoff	90
Layoff, rehiring, and work sharing		Vacations	
Seniority as criterion	89	Three weeks or more	89
Seniority as sole factor	49	Four weeks or more	84
Notice to employees required	50	Five weeks or more	62
No minimum	6	Six weeks or more	22
1-2 days	22	Based on service	90
3-4 days	15	Work requirement for	
5-6 days	17	eligibility	50
7 or more	16	Vacation scheduling by	
Bumping permitted	60	management	87
Manufacturing contracts	74	Working conditions and safety	
Nonmanufacturing contracts	39	Occupational safety and health	84
Recall	82	Hazardous work acceptance	26
Work sharing	18	Safety and health committees	49
Leaves of absence		Safety equipment provided	44
Personal	72	Guarantees against discrimination	
Union	77	Guarantees mentioned	96
Maternity	36	EEO pledges	18

Source: *Collective Bargaining Negotiation and Contracts*, 1986 data.

defined where the production process requires relatively few specific tasks and where training time is designed to be short. Jobs may also be narrowly defined where the sophistication of necessary skills is great, such as in carpentry or electrical work. Typically, manufacturing environments have had a relatively large number of jobs. These jobs are arranged to allow an employee to advance as the result of learning additional skills and/or accumulating seniority. Frequently, more senior workers bid for jobs that have better working conditions and require less physical effort.

Some work rule changes aim at increasing efficiency by utilizing capital goods at a higher level (for example, Teamster drivers handling less-than-full truckload shipments).[1] Others aim at increasing employee flexibility through greater skills and management's ability to assign employees to an increased variety of tasks.

In return for increased job security guarantees, managements have negotiated team-oriented production designs where workers have responsibilities for several tasks and where an employee can be assigned to what would have been a variety of jobs. The GM–UAW agreement for its new Saturn division reduces job classifications substantially.

Work rules that reserve certain responsibilities to certain jobholders reduce efficiency, but they may preserve employment levels. One study of the construction industry found labor costs are increased by about 5 percent by restrictive work rules, and, in terms of their bargaining power, unions appear willing to give up about 5 percent in wages to increase staffing levels by 3 percent.[2] Exhibit 9–1 covers some these issues.

HOURS OF WORK

Hours of work are both a mandatory issue for bargaining and regulated by various federal and state wage and hour laws. As mentioned in Chapter 2, unions' campaign for shorter work hours has been a major bargaining issue since the early 1800s, with the National Labor Union proposing a uniform eight-hour day after the Civil War. The federal government regulated hours of work for civil servants during President Van Buren's administration in 1840 and legislated penalties for employers for overtime beginning in the 1930s.

Federal Wage and Hour Laws

In 1937, Congress passed the Fair Labor Standards Act (FLSA), which regulated wages, hours, and working conditions for private-sector em-

---

[1] Thomas A. Kochan, Harry C. Katz, and Robert B. McKersie, *The Transformation of American Industrial Relations* (New York: Basic Books, 1986), 117–18.

[2] Steven G. Allen, "Union Work Rules and Efficiency in the Building Trades," *Journal of Labor Economics* 4 (1986), pp. 212–42.

EXHIBIT 9-1

Work Rules Shape Up as Major Battleground in U.S. Labor Disputes

Work rules are turning into the next big battleground between management and labor.

Since company profits have risen from the depths of this decade's recession, further wage cuts have become less of an issue. So industry, still eager to cut costs, has turned instead to work rules—everything from the frequency of restroom breaks to who operates which machine. Unions, determined to preserve every remaining job, are digging in.

"Every major strike or labor dispute today has work rules at its core," says Harley Shaiken, a labor specialist at the University of California, San Diego.

Despite work-rule changes' current popularity with management, some labor experts question the saving from the changes. They say that when workers do more tasks—the essence of most work-rule changes—companies have to spend time teaching workers new skills. A Borg-Warner Corp. transmissions unit in Muncie, Indiana, for example, wants to create a single job classification for the workers in one part of its plant. While the company is excited about the prospect, it says that each worker will require 800 hours of training, 10 times more than at present.

Nobody has done exhaustive studies on costs and savings, but companies argue that common sense says the savings are big. Cablec Corp. is a case in point.

The . . . cable maker bought a . . . plant . . . that still ran by rules adopted as long ago as the 1930s. Job categories were so rigid that when somebody classified as a millwright—essentially a mechanic—was told to repair a lift truck, he first had to call somebody classified as an electrician to disconnect the battery cables. And the seniority rules were so stiff that two years ago the plant had to rehire six high-seniority workers before it found someone with the skill to run a complicated cable-insulating machine. The five surplus workers swept floors.

Jobs are at the heart of union resistance to work-rule changes. Union members generally don't defend the most archaic work rules. For example, Ron Davis, the president of the . . . local at Cablec, says the old rule that allowed high-seniority workers off a job "wasn't real productive." But he and other union members fear that eliminating even the bad rules will cost them jobs. TWA says that it will need 39 percent fewer flight attendants during the off-peak season if it gets more work-rule flexibility. And a Chicago-based labor-research group concluded that one third of the jobs lost in northwest Indiana's steel industry between 1981 and 1984 were due to work-rule changes.

"The motive for work-rule changes very often is something other than productivity—it's simply to eliminate people and increase profits," says John Zalusky, an AFL–CIO economist.

ployers involved in interstate commerce. Briefly, the legislation requires employees not performing supervisory, outside sales, or jobs requiring professional training to be paid a 50 percent premium over their regular earnings rate for more than 40 hours per week. This premium requirement covers all employees whose work is of a routine nature or requires close supervision and direction. The legislation also establishes a minimum wage level and prohibits persons under certain ages from working in specific occupations or industries.

Congress had previously enacted the Davis-Bacon and Walsh-Healy Acts, which required overtime payments for employees with similar job duties after eight hours in a given day if they were involved in government contract construction work or the production of manufactured goods for the federal government. The legislation, enacted during the Depression, was designed to stimulate employers to expand their work forces, because effective rates for overtime work were set at 50 percent above the employees' regular hourly rates. Employers would therefore save by hiring more employees rather than paying overtime to existing employees.

Collective Bargaining and Work Schedules

Unions have continually favored reductions of the workweek and workday. The 40-hour week is now typical in many union contracts, but unions have been able to reduce the workweek substantially in certain contracts. For example, Local 3 of the International Brotherhood of Electrical Workers gained a 25-hour workweek during 1962 negotiations in the construction industry. Few electricians worked only 25 hours in a given week, but overtime pay commenced after this threshold.[3]

The AFL–CIO and its constituent nationals have advocated a reduction in the FLSA workweek from 40 to 35 hours.[4] This reduction has a double effect: first, penalizing for overtime after 35 rather than 40 hours, thereby leading to a possible expansion in employment; and second, boosting wages if employers do not hire additional employees.

Entitlements to and Restrictions on Overtime

Contracts usually specify rules for assigning overtime. Overtime is often rotated among workers based on their seniority, balancing hours in the work group before returning to the senior worker to begin a new cycle. Some contracts include provisions allowing employees to refuse more than a specified number of overtime hours per week. Employees

---

[3] See Richard L. Rowan, "The Influence of Collective Bargaining on Hours," in *Hours of Work,* ed. Clyde E. Dankert, Floyd C. Mann, and Herbert R. Northrup (New York: Harper & Row, 1965), pp. 17–35.

[4] John Zalusky, "Shorter Hours—The Steady Gain," *The American Federationist,* January 1978, pp. 12–16.

**Memorandum of Understanding between GM and the UAW on
Mandatory Overtime**

Introduction

The parties recognize that the manufacturing operations of the Corporation are
highly and completely integrated. An interruption at one stage of the production process,
whether during the regular work day, work week, or overtime or other premium hours,
can, and probably will, cause costly interruptions of the process at earlier and/or later
stages. This Memorandum represents an accommodation between the needs of the
Corporation and the rights of individual employes to decline overtime work on occasion
for a variety of individual and personal reasons.

The parties have earnestly sought during negotiations resulting in the contract dated
today, feasible steps that the Corporation might take in scheduling overtime work to
provide employes an opportunity to accept or decline work opportunities during such
periods, and have reached the following understanding, which shall constitute a supplement to the National Agreement.

In order to accommodate the scheduling of overtime in a manner compatible with
changing production requirements, while preserving the right of employes to decline
overtime, Local Plant Management will make an election once each model year to
schedule overtime operations in accordance with Plan A or Plan B below.

Plan A

1. Daily Overtime

Hours in excess of nine (9) hours worked per shift shall be voluntary, except as
otherwise provided in this Memorandum of Understanding, for an employe who shall
have notified Management in accordance with Paragraph 8.

2. Saturday Overtime

Employes may be required to work Saturdays; however, except as otherwise
provided in this Memorandum of Understanding, an employe who has worked two or
more consecutive Saturdays may decline to work the following (third) Saturday provided
(a) he shall have notified Management in accordance with Paragraph 8, and *(b)* he has not
been absent for any reason on any day during the week preceding the Saturday. For
purposes of this Paragraph, Saturday work shall not include hours worked on Saturday by
employes regularly scheduled to work Saturday or any portion thereof as the normal fifth

who have not met this threshold would be subject to discipline for
refusing to work scheduled overtime.

Shift Assignments and Differentials

In organizations where continuous-flow operations are most efficient
(such as chemical manufacturers and refiners) or where product demand levels and plant investment are high enough to justify multishift
operations, contracts specify which employees are entitled to which
work schedules. Provisions may allow employees to transfer shifts as
jobs become available in their specialties if they are more senior than
other eligible employees. Shift arrangements may also be negotiated to
allow rotation across shifts as work periods progress. For example, an
intact shift might work from midnight until 8 A.M. for four weeks,
then rotate to the 8-A.M.-to-4-P.M. shift for four weeks, then move to
the 4-P.M.-to-midnight shift for four weeks.

Innovative Work Schedules

A variety of innovative work schedules has been designed to meet
employee desires and employer requirements. Most have been imple-

FIGURE 9–1 *(concluded)*

day worked such as *(i)* an employe whose shift starts Friday and continues into Saturday, or *(ii)* an employe who is assigned to work on No. 1 Shift (Midnight) operations regularly scheduled to start with the No. 1 Shift (Midnight) Tuesday. In this Memorandum of Understanding, overtime work on Sundays shall be voluntary; provided, however, that *(a)* the employe shall have notified Management in accordance with Paragraph 8, and *(b)* the employe has not been absent for any reason on any day during the week preceding such Sunday, except for a Saturday which he declined to work pursuant to Paragraph 2 above. For purposes of this Paragraph, Sunday work shall not include those hours worked on Sunday which are part of an employe's normal five-day work week (Sunday P.M. through Friday A.M.). . . .

Plan B

4. *Daily Overtime*

Daily hours in excess of ten (10) hours worked per shift and Saturday hours in excess of eight (8) hours per shift shall be voluntary, except as otherwise provided in this Memorandum of Understanding.

5. *Saturday Overtime*

Management shall have the right to designate during a model year period, beginning at the completion of the model launch exemption period stated in Paragraph 10 below, and ending two weeks preceding the announced model buildout, six Saturdays as nonvoluntary overtime work days. All other Saturdays are voluntary, except as otherwise provided in this Memorandum of Understanding, and employes may decline to work any other Saturday during such model year, provided *(a)* he shall have notified Management in accordance with Paragraph 8, and *(b)* he has not been absent for any reason on any day during the week preceding any Saturday which he elects not to work.

6. *Sunday Overtime*

The provisions of Paragraph 3 shall apply.

7. This Memorandum of Understanding shall not apply to employes working on what are normally classified as seven (7) day operations. The International Union may bring to the attention of the Corporation any overtime problems connected with employes on such operations.

Source: *Collective Bargaining Negotiations and Contracts* (Washington, D.C.: Bureau of National Affairs, 1983), p. 96.

mented in nonunion orgnizations, and most have involved the expansion of daily work hours and the shortening of the number of days in the workweek.[5]

Examples of 12-hour shifts leading to more time off are shown in Figure 9–1. In the first schedule, employees receive every other weekend off and work alternate 36 and 48-hour weeks. The second shows a three-on, three-off 36-hour schedule. Both use four work crews.[6]

Unions have opposed longer workday schedules because they have stressed fatigue, safety, and long-term health impact issues in arguing for shorter days. However, evidence suggests worker satisfaction improves and fatigue is not a problem in occupations that are not physically strenuous. Where employees desire to work fewer days and off-job demands in a given day are not great, compressed workweeks may

---

[5] For a complete summary of these innovations, see Herbert G. Heneman III, Donald P. Schwab, John A. Fossum, and Lee D. Dyer, *Personnel/Human Resource Management*, 3rd ed. (Homewood, Ill.: Richard D. Irwin, 1986), pp. 673–77.

[6] Herbert R. Northrup, James T. Wilson, and Karen M. Rose, "The Twelve-Hour Shift in the Petroleum and Chemical Industries," *Industrial and Labor Relations Review*, April 1979, pp. 312–26.

benefit both employers and employees. However, employers should be aware of employee preferences before proposing the issue.[7] The union must also be aware of employee preferences. In one case, a union opposed to compressed work schedules was threatened with decertification by its members if it did not go along with the work change.[8]

Paid Time Off

Paid time off includes holidays, vacations, and other leave periods. These benefits are relatively straightforward, although some restrictions may be placed by management on entitlement or use. For example, employees must normally work the days before and after a holiday to receive holiday pay. Employers may also exercise their discretion regarding vacation schedules. If operations are highly integrated and insufficient numbers of employees are available to continue in the absence of vacation takers, management usually sets aside a period for vacations and shutdowns. Other organizations may require vacations to be taken during slack.

LENGTH OF CONTRACTS

Most contracts cover more than one year, with three years most common. Some contracts provide for wage reopeners during the course of the agreement, especially when cost-of-living agreements are not included. Where management seeks to eliminate them, unions usually demand shorter contracts. Evidence regarding the effects of contract length on other outcomes is relatively sparse. Longer contracts are more likely to have COLAs to insure employees against the uncertainty of wage changes, especially when inflation rates at the time of negotiation are relatively high.[9] Employers try to avoid one-year contracts because they believe such contracts lead to more strikes, more contract administration problems, lower employee morale, and higher and more unpredictable labor costs.[10] However, longer-term contracts may be more difficult to negotiate when the parties are involved in an

[7] See, for example, Myron D. Fottler, Annual Volume "Employee Acceptance of a Four-Day Workweek," *Academy of Management Journal*, 20, 1977, pp. 656–68; and Simcha Ronen and Sophia B. Primps, "The Compressed Work Week as Organizational Change: Behavioral and Attitudinal Outcomes," *Academy of Management Review*, January 1981, pp. 61–74.

[8] Northrup et al., "Twelve-Hour Shift," pp. 320–21.

[9] W. E. Hendricks and Lawrence M. Kahn, "Contract Length, Wage Indexation, and Ex Ante Variability of Real Wages," *Journal of Labor Research* 8 (1987), pp. 221–36.

[10] Sanford M. Jacoby and Daniel J. B. Mitchell, "Employer Preferences for Long-Term Union Contracts," *Journal of Labor Research* 5 (1984), pp. 215–28.

uncertain environment. New agreements were more difficult to negotiate when a long-term agreement was expiring in conditions where
foreign competition was great; where capacity utilization, selling price
of the company's products, and the rate of vacant positions varied
substantially during the contract period; where buyer or seller concentration in the industry was high; among larger employers; and
during periods of high inflation.[11]

MANAGEMENT AND UNION RIGHTS

Most contracts exclusively reserve to management the right to take
actions in areas not constrained by the agreement. Typical reserved
rights include the rights to subcontract work even though it could be
performed within the bargaining unit,[12] to assign bargaining unit work
to supervisors in emergency situations or in training new employees,
to introduce technological changes to improve production efficiency,
and to determine the criteria for plant shutdowns or relocations. When
management does not exclusively reserve these rights, the union is
entitled to bargain during the course of the contract if changes involving job security occur. For example, if a plant shutdown would result in
layoffs, the absence of a clause leaving this determination to management requires bargaining on the effects of the shutdown if the union
requests it.

Contracts also specify the representation rights of the union. Most
relate to the number of union stewards or representatives permitted
within the bargaining unit, their rights to access in various plant areas,
the amount of time off available for union representation activities and
who is responsible for compensating this time, office space, access to
bulletin boards, and access of nonemployee union officials to the
organization.

Management rights clauses also frequently specify rights to direct
the work force, to establish production levels, and to frame appropriate
company rules and policies. The establishment of rules and procedures

---

[11] J. M. Cousineau and R. Lacroix, "Imperfect Information and Strikes: An Analysis
of Canadian Experience, 1967–82," *Industrial and Labor Relations Review* 39 (1986), pp.
377–87.

[12] The Supreme Court decision in *Fibreboard Paper Products* v. *NLRB*, 379 U.S.
203 (1964), requires bargaining by management if the union requests when subcontracting is being considered, unless the union has expressly waived its right in this area.
However, this rule has been relaxed somewhat by *First National Maintenance* v. *NLRB*,
107 LRRM 2705 (U.S. Supreme Court, 1981), and later by the NLRB when it held that
removal of union work to another facility of the company would be permissible if
bargaining had reached an impasse [*Milwaukee Spring Div. of Illinois Coil Spring Co.*,
115 LRRM 1065 (1984), enforced by the U.S Court of Appeals, District of Columbia
Circuit, 119 LRRM 2801 (1985)], or for a legitimate business reason if there were no
antiunion animus [*Otis Elevator Co.*, 115 LRRM 1281 (1984)].

and the direction of the work force form a base for clauses relating to discipline and discharge.

DISCIPLINE AND DISCHARGE

Most contracts specify that employees can be discharged or disciplined for just cause. Some reasons for discharge are spelled out in the contract, and others relate to violations of rules that the employer may promulgate under the power retained in a management rights clause.

Specific grounds in discipline and discharge clauses most often cover intoxication, dishonesty or theft, incompetence or failure to meet work standards, insubordination, unauthorized absence, misconduct, failure to obey safety rules, violations of leave provisions, or general violations of company rules.[13] Committing a violation does not necessarily mean an offender will be automatically discharged but rather will be subject to discipline. However, the organization must be consistent in the way discipline is meted out if it is to successfully defend its disciplinary actions from grievances.

Discipline and discharge clauses may also spell out the due process procedures necessary before discipline can be imposed. Renegotiation of a long-term contract frequently requires disciplinary action taken for offenses before a certain period to be removed from an employee's file.

GRIEVANCE AND ARBITRATION

Grievance procedures are a high-priority bargaining issue for unions because they allow employees to object to unilateral management action during the term of the agreement. For example, assume an employee believes a supervisor unjustly suspended him/her for a work rule violation. Without a grievance procedure, no review of the supervisor's action would take place. Grievance procedures are also useful to management because the aggrieved employee is expected to use this forum when an alleged violation occurs, rather than refusing a work assignment or walking off the job.

Grievance procedures usually specify the person to whom a grievance should be filed, the right of employees to representation at various steps in the process, the path a grievance follows if it cannot be resolved by the parties after it has been filed, and the time limits at each step before some action is required. Chapter 13 presents grievance procedures in considerable detail.

---

[13] For more details, see *Collective Bargaining Negotiation and Contracts* (Washington, D.C.: Bureau of National Affairs, updated as necessary), Tab Section 40.

Most contracts specify that when parties cannot agree on the disposition of a grievance, a third party will arbitrate the dispute and render a decision binding on both parties. The contract specifies how an arbitrator will be selected, how arbitrators are paid, the powers of the arbitrator, and the length of time an arbitrator has to render a decision. Arbitration of contract interpretation disputes are dealt with in Chapter 14.

High grievance rates are associated with decreased productivity. While low morale might be a hypothesized cause, productivity decreases also occur because employees and supervisors are involved during working hours in settling grievances rather than in production.[14]

STRIKES AND LOCKOUTS

Pledges by unions and mangements to avoid strikes and lockouts during the term of the agreement appear in most contracts. Managements frequently demand a no-strike agreement in return for arbitrating unresolved grievances. Unions usually do not give up the right to strike during the contract if management refuses to comply with an arbitration award.

Many contracts require that when unauthorized work stoppages (wildcat strikes) occur the union will take affirmative action to disavow the strike and urge the employees to return to their jobs. If employees strike in violation of the agreement, many contracts specifically indicate that they can be discharged.

Some work stoppages are permitted by contracts including the rights of employees to refrain from crossing picket lines of other unions dealing with the same employer and to refuse to perform struck work.

UNION SECURITY

Because the union is the exclusive representative of employees in the bargaining unit, it desires that they be required to join and pay dues for the representational services the union renders on their behalf. Different levels of union security may be negotiated. Except in states with right-to-work laws, contracts may contain agency or union-shop clauses. The following are definitions of various forms of union security.

---

[14] Casey Ichniowski, "The Effects of Management Practices on Productivity," *Industrial and Labor Relations Review* 40 (1986), pp. 75–89.

1. *Closed shop* requires employers to hire only union members. Although this requirement is illegal, a contract clause can require the employer to offer the union an opportunity to fill vacant assignments. This stipulation occurs most frequently in the construction and maritime industries, in which many employers are relatively small and have relatively short-run demands for certain occupations.

2. *Union shop* requires any bargaining unit employee employed with the firm for a specific length of time (not less than 30 days, 7 days in constuction) to become a union member as a condition of continued employment.

3. *Modified union shop* requires any bargaining unit employee hired after a date specified in the agreement to become a union member within a specific length of time as a condition of continued employment.

4. *Agency shop* requires any bargaining unit employee who is not a union member to pay a service fee to the union for its representation activities.

5. *Maintenance of membership* requires any bargaining unit employee who becomes a union member to remain one as a condition of continued employment as long as the contract remains in effect.

Contracts also frequently provide for a dues "checkoff." Here the employer deducts union dues from members' paychecks and forwards the amount directly to the union, rather than requiring the union to collect dues individually. The process benefits all parties. First, it avoids workplace disruptions necessary for the collection of dues. Second, it insulates employees from union disciplinary action for nonpayment of dues. Third, it ensures a smooth cash flow for the financial operations of the local union.

Unions usually try to obtain the highest form of union security attainable in the negotiating situation, but one might argue that a union or agency shop would not be in the best interests of the individual members. If union membership were not compulsory, those who joined or remained members would see to it that the union accomplished important ends efficiently. State right-to-work laws enable a preliminary test of whether union membership is influenced by the efficiency of the local union, because an individual can choose to join as s/he sees fit. However, one study found that only the costs of a local's operation were lower in right-to-work states; there were no differences in dues levels, provisions of benefits or services, compensation of union officers, or profitability of investments.[15] In most in-

---

[15] James T. Bennett and Manuel H. Johnson, "The Impact of Right-To-Work Laws on the Economic Behavior of Local Unions—A Property Rights Perspective," *Journal of Labor Research*, Spring 1980, pp. 1–28.

stances, right-to-work laws have had little effect on individual decisions associated with union membership. Some evidence shows the proportion of union members in the bargaining unit influences the bargaining power of the union, because wage levels increase with higher representation.[16]

WORKING CONDITIONS AND SAFETY

Working conditions and safety clauses are primarily concerned with the provision of safety equipment, the right to refuse hazardous work, and the creation of joint management–union safety committees. Many of the collective bargaining concerns with health and safety have been superseded by the Occupational Safety and Health Act. Unions are free to negotiate standards of hazard removal higher than what is required in the act.[17]

SENIORITY AND JOB SECURITY

The issue of seniority cuts across several economic and noneconomic bargaining issues. Seniority may entitle employees to higher pay levels or to overtime, preferences on vacation periods, lengths of vacations, eligibility for promotions and transfers, and insulation against layoffs.

At the outset, a distinction should be made between two types of seniority—*benefit status* and *competitive status*. Benefit status seniority is related to the entitlement to organization-wide or bargaining unit-wide benefits established in the contract. For example, if the contract specifies that a vacation length depends on seniority in the organization, then the date of hire (as adjusted by any layoffs or leaves) establishes a benefit status. Most contracts base benefit entitlements on the total length of employment.

Competitive status seniority relates to entitlement to bid on promotions and transfers and to avoid layoffs. Benefit and competitive status seniority occasionally overlap, but the usual pattern accumulates competitive status seniority within a job or department. Assume an employee with five years' total service in the organization bids on an inspection job from a present job in assembly work. If the person gained the inspection job, competitive status seniority among the

---

[16] Sandra Christenson and Dennis Maki, "The Wage Effect of Compulsory Union Membership," *Industrial and Labor Relations Review*, January 1983, pp. 230–38.

[17] For an extended overview of occupational safety and health issues, see Heneman et al., *Personnel/Human Resource Management*, 3rd ed. (Homewood, Ill.: Richard D. Irwin, 1986).

inspectors would begin as of the date of the job change. If a subsequent layoff occurred in which employees with four or fewer years of service on the job were furloughed, this inspector would be laid off. The inspector's benefit status seniority would be five years, but competitive status seniority would begin only from the date of obtaining the inspector job. Competitive status seniority is more likely to be company-wide than department-wide when the employer is small, capital intensive, in a single-employer bargaining unit, and the production technology requires substantial training by the employer.[18]

Occasionally, competitive status seniority systems have a differential impact on women and minorities if they are hired more often into positions that require training and experience before allowing a promotion to a higher-level job. They become more vulnerable to layoff, even though they may have more benefit status seniority than their co-workers who remain within the department during a cutback. We examine the current relationship between civil rights requirements and seniority systems later in this section.

Layoff Procedures

In almost 60 percent of the contracts surveyed in a recent sample, seniority was the sole provision for determining layoff or retention rights during employment cutbacks.[19] In another 30 percent of the contracts, seniority was the determining factor as long as the individual was qualified for the remaining jobs.

Layoffs usually take place in inverse order of seniority, thereby protecting the most senior worker for the longest period. Many contracts specify that layoffs will be determined on the basis of departmental seniority; some permit "bumping," whereby a senior employee is entitled to replace a junior employee in another department or job as long as the senior employee is qualified for it.

Promotions and Transfers

The *CBNC* survey found seniority is less frequently a criterion for promotions and transfers than for layoffs. In about half of all contracts, seniority is the sole or determining factor if qualifications are essentially equal for promotions. For transfers, seniority is also held as a sole or determining factor in half of the contracts.[20]

Depending on the contract, seniority for someone promoted out of

---

[18] J. F. Schnell, "An Ordered Choice Model of Promotion Rules," *Journal of Labor Research* 8 (1987), pp. 159–78.

[19] *Collective Bargaining Negotiation and Contracts*, Tab Section 60.

[20] Ibid., Tab Section 68.

the bargaining unit (for example, to first-line supervision) may continue to be accumulated, may be frozen, or may be lost after a period of time. Employers usually desire clauses protecting accumulated seniority for supervisors as rank-and-file employees may be more willing to vie for promotions where risks of job loss are less if they fail or if employment is later reduced.

Equal Employment Opportunity and Seniority

Title VII of the 1964 Civil Rights Act forbids employers and unions to use race, sex, color, religion, or national origin as a basis for making employment decisions. Except under hiring-hall agreements in the construction and maritime industries, unions have no say in hiring decisions. Union-shop clauses cover workers after they complete a probationary period, not before or at hire. After workers complete a probationary period, the union becomes involved in promotion and transfer decisions through the application of the negotiated contract.

Superficially, seniority requirements are neutral regarding race or sex, and Section 703(h) of Title VII explicitly permits personnel decisions to be made using a seniority criterion:

> Notwithstanding other provisions of this title, it shall not be an unlawful employment practice for an employer to apply different standards of compensation, or different terms, conditions, or privileges of employment pursuant to a bona fide seniority or merit system . . . provided that such differences are not the result of an intention to discriminate because of race, color, religion, sex, or national origin.

Seniority systems and utilization. The Equal Employment Opportunity Commission (EEOC) has generally presumed that if an employer either rejects for employment a larger proportion of a subgroup than majorities or if the proportion of minority or female employment is less than in the relevant labor supply, the imbalances result from discriminatory practices, unless the employer can prove otherwise. Although nondiscriminatory hiring policies have existed since the Civil Rights Act became law, layoffs based on seniority will have a diffential impact on women and minorities if they are more likely to have been recently hired. Is this system racially discriminatory or bona fide under Section 703(h) of Title VII? Table 9-2 is an example of the types of imbalances presumed to be discriminatory.

The Supreme Court and seniority. The Supreme Court has rendered a series of decisions clarifying the requirements for a bona fide seniority system and the rights of unionized employees under this type of system. The Court has held that back pay is not adequate relief for victims of discrimination in unionized jobs because any future decision based on competitive status seniority would trigger a new inci-

TABLE 9–2

Presumed Discriminatory Impact

	Applicants	Hires	Labor market	Firm
Hiring				
Blacks	100	20		
Whites	100	60		
Utilization				
Blacks			20%	5%
Whites			80%	95%

dent in which back pay would be required. Only retroactive seniority from the date of the discriminatory action cures the problem.[21]

An important consideration in the operation of seniority systems is the potential adverse effect that departmental competitive status seniority systems may have on women and minorities, particularly where an individual must irrevocably surrender accumulated competitive status seniority when transferring to another department. How far is Congress's protection of seniority in Section 703(h) to extend? If the effects of decisions based on seniority have adverse effects on women and minorities, can the system still be legal?

In *Teamsters (T.I.M.E.–D.C.)* v. *U.S.*, the government charged that the union and the company discriminated against blacks and Spanish-surnamed applicants and employees in hiring for line (over-the-road) driving positions and that the departmental seniority system in the collective bargaining agreement perpetuated the discrimination.[22] Under the contract, city terminal drivers and other employees lost accumulated seniority when promoted. Their promotional rights were also subordinate to those of laid-off line drivers, who retained recall rights for three years after layoff.

The Court found the company had violated Title VII by virtually refusing to hire minorities for line driver positions. Of the company's 6,472 employees in 1971, 571 (9 percent) were minorities; but of the 1,838 line drivers, only 15 (.8 percent) were minorities. The Court also noted that before 1969, the company had employed only one minority line driver.

The Court examined the effects of the seniority system to determine whether it met the bona fide requirements of 703(h). In this labor agreement, benefit status seniority ran from the date of hire on a

---

[21] *Franks* v. *Bowman Transportation Co.*, 424 U.S. 747 (1976).

[22] *International Brotherhood of Teamsters* v. *U.S.* and *T.I.M.E.–D.C., Inc.* v. *U.S.* (U.S. Supreme Court, 14 FEP Cases 1514); *East Texas Motor Freight System, Inc.* v. *Rodriguez, Teamsters Local Union 657* v. *Rodriguez,* and *Southern Conference of Teamsters* v. *Rodriguez* (U.S. Supreme Court, 14 FEP Cases 1505).

system-wide basis, but competitive status seniority dated from the beginning of one's tenure on a particular job at a particular terminal. Because competitive status seniority did not accrue across jobs, the system discouraged city drivers from bidding for higher-paying line driver jobs, particularly if job security were important for a city driver. The union argued that the seniority system was bona fide; Title VII remedies post-act discrimination; and the union was ready, willing, and able to press for back seniority for post-act victims who availed themselves of the grievance procedure.

The Court held that persons discriminated against since the act took effect were entitled to relief. However, the Court interpreted the wording of 703(h) and the congressional debate behind it to preclude relief from pre-act discrimination. Thus, constructive (or backdated) seniority could not be granted beyond the effective date of Title VII. Persons who accumulated seniority in a job before that date, even as a result of discrimination, could continue to use it for competitive status purposes.

The Court held that the departmental seniority system for jobs within terminals applied equally to majorities and minorities. The system was not negotiated to establish or maintain discrimination. Thus, persons suffering from the effects of pre-act discrimination were not entitled to relief, even though the application of the seniority system *at this time* could reduce their opportunities or discourage their bidding for promotion.[23]

EFFECTS OF UNIONS ON NONWAGE OUTCOMES

Unions influence nonwage outcomes for both the employer and the employee predominantly in labor mobility. The effects involve hiring, promotions and transfers, and turnover and retirement from the organization. Employee satisfaction is also related to union membership. This section explores some recent research on the effects of unions on these types of nonwage outcomes.

Union Influences on Hiring

Lower-skilled workers prefer union jobs. Given this preference, unionization may improve the employer's ability to select more-qualified job applicants. For applicants who do not initially obtain union employ-

---

[23] For an overview of seniority and equal employment opportunity issues, see Marvin J. Levine, "The Conflict between Negotiated Seniority Provisions and Title VII of the Civil Rights Act of 1964: Recent Developments," *Labor Law Journal*, June 1978, pp. 352–63.

ment, the passage of time makes union jobs less attractive because opportunities for promotion within bargaining units are at least partially related to seniority.[24]

Across employers, employment in unionized jobs appears to positively influence wage levels for both black and white males. But the effects appear greater for blacks than for whites and much greater for young blacks. From an overall standpoint, the proportion of unionized employment in an area depresses employment opportunities for younger workers and particularly depresses wages for young black males.[25] But, the proportion of newly hired employees who are minorities is greater in unionized organizations than in comparable nonunion organizations.[26]

Promotions, Transfers, and Turnover

Most contracts specify the methods for filling vacant positions requiring promotions or transfers. In nonunion organizations, unless policy or custom dictates otherwise, the employer is free to devise ad hoc criteria for filling jobs.

Substantial evidence demonstrates turnover in nonunion organizations is larger than in organizations with equivalent jobs where employees are represented by unions. Chapter 6 suggested a relatively stable work force is necessary for a successful organizing campaign. A plausible explanation for lower turnover following unionization would be the stable base preceding it. Evidence suggests, however, that employers with represented work forces are no more likely than other employers to hire applicants who seem innately stable.[27] Lower turnover is also probably related to the fact that wage premiums for taking a unionized job are about 3 to 8 percent, but losses from leaving one are about 7 to 11 percent.[28]

One explanation of union–nonunion differences in quit rates is the inclusion of contract provisions requiring decisions in promotions and transfers to be based on the employees' seniority. Block found the

[24] John S. Abowd and Henry S. Farber, "Job Queues and the Union Status of Workers," *Industrial and Labor Relations Review*, April 1983, pp. 354–67.

[25] Harry J. Holzer, "Unions and the Labor Market Status of White and Minority Youth," *Industrial and Labor Relations Review*, April 1982, pp. 392–405.

[26] Jonathon S. Leonard, "The Effect of Unions on the Employment of Blacks, Hispanics, and Women," *Industrial and Labor Relations Review* 39 (1985), pp. 115–32.

[27] Richard B. Freeman, "The Effect of Unionism on Worker Attachment to Firms," *Journal of Labor Research*, Spring 1980, pp. 29–61.

[28] J. D. Cunningham and E. Donovan, "Patterns of Union Membership and Relative Wages," *Journal of Labor Research* 7 (1986), pp. 127–44.

degree to which the contract required seniority to be given weight in job assignments was likely to be associated with lower turnover rates within industries with strong clauses.[29]

A series of studies on unions and internal mobility concluded that collective bargaining provides employees with a voice in the operation of the organization. With grievance procedures and contract negotiations, employees have methods for changing conditions they judge unsatisfactory. Without collective bargaining, an employee must leave the organization to escape unsatisfactory conditions.[30]

When employees have grievances with their employers in nonunion organizations without established procedures for resolution, they must accept the employer's unilateral action or leave (assuming the action was not unlawful). In a unionized situation, the employee is entitled to due process, and the grievance might be allowed. Any lag time in the grievance process will extend tenure until the grievance is finally decided against the employee. Other inducements to continue tenure in organized firms relate to anticipated progress in the next round of negotiations and perceptions about the likelihood of vacancies for which the individual can qualify by reason of seniority.[31]

Layoff and discharge likelihoods are not changed by unionization,[32] but laid-off unionized employees are much less likely to quit while awaiting recall than are nonunion employees. Thus, in the absence of supplemental unemployment benefit packages, unionized employers should have a cost advantage, because recall costs are lower due to fewer vacancies and training of new employees, which would result from quits. Management can store labor for future demand at relatively minimal costs.[33]

Seniority provisions may also result from management attention toward the interests of senior bargaining unit members (they are much more likely to be represented on negotiating committees than are junior members) and away from the impact of the external labor market on the establishment of employment policy. Thus, where cost differences are not significant and the experience of senior employees is related to productivity, negotiated seniority clauses may benefit

---

[29] Richard N. Block, "The Impact of Seniority Provisions on the Manufacturing Quit Rate," *Industrial and Labor Relations Review*, July 1978, pp. 474–88.

[30] Richard B. Freeman, "Individual Mobility and Union Voice in the Labor Market," *American Economic Review*, May 1976, pp. 361–68.

[31] Freeman, "Effect of Unionism."

[32] Ibid.

[33] James R. Medoff, "Layoffs and Alternatives under Trade Unions in U.S. Manufacturing," *American Economic Review*, June 1979, pp. 380–95.

both the employer and longer-tenure employees. Bargaining unit members are probably more willing to ratify contracts with significant benefits for seniority, because many of them will likely have longer seniority if turnover in union situations is less; unionized employees may also anticipate achieving these benefits in later years.

If seniority clauses actually create opportunities for senior employees, tracking employees over time should demonstrate that union members have more internal job changes than nonunion employees have. Quit rates for white union members are substantially below those of nonunion employees, and transfer and promotion rates are significantly higher. In the samples examined, almost all union members who had remained with the same employer for more than 10 years had made at least one internal job change. Within the sample of union employees, education was negatively related with a bargaining unit promotion but was positively related to a promotion out of the bargaining unit. Promotion likelihoods are greater with more seniority in unionized situations, while they are less in nonunion employment. Unlike the nonunion situations in which women were less likely to receive promotions, gender made no difference in situations where employees were represented.[34]

Retirement Programs

While the level of benefits retirees become entitled to is a wage issue, the age of retirement takes on a nonwage flavor for the individual (even though it has an economic consequence for the employer). In the past, a single retirement age of 65 was established as a general rule across most organizations and within most occupations, but these age rules have changed. For example, the 1979 UAW agreement with the automakers provided that an individual could retire after accumulating 30 years of service (25 in foundries) regardless of age. Although past contracts have specified mandatory retirement at age 65, no new contracts may now be negotiated requiring retirement at any specific age, given the amendments to the Age Discrimination in Employment Act. Thus, employees in the auto industry could choose to retire as early as age 43 (with 25 years in foundry operations) and could not be forced to retire.

Early retirement decisions appear strongly influenced by the retiree's economic expectations and general state of health. The better

---

[34] Craig A. Olson and Chris J. Berger, "The Relationship between Seniority, Ability, and the Promotion of Union and Nonunion Workers," in, *Advances in Industrial and Labor Relations*, ed. David B. Lipsky and Joel M. Douglas (Greenwich, Conn.: JAI Press, 1983), pp. 91–129.

the expectations and the worse the health, the more likely the individual is to retire early.[35] A study of the predictors of planned retirement age suggests married men retire earlier when they expect larger pensions from both private and public sources, when their pensions have a known benefit level, when they are homeowners, when they have earned relatively higher wages, when they are in poorer health, and when they work in jobs where the retirement age is compulsory.[36]

As benefit levels increase and as retirement decisions cover a range of time periods rather than a particular date, greater amounts of retirement planning by individuals and organizations are probable.[37] Many contracts presently in effect offer social security and private pension benefits and tax advantages, which when combined impose an actual cash penalty on one who continues to work after eligibility for social security begins.

Job Satisfaction

Evidence surrounding the effect of union membership on job satisfaction is not at all clear cut. Chapter 6 pointed out that dissatisfaction was a significant predictor of a vote for the union during organizing campaigns.[38] Receiving the benefits that a union might gain is expected to relate to increased job satisfaction, but a large-scale across-sectional study found job satisfaction of union members lower than nonunion employees when other variables were held constant.[39]

Job satisfaction increases for union members whose jobs change as the result of a transfer or promotion but not from a turnover. The reverse was found for nonunion employees: their satisfaction increased with turnover and did not change as the result of internal job movements.[40]

In a cross-sectional study of a national sample, the overall job

---

35 Richard Barfield and James Morgan, *Early Retirement: The Decision and the Experience* (Ann Arbor: Survey Research Center, University of Michigan, 1969).

36 Arden Hall and Terry R. Johnson, "The Determinants of Planned Retirement," *Industrial and Labor Relations Review*, January 1980, pp. 241–54.

37 For an example of the types of information combined to make retirement decisions for U.S. Naval officers (who generally may retire across a 10-year span), see Donald F. Parker and Lee Dyer, "Expectancy Theory as a Within-Person Behavioral Choice Model: An Empirical Test of Some Conceptual and Methodological Refinements," *Organizational Behavior and Human Performance*, October 1976, pp. 97–117.

38 Julius G. Getman, Stephen B. Goldberg, and Jeanne B. Herman, *Union Representation Elections: Law and Reality* (New York: Russell Sage Foundation, 1976), pp. 53–57.

39 Richard B. Freeman, "Job Satisfaction as an Economic Variable," *American Economic Review*, May 1978, pp. 135–41.

40 Olson and Berger, "Relationship between Seniority."

satisfaction of unionized employees was somewhat lower than for nonunion employees; but when various facets of satisfaction were examined, the results varied. Union members were more satisfied with their pay, because they received more and because they valued pay outcomes more than nonunion employees did. Promotion satisfaction was also greater, largely because union members place lower value on promotions than on other union achievements. This result can be partially accounted for by relatively lower pay differentials between jobs in unionized situations. Union members were less satisfied with supervisors and co-workers, largely through lower perceptions of supervisory behavior. They were also less satisfied with their jobs, largely as the result of lower job scope (or less varied tasks) than for nonunion employees.[41] Unions could influence the satisfaction level of employees toward supervisors and the job if they pointed out those features as potential sources of problems that the unions will help employees solve. An adversarial position might be necessary to create the need for continued representation.

Commitment to the Union

Several studies have examined the influence of commitment to an employing organization and its relationship to turnover.[42] The measurement of commitment to a union and the effects of commitment on behavior have also been examined recently. Commitment to a union is reflected in the desire to remain a member, the willingness to exert effort on behalf of the union, and the belief in and acceptance of union goals and values. In a situation where membership was voluntary, commitment to the union appeared related to early involvement and socialization in union activities and continued participation. Satisfied union members were also more likely to be satisfied with management, although the union was seen as more important among less-satisfied employees.[43] Commitment to the union appears related, in decreasing order, to the following factors: loyalty, responsibility to the union, willingness to work for the union, and belief in unionism.[44]

---

[41] Chris J. Berger, Craig A. Olson, and John W. Boudreau, "Effects of Unions on Job Satisfaction: The Role of Work-Related Values and Perceived Rewards," *Organizational Behavior and Human Performance,* 1983, 289–324; for additional confirmatory evidence, see Susan Schwochau, "Union Effects on Job Attitudes," *Industrial and Labor Relations Review* 40 (1987), pp. 209–34.

[42] Richard T. Mowday, Richard M. Steers, and Lyman W. Porter, *Employee–Organizational Linkages: The Psychology of Commitment, Absenteeism, and Turnover* (New York: Academic Press, 1982).

[43] Michael E. Gordon, John W. Philpot, Robert E. Burt, Cynthia A. Thompson, and William E. Spiller, "Commitment to the Union: Development of a Measure and an Examination of Its Correlates," *Journal of Applied Psychology,* August 1980, pp. 479–99.

[44] Robert T. Ladd, Michael E. Gordon, Laura L. Beauvais, and Richard L. Morgan, "Union Commitment: Replication and Extension," *Journal of Applied Psychology,* October 1982, pp. 640–44.

Commitment to the union and to the employer has been demonstrated to be independent. Simultaneous (dual) commitment to the employer and the union has been found to be related to both individual differences[45] and a positive labor relations climate.[46] Union stewards were found to have dual commitment, but generally higher commitment to the union than to the employer. Commitment to the employer was predicted by tenure; perceptions of immobility, supervisor support, promotion opportunities, and influence on the employer; and employment in smaller establishments. Union commitment was related to perceived immobility, belief that the union should use grievances to punish the employer, involvement in union activities and decision making, and employment in larger establishments. High dual commitment was predicted by involvement in union decision making, perceived immobility and influence on the employer, being a woman, and being unskilled. Unilateral commitment to the union was predicted by low economic outcomes, perceived involvement in the union, and lack of support from the employer.[47]

SUMMARY

Nonwage issues in contracts are related primarily to hours of work, lengths of contracts, management rights, union security, and seniority provisions. All of these have economic consequences for the employer and represented employees.

Hours-of-work issues primarily relate to establishing the length of the workday, entitlements to overtime, shift assignments, and the number of days worked during given periods. Recent evidence suggests employers might prefer innovative schedules with fewer days and longer hours in some operations.

Management rights clauses spell out those areas in which management exercises decision-making control. It also establishes the employer's right to make and enforce reasonable rules. Grievance and arbitration clauses provide due process rules when bargaining unit members disagree with management's interpretation and operation of the contract.

Union security clauses provide requirements related to dues payment and membership in the union. Union shops require all bargaining

[45] Cynthia V. Fukami and Erik W. Larson, "Commitment to Company and Union: Parallel Models," *Journal of Applied Psychology* 69 (1984), pp. 367–71.

[46] Harold L. Angle and James L. Perry, "Dual Commitment and Labor-Management Climates," *Academy of Management Journal* 29 (1986), pp. 31–50.

[47] James E. Martin, John M. Magenau, and Mark F. Peterson, "Variables Related to Patterns of Union Stewards' Commitment," *Journal of Labor Research* 7 (1986), pp. 323–36.

unit members to belong to the union, while agency-shop agreements require nonmembers as well as members to pay dues.

Seniority provisions establish entitlements to benefits (benefit status) and employment (competitive status). Benefit status seniority usually dates from hire, while competitive status seniority may begin on entry in a particular job or department. Most contracts use seniority as the prime consideration in deciding layoffs and promotions. Seniority provisions may have adverse impacts on minorities and women during layoffs.

DISCUSSION QUESTIONS

1. Is it to the organization's advantage to enjoy the lower turnover rates that unionization seems to include?
2. Why would union officials likely oppose flexible work hours and other innovative work schedules?
3. What potential problems and benefits are likely with early or flexible retirement programs?
4. Should either unions or managements be concerned with the apparently little effect of higher economic outcomes on overall union member satisfaction?

CHAPTER 10

Contract Negotiations

The negotiation of a labor agreement is of critical importance to both parties. The agreement will govern the relationship between them for a definite contractual period. For the employer, the contract will have cost impacts and constrain management decision making. For the union, it will spell out the rights of union members in their employment relationships.

Why does a contract emerge in the form that it does? How do the parties prepare for bargaining? What influences do the rank and file or the various functional areas within an organization have on the demands made in the negotiations? How does each group organize for bargaining? What constitutes success or failure in negotiations? What sequence of activities usually takes place during negotiations?

In this chapter, we first examine the activities preceding the negotiations themselves, from both union and management perspectives. Then we examine the theory and tactics of the negotiating process. The steps necessary for agreement and ratification are covered. Finally, management's assessment of bargaining is examined.

In reading this chapter, consider the following questions:

1. How do both management and union prepare for negotiations?
2. How are negotiating teams constituted for bargaining?
3. What processes are usually involved in presenting and responding to demands in collective bargaining negotiations?
4. How are agreements reached, and what processes are necessary to obtain approval by the union rank and file for ratification?

Except for initial contracts and unusual financial conditions, the timing of bargaining activities is largely determined by the expiration of a previous contract and the law. Under the law, if either party desires to modify the agreement at its expiration, it must give the other at least 60 days' notice. In all negotiations, initial or otherwise, the parties are required to meet at reasonable times to bargain.

Different strategies may be used across bargaining situations; however, Figure 10-1 portrays the general sequence of activities likely found in the bargaining process. The diagram lays out the basic prenegotiation activities, the proposals and responses in bargaining, and the possible outcomes of bargaining together with settlement procedures.

Both parties have some idea how they would like a new contract to be shaped. They either have taken positions during an organizing campaign or have some experience with an existing agreement. We will examine bargaining activities using Figure 10-1 as a general backdrop.

MANAGEMENT PREPARATION

Because labor is a very large share of the total costs of operating most organizations, management must be well aware of the cost implications of various contract proposals. The more heavily organized the firm, the more attention paid to contract terms. Ironically, less-organized firms should also be aware of contract implications, because benefits won at the bargaining table are frequently passed on to non-organized employees.

Collective bargaining practices have been examined by the Conference Board, a group of collaborating organizations supporting business research projects.[1] The results of the board's research will be followed in examining management preparation.

Department Involvement

In heavily organized firms, the chief executive officer (CEO) generally establishes the limits for possible concessions and targets needed changes for the organization during bargaining. The top industrial relations executive is responsible for coordinating preparations for bargaining and may act as the leading management negotiator. Various functional departments contribute to preparations for bargaining and have interests in seeing certain issues pursued at the bargaining table. Production managers may be interested in work rules and costs. Marketing managers want a contract that will minimize shipping disruptions. Accounting personnel supply many of the cost figures useful for bargaining purposes.

---

[1] Audrey Freedman, *Managing Labor Relations* (New York: Conference Board, 1979).

FIGURE 10–1

Bargaining Process Events

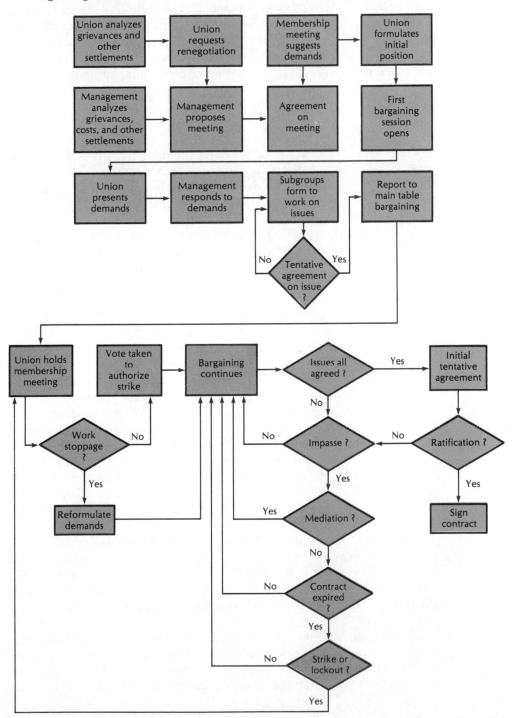

Reviewing the Expiring Contract

The expiring contract is reviewed by top management, the labor relations staff, and first-line supervisors. This review centers on contract language that contributed to cost or operating difficulties over the term of the contract, areas in which frequent grievances were encountered, the results of arbitrations over unresolved grievances, current practices not covered in the contract, and other contract supplements that have an impact on operations.

Preparing Data for Negotiations

Pay and benefit data are necessary and include relevant comparisons, such as rates paid within the industry, local labor market rates for occupations governed by the agreement, settlements gained by unions known as pattern setters, and changes in cost-of-living figures since the last negotiations.

The distribution of the employer's work force in terms of seniority, age, sex, job classification, shift, and race is important. Because entitlement to many benefits is related to seniority, an increasingly senior work force will incur higher benefit costs, even without an increase in benefit levels in a given negotiation. For example, if entitlement to vacations increases from two to three weeks after five years' service, a work force that had 200 employees with three years' seniority at the beginning of a three-year agreement would have 200 with six years at the end (assuming no turnover). This change in seniority would mean an increase of 200 weeks of vacation at the end of the agreement. Possible implications include paying for 200 unworked weeks and hiring four more employees to work the lost production time. Knowing the number of persons on each shift will allow consideration of demands for shift differentials and their costs.

Internal economic data—such as the cost of benefits, participation in discretionary benefit plans (recreation, etc.), overall earnings levels, and the amount and cost of overtime—are important. Management would prefer to negotiate broadly used benefits, because they will improve employees' perceptions of the competitiveness of the compensation program. Competitive overall earning levels are important as some employee groups may feel underpaid. For example, skilled trades employees in industrial plants earn less per hour than their counterparts in contract construction; but they are laid off less frequently for weather or lack of work and thus may have higher gross earnings.

Legal requirements are scrutinized. A union would probably not permit an employer to pay wages or benefits below a legal minimum, but an employer also tracks the implications of legal changes on costs and practices. For example, social security tax increases raise costs without wage increases.[2] Changes in equal employment opportunity laws and regulations may also suggest that employers negotiate changes in promotion and transfer procedures.

An examination of the union's negotiation and ratification procedures is important. The bargaining team needs to know how the union signals concessions and how it drops demands during the process. The length of time necessary for ratification and whether the union usually works after contract expiration are important from a time deadline standpoint.

Information regarding the organization's current level of operations and anticipated future changes will be important in assessing bargaining power on certain issues. For example, if little inventory is available and customer orders have increased recently but customers have different sources available for similar products and services, then a strike might be disastrous.

Identification of Probable Union Demands

Using information from grievances under the expiring contract and feedback from first-line supervision, management may be able to assess the likelihood of certain demands and the likely tenacity of the union during bargaining. In large companies where national-level negotiations will take place, attention to union bargaining conventions should inform management about the issues to which the union has committed itself. Other pattern settlements should offer clues to management.

Costing the Contract

As noted in Chapter 7, the wage and fringe benefits included in the ultimate settlement have a definite cost impact for the organization. To make rational choices among possible demands and to counteroffer with an acceptable package that will minimize its costs, management must accurately cost contract demands.

A variety of costing methods can be used. Some are more sophisticated than others. A good example of a relatively simple approach highlighting many of the issues is portrayed in Figure 10–2.[3] This example shows some of the important dynamics in long-term contracts. For example, social security tax rates and taxable bases may

---

[2] Thomas A. Mahoney, "The Real Cost of a Wage Increase," *Personnel*, May–June 1967, pp. 22–32.

[3] Reed C. Richardson, "Positive Collective Bargaining," in, *Handbook of Personnel and Industrial Relations*, ed. Dale Yoder and H. G. Heneman, Jr. (Washington, D.C.: Bureau of National Affairs, 1979), pp. 7-127–7-129.

FIGURE 10-2

Costing Out Changes in Contract Terms

Changes in costs	Increased cost
1. Direct payroll—annual	
Straight-time earnings—36¢ per hour general increase; 100 employees × 2,080 hours × 36¢	$ 74,800
Premium earnings—second shift established differential—10¢ per hour; 30 employees 2,080 hours × 10¢	6,240
Overtime—overtime cost increased by increased straight-time rate—average straight-time rate increases 39¢; 39¢ × 12,000 overtime hours × .5 overtime rate	2,340
Bonus	None
Other direct payroll cost increases	None
Total increase in direct payroll costs	$ 83,460
2. Added costs directly resulting from higher payroll costs— annual F.I.C.A.—5.85 times increase in average straight-time earnings below $9,000 annual; 100 employees × 36¢ × 5.85% × 2,080 hours	$ 4,380.48
Federal and state unemployment insurance tax—Number of employees × 4,200 × 2.5% tax rate	No change
Workers' compensation (total cost or estimate)	No change
Other	No change
Total additional direct payroll costs	$ 4,380.48
3. Nonpayroll costs—annual	
Insurance—company portion	
Health insurance	No change
Dental insurance	None
Eye care	None
Life insurance—added employer contribution, $100 per year; $100 × 100 employees	$ 10,000
Pension costs—fully vested pension reduced from 25 years and age 65 to 20 years and age 62	
Estimated additional cost	52,000
Miscellaneous	
Tuition reimbursement (addition)	600
Service rewards	No change
Suggestion awards (addition)	350
Loss on employee cafeteria	No change
Overtime meals	No change
Cost of parking lots	No change
Company parties	No change
Personal tools	No change
Personal safety equipment (addition)	1,200
Personal wearing apparel	No change
Profit sharing	No change
Other	No change
Total additional nonpayroll costs—annual	$ 64,150

change during the term of the contract. Unemployment insurance rates may increase or decline, depending on the state of the economy and a firm's individual layoff rate.

Moreover, the implications of certain contract terms are not straightforward and must be examined closely to capture the real cost

FIGURE 10–2 *(concluded)*

Changes in costs	Increased cost
4a. Changes in nonwork paid time	
Holidays—2 new holidays added to 6 already in contract; 100 employees × 8 hours × 2 holidays × $3.96 average new wage	$ 6,336
Vacation—new category added—4 weeks (160 hours annual vacation) with 20 or more years service—former top was 3 weeks after 15 years Average number of employees affected annually: 15 employees × 40 hours @ $3.96 average new wage	2,376
Paid lunch time—paid ½ lunch time added to contract; 100 employees × ½ hour × 236 days worked yearly × $3.96 average new wage	$ 46,728
Paid wash-up time	None
Coffee breaks	No change
Paid time off for union activity—new 1 hour per week per shop steward; 10 shop stewards × $4.20 shop steward average new wage × 1 hour × 52 weeks	2,184
Paid sick leave	None
Paid time off over and above worker's compensation paid time	None
Jury service time off—no change	None
Funeral leave time off—no change	None
Paid time off for safety or training—no change	None
Other	None
Total change in hours paid for but not worked—annual	$ 57,624
4b. Financial data derived from costing out (Items 1–4, above)	
Total increase in contract costs: Item 1 + Item 2 + Item 3	$151,990
Average total increase in contract costs per employee payroll hour: Item 1 + Item 2 + Item 3 ÷ 2,080 hours	.73
Average total increase in direct payroll cost per labor-hour: Item 1 + Item 2 ÷ 2,080 hours ÷ 100 employees	.422
Average total increase in nonpayroll costs per payroll-hour per employee: Item 3 ÷ 2,080 hours ÷ 100 employees	.308
Average total increase in nonwork paid time expense per payroll-hour per employee: Item 4 ÷ 100 employees	.277
Average total increase in direct payroll costs per productive (worked) hour per employee: Item 1 + Item 2 ÷ 1,888 hours ÷ 100 employees	.49
Average total increase in nonpayroll costs per productive (worked) hour per employee: Item 3 ÷ 1,888 hours ÷ 100 employees	.34

Source: Reed C. Richardson, "Positive Collective Bargaining," in *Handbook of Personnel and Industrial Relations,* ed. Dale Yoder and H. G. Heneman, Jr. (Washington, D.C.: U.S. Bureau of National Affairs, 1979), pp. 7-127–7-129.

impacts.[4] First, many firms do not closely track the "roll-up," or amount by which overtime and wage-tied fringes are increased by

---

[4] Michael H. Granof, *How to Cost Your Labor Contract* (Washington, D.C.: Bureau of National Affairs, 1973).

changes in the base rate. Second, granting overtime premiums greater than required by law should cause the firm to consider how controllable its overtime hours are and the degree to which labor cost increases can be passed on to customers. Third, the cost of vacations and holidays are seldom critically examined. For example, vacations for maintenance employees may be essentially costless if their work is postponable and if an excess of staff can accomplish it. On the other hand, production employees' vacations may require scheduling overtime, thereby increasing vacation costs by the premium rate, or hiring an equivalent number of full-time employees. Fourth, relief time may cost more if it is broken up in short periods—some time may be necessary to begin the break and then return to work. This *slippage* will require adding more employees to sustain production volume.[5]

Benefits costing also poses problems for organizations. Pension costs depend not only on a defined contribution requirement in some cases (for example, 5 percent of base wages) but also on experience factors, vesting (personal ownership of benefits) requirements, and possible defined benefit levels at retirement. For example, if the contract provided for vesting of benefits after five years of service but only 20 percent of employees ever accrue five years, the cost of the pension would be far less than the 5 percent of base wages used in the example. Health insurance is generally negotiated to provide a certain level of benefits (for example, all hospital and physician expenses up to $100,000 annually with $250 deductible). Unfortunately, organizations have little control over the premium charged for the benefits. Thus, their future costs can only be estimated.[6]

Organizations may not closely evaluate the costs of salary increases during the term of the agreement. For example, given interest rates and the total amount paid out, agreeing to a wage demand for increases of 50 cents, 50 cents, and 75 cents over a three-year agreement might cost the company less than giving 90 cents, 40 cents, and 30 cents. In the former case, the total increase is $1.75, while the latter is $1.60. But in the former case, an employee would earn 50 cents per hour more for three years ($1.50), 50 cents more for two years ($1.00), and 75 cents more for one year—a total of $3.25 more over the contract period. In the latter case, the employee would get 90 cents more for three years ($2.70), 40 cents for two years ($.80), and 30 cents for one year—a total of $3.80. But postponing increases to give a larger total increase during the agreement raises the base wage rate for subsequent negotiations.[7] Management should also consider the costs of wages and fringes that will be granted to nonunion employees to preserve wage differentials and equity.

---

[5] Ibid., pp. 55–56.
[6] Ibid., pp. 60–69.
[7] Ibid., pp. 83–126.

A detailed example of costing contract demands is given in the introduction to the negotiating exercise at the end of this chapter. Whatever method is used for costing should allow management to calculate the effects of various union proposals quickly and to provide a true estimate of their financial ramifications.

Negotiation Objectives and the Bargaining Team

Contract objectives should support the goals of the organization. For example, if disruptions in production are to be avoided, agreement to clauses providing for arbitration of grievances that cannot be mutually resolved in return for no-strike agreements will serve this purpose. If cost certainty is important, then avoidance of fringe benefits and cost-of-living clauses and inclusion of gainsharing, profit sharing, and/or piece-rate pay plans provide a path to these ends. Exhibit 10–1 is an example of management objectives and preferences in bargaining.

EXHIBIT 10–1

Extracts from Bituminous Coal Operators' Association Bargaining Statement

Today's Reality for UMWA-National Agreement Coal

1981 negotiations between the UMWA and the BCOA for a new National Bituminous Coal Wage Agreement come at a time when the reality of today's depressed economic conditions, particularly in that sector of the coal industry covered by the UMWA-National Agreement, falls far short of tomorrow's promise for the coal industry as America's growing energy source of the future.

- Over 20,000 miners are laid off.
- Many mines have closed, and more are expected to close.
- At least 100 million tons of annual production capacity lies idle for lack of a market, and most of that idle capacity is in the Eastern half of the United States where most UMWA-National Agreement mines are located.

And there are no signs that these crippling conditions, especially in the UMWA-National Agreement sector of the industry, are likely to change very quickly.

* * * * *

Low Productivity

The biggest reason for the failure of the UMWA National Agreement segment of the industry to participate in the growth of the total coal market is the heavy cost burden that low productivity imposes on coal produced under the UMWA-National Agreement. Unless corrective steps are taken now to

EXHIBIT 10-1 *(concluded)*

reduce this cost, coal mined under the UMWA-National Agreement cannot compete effectively in the coal market.

During the period from 1969 to 1979, the United States experienced a period of continuing gains in industrial productivity. Every major industry enjoyed the benefits of a productivity increase; every industry, that is, except one—the coal industry.

If coal from UMWA-National Agreement mines is going to compete in the marketplace with coal from the rest of the industry, it is essential that we get our productivity back where it once was, and improve each year as other industries do. The market world will not pay for our noncompetitive costs. As we negotiate a new UMWA-National Agreement, we are in a position to take major steps toward correcting the situation. The present agreement has many provisions which contribute nothing to the well-being of the coal miner, but do stand in the way of increased productivity, such as those that:

- Restrict full use of expensive equipment in continuous operations.
- Allow employees too much lateral and downward job bidding.
- Restrict use of new employees on equipment.
- Permit largely unrestricted use of paid days off.
- Encourage featherbedding.

* * * * *

Labor Instability

Another major reason, which cannot be overlooked, that has contributed greatly to the erosion of the UMWA-National Agreement share of the coal market has been labor instability—wildcat strikes.

High Employment Costs

In 1970, the coal miner's earnings were 41% higher than the earnings of workers in other industries. By 1980, however, the gap between the coal miner and other workers had widened to a full 63% difference in favor of the coal miner.

Source: *Daily Labor Report,* January 13, 1981, pp. F1-F8.

Bargaining team members often represent areas of particular interest in the contract (for example, production) or have expertise in specific negotiated areas (for example, employee benefits manager). The leader of management's team is frequently the top industrial relations executive of the organization. The CEO may delegate responsibilities for negotiating the contract but may also retain authority to approve the ultimate agreement.

Bargaining Books

A bargaining book is a cross-referenced file enabling a negotiator to quickly determine what contract clauses would be affected by a demand. It also contains the general history of specific contract terms. The book may also contain a code alongside the proposals to indicate their relative importance to management. A bargaining book might contain information on each of these classifications for a given clause:

1. The history and text of the particular clause as it was negotiated in successive agreements.
2. Comparisons of the company's experience with that of other companies in the industry, including comments on similarities and differences.
3. The company's experience with the clause, both in operation and in the grievances arising thereunder.
4. Legal issues pertaining to the clause, including both NLRB determinations and judicial decisions.
5. Points the company would like to have changed with regard to the clause, differentiated into minimum, maximum, and intermediate possibilities.
6. Points the union may have asked for in the past with regard to changes in the clause, the union's justification for the proposed change, and the arguments used by mangement to rebut the union's position.
7. Data and exhibits with regard to the clause, including cost and supporting analysis.
8. Progress with regard to the clause in the current negotiation, together with drafts of various company proposals.[8]

An example of a possible format for a bargaining book is shown in Figure 10–3.

Strike Preparation

As noted, anticipation of a strike or the reduction of vulnerability to a strike may substantially improve managment's bargaining power. Besides the bargaining power issues, the organization needs to plan how it will handle a potentially disruptive situation, particularly if it anticipates continuing operations.

Organizations must determine the costs and benefits of remaining in operation. Labor relations will undoubtedly be troublesome after a

---

[8] Meyer S. Ryder, Charles M. Rehmus, and Sanford Cohen, *Management Preparation for Bargaining* (Homewood, Ill.: Dow Jones-Irwin, 1966), pp. 65–66.

240

FIGURE 10–3

Bargaining Book Format

BARGAINING* ITEMS	PRIORITIES†	RANGE OF BARGAINING OBJECTIVES			INITIAL BARGAINING POSITION‡	EVALUATION RESULTS		
		PESSIMISTIC	REALISTIC	OPTIMISTIC		P	R	O

Collective bargaining by objectives—A guide for data preparation, strategy, and evaluation of bargaining results (blank form)

* Classify items in two groups: financial and nonfinancial.

† Relative priority of each bargaining item to all bargaining items.

‡ Actual visible position taken by parties at opening of negotiation (union initial proposal or company response or counter offer).

Source: Reed C. Richardson, "Positive Collective Bargaining," in *Handbook of Personnel and Industrial Relations*, ed. Dale Yoder and H. G. Heneman, Jr. (Washington, D.C.: U.S. Bureau of National Affairs, 1979), p. 7–116.

contract is negotiated, particularly if replacements have been hired. Additional security may be required, and picket-line observation will be important. Suppliers, customers, and government agencies will require notification if a strike takes place. For important customers, alternative methods of supply—including supply through competitors—may be necessary.

Strategy and Logistics

Finally, the strategies used to move toward an agreement must be constructed. Questions about who has the power to make concessions and the final positions beyond which management will not go must be answered.

Arrangements must be made for a place to hold bargaining meetings. If meetings will be held off the organization's premises, questions regarding costs must be resolved before commencing negotiations. The union will probably prefer a neutral site, given the evidence (explored later in this chapter) that concessions are more difficult for the company to make on its home ground. Figure 10–4 is an example of the time frames and functions involved in preparations for negotiations.

UNION PREPARATION

To some extent, union preparations parallel those of management, but some important distinctions exist. Historically, the union proposes most of the significant changes, and management responds with counterproposals. Thus, the union is usually not well prepared for possible management demands. The union also differs from management in its explicit political nature. Because union officers are elected, they espouse bargaining positions consistent with rank-and-file desires. Unions also solicit input from the membership during preparations. Some of the preparation activities on both national and local levels will be examined.

National-Level Activities

Research departments in national unions are responsible for tracking settlements in contract negotiations. Research is also done to assess the employers' ability to improve economic terms of contracts.

The ability of union members to take strikes is an important issue. If the union were involved in a long strike during recent negotiations, it may not have the resources to provide subsistence strike benefits for a long strike in the present negotiations. The national must also consider the target company's ability to withstand a strike and its vulnerability to competition.

If the negotiations involve many units of a single company or are conducted on an industry-wide basis, the national is usually responsible for negotiating economic issues. The bargaining team usually comprises national officers and officers of some key locals.

Before commencing negotiations, the national union may call a bargaining convention at which delegates from the local unions hear the national's plans for bargaining and propose their own issues. The bargaining convention has two major purposes. First, the rank and file are heard, thus fulfilling the grass-roots political requirements for involvement in the creation of bargaining issues. Second, the union leadership has a forum for publicly committing itself to certain bargaining positions. This commitment strengthens the union's bargaining power, because conceding these committed issues later at the bargaining table will be more difficult.

If the local will carry the major role in bargaining, the national will supply a representative to assist and to ensure that the local negotiates

FIGURE 10-4

Management Planning for Contract Negotiations

	8 to 12 months before contract expires	4 to 8 months	1 to 4 months prior commencement of negotiations
Local unit management	1. Assigns responsibilities for community surveys estimating union demands and employee attitude. 2. Assesses the total corporate community and union compensation/benefit plans. 3. Assesses union/employee motivation and goals for impending negotiations.	1. Develops with division management, corporate E.R., and corporate insurance project alternate benefit proposals that are to be designed and costed. 2. Continues all steps in the planning process.	1. Secures division approval of strategy negotiating plans and cost estimates.
Division headquarters management	1. Assures local unit is preparing for negotiations. 2. Plans through annual financial plan project impact of inventory build-up. Possible settlement costs, etc. 3. Identifies internal responsibilities and relationships (corporate, law, E.R. insurance, benefits, etc.). 4. Keeps corporate employee relations informed.	1. Coordinates the development of strategy and negotiating plan, consulting with corporate employee relations and benefits. 2. Develops with local management, corporate E.R., and insurance project alternative benefit proposals that are to be designed and costed. 3. Makes broad judgment on impact of company and expected proposals in relation to division and corporate goals, strategy, and plans. 4. Evaluates plans to control costs and deviations from plan/strategy.	1. Approves negotiating plan strategy. 2. Clears benefit and corporate policy variances from plan with corporate employee relations. 3. Communicates progress to senior management and corporate employee relations. 4. Approves cost variances from plan. 5. Identifies strike issues.
Corporate employee relations	1. Advises division and local management of union's national position on economics, benefits, and other issues. 2. Counsels on any anticipated conflict with corporate policy, other divisions, etc. 3. Provides available historical information pertinent to planning.	1. Assists division, local management, and corporate insurance in projecting and preparing alternate benefit proposals that are to be designed and costed. 2. Keeps division and local unit informed of any external developments having impact on its planning.	1. Consults with division on strategy and plans; available for on-the-scene assistance or to consult with international union officers; recommends corporate point of view on issues. 2. Approves all variances from corporate personnel policy and benefit plan proposals. 3. Assures that all issues are resolved at the required levels.
Corporate law department	1. Counsels on request.	1. Counsels on request and reviews current contract as required. 2. Approves benefit plan drafts to assure legal compliance.	1. Counsels and drafts contract language on request. 2. Makes counsel available to review contract language before signing.

Source: Audrey Freedman, *Managing Labor Relations* (New York: Conference Board, 1979), p. 24. Copyright © The Conference Board, 1979, used by permission.

During negotiations	Postnegotiations
1. Continues negotiations, clears significant cost variances from plan and division management. 2. Integrates benefit negotiations with all other items. 3. Secures agreement in accord with plan. 4. Agrees with union on method and expense to inform employees of new contract terms.	1. Evaluates previous negotiations against plan within 30 days. 2. Assigns responsibilities for the planning process so as to integrate with the division's plans. 3. Identifies tentative objectives for next contract. 4. Completes wage/benefit adjustment form.
1. Provides in addition to those points in "1 to 4 months" column, identification of "end" position and supports local negotiators in maintaining such position.	1. Evaluates all aspects of the previous negotiations within 45 days. 2. Identifies and communicates all long-range needs to executive management and corporate employee relations. 3. Integrates planning process in the division growth plan.
1. Provides same as "1 to 4 months" column. 2. Identifies to division management potential problems having corporate impact; if necessary, advises corporate management of unresolved major issues.	1. Counsels with union and/or unit management on negotiating experiences and/or evaluation of new contract. 2. Informs other units of results. 3. Initiates needed objectives for study, policy change, or corporate decision.
1. Provides same as "1 to 4 months" column.	1. Reviews new contracts for possible problems; advises division and corporate employee relations.

EXHIBIT 10–2

UAW Approves Outline of 1987 Contract Goals

After a four-day convention dominated by debate on "whipsawing"—the practice by large corporations of forcing workers at one plant to grant concessions or otherwise lose work to employees at another plant—the United Auto Workers overwhelmingly adopts a 1987 collective bargaining program that identifies secure jobs and assured income as "our two highest priorities."

. . . "This union has never supported pitting worker against worker and we're not going to now," said UAW President [Owen] Bieber. But the leadership declines to consider specific resolutions that would condemn whipsawing and the combining of job classifications, a change sought by management to increase flexibility and productivity. Proponents of the resolution point to GM's decision to close an Ohio plant while continuing similar production at a California plant that agreed to implement a "team" concept. Bieber says that the international is "quick to defend local unions," but he comments that it is "not very realistic to say that you'll never change classifications."

UAW recognizes that further contraction of the workforce may be needed, but it wants an "orderly" approach, according to Bieber. Approaches advocated by the union include expansion of 1984 job guarantee provisions to cover plant closings, improved early retirement and retirement bonuses, plant closing moratoriums, and compensatory time off to cope with excessive overtime. Automakers and suppliers also should consider arrangements where they will hire laid-off workers from other UAW-represented firms before they hire from outside, the union said.

Source: *Employee Relations Weekly*, Vol. 5, (April 20, 1987), p. 489.

---

a contract consistent with the national's interest. Exhibit 10–2 is an example of how one national recently opened negotiations.

Local-Level Preparations

At the local level, the negotiating committee is usually elected with the other officers and has responsibility for negotiating contracts and processing grievances. The committee reaches some conclusions about portions of the contract (for example, allocation of overtime) susceptible to more than one interpretation or viewed as inequitable by the membership.

Locals are also served by the national union's field representatives. As a result, members learn about settlements reached by other locals in the same national. They also get more specific indications of issues the national considers critically important to include in all contracts.

The performance of the employer (in terms of profitability, sales, etc.) is general knowledge if the employer is publicly owned and may be used by the union to gauge the level of its economic demands. The union also knows the perishability of the employer's products, its competition and its ability to operate during a strike. The union may also be aware of industry trends to move plants to other geographic regions and the likelihood that the company would introduce labor-replacing equipment if high economic demands were won.

Local unions hold membership meetings before the negotiations to inform the membership about important issues and to solicit more input. These meetings also help determine local members' levels of commitment to bargaining issues in case a strike is called at a later time.

After negotiations are under way, the union usually calls another membership meeting. The negotiating committee reports on the bargaining to the members and requests authorization to call a strike if necessary. The membership traditionally gives overwhelming approval. This vote does not mean a strike *will* occur but rather the bargainers have the authority to call one after the contract expires.

Effects of Union Characteristics on Bargaining Outcomes

Bargaining outcomes could be influenced by such characteristics of the union as its size, union democracy, complexity, propensity for striking, involvement in political activities, level of dues, recent success in organizing relative to the total size of its membership, and the diversity of the workers it represents. When a variety of other characteristics are controlled, wage rates in negotiated agreements appear influenced by national control of the content of bargaining, less control of the bargaining process by the national, smaller sizes of locals in the national union, local union autocracy, membership diversity, little recent organizing, and higher dues. Higher job security outcomes were predicted by smaller national unions, more involvement of the national in the bargaining process, salary levels of union officers, political activity, lower complexity, and lower dues. Overall union democracy is related to higher job security and lower wages. Higher outcomes occur when the union has a relatively small number of large locals organized in several industries. Strikes may enhance outcomes, but present attention to organizing and political activity is related to lower outcomes.[9]

---

[9] Jack Fiorito and Wallace E. Hendricks, "Union Characteristics and Bargaining Outcomes," *Industrial and Labor Relations Review* 40 (1987), pp. 569–84.

NEGOTIATION REQUESTS

Section 8(d) of the Taft-Hartley Act requires the party desiring a renegotiation of the contract (usually the union) to notify the other party
of its intention and to offer to bargain a new agreement. This notice
must come at least 60 days before the end of the contract if the
requesting party intends to terminate the agreement at that time.

The usual management reply is the proposal of a time and place for
negotiations to begin. This time—usually not immediate—often leads
to the initial demands not being made until a month or less before the
expiration date. After notice is served, both parties commence last-
minute preparations for bargaining.

WHAT IS BARGAINING?

Several academic disciplines have undertaken the study of bargaining.
The following is a description of bargaining or negotiating from an
economic perspective:

1. Negotiation takes place if both parties will benefit by an agreement. In labor–management relations, the employer benefits by
   continued operations and the union benefits by better conditions
   for its members.
2. The concessions made by the parties during the negotiations are
   voluntary. The concessions, in number and degree, may be influenced by the magnitude of the demands and the opponent's beliefs
   about the demander's willingness to concede;[10] but any movements made are still voluntary.
3. Negotiations are seen as productive. They may disclose areas of
   agreement or alternatives not previously considered by either
   party.
4. Negotiations as used in labor–management relations are characterized by verbal and/or written demands and concessions. And
   finally, the bargaining process requires competition before the
   benefits available accrue to the parties involved in the bargaining.[11]

Bargaining, in its simplest format, is the communication by both
parties of the terms they require for consummation of a transaction
and the subsequent acceptance or rejection by both of the bargain.

---

[10] Frederik Zeuthen, *Problems of Monopoly and Economic Warfare* (Boston: Rout-
ledge & Kegan Paul, 1930).

[11] John G. Cross, *The Economics of Bargaining* (New York: Basic Books, 1969), pp.
4–6.

Negotiation is the set of techniques used to translate bargaining power into the ultimate settlement.[12]

From a psychological perspective, bargaining may be defined as "the process whereby two or more parties attempt to settle what each shall give and take, or perform and receive, in a transaction between them." For bargaining to be required, the parties must have a conflict of interest in relation to issues jointly affecting them. For most bargaining, the parties are joined in a voluntary relationship. This may not be true in collective bargaining, and the joining is relatively permanent. The activities of the parties include the division of resources and other intangible issues in which the parties have joint interests. The process of negotiation requires the presentation of positions, their evaluation by the other party, and, finally, counterproposals. The process requires a sequential rather than simultaneous mode, because each party must have time to evaluate the other's proposals before responding.[13]

This chapter and book are not primarily concerned with bargaining per se, but rather with collective bargaining. A more specific definition from a behavioral perspective includes the following:

1. Collective bargaining includes a variety of issues, some generating conflict between the parties and others requiring collaboration to accommodate the separate interests of both.
2. The attitudes and feelings of the bargainers play a part in the outcome of the negotiations over and above what occurs as a result of the rationally defined attributes of the parties. Further, the parties do not come together only for this negotiation but must maintain an ongoing relationship. Thus, the results of the bargaining situation have an impact on the long-run characteristics of the bargaining relationship.
3. The bargainers are often acting on behalf of others rather than for their own ends. They are representing constituents who evaluate their performance and may affect their tenure in negotiating positions.[14]

Thus, the bargaining process involves parties who have mutual interests in reaching agreement on a variety of issues. The negotiators represent others who stand to have their positions altered as a result of the bargaining. Personal characteristics of the bargainers, as well as the

[12] Carl M. Stevens, *Strategy and Collective Bargaining Negotiations* (New York: McGraw-Hill, 1963), pp. 2–4.

[13] Jeffrey Z. Rubin and Bert R. Brown, *The Social Psychology of Bargaining and Negotiation* (New York: Academic Press, 1975), pp. 2–18.

[14] Richard E. Walton and Robert B. McKersie, *A Behavioral Theory of Labor Negotiations* (New York: McGraw-Hill, 1965), pp. 3–4.

innate power of the organizations they represent, are likely to have an impact on the outcome.

Attributes of the Parties

Much has been speculated about bargaining power properties related to the personalities of bargainers, but virtually no research on the effects of personal attributes on labor negotiations has been reported. However, some general conclusions have been reached on individual and contextual factors related to bargaining behavior in a variety of situations.

The social components of bargaining influence behavior. Labor negotiations are seldom conducted in complete privacy. Although the general public and most union and management constituents are excluded, the negotiating teams witness the behavior of all parties involved. This contextual aspect is important because evidence suggests audiences make it more difficult for bargainers to make concessions. This difficulty is increased if the bargainer has a high degree of loyalty to the group or if the group has a strong commitment to the bargaining issue. If concessions are made and if the other party views the concession as a sign of weakness, retaliation is likely in subsequent negotiations.[15] Two tactical suggestions result from these findings. First, to promote an opponent's willingness to concede, the bargainer's response to an opponent's concession should be a simultaneous concession on another area important to them or indicate that a major concession requires hard bargaining. Second, the negotiator should be aware that public commitment to an issue will reduce the degree to which objective data can modify the position. However, the skilled negotiator must be aware that public commitment may simply be a tactic to justify support for an issue not really viewed as important.

A number of aspects related to the bargaining environment, the perceptions of the bargainers, and the complexity of the negotiations are important. Aspects of neutrality in the bargaining environments are important. There appears to be little willingness to make concessions if the negotiations are conducted on one's home ground, so unions are advised to bargain away from the plant. In addition to the setting, the perception of the opposition's characteristics is important. If the opponent is perceived through status or other attributes as nondeferring, then gaining concessions will not be sought as vigorously. As more issues are injected into bargaining, two processes are likely to occur. The first process, "logrolling" (trading off blocks of apparently dissimilar issues; for example, union shop for a wage in-

---

[15] Ibid., pp. 43–54.

crease), occurs frequently. Second, a sequence of offers, counteroffers, and issue settlement will result from bargaining on numerous issues.[16]

The interaction of personality and context variables affects the bargaining relationships. This interaction includes interpersonal orientation, motivational orientation, and power. Interpersonal orientation reflects responsiveness to others; reacting to, being interested in, and appreciating variations in another's behavior.[17] Motivational orientation refers to whether one's bargaining interests are individual (seeking only one's own interest), competitive (seeking to better an opponent), or cooperative (seeking positive outcomes in the interests of both).[18] Power refers to the range of bargaining outcomes through which the other party may be moved.[19]

Interpersonal orientation appears somewhat related to individual differences. Motivational orientation may be affected by attitudes toward bargaining, the structuring of rewards and their attainability, and the roles bargainers may be told to take by their constituents.[20] Discrepancies between the parties in their amounts of power and in their amounts of absolute power (ability to inflict loss on the other) are also important parameters.[21]

Given these individual differences and contextual variables, bargaining effectiveness should be greatest when interpersonal orientation is high, motivational orientation is cooperative, and power is equal and low.[22] The interaction of these variables may have no effect on how the parties independently decide to structure their negotiating teams. Much of the structuring must depend on the goals of a party (for example, to break new ground on productivity issues requiring cooperation) and on beliefs about the tactics an opponent may use (for example, assigning low-interpersonal-orientation bargainers to a team).

The type and levels of concessions from a party convey important information about the party's true position. For example, a series of concessions on a given issue followed by no subsequent movement could signal that the party's resistance point has been approached. Negative concessions or a retreat toward an original position may signal the toughening of a stand. Concessions appearing to reward the requester's behavior may well increase cooperation between the parties and may strengthen the role of an attractive counterpart to the requester's constituency.[23]

---

[16] Ibid., pp. 130–56.
[17] Ibid., p. 158.
[18] Ibid., p. 198.
[19] Ibid., p. 213.
[20] Ibid., pp. 201–13.
[21] Ibid., pp. 213–33.
[22] Ibid., pp. 256–57.
[23] Ibid., pp. 276–78.

Perceptions of Bargainers

Besides the personal attributes of the parties, the negotiators form perceptions about the bargaining situation. A variety of characteristics may influence the willingness to concede and, thus, the outcome of negotiations. One characteristic considered by bargainers relates to perceived strategic power. A bargainer would have high strategic power if (1) agreement is less advantageous for the bargainer than it is for the opponent, and (2) more ways exist to satisfy the bargainer's needs than to satisfy the opponent, (3) more credible threats can be made by the bargainer than by the opponent, (4) maintenance of the bargaining relationship is more important to the opponent, and (5) the opponent is under heavier time pressure.[24]

Within this framework, one example of condition (1) is an organization with a large backlog of orders. The company might be more motivated to settle, because large profits would be lost. Relatively little pressure might exist for the union, because it might reasonably believe lost wages would be made up with overtime when the plant reopened. As an example of condition (2), a conglomerate organization or one that is struck in one of many plants would have a distinct bargaining advantage. Condition (3) could involve beliefs that threatened actions will be taken. It reinforces the idea that a strike may have value for future bargaining situations. In condition (4), unions are expected to be more responsive because the bargaining process is necessary to maintain the relationship. Finally, condition (5) relates to organizations dealing in perishable goods, such as food producers and transportation companies (Christmas travel forgone due to strikes). Such companies are under greater pressure to settle on the union's terms.

THEORIES OF BARGAINING TACTICS

Bargaining takes place because either or both parties are unwilling to agree to the other's demands. The following six rules govern the conduct of bargaining.

Rule 1 states an impending contract expiration is necessary for the commencement of bargaining. During the course of the agreement, the parties have essentially agreed not to bargain, so the anticipated expiration serves as an enabling process for the renewal of bargaining.

Rule 2 states the initial bargaining demand should be large. Even though both parties are fairly certain that the initial positions are at

---

24 John M. Magenau and Dean G. Pruitt, "The Social Psychology of Bargaining: A Theoretical Synthesis 1," in *Industrial Relations: A Social Psychological Approach*, ed. Geoffrey M. Stephenson and Christopher J. Brotherton (New York: John Wiley & Sons, 1979), pp. 197–99.

substantial variance from what each is willing to settle for, the large initial demand creates substantial room for bargaining and allows relatively large concessions when the time is right.

Rule 3 explains the negotiating agenda is determined by the initial demands and counterproposals. In other words, the issues initially raised by the parties constitute the focus of the bargaining. Additions to the initial agenda are seldom made, and offers made in regard to these items can seldom be effectively retracted.

Rule 4 is the strike or lockout deadline rule. Stevens notes this rule precludes strikes before a certain time and requires notice that a strike is possible after this point.

Rule 5 provides for a termination of negotiations as the result of an agreement. Within this rule may be a requirement that unresolved issues be arbitrated or operations continued to preclude an emergency while an agreement is reached.

Rule 6 requires the parties to negotiate in good faith. To do this, the parties must respond to each other's demands and take no unilateral action to change the existing conditions prior to the end of negotiations.[25]

Bluffing

A good deal of attention has been given to bluffing in contract negotiations. In most negotiations, neither party expects to win its initial demands. Further, the other party knows a demand is greater than the expected settlement. If so, what benefit accrues from overstating demands? And does this condition ultimately lead to a splitting of the differences between the parties? If so, then making extreme demands of an opponent faced with some minimum level that must be met should lead to larger gains for the demander.

Bluffing serves several valuable purposes in negotiating. First, if one stated a final position first, conceding from this position would be unreasonable. A failure to concede would destroy the ongoing relationship required in collective bargaining. Bluffing also allows a bargainer to test the firmness of an opponent's demands without a full commitment to a settlement. Thus, more is learned about the opponent's expectations through the bluffing process.[26]

If bluffing is a process used to gain information for a final settlement, the union may reasonably make extreme demands, particularly on financial issues, because it lacks much of management's information regarding its ability to pay. When management has a good deal of information on a settlement point, its initial offer may be close to its expected settlement point. An examination of contract settlements

---

[25] Stevens, *Strategy*, pp. 27–56.
[26] Cross, *Economics of Bargaining*, pp. 169–80.

between the Tennessee Valley Authority and unions representing its employees shows final agreements on economic issues are closer to management proposals than to union proposals in most instances. However, if management is pressured by outside forces, settlements tend to be closer to the union's position.[27] But the union runs a risk in making very high demands, because these demands may increase management's cost expectations and lead to a strike over points the union may ultimately be willing to concede.[28]

BEHAVIORAL THEORIES OF LABOR NEGOTIATIONS

Four behavioral components are involved in bargaining. *Distributive bargaining* takes place when the parties are in conflict on a particular issue and when the outcome will be a loss for one party and a gain for the other.[29] Suppose the union wants a 60-cent hourly increase, and the parties ultimately settle for 30 cents. The 30-cent increase is a gain to the union and a loss to the company, which is not to say the loss is greater than the company expected, however. The company may have felt a settlement for anything less than 35 cents would be better than it expected to win. Distributive bargaining simply means some resource is in fixed supply, and one's gain is the other's loss as to that resource.

Since distributive bargaining involves the division of outcomes on a bargaining issue, much of the activity is related to providing the opponent with information as to the importance of a particular position, the likelihood of future movement on that position, and the trade-offs possible for a concession on the position. Through the bargaining itself, both sides may pick up cues as to where the other is willing to settle. An important part of this process is identifying the finality of commitment a bargainer attaches to a position. Figure 10–5 portrays various management and union commitment statements and analyzes their finality, specificity, and consequences for ignoring them.

Integrative Bargaining

The second component is *integrative bargaining*, which takes place when the parties face a common problem.[30] For example, a company may be experiencing above-average employee turnover. As a result, union membership may be eroded, and union officials may have to

---

[27] Roger C. Bowlby and William R. Schriver, "Bluffing and the 'Split-the-Difference' Theory of Wage Bargaining," *Industrial and Labor Relations Review*, January 1979, pp. 161–71.

[28] Henry S. Farber, "The Determinants of Union Wage Demands: Some Preliminary Empirical Evidence," *Proceedings of the Industrial Relations Research Association*, 1977, pp. 303–10.

[29] Walton and McKersie, *Behavioral Theory*, p. 4.

[30] Ibid., p. 5.

spend an inordinate amount of time recruiting new members from the workers hired as replacements. Both parties may seek a solution to their joint problem by attacking the causes of turnover existing in their present or previous agreement.

Integrative bargaining occurs in contexts where both management and union accommodate the needs of the other without cost or through a simultaneous gain. These contexts frequently involve management's desires to improve flexibility and unions' simultaneous desires for increased job security.[31]

Attitudinal Structuring

Attitudinal structuring relates to the activities the parties engage in to create such atmospheres as cooperation, hostility, trust, and respect.[32] The process primarily involves changing the parties' attitudes, expecting changed attitudes to change predispositions to act.

The relationship patterns occurring between labor and management will have an effect on or be a result of one party's action toward the other, beliefs about legitimacy, level of trust, and degree of friendliness.[33] As a result of these attitudinal dimensions (shown in Figure 10–6), the predominant patterns fall within the categories of conflict, containment-aggression, accommodation, cooperation, and collusion.

Conflict occurs when both parties seek to destroy the other's base. Neither acknowledges the legitimacy of the other, and activities are pursued to interfere with the other's existence. Containment-aggression occurs when either or both sides demonstrate a high degree of militancy while recognizing the other's right to exist. Accommodation takes place when each party accords the other a legitimate role and allows the other to represent its position as a legitimate interest. Cooperation occurs when the other's position is seen as completely legitimate and when common issues are of simultaneous concern to both parties. Collusion takes place when both join to subvert the goals of the parties they represent.[34] Collusion occurs when mangement covertly assists a union to organize in return for a nonmilitant stance on bargaining.

Intraorganizational Bargaining

Intraorganizational bargaining involves achieving agreement within one of the bargaining groups.[35] For example, a management bargainer's efforts might convince fellow management representatives that a 40-

---

31 Ibid., pp. 129ff.
32 Ibid., p. 5.
33 Ibid., pp. 184–280.
34 Ibid., pp. 186–88.
35 Ibid., p. 5.

FIGURE 10-5

Interpretative Comments about the Degree of Firmness in Statements of Commitments

Statement of commitment (1)	Degree of finality of commitment to a position (2)	Degree of specificity of that position (3)	Consequences or implications associated with a position (the threat) (4)
From a negotiation involving a middle-sized manufacturing plant in 1953: "We have looked very seriously and must present this (10-cent package) as our final offer."	The statement "must present this as our final offer" is not as strong as, for example, "this is our final offer." The strength of the word "final" is somewhat hedged by the more tentative phrase "must present this as."	The reference to the "10-cent package" was fairly specific.	No reference to the consequences. What the other party is expected to associate with the company's position would depend on the company's reputation or other confirming tactics. It would seem to imply that company is ready to take a strike.
A union replied later, "The membership disagreed" with the company's economic proposal. "The present contract will not extend beyond 12:00 tonight."	Significantly, the membership was reported as only having "disagreed"; it did not "reject."	Reference to "economic proposal" is not specific. Hence the degree of disagreement is unclear.	By stating "the present contract will not extend," they do not state that there would be a strike. And in the particular context it was not clear that they would strike.
From the public statements regarding the 1955 negotiations between the UAW and the Ford Motor Company: Henry Ford II suggested alternate ways of achieving security "without piecemeal experimenting with dangerous mechanisms or guinea pig industries. . . ." This was a statement of opposition to the union's GAW proposal.	The statement contained no hint about the finality of his commitment of opposition.	The phrase "piecemeal experimenting . . ." clearly avoided reference to just what was objected to.	There were no references to the consequences to be associated with ultimate failure to agree.

From the transcripts of a negotiation in the oil industry: Management stated, "If you say now or never or else (on a wage increase demanded by the union), I would say go ahead; we are prepared to take the consequences."	This was an explicit, binding commitment.	The company's position was also clear in this instance—it was not prepared to make any concession on the issue at hand.	Company was indicating its readiness for a work stoppage.
Later the union spokesman replied, "My advice to your employees will be not to become a party to any agreement which binds them to present wages."	Regarding what the union leader's advice will be, that is final. It says nothing about the finality of that position of the party, however.	The advice "not to become a party to any agreement which binds them to present wages" is hardly specific. Any increase would meet the test of this statement. In fact, even a reopening clause would avoid "binding the union to present wages."	Although at first glance this statement seems to commit the union to a wage increase "or else," it leaves them the option of continuing with no contract and with signing a contract which has a way of adjusting wages in the future. The context did nothing to clarify just what consequences were to be associated with the union's position.
"I don't believe that they (the rest of the union committee) can recommend acceptance" (of the company's offer).	"I don't believe" is more tentative than "I know they cannot."	"I don't believe that they can recommend acceptance" leaves unanswered whether the union committee would recommend that the membership not accept the offer or merely make no recommendation. Moreover, the reference is only to the company's *offer as it now stands*.	Not specified here, but the union had begun to refer to economic sanctions.

Source: B. M. Selekman, S. K. Selekman, and S. H. Fuller, *Problems in Labor Relations*, 2nd ed. (New York: McGraw-Hill, 1958), pp. 221, 226, 233; Material from these pages used in formulating table by Richard E. Walton and Robert B. McKersie in *A Behavioral Theory of Labor Negotiations* (New York: McGraw-Hill, 1965), pp. 96, 97. Copyright © 1965 McGraw-Hill. Used with the permission of McGraw-Hill Book Company.

FIGURE 10-6

Attitudinal Components of the Relationship Patterns

Pattern of relationship

Attitudinal dimensions	Conflict	Containment-aggression	Accommodation	Cooperation	Collusion
Motivational orientation and action tendencies toward other	Competitive tendencies to destroy or weaken		Individualistic policy of hands off	Cooperative tendencies to assist or preserve	
Beliefs about legitimacy of other	Denial of legitimacy	Grudging acknowledgment	Acceptance of status quo	Complete legitimacy	Not applicable
Level of trust in conducting affairs	Extreme distrust	Distrust	Limited trust	Extended trust	Trust based on mutual blackmail potential
Degree of friendliness	Hate	Antagonism	Neutralism—courteousness	Friendliness	Intimacy—"sweetheart relationship"

Source: Richard E. Walton and Robert B. McKersie, *A Behavioral Theory of Labor Negotiations* (New York: McGraw-Hill, 1965), p. 189. Copyright © 1965 McGraw-Hill. Used with the permission of McGraw-Hill Book Company.

cent raise is necessary to avoid a strike, although management had determined previously that the union would likely settle for 35 cents. Intraorganizational bargaining also refers to the activities of union negotiators in selling an agreement to the union's membership.

On the union side, the negotiating team must be able to sell an agreement to the rank and file once it's been reached. To do this, the team has to be sensitive to the demands of the membership while balancing the competing needs of subgroups within the union. One tactic used by union negotiators is estimating some reasonable range of contract outcomes to the membership. Suggestions that excessive demands could damage the nature of the bargaining relationship (see attitudinal structuring) can help to moderate initial demands.

Another tactic, used particularly by management, limits participation of those likely to take militant stances or likely to be unwilling to modify positions as bargaining continues. This way, the management negotiator is freer to respond during the bargaining process.[36]

Use of the Components in Bargaining

The four bargaining processes and their degree of use may result from certain preexisting conditions and the behaviors of the negotiators.[37] Figure 10–7 shows the predictors of the processes. Conditions such as high bargaining power are expected to be related to early commitment to a firm position. This, in turn, should lead toward the use of distributive bargaining.

Questionnaire information gathered from union and management negotiators on their perceptions of negotiations in which they were involved suggests distributive bargaining success was influenced by bargaining power, low probability of a work stoppage, clarity in stating issues, and the opponent's behavior when discussing the basis for its position. Integrative bargaining success depended on conditions of trust, support, and friendliness by the opponent and a clear statement of issues with open discussion and plentiful information. Success in attitudinal structuring was related to management respect for the union, generally constructive relationships toward management, and a lack of criticism of the opponent. Intraorganizational bargaining success depended on the confidence bargainers had in their constituents' endorsement and the high perceived costs of a stoppage. Behaviors relevant to success related to team solidarity and low outside pressures.

---

36 Ibid., pp. 281–340.

37 Richard B. Peterson and Lane Tracy, "Testing a Behavioral Theory Model of Labor Negotiations," *Industrial Relations*, February 1977, pp. 35–50.

FIGURE 10–7

Model of Conditions and Behaviors Related to Walton and McKersie's Four Goals of Bargaining

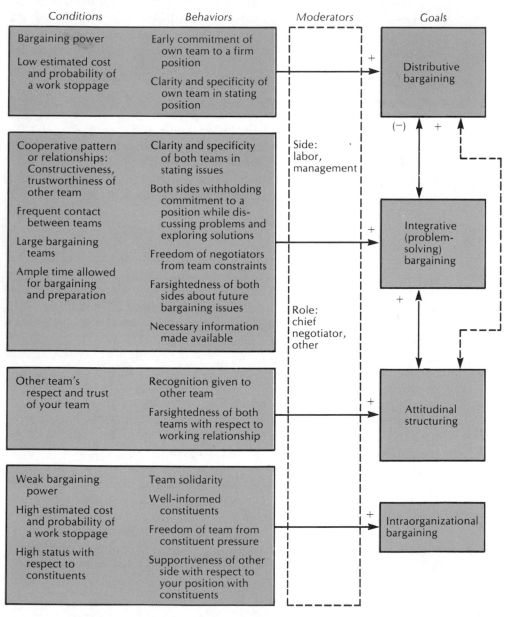

Source: Richard B. Peterson and Lane Tracy, "Testing a Behavioral Theory Model of Labor Negotiations," *Industrial Relations*, February 1977, p. 17.

NEGOTIATIONS

This section examines the activities involved in bargaining a new contract. Issues covered include tactics, information requirements, and union and management requirements for agreements. The Taft-Hartley Act requires the parties to meet at reasonable times and places and to bargain in good faith over issues involving wages, hours, and terms and conditions of employment.

Initial Presentations

Although not legally required, the party requesting changes in its favor customarily presents its demands first. Thus, the union will present demands when seeking improvements and management will do so when seeking concessions. At this presentation, the side taking the initiative will specify all areas of the contract in which changes are desired. This initial session also allows the union to get onto the table all grievances or positions developed through the membership meetings. The union does not expect to gain all of these changes; but, as a political organization, it has an obligation to state the positions of individual members. It also creates new bargaining positions that alert management to expect more vigorous future demands in these areas.

Management may not reply to the union's demands at the initial session, but it will respond early in the negotiations. Its response is usually substantially below what it would be willing to settle for. If management adheres to or refuses to move past its original position, it must provide information if asked by the union to support those positions based on an inability to pay.[38]

Bargaining on Specific Issues

If the issues are complex or the company is large, the negotiating committee and company representatives will frequently divide themselves into subcommittees to negotiate specific issues. For example, the contract language on work standards may be handled by a subgroup of production employees or union stewards and production supervisors.

Usually the subgroups do not have the authority to finalize the issues they discuss because these issues form part of a trade-off package, but they may bring tentative agreements or positions back to the main table for consideration.

---

[38] *NLRB* v. *Truitt Mfg. Co.*, 351 U.S. 149 (U.S. Supreme Court, 1956).

At the main table, issues not forming part of a combined package or be used as trade-offs may be initialed by the parties as finalized for the ultimate agreement. Thus, the final settlement is not necessarily a coalescence on all issues simultaneously but rather a completion of negotiations on final areas in which disagreement existed.

In most negotiations, nonwage issues—union security clauses, seniority provisions, work rules, and the like—are decided first. Wage and benefit issues are often settled as a package near the end of negotiations. As noted earlier in discussing the certainty of outcomes and the potential costs of package characteristics, wages and benefits are issues that management must consider carefully.

TACTICS IN DISTRIBUTIVE BARGAINING

Each party enters the negotiations with certain positions it hopes to win. Management may have an economic position it wants to protect. The union may have specific wage and benefit demands it perceives as achievable. Bargaining is the process by which the two parties influence the perceptions of the other to adopt their positions as a final outcome.

The following represents the types of tactics both parties use to influence the resistance points of their opponents through information transmission in bargaining:

"I do not think you really feel that strongly about the issues you have introduced."

"I believe a strike will cost you considerably more than you are willing to admit."

"I believe a strike will cost me almost nothing in spite of your statements to the contrary."

"I feel very strongly about this issue regardless of what you say."[39]

Besides the preparations that take place before negotiations, certain tactics may be used during negotiations to assess the actual point at which an opponent would prefer to settle. Addressing questions to various members of the negotiating team may gain an overall flavor of the important issues through their responses. To highlight the importance of a particular issue, the party proposing it may provide detailed information that clearly establishes its position. For example, a firm faced with a large wage demand may provide a volume of data on the wage costs of its competition and its inability to pass through cost increases to its consumers.

One tactic gets the opponent to see that its demands will not result in as positive an outcome as it expects. For example, a demand for

---

[39] Walton and McKersie, *Behavioral Theory*, p. 60.

more paid time off may be seen by the union as a way to increase employment, but the company may show that the increased costs will result in replacement of existing workers with robots.

Another successful tactic changes the costs of a strike for an opponent. For example, a strike by the UAW is much more critical if it is close to a new model year when auto companies do not have inventories of vehicles ready for delivery (as they would have in the spring). Employers may build up inventories before contract expirations by working at full capacity or by scheduling overtime to reduce the potential costs of a strike.

Committing to a Position

Commitment to a position can be a powerful bargaining tool. If the opposition perceives no more movement will be made on a specific issue, it may then be willing to concede to the offered point if within its settlement range. Three components of a position signal commitment: finality (communication content indicating no further movement will be made), specificity (the clarity of the position), and the consequences (the contingent outcomes, such as a strike that will occur if the demand is not accepted as proposed).[40]

Several tactics may telegraph commitment to the opposition. Most relate to the question of consequences. For example, the union's strike authorization vote signals its commitment to management. A company making preparations for closing operations or refusing to accept new orders signals to the union that it is prepared to call the union's bluff on its bargaining positions.

Consider the 1981 Federal Aviation Administration–Professional Air Traffic Controllers Organization dispute in which President Reagan committed management to a position that it would not bargain during a strike (finality) and that all strikers must return to work within 48 hours (specificity) or be permanently severed from federal employment (consequences).

SETTLEMENTS AND RATIFICATIONS

When the negotiators have reached agreement on a new contract, the union team still has some responsibilities to fulfill before the final agreement is signed. In most unions, two hurdles remain to be cleared before the tentative agreement becomes permanent. First, the international union must approve the agreement, which ensures a local will not negotiate an agreement substantially inferior to other contracts in

---

[40] Ibid., p. 93.

the international or other unions. Second, most unions require a referendum to be held among the bargaining unit's membership to ratify
the contract. To do this, the bargaining team conducts a membership
meeting and explains the contract gains won in negotiations. The team
then generally recommends settlement, and the members vote to accept or reject.

If the negotiating committee recommends acceptance, the membership nearly always votes to ratify. However, some exceptions occur.
In a study of mediated negotiations in which contract rejection occurred, only about 30 percent followed a unanimous recommendation
by the bargaining committee to accept the contract.[41] Table 10-1
presents reasons for contract rejections found in the study, and Figure
10-8 shows the mechanisms related to rejection. These include an

TABLE 10-1

Factors Involved in 41 Contract-Rejection Cases

Factor	Frequency of occurence among cases*
Management rejection	1
Local–international conflict	5
Committee membership gap†	10
Lack of recommendation	28
Union elections	4
Other union(s) in plant	4
Other union(s) outside	13
Plant move impending	1
Youth versus age	6
Skilled versus unskilled	1
Poor labor-management relations	9
Company-employee gap‡	1
Misunderstanding of provisions	3
Rejection of unanimous recommendation§	12
Leadership imposed settlement	2
Racial factors	2
Uncoordinated committee	1
Refusal of anything	3
Engineered rejection	2
New leaders—no control	2
Weak union leadership	2

* In many cases, more than one factor was involved.

† No membership consensus was derived.

‡ Management was unaware of employee priorities.

§ In these cases, no discernible factor was present.

Source: Donald R. Burke and Lester Rubin, "Is Contract Rejection a Major Collective Bargaining Problem?" *Industrial and Labor
Relations Review*, January 1973, p. 831.

---

[41] Donald R. Burke and Lester Rubin, "Is Contract Rejection a Major Collective
Bargaining Problem?" *Industrial and Labor Relations Review*, January 1979, pp. 820–33.

FIGURE 10–8

Typology of Variables in Contract Rejection

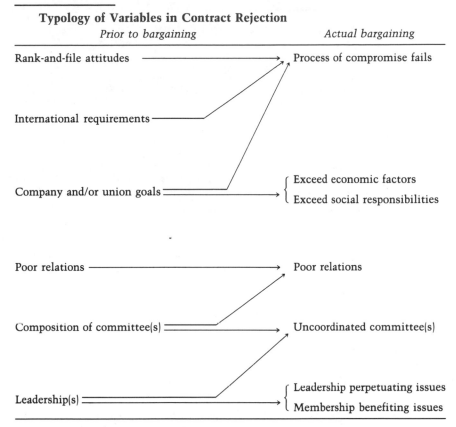

Prior to bargaining	*Actual bargaining*

Rank-and-file attitudes ⟶ Process of compromise fails

International requirements

Company and/or union goals ⟶ { Exceed economic factors / Exceed social responsibilities

Poor relations ⟶ Poor relations

Composition of committee(s) ⟶ Uncoordinated committee(s)

Leadership(s) ⟶ { Leadership perpetuating issues / Membership benefiting issues

Source: Donald R. Burke and Lester Rubin, "Is Contract Rejection a Major Collective Bargaining Problem?" *Industrial and Labor Relations Review*, January 1973, p. 831.

inability to alter positions through bargaining, final positions outside the opponent's settlement range, hostile relationships between the parties, poor coordination in bargaining, or a failure to correctly estimate the priorities of the membership. Contract rejection has recently occurred in several major concession bargaining situations, even after the national union recommended the agreement. Exhibit 10–3 displays some recent major examples.

When the negotiating committee unqualifiedly recommends ratification but the contract is rejected, union negotiators are placed in a precarious position. Management may rightfully question whether the union actually speaks for the rank and file. During the negotiations, management may have conceded on issues of seeming importance to the bargainers but of questionable relevance to the rank and file. The negotiating committee also may have difficulty selling a subsequent settlement to the membership because its credibility was undermined by the earlier rejection.

EXHIBIT 10–3

Major Recent Contract Rejections

WHERE WORKER DISSENT IS CAUSING PROBLEMS	
Union Employer	Dispute
1983	
Auto Workers General Motors (Van Nuys, Calif.)	4,400-member Local 645 delays for three years work-rule changes proposed by GM and UAW leaders
1984	
Food & Commercial Workers Kroger (Pittsburgh)	Kroger sells 45 stores after 2,800 members of Local 23 turn down wage and work-rule concessions accepted by their leaders
1985	
Electronic Workers (IUE) General Electric (Lynn, Mass.)	The 8,500 members of Local 201, unhappy with proposed concessions in their national contract, vote out the local's executive board
Teamsters Richard A. Shaw Inc. Watsonville Canning (Watsonville, Calif.)	Local 912's 1,700 members resist wage concessions, leading to a strike in defiance of local leaders
Food & Commercial Workers Hormel (Austin, Minn.)	1,500-member Local P-9 rejects wage cuts in defiance of international union. Hormel breaks the ensuing strike, and the local sues its parent union, which has put P-9 in trusteeship
1986	
State, County & Municipal Employees City of Detroit	7,000 members of Michigan Council 25 reject a wage deal accepted by their leaders, forcing continuation of a strike begun on July 16
DATA: BW	

Source: *Business Week,* August 11, 1986, p. 72.

Occasionally, management will question whether the bargaining committee is representing the true wishes of the rank and file. Management bargainers may suggest a package be submitted to the membership for ratification. The company may not insist on taking a proposal to the membership, however, because this is not a mandatory bargaining issue.[42] If the negotiating committee is reasonably certain a proposal will be rejected, it may encourage the membership to reject so as to strengthen its bargaining position by putting management on notice that its position is not acceptable.

Nonagreement

Occasionally, the parties may fail to reach an agreement, either before or after the contract expires. A variety of activities may then occur, including mediation, strikes, lockouts, replacements, management's implementation of its last offer, and arbitration. Impasses in negotiations lead to very complex issues, which will be detailed in the next chapter.

CHANGES IN BARGAINING OUTCOMES IN THE 1980s

The last several years have seen major changes in the objectives of managemenet in collective bargaining. Figure 10–9 shows changes in management's nonwage objectives in bargaining between 1978 and 1983. Over this period, managements substantially reduced their willingness to give on virtually all objectives and expected to get improvements on all. A large share of companies have recently requested changes in their contracts before the scheduled expiration dates. Table 10–2 indicates major types of changes requested and the rate at which companies were successful in obtaining them. Generally, unions responded most frequently by asking for greater job security, limits on subcontracting, or some form of profit-sharing or gainsharing program. They were most successful in obtaining job security and gainsharing but very unsuccessful in obtaining subcontracting limits.[43]

Previous evidence has shown that companies vulnerable to strikes or struck in the past are more likely to settle above their wage targets. This trend lends credence to the suggestion that striking may constitute an investment in bargaining power for the union. Companies emphasizing union containment goals as well as bargaining goals are

---

[42] *NLRB* v. *Wooster Division of Borg Warner Corp.*, 356 U.S. 342 (1958).

[43] Audrey Freedman, *The New Look in Wage Policy and Employee Relations* (New York: Conference Board, 1985), pp. 10–15.

FIGURE 10–9

Shift in Management's Nonwage Objectives between 1978 and 1983

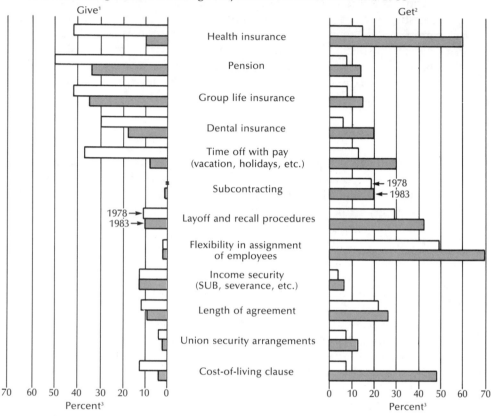

[1] Proportion of companies that were willing to use a specific item in trade for another item.

[2] Proportion of companies that wanted to tighten existing provision or get a more favorable one.

[3] 100% = all companies with the same bargaining unit for both years, with an objective in the subject area in 1978 and in 1983. (e.g. Health benefits, 130 companies; subcontracting, 86 companies.)

Source: Audrey Freedman, *The New Look in Wage Policy and Employee Relations* (New York: Conference Board, 1985), p. 15.

more likely to achieve their targets.[44] However, one must not necessarily attribute a hard-line approach to success in bargaining, because a heavily unionized firm cannot readily have a credible containment policy. Containment may be related to relatively small proportions of employees being unionized, which, in turn, increases bargaining leverage.

---

[44] Freedman, *Managing Labor Relations*, p. 48.

TABLE 10-2

Management Requests for Changes in Union Contract before Expiration Date (largest bargaining unit in 133 companies reporting early openings)

Proposed Change	Number of Companies Proposing Change[a]	Percent of All Early Openings	Proportion of Proposed Changes Accomplished
			(% of col. 1)
Defer ("freeze") or delay scheduled wage increases	68	51	60
Reduce wages	38	29	66
Established lower wage rates for new hires	40	30	80
Reduce fringe benefits	53	40	66
Reduce paid time off	38	29	79
Change work rules	76	57	76
Cost-of-living adjustment (COLA)			
Defer or delay effective adjustment	39	29	72
Eliminate entire clause	23	17	48
Modify formula	17	13	65
Divert COLA	15	11	93

[a] Multiple responses.

Source: Audrey Freedman, *The New Look in Wage Policy and Employee Relations* (New York: Conference Board, 1985), p. 12.

SUMMARY

Managements prepare for bargaining by gathering internal and comparative data, including employee distributions by job, seniority, shift, and the like. Other data relate to wage rates granted in other negotiations, local labor market rates, and the like. Many different functional departments contribute to obtaining information and formulating a management negotiating position. Contract terms that may be renegotiated must be costed to assess their relative financial impacts on the employer. Bargaining books assist in negotiations.

Unions prepare for bargaining by determining what their memberships view as important issues. The political nature of unions requires attention be given to interests of major groups of employees. National-level preparation involves the collection and analysis of data, while local-level preparation formulates bargaining positions and involves members in forming a negotiating team.

Bargaining takes place in situations when both parties expect the act of bargaining to improve their positions. One side may expect an improvement in benefits, while the other gains certainty through the contracting process. Attributes of the bargaining situation and the personalities of the parties involved influence the outcomes of the process. Bluffing in bargaining appears important because it allows the parties to explore the significance and reasons behind demands without initially stating positions they might want to retreat from later.

Collective bargaining is suggested to have four components: distributive bargaining (one's gain is the other's loss), integrative bargaining (a settlement improves both parties' positions), attitudinal structuring (attempts to create atmospheres likely to obtain desired concessions), and intraorganizational bargaining (the parties try to convince constituents within their own organizations to change positions).

Bargaining usually begins with the party seeking a change presenting its positions. Changes will frequently be handled sequentially, although logrolling occurs on occasion. Following an agreement, the union's members must ratify the tentative agreement. Failure to ratify appears primarily related to difficulties in attitudinal structuring and intraorganizational bargaining.

DISCUSSION QUESTIONS

1. To what extent should management allow the union to select the components of an economic package in a contract negotiation?
2. What balance should exist between local- and national-level influences in negotiations? Should this balance differ by bargaining issue?
3. How could an opponent in bargaining overcome what appears to be a strong commitment to an issue by its opposite member?
4. What strategies should management use in bargaining when a settlement unanimously recommended by the union's bargaining team is rejected?
5. Why would it be harder for heavily unionized organizations to settle on their bargaining targets than those with a small proportion of employees unionized?
6. What attitudinal structuring and intraorganizational bargaining tactics would be different for integrative as compared to distributive bargaining?

CASE

Negotiating Exercise

This mock negotiating exercise will help you develop an appreciation of and insight into principles and problems of collective bargaining, with special emphasis on contract negotiation. Using the information covered to this point in the text, you will act as a member of a union or management bargaining team in formulating its strategies and tactics for negotiations. Following a more detailed approach to contract costing and the instructions for the exercise, a copy of the expiring contract between General Materials & Fabrication Company (GMFC) and Local 384 of the United Steelworkers of America will be presented.

A. Contract Costing

Contract costing is not straightforward. The cost changes often depend on changes in employee seniority, how increased vacations are handled, and similar issues not directly associated with the amount of an hourly wage increase. A simple costing example will be created so you can see the effects. Assume a bargaining unit containing 100 employees will renegotiate its contract. Five pay grades presently have pay rates, given length of service *in the organization*, as shown in Table MN-1.

The 100 employees are distributed by grade and seniority, as shown in Table MN-2.

Table MN-3 shows the historic turnover rates (proportion of employees who quit or retire in a given year) of bargaining unit employees by grade and seniority level.

The organization presently has a retirement plan providing for full vesting of benefits at five years' service. Employees who quit before

TABLE MN-1

Pay Rates

			Seniority		
Grade	< 1 Yr.	1-2 Yr.	3-5 Yr.	6-10 Yr.	> 10 Yr.
1	5.50	6.00	6.50	6.50	6.50
2	6.50	7.00	7.50	8.00	8.00
3	7.50	8.00	8.50	9.00	9.50
4	8.50	9.00	9.50	10.00	10.50
5	9.50	10.00	10.50	11.00	11.50

TABLE MN-2

Employment Levels

Grade	Seniority					Total
	< 1 Yr.	1-2 Yr.	3-5 Yr.	6-10 Yr.	> 10 Yr.	
1	8	2				10
2	2	4	14			20
3		5	15	20	5	45
4			3	6	6	15
5				2	8	10
Total	10	11	32	28	19	100

accruing five years of service lose their benefits. The plan is presently fully funded to provide for pensions for present employees, taking anticipated turnover into account. The retirement program provides that employees will receive an equivalent of 5 percent of their gross pay (regular and overtime) contributed to their pension funds. The health care program provides hospital and medical coverage paid by the employer. Twenty-five percent of the employees are single and without dependents. The other 75 percent have families, but of these, 5 percent are families in which both the husband and wife are employed by this company, so premiums need not be paid for both. Health care premiums are presently $150 per month for single employees and $250 per month for those with dependents. Premiums are expected to increase 15 percent next year for both single and family policies.

Under the contract, overtime is apportioned (within grade) on the basis of seniority, with each employee entitled to five hours of overtime before the next-junior employee in that grade is entitled. If all employees within the grade have received the overtime, the cycle is repeated. During the last year, overtime was available in the following numbers of hours by grade: grade 1, 520 hours; 2, 840; 3, 1,640; 4,

TABLE MN-3

Turnover Rates

Grade	Seniority				
	< 1 Yr.	1-2 Yr.	3-5 Yr.	6-10 Yr.	> 10 Yr.
1	.25	.10	.10	.10	.10
2	.10	.05	.05	.00	.00
3	.05	.05	.05	.00	.02
4	.00	.00	.00	.00	.03
5	.00	.00	.00	.00	.10

TABLE MN–4

Hours of Overtime

Grade	< 1 Yr.	1-2 Yr.	Seniority 3-5 Yr.	6-10 Yr.	> 10 Yr.	Total
1	51.25	55.00				520
2	40.00	40.00	42.86			840
3		35.00	35.00	37.00	40.00	1,640
4			65.00	67.70	70.00	1,020
5				75.00	78.75	780

1,020; and 5, 780. The overtime premium for all of these hours was 50 percent. Table MN-4 shows the average number of hours of overtime per employee by seniority and grade level during the past year.

All employees receive nine paid holidays and three paid sick days. The average employee takes two of these days, with no variation across grades or seniority levels. Vacations are tied to length of service. Employees with less than one year's service are not entitled to vacations and do not accrue vacation time. Those with 1 to 2 years are entitled to one week; 3 to 5 years, two weeks; 6 to 10 years, three weeks; and more than 10 years, four weeks.

All employees are presently working on one shift, and all have two paid break periods of 10 minutes each in the morning and afternoon.

Table MN-5 shows the average wage cost per employee by grade and seniority level under the expiring contract. It is calculated by multiplying the wage rate by 2,080 (the number of hours in a normal work year) plus the number of overtime hours from the appropriate cell in Table MN-4 times 1.5 (to account for the overtime premium rate).

Social security tax rates are 7.51 on the first $45,000 (1988) of income; unemployment insurance is 4 percent on the first $10,000 of earnings; and worker's compensation insurance premiums are 1.2 per-

TABLE MN–5

Average Wage Cost per Employee

Grade	< 1 Yr.	1-2 Yr.	Seniority 3-5 Yr.	6-10 Yr.	> 10 Yr.
1	$11,863	$12,975	$13,520	$13,520	$13,520
2	13,910	14,980	16,082	16,640	16,640
3	15,600	17,060	18,126	19,220	20,330
4	17,680	18,720	20,686	21,816	22,943
5	19,760	20,800	21,840	24,118	25,278

TABLE MN-6

Pension Vesting Probabilities

Grade	< 1 Yr.	1-2 Yr.	Seniority 3-5 Yr.	6-10 Yr.	> 10 Yr.
1	0.6075	0.8000	0.9000	1.0000	1.0000
2	0.8123	0.9000	0.9500	1.0000	1.0000
3	0.8574	0.9000	0.9500	1.0000	1.0000
4	1.0000	1.0000	1.0000	1.0000	1.0000
5	1.0000	1.0000	1.0000	1.0000	1.0000

cent of total payroll. With pensions vesting in five years, the pension contribution for persons with less than six years' service must be multiplied by the likelihood that they will remain for that period to get the total contribution required. Table MN-6 is a matrix of probabilities of an employee remaining long enough to receive vested benefits.

Present pension costs by grade and seniority (Number of employees × Wage cost × Retention factor) are shown in Table MN-7.

Present wage costs [straight time (2,080 hours per year) and overtime at time and a half] are obtained by multiplying the cells in Table MN-2 by corresponding cells in Table MN-5. The results are shown in Table MN-8.

The total labor costs in the last year of the expiring contract were:

Wages	$1,858,046
Pension contributions	88,550
Social security (.0751 × Wages)	139,539
Unemployment insurance (.04 × $10,000 × Number of employees)	40,000
Worker's compensation (.012 × Wages)	22,297
Health insurance (25 singles × $150 × 12 months)	45,000
Health insurance (75 families × $250 × 12 months)	225,000
(Less health insurance for five husband–wife duplications)	(15,000)
Total	$2,403,432

TABLE MN-7

Total Pension Costs

Grade	< 1 Yr.	1-2 Yr.	Seniority 3-5 Yr.	6-10 Yr.	> 10 Yr.	Total
1	$2,883	$1,038	$ 0	$ 0	$ 0	$ 3,921
2	1,130	2,696	10,695	0	0	14,521
3	0	3,839	12,915	19,220	5,083	41,055
4	0	0	3,103	6,545	6,883	16,530
5	0	0	0	2,412	10,111	12,523
Total	4,013	7,573	26,713	28,176	22,077	88,550

TABLE MN–8

Total Wage Costs

Grade	< 1 Yr.	1–2 Yr.	3–5 Yr.	6–10 Yr.	> 10 Yr.	Total
			Seniority			
1	$ 94,903	$ 25,950	0	0	0	$ 120,853
2	27,820	59,920	$225,150	0	0	312,890
3	0	85,300	271,894	$384,390	$101,650	843,234
4	0	0	62,059	130,893	137,655	330,607
5	0	0	0	48,235	202,228	250,463
Total	$122,723	$171,170	$559,103	$563,518	$441,533	$1,858,046

For the coming year, assume a set of contract demands as follows:

1. A 50-cent across-the-board wage increase.
2. Five cents additional per grade from grade 2 on.
3. A 6-percent pension contribution.
4. One week additional vacation for all employees with more than five years' service.

Assume normal turnover takes place over the next year and that all terminees and retirements are replaced at Grade 1 and present employees are promoted to fill the vacancies left. Five employees will be lost: grade 1, less-than-1-year group, two; grade 2, 3–5-year group, one; grade 3, 3–5-year group, one; and grade 5, over-10-year group, one. Each employee will also increase one year in seniority. Assume employees are relatively evenly distributed within seniority groups and promotions are most often given to the most senior person applying, but in only two thirds of the cases is the most senior person eligible. The vacation demand will result in the loss of 56 weeks' work. Assume an additional employee must be hired at grade 1 to make up for 42 weeks of the loss and the other 14 weeks must be worked as overtime, evenly

TABLE MN–9

Returning Employees

Grade	< 1 Yr.	1–2 Yr.	3–5 Yr.	6–10 Yr.	> 10 Yr.	Total
			Seniority			
1	6	2	0	0	0	8
2	2	4	13	0	0	19
3	0	5	14	20	5	44
4	0	0	3	6	6	15
5	0	0	0	2	7	9
Total	8	11	30	28	18	95

TABLE MN–10

Seniority Level with Promotions and New Hires

| | | Seniority | | | | |
Grade	< 1 Yr.	1-2 Yr.	3-5 Yr.	6-10 Yr.	> 10 Yr.	Total
1	6	5	0	0	0	11
2	0	6	12	2	0	20
3	0	2	12	23	8	45
4	0	0	2	6	7	15
5	0	0	0	2	8	10
Total	6	13	26	33	23	101

distributed among employees in grades 3 to 5 according to seniority rules. This results in 560 additional hours, with 200 hours apportioned to grade 5 and 180 each to grades 3 and 4. At the end of the contract year, the grade and seniority matrix (after turnover) could look as shown in Table MN-9.

Table MN-10 shows the seniority level and distribution of employees after promotions have been made and new hires added.

If the union wins its demands, the new wage rates would be as shown in Table MN-11, given the union's wage demands.

Overtime for the coming year (assuming same as last year except for additional hours necessary if the vacation demand is won) is shown in Table MN-12.

Table MN-13 shows the average wage cost per employee for straight time and overtime, given the proposed demands.

Multiplying Table MN-10 by Table MN-13 yields the total wage cost (less fringes) under the new contract. The results are shown in Table MN-14.

Multiplying the turnover probability table (Table MN-6) by the total wages in Table MN-14 gives the pension costs under the new contract as 6 percent. These are shown in Table MN-15.

TABLE MN–11

Post-Negotiation Pay Rates

| | | Seniority | | | |
Grade	< 1 Yr.	1-2 Yr.	3-5 Yr.	6-10 Yr.	> 10 Yr.
1	$ 6.00	$ 6.50	$ 7.00	$ 7.00	$ 7.00
2	7.05	7.55	8.05	8.55	8.55
3	8.10	8.60	9.10	9.60	10.10
4	9.15	9.65	10.15	10.65	11.15
5	10.20	10.70	11.20	11.70	12.20

TABLE MN–12

Post-Negotiation Overtime Distribution

Grade	< 1 Yr.	1-2 Yr.	3-5 Yr.	6-10 Yr.	> 10 Yr.	O/T Hours
1	45	50				520
2		40	42.5	45		840
3		40	40	40	42.5	1,820
4			80	80	80	1,200
5				95	98.75	980

TABLE MN–13

Post-Negotiation Wage Cost per Employee

Grade	< 1 Yr.	1-2 Yr.	3-5 Yr.	6-10 Yr.	> 10 Yr.
1	12,885	14,008	14,560	14,560	14,560
2	14,664	16,157	17,257	18,361	17,784
3	16,848	18,404	19,474	20,544	21,652
4	19,032	20,072	22,330	23,430	24,530
5	21,216	22,256	23,296	26,003	27,183

TABLE MN–14

Post-Negotiation Total Wage Cost

Grade	< 1 Yr.	1-2 Yr.	3-5 Yr.	6-10 Yr.	> 10 Yr.	Total
1	77,310	70,038	0	0	0	147,348
2	0	96,942	207,086	36,722	0	340,751
3	0	36,808	233,688	472,512	173,215	916,223
4	0	0	44,660	140,580	171,710	356,950
5	0	0	0	52,007	217,465	269,472
Total	77,310	203,788	485,434	701,821	562,390	2,030,743

Pension costs increase by $28,509 (or 32 percent more than under the expiring contract) due to increased seniority, which leads to a greater likelihood of staying combined with the 20 percent increase in contribution rates. Following are the total costs in the first year of a new contract:

TABLE MN-15

Post-Negotiation Total Pension Costs

Grade	< 1 Yr.	1-2 Yr.	3-5 Yr.	6-10 Yr.	> 10 Yr.	Total
			Seniority			
1	2,818	3,362	0	0	0	6,180
2	0	5,235	11,804	2,203	0	19,242
3	0	1,988	13,320	28,351	10,393	54,051
4	0	0	2,680	8,435	10,303	21,417
5	0	0	0	3,120	13,048	16,168
Total	2,818	10,584	27,804	42,109	33,743	117,059

Wages	$2,030,743
Pension contributions	117,059
Social security	152,509
Unemployment insurance (101 employees)	40,400
Worker's compensation insurance	24,369
Health insurance (26 singles, 15% increase)	53,820
Health insurance (75 families, 15% increase)	258,750
(Less health insurance for 5 husband–wife	
duplications, 15% increase)	(17,250)
Total	$2,660,099

Under the proposed new contract, total labor costs would increase by 11.1 percent, even though average straight-time percentage wage increases would rise by grade and seniority level as shown in Table MN-16.

B. Approach

Assume the following contract is due to expire soon and the union has made a timely notification to management that it desires renegotiations. Your responsibility is to negotiate a new contract. Following are the demands of both labor and management and supplemental information that will be of help in choosing contract demands.

TABLE MN-16

Post-Negotiation Percentage Wage Increases

Grade	< 1 Yr.	1-2 Yr.	3-5 Yr.	6-10 Yr.	> 10 Yr.
			Seniority		
1	8.6	8.0	7.7	7.7	7.7
2	5.4	7.9	7.3	10.3	6.9
3	8.0	7.9	7.4	6.9	6.5
4	7.6	7.2	7.9	7.4	6.9
5	7.4	7.0	6.7	7.8	7.5

C. Demands

1. The union may formulate its demands from the following set, including all items from *a* through *d* and choosing any four from *e* through *k:*
    a. A general wage increase of 75 cents per hour during each year of the contract, plus an additional 50 cents per hour at the effective date.
    b. The company will neither subcontract work that the bargaining unit is capable of performing nor close the plant or move any of its operations during the life of the agreement.
    c. A 50-cent additional increase will be given to maintain wage differentials for employees outside of the Assembler A and B classifications.
    d. The amount of COLA (three cents per hour for each one-point increase in the consumer price index) forgone in the recent concessions will be added to the base wage rate at the end of the expiring contract, and the two-tier wage plan will be abolished, with lower-tier employees immediately increased to the pay rates of upper-tier employees.
    e. The A jobs appear to be male-dominated occupations, while the B jobs are female-dominated occupations. Because they appear to be of comparable worth to the organization, A and B jobs will be merged, with grade 61 being equated to grade 7, 62 with 8, and so on. The B classification will be eliminated following the merger.
    f. Vacations will be increased one week for employees with eight or more years of service.
    g. The company's pension contribution will be increased from 5 percent of straight-time earnings to 6 percent of straight and overtime earnings. Vesting of benefits will begin at 50 percent for employees who have been employed three years and increase at 16⅔ percent per year until fully vested.
    h. A union-shop clause will be implemented, with membership required after 60 days of employment.
    i. Double-pay will be given for all overtime after nine hours in a day and for all Sunday or holiday work.
    j. Company-paid dental and optical insurance will be provided.
    k. The addition to wages for each one-point increase in the consumer price index will be raised from three cents to five cents.
2. The company's offers and demands will be formulated from the following list. All demands between *a* and *d* will be included in the offer, and any four demands between *e* and *k* may be included:
    a. The length of the agreement will be three years.
    b. Management shall have the right to subcontract or move to another plant any work without consulting the union.
    c. Wage increases of 25 cents, 35 cents, and 40 cents will be given

at the beginning of each year of the contract to graded employees. Employees in jobs with defined titles will receive increases of 3 percent, 4 percent, and 4½ percent at the beginning of each year of the contract.

d. The cost-of-living allowance (Section 7.02), which was suspended during the concessions, will be eliminated.

e. The two-tier wage plan negotiated into the previous agreement will be continued. Newly hired employees will begin at $1.25 below present employees. Wage increases to new employees will occur as negotiated for all employees.

f. Persons promoted to supervisory positions will continue to accrue seniority within the bargaining unit following their promotion.

g. Jobs will be consolidated into six different levels. Employees will be expected to be proficient in the duties included in all present jobs within each of the levels within six months after the effective date of the agreement. Level 1 includes all employees whose wage rates were at or below $7.50 per hour at the beginning of the last contract; level 2, those at or below $8.00; level 3, those at or below $8.50; level 4, those at or below $9.00; level 5, those at or below $9.50; and level 6, those above $9.50. Promotions to higher job levels will require demonstration of skills required by the next level and at least one year of service at the level immediately below. Persons in jobs at each level will be expected to demonstrate skills associated with all jobs at that level.

h. Employees will pay the first $500 of health care costs annually before the company-paid health care plan will begin to pay benefits.

i. All promotions will be determined by merit and ability alone. Seniority will continue to be used for layoffs and recalls.

j. Bargaining unit members who elect to join the union must maintain membership during the life of the agreement. With each contract expiration, individuals who had been members will be free to withdraw during the first week of the subsequent agreement.

k. The losing party in arbitration shall be responsible for all expenses of the arbitration procedure.

D. Organization for Negotiations

Each labor team will be headed by a chief negotiator. One member of labor's team should assume the role of international representative. Team sizes should be not less than three nor more than eight. Each management team will be headed by the plant labor relations director and may include experts from other functional areas—manufacturing, accounting, shipping, and so forth. Management team sizes should be about the same as labor's.

Before negotiations, each team should:

1. Construct its demand or offer package and identify the relative priority of the issues it is including.
2. Identify issues it would be willing to trade off.
3. Develop bargaining books tying demands to provisions in the present contract. Identify for each demand a desired settlement position, an expected settlement position, and a maximum concession position before bargaining.
4. Cost the provisions of the contract that would be changed. (Both parties should do this.)
5. Identify and develop strategies and tactics to be used during the negotiations. Structure the roles of each member.

E. Negotiations

1. At the first bargaining session, labor and management shall first agree on an agenda and order of presentation. If a mutually satisfactory agenda cannot be achieved, the following may be used:
   a. Each demand or offer will be presented separately, with the other party responding. Normally, where both sides will make offers on the same issue, the union will present its demand first.
   b. All demands will be presented and responded to before any concession is made.
2. As you begin to bargain, you should remember that once a concession is made, it is very difficult to retract it. Thus, carefully consider changes in your positions before announcing them.
3. During the process, it is often beneficial to suspend face-to-face negotiations to hold a caucus of your bargaining group to consider a demand or concession.
4. As you negotiate, consider the impact of the bargaining outcomes you attain on the bargaining relationship after the contract is signed. Is this a concession the other side can live with?
5. After the contract is agreed to, management must determine the final cost impact of the agreement, and the union must develop a strategy for gaining rank-and-file ratification.

F. Additional Information

1. The terms of the contract may have some cost impact outside of the bargaining unit, because improved fringe benefits are usually passed on to nonunion white-collar workers.

TABLE MN–17

Overtime Hours Worked under the Expiring Agreement

	Production (A and B)			Nonproduction (maintenance and craft)		
	1986	1987	1988	1986	1987	1988
Saturdays (nine hr. shift)	90	99	135	18	27	45
Weekday 9th hours	58	73	86	5	17	38
Holidays (eight hours)	0	0	0	0	0	4
Sundays (eight hours)	0	0	0	2	0	8
Miscellaneous overtime, not elsewhere classified	0	0	4	5	4	16
Total	148	172	225	30	48	111

2. Over the last contract, the average amount of overtime per year has been distributed as shown in Table MN–17.

3. The plant has experienced serveral layoffs since 1981. The plant population at the end of 1980 was 1,208, the largest ever achieved. In 1981, the production work force was cut by 20 percent in January and another 20 percent in March. In April 1982, 10 percent were recalled, with an additional 10 percent in October 1982 and a final 10 percent in May 1983. Maintenance and craft employment were cut 10 percent in January 1981, 10 percent in March 1981, 10 percent in June 1981, and 10 percent in September 1981. Recalls of 10 percent were made in January 1982, 10 percent in June 1982, and 10 percent in May 1983. Of those who were laid off, all have been recalled except five employees with less than one year of service at the time of the layoffs. The present seniority list (as of March 1, 1986) is shown in Table MN–18. Turnover includes quits, retirements, and promotions and transfers out of the bargaining unit. All employees who have reached 30 years of service in the bargaining unit have retired when they became eligible.

4. The B job classification consists of 92 percent women, while the A job classification consists of 98 percent men.

5. The plant has been located in Central City for almost 40 years, but it expanded rapidly during the early to middle 1970s. No expansion is planned for the Central City facility at present. The company does have other similar operations in the United States and abroad, and one relatively new plant in the Sun Belt is unorganized.

6. Presently, 986 bargaining unit members belong to the union.

7. The average arbitration case cost the company and the union $5,000 each during the last contract. Arbitrators heard 24 cases and ruled for the company in 17, for the union in 7.

TABLE MN–18

Seniority of Employees and Turnover Rates by Length of Service (seniority list as of March 1, 1986)

Years of seniority	Number of employees	Cumulative number	Percent turnover
30	2	2	100.0
29	3	5	1.0
28	3	8	1.0
27	4	12	1.0
26	20	32	1.0
25	25	57	1.0
24	17	74	1.0
23	18	92	1.0
22	20	112	1.0
21	16	128	1.0
20	14	142	1.0
19	9	151	1.0
18	11	162	1.0
17	13	175	1.0
16	101	276	1.0
15	143	419	1.0
14	105	524	1.0
13	117	641	1.0
12	27	668	1.0
11	61	729	1.0
10	96	825	1.0
9	68	893	1.5
8	18	911	2.0
7	59	970	2.5
6	8	978	3.0
5	2	980	4.0
4	0	980	5.0
3	0	980	6.0
2	7	987	8.0
1	9	996	10.0
<1	6	1002	30.0

8. Table MN–19 gives a distribution of employees by job and seniority.

9. Productivity changes over the last five years have been as follows: 1984, up 5 percent; 1985, up 3 percent; 1986, up 5 percent; 1987, up 4 percent; and 1988, up 5 percent.

10. You should consider the costs of health fringes, social security and other wage-tied benefits, and changes in the consumer price index (if applicable) when costing contract terms.

11. For wage-comparison purposes, GMFC operations are in Standard Industrial Classification (SIC) codes 3441 (Fabricated Structural Metals), 3443 (Fabricated Plate Work), 3531 (Construction Machinery and Equipment), and 3537 (Industrial Trucks, Tractors, Trailers, and Stackers).

12. Recent selected financial information for this location is shown in Table MN–20.

TABLE MN–19

Seniority Level by Job at End of Expiring Contract

Years of seniority

Data at end of contract	No. employees	<1	1	2	3	4	5	6	7	8	9	10	11	12	13	14	15	16	17	18	19	20	21	22	23	24	25	26	27	28	29	30	Tot.
Assembler B, grade 61	12	2	4	2	0	0	1	3	0	0	0	0	0	0	0	0	0	0	0	0	0	0	0	0	0	0	0	0	0	0	0	0	12
Assembler B, grade 62	87	0	0	0	0	0	0	0	20	6	24	33	4	0	0	0	0	0	0	0	0	0	0	0	0	0	0	0	0	0	0	0	87
Assembler B, grade 63	83	0	0	0	0	0	0	0	0	0	0	0	19	9	40	15	0	0	0	0	0	0	0	0	0	0	0	0	0	0	0	0	83
Assembler B, grade 64	67	0	0	0	0	0	0	0	0	0	0	0	0	0	0	21	46	0	0	0	0	0	0	0	0	0	0	0	0	0	0	0	67
Assembler B, grade 65	48	0	0	0	0	0	0	0	0	0	0	0	0	0	0	0	3	34	4	4	3	0	0	0	0	0	0	0	0	0	0	0	48
Assembler B, grade 66	28	0	0	0	0	0	0	0	0	0	0	0	0	0	0	0	0	0	0	0	0	5	5	7	6	5	0	0	0	0	0	0	28
Assembler B, grade 67	17	0	0	0	0	0	0	0	0	0	0	0	0	0	0	0	0	0	0	0	0	0	0	0	0	1	9	7	0	0	0	0	17
Assembler A, grade 7	11	3	4	4	0	0	0	0	0	0	0	0	0	0	0	0	0	0	0	0	0	0	0	0	0	0	0	0	0	0	0	0	11
Assembler A, grade 8	119	0	0	0	0	0	1	4	30	9	34	41	0	0	0	0	0	0	0	0	0	0	0	0	0	0	0	0	0	0	0	0	119
Assembler A, grade 9	80	0	0	0	0	0	0	0	0	0	0	7	32	14	27	0	0	0	0	0	0	0	0	0	0	0	0	0	0	0	0	0	80
Assembler A, grade 10	95	0	0	0	0	0	0	0	0	0	0	0	0	0	31	52	12	0	0	0	0	0	0	0	0	0	0	0	0	0	0	0	95
Assembler A, grade 11	66	0	0	0	0	0	0	0	0	0	0	0	0	0	0	0	60	6	0	0	0	0	0	0	0	0	0	0	0	0	0	0	66
Assembler A, grade 12	47	0	0	0	0	0	0	0	0	0	0	0	0	0	0	0	0	45	2	0	0	0	0	0	0	0	0	0	0	0	0	0	47
Assembler A, grade 13	37	0	0	0	0	0	0	0	0	0	0	0	0	0	0	0	0	0	5	5	5	7	8	7	0	0	0	0	0	0	0	0	37
Assembler A, grade 14	23	0	0	0	0	0	0	0	0	0	0	0	0	0	0	0	0	0	0	0	0	0	3	9	8	3	0	0	0	0	0	0	23
Assembler A, grade 15	13	0	0	0	0	0	0	0	0	0	0	0	0	0	0	0	0	0	0	0	0	0	0	0	0	4	9	0	0	0	0	0	13
Assembler A, grade 16	9	0	0	0	0	0	0	0	0	0	0	0	0	0	0	0	0	0	0	0	0	0	0	0	0	0	0	6	3	0	0	0	9
Tool and model maker	2	0	0	0	0	0	0	0	0	0	0	0	0	0	0	0	0	0	0	0	0	0	0	0	0	0	0	0	0	1	0	1	2
Tool and die maker	5	0	0	0	0	0	0	0	0	0	0	0	0	0	0	0	0	0	0	0	0	0	0	0	0	0	1	1	1	0	1	1	5
Systems control tech.	1	0	0	0	0	0	0	0	0	0	0	0	0	0	0	0	0	1	0	0	0	0	0	0	0	0	0	0	0	0	0	0	1
Jig grinder operator	4	0	0	0	0	0	0	0	0	0	0	0	0	0	0	0	0	1	1	1	1	0	0	0	0	0	0	0	0	0	0	0	4
Meas. and control tech.	1	0	0	0	0	0	0	0	0	0	0	0	0	0	0	0	0	0	0	0	0	0	0	0	0	0	0	0	0	1	0	0	1
Inst. maint. tech.	2	0	0	0	0	0	0	0	0	0	0	0	0	0	0	0	1	1	0	0	0	0	0	0	0	0	0	0	0	0	0	0	2
Electrician	2	0	0	0	0	0	0	0	0	0	0	0	0	0	0	0	0	0	1	1	0	0	0	0	0	0	0	0	0	0	0	0	2
Machinist	13	0	0	0	0	0	0	0	0	0	0	0	0	0	0	3	4	2	0	0	0	0	0	1	1	1	1	0	0	0	0	0	13
Refrig. and AC mech.	2	0	0	0	0	0	0	0	0	0	0	0	0	0	0	1	1	0	0	0	0	0	0	0	0	0	0	0	0	0	0	0	2
Steamfitter	2	0	0	0	0	0	0	0	0	0	0	0	0	0	0	1	1	0	0	0	0	0	0	0	0	0	0	0	0	0	0	0	2
Devel. electr. tech.	5	0	0	0	0	0	0	0	0	0	0	0	0	0	1	1	2	1	0	0	0	0	0	0	0	0	0	0	0	0	0	0	5
Welder	13	0	0	0	0	0	0	0	0	0	0	0	0	0	2	2	3	2	2	1	1	0	0	0	0	0	0	0	0	0	0	0	13
Millwright mechanic	5	0	0	0	0	0	0	0	0	0	0	0	0	0	0	0	1	1	1	1	1	0	0	0	0	0	0	0	0	0	0	0	5
Maintenance mechanic	6	0	0	0	0	0	0	0	0	0	0	0	0	0	0	1	1	1	1	1	1	0	0	0	0	0	0	0	0	0	0	0	6
Millwright	7	0	0	0	0	0	0	0	0	0	0	0	0	0	1	1	1	1	1	1	1	0	0	0	0	0	0	0	0	0	0	0	7
Precision grinder	2	0	0	0	0	0	0	0	0	0	0	0	0	0	0	0	1	1	0	0	0	0	0	0	0	0	0	0	0	0	0	0	2
Lay. and setup worker	6	0	0	0	0	0	0	0	0	0	0	0	0	0	0	1	1	1	1	1	1	0	0	0	0	0	0	0	0	0	0	0	6

Job title	Total
Painter	3
Profile mill operator	2
Machinist trainee	1
Capital assy. worker	3
Weldment finisher	2
Metal fabricator	4
Grinder operator	7
Milling machine oper.	4
Lathe operator	4
Cabinet maker	2
Head assembly worker	1
Locksmith	1
Specialist	1
Devel. assembler	1
Oiler	7
Steelroom handlers	2
Machine operator	4
Head stockroom clerk	2
Yard worker	1
Stock service worker	1
AC cleaner	1
Truck driver	2
Experimental assembler	1
Tool crib attendant	3
Trades helper	2
Stockroom clerk	2
Assembler	1
Waste hauler	2
Yard laborer	1
Janitor	14
Total by seniority level	**1,002**

TABLE MN-20

Selected Financial Information for This Location

	Income statement (000s)				
	1984	*1985*	*1986*	*1987*	*1988*
Net Sales	98,513	102,019	103,489	108,019	127,864
Deductions					
Cost of materials	50,968	54,234	57,381	59,898	74,890
Depreciation	4,488	4,160	3,818	3,475	3,214
Compensation	30,949	31,919	33,098	34,150	35,293
Interest expense	998	1,173	1,419	1,626	1,721
Extraordinary charges	0	0	1,234	0	0
Profit sharing	1,111	1,053	654	887	1,275
Income before taxes	10,000	9,480	5,885	7,983	11,471
Provision for taxes	4,400	4,171	2,590	3,193	4,588
Net income	5,600	5,309	3,296	4,790	6,883
	Balance sheet (simple)				
Current assets	2,980	3,960	2,741	2,093	• 4,567
Plant and equipment	64,289	65,086	65,827	66,219	67,086
(Less: Accumulated depreciation)	23,489	27,649	31,467	34,942	38,156
Investments	175	10,675	20,325	31,225	40,065
TOTAL ASSETS	43,955	52,072	57,427	64,596	73,562
Current liabilities	1,391	2,349	1,824	2,026	3,108
Long term debt	10,500	12,350	14,934	17,111	18,113
Retained earnings	32,064	37,373	40,669	45,459	52,341
TOTAL LIABILITIES AND CAPITAL	43,955	52,072	57,427	64,596	73,562
	Employment				
Avg. number of employees	1,249	1,208	1,195	1,174	1,153
Bargaining unit employees	1,041	1,026	1,015	1,008	1,002

AGREEMENT

between

GENERAL MANUFACTURING & FABRICATION COMPANY

CENTRAL CITY, INDIANA

and

LOCAL 384, UNITED STEELWORKERS OF AMERICA

AFL–CIO/CLC

Effective March 1, 1986

CONTENTS

ARTICLE 1. PURPOSE

1.01   It is the intent and purpose of the parties hereto that this Agreement will promote and improve industrial and economic relations between the employees and the COMPANY, and to set forth herein a basic agreement covering rates of pay, hours of work, and other conditions of employment to be observed by the parties and to insure the peaceful settlement of disputes and to prevent stoppages of work.

ARTICLE 2. RECOGNITION

2.01   The COMPANY recognizes Local Union No. 384, United Steelworkers of America, AFL–CIO/CLC, as the exclusive bargaining agent for all hourly paid employees designated in the bargaining unit by the National Labor Relations Board for the Central City plant and warehouses, which includes all production and maintenance employees including machine shop employees and receiving department and warehouse employees but excluding boiler room employees, clerical employees, watchpersons, guards, assistant supervisors, supervisors, and any other supervisory employees with authority to hire, promote, discharge, discipline, or otherwise effect changes in the status of employees or effectively recommend such action.

2.02   Any employee who is a member of the UNION on the effective date of this Agreement shall, as a condition of employment, maintain his/her membership in the UNION to the extent of paying membership dues.

2.03   Any employee who on the effective date of this Agreement is not a member of the UNION shall not be required to become a member of the UNION but shall be required to pay an amount equal to the UNION's regular monthly dues. Any such employee, however, who during the life of the Agreement joins the UNION must remain a member as provided in Section 2.02.

ARTICLE 3. CHECKOFF OF UNION DUES

3.01   Upon individual authorization from members, monthly UNION DUES in an amount to be determined by the UNION shall be deducted by the COMPANY from each member's first pay in each month. Such sums shall be forwarded by the COMPANY to the financial secretary of the UNION before the 15th day of the month.

ARTICLE 4. MANAGEMENT

4.01   The UNION and its members recognize that the successful and efficient operation of the business is the responsibility of management and that management of the plant and the direction of the working force is the responsibility of the COMPANY, provided, in carrying out these management functions, the COMPANY does not violate the terms of this Agreement.

4.02   The COMPANY retains the sole right to discipline and discharge employees for cause, provided that in the exercise of this right it will not act wrongfully or unjustly or in violation of the terms of this Agreement.

ARTICLE 5. REPRESENTATION

5.01   The UNION shall designate a UNION COMMITTEE of no more than 10 members who shall represent the UNION in meetings with the COMPANY, with no more than 7 employees actively working in the plant as members of the committee.

5.02   The COMPANY agrees that during meetings held with management members of the UNION required to attend shall be paid at their regular hourly base rate plus their departmental incentive for all time lost from their regularly assigned work schedule.

ARTICLE 6. HOURS

6.01   *Work day.*   A day starts at the beginning of the first shift and ends at the close of the third shift. The first shift is any shift that starts after midnight. Normally the first shift starts at 7:00 A.M. or 8:00 A.M. Present shift schedules will continue unless changes are mutually agreed to by the COMPANY and the UNION.

6.02   *Payroll week.*   The payroll week starts at the beginning of the first shift on Monday and ends at the end of the third shift on Sunday.

6.03   *Daily overtime.*   Time and one half shall be paid for all hours worked in excess of eight in any one day. Time and one half shall be paid for all hours worked in excess of eight in any 24-hour period whenever provisions of the Walsh-Healy Act apply.

6.04   *Weekly overtime.*   Time and one half shall be paid for all hours worked in excess of 40 in any one payroll week for which overtime has not been earned on any other basis.

6.05   *Saturday work.*   Time and one half shall be paid for work performed on Saturday between the hours of 7:00 A.M. or 8:00 A.M. Saturday to 7:00 A.M. or 8:00 A.M. on Sunday.

6.06   *Sunday work.*   Double time shall be paid for work performed on Sunday between the hours of 7:00 A.M. or 8:00 A.M. Sunday to 7:00 A.M. or 8:00 A.M. Monday.

6.07   *Consecutive hours over 8.*   Time and one half shall be paid for all hours worked over 8 but less than 12.

6.08   *Consecutive hours over 12.*   Double time shall be paid for all consecutive hours worked over 12.

6.09   *Distribution of overtime.*   Overtime shall be distributed on an equitable basis within the department in a manner to be decided by the supervision and the UNION representatives in that department, giving consideration to seniority and ability to perform the work. Refused overtime hours shall be credited as overtime hours worked for purposes of distributing overtime.

6.10   *Shift premium.*

      a.   A shift premium of 30 cents per hour will be paid to all employees for all hours worked on a particular day if 50 percent or more of the hours worked on that day fall between the hours of 3:00 P.M. and 11:00 P.M.

      b.   A shift premium of 40 cents per hour will be paid to all employees for all hours worked on a particular day if 50 percent or more of the hours worked on that day fall between the hours of 11:00 P.M. and 7:00 A.M.

      c.   The incentive premium will not be applied to the shift premium.

6.11   *Holidays.*

      a.   After completion of the probationary period an hourly employee not working on the holiday will be granted holiday benefit consisting of eight hours' straight-time pay at his/her regular hourly base rate on the following holidays:

New Year's Day	Thanksgiving
Memorial Day	Christmas
Independence Day	December 24
Labor Day	December 31
Floating Holiday	

b. Double time in addition to the holiday pay, as stated in Section 6.11a, will be paid for all hours worked on the above holidays.

c. The floating holiday will be designated by the COMPANY. The UNION will be notified at least 90 days prior to the day set by the COMPANY.

d. A holiday starts at the beginning of the first shift and ends at the close of the third shift. When one of these holidays falls on Sunday, the holiday shall be observed on Monday. When one of these holidays falls on Saturday, the holiday shall be observed on Friday.

e. To be eligible, the employee must be at work on the days for which he/she is scheduled prior to the holiday and following the holiday unless absence is established for any of the following reasons:

1. Unavoidable absence caused by sickness or injury.
2. Emergencies in the immediate family.
3. Any other justifiable absence previously approved by his/her supervisor.

ARTICLE 7. WAGES

7.01 Effective March 1, 1986, all hourly rates will be contained in the Appendix.

7.02 Effective March 1, 1987, all hourly rates will be increased by $.35.

7.03 Effective March 1, 1988, all hourly rates will be increased by $.40.

7.04 Effective March 1, 1982, all cost-of-living adjustments contained in previous Agreements are suspended.

7.05 Effective March 1, 1982, 10 percent of profits (net income before provision for income taxes) generated by the plant for the calendar year ending on December 31, 1982, and continuing thereafter on December 31 of each calendar year will be divided among members of the bargaining unit. Each employee will receive an amount equal to his/her hours worked divided by the total number of hours worked by the bargaining unit during the calendar year times the profit proportion (if any). Profit-sharing payments will be made not later than January 31 of the following year for distributions earned for the preceding calendar year.

7.06   *Job classification plan.* The principle of like pay for like work shall prevail. The rates for production jobs throughout the plant shall continue to be established or reviewed by the COMPANY and the UNION after careful rating under the job classification plan in proportion to all factors of skill, responsibility, effort, and working conditions of each individual job. When a new job is established or the duties and responsibilities of any job have changed sufficiently to place that job in a different pay bracket, a special job rating to determine the proper rate will be made no later than 30 days from the rating request. A special form for this purpose will be supplied by the COMPANY.

7.07   *Rates retained above classified rates.*

    a. If, as a result of job classification, the classified rate for a job is lowered, the employee on the job will retain his/her current rate for that job. In the event of a wage increase, he/she will participate to the extent that it does not bring his/her rate above the classified rate. Future transfers, promotions, and demotions will conform to the new rate schedule established as a result of job classification. If the higher rate is established as a result of job classification, the employee on the job will advance to the proper classified rate as provided in Section 7.06 unless the job increases two pay grades, in which case it will be posted.

    b. An employee who retains a rate above the classified rate on a job that has been reclassified will be expected to accept promotion to a higher classified job within his/her department in accordance with his/her seniority when a vacancy occurs and he/she is considered qualified to handle the job. In the event the employee who is offered the promotion chooses to remain on his/her present job, he/she will receive the new rate for his/her job on the following Monday, except in cases where the promotion would result in changing from a fixed day shift to a shift operation.

7.08   *New employees.* Employees hired after March 1, 1986, shall be paid at $1.25 per hour less than the rates for their jobs stated in the appendix to this Agreement during the life of this Agreement.

7.09   ***Promotional increases.***   When an employee is promoted to a higher-classified job, he/she will receive the classified rate for the job the first Monday on or after his/her promotion. Employees hired on or after March 1, 1986, will receive $1.25 per hour less than the classified rate.

7.10   ***Temporary service in higher jobs.***

      a.   Temporary work or part-time service in a higher-classified job for periods of less than one full payroll week will not be classified as a promotion or a change in classification. Wherever possible, departmental seniority will be given due consideration in assigning such temporary work.

      b.   When an employee has worked temporarily on a higher-classified job for 50 percent or more of his/her scheduled hours in the week, he/she will receive the higher rate during the week. When an employee is assigned temporary work in a higher classification, he/she shall, whenever possible, be allowed to complete 50 percent or more of the week on the higher-classified job.

7.11   ***Transfers to lower jobs.***   When an employee is permanently transferred to a lower-classified job, he/she will receive the rate for the lower classification the first Monday on or after transfer to the lower-classified job.

7.12   ***Temporary service in lower jobs.***   The COMPANY agrees that, while an employee is assigned temporarily to a lower-classified job, he/she shall receive his/her regular higher-classified rate.

7.13   ***Temporary transfers between departments.***   When in the interest of effective and economical operation or as a means of deferring layoffs, it is desirable to transfer employees temporarily from one department to another, such temporary transfers may be made for a maximum period of four weeks, if mutually agreeable to both the COMPANY and the UNION. Wherever possible, departmental seniority will be given due consideration in determining employees to be transferred. The UNION agrees to cooperate with the COMPANY in arranging such temporary interdepartment transfers. The COMPANY agrees not to request temporary interdepartment transfers except in the interests of efficient and economical operation or as a means of deferring layoff.

7.14   ***Employee reporting and no work available.*** Employees reporting for work according to their regularly assigned work schedules without being notified in advance not to report and work is not available shall be allowed a minimum of four hours' pay at the employees' regular straight-time hourly base rate except in cases beyond the control of the COMPANY.

7.15   ***Call-in pay.*** Employees who have been recalled to work after they have completed their regularly scheduled shift and have left the plant shall be given a minimum of four hours' work if they so desire. If four hours' work is not available, the employee shall be paid the hours worked according to the wage and premium pay policy, and the remainder of the four hours not worked shall be paid at the employee's regular straight-time hourly rate.

7.16   ***Jury duty.*** The COMPANY agrees to pay the difference between jury duty pay and the employee's straight-time hourly base rate earnings when called for jury duty. When called, the employee will be scheduled to work on the first shift whenever possible. The employee shall be required to report for work whenever he/she is able to work four consecutive hours or more of the first shift.

ARTICLE 8. SENIORITY

8.01   ***Plant seniority.*** Plant seniority shall be determined from the employee's earliest date of continuous employment with the COMPANY and shall apply to divisional and plant layoffs and plant recalls after layoff.

8.02   ***Departmental seniority.*** Departmental seniority shall be determined from the employee's earliest date of continuous employment in the department and shall apply to promotions, demotions, and reductions in force within the department.

8.03   ***Termination of seniority.*** Seniority shall terminate for the following reasons:

     a. Voluntary resignation.

     b. Discharge for proper cause.

     c. Absence for three successive working days without notice, unless satisfactory reason is given.

     d. Failure to report to work after layoff within five working days after being notified by registered letter (return receipt requested) at the employee's last available address, unless satisfactory reason is given. A copy of the written offer shall be sent to the UNION.

8.04 **Employees on layoff.**

a. Employees who are or shall be laid off due to lack of work and later reemployed shall retain their seniority as of the time of the layoff but will not accumulate seniority during the layoff period. If an employee after the first six months of layoff declines to return to work when contacted by the production personnel office regarding an opening, his/her seniority rights shall be terminated.

b. Employees shall be given three working days' notice of impending layoff from the plant or three days' pay in lieu thereof.

8.05 **Probationary employees.**

a. A new employee shall be on probation without seniority for 40 days actually worked after date of employment by the COMPANY, during which period the COMPANY shall determine the employee's ability to perform satisfactorily the duties and requirements of the work. Layoff or discharge of an employee during such probationary period shall not be subject to the grievance procedure.

b. Upon satisfactorily completing the probationary period, the employee will be placed on the department's seniority list, and his/her departmental seniority shall date from the beginning of the probationary period. If an employee is transferred to another department during his/her probationary period, his/her departmental seniority shall date back to the date of transfer to the new department upon completion of the probationary period.

8.06 **Promotions and vacancies.** When vacancies are to be filled and increases are to be made in the work force, it shall be done on the following basis:

a. Departmental postings.

1. When vacancies occur in a department, notices shall be posted by the COMPANY for three working days in the department in which the vacancy occurs and a copy of the posting provided to the UNION representatives of the department. Any employee in the department

wishing to fill the vacancy shall make written application on the form provided by the COMPANY containing the following information: *(a)* department and location, *(b)* date and hour of posting, *(c)* serial number of notice, *(d)* job title and classified rate of vacant job, *(e)* date job becomes effective, and *(f)* date and hour of closing time for application.

2. The employee making application with the most departmental seniority shall be given the job, provided he/she is qualified and has the experience to handle the job.

b. ***Plant postings.*** In the event the vacancy is not filled from the employees in the department as outlined above, the COMPANY agrees to post the vacancy in the plant entrances for three working days, and employees will be selected in accordance with Section 8.06a-2. To expedite the processing time, the opening adjudged to be the resulting vacancy may be posted concurrently with the departmental posting. To be eligible for consideration, an employee must make written application on the form provided for the purpose, a copy of which shall be retained by the production personnel office and a copy to be given to the UNION. The rate of pay for the job and the date the employee's seniority shall commence in the new department will be included in the posting.

c. Transfers between "A" and "B" seniority groups will not be allowed.

d. A qualified applicant shall be given a chance to qualify on the job by a fair trial. Any employee who is disqualified for any reason may have his/her qualifications acted upon in accordance with the grievance procedure.

8.07 ***Transfers.***

a. When an employee leaves his/her department to accept a job in another department, his/her seniority rights in the department that he/she left shall not be forfeited for a period of 90 days. If the employee chooses to return to his/her home department (home department is where he/she has recall and return rights) within 90 days from the date of such transfer, he/she shall be returned to his/her former job not later than the third Monday following his/her request, provided he/she has enough seniority; otherwise he/she will be placed in a classification to which his/her seniority entitles him/her, provided it is not higher than the job grade he/she left. If he/she requests transfer to another department within 12 months of his/her return to his/her home department, he/she shall, upon being transferred, forfeit all departmental seniority rights.

b. When an employee has been reduced from his/her home department and is working in another department, he/she may sign plant postings, but the above clause does not apply.

c. If an employee signs a plant posting and during the 90-day period in that job signs another plant posting, he/she has the original 90 days to return to his/her home department but has no right of return to the second department he/she left.

8.08 *Layoffs.*

a. *Departmental.* When the number of employees in a department is reduced, reduction to lower jobs or layoffs shall be made on the basis of departmental seniority, providing those remaining are qualified to perform the work.

b. *Divisional.* The employee ultimately laid off from a department shall be entitled to bump into the department of the least-senior employee in the division on the basis of plant seniority, provided he/she has the necessary qualifications to perform the job to which he/she is assigned. In multiple reductions involving the displacement of employees in the department in which reduction is taking place, the employees with the most departmental seniority of those on the original reduction schedule will be retained in the department, providing employees in the reducing department do not have sufficient plant seniority to allow them to remain in the division. Others reduced from the department will be assigned to one or two shifts according to plant seniority. Upon notification to the production personnel department, special shift requests will be given consideration.

c. *Plant.* The employee laid off from his/her division shall be entitled to bump into the department of the least-senior employee in the plant, providing the claiming employee has the necessary qualifications to perform the job to which he/she is assigned and has more than six months of plant seniority to his/her credit. In case any of the jobs vacated by the least-senior employees in the plant are on a one- or two-shift basis as opposed to the ordinary three-shift basis, the employees being laid off from a division who have the most plant seniority shall automatically be given these one- or two-shift jobs. Upon notification to the production personnel department, special shift requests will be given consideration.

d. The employee so reduced or transferred shall accept, according to his/her seniority, the position vacated to make room for him/her. The supervisor shall have the right to place the crew as he/she sees fit on jobs carrying the same classified rate in all cases of emergencies and vacancies, taking into account the most efficient utilization of his/her working force.

e. When a classification is eliminated, the employee(s) occupying that classification may exercise his/her seniority to claim any classification within the department to which his/her seniority entitles him/her. The employee(s) then affected will follow the normal layoff procedure.

f. Bumping shall not be allowed between "A" and "B" seniority groups.

8.09 ***Recall after layoff.***

a. When it is necessary to employ additional employees, employees laid off due to lack of work will be recalled in order of their plant seniority, providing they are qualified to handle the jobs, before new employees are hired.

b. When an employee is recalled after layoff for a job in another department and accepts, he/she will retain his/her home departmental seniority until such time as he/she declines an opportunity to return to his/her home department, subject to Section 8.07. If a laid-off employee declines, he/she shall remain on recall to his/her home department for a period not to exceed six months after layoff date. If, during the six months' period, the employee wishes to be considered for an opening in another department, he/she may do so by notifying the production personnel office. Thereafter, he/she must return to work when offered employment by the COMPANY or his/her seniority will be terminated.

8.10   *Leaves of absence.*

    a. Members of the UNION, not to exceed three in number at any one time, shall be granted leaves of absence for the duration of this Agreement to work directly for the local UNION. It is further agreed that four additional leaves shall be granted to any employees of the COMPANY covered by this Agreement who have been or who may in the future be elected to or appointed to a full-time office in the international union or the state federation of labor, AFL–CIO, providing that such leaves do not exceed the duration of this Agreement. Upon being relieved of their official positions, they will be entitled to full seniority rights as though they had been employed by the COMPANY continuously.

    b. Employees, not to exceed 1 percent of the UNION's membership, who are members of the UNION when delegated or elected to attend a UNION convention or conference shall be granted such leaves of absence as may be necessary, providing reasonable notice is given the COMPANY.

    c. Any employee elected to or appointed to any federal, state, or city public office shall be granted a leave of absence during the period he/she is actively engaged in such service.

    d. *Maternity leave.*

        1. An employee who becomes pregnant will be granted a leave of absence upon request at any time during pregnancy and extending for three months after the birth of the child. Where leave of absence is taken, such employee shall not lose seniority that was acquired before the beginning of such leave of absence.

        2. All employees placed on maternity leave of absence shall have their seniority dates adjusted upon their return by an amount of time equal to the number of days absent prior to and after the birth of the child.

8.11   **Supervisory and other salaried positions.**

    a. It is recognized that all supervisory employees are

representatives of management and the assignment of their duties, promotions, demotions, and transfers is the responsibility of the COMPANY and cannot be determined on the basis of seniority.

b. Any supervisory employees, including quality supervisors, promoted from any hourly job shall maintain seniority as follows:

1. Hourly employees promoted to supervisory positions prior to January 1, 1980, shall continue to accumulate seniority while holding a supervisory position.

2. Hourly employees promoted to a supervisory position after January 1, 1980, shall accumulate seniority until such a time that he/she holds a supervisory position continuously for six months. After six continuous months his/her seniority in the bargaining unit shall be frozen as of the date of promotion. If later reduced to an hourly job, he/she shall be assigned to the job to which his/her accumulated or frozen seniority entitles him/her in the department that he/she left to become a supervisor, providing he/she is qualified to perform the job and providing the job is not in a higher job grade than the job he/she left to become a supervisor. No supervisor as herein defined shall have posting privileges until 30 days following his/her reassignment to an hourly production job. In return for protecting an employee's seniority while he/she is in a supervisory position as well as allowing him/her the right to claim a job in the bargaining unit if reduced from his/her supervisory position, supervisors who are reduced to hourly jobs shall become members of the UNION within 30 days.

c. Supervisory and other salaried employees will not perform the work of hourly production employees except in cases of emergency.

ARTICLE 9. GRIEVANCE PROCEDURE AND NO–STRIKE AGREEMENT

9.01 ***Departmental representatives.*** The UNION may designate representatives for each section on each shift and in each department for the purpose of handling grievances that may arise in that department. The UNION will inform the production personnel office in writing as to the names of the authorized representatives. Should differences arise as to the intent and application of the provisions of this Agreement, there shall be no strike, lockout, slowdown, or work stoppage of any kind, and the controversy shall be settled in accordance with the following grievance procedures.

9.02 ***Grievances.***

Step 1. The employee and the departmental steward, if the employee desires, shall take the matter up with his/her supervisor. If no settlement is reached in Step 1 within two working days, the grievance shall be reduced to writing on the form provided for that purpose.

Step 2. The written grievance shall be presented to the supervisor or the general supervisor and a copy sent to the production personnel office. Within two working days after receipt of the grievance, the general supervisor shall hold a meeting, unless mutually agreed otherwise, with the supervisor, the employee, and the departmental steward and the chief steward.

Step 3. If no settlement is reached in Step 2, the written grievance shall be presented to the departmental superintendent, who shall hold a meeting within five working days of the original receipt of the grievance in Step 2 unless mutually agreed otherwise. Those in attendance shall normally be the departmental superintendent, the general supervisor, the supervisor, the employee, the chief steward, departmental steward, a member of the production personnel department, the president of the UNION or his/her representative, and the divisional committeeperson.

Step 4. If no settlement is reached in Step 3, the UNION COMMITTEE and a national representative of the UNION shall meet with the MANAGEMENT COMMITTEE for the purpose of settling the matter.

Step 5. If no settlement is reached in Step 4, the matter shall be referred to an arbitrator. A representative of the UNION shall meet within five working days with a representative of the

COMPANY for the purpose of selecting an arbitrator. If an arbitrator cannot be agreed upon within five working days after Step 4, a request for a list of arbitrators shall be sent to the Federal Mediation and Conciliation Service. Upon obtaining the list, an arbitrator shall be selected within five working days. Prior to arbitration, a representative of the UNION shall meet with a representative of the COMPANY to reduce to writing wherever possible the actual issue to be arbitrated. The decision of the arbitrator shall be final and binding on all parties. The salary, if any, of the arbitrator and any necessary expense incident to the arbitration shall be paid jointly by the COMPANY and the UNION.

9.03   In order to assure the prompt settlement of grievances as close to their source as possible, it is mutually agreed that the above steps will be followed strictly in the order listed and no step shall be used until all previous steps have been exhausted. A settlement reached between the COMPANY and the UNION in any step of this procedure shall terminate the grievance and shall be final and binding on both parties.

9.04   The arbitrator shall not have authority to modify, change, or amend any of the terms or provisions of the Agreement or to add to or delete from the Agreement.

9.05   The UNION will not cause or permit its members to cause or take part in any sit-down, stay-in, or slowdown in any plant of the COMPANY or any curtailment of work or restriction of production or interference with the operations of the COMPANY.

9.06   The UNION will not cause or permit its members to cause or take part in any strike of any of the COMPANY's operations, except where the strike has been fully authorized as provided in the constitution of the international union.

ARTICLE 10.   VACATIONS

10.01   The vacation year shall be from April 1 to and including March 31. Wherever possible, however, vacations shall be taken before December 31 of any one year. Vacations for any two years shall not be taken consecutively.

10.02   ***One week's vacation.***   One week's vacation with pay (see Section 10.07) will be granted to an employee who has accumulated 12 months or more of service credit prior to September 30 of the vacation year, provided he/she has accumulated a minimum of 6 months' service credit during the 12-month period immediately preceding April 1 of the vacation year and is actively working on or after April 1 of the vacation year.

10.03   ***Two weeks' vacation.***   Two weeks' vacation with pay (see Section 10.07) will be granted to an employee who has accumulated 36 months or more of service credit by December 31 of the vacation year, provided he/she has accumulated a minimum of 6 months' service credit during the 12-month period immediately preceding April 1 of the vacation year and is actively working on or after April 1 of the vacation year.

10.04   ***Three weeks' vacation.***   Three weeks' vacation with pay (see Section 10.07) will be granted to an employee who will complete 120 months or more of service credit by December 31 of the vacation year, provided he/she has accumulated a minimum of 6 months' service credit during the 12-month period immediately preceding April 1 of the vacation year and is actively working on or after April 1 of the vacation year.

10.05   ***Four weeks' vacation.***   Four weeks' vacation with pay (see Section 10.07) will be granted to an employee who will complete 180 months or more of service credit by December 31 of the vacation year, provided he/she has accumulated a minimum of 6 months' service credit during the 12-month period immediately preceding April 1 of the vacation year and is actively working on or after April 1 of the vacation year.

10.06   ***Five weeks' vacation.***   Five weeks' vacation with pay (see Section 10.07) will be granted to an employee who will complete 300 months or more of service credit by December 31 of the vacation year, provided he/she has accumulated a minimum of 6 months' service credit during the 12-month period immediately preceding April 1 of the vacation year and is actively working on or after April 1 of the vacation year.

10.07   One week of vacation pay shall consist of 40 hours' pay at the employee's regular straight-time hourly base rate plus the average incentive percentage of the eight weeks prior to April 1 of the department in which he/she is working at the time the vacation is taken.

10.08   If a holiday recognized with this Agreement falls within an employee's vacation period, he/she shall be granted an extra day of vacation, provided the employee is eligible for holiday pay on that holiday.

10.09   Any employee who is discharged for proper cause will not be eligible for vacation.

10.10   Vacations shall be granted at such times of the year as the COMPANY finds most suitable, considering both the wishes of the employee according to plant seniority and the requirements of plant operation.

10.11   Employees who are laid off will be granted the vacation to which they are otherwise ineligible if they have worked a minimum of 1,600 straight-time hours since the previous April 1.

ARTICLE 11.   SICK LEAVE

11.01   ***Employees with one- to five-year service credit.*** Employees who have accumulated 12 months but less than 60 months of service credit shall be entitled to a maximum of four working days' sick leave (32 hours straight-time pay at the employee's regular hourly base rate) in any one year calculated from April 1 to March 31, inclusive. Such benefits, not to exceed eight hours in any day, will apply only to time lost from scheduled work for reasons of personal illness or injury except that no benefits will be paid for the first two scheduled working days of any period of such absence.

11.02   ***Employees with five or more years of service credit.***

    a. *Eligibility.* A five-year employee who has accumulated 60 months of service credit will receive the difference between sickness and accident insurance or worker's compensation benefits for which he/she is eligible and his/her regular hourly base rate for time lost due to unavoidable absence as defined in Section 11.02e, which occurs during the first 40 hours he/she is scheduled to work in any week, not to exceed 8 hours in any one day, and subject to Section 11.02d.

    b. *Amount of benefits.* The benefits made available each year shall be 80 hours. The year starts April 1. Combined benefits on any day of qualified absence shall total the amount equal to the number of qualified hours multiplied by the employee's base rate. In no instance shall this payment total more than base rate earnings of 8 hours per scheduled work day nor more than base rate earnings of 40 hours per scheduled work week. In other words, the COMPANY shall supplement with sick leave pay ments any compensation or insurance payments from a company-financed private or government plan with an amount of money sufficient to make the combined total payment equal to 8 hours of base rate pay per day of qualified absence or 40 hours per week of qualified absence.

1. If the employee qualifies for compensation from a company-financed private or governmental plan, his/her available sick leave benefits will be charged 19.9 hours per 40-hour week or 49.8 percent of the eligible working hours absent for part weeks. If the employee does not qualify for compensation from a company-financed private or governmental plan, his/her available sick leave benefits will be charged with 100 percent of the eligible working hours absent.

c. *Accumulation.*

1. Sick leave benefits unused in any year of the plan may be accumulated for possible use in the next two years. When fourth-year benefits become available, the unused benefits from the first year automatically cancel and so on for each succeeding year. Order of sick leave usage is, first, the current year's benefits and second, the oldest year's benefits. Employees out sick before April 1 whose absence due to that illness extends through April 1 will first use those benefits that were available at the commencement of the absence.

d. *Waiting period.* There shall be no waiting period for the first five days (40 hours) of sick leave usage in a benefit year. However, no benefits shall be payable for the first normally scheduled working day in any period of absence commencing thereafter.

e. Unavoidable absence is defined as follows:

1. Unavoidable absence caused by sickness or injury.
2. Emergencies in the immediate family.

f. Immediate family shall consist of the following with no exceptions:

Spouse	Son	Sister
Mother	Daughter	Mother-in-law
Father	Brother	Father-in-law

In addition, the death of the employee's grandfather or grandmother will be recognized as an emergency in the immediate family to the extent of allowing one day's benefit, provided it is necessary that he/she be absent.

11.03   *a.* A 15-year hourly employee will receive straight-time pay at his/her regular hourly base rate for time lost due to hospitalization in a recognized hospital or convalescence thereafter that occurs during the first 40 hours he/she is scheduled to work in any week not to exceed 8 hours in any day. The total amount of such allowance will not exceed 80 hours in any one year, calculated from year to year. Benefits provided in this paragraph will not apply to days of unavoidable absence for which benefits are paid under the provisions of Section 11.02.

   b. A 25-year hourly employee will receive straight-time pay at his/her regular hourly base rate for time lost due to hospitalization in a recognized hospital or convalescence thereafter that occurs during the first 40 hours he/she is scheduled to work in any week not to exceed 8 hours in any day. The total amount of such allowance will not exceed 160 hours [an additional 80 hours to *(a)* above] in any one year, calculated from year to year. Benefits provided in this paragraph will not apply to days of unavoidable absence for which benefits are paid under the provisions of Section 2 above.

11.04   In order to obtain these benefits, the employee shall, if required, furnish his/her supervisor satisfactory reason for absence.

11.05   The COMPANY and the UNION agree to cooperate in preventing and correcting abuses of these benefits.

ARTICLE 12.   GENERAL

12.01   ***Bulletin boards.*** The COMPANY shall provide bulletin boards that may be used by the UNION for posting notices approved by the industrial relations manager or someone designated by him/her and restricted to:

   a. Notices of UNION recreational and social affairs.
   b. Notices of UNION elections.
   c. Notices of UNION appointments and results of UNION elections.
   d. Notices of UNION meetings.
   e. And other notices mutually agreed to.

12.02   ***Relief periods.***
  a. Relief periods of 25 minutes for every eight-hour work period will be on COMPANY time at such times in each department as will be most beneficial to the employees and the COMPANY. A lunch period on COMPANY time may be substituted for relief period, provided the total time allowed for lunch and relief period in an eight-hour work period does not exceed 25 minutes.
  b. The relief and lunch periods in each department will be determined by the department supervisors and the UNION stewards, considering both the wishes of the employees and the requirements of efficient departmental operations.

12.03   All benefits now in effect and not specifically mentioned in this Agreement affecting all hourly paid employees of the COMPANY shall not be terminated for the duration of this Agreement.

12.04   ***Sickness and accident.*** The COMPANY agrees to maintain its current sickness and accident insurance plans, as amended, effective December 1, 1985. Benefits begin one month after the sickness and accident initially occurred and continue for six months. Benefits will be equal to 60 percent of the employee's straight-time wage at the time of the sickness or accident.

12.05   ***Long-term disability plan.*** Subject to the provisions and qualifications of the long-term disability plan, there will be available monthly income benefits commencing after 26 weeks of continuous disability and continuing until recovery or death but not beyond the normal retirement date. The monthly amount will be $25 per $1,000 on the first $10,000 of group life insurance.

12.06   ***Group life insurance.***
  a. The COMPANY will pay for the first $1,000 of group life insurance available to employees. Employees will have the option of purchasing an additional amount of insurance in accordance with their earnings class schedule.
  b. The present permanent and total disability benefit is replaced by a disability waiver-of-premium provision under which coverage will be continued during periods of total disability, while long-term disability payments are being made, but reduced each month by the amount of the long-term disability benefit. Reductions will cease when the amount of

insurance in force is equal to the greater of *(a)* 25 percent of the original amount or *(b)* the employee's post-retirement life amount calculated as of the date of commencement of LTD payments. Coverage will be reduced to the latter amount at the earlier of *(a)* normal retirement age or *(b)* commencement of any income under ERI.

12.07   *Retirement income plan.*
  a. The COMPANY will contribute an amount equal to 5 percent of each employee's straight-time earnings to the retirement trust fund administered by Commonwealth National Bank, Central City, Indiana.
  b. The COMPANY will provide for 100 percent vesting in pension benefits after five (5) years' service.
  c. Contributions and any investment income earned on them that are forfeited by employees who terminate prior to the vesting of pension benefits will be returned to the COMPANY.

12.08   The COMPANY will contract with Indiana Blue Cross-Blue Shield to provide hospitalization and medical insurance for all employees and their family members residing at home (except children over 21). The COMPANY will pay all premiums necessary to provide full coverage of necessary surgical, medical, and hospital care under Blue Cross-Blue Shield fee schedules when performed in a participating hospital.

12.09   Departmental agreements between COMPANY and UNION representatives shall not supersede provisions contained in this Agreement should controversies arise. In no case, however, shall any retroactive adjustment be made if and when such a departmental agreement is cancelled. Wherever possible, the UNION shall receive a copy of the agreement.

12.10   *Safety.*
  a. The COMPANY will make reasonable provisions for the safety and health of the employees of the plant during the hours of their employment. Such protective devices and other safety equipment as the COMPANY may deem necessary to protect employees from injury properly shall be provided by the COMPANY without cost to the employees. The supervisor in each department will arrange for this equipment.
  b. Gloves and uniforms required on such jobs and in

       such departments as the COMPANY may deem necessary shall be furnished and maintained by the COMPANY.

c. The UNION agrees in order to protect the employees from injury and to protect the facilities of the plant that it will cooperate to the fullest extent in seeing that the rules and regulations are followed and that it will lend its wholehearted support to the safety program of the COMPANY.

d. Rotating UNION departmental representatives chosen by the UNION will participate in periodic safety inspections conducted by departmental supervision and safety staff.

e. The COMPANY agrees that it will give full consideration to all suggestions from its employees of their representatives in matters pertaining to safety and health, including proper heating and ventilation, and if these suggestions are determined to be sound, steps will be taken to put them into effect.

f. It shall be considered a regular part of each employee's regular work to attend such safety meetings as may be scheduled by the COMPANY. Hours spent at safety meetings will be compensated for as hours worked.

g. It is understood that the COMPANY shall not be required to provide work for employees suffering from compensable or other injuries; the COMPANY, however, will offer regular work that may be available to such employees, provided that they can perform all duties of the job.

12.11   Other than for the recall provisions of the Agreement and the privileges accorded an employee under the COMPANY group insurance plans, employees on layoff shall not be entitled to the benefits of this Agreement.

12.12   ***Supplementary unemployment benefit plan.***

a. *Objective.* To provide a greater measure of income protection during periods of unemployment for all eligible employees by supplementing state unemployment benefit payments.

b. *Suspension of plan.* Due to the financial difficulties recently experienced by the COMPANY, the supplementary unemployment benefit plan is suspended for the duration of this Agreement.

c. *Reinstatement of plan.* When and if the supplementary unemployment benefit plan is reinstated, the level of benefits, and length of service requirements for eligibility to receive benefits, entitlement to reinstatement of benefits, and methods for obtaining benefits will be determined through negotiations between the COMPANY and the UNION.

12.13 In the event any section or any article of this Agreement shall be found to be illegal or inoperable by any government authority of competent jurisdiction, the balance of the Agreement shall remain in full force and effect.

12.14 *Nondiscrimination agreement.*

   a. The COMPANY and the UNION agree that the provisions of this agreement shall apply to all employees covered by the Agreement without discrimination, and, in carrying out their respective obligations, it neither will discriminate against any employee on account of race, color, national origin, age, sex, or religion.

   b. In an effort to make the grievance procedure a more effective instrument for the handling of any claims of discrimination, special effort shall be made by the representatives of each party to raise such claims where they exist and at as early a stage in the grievance procedure as possible. If not earlier, a claim of discrimination shall be stated at least in the third-step proceedings. The grievance and arbitration procedure shall be the exclusive contractual procedure for remedying discrimination claims.

ARTICLE 13. RENEWAL

13.01 This Agreement shall become effective as of March 1, 1986, and shall continue in full force and effect until 11:59 P.M., February 28, 1989, and thereafter from year to year unless written notice to modify, amend, or terminate this Agreement is served by either party 60 days prior to the expiration of this Agreement, stating in full all changes desired.

13.02 After receipt of such notice by either party, both parties shall meet for the purpose of negotiating a new agreement within 30 days from the date of service of said notice, unless the time is extended by mutual agreement.

APPENDIX

Job title	Wage rate	Job title	Wage rate
Assembler B, grade 61	7.65	Maintenance mechanic	10.24
Assembler B, grade 62	7.715	Millwright	10.24
Assembler B, grade 63	7.78	Precision grinder	10.24
Assembler B, grade 64	7.845	Layout and setup worker	10.15
Assembler B, grade 65	7.91	Painter	10.15
Assembler B, grade 66	7.975	Profile mill operator	9.82
Assembler B, grade 67	8.04	Machinist trainee	9.82
Assembler A, grade 7	8.155	Capital assembly worker	9.63
Assembler A, grade 8	8.25	Weldment finisher	9.63
Assembler A, grade 9	8.345	Metal fabricator	8.55
Assembler A, grade 10	8.44	Grinder operator	8.55
Assembler A, grade 11	8.535	Milling machine operator	8.55
Assembler A, grade 12	8.63	Lathe operator	8.55
Assembler A, grade 13	8.725	Cabinet maker	8.55
Assembler A, grade 14	8.82	Head assembly worker	8.48
Assembler A, grade 15	8.915	Locksmith	8.41
Assembler A, grade 16	9.01	Specialist	8.32
Tool and model maker	10.99	Developmental assembler	8.18
Tool and die maker	10.78	Oiler	8.13
Systems control technician	10.60	Steelroom handler	8.105
Jig grinder operator	10.51	Machine operator	8.105
Measurement and control technician	10.42	Head stockroom clerk	8.105
		Yard worker	7.98
Instrument maintenance technician	10.42	Stock service worker	7.98
Electrician	10.42	Air conditioning cleaner	7.98
Machinist	10.33	Truck driver	7.82
Refrigeration and air conditioning mechanic	10.33	Experimental assembler	7.85
		Tool crib attendant	7.85
Steamfitter	10.33	Trades helper	7.85
Development electronics technician	10.33	Stockroom clerk	7.85
		Assembler	7.635
Welder	10.24	Waste hauler	7.61
Millwright mechanic	10.24	Yard laborer	7.61
		Janitor	7.565

CHAPTER 11

Impasses and Their Resolution

All negotiations do not result in an agreement. If a person is looking for a car and the dealer is unwilling to sell at the highest offer, a sale is not made. The same thing happens in labor–management negotiations when management and the union cannot agree on the terms of a new contract. This inability to agree is called an impasse. Unlike the car purchase situation, the union is not free to seek a new employer to deal with, and the company must still be willing to negotiate with the union representing its employees.

Most negotiations do not result in an impasse. The parties usually find a common ground for settlement, and strikes or interventions by third parties are not required. Recent data show that for the early 1980s about 24 million workdays per year were lost to strikes—only about .11 percent of total time available.[1]

This chapter examines the causes of impasses, the tactics available to either side after an impasse is reached, and the interventions of third parties. This chapter focuses on the private sector. Public-sector impasse resolution procedures, which are generally more complex and often applicable only to certain occupational classifications, are covered in Chapter 15.

In reading this chapter, attention should be focused on these issues:

1. What differences exist in the way impasses are handled in organizations covered by the Railway Labor Act?
2. What actions can labor and management legally take when an impasse is reached?

---

[1] *Monthly Labor Review*, March 1984, p. 103.

3. What is involved in the mediation process?
4. What steps do private enterprise and labor take to reduce the incidence of impasses?

IMPASSE DEFINITION

A bargaining impasse occurs when the parties are unable to move further toward settlement. The impasse may result because the settlement ranges of both parties are nonoverlapping—the least the union is willing to take is more than the most the employer is willing to offer. It may also result because the parties have been unable or unwilling to communicate enough information about possible settlements for an agreement to be reached. The first type of impasse is relatively more difficult to overcome, because it requires either or both parties to adjust their settlement ranges to reach a solution. The second type may be helped by outside parties facilitating communication and keeping the parties working toward a settlement.

Impasses resolved with the help of third parties are dealt with first by examining the procedures used to open communications, allow reassessment and adjustment of bargaining stances, and lead toward settlement. Because employees in most public-sector jobs are precluded by law from striking (although plentiful evidence demonstrates the law's general unenforceability), the use of third parties is more prevalent there. The general types of third-party interventions used across both public and private sectors are covered here, and their application in public jurisdictions is explained in greater detail in Chapter 15.

THIRD–PARTY INVOLVEMENT

Three major types of third-party interventions are mediation, fact-finding, and arbitration. Each becomes progressively more constraining on the freedom of the parties; but in most private-sector negotiations (except for health care organizations covered under federal legislation) the parties have to agree voluntarily before any third-party involvement can be imposed on them. The only major exception involves national emergency disputes under the Taft-Hartley Act, in which outside fact-finding is required. However, Taft-Hartley procedures have not been imposed during the 1980s.

MEDIATION

In mediation, a neutral third party attempts to assist the principals toward reaching agreement. The procedures used are tailored to the situation and aimed at maintaining communications and pointing out settlement cues the parties may have missed.

While some parties use mediation as a matter of course, the mediator is frequently dealing with a situation where the parties have been unable to reach an agreement on their own. Mediation may not be requested until an impasse has been reached and negotiations have broken off. The mediator may have trouble not only in getting a settlement but also in getting the sides back together to bargain. As a show of bargaining strength, both sides may refuse to propose a bargaining session; and as the coverage on behavioral issues in bargaining showed in Chapter 10, if one side appeared willing to reopen bargaining, the other might interpret that willingness as weakness.

The mediator must ultimately get the parties face to face to reach a settlement, but often many sessions will be held between the mediator and a party to assess possibilities of movement. Changing the location of a meeting to the mediator's office may increase the mediator's strength in the process. Mediation requires the parties to continue to communicate and negotiate, but not at an intensity leading to a hardening of positions.[2]

Because the parties have reached an impasse, the mediator not only has to keep communications open but also must move the parties toward settlement, if possible. Mediators apparently use one of two approaches. In the public sector, where bargainers may be less experienced, mediators may try to create an acceptable package by obtaining the facts in dispute and the priorities of the parties regarding a settlement. With this information, mediators then attempt to "make a deal" both parties can accept. In private-sector mediation involving federal mediators, settlements are "orchestrated" through exchanging information to build a settlement the parties recognize as acceptable. Mediators let the parties establish their own priorities and help them prepare proposals in the negotiation process.[3]

To get an assessment of settlement possibilities, the mediator may try out hypothetical settlements to see the parties' reactions. The relative rigidity of a party's position must also be assessed so the mediator knows whether the party is willing to compromise on given issues. As a strike deadline approaches, the mediator must communicate assessments of the likelihood of a strike, the possible settlement packages available, and the costs of striking versus settling on one of the present proposals.

A few excerpts from Ann Douglas's classic work on mediation helps show the role of the mediator in resolving disputes.[4] In Exhibit

---

[2] William E. Simkin, *Mediation and the Dynamics of Collective Bargaining* (Washington, D.C.: Bureau of National Affairs, 1971).

[3] Deborah M. Kolb, "Strategy and the Tactics of Mediation," *Human Relations*, 1983, pp. 247–68.

[4] Ann Douglas, *Industrial Peacemaking* (New York: Columbia University Press, 1962).

EXHIBIT 11-1

M: Well, look, fellows, to get this started, I don't know how much I rea— how much time I really need with you. I had a pretty good idea last time of just what you wanted, what were the basic demands, and most prob'ly, I have more work to do with the company at this point than with you. However, I do want to do one thing tonight. I wanta go over with you what the company has responded with respect to each of the nine basic demands you substituted, plus get your thinking on each of the company's counterproposals. Now, before we get into that, I want to spend a minute or two with something else. I wanta remind you of something I used as a comparison of one of the early cases we had. You recall at that time I said that, in a sense, we all do bargaining in one form or another on many occasions, and I used the example of any one of you who might have an automobile that ya wanted to sell. What ya did was dress the thing up, make it look as attractive as possible, and put the highest price you felt you could reasonably ask on it. When a prospective purchaser came around, you gave him the best sales talk you could give, but ordinarily you did not expect he was going to say "Yes." Ya expected he was going to haggle a little bit, and when he did, ya tried to think up some arguments to counter those that he advanced. Ya try to indicate to him that the lower price he was offering was not a proper price. Maybe you would even go back in the garage and dig up another spare tire or something else to make the car a little bit more attractive, and you would keep on haggling with him over price. And eventually he would offer something that was worthwhile to you, for which you would make the swap. Now, in that sort of thing, you didn't get overly mad. Ya took it as part of the game you were playing. I'm not saying, that in collective bargaining, where you're dealing with—with much more serious things, and things which are not quite within your control as is the sale of an automobile. You can either sell it or not sell it; you don't have to. With a contract, though, ya do have to conclude it, and ya have some compulsion here which was not present in any individual bargaining you might do over a personal effect. But there are a lot of elements of sameness; and just as you would do in a private transaction, so, in part, you must do here. When you make a proposal, until ya come right down to the end of the wire, where ya have most everything settled and it's a matter of saying "Yes" or "No" to a couple of final propositions, ya got to expect that what you're going to get is a tentative "Maybe," usually ah— to which is usually added a couple of other propositions, and it becomes a switch back and forth, a jockeying to try and get the most of what you want, knowing that the company is going to do the same thing. Now, I mention these things because I want to remind you that last time I said that I did not think

---

11-1, the mediator gives the union caucus some background on negotiating to make them see the processes necessary to reach a settlement. (**M** stands for the mediator; **U1** is the union's chief negotiator; **U2** is second in line; and so forth. **C1, C2,** and so on are company negotiators).

In Exhibit 11-2, the mediator meets with company negotiators. He asks them to examine positions, sees where movement can be made,

EXHIBIT 11-1 *(concluded)*

the company counterdemands, which you felt pretty strongly about, were
things to get too seriously concerned with, for, as far as I knew at that point—
they may be, but as far as I know, they do not represent a final company
position. If they did, then I think that you would be logically entitled to say—
and holler every sort of implication you could think of. But I don't think that
that's what they represent. I think what is called for after this is some further
thinking, some further proposals on your part. What I want to do is to find out,
how much that the company offered in connection with the counterproposals
they made to your nine proposals is acceptable to you, either as they have
stated it or in some modified form. I want to find out, secondly, what there is
in the company's additional nine proposals you think have any merit or that
you're willing to go along with, either as they stated or in some modified form.
This for my information. Tomorrow I have to do the same thing with management. How much of what the union—of what they said in their counterproposals did they say for bargaining purposes, how much closer to what
they know the union wants are they willing to go?—that, again, is confidential
with me. When I have those two things, then I can see how really far apart you
are, and it becomes a problem, then, of trying to get you to go a little bit this
way on that business, gettin' the company to go a little bit your way on some
other matter, until we reach the point where it looks like we have something
that is an agreeable thing with you, something that's agreeable with them. And
the only way we can do that is through this point-by-point discussion. I want
to repeat that what you have to say concerning it is between you and I.
Concessions that you tell me you are prepared to make are not told to the
company. Concessions the company tell me they are prepared to make are not
told to you at this point. For what you will be willing to do, what they will be
willing to do will be perhaps to make concessions on one item, providing they
get a counter-, or you get a counter-, concession on another item. So until the
whole thing is squared up, I have to be the repository of your confidence and of
theirs. So, to get to this, then (pause), let's start with their response in connection with No. 1, two-year contract. And this is what I want to know. If you
gave them a two-year contract, what would you want in return? Of what
advantage is it to you to say, "We'll give you a two-year contract"? What can
you get out of them in return?

Source: Ann Douglas, *Industrial Peacemaking* (New York: Columbia University Press, 1962),
pp. 56–58.

and stresses the difficulties that lie ahead. Notice he refuses to tip his
hand about information he may have on the union's position.

Returning to the union caucus, the mediator is still not specific
about the positions taken by management but does say a gap exists in
the settlement range. He also continues his lessons on bargaining in
Exhibit 11–3.

The exchanges depicted in the exhibits and the crisis atmosphere

EXHIBIT 11–2

From the Second Management Caucus with the Mediator:

M: Well, what I'd like to do today is go over the company's counterproposals to the union's proposals and see how much it means, actually,
how much room there is to move around in connection with the various points
you have made, and I want this for my own information. I've already discussed
a good bit of this with the union, so I have some notions on what they will and
will not do. I wanta get similar notions from you and see whether or not
actually you're really closer together than you appear on the surface. I'll say
this pretty frankly, that quite probably there's goin' ta have ta be a lot of
shaking down before you get to an agreement. The union is undoubtedly
holding out for more now than you're prepared to give, and they're going to
have to come down (*C2:* Uh-huh) in a number of respects.

C2: Any particular areas?

M: U1—(slight pause) I won't say now. Just (*C2:* Uh-huh) as a general
position, they would appear to be holding to some things which are unlikely to
come their way. I mention this because I think in part they're holding to them
out of a belief that you, in your counterproposals, have advanced some rather
unreasonable notion.

C1: You mean unreasonable to them.

M: Oh, of course (laughing). Not to me, never? (*C1, C2,* and *M* all laugh)
Not for recording on tape.

M: No, but I expect to get at least part of it today.

C1: What you're tryin' to do is find out where the soft spots are.

M: Yeah, and without presenting as notions the union might have to you,
I shall discuss these things from the point of view of softening your position.
Again I say that this is between us and for my information to see where I can
then approach the union to get them to do likewise, and if we can get enough of
that done, why, the thing may not look quite as black as it appears to the union
to be.

Source: Ann Douglas, *Industrial Peacemaking* (New York: Columbia University Press, 1962),
p. 91.

in which mediators operate require a special mix of experience, talents,
and behaviors.

Mediator Behavior and Outcomes

While the mediation scenarios presented in the exhibits cast the mediator in the roles of teacher and communicator, not all mediations
follow this approach. Mediators may be either "deal makers" or "orchestrators," with the former approach used most often by mediators

EXHIBIT 11–3

From the Mediator's Third Caucus with the Union:

U1: What's their attitudes on—their position as to our minimum demand? Are they altering those?

M: Well, you have their counterproposal, which is very definitely not acceding to your minimum demand. See, I—I don't understand minimum demand (*U1:* Well, you gotta remember that—)—what you mean by minimum demands. If you have to have everything such as this, then there's no room for bargaining.

U1: No. But we'd like to know if their counterproposal to ours is their final position.

M: Well, I just explained it. I've just told you the answer to that.

U2: Which?

M: That I've found that there is things in their position (*U2:* That's what—) that are bargainable (*U2:* Well—), which merely means that they are not saying to you, or they're not saying to me that "What we have answered the union is as far as we'll go."

U2: See what's happened, U1? We—when we went through—pract'ly went through all of these here and gave 'em our minimum demands, now what they're doin' is just knockin' them down to where—

U1: Yeah!

U2: The way it is now, we want all of ours.

U3: That's were the stalemate is.

M: No! The stalemate is that after you gave the company this offer, the company made a counteroffer and then you quit bargaining.

U1: We didn't quit bargaining. They did.

U3: They did.

M: All right. There was no cause for further reaction on your part directly to what they had said and that's what I am trying to get. Ordinarily in these things, it's a series. You demand, they reply; you demand, they reply; you demand, they reply; you demand, they reply. Somewhere in there—and this is exactly the way it looks—you start here with your demand. They reply. Then on down, each counterdemand is met with a counterreply until you reduce the difference (*U2:* Well, the—) the point where you reach an agreement. Now—

U4: Fact, all the time we're in there, M, we're t—all the time we were talking about their proposals. We hardly, if ever, mentioned our own proposals, because we figured when they got through we'd have our chance, and we never got our chance to talk.

U5: (Over *U4* above) U4, as far as language is—is concerned, the whole thing is in a package and what—C1 is sittin' back, little ah—oh, one of these here chess players with the idea he just—he can take and move us fellows like we's just pawns or somethin' there. He just tryin' to—

EXHIBIT 11-3 *(concluded)*

U4: We never ran into that before. I mean—

M: (Over *U4* above) Well, look. How—how would you propose that you go about—about reaching an agreement? What's your idea of how you do these things?

U1: They never once discussed any of our demands, never (*M:* Well—), and that's what we were asking for. (*M:* And—) Uh—

M: If they didn't discuss them, it was because you didn't insist on it, because you certainly have a right to discuss your own demands. (*U1:* We insisted on those.) If you start, then they got to respond. You'll haggle back and forth until you get what is reasonably satisfactory. Now, when you tell me that you'll take 4 cents plus—4-cent improvement factor each year plus the cost-of-living adjustment, I am not going to tell them that. If anything, I might tell 'em, well, you'll take 10 cents plus their—no, I won't tell them you'll take. I'll ask them, "Well, what do you say—give 'em 10 cents plus the cost-of-living, huh?" to give me some room to move around. I gotta bargain with them, so I can't—I'm not gonna give them minimums. (Laughs) I'll stretch the minimum so I can come back a little bit.

Source: Ann Douglas, *Industrial Peacemaking* (New York: Columbia University Press, 1962), pp. 59–60.

who feel their clients are inexperienced in negotiations. Research has found deal makers are more likely than orchestrators to run into problems in consummating their deals and getting agreements.[5]

Other variables suggested as influencing mediator behavior and bargaining outcomes revolve around the intensity of the dispute and the intensity of the mediator's activities. Dispute intensity reduces the likelihood that a mediator can achieve a settlement, particularly for impasses involving the employer's inability to pay the increase demanded. Mediators appear more effective in achieving settlements when they act aggressively and in cases where negotiations have broken down.[6] Intense impasses characterized by such conditions as a new bargaining relationship, dislike between key negotiators, conflict within the management or union team, high union strength, pattern bargaining, and an inability to pay appear more frequently assisted in resolution by mediators who become intensely involved in the process. High-intensity mediation includes a willingness to get true feelings before the parties and to discuss the real costs of the proposed pack-

---

[5] Deborah M. Kolb, "Roles Mediators Play: Contrasts and Comparisons in State and Federal Mediation Practice," *Industrial Relations*, Winter 1981, pp. 1–17.

[6] Thomas A. Kochan and Todd Jick, "A Theory of the Public-Sector Mediation Process," *Journal of Conflict Resolution*, June 1978, pp. 209–41.

ages. Low-intensity mediation appears more successful when the impasse also is low intensity.[7]

Mediation may lead toward settlement by (1) reducing hostility through focusing on bargaining objectives, (2) enhancing understanding of the opponent's position, (3) adjusting the negotiating format through chairing, subcommittee creation, and the like, (4) assuming the risk in exploring new solutions, (5) affecting perceptions regarding the cost of the conflict, and (6) contributing to face-saving that facilitates concessions.[8] A study examining reactions of managements and unions to mediated settlements found that management felt mediator expertise and impartiality increased the likelihood of settlements, while the union attributed settlements to mediator neutrality and persistence. Mediation strategies most often cited by management as facilitating settlement included discussions of costs of disagreement, suggestions of face-saving proposals, and gains in the parties' trust. Unions said changing expectations and devising an improved negotiating framework hastened settlement.[9]

Although mediation is an art, the behaviors of mediators and the levels or types of disputes could be classified. If this were done, a mediator could select an appropriate style to match the intensity of the negotiations to exert the greatest likelihood of a settlement. Alternatively, mediators whose styles best fit the impasse could be assigned to the case at hand.[10]

Mediator Backgrounds and Training

No specific requirements are needed for selection as a mediator or for appointment to the Federal Mediation and Conciliation Service. This is not to say FMCS mediators are not carefully selected or are untrained. Persons with experience in negotiating contracts are preferred, regardless of whether they were on the side of managements or unions in the past.

One report finds less than half of the mediators studied have college degrees, but they do have experience. In 1969, 69 percent of 295 FMCS mediators had significant experience as management or union

---

[7] Paul F. Gerhart and John E. Drotning, "Dispute Settlement and the Intensity of Mediation," *Industrial Relations*, Fall 1980, pp. 352–59.

[8] Ahmad Karim and Richard Pegnetter, "Mediator Strategies and Qualities and Mediation Effectiveness," *Industrial Relations*, Winter 1983, pp. 105–14.

[9] Ibid.

[10] For arguments supporting this viewpoint, see Janette Webb, "Behavioral Studies of Third-Party Intervention," in *Industrial Relations: A Social Psychological Approach*, ed. Geoffrey M. Stephenson and Christopher J. Brotherton (New York: John Wiley & Sons, 1979), pp. 309–31; and James A. Wall, Jr., "Mediation: A Categorical Analysis and a Proposed Framework for Future Research," *Academy of Management Proceedings*, 1980, pp. 298–302.

negotiators, and an additional 25 percent had been neutrals in labor relations disputes. Mediators in the FMCS are most often over age 45, and many have long experience in the service.[11]

A new FMCS mediator generally begins with a two-week training program in Washington and then is sent to a regional office to learn procedures and to work with experienced mediators. By the end of the first year, a first case has probably been assigned. Summaries and specialized training supplement experience as the mediator is assigned to increasingly complex cases.

Mediator Activity

Under the Taft-Hartley Act, employers and unions are required to notify the FMCS 30 days before the expiration of a contract when negotiations are under way and an agreement has not been reached. Table 11-1 shows the notifications and caseload for the FMCS during fiscal years 1980–85. The figures indicate the FMCS is involved in just under 23 percent of cases in which 30-day notifications had been received. The proportion of cases requiring assistance and the caseload has remained about the same over several years, as Table 11-2 indicates.

TABLE 11-1

Analysis of Dispute Notifications (number of dispute notifications received by FMCS for the years 1980 through 1985)

Receipt of Notifications	Fiscal 1980	Fiscal 1981	Fiscal 1982	Fiscal 1983	Fiscal 1984	Fiscal 1985
Notifications received during the year	106,382	97,449	75,167	101,541	98,770	108,751
30-day notices required by the LMRA	98,927	90,802	68,683	94,287	93,202	105,591
Requests from union and/ or company	4,109	3,655	4,576	5,426	3,667	1,168
NLRB and FLRA Certifications	3,338	2,989	1,907	1,767	1,896	1,803
Intercessions by FMCS	8	3	1	61	5	5
* Public sector board requests	—	—	—	—	—	184
Pending at close of previous year	6,257	6,089	5,607	6,803	6,049	5,892
Total dispute notifications processed	112,639	103,538	80,774	108,344	104,819	114,643

(* Data for years prior to 1985 were included in other figures.)

Source: U.S. Federal Mediation and Conciliation Service, *Thirty-Eighth Annual Report* (Washington, D.C.: Government Printing Office, 1986) p. 30.

---

[11] Simkin, *Mediation*, pp. 57–69. Recent work suggests this pattern has not changed. See Kolb, "Roles Mediators Play."

TABLE 11-2

Analysis of Assigned Mediation Cases (number of closed dispute, preventive mediation and public information cases for fiscal years 1980 through 1985)

Type of case	1980	1981	1982	1983	1984	1985
Total	23,723	20,923	17,693	20,466	22,376	24,518
Dispute cases	21,506	19,125	16,283	18,584	20,921	22,736
Joint meeting	10,299	9,297	7,908	8,617	9,052	8,019
Nonjoint meeting	11,207	9,828	8,375	9,967	11,869	14,717
Preventive Mediation	1,132	924	619	1,006	730	960
Public Information	1,085	874	791	876	725	822

Source: U.S. Federal Mediation and Conciliation Service, *Thirty-Eighth Annual Report* (Washington, D.C.: Government Printing Office, 1986) p. 26.

Thus, most cases are settled without the intervention of mediators. Data from the FMCS *Annual Report* series show mediation is used more frequently when the parties are negotiating their first contract and when the term of the contract is for three years. Thus, the inexperience of the negotiators and/or the permanency of the agreement terms appear to inhibit the parties from agreeing without outside assistance.

Mediation is one method of third-party intervention in labor disputes. It's an active process of keeping the parties together using a neutral approach. Mediation allows the parties to settle on their own terms when they have been unable to do so on their own.

FACT-FINDING

Fact-finding has a long history in U.S. labor relations. In the 19th century, fact-finding was used for fixing the blame on one party rather than finding the underlying causes of the dispute.[12] Present-day fact-finding involves a neutral party's study of the issues in a dispute and the rendering of a public recommendation of a reasonable settlement.[13]

Fact-finding requires using neutrals who act on behalf of the public.[14] When used in the private sector, if the fact-finder's published

---

[12] Thomas J. McDermott, "Fact-Finding Boards in Labor Disputes," *Labor Law Journal*, 1960, pp. 285–304.

[13] Charles M. Rehmus, "The Fact-Finder's Role," *The Proceedings of the Inaugural Convention of the Society of Professionals in Dispute Resolution*, October 1973, pp. 34–44.

[14] Jean T. McKelvey, "Fact-Finding in Public Employment Disputes: Promise or Illusion?" *Industrial and Labor Relations Review*, July 1969, p. 529.

findings are not adopted in a settlement, the parties are free to return to bargaining as they see fit.

In the United States, fact-finding has been used in two major types of disputes. The first is covered by the Taft-Hartley emergency disputes requirements (in which fact-finding has been relatively ineffectual). The second is in railroad disputes where presidential emergency boards have been created under the Railway Labor Act.[15] Fact-finding in the public sector is covered in Chapter 15.

Taft-Hartley Fact-Finding

Section 206 of the Taft-Hartley Act specifies that in the case of a national emergency dispute, the president may name a fact-finding board to prepare a report. No recommendations are made in the report, which is filed with the FMCS. Under Section 208, after the fact-finders have made their report, the president can ask a federal district court to enjoin a strike or lockout if *the court* finds the dispute falls within the national emergency criteria. Thus, use of the fact-finding board appears redundant, because a court must conclude an emergency exists.

The use of Taft-Hartley fact-finding boards has diminished over time.[16] Their determinations were generally reflected in the federal court's granting of injunction, but neither the reports nor the injunctions appeared to succeed in resolving impasses.

Railway Labor Boards

Presidential emergency boards may have succeeded in resolving impasses in critical transportation disputes. Issues facilitated in rail disputes by fact-finders include the settlement of nonoperating craft job security issues, recommendations made on phasing out the fireman job in diesel engines, and the introduction of new equipment in the airline industry.[17]

On the other hand, the availability of fact-finding may lead to increasing numbers of railroad negotiations being designated emergencies. Further, the boards may not have been very independent (more likely politically expedient), and the existence and use of boards may have reduced the parties' willingness to bargain.[18]

---

[15] Rehmus, "Fact-Finder's Role," pp. 35–36.

[16] Charles M. Rehmus, "The Operation of the National Emergency Provisions, 1947–1954," in *Emergency Disputes and National Policy*, ed. Irving Bernstein, Harold L. Enarson, and R. W. Fleming (New York: Harper & Row, 1955), pp. 261–68.

[17] Rehmus, "Fact-Finder's Role," p. 36.

[18] Herbert R. Northrup and Gordon F. Bloom, *Government and Labor* (Homewood, Ill.: Richard D. Irwin, 1963), pp. 327–30.

Fact-Finding and the Issues

Private-sector fact-finders are relatively unsuccessful on matters related to distributive bargaining. They have little authority to make more than recommendations and can do little to keep the parties together. Neither labor nor management may accord legitimacy to an outside group in determining or recommending what either is entitled to.

On the other hand, presidential emergency board fact-finders appear to have had some success in integrative bargaining areas. Employers and unions in the rail industry have been faced with many problems where innovations raised job security issues for the union and survival issues, given competition, for management if they were not implemented. In general, convening boards to propose solutions has been necessary, and the proposal by a neutral group may legitimize possible avenues toward resolution enough so that the parties can implement them without bearing as great an individual responsibility to their constituents. Thus, fact-finding boards allow integrative bargaining through the proposal of solutions and encourage intraorganizational bargaining by legitimizing positions the principal negotiators may be willing to raise but see as unacceptable to the memberships.

INTEREST ARBITRATION

Interest arbitration is an impasse resolution method that has seen considerable use in various forms in the public sector. Arbitration differs substantially from mediation and fact-finding. While mediation assists the parties to reach their own settlement, arbitration hears the positions of both and decides on binding settlement terms. While fact-finding would recommend a settlement, arbitration dictates it.

Two major types of arbitration are central to labor relations—*rights* and *interest*. According to the Supreme Court, interest arbitration occurs when no agreement exists or a change is sought and when the parties have an interest in the outcome because the contract will specify future rights. Rights arbitration involves the interpretation of an existing agreement to determine which party is entitled to a certain outcome or to take a certain action.[19]

In the United States, interest arbitration was used by the National War Labor Board during World War II and has been imposed, essentially, on the railroad industry by Congress on a number of occasions since the 1960s. The imposition of interest arbitration eliminates the parties' needs to settle on their own because a settlement is certain

---

[19] *Elgin, Joliet, & Eastern Railway Co.* v. *Burley*, 325 U.S. 71 (1945).

through outsiders if an impasse is reached. A great deal of controversy surrounds whether the availability and use of interest arbitration has a "narcotic" effect. The findings will be explored in greater detail in Chapter 15.

REVIEW OF THIRD-PARTY INVOLVEMENTS

Of the three methods of third-party involvements, only one—arbitration—guarantees a solution to an impasse. But, for various reasons, arbitration to decide interest issues has not been embraced by the private sector. Fact-finding also has a relatively checkered past. It has generally been *imposed* on the parties, who are then free to ignore its recommendations. Actually, no facts are involved in fact-finding, only values associated with the possible positions taken on outcomes in the dispute. Mediation is neutral in the sense that it generally requires the parties to bargain their own terms. It has been relatively successful in keeping parties at the table, given the FMCS load and success rate reported earlier.

The FMCS has, however, been involved in quasi-fact-finding or arbitration. When an impasse is apparent, rather than the bargaining power in major disputes determining the outcome, the parties have been brought to Washington, and deadlines for settlement strongly implied as government action was threatened.

Strikes and lockouts account for relatively little lost time compared to employee absences. A strike or lockout is a relatively small price to pay to preserve the right and obligation of the parties to settle their own differences. Ironically, however, advocates of free collective bargaining find themselves modifying well-thought-out positions when faced with the pressures of public office. For example, Exhibit 11–4A contains a quote from a paper by George Shultz, then professor of economics at the University of Chicago. Compare it with a later pronouncement in the 1970 rail negotiations, when he was secretary of labor (Exhibit 11–4B).

Sometimes the parties do not use or have mediation, fact-finding, or arbitration imposed. And sometimes mediation and fact-finding fail to break impasses. Strikes pressure the employer to settle on the union's terms. Lockouts or hiring replacements try to get the union to settle on the employer's terms. We will examine the use, effectiveness, and legality of each.

STRIKES

The four major types of strikes all have one thing in common: a withholding of effort by employees. An *economic strike* occurs as a

EXHIBIT 11–4A

Shultz's Differing Positions on National Emergency Strikes

"Now, perhaps you will say that the recent longshore strike, in which Taft-Hartley injunction was used, is a case against me. That may be, but I think it is worth noting that the president sought and got an injunction against such a strike on the grounds that, if the strike were permitted to occur, it would create a national emergency. But after the injunction expired, a strike did run for over one month and what did people talk about? All I read about in *The Wall Street Journal* was the bananas; you are not going to get bananas, they are doubling in price. My, oh my, should we throw away our freedoms for a handful of bananas? Just for fun, I ordered bananas with my shredded wheat to see if they would come. The waiter didn't even give me an argument, he brought the bananas. Or a banana, I should say. Maybe he only had one. This is not to deny the genuine economic hardship and public inconvenience that can be caused by a prolonged strike on the docks or in some other industries. But the allegations of hardship need the closest scrutiny, and the true costs must be balanced against the price of intervention."

Source: George P. Shultz, "Strikes: The Private Strike and Public Interest," selected paper no. 8, Graduate School of Business, University of Chicago, 1963.

EXHIBIT 11–4B

Following is the Text of the Telegram to the Presidents of the Unions and the Designated Presidents of a Smaller Number of Railroads that Represent 76 Rail Carriers: *(Official Text)*

It is apparent that the nation is threatened with an imminent railroad work stoppage because of a breakdown in labor contract negotiations between the industry and the shopcraft unions. The adverse effect on the nation coupled with the relatively narrow nature of the unresolved issue in dispute make it imperative that every reasonable step be taken to avoid such an occurrence. Accordingly, please advise me immediately of your agreement to proceed as follows:

1. The parties will not engage in any strike or lockout for the next seven days.
2. You and presidents of the other affected unions will meet with me and designated railroad company presidents on Monday, February 2, at 2 P.M. to explore further avenues of dispute settlement."

Source: Secretary of Labor Telegram reported in *Daily Labor Report* (Washington, D.C.: Bureau of National Affairs, January 30, 1970), p. A-9.

result of a failure to agree on the terms of a contract. It is called to place pressure on the employer to settle on the union's terms. The union believes the cost of the strike (both economic and political) will be less to it than to the employer, and the benefits of the expected solution are greater than the costs. Just because it is called an *economic strike* does not mean the issues in dispute always involve wages. An economic strike can occur over any of the mandatory bargaining issues mentioned in the labor acts. But if a union insists on going to impasse and strikes over permissive issues, it commits an unfair labor practice.[20] An economic strike involves unique rules, which are explained later.

Unfair labor practice strikes protest illegal conduct by the employer. If the employer has committed illegal acts, the employees' right to strike in protest and to be reinstated after the strike's conclusion is absolutely protected by NLRB and court interpretations of the labor acts. A *wildcat strike* is an unauthorized strike occurring during the term of the contract. Employees may face disciplinary action if their strike breaches a no-strike clause. A *sympathy strike* occurs when one union strikes in support of another's strike. These strikes take place where more than one union represents employees in a single establishment. Although no dispute exists between the sympathetic union and the employer, the union's right to support another is guaranteed by the Norris-LaGuardia Act, *even if* its present contract contains a no-strike clause and provides for the arbitration of unresolved grievances.[21]

Strike Votes and Going Out

As noted in Chapter 10, the union generally takes a strike vote sometime during negotiations to strengthen its bargaining position. This does not mean a strike will be called, only that the union may go out on strike at the contract's expiration. A local union usually needs the approval of its parent international to strike. If it strikes without this approval, local officers and the local union may be disciplined, the international may place the local under trusteeship, or strike benefits may not be paid.

Unions generally require members to participate in strike activities, such as picketing, to receive strike benefits. The union may also discipline members who refuse to strike. Evidence suggests a strike might increase the cohesiveness and solidarity of the union. A study examining attitudes of union members involved in a strike queried UAW members four times during 1976 and 1977 regarding their perceptions during contract negotiations. During these talks, Ford was struck but General Motors and Chrysler were not. While on

---

[20] *Detroit Resilient Floor Decorators Union*, 136 NLRB 756 (1962).

[21] *Buffalo Forge Co.* v. *United Steelworkers of America, AFL–CIO*, 92 LRRM 3032 (U.S. Supreme Court, 1976).

strike, Ford employees' attitudes toward their international union and its leaders were more positive than prior to the strike and more positive than fellow union members at GM and Chrysler.[22]

Picketing

One of the first and most pervasive activities occurring during a strike is picketing. In picketing, the union informs the public about the existence of a labor dispute. The appeal may ask others to refrain from business dealings with the struck employer during the dispute. Before Norris-LaGuardia, state laws and federal courts frequently enjoined picketing. Since then, federal courts have been unable to enjoin these activities unless a clear and present danger to life or property resulting from actions of the strikers could be shown. States may not restrict peaceful picketing because it is protected by the First Amendment.[23] Some restrictions, however, have been imposed on recognitional picketing in amendments to the labor acts.

To be protected from employer reprisals, employees must publicize their involvement in a labor dispute when they picket or inform the public. For example, the Supreme Court decided a group of TV technicians could be discharged for passing out handbills that questioned the quality of local TV coverage at the struck stations because the handbills did not also state the employees were involved in a labor dispute.[24]

The site and manner of the picketing is also of concern, because the union can be accused of illegal secondary activity in certain instances. The next sections examine various types of picketing activity. Legal picketing is not necessarily associated only with strikes, but may also involve informational and recognitional activities.

Common situs picketing. The place at which picketing occurs may affect secondary employers and the expected benefits associated with picketing. This issue is of great importance in the construction industry, where a prime contractor and several subcontractors may work simultaneously on a common site. Each utilizes different trades, may or may not be unionized, and may have different wages, terms, and expiration dates in contracts. If unions strike in sympathy with a primary dispute and if a dispute exists with one contractor, a whole site may be shut down.

A primary employer is involved in the dispute, and a neutral employer is affected by the picketing activity of the primary's employ-

---

[22] Ross Stagner and Boaz Eflal, "Internal Union Dynamics during a Strike: A Quasi-Experimental Study," *Journal of Applied Psychology*, February 1982, pp. 37–44.

[23] *Thornhill* v. *Alabama*, 310 U.S. 88 (1940).

[24] *NLRB* v. *Local Union 1229, International Brotherhood of Electrical Workers*, 346 U.S. 464 (1953).

ees. The rules governing common situs picketing in construction were laid down in 1951 in the *Denver Building Trades Council* cases.[25] Picketing began when the union learned that the prime contractor on the site had employed a nonunion subcontractor. One object of the picketing was to force the general contractor to drop the sub. When the picketing began, all other union workers refused to cross the picket line. The prime contractor maintained the dispute was with the subcontractor and general picketing of the site was an illegal secondary boycott designed to force neutral parties to cease their dealings with the sub. The court agreed, and since that time, construction unions are forbidden to picket sites for the purpose of forcing a primary employer to cease doing business with a nonunion subcontractor. The usual practice at construction sites is to establish reserved gates for each employer. Primary dispute pickets may then patrol only the gate of their employer.

Ambulatory site. Sometimes the objects of a strike move from place to place, such as a ship being struck by a seafarers' union. In one case, when the ship was moved to a dry dock for repairs, the union sought to picket by the ship. The dry dock management refused to allow this, and a picket line was set up at the entrance to the dock. The NLRB ruled that such picketing would be legal if (1) the object is currently on the secondary employer's site, (2) the primary employer continues to engage in its normal business, (3) the picketing is reasonably close to the strike object, and (4) the picketing discloses that the dispute is with the struck employer and not the site owner.[26]

Multiple-use sites. In the past, an employer's site was usually easily identified. But recent changes in retailing, for example, have blurred this concept. The enclosed shopping center makes picketing a primary employer without disrupting secondary businesses difficult. And, the employer has usually leased the site from another company that owns the shopping mall.

The Supreme Court originally held that a mall owner could prohibit pickets from publicizing a labor dispute with one of the stores located in the mall.[27] However, the Court recently reversed itself in holding that a union does not interfere with a neutral owner and other stores by peacefully informing the public about a labor dispute with one of the stores within the mall.[28]

Slowdowns

The incidence of strikes declined markedly during the middle 1980s. Employers have occasionally replaced economic strikers and have be-

---

[25] *NLRB* v. *Denver Building Trades Council*, 341 U.S. 675 (1951).

[26] *Sailor's Union of the Pacific (Moore Dry Dock Co.)*, 92 NLRB 547 (1950).

[27] *Hudgens* v. *NLRB*, 91 LRRM 2489 (U.S. Supreme Court, 1976).

[28] *Edward J. DeBartolo Corp.* v. *Florida Gulf Coast Building and Construction Trades Council and NLRB*, U.S. Supreme Court, No. 86-1461, 1988.

come more automated and thus better able to operate for extended periods with only supervisory employees. Unions, for their part, are increasingly using slowdowns to put pressure on employers to settle contracts. A slowdown most often involves "working to rules." Employees refuse to perform activities outside of their job descriptions, follow procedures to the letter, and refuse overtime and other employment duties that might be voluntary. Because they are complying with the contract and company work rules, they can seldom be disciplined.[29]

Corporate Campaigns

Corporate campaigns are a relatively recent innovation. In a corporate campaign, the union and its consultants look for points where the employer might be vulnerable and exert pressure on those points to support the collective bargaining effort. A corporate campaign successfully forced the J. P. Stevens Company to negotiate a first contract with the Clothing and Textile Workers, who had won representation rights several years earlier.

The first phase of a corporate campaign involves a detailed exploration of the corporation's business together with research to uncover any possible regulatory violations recorded by government agencies, such as the Environmental Protection Agency or the Occupational Safety and Health Administration. The campaign will also determine what other corporations are closely linked as suppliers, customers, financial backers, and the like.

The second phase involves publicity of material detrimental to the employer's interests and supportive of the union's demands. The campaign tries to get outsiders in the dispute to put pressure on the employer to settle with the union, and especially to settle on terms beneficial to the employees. Some of the activities may help to motivate consumer boycotts.[30]

Shutdowns

A variety of responses are available to the employer when struck. These responses generally fall into three categories: (1) shut down the affected area, (2) continue operating, or (3) contract out work for the duration. Each has its own consequences and can cause retaliatory action.

---

[29] "Labor's Shift: Finding Strikes Harder to Win, More Unions Turn to Slowdowns," *The Wall Street Journal*, May 22, 1987, pp. 1, 6; see also a new publication for union members, *The Inside Game: Winning with Workplace Strategies*, Industrial Union Department, AFl–CIO, 1987.

[30] Harold Datz, Leo Geffner, Joseph M. McLaughlin, and Susan Kellock, "Economic Warfare in the 1980s: Strikes, Lockouts, Boycotts, and Corporate Campaigns," *Industrial Relations Law Journal* 9 (1987), pp. 82–115.

Shutdowns are designed to have the least consequences in terms of union activity. But a shutdown has consequences the employer would like to avoid. First, revenues from production are lost during this period. Second, the company may find competitors gearing up to take over the lost production, thus permanently reducing its market share. Third, if a firm is a sole supplier, the users of its product may encourage others to enter the market as alternative sources of supply, thus reducing the possibilities of temporary shortages. And fourth, during periods of scarcity, the firm may lose its suppliers as they fill orders from more reliable customers.

Continued Operations

Continued operations may be accomplished by two strategies. Neither is relished by the union, but the second will almost certainly lead to some militant union action. The first strategy is to continue operations using supervisors and other nonproduction workers, which is feasible if the firm is not labor intensive and if maintenance demands are not high. Automated and continuous-flow operations, such as found in the chemical industry, fall into this category. One difficulty encountered later if this strategy is used is that supervisory–employee relations may be strained following the strike because the supervisor's work may have enabled the company to prolong the strike.

The second strategy is to hire replacements for the strikers. Because this action places the strikers' jobs in direct jeopardy, difficulties usually result. During the early 1980s, employers were much more likely to continue operations by hiring replacements, given their ready availability when unemployment was high. Exhibit 11–5 describes the responses of some employers to recent work stoppages. The ability of the company to attract replacements substantially reduces the bargaining power of the union. Strike replacements face a possible difficult position: they are reviled as "scabs" by the strikers (see Exhibit 11-6 for a definition almost invariably used when strike replacements are hired) and, due to low seniority, may find themselves vulnerable to layoff after a new contract is signed. On the other hand, if the employer can operate without settling the strike for a year, the new employees may succeed in decertifying the union representing the strikers.

Rights of Employers

A strike would be a true economic strike if the company bargained in good faith to an impasse. Then, if either the company or the union refused to move further, the gulf would remain permanently, and new employees would have to be hired to remain in business. Employers can legally replace economic strikers, and operations can then re-

EXHIBIT 11-5

More Firms Get Tough and Keep Operating in spite of Walkouts

To an increasing number of companies, "strike" is no longer a frightening word. These companies are prepared to continue operating right through a labor walkout.

The latest example is Continental Airlines, which decided to keep flying on a curtailed schedule despite strikes by its pilots, flight attendants, and ground personnel. When the Machinists union struck Continental last summer, the carrier immediately hired replacements. And when the company recently filed a bankruptcy petition to bail itself out of its labor and financial problems, it rehired about 35 percent of its former work force at drastically reduced pay, and then resumed flights.

Operating during strikes is nothing new for many companies. . . . But now many labor-intensive concerns are adopting the strategy as a continuation of the hard-nosed concession bargaining pressed during the recession. Companies that have chosen to operate despite strikes recently have included, in addition to Continental, Phelps Dodge Corp., Magic Chef, Inc., and Whirlpool Corp.

Labor experts say the time is ripe for such aggressive management tactics . . . "We have a president who says let's confront them, fire them, and keep on rolling. That makes it legitimate to operate during strikes, and private employers have followed the lead," says John Zalusky, an economist in the AFL-CIO's research department.

sume.[31] However, strike replacements become members of the bargaining unit and are represented by the striking union. Decertification is necessary to remove the bargaining representative.

Rights of Economic Strikers

If replacements are hired, the strikers may still get their jobs back. First, if they unilaterally offer to return to work and if their jobs or others for which they are qualified are unfilled, refusing to rehire them would be an unfair labor practice because a strike is protected by Section 7. Second, if employees ask for reinstatement when the strike is concluded, they are entitled to their jobs, if open, or to preference for rehiring when positions become open.[32] However, employers are not required to reinstate employees involved in breaking rules during the

---

[31] *NLRB* v. *MacKay Radio & Telegraph*, 304 U.S. 333 (1938).
[32] *NLRB* v. *Fleetwood Trailer Co., Inc.*, 389 U.S. 375 (1967).

EXHIBIT 11-6

What Is a Scab?

After God had finished the rattlesnake, the toad, and the vampire, he had some awful substance left with which He made a *scab*. A *scab* is a two-legged animal with a corkscrew soul, a water-logged brain, and a combination backbone made of jelly and glue. Where others have hearts, he carries a tumor of rotten principles.

When a *scab* comes down the street, men turn their backs, and angels weep in heaven, and the devil shuts the gates of hell to keep him out. No man has a right to *scab* as long as there is a pool of water deep enough to drown his body in, or a rope long enough to hang his carcass with. Judas Iscariot was a gentleman compared with a *scab*. For betraying his Master, he had character enough to hang himself. A *scab hasn't!*

Esau sold his birthright for a mess of pottage. Judas Iscariot sold his Savior for thirty pieces of silver. Benedict Arnold sold his country for a promise of a commission in the British Army. The modern strikebreaker sells his birthright, his country, his wife, his children, and his fellow men for an unfulfilled promise from his employer, trust, or corporation.

Esau was traitor to himself, Judas Iscariot was a traitor to his God. Benedict Arnold was a traitor to his country.

A strikebreaker is a traitor to his God, his country, his family, and his class!

Source: Philip S. Foner, *Jack London, American Rebel* (New York: Citadel Press, 1947), pp. 57-58.

---

strike, such as sabotage and picket line violence. But discharges must be for cause, and the grievance procedure would be open for hearing disputes over these discharges.

Contracting Out

For the employer with several major customers whose business demands work on a fixed schedule, a strike can have serious consequences, particularly if competitive firms offer the same services. One strategy open to the struck employer is to arrange for a competing firm to handle the work temporarily.

On its face, this strategy seems foolproof: no problems exist with strikebreakers and the union, and the customers get their work done on time by a subcontractor. It is not foolproof, however. If the subcontractor is unionized, its employees can legally refuse to perform the subcontracted work when the struck employer has initiated the order. Such refusals are allowed under the so-called *ally doctrine*.

As one example, a printing firm responsible for providing Sunday supplements to newspapers was struck by its employees. To maintain its ability to meet the weekly schedule, it subcontracted the work to another firm. When the second firm's employees learned why they were doing the work, they refused to perform it. The first employer charged that this was a secondary boycott, but the NLRB reasoned the dispute became primary through the handling of the struck work for the primary employer.[33]

An exception to the ally doctrine is granted to health care organizations. Sick patients can't be made to wait for care until a strike is over. Hospitals accepting struck work (patient care) cannot risk the extension of the strike to their facilities. Congress recognized these problems by modifying Section 8 (b)(4) of the Taft-Hartley Act to apply to health care facilities. If a hospital is struck and another health care facility supplies an occasional technician to assist the struck facility, an ally relationship is not established. On the other hand, if shifts of LPNs were provided by a group of hospitals, they would become allies. Thus, the magnitude of the assistance is the determinant factor in whether a union could take action against an assisting organization.

Evidence on the Incidence and Effects of Strikes

Strikes are popularly viewed as counterproductive. Those not directly involved might be inconvenienced, and often a winner is not apparent. Companies lose profits on lost sales, and workers lose wages that take years to make up even if the strike secured a wage rate higher than offered before the walkout. But striking or taking a threatened strike may be a long-term investment. If a union never takes militant action to support its demands, the employer may doubt the credibility of its threats. Short strikes may be a relatively low-cost investment in gaining action on larger future demands. From a management standpoint, taking a strike may be necessary for gaining union permission to introduce new work methods or for lowering union expectations.[34]

A number of studies identify the variables associated with the incidence and duration of economic strikes. From an overall standpoint, declines in real wages or a failure to win wage increases comparable to other collective bargaining situations increases the likelihood of strikes.[35] As unemployment increases, the incidence of strikes drops, but their duration increases;[36] however, defensive

---

[33] *Blackhawk Engraving Co.*, 219 NLRB 169 (1975).

[34] For arguments supporting this position, see Charles R. Greer, Stanley A. Martin, and Ted E. Reusser, "The Effect of Strikes on Shareholder Returns," *Journal of Labor Research*, Fall 1980, pp. 217–29; and Martin J. Mauro, "Strikes as a Result of Imperfect Information," *Industrial and Labor Relations Review*, July 1982, pp. 522–38.

[35] See Orley Ashenfelter and George E. Johnson, "Bargaining Theory, Trade Unions, and Industrial Strike Activity," *American Economic Review*, March 1969, pp. 35–49; and Daniel J. B. Mitchell, "A Note on Strike Propensities and Wage Developments," *Industrial Relations*, Winter 1981, pp. 123–27.

[36] See John Kennan, "Pareto Optimality and the Economics of Strike Duration," *Journal of Labor Research*, Spring 1980, pp. 77–94; and Bruce E. Kaufman, "The Determinants of Strikes over Time and across Industries," *Journal of Labor Research*, Spring 1983, pp. 159–75.

strikes to avoid give-backs increase.[37] Urban, southern, and female-dominated bargaining units are less likely to strike.[38] Unions in high-injury industries strike more frequently.[39] Stability in employing and union organizations is associated with a lower incidence of strikes.[40] Environmental stability in the employer's supplier markets is related to lower strike activity.[41] Declining real wages and location in a right-to-work–law state are also related to higher strike incidence levels.[42] Strikes in previous periods apparently reduce the possibility of strikes during subsequent negotiations.[43] The greater the involvement of the rank-and-file employee, the greater the propensity to strike, as shown in increases in strike activity following passage of the Landrum-Griffin Act, which increased guarantees of union democracy.[44] Younger members appear more willing to be militant, while personal hardship decreases militancy.[45] Economic strikes in the auto industry were more prevalent during periods of low productivity, while intracontractual strike frequency was higher during periods of increasing productivity.[46] Whether worker militancy is related to both higher strike rates and lower productivity is hard to establish, however.

The duration of strikes and their settlement appear related to a number of variables. The costs do not necessarily increase at the same rate as the duration. For the employer, strike costs for a short strike may be small if shipments can be made from inventory or if customers have stocked up in anticipation. As the strike lengthens, costs associated with forgone orders increase rapidly, and long-run costs are ultimately incurred as market share is lost to more reliable competitors. For the union member, direct marginal costs rise rapidly as savings are exhausted and as the disparity between strike benefits and wages

[37] Michele I. Naples, "An Analysis of Defensive Strikes," *Industrial Relations* 26 (1987), pp. 96–105.

[38] Kaufman, "Determinants of Strikes."

[39] J. Paul Leigh, "Risk Preferences and the Interindustry Propensity to Strike," *Industrial and Labor Relations Review*, January 1983, pp. 271–85.

[40] Bruce E. Kaufman, "The Determinants of Strikes in the United States: 1900–1977," *Industrial and Labor Relations Review*, July 1982, pp. 473–90.

[41] J. M. Cousineau and R. Lacroix, "Imperfect Information and Strikes; An Analysis of Canadian Experience, 1967–1982," *Industrial and Labor Relations Review* 39 (1986), pp. 539–49.

[42] Cynthia L. Gramm, "The Determinants of Strike Incidence and Severity: A Micro-Level Study, *Industrial and Labor Relations Review* 39 (1986), pp. 361–76.

[43] J. F. Schnell and Cynthia L. Gramm, "Learning by Striking: Estimates of the Teetotaler Effect," *Journal of Labor Economics* 5 (1987), pp. 221–41.

[44] Ashenfelter and Johnson, "Bargaining Theory."

[45] James E. Martin, "Predictors of Individual Propensity to Strike," *Industrial and Labor Relations Review* 39 (1986), pp. 214–27; see also Alan W. Black, "Some Factors Influencing Attitudes toward Militancy, Solidarity, and Sanctions in a Teachers' Union," *Human Relations* 36 (1983), pp. 973–85.

[46] Sean Flaherty, "Strike Activity, Worker Militancy, and Productivity Change in Manufacturing, 1961–1981," *Industrial and Labor Relations Review* 40 (1987), pp. 585–600; and "Strike Activity and Productivity Change: The U.S. Auto Industry," *Industrial Relations* 26 (1987), pp. 174–85.

becomes apparent. Strikes last longer when union members have relatively low debt-to-income ratios.[47] When strike issues are most strongly related to plant administration and job security issues, strikes seem to be of shortest duration. General wage change disputes result in longer strikes, with the average length from 7 to 15 days.[48] Renegotiation strikes are almost always over economics (85 percent of cases), while intracontract strikes are almost always noneconomic (90 percent of cases). The median duration of renegotiation strikes in one studied sample was 15 days, while the median for intracontract strikes was just 3 days.[49] Ironically, the shorter the strike, the more easily it appears to be settled. Almost 13 percent of strikes are settled in the first day. At the 10-day duration, the rate drops to 4.8 percent; at 30 days, to 3.2 percent; and at 50 days, only 2.4 percent of the remaining strikes are settled. The data show once a strike has exceeded this length, the probability of settling does not particularly change, indicating the costs of continuing the strike for both sides after this time do not change relative to the other.[50]

Wildcat strikes most frequently involve plant administration issues and generally last three days or less. They are predicted by high unionization rates within the industry, unsafe working conditions, low inventories, a liberal political environment, and a moderate degree of bargaining experience. Factors inhibiting wildcat strikes are the employer's likelihood of filing an unfair labor practice charge, unemployment rates, high real wages in the industry, the percent of women in the bargaining unit, location in the South, and a long-term bargaining relationship.[51]

In an examination of the perceived results of striking, chief negotiators felt management appeared to gain more from strikes than did unions. The ability to remain in operation and/or to have a large proportion of a plant's employees involved in the strike increased management's perceived advantage.[52]

Some have argued that strikes are strictly random events not known before their occurrence. If this were the case, outsiders who could be hurt or benefit from strikes could not take any action to insulate themselves. During the 1960s and early 1970s, steel customers traditionally stocked up before contract expiration dates in the expectation of strikes, due to past experience with steel negotiations

---

[47] Gramm, "Determinants of Strike Incidence."

[48] Kennan, "Pareto Optimality."

[49] Sean Flaherty, "Contract Status and the Economic Determinants of Strike Activity," *Industrial Relations*, Winter 1983, pp. 20–33.

[50] Kennan, "Pareto Optimality."

[51] Dennis M. Byrne and Randall H. King, "Wildcat Strikes in U.S. Manufacturing, 1960–1977," *Journal of Labor Research* 7 (1986), pp. 387–401.

[52] Arie Shirom, "Strike Characteristics as Determinants of Strike Settlements: A Chief Negotiator's Viewpoint," *Journal of Applied Psychology*, February 1982, pp. 45–52.

and strikes. Recent studies of shareholder behavior suggest investors anticipate strikes, because the rates of return on shares of struck companies decline in value *before* incontrovertible evidence that a strike will take place. Investors also appear to discount stocks as the duration increases over relatively short runs.[53] However, only about one third of the total decline in share price is discounted before the strike is announced.[54] Very long strikes appear related to situations in which firms have done better than average before the strike (ability to pay), and investors bid these stocks up after the strike (perhaps anticipating that management gained major concessions).[55]

Depending on which data are examined, one could argue that involvement in strikes is higher than we've suggested. This chapter's introduction noted that time lost due to strikes was not large in comparison to total time worked. Evidence suggests, however, about 15 out of every 100 workers covered by a contract strike in a given year for some period.[56] The relatively low number of days lost and the decline in the percentage of days lost may be attributed to short durations of strikes and the declining percentage of employees covered by collective bargaining agreements.

Overview

Strikes can be powerful weapons if an employer has few options in terms of remaining open. They are not without their risks, however, because economic strikers can legally be replaced and some positive movement by the union may be necessary to resume bargaining.

One other weapon open to unions is generally used only in extreme cases—the boycott.

BOYCOTTS

The boycott has been used infrequently and has obtained mixed results. As noted in Chapter 2, the Danbury Hatters' and Buck's Stove boycotts were declared violations of the Sherman Antitrust Act, leaving the unions responsible for treble damages. Later legislation exempted unions from antitrust provisions, but the boycott is still infrequently used.

There are a number of reasons for this lack of use: (1) a boycott requires a great deal of organization and publicity to alert customers,

---

[53] George R. Neumann, "The Predictability of Strikes: Evidence from the Stock Market," *Industrial and Labor Relations Review*, July 1980, pp. 525–35.

[54] Brian E. Becker and Craig A. Olson, "The Impact of Strikes on Shareholder Equity," *Industrial and Labor Relations Review* 39 (1986), pp. 425–38.

[55] Greer et al., "Effect of Strikes."

[56] Mitchell, "Note on Strike Propensities."

(2) customers may not be sympathetic to union demands unless a clear-cut social issue is involved, (3) keeping a legal primary boycott from having secondary ramifications is sometimes difficult, and (4) the effects of a boycott are not turned off as easily as those of a strike, because the public may continue to identify the producer with poor labor relations after a settlement.

One boycott technique informs the general public of a labor dispute at a location where the struck business's products are sold. However, this type of activity risks being declared a secondary boycott.

Consider the following: A major TV and radio receiver manufacturer is struck by its production employees. In an attempt to pressure the employer to settle, the union pickets retail stores selling the TV sets. Their signs read, "Don't shop here. This store sells XYZ TV sets produced under unfair conditions. ABC union on strike for justice against XYZ." On the other hand, suppose the union uses a different message on its signs: "ABC on strike against XYZ Co. Don't buy an XYZ TV while shopping here today. ABC has no dispute with this store." Are both strategies legal? Only the second is. In the second instance, the picket calls attention to the labor dispute and the struck product but does not ask persons to boycott the neutral store. If the union follows the second strategy and does not impede customers or deliveries, the action is considered primary and legal.[57]

Recently, boycotts have been used against Adolph Coors Company (to force recognition) and J. P. Stevens & Co., Inc. (to force recognition and bargaining on initial contracts). The Coors boycott probably had some effect on the ultimate willingness of the firm to recognize the union, but the J. P. Stevens action was much more difficult because many of its products are sold under labels that are difficult to identify with the employer.

An unanswered issue in boycotts is what responsibility unions have to the secondary employer who handles the goods. In a case involving J. P. Stevens products in a large department store, the impact may be minimal. But if the employer handled primarily J. P. Stevens products and the boycott was successful, the impact could be great.

The question of degree of impact was dismissed as an improper test of the legality of a boycott affecting a secondary employer in the *Tree Fruits* case but was raised again in a case where the impact of a successful boycott was much greater on the employer. Steelworkers Local 14055 struck the Bay Refining division of Dow Chemical Company at Bay City, Michigan, in 1974. Among other company products, gasoline produced by the struck refinery was marketed through Bay gasoline stations in Michigan. To put pressure on Dow, pickets informed customers in heavily unionized areas that Dow supplied Bay

---

57 *NLRB* v. *Fruit & Vegetable Packers Local 760*, 377 U.S. 58 (1964).

gasoline and asked consumers not to buy it when patronizing Bay stations. Over 80 percent of station revenues resulted from gasoline sales, so where the boycott was effective, the impact on the secondary employer was great. Because gasoline refining was only a small part of Dow's business, any sales loss would have been minimal. Furthermore, the gasoline could easily have been marketed through other firms. The appeals court dismissed unfair labor practice complaints against the Steelworkers because the *Tree Fruits* case said impact was not a proper test. The Supreme Court, however, reopened the issue by overruling the appeals court and remanding the issue to the NLRB. But the board did not reconsider its decision because Local 14055 had been disestablished.[58] Thus, the impact test has not been decided.

A Supreme Court decision has reduced a union's power to use the boycott as a political statement. The Court found that the International Longshoremen's Association's refusal to handle Russian goods following its invasion of Afghanistan constituted an illegal secondary boycott even though no primary dispute existed with the dockworkers' employer.[59]

So far, coverage of impasses has primarily involved union initiatives. One tactic has also been used by employers—the lockout. Although the strike has been protected since Norris-LaGuardia, the lockout has a much murkier legal background.

LOCKOUTS

Lockouts can be thought of as the flip side of the strike coin. After passage of the Wagner Act, the NLRB declared lockouts unfair labor practices. The board said the use of lockouts interfered with employees' rights to engage in protected concerted activities. As such, any refusal to provide work as the result of a labor dispute presumably related to and interfered with workers' protected rights. Over time, this broad approach has been redefined by specific situational variables and court interpretations. Three distinct types of situations have been defined in which lockouts are legal if specific conditions are met: (1) perishable goods, (2) multiemployer bargaining units, and (3) single-employer units.

---

[58] *Daily Labor Report* (Washington, D.C.: Bureau of National Affairs, May 5, 1977), p. A-4.

[59] *International Longshoremen's Association, AFL–CIO v. Allied International, Inc.*, No. 80-1663, U.S. Supreme Court, 1982; for a critique of this decision, see John Rubin, "The Primary–Secondary Distinction: The New Secondary Boycott Law of *Allied International, Inc.* v. *International Longshoremen's Association*," Industrial Relations Law Journal, 1984, pp. 94–124.

Perishable Goods

An employer dealing with perishable goods is frequently at the mercy of the union. For example, in 1976 the California vegetable canners were struck just before the harvest. Because their revenues depended on packing and selling the produce when it was available, a strike during the pack itself would have caused the produce to rot. Thus, great pressure for a quick settlement was placed on the employers.

Similar situations occur when the employer's goods and services are perishable but the employer has more control over their perishability. For a packer, the timing of the crop's maturity is not within the firm's control. On the other hand, a brewer can decide when to start a new batch of beer, and a contractor can elect when to begin a tract of houses. In the brewer's case, if the beer is started, it must be bottled on a certain date or the batch will spoil, resulting in immediate economic loss. For the contractor, customers may become dissatisfied with the waiting period on an unfinished house and spread their displeasure by communicating to others. Thus, the long-term business interests of the contractor and the short-term economic losses suffered by the brewer can only be minimized by capitulating to the union on its terms. The lockout is a legitimate employer tactic to neutralize or decrease union power in situations involving perishable goods when it is done to avoid economic loss[60] or to preserve customer goodwill.[61]

Multiemployer Lockouts

Frequently, several small employers engaged in the same business have employees represented by the same union. The union has a high degree of bargaining power when dealing with a single employer, because a strike against one employer leaves its business vulnerable while the other unstruck companies remain open for customers. To get back into business, the employer may settle on terms favorable to the union. After settlement, the union selects its next target and, in a whipsaw manner, wins increasingly favorable settlements. To counteract this union tactic, the employers may band together and bargain as one. But what happens if the union only takes strike action against one employer or attempts to break the solidarity of the group by using a whipsaw strategy? Is a lockout then an appropriate and legal weapon for the multiemployer group?

In the *Buffalo Linen* case, the Supreme Court held that when one member of a multiemployer unit is struck and the remaining members lock out their employees, the lockout is defensive in nature, and

---

[60] *Duluth Bottling Association*, 48 NLRB 1335 (1943).
[61] *Betts Cadillac-Olds, Inc.*, 96 NLRB 268 (1951).

without its use the continued integrity of the bargaining unit could not be assured.[62]

Buffalo Linen explicitly recognizes the lockout's legality in multi-employer units when an impasse in bargaining is reached and a strike follows against one of the members. As we learned earlier, employers involved in economic strikes are free to replace strikers. On the other hand, can an employer lock out its employees and temporarily replace them for the duration of the lockout to continue operations? The Court ruled multiemployer groups could.

In *NLRB* v. *Brown*, a group of retail food stores were bargaining with their clerks. When an agreement could not be reached, the clerks struck one store, and the other employers responded by locking out their clerks. All stores continued operating, using temporary replacements. When an agreement was reached, the replacements were discharged, and the clerks were reinstated. The Supreme Court held the action was legal and simply one of a permissible group of economic weapons the parties might use in convincing the other to agree to its bargaining positions. The legitimate interest of the group in continuing multiemployer bargaining, given the tactics used here, outweighed any harm done to the employees through their loss of wages.[63]

Single-Employer Lockouts

If a union negotiates with a single employer, a lockout cannot be justified as a weapon to forestall whipsaw effects, because a whipsaw requires a multiemployer group. Thus, the question of whether a lockout interferes with employee rights to engage in concerted activities must be much more closely scrutinized for single employers.

In a case involving no impasse or imminent strike, Quaker State Oil followed through with its threats to shut down its operations, even though the union had given written assurances that its members would continue to work while bargaining continued. The NLRB held the lockout by the company was coercive in nature, because the union had always abided by its word on continued work in the past and the threat and action were taken before an impasse was reached.[64]

The flagship decision in the single-employer lockout area was handed down by the Supreme Court the same day it established the prevailing precedent in multiemployer lockouts (*NLRB* v. *Brown*).[65] American Ship Building operated four shipyards on the Great Lakes. Most of the work involved ship repair on a schedule during the winter

---

[62] *NLRB* v. *Truck Drivers' Local 449*, 353 U.S. 87 (1957).

[63] *NLRB* v. *Brown*, 380 U.S. 278 (1965).

[64] *Quaker State Oil Refining Corp.*, 121 NLRB 334 (1958).

[65] *American Ship Building Co.* v. *NLRB*, 380 U.S. 300 (1965).

months and emergency problems encountered during the heavy summer shipping season.

The company bargained with eight different unions and had experienced strikes during contract negotiations several times. In 1961, it feared a repeat of this practice, especially likely to occur when a ship entered its yards for emergency repairs or during the winter when workloads were heaviest. On August 11, after a bargaining impasse was reached and 10 days after the contract expired, the Chicago yard was shut down, the Toledo work force was reduced to two, and the Buffalo work force was gradually laid off as work was completed. The Lorain, Ohio, facility remained open to work on a major project.

The NLRB viewed this action as illegal, believing it was done only to enhance a bargaining position. The Supreme Court overruled the board, holding the employer does not necessarily discriminate against union membership or coerce workers in the exercise of their rights by the use of lockouts. The Court held the lockout was the corollary of the strike and unions had no legislated right to determine the starting date and duration of a work stoppage. Justice Goldberg suggested in his concurring opinion that the legality of lockouts should be assessed in relation to the length, character, and prevailing relationships in the bargaining relationship. For instance, a refusal to bargain simply to gain an impasse allowing the use of a lockout would be unlawful.

Recently, the NLRB substantially liberalized rules for single employers in holding that temporary replacements can be hired to bring pressure on the union after a lockout has been imposed.[66]

BANKRUPTCIES

While bankruptcies are not the same as impasses, several organizations have used them to end impasses over concessions or simply to escape existing collective bargaining agreements without negotiations. Bankruptcy law allows companies to abrogate contracts with suppliers and renegotiate on more favorable terms. Under Chapter 11 of the bankruptcy laws, the firm cannot cease operations but may gain protection from its creditors while trying to reorganize. Bankruptcy courts oversee the changes made to contracts to safeguard the interests of both the creditors and the debtor-in-possession.

When companies attempt to abrogate labor agreements, unions have generally reacted by filing refusal-to-bargain charges with the NLRB. The NLRB has generally upheld these complaints and ordered the companies to reinstate the contract, pending the negotiation of a

---

[66] *Harter Equipment, Inc.*, 122 LRRM 1219 (1986).

revised agreement. Bankrupt companies, however, have sought protection from the bankruptcy courts, arguing that labor agreements do not differ from other supplied contracts that the firms have made and can be abrogated under the same authority.

Early in 1984, the Supreme Court ruled bankruptcy courts may approve the rejection of collective bargaining agreements if the debtor-in-possession shows that their continued operation is burdensome to the business. The bankrupt firm may also unilaterally modify the terms after filing for bankruptcy but before formal approval is received from the bankruptcy court.[67]

Some have argued that the relatively liberal provisions of Chapter 11, which do not require present insolvency, and the Supreme Court decision allowing the abrogation of labor agreements will lead to some "going concerns" electing to file bankruptcy to escape labor agreement terms unavoidable through collective bargaining. Fundamental conflicts between labor legislation and bankruptcy law lead to controversy whenever bankruptcy is declared.[68] Congress may act in the future to clarify the status of labor agreements, vis-à-vis other contracts, that reorganizing firms have made.

SUMMARY

Impasses occur when the parties fail to reach an agreement during negotiations. Several methods are used to break impasses. The parties may strike or lock out, agree to mediation, or invoke interest arbitration.

Mediation is a process of bringing the parties together through a third party who helps to reopen communications, clarify issues, and introduce a realistic approach to bargaining issues that continue to separate the parties. Interest arbitration turns the dispute over to a neutral who decides what the final settlement should be.

Typical tactics used by unions in impasses include strikes, picketing, boycotts, and corporate campaigns. Employers respond by hiring replacements, locking out employees, or declaring bankruptcy.

Strikes usually occur as the result of a disagreement on the terms of a new agreement. These strikes are called economic strikes. Other strikes occur over unfair labor practices, in sympathy with other unions, and in violation of no-strike clauses. The strikers' rights to employment in each category have been clearly defined by the courts.

---

[67] *NLRB* v. *Bildisco & Bildisco*, 115 LRRM 2805, U.S. Supreme Court, 1984.

[68] For further details, see Thomas R. Haggard and Mark S. Pulliam, *Conflicts between Labor Legislation and Bankruptcy Law*, Labor Relations and Public Policy Series, No. 30 (Philadelphia: Industrial Relations Unit, The Wharton School, University of Pennsylvania, 1987).

Lockouts involve a refusal to provide work. Although strikes can occur anytime after the termination of the contract, lockouts seldom occur because the employer loses revenues when not in operation. Most lockouts involve multiemployer bargaining units whose members seek to preserve the bargaining relationship by countering the strike of a single member.

Strikes occur more often when unions have failed to keep up with relevant comparison settlements. Good economic conditions are also associated with more strikes. The duration of strikes is longer if economic issues are the major concern.

Bankruptcies have been used increasingly by employers to abrogate labor agreements. Present interpretations of bankruptcy laws permit employers who undergo reorganization to unilaterally dissolve labor agreements just as they do other contracts.

DISCUSSION QUESTIONS

1. Why don't more firms use lockouts to break impasses?
2. What conditions are necessary for mediation to assist in settling an impasse?
3. Do you feel the present rights given to strikers by the NLRB are appropriate? Should they be greater or decreased?
4. What are the potential consequences for labor relations of the present interpretation of the bankruptcy statutes?

CASE

GMFC Impasse

Assume you are director of industrial relations for GMFC. The company and the union have failed to agree on a new contract, and the old contract expired last week. Two issues are unresolved, and no movement has been made on these for more than 10 days. The union is demanding 10 cents an hour more than the company is willing to offer, and management continues to demand some co-payment by employees for medical care. This is the first negotiation in 15 years in which a new contract has not been ratified before the expiration of the old one.

Local 384 voted a strike authorization for its leadership about a month ago, but they have not indicated yet whether they intend to strike. In your organization, production managers are lobbying for a lockout to avoid material losses if the heated steel-treating process must be shut down rapidly. Marketing managers want production maintained to meet orders scheduled for shipment. They argue the union doesn't intend to strike because it hasn't already done so.

In the executive council meeting this morning, financial officers briefed the top executives of GMFC and indicated the company could accept a wage settlement of 5 cents an hour more, but only if this were a firm figure and not subject to increases over the term of the contract. Unfortunately, the union appeared adamant that it will not agree to any health care co-payment.

It is now your turn to recommend strategy to the company in this impasse. Considering the evidence, what course of action should the company take? Outline the action, including processes used and timetables. Consider the possibility that your strategy will trigger a strike or other union activity.

CHAPTER 12

Union–Management Cooperation

Many labor relations practices are adversarial—organizing, bargaining over wages, disputing contract interpretation, and the like. But, it has been increasingly argued that unions and managements can achieve improved outcomes for both through cooperation. As noted earlier, the bargaining unit depends on employment for its existence. If the viability of the employer is threatened and the union perceives this threat as credible, both are likely to cooperate to devise a survival strategy. Recent union concessions in many of the nation's primary industries were rooted in the recognition that union members' jobs were on the line.

This chapter explores the mechanisms and programs involved in union–management cooperation, including regional labor–management cooperation projects, joint union–management productivity programs, gainsharing programs, and innovative methods for improving negotiations. In reading this chapter, consider the following questions:

1. How are the mechanisms required for problem solving different than those for adversarial situations?
2. When do cooperative projects become incorporated into the contract, and when are they operated by more informal relationships?
3. What are some results of cooperative programs? Are they equally likely to lead to successes for both unions and managements?
4. What types of outside assistance might be necessary for unions and managements to implement cooperative programs?

INTEGRATIVE BARGAINING

Integrative bargaining is defined as a set of activities leading to the simultaneous accomplishment of unconflicting objectives for both parties. The objectives are related to the solution of a common problem.[1] Conflict occurs when parties have different goals and either the sharing of resources or the interdependencies of tasks leads to the blockage of one party's goal attainment if the other party pursues a certain course.[2] For example, shared resources may be available hours of work, and different goals may be premium earnings for the union and high profits for management. One's accomplishment will interfere with the other's.

Integrative bargaining takes place when the accomplishment of one party's goal will not block the accomplishment of the other's. Integrative issues may not be immediately known to the parties or may emerge as the result of distributive bargaining's failure to achieve the goals the parties anticipated for themselves.

Two major types of integrative solutions are suggested. The first is a situation in which both parties experience an absolute gain over their previous positions. As an example, the West Coast dockworkers achieved permanent job security in return for the maritime industry's ability to introduce technological changes in the 1960s.[3] This bargain allowed the industry to reduce costs and guaranteed longshore workers a base earnings level because of a guaranteed number of hours of work. Second, integrative bargaining may occur when both parties sacrifice simultaneously (in distributive bargaining, one's gain is the other's loss).[4] Auto industry concessions reduced labor costs enough in several situations to keep open certain plants that had been considered for closure, thus increasing the likely job security of many auto workers.

Change processes within union–management situations may require certain conditions to exist. Increasing internal or external pressures should lead to the consideration of new joint ventures. Multiple constituencies within the union and/or management would stimulate new efforts to arrive at innovative procedures for dealing with joint problems. Where the normal collective bargaining process and its attention to crisis situations is used exclusively, innovation is less likely. Joint commitments are more likely when a program is seen as accomplishing important ends for both and when both are willing to make some compromises on the level of goal accomplishments they

[1] Richard E. Walton and Robert B. McKersie, *A Behavioral Theory of Labor Negotiations* (New York: McGraw-Hill, 1965), p. 5.

[2] Stuart M. Schmidt and Thomas A. Kochan, "Conflict: Toward Conceptual Clarity," *Administrative Science Quarterly*, 1972, pp. 359–70.

[3] Max D. Kossoris, "1966 West Coast Longshore Negotiations," *Monthly Labor Review*, October 1966, pp. 1073–4.

[4] Walton and McKersie, *Behavioral Theory*, pp. 128–29.

desire. Programs should allow early measurable progress toward goal attainments to maintain support for both constituencies. Benefits of the program must be experienced by many of each group's members, and these benefits should not detract from the accomplishment of other important goals. Programs should be insulated from the formal bargaining process, and the usual methods for distributive bargaining would be expected to continue.[5]

A three-step integrative bargaining model requires that; (1) the problem as perceived by each party is identified, and each conveys information germane to the problem; (2) the parties discover how they will reach their individually important goals simultaneously; (3) the parties compare and evaluate the alternatives for reaching simultaneous goals to determine the course having the greatest benefits to both.[6]

Several conditions are necessary for facilitating problem solving. First, the parties must be jointly motivated to reach a solution. Second, communications between the two parties must reveal as much information addressing the problem as possible. Third, the parties must have created a climate in which they can trust each other to deliberate over the issues without taking advantage of information disclosed.[7]

Paradoxically, integrative bargaining is most appropriate in both immediate and long-run problem situations. For example, an integrative solution may be appropriate when a particular contract issue causes grievances during the term of the agreement. Rather than waiting until the next negotiation, addressing the problem immediately may lead to positive outcomes for both parties. On the other hand, anticipated consequences of changes in technology may be long run and require the parties to enter into an open-ended relationship extending beyond the contract period.

Recognize, however, that success in problem solving and integrative bargaining does not necessarily create an idealistic long-run relationship between the parties. Not many of the integrative bargaining arrangements concluded during the 1960s have continued to the present time.[8] Perhaps integrative bargaining results from the recognition that a major change faces an organization or industry (for example, survival), and the integrative solutions necessary to solve the employ-

---

[5] Thomas A. Kochan and Lee Dyer, "A Model of Organizational Change in the Context of Union–Management Relations," *Journal of Applied Behavioral Science,* 1976, pp. 59–78.

[6] Walton and McKersie, *Behavioral Theory,* pp. 137–39.

[7] Ibid., pp. 139–43.

[8] See, for example, a major work examining integrative solutions of the 1950s and 1960s by James A. Henderson, Edward R. Hintz, Jr., Jerry V. Jarrett, Robert G. Marbut, William J. White, and James J. Healy (eds.), *Creative Collective Bargaining: Meeting Today's Challenges to Labor–Management Relations* (Englewood Cliffs, N.J.: Prentice-Hall, 1965), and try to find how many are still in operation.

ment problems associated with the major change form a platform for subsequent distributive bargaining.

MODELS OF COOPERATION

The usual union–management relationship is adversarial. Cooperation requires structures other than those involved in contract negotiations. One model of cooperation is equivalent to the normal collective bargaining model, with union and management representatives determining the outcomes to pursue. The other model includes management and the employee representatives (some of whom may be elected by union members). The greatest difficulty in the first model is determining which issues should be handled by the collective bargaining process and which should be handled in a joint problem-solving manner. In the second, the union may lose power because nonunion constituents become a part of the employee involvement process.[9]

The employee representatives in a cooperative system may be more effective if they are also union representatives when the collective bargaining relationship is successful but not when it is perceived as unsuccessful. When the normal collective bargaining relationship is to be retained, cooperative groups will be advisory; but when management and employee representatives are included outside the bargaining relationship, they must have the power to implement solutions to be effective.[10]

A great deal of evidence strongly supports the premise that U.S. employers are basically opposed to unions, particularly to union involvement in decision making of any kind.[11] Recently, however, there has been an increasing number of collaborative initiatives outside the collective bargaining agreement and integrative bargains within the contract to enhance firm performance and improve job security.[12] Given management's long-standing antipathy toward unions, it's reasonable to expect collaboration to be pursued only where improved performance is an expected result.

Cooke has proposed a model of the impact of collaboration on performance. The model (shown in Figure 12-1) suggests that the

9 Jeanne M. Brett, "Behavioral Research on Unions and Union–Management Systems," in *Research in Organizational Behavior*, ed. Barry M. Staw and Larry L. Cummings (Greenwich, Conn.: JAI Press, 1980), pp. 201–4.

10 Ibid., pp. 204–7.

11 David Lewin, "Industrial Relations as a Strategic Variable," in *Human Resources and the Performance of the Firm*, ed. Morris M. Kleiner, Richard N. Block, Myron Roomkin, and Sidney W. Salsburg (Madison, Wis.: Industrial Relations Research Association, 1987), pp. 1–41.

12 Thomas A. Kochan, Harry C. Katz, and Robert B. McKersie, *The Transformation of American Industrial Relations* (New York: Basic Books, 1986).

FIGURE 12-1

Implicit Model of the Impact of Collaboration on Performance

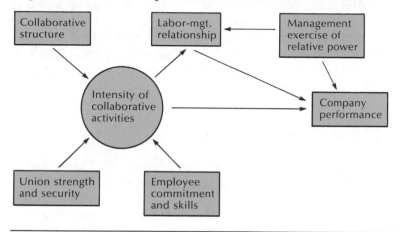

Source: William N. Cooke, "Improving Productivity and Quality: Juxtaposing Relative and Collaborative Power," unpublished paper, Ann Arbor: Graduate School of Business Administration and Joint Labor-Management Relations Center, University of Michigan, 1988, p. 8.

intensity of collaborative activities, the underlying union-management relationship, and management's exercise of relative power all influence performance. The union–management relationship is enhanced positively by intense collaboration and negatively by the exercise of management power in, for example, substituting capital for labor. Intensity depends on a collaborative structure, the commitment and skill of employees, and union strength and security.

Team-based efforts actively involved in problem identification and solution are seen as enhancing collaborative intensity more than broad-based committee activity. The union's strength and security should reduce member suspicions about possible management cooptation. Strong unions may also reduce the relative power of management, thus worsening union-management relations. Skills and commitment may be enhanced in more senior employees, who understand the production process; however, they may be less accustomed to and have greater antipathy toward collaboration with a historical adversary.[13]

Methods of Cooperation

Most of the rest of this chapter examines a variety of methods of cooperation. The assumptions associated with various types of cooper-

[13] William N. Cooke, "Improving Productivity and Quality: Juxtaposing Relative and Collaborative Power," unpublished paper (Ann Arbor: Joint Labor-Management Relations Center, University of Michigan, 1988).

ation, the mechanisms used to achieve cooperation, the union and management personnel involved, and the results of the cooperative efforts are covered. To do this, several generic types of approaches to improving labor–management cooperation, including area-wide labor–management committees, improvement of the atmosphere in contract negotiations, productivity improvement and employee involvement plans, quality-of-work-life programs, and employee stock ownership plans are examined.

AREA–WIDE LABOR–MANAGEMENT COMMITTEES

Area–wide labor–management committees (AWLMC) are jointly sponsored organizations created in particular geographic areas or industries. They neither engage in collective bargaining nor form multiemployer or multiunion bargaining units. Instead, they serve as advisory units to deal with employment issues jointly experienced by their constituents.

AWLMCs have almost always been created as a result of significant employment problems. To this point, they have been concentrated in the Northeast and Midwest in areas with significant declines in employment and in industries declining or lagging in growth. There may have been a history of plant closings and parent companies expanding elsewhere. High wages and/or union–management relations problems may have led to some of the employment problems.

The primary assumption behind the creation of AWLMCSs is that labor and management's peer members may place pressure on each other to identify sources of employment problems and use cooperative methods for reducing or avoiding conflict. The identification of joint issues, such as reduced profits and declining job security, may lead to joint efforts to resolve them.

AWLMCs are typically managed by an executive director hired by a coalition of top-level business and union leaders in an area or industry. Approximately equal numbers of members are from labor and management. The AWLMCs engage in four major types of activities: (1) sponsoring social events to improve labor–management communications, (2) establishing labor–management committees in local plants, (3) providing assistance in negotiations, and (4) fostering local economic development.[14] These activities aimed at creating an environment in which problems can be solved and an outward appearance of labor and management cooperation for the betterment of both.

---

[14] Richard D. Leone, *The Operation of Area Labor-Management Committees*, (Washington, D.C.: U.S. Department of Labor, Labor-Management Services Administration, 1982).

The effectiveness of AWLMCs is difficult to assess because in many areas they do not encompass all employers and all employers are not facing the same types of problems. In Buffalo, New York, in-plant committees were established to facilitate negotiations in a utility company having a 17-week strike and in four cargo-handling firms facing declining shipping volumes. Progress toward the negotiating and cargo volume objectives was achieved.

In Jamestown, New York, several committees were begun in small- to medium-size plants. The community had little success in involving the two largest local employers. Early evidence suggests in-plant committees were successful in improving productivity and reducing overhead; but because inadequate attention was paid to implementation and gaining agreement on the effects of changes, many of the efforts foundered.

Generally speaking, the evidence suggests AWLMCs need the backing of major employers who have visibility in the community and a competent executive director who is willing and able to stay in the post for an extended period to accomplish their goals.[15]

JOINT LABOR–MANAGEMENT COMMITTEES

An examination of the joint labor–management committee (JLMC) in the retail food industry indicates the forum involving top union and management leaders has helped managers understand the na-tional–local union relationship in a decentralized industry. Successful projects have involved research in occupational safety and health is-sues, the introduction of new technology, health care cost con-tainment, and competitiveness issues.[16] Generally, JLMCs are imple-mented in industries with many employers and a dominant union with locals in many employers and locations.

RELATIONS BY OBJECTIVES

The FMCS has begun a pilot program called relations by objectives (RBO) to assist bargaining relationships that have had chronic negotiat-ing difficulties. The program is designed to increase the skills of union and management negotiators in communication, mutual goal setting, and goal attainment. These programs assume that improving problem-solving skills and obtaining increased information will enable each side to better appreciate the other's positions and to specify the issues

---

[15] Ibid.; and Robert W. Ahern, "Discussion of Labor-Management Cooperation," *Proceedings of the Industrial Relations Research Association*, 1982, pp. 201–6.

[16] Kochan et al., *Transformation*, pp. 182–89.

over which negotiations should take place. The techniques bring union and management members together outside of the negotiating situation to mutually plan actions to reduce future conflict.

Initial experiments with RBO were conducted where bargaining had experienced severe difficulties in the past. However, both managements and unions were motivated to improve relations due to disruptions in production and union members' impatience over failure to solve contract disputes and grievances without strikes. Members of bargaining committees for both sides were taken off-site and taught problem identification and solving skills. Then, mixed groups were given practice in problem solving. After the training, joint labor–management committees monitored progress within the RBO programs, and some reduction in friction was reported.[17]

However, the efficacy of third-party intervention programs for the reduction of strikes has been questioned. In a continuation of the work begun on wildcat strikes in the coal mining industry, it was suggested that the organizational development approach inherent in RBO is inappropriate for collective bargaining. The elimination of conflict is inconsistent with collective bargaining. The parties might be better off to construct a system allowing the conflict to be resolved in a structured manner, written out and known by both parties prior to conflicts.[18]

WORKPLACE INTERVENTIONS

The prevalence of joint programs varies widely across manufacturers. Table 12–1 shows the prevalence of a variety of joint programs among over 200 company and union situations. Of these, quality and productivity issues seem the most frequently addressed by workteam-based programs, while productivity and labor–management climate are more frequently handled by committee-based structures. Programs were generally initiated by the company without outside assistance. Where outside assistance was used, U.S. government agency support was most frequently cited.[19]

A variety of workplace interventions have been implemented in American industry. Figure 12–2 summarizes key program dimensions across intervention names for six major types of methods. The meth-

---

[17] Denise T. Hoyer, *Relations by Objectives: An Experimental Program of Management–Union Conflict Resolution,* unpublished doctoral dissertation (Ann Arbor: University of Michigan, 1982).

[18] Jeanne M. Brett, Stephen B. Goldberg, and William Ury, "Mediation and Organizational Development: Models of Conflict Management," *Proceedings of the Industrial Relations Research Association,* 1980, pp. 195–202.

[19] William N. Cooke, "Labor–Management Collaboration: New Partnerships or Going in Circles," unpublished manuscript (Ann Arbor: University of Michigan, 1988).

TABLE 12-1

Type and Extent of Joint Programs Across Manufacturing

Type of program	Percent of plants with program*
Quality circles	31
Quality of work life/employee involvement	19
Work teams	18
Productivity committees	17
Labor-management committees	15
Scanlon or other gainsharing (with employee involvement)	7
Employee stock ownership (with employee involvement)	6
Profit sharing (with employee involvement)	6
Other than above	12

* Based on 194 company responses and 40 unique union responses.

Source: William N. Cooke, "Improving Productivity and Quality: Juxtaposing Relative and Collaborative Power," unpublished paper, Ann Arbor: Graduate School of Business Administration and Joint Labor-Management Relations Center, University of Michigan, 1988, 4.

ods can be divided roughly into two different types: gainsharing and nongainsharing. Gainsharing occurs when labor becomes more productive following an intervention than it was during a base period and when the economic gains are shared with labor. Nongainsharing approaches may involve a changed reward structure (primarily nonmonetary) as part of the intervention, but no contingency between productivity and pay is established. The figure summarizes each intervention method's guiding philosophy, primary change goal, degree of worker participation, role of supervisors and management, any bonus formulas, role of the union, and other method characteristics.

Scanlon, Rucker, and Impro-Share plans are explicitly designed to improve productivity. Scanlon and Rucker plans depend on employee suggestions; the Scanlon plan allows employee groups to screen and implement suggestions, while management controls the suggestion system in Rucker plans. The Impro-Share plan shares savings resulting from improvements in individual performance over an engineered standard and allows employers to make "buy outs" or productivity improvements if new technologies are introduced. Quality circles enable employees to solve production problems and implement solutions. No bonus is explicitly tied to improvements; however, under Japanese systems, all employees share in bonuses resulting from the organization's performance at six-month or yearly intervals. Labor-management committees are often formed to deal with pervasive employment problems within the organization. Quality-of-work-life programs aim at improving the workplace environment and increasing the satisfaction of employees, with productivity changes as a welcomed by-product if they are positive.

The current preoccupation by American managers with Japanese methods is useful for a reexamination of these approaches. But Ameri-

FIGURE 12-2

Comparative Analysis of Six Workplace Interventions

Intervention

	Gainsharing		
Program dimension	*Scanlon*	*Rucker*	*Impro-Share*
Philosophy/theory	Org-single unit; share improvements; people capable/willing to make suggestions, want to make ideas	Primarily economic incentive; some reliance on employee participation	Economic incentives increase performance
Primary goal	Productivity improvement	Productivity improvement	Productivity improvement
Subsidiary goals	Attitudes, communication, work behaviors, quality, cost reduction	Attitudes, communication, work behaviors, quality, cost reductions	Attitudes, work behaviors
Worker participation	Two level of committees: screening (1), production (many)	Screening (1), production (1) (sometimes)	Bonus committee
Suggestion making	Formal system	Formal system	None
Role of supervisor	Chair, production committee	None	None
Role of managers	Direct participation in bonus committee assignments	Ideas coordinator evaluates suggestions, committee assignments	
Bonus formula	$\dfrac{\text{Sales}}{\text{payroll}}$	$\dfrac{\text{Bargaining unit payroll}}{\text{Production value (sales-materials, supplies, services)}}$	$\dfrac{\text{Engineered std.} \times \text{BPF}}{\text{Total hours worked}}$
Frequency of payout	Monthly	Monthly	Weekly
Role of union	Negotiated provisions, screening committee membership	Negotiated provisions, screening committee membership	Negotiated provisions
Impact on management style	Substantial	Slight	None

Source: Michael Schuster, *Union-Management Cooperation: Structure, Process, and Impact* (Kalamazoo, Mich.: W. E. Upjohn Institute for Employment Research, 1984), p. 73.

	No gainsharing	
Quality circles	Labor–management committees	Quality-of-work-life projects
People capable/willing to offer ideas/make suggestions	Improve attitudes; trust	Improve working environment (physical, human, systems aspects)
Cost reduction, quality	Improve labor–management relations, communications	Improve psychological well-being at work; increase job satisfaction
Attitudes, communication, work behaviors, quality, productivity	Work behaviors, quality, productivity, cost reductions	Attitudes, communication, work behaviors, quality, productivity, cost reduction
Screening (1), circles (many)	Visitor sub-committees (many)	Steering committees; ad hoc to work on problem; informal
Context of committee	None, informal	Possibly informal, depending on project
Circle leaders	None	No direct role
Facilitator evaluates proposed solutions	Committee members	Steering committee membership
All savings/improvements retained by company	All savings/improvements retained by company	All savings/improvements retained by company
Not applicable	Not applicable	Not applicable
Tacit approval	Active membership	Negotiated provisions, steering committee membership
Somewhat	Somewhat	Substantial

can managers have often tended to implement bits and pieces of methods without understanding the underlying foundations necessary for their success. For example, quality circles do not exist in a vacuum. A support system in which a supervisor is a team leader, where employees sense management's commitment to their individual goals, and where members work as equals on a common problem are necessary cultural props for participatively based systems to work.[20]

The Scanlon Plan

The genesis of the Scanlon plan took place in the late 1930s in an obsolete steel mill. With profits close to zero and employees demanding higher wages and better working conditions, their union leader, Joseph Scanlon, saw that gaining the demands would force the company out of business. To meet the profit goals of the company and the wage and working condition demands of the employees, he proposed the parties work together to increase productivity while postponing a wage increase. But at a later date, if productivity were improved, the gains would be shared with the workers. The program's two underlying foundations are participation by all organization members and equity in reward distribution.[21]

The participation system is based on a recognition that abilities are widely distributed in the organization and that change in the organization's environment is inevitable. Because change occurs and because persons at all levels may have solutions to problems or may suggest changes to improve productivity, the system includes an open suggestion procedure. These suggestions are evaluated and acted on by joint-management committees who make recommendations up the line. Figure 12–3 details the typical composition of a committee and its actions.

A suggestion is evaluated by the production committee of a given work unit. If the suggestion is implementable and has merit in that unit, the production committee can place it into effect. If the suggestion is questionable or has wide impact, it is forwarded to the screening committee (comprising executives and employee representatives) for evaluation and possible implementation.

The screening committee also has the responsibility of determining the level of the bonus paid each month or quarter. The bonus is generally calculated by comparing the usual share of product costs attributed to labor against the most recent actual costs. For example, if

---

[20] See Nina Hatvany and Vladimir Pucik, "Japanese Management Practices and Productivity," *Organizational Dynamics*, Spring 1981, pp. 4–21; and William Ouchi, *Theory Z* (Reading, Mass.: Addison-Wesley Publishing, 1981).

[21] Carl F. Frost, John H. Wakely, and Robert A. Ruh, *The Scanlon Plan for Organization Development: Identity, Participation, and Equity* (East Lansing: Michigan State University Press, 1974), pp. 5–26.

FIGURE 12-3

Scanlon Plan Production Committee

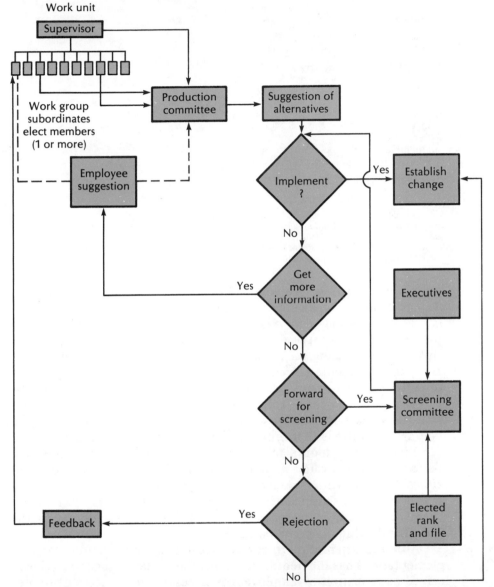

on the average each $1 of sales has traditionally required 30 cents' worth of labor, then any improvement to, say 29 or 25 cents would represent a productivity improvement. Table 12-2 represents a simple formula in which labor costs are 30 percent of the total production value.

Company-wide and individual bonuses can be calculated after the

TABLE 12–2

Simple Labor Formula

Sales	$ 98,000
Returned goods	3,000
Net sales	95,000
Inventory +	5,000
Production value	$100,000
Labor bill	
Wages	$ 16,000
Salaries	8,000
Vacations and holidays	1,800
Insurance	1,700
Pensions	500
Unemployment	500
F.I.C.A.	1,500
Total labor bill	$ 30,000
Ratio	

Source: Carl F. Frost, John H. Wakeley, and Robert A. Ruh, *The Scanlon Plan for Organization Development: Identity, Participation, and Equity* (East Lansing: Michigan State University Press, 1974), p. 103.

screening committee receives operating results for the previous period. Table 12–3 gives an example of a company and an employee report.

The plan's major purposes are to increase the rewards to both parties for productivity gains, encourage and reward participation, and link rewards to employee performance. The system focuses on productivity improvements associated with lower *labor* costs—a factor more directly within workers' control. Thus, the behavior–outcome relationship is higher than profit sharing or other similar types of gain-sharing systems. Productivity gains are shared across work groups, encouraging solutions that mutually benefit several departments.

When one Scanlon plan was intensively tracked over a nine-year period, the investigators found it had failed to pay a bonus only 13 times. Further, while productivity changes and productivity improvements were not significantly better, their direction was up. Employment at the site decreased over time but not as rapidly as in the industry in which it participated.[22]

Although attempting to compare results across Scanlon plan implementations has inherent limitations, the evidence suggests: (1) perceived participation by employees is necessary for successful implementation, (2) company or plant size does not appear to be a factor in plan success, (3) managerial attitudes toward the plan predict its success, (4) successful implementation takes a considerable period of time, (5) plans are more successful where expectations are high but

[22] Christopher S. Miller and Michael Schuster, "A Decade's Experience with the Scanlon Plan: A Case Study," *Journal of Occupational Behavior* 8 (1987), pp. 167–74.

TABLE 12–3

Bonus Report

a.	Scanlon ratio	0.40/1.00
b.	Value of production	$100,000
c.	Expected costs ($a \times b$)	40,000
d.	Actual costs	30,000
e.	Bonus pool ($c - d$)	10,000
f.	Share to company—20% ($e \times 0.20$)	2,000
g.	Share to employees—80% (adjusted pool) ($e \times 0.80$)	8,000
h.	Share for future deficits—25% of adjusted pool ($g \times 0.25$)	2,000
i.	Pool for immediate distribution ($g - h$)	6,000
j.	Bonus for each employee* as a percentage of pay for the production period ($i \div d$)	20%

The June pay record might look like this for a typical employee:

Name	Monthly pay for June	Bonus percent	Bonus	Total pay
Mary Smith	$900	20%	$180	$1,080

* This example assumes all employees are participating in the plan at the time this bonus is paid; for example, there has been no turnover and no employees are in their initial 30-, 60-, or 90-day trial periods.

Source: Modified from Carl F. Frost, John H. Wakeley, and Robert A. Ruh, *The Scanlon Plan for Organization Development: Identity, Participation, and Equity* (East Lansing: Michigan State University Press, 1974), p. 15.

realistic, (6) a high-level executive must be a leader in the implementation for it to be successful, and (7) the type of production technology used does not appear related to success or failure.[23]

Rucker Plans

Rucker plans have some of the participative elements of the Scanlon plan, but management usually has an idea coordinator who handles the suggestion process. The bonus formula is calculated in much the same way as the Scanlon plan except it allows employees also to share in savings in materials and other purchases for production. On the other hand, their increased costs, even in the face of improved productivity, could result in an inability to pay bonuses. Rucker plans might be suggested for an organization that is not ready to participate to the degree a Scanlon plan requires, but they may be difficult to obtain in a collective bargaining agreement.[24]

Impro-Share

Impro-Share is an individually oriented plan tying improved performance to an individual's pay. While consultative management is sug-

---

[23] J. Kenneth White, "The Scanlon Plan: Causes and Correlates of Success," *Academy of Management Journal*, June 1979, pp. 292–312.

[24] Michael Schuster, *Union–Management Cooperation: Structure, Process, and Impact*, (Kalamazoo, Mich.: W. E. Upjohn Institute for Employment Research, 1984).

TABLE 12-4

Conditions Favoring Gainsharing Plans

Characteristic	Favorable condition
Size	Less than 500 employees
Age	Old enough so that learning curve has flattened and standards can be set based on performance history
Financial measures	Simple, with a good history
Market for output	Good, can absorb additional production
Product costs	Controllable by employees
Organizational climate	Open, high level of trust
Style of management	Participative
Union-management relationship	Cooperative
Overtime history	Limited to no use of overtime in the past
Seasonality of business	Relatively stable across time
Work floor interdependence	High-to-moderate interdependence among jobs
Capital investment plans	Little investment planned
Product stability	Few product changes
Comptroller/CFO	Trusted, able to explain financial measures
Communication policy	Open, willing to share financial results
Plant manager	Trusted, committed to plan, able to articulate goals and ideals of plan
Management	Technically competent, supportive of participative management style, good communications skills, able to deal with suggestions and new ideas
Work force	Technically knowledgeable, interested in participation and higher pay, financially knowledgeable and/or interested
Plant support services	Maintenance and engineering groups competent, willing, and able to respond to increased load

Source: Adapted from E. E. Lawler, *Pay and Organizational Development* (Reading, Mass.: Addison-Wesley Publishing, 1982), p. 144.

gested in the plan, union participation is minimal except through a bonus committee responsible for determining some of the aspects of the bonus formula. The bonus formula is somewhat complex, but the result subtracts the actual hours an employee works from the "base value earned hours" of his/her productivity. If the result is positive, the employee's share (say, 50 percent) is divided by the actual number of hours worked to obtain a bonus percentage. For example, if an employee worked 1,000 hours during a period and the base value earned hours were 1,100 with a 50 percent share, the Impro-Share bonus would be 5 percent.

Impro-Share allows the organization to pinpoint incentives toward specific jobs or groups and decreases competitors' ability to determine wage costs based on bonus formulas. However, employees have difficulty calculating what they will receive.[25] Table 12-4 lists characteristics improving the likelihood of a gainsharing program's success.

---

[25] Ibid.

EXHIBIT 12-1

Typical Characteristics of Quality Circles

Objectives:
  To improve communication, particularly between line employees and management.
  To identify and solve problems.

Organization:
  The circle consists of a leader and 8 to 10 employees from one area of work. The circle also has a coordinator and one or more facilitators who work closely with it.

Selection of circle members:
  Participation of members is voluntary.
  Participation of leaders may or may not be voluntary.

Scope of problems analyzed by circles:
  The circle selects its own problems.
  Initially, the circle is encouraged to select problems from its immediate work area.
  Problems are not restricted to quality but also include productivity, cost, safety, morale, housekeeping, environment, and other spheres.

Training:
  Formal training in problem-solving techniques is usually a part of circle meetings.

Meetings:
  Usually one hour per week.

Awards for circle activities:
  Usually no monetary awards are given.
  The most effective reward is the satisfaction of the circle members from solving problems and observing the implementation of their own solutions.

Quality Circles

Quality circles (QCs) are a nongainsharing workplace intervention method. QCs are teams of employees supported by management who periodically meet to focus attention on product and service quality or other issues. In both union and nonunion settings, the leaders or facilitators in the QCs typically have not been the supervisors of the work group, particularly where the circle cuts across functional areas (for example, production and quality assurance). Exhibit 12-1 shows the typical characteristics of QCs. Until recently, little direct evidence on the effects of QCs in union situations in the United States has been obtained. However, a recent study found the opportunity for participation in quality circles was most attractive to employees who were younger; believed the union should be involved; less likely involved in union activities; more often involved in on-the-job activities, such as suggestion programs; desired more participation; and had more information on quality circles. The results of the study suggest unions should not be concerned about employee involvement programs as a means for weakening union control, but rather employees will identify increasingly with the company if the union doesn't support an opportunity for interested employees to be involved.[26]

Labor–Management Committees

Labor–management committees are most often the plant-level corollary of the AWLMC. They tend to focus on particular problems of the organization if labor–management relations have been deteriorating and may lead to one of the more formal plans previously described. Representatives and methods are determined on an ad hoc basis. Their success probably depends on the degree to which the parties can focus on joint problems threatening their mutual interests.

Quality-Of-Work-Life Programs

Quality of work life (QWL) represents not only job satisfaction but also an opportunity for growth and self-development, freemom from tension and stress, and an avenue to the fulfillment of basic needs.[27] Work environments offering security, equity in treatment, opportunities for individual adaptations, and democracy are assumed to be of high quality.[28] Where QWL programs have been implemented, integrative bargaining methods have been used to begin the programs. The actual QWL experiment is frequently conducted outside the contract, or the contract itself is suspended within the unit in which changes are taking place.

From an overall standpoint, QWL programs apparently include three components: (1) improving climate, (2) generating commitment, and (3) implementing change. However, three alternative developmen-

[26] Anil Verma and Robert B. McKersie, "Employee Involvement: The Implications of Noninvolvement by Unions," *Industrial and Labor Relations Review* 40 (1987), pp. 556–68.

[27] Edward E. Lawler, "Measuring the Psychological Quality of Working Life: The Why and How of It," in *The Quality of Working Life* vol. 1, ed. Louis E. Davis and Albert B. Cherns (New York: Free Press, 1975), pp. 124–25.

[28] Neal Q. Herrick and Michael Maccoby, "Harmonizing Work: A Priority Goal of the 1970s," in *The Quality of Working Life*, vol. 1, ed. Louis E. David and Albert B. Cherns (New York: Free Press, 1975), pp. 64–66.

tal patterns involving these three components exist. In planned programs, climate and commitment lead to change; in evolved programs, climate leads to change, which leads in turn to commitment; and in induced programs, change leads to appropriate climate and commitment.[29]

A number of QWL experiments have been conducted, with mixed results. Many have taken place in the auto industry and have involved the UAW and supplier organizations or General Motors. In one case, Rockwell International agreed a new plant would establish work teams and give employees wider responsibilities. Employees would participate in determining work rules and production standards. Mechanisms were developed to resolve as many grievances as possible on a supervisor–employee level.[30] At Harman International in Bolivar, Tennessee, automobile mirror production workers were given the options of leaving when their day's production quota was completed, working a full eight hours at piece rates, taking training for other jobs provided by the company, or taking another job with another employer.[31]

These QWL programs aim at improving outcomes for both employees and the employer. More satisfying work, better economic outcomes, and more say in work methods and production rates may increase employees' overall feelings about the quality of their employment. Employers may gain through reductions in absences, accidents, and strikes; improved productive volume and quality; enhanced abilities to transfer workers as skills improve; and reduced downtime to equipment.[32]

Because a good deal of controversy arises among both employers and unions about the necessity for QWL programs and the ways in which they should be implemented, research on the preferred methods for starting programs is important. Union leaders prefer handling QWL programs jointly outside of the collective bargaining agreement.[33]

Although evidence on the effectiveness of QWL programs is not in yet, isolated examples are now beginning to be reported, including a series of publications indicating results of QWL and other labor-management cooperation programs.[34] Some major companies

---

[29] Robert W. Keidel, "QWL Development: Three Trajectories," *Human Relations,* 1982, pp. 743–61.

[30] Edgar Weinberg, "Labor–Management Cooperation: A Report on Recent Initiatives," *Monthly Labor Review,* April 1976, pp. 13–22.

[31] Michael Maccoby, "Changing Work," *Working Papers,* Summer 1975, pp. 43–55.

[32] Barry A. Macy and Philip H. Mirvis, "A Methodology for Assessment of Quality of Work Life and Organizational Effectiveness in Behavioral-Economic Terms," *Administrative Science Quarterly* 1976, p. 214.

[33] Lee Dyer, David B. Lipsky, and Thomas A. Kochan, "Union Attitudes toward Management Cooperation," *Industrial Relations,* May 1977, pp. 163–72.

[34] U.S. Department of Labor, Labor Management Services Administration, *Labor-Management Cooperation: Recent Efforts and Results* (Washington, D.C.: U.S. Government Printing Office, 1982).

have implemented broad programs on an organization-wide basis; but, some of the plants in which these programs were inaugurated have had difficulties sustaining them through the recent auto industry concessions.

A preliminary study of some results of the GM–UAW QWL projects in 18 plants has been reported. The study examined aspects of industrial relations performance, quality, productive efficiency, and QWL components. From a labor relations perspective, measures of grievances, discipline, absenteeism, number of local contract demands, and negotiating time were significantly related. Grievances and absenteeism also tended to rise during periods of strong demand for automobiles. Product quality and productivity-efficiency measures were negatively related to industrial relations problems. Managerial attitudes were positively related to both labor relations and productivity-efficiency measures. Evidence also suggests QWL programs were associated with higher product quality and reduced grievance rates. Absenteeism, ironically, was associated with higher quality, possibly because less-careful workers were absent more often. QWL program ratings were not associated with productivity-efficiency changes.[35]

Research on the Effects of Cooperation across Organizations

A study of several hundred organizations has yielded important information on the effects of various contextual and cooperative structures on productivity and quality. The more active that team-based programs are, the greater their effect. Top union leader participation is important as well. Larger plants have more difficulty improving productivity through cooperative efforts. Technology changes improve productivity at a rate faster than any negative effects from unilateral management implementation. Higher union security predicts more positive results. Subcontracting apparently reduces the possibility of gains, as do situations where layoffs occur more frequently. Interestingly, the larger the proportion of women in the work force, the greater are productivity gains.[36]

Research on the Long-Run Effects of Cooperation

Surprisingly little research on the long-run effects of union-management cooperation has been reported. However, a recent study of several different types of union–management cooperation initiatives now begins to offer some evidence of the effects.[37]

---

[35] Harry C. Katz, Thomas A. Kochan, and Kenneth R. Gobeille, "Industrial Relations Performance, Economic Performance, and QWL Programs: An Interplant Analysis," *Industrial and Labor Relations Review*, October 1983, pp. 3–17.

[36] Cooke, "Improving Productivity and Quality."

[37] Schuster, *Union–Management Cooperation.*

Large differences are apparent in the philosophies underlying cooperation projects. Scanlon and quality circle programs have the greatest participation, while Rucker and Impro-Share programs are mostly associated with economic incentives. The plans cannot substitute for good management, but where that does not exist, labor–management committees can be a springboard for progress. In the absence of management's commitment to participation, Scanlon and other types of high-participation programs will fail. Critical factors for the ongoing success of the programs are the training and commitment of supervisors and the construction and understanding of the bonus formulas.

Companies and unions generally begin the programs to improve labor relations, to increase the amount of compensation available, and so on. Whatever the parties' motives might be, they will influence the type of cooperation plan chosen. Gainsharing influences productivity more than labor–management committees or QWL programs. And no matter which method is chosen, it will not be necessary if traditional collective bargaining methods are successful. Companies and unions both appear to bargain rather than use cooperative alternatives unless difficulties arise in accomplishing their goals.

A study of cooperation in 23 sites found productivity improvements in 12 and no change in 10 others. In 16 of the sites, the subsequent experience enabled union members to earn bonuses supplementing what they would have earned solely as a result of collective bargaining. Evidence suggests bonus levels are directly influenced by the rate of suggestions generated by the employees.[38] Employment levels are relatively unaffected by cooperative programs, and labor relations are seen as improved.[39]

Finally, evidence suggests the productivity improvements are associated primarily with a one-shot increase rather than a long, steady improvement. And, the workplace intervention most likely to produce the productivity improvement appears to be the Scanlon plan.

EMPLOYEE STOCK OWNERSHIP PLANS

Employee stock ownership plans (ESOPs) were first permitted by the Employee Retirement Income Security Act (ERISA) of 1974. Under the legislation, employees may participate in the ownership of their employing firms through profit sharing, productivity improvements, or subtractions from their wages. Since the early 1980s, several companies (such as Chrysler Corporation, Eastern Air Lines, and National

---

[38] Michael Schuster, "The Scanlon Plan: A Longitudinal Analysis," *Journal of Applied Behavioral Science*, 1984, pp. 23–38.

[39] Michael Schuster, "The Impact of Union–Management Cooperation on Productivity and Employment," *Industrial and Labor Relations Review*, April 1983, pp. 415–30.

Steel Corporation) have agreed to give employees stock in the firm in exchange for labor concessions. In some companies, like Rath Packing, the employees became majority owners.

Employee ownership began in relatively small-sized companies and in subsidiaries of larger companies that were up for sale or potential closure. Some evidence suggests employee-owned companies are more profitable than others. Managers in these companies believe employee attitudes are better and this is partially related to the breadth of employee participation in ownership.[40]

Employee ownership sometimes occurs as a result of progressively declining organizational performance. Rath Packing in Waterloo, Iowa, is an example in which a local labor–management committee helped arrange a government grant that provided loans for new equipment while employees bought 60 percent of the company through wage reduction contributions.[41] The company was able to move into the black for a short while but has since gone bankrupt due to continued cost pressures on the older segments of the meat-packing industry.

SUMMARY

Cooperation between unions and managements takes place in the specification of the bargaining relationship regarding the working environment of employees and the goals of employers. The mechanism for establishing cooperative relationships is integrative bargaining. This approach differs from distributive bargaining in that both parties are jointly seeking a solution to a problem instead of contesting for an outcome.

In the United States, cooperation usually occurs outside of the negotiated relationship but involves representatives of the union and management. Experiments have involved improving the bargaining relationship through such programs as relations by objectives or workplace interventions such as gainsharing plans (the Scanlon plan, Rucker plan, and Impro-Share) and nongainsharing interventions (labor–management committees, quality circles, and quality-of-work-life programs).

Employee stock ownership plans aim to increase employee commitment to the company through the long-run improvement of the value of ownership gained through higher productivity.

Evidence suggests increasing numbers of companies are implementing (with unions) team-based action groups to improve productiv-

---

[40] Michael Conte and Arnold S. Tannenbaum, "Employee-Owned Companies: Is the Difference Measurable?" *Monthly Labor Review*, July 1978, pp. 23–28.

[41] Warner Woodworth, "Collective Bargaining: Concessions or Control?" *Proceedings of the Industrial Relations Research Association*, 1982, pp. 418–24.

ity and quality. Perceived productivity seems to increase most where the union is secure, where top union officials are involved in the process, and where significant numbers of union members are involved in team-based activities. Employer introduction of new technology continues to lead the way in improving productivity.

DISCUSSION QUESTIONS

1. Why would including such programs as QWL in the collective agreement be difficult?
2. Under what conditions would a Scanlon plan likely be effective over relatively long time periods?
3. What are the potential long-run problems for unions in agreeing to productivity bargaining programs?
4. Should unions be guaranteed a seat on an organization's board of directors?

CASE

Continuing or Abandoning the Special-Order Fabrication Business

It is about three months since the effective date of the GMFC–Local 384 contract. In GMFC's executive council meeting this morning, financial officers made their report of an in-depth study on the profitability of the special-order fabrication operations. Their recommendation was that GMFC take no more orders for this area and, when present commitments were shipped, close down the operation. Their data showed the operations were losing money two out of the last three years, and they argued the Speedy-Lift assembly lines could be expanded into that area for meeting the increasing demand for GMFC forklift trucks.

Top-level management in the special-order fabrication operations conceded that profits, when earned, were low but pointed out that, from a return-on-investment standpoint, they had been among the best in the company during the 1968–73 period. Besides, they argued many of the special orders were from some of the largest customers in the standard product lines, and GMFC could ill afford to lose that business if it was dependent on occasional custom orders as well.

The finance people reiterated their recommendations to terminate the operation, pointing out that labor costs had risen over the last several contracts and, due to the custom nature of the work, productivity gains had been small because new technologies could not be introduced.

After both sides presented their final summations, the chief executive officer announced that the firm should make preparations necessary to terminate operations. After the announcement, the industrial relations director pointed out that GMFC would have to negotiate the termination with Local 384. The union might demand severance pay, job transfers, and so forth. The point was also raised that this decision offered the union and the company the opportunity to devise a method for reducing and controlling labor costs.

The CEO designated the vice president of finance, the general manager of special-order fabrications, and the industrial relations director as the bargaining team to present the company's decision and bargain a resolution. The CEO made it clear that the company intended to abandon these operations but could reverse its position with the right kind of labor cost reductions.

Although this meeting was not publicized, Local 384's leadership had been concerned about the special-order fabrications area for some time. Management had frequently grumbled about low productivity, and stewards were frequently harassed about alleged slowdowns. Union members in the shop often grieved about work rule changes. The stack of piled-up grievances, coupled with management's inaction on them, led the leadership to request a meeting with the industrial relations director to solve the problems.

Directions

1. Rejoin your original labor or management bargaining team.
2. Reach an agreement for continuation or termination of the special-order fabrication operations.
   a. Company negotiators must reduce labor costs by 10 percent and stabilize them for project bids if operations are to continue (labor costs are 30 percent of the total costs, and ROI would be 7 percent if costs were cut by 10 percent).
   b. Union members are unwilling to have their pay rates cut.
   c. All employees in this area are grade 15 or 16 production workers, and most have more than 20 years' experience.
3. Use the agreement you previously reached or the contract in Chapter 10 to specify current terms for these workers.

CHAPTER 13

Contract Administration

After the contract is negotiated and ratified, the parties are bound by its terms. But the parties may interpret contract clauses differently, so mechanisms are needed to resolve disputes. Almost all contracts contain a grievance procedure to resolve intracontractual disputes. This chapter aims primarily at identifying the types and causes of disputes and the means for resolving them within the contract.

In reading this chapter, keep the following questions in mind:

1. What areas of disagreement usually emerge while the contract is in effect?
2. What actions by the parties are violations of the labor acts?
3. To what extent are disagreements solved by bargaining or by evaluating the merits of a given issue?
4. What obligation does the union owe its individual members in grievance processing?

THE DUTY TO BARGAIN

The parties do not end their obligation to bargain by concluding an agreement. The NLRB and the courts have interpreted the duty to bargain to cover the entire labor relationship from recognition onward. Any differences in opinion regarding wages, hours, or terms and conditions of employment must be mutually resolved. Most often the parties negotiate a grievance procedure to handle disagreements during the term of the contract.

Management generally takes the initiative in contract administration. It determines how it will operate its facilities, and the union reacts if it senses a result inconsistent with its interpretation of the contract.

When management makes a change in its operations and a grievance procedure exists, employees are expected to conform to the change and file grievances if the change is considered unjust, rather than to refuse the order. If the latter occurs, employees can rightfully be discharged for insubordination even if the management practice was found to be in violation, unless the violation was flagrant.

ISSUES IN CONTRACT ADMINISTRATION

A number of issues are the focus of disputes during the life of the contract. These disputes result from initiatives taken by the employer. The employer generally does not file a grievance when the union or a worker allegedly violates the contract; it simply takes some action and waits for the union to respond. For example, if a worker swears at a supervisor, the company may suspend him/her for five days. The company does not contact the union and ask it to discipline its members. If the union feels this is unjust, it protests the action through a grievance. Some of the major contract areas leading to grievances will be examined next.

Discipline

One of the most frequently disputed issues relates to discipline imposed by the employer for infractions of rules. Discipline can take the form of demotions, suspensions, and discharges. Frequently, discipline is meted out for insubordination, dishonesty, absenteeism, rule violations, or poor productivity. A discharge is the industrial equivalent of "capital punishment" and will very often result in a grievance regardless of its ultimate merit, because political solidarity often requires the union to extend itself in trying to save a member's job.

Unions are frequently concerned about possible arbitrariness in the employer's discipline system. For example, if absences are not dealt with consistently, an employee disciplined for absenteeism may pursue a grievance because others have not been disciplined for this in the past.

Incentives

A contract will occasionally have an incentive scheme where employees are paid by the piece or receive bonuses for productive efficiency. Frequently, these contracts establish groups of jobs that work on incentive rates and identify others that don't. If an employee is moved from an incentive job to a nonincentive job, wages will probably decrease as a result. If the job seems highly similar to the incentive job, grievances may result. A grievance might also result if the assignment is considered arbitrary or punitive.

Problems also arise if a new production process is introduced and management seeks to establish higher base rates or time standards before incentive earnings begin. New standards must be bargained collectively.

Work Assignments

A variety of job classifications might create disputes as to which job classification is entitled to perform certain work. For example, assume an electrical generating plant powered by coal-fired boilers for steam generation has a boiler shut down for rebricking. To do this, a wall has to be knocked down with some care to avoid damaging other boiler parts. Who should do the work? If a general helper category existed, these helpers might do the work under a supervisor's direction. On the other hand, because some care is required and the work is preparatory to rebricking, the job could rightfully be assigned to skilled masonry workers. The company may assign the job to the helpers because the cost is less and the skill requirements are believed to be low. But the masons may feel the task is an integral part of their job and so file a grievance. This is essentially a job security issue.

Individual Personnel Assignments

These grievances are most often related to promotion, layoffs, transfers, and shift assignments. Most contracts specify that seniority, seniority and merit, or experience on a particular job will be the governing factor in personnel assignments. Disputes often relate to layoffs and shift preference. Persons who are laid off may feel they are entitled to the jobs of more junior workers in another department who have been retained. While contracts normally specify that persons must be qualified for a job if they are "bumping" junior employees, opinions may differ as to whether the claimed qualifications are actually possessed.

Hours of Work

Grievances in this area relate to overtime requirements and work schedules. For example, if the firm has maintained an 8-A.M.-to-4-P.M. shift to mail customer orders and finds its freight companies have moved their shipping schedule from 4 P.M. TO 3 P.M., then a 7-A.M.-to-3-P.M. shift would better meet its needs. However, the change will affect employees, and grievances may result.

Supervisors Doing Production Work

Most contracts forbid supervisors to do production work except when demonstrating the job to a new employee or handling an emergency. Absence of an employee is usually not considered an emergency. Like the work assignment area, this is basically a job security issue.

Production Standards

Management and the union will often have agreed on the rate of output in assembly-line technologies or the underlying standard for an incentive in piece-rate output. If management speeds up the line or re-engineers the standards, then more effort is required for the same amount of pay, and grievances often result.

Working Conditions

These issues often relate to health and safety concerns. For example, if the workers believe excessive amounts of fumes are present or if an existing convenience such as heating fails, grievances often result.

Subcontracting

Unless the contract specifically allows the company complete discretion in subcontracting, any work done by bargaining unit members may not be subcontracted without first bargaining with the union.[1] Subcontracting can affect job security, and if a grievance results, management would be involved in a refusal to bargain if it did not discuss the subcontracting issue.

Past Practice

Often, practices involving labor and management are not written into a contract but are considered by the union to be obligations. For example, the company may operate a cafeteria or vending machines so

---

[1] The Supreme Court decision in *Fibreboard Paper Products* v. *NLRB*, 379 U.S. 203 (1964), requires bargaining by management if the union requests when subcontracting is being considered, unless the union has expressly waived its right in this area; however, this rule has been relaxed somewhat by *First National Maintenance* v. *NLRB*, 107 LRRM 2705 (U.S. Supreme Court, 1981), and later by the NLRB when it held removal of union work to another facility of the company would be permissible if bargaining had reached an impasse [*Milwaukee Spring Div. of Illinois Coil Spring Co.*, 115 LRRM 1065 (1984), enforced by the U.S. Court of Appeals, District of Columbia Circuit, 119 LRRM 2801 (1985)], or for a legitimate business reason if there were no antiunion animus [*Otis Elevator Co.*, 115 LRRM 1281 (1984)].

workers can obtain meals at costs below those of commercial operations. If the employer closes the cafeteria, the union may grieve even though no contract language mentions the cafeteria, and management must respond.[2] If stopping work 15 minutes prior to the end of a shift to wash up is common practice, then extending working time to the shift's end is a change in past practice.

Rules

Employers occasionally institute rules to improve efficiency or to govern the work force. Many contracts establish the employer's right to do so under the management rights clause. Employees may grieve the establishment of rules as altering a term or condition of employment. For example, employer changes requiring random drug testing or prohibiting or sharply restricting smoking might be grieved as changing a term or condition of employment.

GRIEVANCE PROCEDURES

Most contracts specify procedures for resolving interpretive disagreements. While contracts vary, most procedures contain four or five steps. In the absence of a grievance procedure, the employee is still entitled to press grievances individually under guarantees contained in Section 9 of the Taft-Hartley Act. Employees may also file grievances if the contract has such a procedure, but as a practical matter they generally do not, leaving the union the right to participate in the process.

Steps in the Grievance Procedure

The usual steps in the grievance procedure are as follows:

Step 1. This step varies considerably across companies. In some, an employee who believes the company has violated the contract (grievant) complains to the union steward, who may accept or assist in the writing of a grievance. Then, the steward presents the grievance to the grievant's supervisor, who has the opportunity to answer or adjust it.

In some companies, few grievances are settled at step 1; the company will not delegate this power to supervisors because their decisions can be used later as precedents in similar grievances filed by the union. Thus, the supervisor simply "denies" the grievance and refuses the relief asked. In other companies, the grievant orally presents the complaint directly to the supervisor, and settlements can be negotiated

---

[2] *Ford Motor Co.* v. *NLRB*, No. 77-1806, U.S. Supreme Court, 1979.

FIGURE 13-1

Example of a Written Grievance

"I have just been given a job review, as a result of which I am now on the second highest eligibility list as against the top list. I now want clear and accurate answers with supporting information to the following questions:

"(1) Why was this job review given five months after its effective date and on the day before my vacation?

"(2) Why change my rating for 'manner and interest' from excellent to good? It was admitted that I am excellent in this category, but only to those whom I think will buy, and that the reviewer did not know of any mistakes in judgment I had made.

"(3) Why change 'alertness to service' from excellent to good? Since I was told by the reviewer that I was too 'selective' in both this and the previous category, I think that (a) one or the other should be eliminated, or (b) perhaps they should be combined, or (c) both reviewer and employees should be made aware of whatever difference there may be.

"(4) Why change 'cooperation' from excellent to good? Since I was told that my cooperation with the other eight people in the department was excellent, I should like to know exactly what incidents took place and who was involved, resulting in this change.

"It also seems that there is a clear, consistent pattern of downgrading everyone in the department from their previous ratings and that job reviews will be given just prior to going on vacation. It is my distinct impression that the present reviewers not only are ignorant of previous reviews but also feel that they do the job much better than the previous reviewers. If they can't come up with some better reasons for the changes than those I have heard, then I think they are doing a remarkably poor job."

Source: Maurice S. Trotta, *Handling Grievances: A Guide for Labor and Management* (Washington, D.C.: Bureau of National Affairs, 1976), pp. 141-42.

immediately. Figure 13-1 is an example of a fairly complex grievance at its first step.

Some evidence indicates supervisory style characteristics have an impact on grievance rates and the ultimate disposition of grievances. In a study of grievances and supervision in a large component manufacturing plant, autocratic supervisors had lower grievance rates in general and less discipline, overtime, and supervisor-related grievances than democratic supervisors. Management was also less likely to reverse grievance settlements at higher levels for autocratic supervisors.[3] In some situations, stewards may be well versed in the contract if they are experienced and if contract administration is their full-time job. But generally, both supervisors and stewards do not understand the contract well. About 70 percent of grievances examined in one study were screened by the steward, and about half used their authority to adjust grievances. If the stewards are trained, the training is equally likely to have been provided by the employer or the union.[4]

[3] Robert L. Walker and James W. Robinson, "The First-Line Supervisor's Role in the Grievance Procedure," *Arbitration Journal*, December 1977, pp. 279-92.

[4] Steven Briggs, "The Steward, the Supervisor, and the Grievance Process," *Proceedings of the Industrial Relations Research Associations*, 1981, pp. 313-19.

Step 2. Most grievances have been settled after this step. If the grievance is denied at step 1, then the steward will present it to a plant industrial relations representative. Both are very familiar with the contract, and both are aware of how grievances have been settled in the past. In most routine cases, the company is also willing to let the IR representative apply and create precedents.

Step 3. If the grievance is likely to have major precedent-setting implications or involves possibilities of major costs, then the IR representative may deny it and send it to step 3. The participants at step 3 may vary substantially depending on the contract. Typical arrangements would include the following: the grievance may be settled locally, with the union represented by its local negotiating committee and management by its top IR manager or plant manager; or in more complex situations or in larger firms, the parties may be an international union representative with or without the local negotiating committee and a corporate-level IR director. A fair share of unresolved grievances are settled at this level.

Step 4. When a grievance is unresolved at the third step, the parties submit the dispute to a neutral arbitrator, who hears evidence from both sides and renders a decision in favor of one side. A number of methods for choosing an arbitrator are available. First, the parties may designate the name of a permanent arbitrator in their contract. Second, the parties may petition a private agency, such as the American Arbitration Association, for an arbitration panel. A panel consists of an odd number of members (usually five) from which each party rejects arbitrators in turn until one remains. He or she becomes the arbitrator unless one party objects, in which case a new panel is submitted. Third, the same process may be followed by petitioning the Federal Mediation and Conciliation Service (FMCS), which also supplies panels of arbitrators listed by this agency. A hearing date is set, and the arbitrator renders a decision sometime after the evidence is presented. We will examine arbitration as a separate topic in the next chapter. Figure 13–2 is an example of a contract clause dealing with grievance handling.

Time Involved

Generally, contracts aim for a speedy resolution of grievances. Typical contracts allow 2 to 5 days for resolution at the first two steps and 3 to 10 days at step 3. If management denies the grievance at this point, then the union has 10 to 30 days to demand arbitration. If the union doesn't, the dispute may not be arbitrable later because it was not referred to arbitration in time. After arbitration is demanded, the time frame is less rigid because an arbitration panel must be requested and received, an arbitrator selected, hearing dates arranged and the hearing held, and the final award written and rendered. While an arbitrated

FIGURE 13–2

Grievance Procedure Clause

9.02   *Grievances*

Step 1   The employee and the departmental steward, if the employee desires, shall take the matter up with his supervisor. If no settlement is reached in step 1 within two working days, the grievance shall be reduced to writing on the form provided for that purpose.

Step 2   The written grievance shall be presented to the supervisor or the general supervisor and a copy sent to the production personnel office. Within two working days after receipt of the grievance, the general supervisor shall hold a meeting, unless mutually agreed otherwise, with the supervisor, the employee, the departmental steward, and the chief steward.

Step 3   If no settlement is reached in step 2, the written grievance shall be presented to the departmental superintendent, who shall hold a meeting within five working days of the original receipt of the grievance in step 2 unless mutually agreed otherwise. Those in attendance shall normally be the departmental superintendent, the general supervisor, the supervisor, the employee, the chief steward, departmental steward, a member of the production personnel department, the president of the UNION or his representative, and the divisional committeeman.

Step 4   If no settlement is reached in step 3, the UNION COMMITTEE and an international representative of the UNION shall meet with the MANAGEMENT COMMITTEE for the purpose of settling the matter.

Step 5   If no settlement is reached in step 4, the matter shall be referred to an arbitrator. A representative of the UNION shall meet within five working days with a representative of the COMPANY for the purpose of selecting an arbitrator. If an arbitrator cannot be agreed on within five working days after step 4, a request for a list of arbitrators shall be sent to the Federal Mediation and Conciliation Service. Upon obtaining the list, an arbitrator shall be selected within five working days. Prior to arbitration, a representative of the UNION shall meet with a representative of the COMPANY to reduce to writing wherever possible the actual issue to be arbitrated. The decision of the arbitrator shall be final and binding on all parties. The salary, if any, of the arbitrator and any necessary expense incident to the arbitration shall be paid jointly by the COMPANY and the UNION.

dispute could conceivably be resolved in two months or less, the time lapse is considerably longer in most cases. Figure 13–3 presents the flow of decisions in a typical grievance process.

METHODS OF DISPUTE RESOLUTION

Disputes that cannot be resolved by negotiations between the parties are handled in two major ways: arbitration and strikes. Arbitration is used far more often, but strikes are traditionally used by some unions or in some types of disputes.

378

FIGURE 13–3

Grievance Procedure Steps

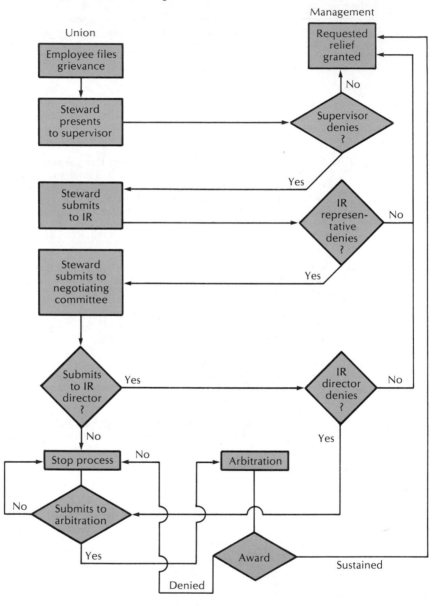

Striking over Grievances

Disputes in which time is of the essence are most likely to involve strikes. Arbitration usually involves a considerable time lag, and so certain unions (such as construction unions) seldom use arbitration because their members frequently work short periods for a given employer. By the time a grievance is arbitrated, the job would be completed, with the employer dictating the working conditions.

The same holds for grievances over safety and working conditions in industrial situations where employers enjoy a stable employment relationship. When these conditions occur, a strike may be used by the union to force the company to interpret the contract as it demands. With a contract in effect, these strikes may or may not be breaches of the agreement and may or may not be enjoinable by the courts.

Wildcat Strikes

If the union and management have negotiated a no-strike clause, a strike during the agreement period is a *wildcat strike*, because it contradicts the contract and is unauthorized by the parent national union. Wildcats are more prevalent in certain industries, particularly rubber,[5] wood by-products,[6] and coal.[7]

Recent research has reported on characteristics associated with wildcat strikes in the coal-mining industry. High-strike mines were larger than low-strike mines, perhaps reflecting the increased formality of grievance handling in large mines. Mines with better working conditions were no less likely to have wildcat strikes, but supervisory friction appeared related to wildcat strikes. Strikes were higher where miners perceived their supervisors as being unable to handle grievances and in mines where disputes could not be dealt with locally. Confidence in the grievance-handling procedure, however, did not relate to strike incidence rates. Miners at both high-and low-strike mines felt strikes resolved disputes in the miners' favor, but high-strike-incidence rates appeared related to perceptions that this was the best method for getting management to listen.[8]

When companies agree to submit unresolved grievances to arbitration, they are giving up some of their initiative in changing conditions. As a quid pro quo, they usually demand and win a no-strike clause. Under that provision, the union agrees not to strike during the term of the contract, because it has an arbitral forum available. But what if the union does strike? Does the company have a legal recourse? The answer was no for a number of years. The Supreme Court interpreted the Norris-LaGuardia Act in an absolute manner, holding unions could

---

[5] James W. Kuhn, *Bargaining in Grievance Settlement* (New York: Columbia University Press, 1961).

[6] David R. Hampton, "Fractional Bargaining Patterns and Wildcat Strikes," *Human Organization*, Fall 1967, pp. 100–9.

[7] Jeanne M. Brett and Stephen B. Goldberg, "Wildcat Strikes in Bituminous Coal Mining," *Industrial and Labor Relations Review*, July 1979, pp. 465–83.

[8] Ibid.

not negotiate away protections included in the legislation.[9] But this interpretation was modified in the *Boys Market* case, in which the Supreme Court held where a bona fide no-strike clause existed with a grievance procedure available and where the union had not sought to arbitrate its dispute, federal courts could enjoin a wildcat strike in violation of the contract.[10] The Court explained it would not apply this doctrine when the employer had been unwilling to include an arbitration agreement along with the no-strike clause.

Discipline for Wildcat Strikes

One question frequently encountered asks what tool management has to counteract a wildcat strike. First, if the strike were over an unfair labor practice and the union were correct in its judgment that the action was illegal, the strike would be protected concerted activity under the labor acts, and the employer could not legally retaliate. But if the strike were in violation of a no-strike clause, several factors would come into play.

Recall that both the national and local unions participate in the ratification of the agreement. Both also share in the joint responsibility for enforcing it. Unfortunately for management, it can gain little in damages unless the union leadership clearly fomented the strike.[11] However, if the union demands that its members return and they fail to obey, they may be subject to union discipline as well as to employer retaliation. But employers cannot sue individual union members for breach of contract for violating a no-strike clause.[12]

Mediation of Grievances

As noted earlier, wildcat strikes have been a troublesome feature of labor relations in coal mining. An experiment in the mediation of grievances found costs and time to settlement reduced by using a mediation-like process to deal with contract disputes. A large share of the grievances headed for arbitration were settled with the help of mediation. The union, in particular, was highly satisfied with mediation, especially as it related to the union's belief regarding the mediator's understanding of the grievance. Mediation may allow the parties to uncover and deal with the real reason for the conflict rather than to require framing the reason as a specific contract violation. Mediation did not appear to increase the likelihood of settlements at lower levels

---

[9] *Sinclair Refining Co.* v. *Atkinson,* 370 U.S. 195 (1962).

[10] *Boys Markets, Inc.* v. *Retail Clerks Union Local 770,* 398 U.S. 235 (1970).

[11] *Carbon Fuel Co.* v. *United Mine Workers,* 444 U.S. 212 (1979).

[12] *Complete Auto Transit* v. *Reis,* 107 LRRM 2145, U.S. Supreme Court, 1981.

and was used for neither discharge grievances nor for those involving financial claims of more than $5,000.[13]

EMPLOYEE AND UNION RIGHTS IN GRIEVANCE PROCESSING

One important issue in grievances concerns an employee's right to union representation in disciplinary proceedings. For example, if a supervisor suspected an employee was quitting early and if this offense normally merited a suspension, can the supervisor confront and interrogate the employee without granting union representation for the employee? The Supreme Court ruled that employees suspected of offenses that could result in disciplinary action are entitled to union representation if they request it.[14] The employer cannot proceed with the interrogation unless a union steward is present to advise its member.

To What Is the Employee Entitled?

Of course, not every grievance constitutes a bona fide contract violation, and not every legitimate grievance is worth pursuing to arbitration. For example, suppose a supervisor performed bargaining unit work during a rush—but not emergency—period. The union may have a legitimate grievance, and the workers might be entitled, as a group, to pay for the period the supervisor worked. But if it's an isolated incident, simply bringing the grievance to management's attention should reduce the likelihood of its recurrence, even if management denies the relief requested.

Cases involving individuals also vary in terms of the merits of particular fact situations. For example, a discharge case is more serious than one in which a grievant claims entitlement to two hours' pay for overtime given to another. How far is the individual union member able to go in pursuing a grievance or in forcing the union to process it through arbitration if necessary? This subject is not entirely resolved, but some direction is available through opinions of legal and labor experts and court discussions. The issue is referred to as *individual rights* and *fair representation*. In our discussion, the latter term is applied to the vigor of the union's advocacy, not necessarily to its competence (the competence issue is covered in Chapter 14). A vigorous approach by the union in the face of management opposition will inevitably cause an unresolved grievance to arrive at arbitration.

---

[13] Stephen B. Goldberg and Jeanne M. Brett, "An Experiment in the Mediation of Grievances," *Monthly Labor Review*, March 1983, pp. 23–30.

[14] *NLRB* v. *J. Weingarten, Inc.*, 420 U.S. 251 (1975).

Occasionally, an employer disciplines an employee for a rule violation more harshly than similar offenders were punished prior to union activity. If the individual charges the company with violating his or her rights to engage in union activity, the NLRB will apply the following test. First, the General Counsel for the board must make a prima facie case that the discipline was motivated by the employee's union activity. Then, the employer could rebut an unfair labor practice charge if it can show the same punishment would have taken place in the absence of union activity.[15]

Fair Representation

The whole question of fair representation is a very complex issue in which the rights and duties of those involved are not completely spelled out. Generally, however, the representation rights of nonunion employees are substantially less, unless the employer grants those rights by policy.[16] All employees, represented or not, are able to seek redress for employer actions violating civil rights, wage and hour, or health and safety laws; but in other areas, unrepresented employees have no legal right to review an arbitrary decision.

Individual Rights under the Contract

A relatively long string of decisions have come down regarding individual rights under collective bargaining agreements.[17] Major decisions prior to passage of the Taft-Hartley Act helped specify the rights of groups or minorities in grievance processing.

In *Elgin, Joliet, and Eastern Railway* v. *Burley,* the Supreme Court held an employer is not immune from an employee's action simply because the employee's union concedes a grievance.[18] The employees must have authorized the union to act for them, and some vigorous defense must be shown. Because the union is the exclusive bargaining agent for all employees, the courts will watch to ensure that all classes and subgroups are entitled to and receive equal protection and advocacy from their representatives.

Passage of the Taft-Hartley Act enables employees to file grievances directly to employers, even if represented. However, employers

---

[15] *Wright Line,* 251 NLRB No. 150 (1980).

[16] Jack Stieber, "The Case for Protection of Unorganized Employees against Unjust Discharge," *Proceedings of the Industrial Relations Research Association,* 1979, pp. 155–63.

[17] For an excellent treatment of the legal issues involved, see Herbert L. Sherman, Jr., *Labor Relations and Social Problems: Unionization and Collective Bargaining* (Washington, D.C.: Bureau of National Affairs, 1972), pp. 184–97.

[18] 325 U.S. 711 (1945).

cannot process their grievances in the absence of union observation, if demanded by the union, or adjust the grievance in a manner inconsistent with the contract. For example, if the contract entitles senior employees to promotions, a junior employee cannot personally insist on receiving a promotion to which a senior employee is entitled.

An individual's rights under the contract are not widely established, given the Taft-Hartley additions. Three possible positions might be suggested: (1) individuals have a vested right to use the grievance procedure through arbitration if they choose; (2) individuals should be entitled to grievance processing for discharge, seniority, and compensation cases; and (3) the union as a collective body should have freedom to decide what constitutes a meritorious grievance and how far the grievance should be pursued.[19]

A number of NLRB and Supreme Court decisions since 1960 have helped clarify somewhat the requirements for fair representation. Prior to these decisions, there was a crazy-quilt approach to the issue. In one decision, the court refused to consider an employee's unfair representation complaint when the union had bargained away her contractual rights.[20] Another state court decision held an employee was entitled to demand arbitration.[21] If a court were to grant relief to an employee who had not gone through the contractual procedures, the employer could rightfully claim the worker would use whatever forum was thought to offer the best chance for winning. As we will see later, the courts generally defer to a final arbitration award; so, if every grievant were entitled to have a grievance formally settled, going to arbitration on all grievances rather than to court would be to the employer's advantage from a cost standpoint.

However, some considerations must be made here to lessen the likelihood of wholesale court action. First, the company and the union would prefer to settle grievances early to gain certainty for their actions. Second, arbitration costs are borne jointly by the company and the union, not the individual employee. Therefore, going to court assumes greater risks of costs, even if the court agrees to entertain the action, than using the grievance procedure to arbitration.

However, several precedents reduce the likelihood of court involvement in grievance resolutions. The first is *Miranda Fuel Company*.[22] In that case, an employee was given permission to start his vacation before the contractual date. Then, when he returned late due to illness, other bargaining unit members demanded the union require

---

[19] Benjamin Aaron, "The Individual's Legal Rights as an Employee," *Monthly Labor Review*, 1963, pp. 671–72.

[20] *Union News Co.* v. *Hildreth*, 295 F. 2nd 658 (U.S. Court of Appeals, 6th Circuit, 1961).

[21] *Donnelly* v. *United Fruit Co.*, 40 N.J. 61 (1963).

[22] 140 NLRB 181 (1962).

he be discharged. The NLRB ruled this was an unfair labor practice because the union acquiesced to the majority demand even though the discharged employee had seniority. The case was not taken to higher court but is in line with a subsequent Supreme Court decision.

The second case involved the merger of two companies.[23] Here the same union represented employees of the acquired and surviving companies. After the merger, the union credited the seniority of the workers from the acquired company rather than beginning it at the acquisition date. Several employees from the surviving company claimed they had been unfairly represented because their union had granted seniority to new employees with the other firm. The Supreme Court held the employees must use Taft-Hartley remedies for breach of contract rather than state court actions to gain redress for unfair representation.

In *Vaca* v. *Sipes*, an employee returning from sick leave was discharged because the employer felt he was no longer capable of holding a job.[24] A grievance was filed and the union pressed his case, obtaining medical evidence and requesting he be given a less physically demanding job. The doctors' reports conflicted on the question of whether the discharged employee could safely continue working. Although the union vigorously pursued the grievance through the final prearbitration step, it did not demand arbitration when the company refused to reinstate the grievant.

The grievant sued his union for unfairly representing him and also sued his employer for breach of contract. The Court held an employee may not go directly to court on a grievance unless the remedies provided by the contract have been exhausted, except in cases where the employer and/or the union have clearly refused to use these remedies. If the grievant contends the union has inadequately represented him or her, then he or she must prove this. The Court found individual bargaining unit members have no inherent right to invoke the use of arbitration. As the representative of all bargaining unit members, the union is at once both an advocate and an agent that must decide whether certain claims are frivolous or inconsistent with past practice or contract interpretation. If the union weighs the merit of the grievance and treats the grievant similarly to others in the same situation, then this is not unfair representation.

An appeals court decision has the potential for placing the union "between a rock and a hard place."[25] In this case, the contract provided that promotions would be based on seniority and merit. When the

---

[23] *Humphrey* v. *Moore*, 375 U.S. 335 (1964).

[24] 386 U.S. 171 (1967).

[25] *Smith* v. *Hussman Refrigerator Co. & Local 13889, United Steelworkers of America* (U.S. Court of Appeals, 8th Circuit, 1979); certiorari denied by U.S. Supreme Court, 105 LRRM 2657 (1980).

company promoted junior employees, the union processed the grievances of senior employees to arbitration. The arbitrator ruled the senior employees were entitled to the jobs. The junior employees who had been displaced sued their union for failing to represent their positions in the arbitration. The court held the union owed equal obligations to both groups. Although the union certainly pressed for seniority as the only basis for promotion during the contract negotiations, it later must represent management's position as well because the contract provides benefits to two potential groups with opposite interests.

A recent fair representation case extends the liability for damages to the union. If an employee can prove the employer violated the collective bargaining agreement to the employee's detriment and if the union dealt with the grievance in an arbitrary and capricious manner, the employee can collect damages from both. The employee collects damages from the employer up to the point at which the union fails to process a meritorious claim and from the union until relief is granted.[26]

A review of Supreme Court cases dealing with representation has extracted the following six principles: (1) employees have the right to have contract terms enforced to their benefit; (2) the individual employee has no right to insist on his or her personal interpretation of a contract term; (3) no individual can require the union to process a grievance to arbitration, but each should have equal access to grievance procedures; (4) settlement on the basis of personal motives by union officials constitutes bad faith; (5) the individual should have a grievance decided on its own merits, not horse-traded for other grievance settlements; and (6) while the union is entitled to judge the relative merit of grievances, it must exercise diligence in investigating the situation that led to the grievance.[27]

GRIEVANCES AND BARGAINING

As noted in the chapters on union structure, organizing, and negotiation, the processes involved can be specified, but the actual behavior does not always exactly duplicate the model. The grievance procedure, as described, provides a method for resolving disputes over the contract's meaning. The process consigns the union to the role of responding to management's actions and management to the role of initiating

---

[26] *Bowen* v. *U.S. Postal Service,* 112 LRRM 2281, U.S. Supreme Court, 1983.

[27] Clyde W. Summers, "The Individual Employee's Rights under the Collective Agreement: What Constitutes Fair Representation?" in *Duty of Fair Representation,* ed. Jean T. McKelvey (Ithaca: New York State School of Industrial and Labor Relations, Cornell University, 1977), pp. 60–83.

some action leading to the dispute. Grievance resolution has been dealt with as a serial process, from both the steps involved (which duplicate reality rather closely) and the presentation order (first in, first out; which is an unlikely duplication). This section looks at grievances from a political standpoint and as a bargaining tool.

Union Responses to Management Action

In many cases, grievances have a number of ramifications for the union. A novel grievance may establish a precedent for or against the union if it is arbitrated. In the past, the situation may have been informally handled on a case-by-case basis usually favorable to the union, but now the risks of losing may be too great. Other grievances may lead to internal disputes, such as entitlements to work or overtime. Politically powerful minorities within the union may also need accommodation. Six considerations guide the union negotiating committee in determining what priority and attention should be given to particular grievances.

1. The immediate interests of the union as an organization in recognition and collective bargaining.
2. The immediate interests of the individual employee who will be directly affected by the grievance settlement.
3. The immediate interests of other employees as individuals or as a group who may be directly or indirectly affected by the grievance settlement.
4. The future interests of the union as an organization and of the employees as individuals or as a group, as affected by the law-making or precedent aspects of the grievance settlement.
5. The political interests of present union officers.
6. The political interests of aspiring union officers.[28]

Besides the responses of union officials to grievances, the rank-and-file members may engage in tactics affecting the grievance process. If a large number of grievances build up or if the settlement of grievances is slow (particularly those alleging a continuing violation), then pressure tactics like slowdowns, quickie strikes, and "working to rules" may be used to pressure management to settle or grant the grievances.[29] Thus grievants might not passively wait for the ultimate response but rather use tactics to speed a favorable settlement.

---

[28] Cyrus F. Smythe, "The Union as Arbitrator in Grievance Processing," *Personnel*, July–August 1963, p. 50. Copyright © American Management Association.

[29] Kuhn, *Bargaining*.

Fractional Bargaining

Because most grievances concern an individual employee or a single work group and relate only to one or a few contract terms, tactics aimed at modifying the practice of contract administration are called *fractional bargaining*.[30] Fractional bargaining affects work groups in the same way that an employer with multiple bargaining units suffers a reduction in bargaining power. An organization consists of interdependent parts, and one part being embroiled in disputes that lessen its productivity will affect the remainder.

Fractional bargaining occasionally poses problems for the union because one critical group may win grievances that others fail to achieve. If a union negotiating committee stops the grievances of a powerful small group, internal political pressures will increase. A steward of a powerful small group may successfully pressure for settlement at lower levels to avoid local officer involvement. The company may accede to this pressure to lessen chances of production disruption.

Management may also take the initiative by assigning work to political opponents of the existing union leadership and by handling some disciplinary cases by the book and being lenient with others. These practices may increase the internal political pressures within the union and cause more of its energies to be devoted to healing these rifts rather than to additional grievance activity. Thus, as in contract negotiations, each side pressures the other, but some mutual accommodation enabling survival of both is usually reached.

Union Initiatives in Grievances

The union may take the initiative with grievances in a number of ways. The union steward may solicit grievances, looking for situations where the rank and file see a contract violation.[31] For a grievance to be filed, a violation need not actually occur—only the belief that one did and a linking of that belief to some contract clause. If the union believes it has problems with one area or supervisor, it may simply flood management with grievances. These create work for management, because they must be answered in a certain time under the contract. If higher management has to spend more time on grievances, it may simply tell supervision to "clean up its act," usually resulting in a more lenient approach to demonstrate to management that supervision has "cured" the grievance problem.

Union stewards may also stockpile grievances to use as threats or

---

[30] Ibid., p. 79.
[31] Ibid., p. 14.

trade-offs for larger issues. If an important point comes up that the steward wants for that constituency, the supervisor may simply be told informally that unless a change is made, grievances on a variety of matters will be filed with higher-ups later in the day.

In large plants, the union steward has a distinct advantage over the supervisor. Many contracts specify that the steward is a full-time union representative although paid by the company. As such, a steward's full-time work involves contract administration, while the supervisor is responsible for personnel, equipment, production, and other matters. The two are usually no match on interpreting the contract, because the contract is a much more integral part of the steward's job and the steward has studied it in far greater detail.

The steward's personality may also play a role in grievance processing. One study found stewards who informally settled grievances with supervisors were likely to have higher needs for autonomy, affiliation, and dominance than those who used formal processes. The study also found stewards who were higher in needs for achievement and dominance were involved in greater numbers of grievances.[32] In another study among the same group of stewards, higher commitment to the union predicted higher grievance activity levels, while higher company commitment and job satisfaction were related to lower grievance activism.[33]

Grievance rates within unions appear related to inexperience among union representatives, union policies that influence grievance filing, and time periods close to negotiations or political choice within the union.[34]

Grievance Types

From an overall standpoint, grievances can be separated into two major categories: (1) those influencing the job security of individual workers (discipline and discharge cases) and (2) those involving groups of workers in job assignments, work standards, or other precedent-setting issues. The first set tends to be handled in the straightforward manner we described earlier, while the latter is more subject to fractional bargaining tactics.

---

[32] Dan R. Dalton and William D. Todor, "Manifest Needs of Stewards: Propensity to File a Grievance," *Journal of Applied Psychology*, December 1979, pp. 654–59.

[33] Dan R. Dalton and William D. Todor, "Antecedents of Grievance-Filing Behavior: Attitude/Behavioral Consistency and the Union Steward," *Academy of Management Journal* 25 (1982), pp. 158–69.

[34] Chalmer E. Labig, Jr., and Charles R. Greer, "Grievance Initiation: A Literature Survey and Suggestions for Future Research," *Journal of Labor Research* 9 (1988), pp. 1–27.

LOGJAMS IN GRIEVANCE PROCESSING

As noted in the next chapter, most of the reported recent innovations relate to the final step—arbitration—rather than to earlier points. One complaint made by union officials is that grievances are seldom handled at lower levels but instead are "bucked up the line" for fear of a supervisor setting a precedent.[35] With this kind of problem or through poor relations between the company and the union, the grievance procedure can become clogged, with unsettled grievances leading to disruptive tactics by the union and a lack of responsiveness by management.

A study of congested grievance procedures concluded most problems occur in large industrial organizations.[36] One aircraft manufacturer had a backlog of 6,000 cases awaiting arbitration. Most of the arbitrators who saw this type of load mentioned faults in both the management and the union, inclining to blame the union more. Following is a list of the reasons arbitrators ascribed as union and management causes for clogging grievance procedures.

1. Refusal of international and local union officers to screen out the grievances, feeling most complaints should be taken to arbitration to satisfy the grievants.
2. A provision in the constitution under which the union cannot pass a resolution without unanimous approval of the numerous locals and, therefore, cannot pass the legislation required to control the affairs of these locals.
3. A shop committee, in order to perpetuate itself, first looks for trouble and files grievances at the drop of a hat.
4. A local union riddled with factional strife. "The local was large . . . and its treasury bountiful." The committee could not refuse to arbitrate weak grievances for fear that the opposition would make political capital.
5. Union investigation is initially poor and continues to be so, poor steward training, newly changed officers, and so on.

The following is a second set of causes that lie within the management organization.

6. Company hard line, called for by operating people, on practically all grievances; industrial relations people have weak status in

---

[35] Kuhn, *Bargaining*, p. 10.

[36] Arthur M. Ross, "Distressed Grievance Procedures and Their Rehabilitation," in *Labor Arbitration and Industrial Change, Proceedings of the 16th National Academy of Arbitrators*, ed. Mark L. Kahn (Washington, D.C.: Bureau of National Affairs, 1963), pp. 104–132.

corporate setup and do not attempt to educate the operating people.

7. Top-line management did not back up the industrial relations people. As a result, the IR people preferred to pass the buck to the arbitrator.[37]

Other causes of high unresolved grievance rates included rapidly changing jobs due to technological change, a bad bargaining relationship perpetuated from an acrimonious organizing campaign, and complicated contract language or job evaluation systems.[38]

When the load gets too high, grievances may not be decided for a year or more. Four types of solutions are most frequently used to deal with this backlog.[39] First is the mass grievance settlement ("fire sale"), in which the union and management horse-trade grievances. This trading may lead to the setting of precedents both parties would prefer to avoid and might encourage the filing of nonmeritorious grievances. It also has unfair representation ramifications. Second, a screening procedure involving the company and the union could concede or withdraw grievances likely to be nonwinnable at arbitration. Third, nonlocal, high-level company and union officials would handle the screening process. Fourth, procedural changes (like scheduling arbitration of grievances on a "first in, first out" basis rather than on the political explosiveness of an issue) may reduce the stockpiling of cases awaiting arbitration.

One other successful approach in reducing grievances is keeping them at the oral or informal stage long enough to settle them on the shop floor. A study of the experience of International Harvester and the UAW reported that at one plant, the grievance rate was so high that on the average each employee submitted one written grievance per year. To alleviate the huge buildup, the company and the UAW agreed to keep grievances oral as long as possible, reducing their formality. If higher-level management or union officers were necessary to help resolve a grievance, they were brought to the shop floor rather than having a written grievance brought to them. The backlog of grievances evaporated as the system became operational.[40]

Another way companies and unions can reduce problems in resolving difficult grievances is to agree that the solution to the existing grievance will be without prejudice. This means no precedent value can be associated with it if another grievance of the same type occurs in the future.

---

[37] Ibid., pp. 107–18.

[38] Ibid., pp. 108–19.

[39] Ibid., pp. 111–13.

[40] Robert B. McKersie and William W. Shropshire, Jr., "Avoiding Written Grievances: A Successful Program," *Journal of Business*, April 1962, pp. 135–52.

WHO FILES GRIEVANCES?

Individuals initiate grievances. This section examines whether individual characteristics are associated with more frequent use of the process. In the International Harvester study, the forge department in one plant, comprising 6 percent of its population, filed 22 percent of the grievances.[41] This does not necessarily mean the group abused the procedure, only that its incidence rate was higher.

In a study of grievants in a heavy-machinery manufacturer, grievants were more active union members, more often absent or tardy, more highly educated than other employees, and earned less and had fewer pay increases.[42] In another study, nongrievants were more likely to be minorities, nonveterans, and young employees. Supervisors with more grievances had longer processing times and more group grievances, but their grievances were reversed less often by higher management. Experienced stewards filed fewer grievances and had a more favorable settlement rate.[43] Maturity in office may mean stewards do not solicit nonmeritorious grievances and are more skillful in gaining favorable settlements.

A study examining more than 4,000 grievances found grievants had received more wage increases, were younger, were better educated, had more derogatory information in personnel files, had fewer sick leaves, were more likely to be handicapped, were laid off more, had more promotions and demotions, were more often absent, and were more likely to request other leaves. Disciplinary grievants were younger, better educated, more likely to file grievances, more often terminated or suspended, and more likely to have refused promotions. They also had fewer commendations, more derogatory personnel file material, more arrests, more sick leaves, and more absences.[44]

Generally speaking, demographic and job-related aspects are poor predictors of grievance activity.[45] However, a recent attitudinal study that examined employees across many organizations found grievants more likely to have lower job satisfaction, higher satisfaction with the union, and to be an active participant in union affairs.[46] Another study using this same sample found employees whose job satisfaction de-

[41] Ibid., p. 138.

[42] Howard A. Sulkin and Robert W. Pranis, "Comparison of Grievants with Non-grievants in a Heavy-Machinery Company," *Personnel Psychology*, Summer 1967, pp. 111–19.

[43] Philip Ash, "The Parties to the Grievance," *Personnel Psychology*, Spring 1970, 13–38.

[44] John Price, James Dewire, John Nowack, Kenneth Schenkel, and William Ronan, "Three Studies of Grievances," *Personnel Journal*, January 1976, pp. 32–37.

[45] Labig and Greer, "Grievance Initiation."

[46] Robert E. Allen and Timothy J. Keaveny, "Factors Differentiating Grievants and Nongrievants," *Human Relations* 38 (1985), pp. 519–34.

clined during the four years between the two waves of the study, who were in larger plants, who perceived themselves as expending lower effort, and who anticipated working for the same employer in five years filed more grievances. Factors relating to perceived union effectiveness, poor or changing working conditions, or the openness of the supervisor did not influence grievance-filing behavior.[47]

EFFECTS OF GRIEVANCES ON EMPLOYERS AND EMPLOYEES

Both employers and employees may be influenced by the filing, processing, and outcome of grievances. A study of grievances in a government agency found that filing two grievances within one rating period was associated with receiving a lower performance rating. However, winning or losing the grievance was not associated with the rating. Employees who grieved were no more likely to transfer; however, employees who filed a second grievance were more likely to receive a disciplinary sanction, and a second negative adjustment to a grievance was associated with an increased probability of quitting. From the employer's standpoint, grievance filing was associated with higher absenteeism and fewer production hours.[48]

From the perspective of the ongoing bargaining relationship between the parties, grievance levels might be expected to be associated with a more conflictual labor relations climate. Evidence across 118 bargaining units in 1976–77 followed up by a study of 18 units in 1979–80 found high grievance rates associated with conflictual rather than cooperative labor relations.[49]

A study of public-sector management and union representatives found explicit performance and disciplinary standards associated with higher grievance rates. Rivalry between unions representing employees within the same employer increased grievances. Positive management attitudes and a willingness to compromise by management were related to lower rates, but consultation with the union about items of mutual interest did not reduce grievances.[50]

The resolution of a grievance provides information to the parties

[47] Brian Klaas and Gregory G. Dell'Omo, "The Determinants of Grievance-Filing Behavior: A Psychological Perspective," paper presented at the Academy of Management Meetings, Anaheim, Calif: 1988.

[48] Brian S. Klaas, Herbert G. Heneman III, and Craig A. Olson, "Grievance Activity and Its Consequences; A Study of the Grievance System and Its Impact on Employee Behavior," unpublished paper (Columbia: University of South Carolina, 1988).

[49] Jeffrey Gandz and J. David Whitehead, "The Relationship between Industrial Relations Climate and Grievance Initiation and Resolution," *Proceedings of the Industrial Relations Research Association,* 1981, pp. 320–28.

[50] Chalmer E. Labig, Jr., and I. B. Helburn, "Union and Management Policy Influences on Grievance Initiation," *Journal of Labor Research* 7 (1986), pp. 269–84.

that might assist the resolution of subsequent cases at lower levels. Evidence suggests only management used prior decisions as a basis for their initial decisions on a grievance. The higher the level of settlement of a grievance, the more likely the parties to use formal settlements of previous grievances as settlements. Earlier decisions are used most frequently as precedents in discipline and work assignment cases.[51] (Note management may settle grievances to the benefit of the grievant and the union "without precedent" for subsequent similar cases.)

This review suggested that employees who frequently grieve do not necessarily have better work outcomes. But what effect do grievances have for employers? Each grievance requires time for settlement, which involves stewards, the grievant, and supervisors at the first step; industrial relations representatives, international union representatives, and the union negotiating committee at subsequent steps; and attorneys or representatives, witnesses, and an arbitrator at arbitration. A recent study of 10 paper mills (9 unionized and 1 nonunion) found higher grievances associated with lower plant productivity. The presence of a grievance procedure (only in the union mills) was associated, however, with higher productivity, perhaps because employees had an outlet for complaints that would operate while production took place.[52]

SUMMARY

Contract administration is the joint activity in which labor and management spend the most time. Not only do the parties respond voluntarily to differences in contract interpretation, but they also must, by law, bargain with each other on practices related to mandatory items over the life of the contract.

Both sides must deal with a variety of issues; job security, seniority, and discipline are among the most important. Methods for handling disputes involve the presentation and resolution of grievances in a step-wise manner, culminating in arbitration if necessary.

Unions must represent employees in a consistent manner in grievance proceedings, and employees who can show they were not accorded fair treatment may hold the union and the employer in breach of contract.

All grievances are not equally meritorious, and many are processed for political purposes. Some grievance processing arises to modify

[51] Thomas R. Knight, "Feedback and Grievance Resolution," *Industrial and Labor Relations Review* 39 (1986), pp. 585–98.

[52] Casey Ichniowski, "The Effects of Grievance Activity on Productivity," *Industrial and Labor Relations Review* 40 (1986), pp. 75–89.

contract applications within different work groups. Other times, labor and management horse-trade a backlog of grievances.

Grievants have been found less satisfied with their jobs, more satisfied with their unions, and more involved in union activities. They are also more likely to grieve if they see fewer alternatives (such as quitting) available to them. Grievances, in general, do not lead to stronger positive outcomes for employees. Employers with high grievance rates appear to have slightly lower productivity.

DISCUSSION QUESTIONS

1. Should management be required to consult with the union about discipline before it is imposed rather than simply providing for grievance processing after its imposition?

2. Should unions be allowed to drop an employee's grievance if the employee desires arbitration?

3. How does the grievance procedure make subtle changes in the meaning of the contract possible over time?

4. What are the advantages and disadvantages of a program to reduce the number of written grievances?

CASE

Carolyn Foster had just returned to her office from the weekly plant IR representatives' meeting. Her secretary had left a note to call George Lowrey, the superintendent of the forklift assembly operation. She called back and immediately recognized from the seriousness of George's tone that a major problem must be brewing in his area. They both agreed she would come right over.

After George had welcomed her into his office, he leaned forward and, putting his chin in his hands, said, "Carolyn, I feel like I'm sitting on a powder keg here. Last year we put in the new Simplex Process assembly line for our forklifts. It had a rated capacity of 35 units an hour. When we installed it, we started up at 28 units, which is the same as the old line, to shake it down and get the bugs out. The new line automates more of the assembly, so each worker has less of a physical demand than before. Well, last week we figured we had everything ironed out on the bugs, so we raised the speed to 35. We figure each worker has to put out about the same amount of effort as under the old system.

"This morning, Ed Zeller, the shop steward, and three of my general supervisors came in, all arguing. Zeller had a fistful of grievances and was yelling about a 'speedup.' Anyway, the upshot is that he wants the job reclassified under Section 7.04 of the contract because he says effort and working conditions have changed.

"Carolyn, we can't give them a penny more and remain competitive. Besides that, if they get a raise, the whole plant will paper us with classification grievances. Zeller is running for union president because Matt Duff is retiring, and if he's successful with this grievance, he's a shoo-in. All we need for a long strike over some penny-ante issue is a bunch of hotheads like him running the show. What can you do to help me?"

Carolyn had been busy taking notes about the problem. She asked, "Do you have the grievances?" George nodded and handed them to her. Then she said, "I'll study the grievances, the contract, and the union situation and get back to you in time for us to plan a step 3 response. I'll be back to you this afternoon."

Directions

1. Draft a strategy for the company to follow. Take into account the immediate problem and the possibilities of precedents being set by your action. List the advantages and disadvantages of your chosen strategy.

2. Prepare a scenario in which your response is presented to Ed Zeller. How is he likely to react? What steps do you expect him to take as a result of your response?

3. What conditions do you consider necessary for these grievances to be resolvable at step 3?

CHAPTER 14

The Arbitration of Grievances

This chapter is about the final step in most grievance procedures—arbitration. Arbitration is not solely a labor relations process, and within labor relations it does not deal solely with grievances. This chapter covers the definition of arbitration, its legal place in labor relations, the process itself, difficulties associated with the practice of arbitration, and results associated with arbitration of employee discharge and discipline cases.

In reading this chapter, consider the following questions:

1. What influences have the Supreme Court's decisions had on arbitration?
2. How is arbitration aided or interfered with by the NLRB?
3. What procedures are used during arbitration?
4. What problems do critics of arbitration point out?

WHAT IS ARBITRATION?

Arbitration is a quasi-judicial process in which the parties agree to submit an unresolved dispute to a neutral third party for binding settlement. Both parties submit their positions, and the arbitrator decides which party is entitled to what types of relief. This chapter is concerned with labor arbitration, but the method is also applied to disputes between buyers and sellers, contractors and real estate developers, and doctors and patients.

Two major types of labor arbitration are *interest* and *rights*. This chapter is primarily concerned with rights arbitration. The next chapter covers interest arbitration. The Supreme Court distinguishes between interest and rights arbitration this way:

The first relates to disputes over the formation of collective agreements or efforts to secure them. They arise where there is no such agreement or where it is sought to change the terms of one, and therefore the issue is not whether an existing agreement controls the controversy. They look to the acquisition of rights for the future, not to assertion of rights claimed to have vested in the past.

The second class, however, contemplates the existence of a collective agreement already concluded or, at any rate, a situation in which no effort is made to bring about a formal change in terms or to create a new one. The dispute relates either to the meaning or proper application of a particular provision with reference to a specific situation or to an omitted case. In the latter event the claim is founded upon some incident of the employment relation, or asserted one, independent of those covered by the collective agreement . . . . In either case the claim is to rights accrued, not merely to have new ones created for the future.[1]

Thus, rights arbitration applies to interpreting and applying the terms of an existing contract, and interest arbitration decides future issues that have not been resolved.

DEVELOPMENT OF ARBITRATION

Arbitration was suggested by the Knights of Labor as a preferred method for the resolution of interest differences. However, no legislation mandates arbitration to settle any labor dispute in the private sector in the United States. The use of rights arbitration in the United States got its biggest boost from the National War Labor Board during World War II. Labor and management were required to include clauses providing for arbitration of possible disputes arising within the term of the contract.[2] A string of Supreme Court and NLRB cases decided since the 1950s has established the role and scope of arbitration.

Lincoln Mills

Lincoln Mills was the first case establishing arbitration as the final forum for contract disputes.[3] In *Lincoln Mills*, the Supreme Court held Section 301 of the Taft-Hartley Act required federal courts to enforce agreements between labor and management, including those providing for the arbitration of future grievances. If the contract called for arbitration and if the court agreed with the arbitrator, the award would be enforced by the court if either party failed to comply with it.

---

[1] *Elgin, Joliet & Eastern Railway Co.* v. *Burley*, 325 U.S. 711 (1945).

[2] Frank Elkouri and Edna Asper Elkouri, *How Arbitration Works*, 3rd ed. (Washington, D.C.: Bureau of National Affairs, 1973), p. 15.

[3] *Textile Workers Union* v. *Lincoln Mills*, 355 U.S. 448 (1957).

Steelworkers' Trilogy

The most important set of cases involving the status of rights arbitration was decided by the Supreme Court in 1960.[4] The question facing the Court was whether arbitrators' decisions were subject to judicial review. The Court essentially said no in this set of decisions, laying down three basic protections for arbitration. First, arbitration clauses require the parties to arbitrate unresolved grievances. Second, the substance of the grievance and its arbitrability is to be determined by the arbitrator, not the courts. And third, if an arbitration clause exists, unless the dispute is clearly outside the scope of the contract, the courts will order arbitration. The decisions state that the arbitrator is presumed to have special competence in labor relations and is thus better able than courts to resolve labor disputes.

In the *Warrior & Gulf* case, the Court held where a broad arbitration clause is included in the contract, even a dispute not covered in other sections is arbitrable. In this case, the employer subcontracted work while the firm's employees were in a partial layoff status. While lower courts held subcontracting to be a potential management right, the Supreme Court held the broad arbitration agreement coupled with the no-strike provision brought the dispute within the arbitral arena.

The *American Manufacturing* case involved an employee who had been disabled and had accepted worker's compensation. Later, his doctor certified his ability to return to work. When the company refused to reinstate him, he grieved, and the company refused to process the grievance, claiming it was frivolous. The Supreme Court, however, ordered arbitration.

The *Enterprise Wheel* case involved several employees who had been fired for walking out in protest of the firing of another employee. After the company refused to arbitrate the discharge grievances, the federal district court ordered it. The arbitrator reinstated the employees with back pay for all but 10 days' lost time. The award was rendered five days after the contract expired, but the Supreme Court ordered the company to comply.

The following four propositions follow from the decisions in the Steelworkers' Trilogy.

1. The existence of a valid agreement to arbitrate and the arbitrability of a specific grievance sought to be arbitrated under such an agreement are questions for the courts ultimately to decide (if such an issue is presented for judicial determination) unless the parties have expressly given an arbitrator the authority to make a binding determination of such matters.
2. A court should hold a grievance nonarbitrable under a valid agree-

---

[4] *United Steelworkers of America* v. *Warrior & Gulf Navigation Co.*, 363 U.S. 574; *United Steelworkers of America* v. *Enterprise Wheel and Car Corp.*, 363 U.S. 593; and *United Steelworkers of America* v. *American Manufacturing Co.*, 363 U.S. 564 (1960).

ment to use arbitration as the terminal point in the grievance procedure only if the parties have clearly indicated their intention to exclude the subject matter of the grievance from the arbitration process, either by expressly so stating in the arbitration clause or by otherwise clearly and unambiguously indicating such intention.

3. Evidence of intention to exclude a claim from the arbitration process should not be found in a determination that the labor agreement could not properly be interpreted in such manner as to sustain the grievance on its merits, for this is a task assigned by the parties to the arbitrator, not the courts.

4. An award should not be set aside as beyond the authority conferred upon the arbitrator, either because of claimed error in interpretation of the agreement or because of alleged lack of authority to provide a particular remedy, where the arbitral decision was or, if silent, might have been the result of the arbitrator's interpretation of the agreement; if, however, it was based not on the contract but on an obligation found to have been imposed by law, the award should be set aside unless the parties expressly authorized the arbitrator to dispose of this as well as any contract issue.[5]

These decisions enable arbitrators to determine, first, whether a dispute is arbitrable; and second, if arbitrable, to decide what the award should be, free from federal court intervention.[6]

The Steelworkers' Trilogy protects a union's right to insist on arbitration and to have arbitral awards enforced without review by the courts. But could management also expect the same treatment, particularly if it agreed to arbitrate and received a favorable award and the union struck to prevent enforcement (given that the Norris-LaGuardia Act broadly prevents federal courts from enjoining most labor organization activities, including strikes for any purpose as long as they did not threaten life or property)?

The 1962 Trilogy

The 1962 trilogy involves the requirement for arbitrating damages for violation of a no-strike clause rather than taking the disputes directly to the federal courts.[7] The *Drake* decision held management should request arbitration when a no-strike clause exists to determine whether the contract has been violated. In the *Sinclair* cases, the Court held the federal courts could not enjoin a strike in violation of a no-strike clause because the Norris-LaGuardia Act prevented injunctions against labor activities.

---

[5] Russell A. Smith and Dallas L. Jones, "The Supreme Court and Labor Dispute Arbitration," *Michigan Law Review* March 1965, pp. 759–60.

[6] Ibid., p. 761.

[7] *Sinclair Refining Co.* v. *Atkinson*, 370 U.S. 195 (1962); *Atkinson* v. *Sinclair Refining Co.*, 370 U.S. 238 (1962); and *Drake Bakeries* v. *Local 50*, 370 U.S. 254 (1962).

The decision in *Sinclair* v. *Atkinson* raised an important consideration for employers and for the interpretation of no-strike clauses. Without the opportunity for court enforcement, nothing would penalize a union for striking over a grievance if an arbitrator ruled against it or for striking rather than using the agreed grievance procedure. But the Supreme Court has reversed itself on this issue. *Boys Markets* later held a strike in violation of a no-strike clause prior to arbitration is enjoinable if the company is willing to arbitrate the dispute.[8]

Recent Supreme Court Decisions on Arbitration

Two cases involving arbitration procedures and awards have modified (in one case) and reaffirmed (in the other) the basics of the Steelworkers' trilogy. In the first case, the company and the union could not agree on whether the disputed situation involved the contract. The union argued a decision on coverage should be made by the arbitrator after appointment, while the company maintained arbitrability should be up to the courts. The Supreme Court agreed with the company and declared the courts ultimately have the responsibility for determining the arbitrability of contract disputes. This does not mean an arbitrator cannot rule on arbitrability, but the decision would be subject to court review, and, if a dispute existed, one of the parties could petition the courts to decide arbitrability before the case was heard.[9]

The second case involved a situation in which an arbitrator had reinstated an employee who had been fired for smoking marijuana. The company appealed the decision, which was later overturned by the courts as inconsistent with public policy on drug use. The Supreme Court reversed, however, holding in the absence of fraud or dishonesty, courts may not review a decision on its merits, or for errors of fact, or possible contract misinterpretations. Further, to overturn an award on the basis of public policy, the court must show that the policy is well defined, dominates the interests of the employee or employer, and has a history of laws and legal precedents to support it.[10]

NLRB Deferral to Arbitration

Occasionally, a dispute involves both a grievance and an unfair labor practice charge. For example, certain work that seems to belong to bargaining unit members may have been given to nonunion employees outside the bargaining unit. The grievance would allege a violation of

---

[8] *Boys Markets, Inc.* v. *Retail Clerks Union Local 770*, 398 U.S. 235 (1970).

[9] *AT&T Technologies, Inc.* v. *Communications Workers of America*, 106 Supreme Court, 1415 (1986).

[10] *United Paperworkers International Union, AFL-CIO* v. *Misco, Inc.*, 108 Supreme Court 364 (1987).

the contract on work assignments, and the union might charge the employer with discrimination based on union membership. To prevent "forum shopping" and to reduce its caseload, the NLRB has adopted rules for deferring to arbitration in cases in which a contract violation and an unfair labor practice are alleged simultaneously.

In developing its policy, the NLRB first held that where a grievance also alleged an unfair labor practice and the arbitration award had been adverse to, say, the union, the union could not then pursue the unfair labor practice.[11] The board decreed it would defer to arbitral awards if the parties had agreed in the contract to be bound by the decisions, the proceedings were fair and regular, and the results were consistent with the provisions of the labor acts.

In 1971, the board went a step further by deferring hearings on pending unfair labor practice charges until the arbitration had been completed, as long as the process met the requirements it had spelled out in *Spielberg*.[12] In early 1977, the NLRB retreated somewhat from the *Collyer* doctrine. In two cases decided the same day, the board limited deferral to cases where the alleged unfair labor practice is not a violation of an employee's Section 7 rights.[13] Ironically, a study of several cases in which the board deferred to arbitration in 1977 through 1978 in the Detroit region, unfair labor practices that involved violations of Section 7 rights were seldom incompatible with board decisions, while refusal to bargain unfair labor practices was frequently incompatible. Also, unions frequently received more favorable treatment from arbitrators than they would have before the NLRB.[14]

Arbitration and Grievance Settlement

The federal courts and the NLRB generally defer to arbitration. As stated in the Steelworkers' trilogy, the adjustment of grievances is best handled through the arbitration process because the system was chosen by the parties and is within the special expertise of the labor arbitrator. These decisions encourage the parties to devise and use processes to settle their disputes. Arbitration, as a means of settlement, is considered binding on the parties and will be left undisturbed by the courts.

---

[11] *Spielberg Manufacturing Co.*, 112 NLRB 1080 (1955).

[12] *Collyer Insulated Wire Co.*, 192 NLRB 150 (1971).

[13] *Roy Robinson Chevrolet*, 228 NLRB 103 (1977); *General American Transportation Corporation*, 228 NLRB 102 (1977).

[14] Benjamin W. Wolkinson, "The Impact of the *Collyer* Policy of Deferral: An Empirical Study," *Industrial and Labor Relations Review* 38 (1985), pp. 377–91.

Exceptions to Deferral

Although the Supreme Court led the way in endorsing arbitration as the final step in contract disputes and the NLRB allowed arbitrators to decide cases simultaneously alleging violations of federal labor relations law and the contract, two cases have set limits on deferral.[15] These cases indicate individual rights granted under other statutory employment laws cannot be decided in an arbitral procedure if a party objects to the outcome. Thus, if the grievant is dissatisfied with an arbitrator's ruling, the case could be started again by complaining to the appropriate federal compliance agency.

In *Alexander*, a black maintenance employee bid on a skilled job. After his promotion, he was warned that his performance was not up to standards; and, after completing the probationary period (during which his right to revert to his former position expired), Alexander was terminated. He charged his termination had been racially motivated. However, the arbitrator ruled it had been performance motivated and upheld the decision.

Alexander complained to the Equal Employment Opportunity Commission (EEOC). During the early part of the process, the company refused to conciliate because the arbitrator had ruled in its favor. The district court dismissed the suit because the contract had an EEO clause and the arbitrator had ruled. Ultimately appealed to the Supreme Court, the case was remanded when the Court ruled the law would not permit deferral to an arbitral award. On remand, the district court determined Alexander had been discharged for performance reasons.

Employers and unions could still use arbitration in discrimination cases if a grievance alleged a violation of *both* the contract and the law. An appropriate procedure would require the grievance to involve only a single individual, to charge only the employer with discrimination, and to not argue the contract itself is discriminatory. Individuals would be entitled to counsels of their own choosing, and a transcript would be kept. Arbitrators would be required to render their awards in writing. Thus, courts might be willing to defer to the award on a case-by-case basis because the procedure would meet the suggested Supreme Court requirements indicated in *Alexander*.[16]

Few EEO grievances are relitigated, and, where they are, arbitrators' awards have seldom been overturned or modified. A survey

---

[15] *Alexander* v. *Gardner-Denver Co.*, 415 U.S. 36 (1974); and *Barrentine* v. *Arkansas-Best Freight System*, 2 WH Cases 1284, U.S. Supreme Court, 1981.

[16] Harry T. Edwards, "Arbitration as an Alternative in Equal Employment Disputes," *Arbitration Journal*, December 1978, pp. 23–27.

of attorneys who are management or union advocates suggests they prefer greater attention to procedural aspects of arbitration rather than the extension of Title VII law to the adjudication of the grievance.[17]

In some public-sector situations, employees are subject to both the labor agreement and rules of administrative agencies. A recent Supreme Court decision requires arbitrators to apply the same standards as administrative bodies in deciding employee performance cases.[18] This prevents the grievant from shopping for the most hospitable forum.

ARBITRATION PROCEDURES

This section examines the processes leading to arbitration, the selection of an arbitrator, the conduct of the arbitration hearing, the preparation and rendering of an award, and the magnitude of arbitration in the United States.

Prearbitration Matters

The parties have specified in their contract how a dispute goes to arbitration. Normally, cases are handled through the preceding steps of the process. At the last step, if management denies the grievance or fails to modify its position sufficiently for the union to agree, the union can then demand arbitration.

If the parties have bargained some concessions prior to arbitration, these concessions do not necessarily become the basis from which the arbitrator works. In most cases, the parties can return to their own initial positions without establishing precedents. Also, in cases settled prior to arbitration, the company may explicitly state in its settlement offer to the union that it will not consider the granting of that specific grievance as precedent setting.

The contract usually specifies time periods for each step. For example, a grievance usually must be filed within five days of its occurrence. A first-line supervisor may have three days to answer it, and so on up the line. If management denies the grievance at the last prearbitration step, the union has a certain time period to demand arbitration. If it does not exercise its rights within this time period, management's decision becomes final.

---

[17] Michele M. Hoyman and Lamont E. Stallworth, "Arbitrating Discrimination Grievances in the Wake of *Gardner-Denver*," *Monthly Labor Review*, October 1983, pp. 3–10.

[18] *Cornelius* v. *Nutt*, 472 U.S. 648 (1985).

Selection of an Arbitrator

Procedures for selecting an arbitrator are in the contract. The usual forms for arbitration hearings are either to (1) use a single impartial arbitrator who hears the evidence and renders an award or (2) have a tripartite board consisting of company and union representatives and an impartial chairperson. Procedures to obtain an arbitrator are specified by the contract. In large organizations or where a long-term bargaining relationship has existed, the contract may name a specific individual or group of persons from whom arbitrators are selected. When a specific individual is named, the position is called a *permanent umpire.* Permanence, however, is relative, because the arbitrator continues to serve only as long as both parties rate performance satisfactory. Permanent umpires may be more vulnerable with a militant union that presents less meritorious cases than with a union that saves arbitration for very important issues. The arbitrator would likely, in dealing with a militant union, rule much more frequently for management; as a result, the union might rate performance unsatisfactory quite soon.[19]

A second and more common type of selection is the *ad hoc* arbitrator, who is appointed to hear only one particular case or set of cases. The appointment expires when the award is rendered, and the company and the union may coincidentally appoint other ad hoc arbitrators to hear unrelated cases at or near the same time.

Both methods of arbitrator selection have advantages and disadvantages. Less may be known about an ad hoc arbitrator, although some information about potential arbitrators is usually available through resumes, previously published decisions, fields of expertise, and so on. But the appointment constitutes no continuing obligation by the parties. The permanent umpire has a better grasp of the problems the parties encounter because of continuing experience with both. But because the relationship is continuous, whether the umpire will engage in award splitting may always be open to question.

In a study of arbitrator acceptability based on the caseloads they carried, the visibility of the arbitrator rather than personal background or practice characteristics was the factor most highly related to caseload. Also particularly important for acceptability were a listing with referral agencies, publication of awards, membership in professional organizations, and background as a permanent umpire.[20] Another study suggests managements and unions should not pay too much

[19] Robben W. Fleming, *The Labor Arbitration Process* (Urbana: University of Illinois Press, 1965), pp. 219–20.

[20] Steven S. Briggs and John C. Anderson, "An Empirical Investigation of Arbitrator Acceptability," *Industrial Relations,* Spring 1980, pp. 163–74.

EXHIBIT 14–1

Gaining Acceptability as an Arbitrator

"Paul, you've been an active arbitrator for over 25 years. For several of those years arbitration was your principal means of livelihood. You're an old-timer. How did you get started?"

"Like many if not most of the old-timers, I started with the War Labor Board. I was a graduate of the Wharton School at the University of Pennsylvania and studied under Prof. George W. Taylor. When Dr. Taylor was appointed in 1942 to be vice chairman of the War Labor Board, he recruited a number of his students to the WLB, including me."

"Did most of the WLB staff continue as arbitrators after the war?"

"No, only a small fraction survived the rough-and-tumble of voluntary arbitration in the postwar years. Throughout this book, Pete, we've frequently referred to the 350 members of the National Academy of Arbitrators who do most of the arbitrating. 'Mainline' arbitrators, they're often called, to distinguish them from 'fringe' arbitrators trying to get into the main current."

"At what point did you personally cease to be a fringe arbitrator and consider yourself a mainliner?"

"Not on any one single case, I can assure you. A fringe arbitrator can be broken by a bad opinion on just one arbitration, but becoming a mainliner is a process rather than the result of a single spectacular case."

"Is there any condition or status you can describe which clearly defines a mainline arbitrator?"

"When you put it that way, Pete, I can make the line of demarcation between a fringe arbitrator and a mainliner quite distinct. When I was a fringe arbitrator, the losing party would scrutinize my opinion to find out where *I* was wrong. I knew I had arrived at the mainline stage when in many cases the loser would study my opinion to find out where *he* was wrong."

Source: Paul Prasow and Edward Peters, *Arbitration and Collective Bargaining: Conflict Resolution in Labor Relations* (New York: McGraw-Hill, 1970), pp. 284–85.

attention to the personal background characteristics of arbitrators in making choices for a particular case because these characteristics account for little variance in arbitrators' rulings for the union or the company.[21] Exhibit 14–1 reports a conversation between two experienced arbitrators on gaining acceptability.

Sources and Qualifications of Arbitrators

There are no absolute qualifications to hold an appointment as an arbitrator. Any one of us could simply declare ourself to be an ar-

---

[21] Herbert G. Heneman III and Marcus H. Sandver, "Arbitrators' Backgrounds and Behavior," *Proceedings of the Industrial Relations Research Association,* 1982, pp. 216–23.

bitrator and seek appointments. However, an arbitrator must be selected by the parties to a grievance, and the parties might evaluate our qualifications differently than we do. So then, where do arbitrators come from? Unfortunately and somewhat tritely, arbitrators are those who have arbitrated. Parties involved in ad hoc arbitration want someone with experience and expertise, because some of the participants have done little arbitrating and need an experienced arbitrator to assist them in procedural matters. They also look for someone with a background in handling the particular disputed area. For parties with much experience in arbitration, a permanent umpire may be named, but this individual is likely to have an outstanding reputation in arbitration.

Arbitrators are generally from two groups, with the first increasingly used. The first group consists primarily of attorneys whose full-time occupation is labor arbitration. The second source is academics who teach labor law, industrial relations, and economics.

Another source of arbitrators is new entrants. However, many offer their services but are never chosen. One method for getting started is to serve an informal apprenticeship under an experienced arbitrator, gaining practice in writing decisions and learning hearing techniques. This exposure with a highly regarded neutral may lead to later appointments. Another method is to attend training courses for arbitrators; however, presently few of these are available. A few recent training programs have been successful, particularly for minority arbitrators.[22] Evidence suggests arbitrator acceptability of those who complete training is quite high.

Presently, three major sources or bodies refer arbitrators in the United States. Each serves a slightly different function, but all have interests in providing arbitrator services in labor disputes.

National Academy of Arbitrators

The National Academy of Artibrators consists of the most highly regarded arbitrators in the country. Membership is limited to active arbitrators who are invited to join. The academy holds meetings and conventions and issues proceedings, which comment on current difficult problems in arbitration and offer alternative solutions. For example, its membership has offered a variety of approaches in handling arbitration of matters having racial overtones, given the *Alexander* v. *Gardner-Denver* decision.[23] The group largely comprises full-time arbitrators, law school professors, and professors of industrial relations in major universities.

---

[22] William A. Nowlin, "Arbitrator Development: Career Paths, Model Program, and Challenges," *Arbitration Journal* 43 (1988), pp. 3–13.

[23] Harry T. Edwards, "Arbitration of Employment Discrimination Cases: A Proposal for Employer and Union Representatives," *Labor Law Journal*, May 1976, pp. 265–77.

The academy does not offer arbitration panels to disputants, but its directory provides a source of recognized, highly qualified arbitrators the parties can contact directly.

American Arbitration Association

Many contracts specify that the parties will use the services of the American Arbitration Association (AAA) for its unresolved grievances. The AAA does not employ arbitrators but acts more as a clearinghouse to administer matters between the parties and the arbitrators.

For example, if a contract specified AAA as the organization to assist in choosing an arbitrator to resolve a dispute, the process would proceed like this: First, AAA is notified that an unresolved contract dispute exists. AAA responds with a list of arbitrators (usually five, and almost always an odd number). The arbitrators may have particular expertise in the disputed area (for example, job evaluation) or may practice in a particular geographic area. Second, names are rejected alternately until only one remains. This person will be the nominee unless either party objects. In that case, AAA will send out another panel. As a rule of thumb, referral agencies usually refuse to send more than three panels for any dispute. Third, after a name has been agreed on, AAA will contact the appointee to offer the dispute, and the appointee in turn will accept or decline. If accepted, arrangements are made directly with the parties for a hearing date. Fourth, AAA will provide hearing facilities and court reporters if the parties request. Finally, AAA follows up to see what decisions were rendered.

Federal Mediation and Conciliation Service (FMCS)

The FMCS maintains a roster of arbitrators from which it can select panels. The arbitrators are not FMCS employees but rather private practitioners. If FMCS assistance is specified in a contract, it would provide panels as AAA does but would not have reporting or facilities assistance available.

FMCS screens persons who seek listing with it as arbitrators. People with obvious conflicts of interest (union organizers, employer labor consultants, and the like) are not included, and listees who fail to be selected over a period of time are purged from subsequent lists.[24] Exhibit 14–2 contains some of the requirements for being listed.

FMCS follows up on referral by requiring appointed arbitrators to render awards within 60 days of the hearing's close and the receipt of posthearing briefs.

Once the arbitrator has been selected, processes related to the scheduled hearing itself begin. From a time standpoint, the procedure

---

[24] *Code of Federal Regulations,* Title 29, Chapter 12, Part 1404.

EXHIBIT 14-2

Requirements for Listing as an Arbitrator with the FMCS

§1404.5 Listing on the Roster; Criteria for Listing and Retention

Persons seeking to be listed on the Roster must complete and submit an application form which may be obtained from the Office of Arbitration Services. Upon receipt of an executed form, OAS will review the application, assure that it is complete, make such inquiries as are necessary, and submit the application to the Arbitrator Review Board. The Board will review the completed applications under the criteria set forth in paragraphs *(a)*, *(b)*, and *(c)* of this section, and will forward to the Director its recommendation on each applicant. The Director makes all final decisions as to whether an applicant may be listed. Each applicant shall be notified in writing of the Director's decision and the reasons therefore.

(a) General Criteria. Applicants for the Roster will be listed on the Roster upon a determination that they:

(1) Are experienced, competent, and acceptable in decision-making roles in the resolution of labor relations disputes; or

(2) Have extensive experience in relevant positions in collective bargaining; and

(3) Are capable of conducting an orderly hearing, can analyze testimony and exhibits, and can prepare clear and concise findings and awards within reasonable time limits.

(b) Proof of Qualification. The qualifications listed in paragraph *(a)* of this section are preferably demonstrated by the submission of actual arbitration awards prepared by the applicant while serving as an impartial arbitrator chosen by the parties to disputes. Equivalent experience acquired in training, internship or other development programs, or experience such as that acquired as a hearing officer or judge in labor relations controversies may also be considered by the Board.

(c) Advocacy—(1) Definition. An advocate is a person who represents employers, labor organizations, or individuals as an employee, attorney, or consultant, in matters of labor relations, including but not limited to the subjects of union representation and recognition matters, collective bargaining, arbitration, unfair labor practices, equal employment opportunity, and other areas generally recognized as constituting labor relations. The definition includes representatives of employers or employees in individual cases or controversies involving worker's compensation, occupational health or safety, minimum wage, or other labor standards matters. The definition of advocate also includes a person who is directly associated with an advocate in a business or professional relationship as, for example, partners or employees of a law firm.

(2) Eligibility. Except in the case of persons listed on the Roster before November 17, 1976, no person who is an advocate, as defined above, may be listed. No person who was listed on the Roster at any time who was not an advocate when listed or who did not divulge advocacy at the time of listing may continue to be listed after becoming an advocate or after the fact of advocacy is revealed.

EXHIBIT 14–2 *(concluded)*

(d) Duration of Listing, Retention. Initial listing may be for a period not to exceed three years, and may be renewed thereafter for periods not to exceed two years, provided upon review that the listing is not cancelled by the Director as set forth below. Notice of cancellation may be given to the member whenever the member:

(1) No longer meets the criteria for admission;

(2) Has been repeatedly and flagrantly delinquent in submitting awards;

(3) Has refused to make reasonable and periodic reports to FMCS, as required in Subpart C of this part, concerning activities pertaining to arbitration;

(4) Has been the subject of complaints by parties who use FMCS facilities and the Director, after appropriate inquiry, concludes that just cause for cancellation has been shown.

(5) Is determined by the Director to be unacceptable to the parties who use FMCS arbitration facilities; the Director may base a determination of unacceptability on FMCS records showing the number of times the arbitrator's name has been proposed to the parties and the number of times it has been selected.

No listing may be canceled without at least 60 days' notice of the reasons for the proposed removal, unless the Director determines that the FMCS or the parties will be harmed by continued listing. In such cases an arbitrator's listing may be suspended without notice or delay pending final determination in accordance with these procedures. The member shall in either case have an opportunity to submit a written response showing why the listing should not be cancelled. The Director may, at his discretion, appoint a hearing officer to conduct an inquiry into the facts of any proposed cancellation and to make recommendations to the Director.

---

involves three distinct phases: prehearing, hearing, and posthearing processes.

Prehearing

Elkouri and Elkouri detail a number of steps both parties should go through before an arbitration hearing:

a. Review the history of the case as developed at the prearbitral steps of the grievance procedure.

b. Study the entire collective agreement to ascertain all clauses bearing directly or indirectly on the dispute. Also, comparison of current provisions with those contained in prior agreements might reveal changes significant to the case.

c. So as to determine the general authority of the arbitrator, and accordingly the scope of the arbitration, examine the instruments used to initiate the arbitration.

d. Talk to all persons (even those the other party might use as witnesses) who might be able to aid development of a full picture of the case, including different viewpoints. You will thus better understand not only your own case but your opponent's as well; if you can anticipate your opponent's case, you can better prepare to rebut it.

e. Interview each of your own witnesses *(a)* to determine what they know about the case; *(b)* to make certain they understand the relation of their testimony to the whole case; *(c)* to cross-examine them to check their testimony and to acquaint them with the process of cross-examination. Make a written summary of the expected testimony of each witness; this can be reviewed when the witness testifies to ensure that no important points are overlooked. Some parties outline in advance the questions to be asked each witness.

f. Examine all records and documents that might be relevant to the case. Organize those you expect to use and make copies for use by the arbitrator and the other party at the hearing. If needed documents are in the exclusive possession of the other party, ask that they be made available before or at the hearing.

g. Visit the physical premises involved in the dispute to visualize better what occurred and what the dispute is about. Also, consider the advisability of asking at the hearing that the arbitrator (accompanied by both parties) also visit the site of the dispute.

h. Consider the utility of pictorial or statistical exhibits. One exhibit can be more effective than many words, if the matter is suited to the exhibit form of portrayal. However, exhibits which do not "fit" the case and those which are inaccurate or misleading are almost certain to be ineffective or to be damaging to their proponent.

i. Consider what the parties' past practices have been in comparable situations.

j. Attempt to determine whether there is some "key" point upon which the case might turn. If so, it may be to your advantage to concentrate upon that point.

k. In "interpretation" cases, prepare a written argument to support your view as to the proper interpretation of the disputed language.

l. In "interests" or "contract-writing" cases, collect and prepare economic and statistical data to aid evaluation of the dispute.

m. Research the parties' prior arbitration awards and the published awards of other parties on the subject of the dispute for an indication of how similar issues have been approached in other cases.

n. Prepare an outline of your case and discuss it with other persons in your group. This ensures better understanding of the case and will strengthen it by uncovering matters that need further attention. Then too, it will tend to underscore policy and strategy considerations that may be very important in the ultimate handling of the case. Use of the outline at the hearing will facilitate an organized and systematic presentation of the case.[25]

In addition to these steps, the parties may continue to meet to seek a settlement or to reduce the time necessary to settle a case. Just because a case has been submitted to arbitration does not mean an arbitrator will ultimately determine the outcome. Anytime during the prehearing phase, the party initiating the arbitration may withdraw it with the consent of the other party. Frequently, the contract will specify how this is to be done, whether the withdrawal is "with prejudice" (nonresubmittable), and whether its withdrawal is precedent setting. The parties may also stipulate certain facts in the case, agree on applicable contract terms, and prepare joint exhibits. Evidence suggests settlement prior to arbitration after a case has been scheduled to be heard occurs more frequently when the parties' representatives are not attorneys.[26]

Hearing Processes

The actual hearing may take many forms. From the most simplified standpoint, a case may be completely stipulated, with the arbitrator simply ruling on an interpretation of the written documents submitted. This option is not entirely up to the parties, however, because the arbitrator may insist on calling witnesses and examining evidence on site.

Representatives of the Parties

The parties' positions may be advocated by anyone of their choosing, which means the representatives may be attorneys, company or union officials, the grievant, and so on. In most cases involving smaller companies, a national union field representative or local union officer and an industrial relations director or personnel officer are the advocates. Attorney representation and so-called equal qualifications across advocates are not required. Parties appear to be at an advantage in winning cases when they are represented by an attorney and the other side is not. When only one side retains an attorney, it is more frequently management.[27]

---

[25] Elkouri and Elkouri, *How Arbitration Works*, pp. 198–99.

[26] Clarence R. Deitsch and David A. Dilts, "Factors Affecting Pre-Arbitral Settlement of Rights Disputes: Predicting the Methods of Rights Dispute Resolution," *Journal of Labor Research* 7 (1986), pp. 69–78.

[27] Richard N. Block and Jack Stieber, "The Impact of Attorneys and Arbitrators on Arbitration Awards," *Industrial and Labor Relations Review* 40 (1987), pp. 543–55.

Presentation of the Case

Because the union generally has initiated the grievance, it has the responsibility to proceed with the case, except in discipline and discharge cases. A union presents joint exhibits relevant to its case, presents its own exhibits, and calls witnesses as necessary. During this period, management's representative may object to exhibits and cross-examine witnesses. When the union has completed its case, management offers its evidence in a similar manner. The rules of evidence in arbitration cases are more liberal than those in courts of law. These differences will be examined shortly.

At the end, both sides may have an opportunity to present closing arguments. During the earlier presentation, the arbitrator may question witnesses but is not required to do so.

Posthearing

Following the hearing, the parties may submit additional material in the form of briefs to support their positions. If these are received, the arbitrator will study the evidence, take the briefs into account, and perhaps examine similar cases in which arbitrators were called on for an award.

The arbitrator then prepares an award and forwards it to the parties for implementation. In some cases, the arbitrator maintains jurisdiction until the award has been completely implemented in case additional proceedings are necessary to iron out differences in application.

The receipt of evidence at the hearing and the form and preparation of the award are examined next.

Evidentiary Rules

In arbitration where AAA rules apply, Rule 28 states: "The arbitrator shall be the judge of the relevancy and the materiality of the evidence offered, and conformity to legal rules of evidence shall not be necessary."[28] However, arbitrators must weigh the relevance or credibility of evidence when considering a grievance.

Two basic types of evidence are *direct* and *circumstantial*. Direct evidence is information specifically tying an individual to a situation. The search for the "smoking gun" is an attempt to find direct evidence. Circumstantial evidence suggests a connection between events and an individual. For example, if shortages in a cash register occur only when

---

[28] 30 LA 1086, 1089.

one particular employee is scheduled, that circumstance, when connected with others, may establish guilt.

Evidence is relevant if it addresses the issue at hand. For example, if an arbitrator hears a case involving drinking on the job, evidence related to the subject's work assignment is not highly relevant. The evidence must also be material. For example, testimony that the subject bought a six-pack of beer the week before the alleged offense has little impact on establishing a connection with the offense.

In arbitration hearings, the union must prove management violated the contract, except in discipline cases. The level of proof required in discipline cases may vary among arbitrators, but it is usually greater if the potential consequences to the employee are more severe.

Generally speaking, employees are expected to know that published rules apply, and prior written warnings they received were correctly given unless challenged. Past discipline may be used to corroborate that an employee committed this type of offense; but the longer the time since the discipline, the less weight it is usually given.

If evidence shows another arbitrator has ruled on the same issue in this company and no contract changes have occurred in the area, the present arbitrator will probably rule the issue has already been decided. In discipline cases where criminal proceedings have also taken place, the arbitrator is not bound by the same rules for obtaining evidence that prove the offense beyond a reasonable doubt.

Arbitrators must also assess the credibility of witnesses. Persons who have little inherent interest in the case might be considered more credible, and one's reputation for honesty may also be considered.[29]

Occasionally, one party will have information that would aid the other in the preparation of a case. Four rules have been suggested for the production of material held by one party: (1) if the arbitrator requests it; (2) if refused, the arbitrator may weigh the refusal as he/she sees fit in the award; (3) the document or information could be used to attack the credibility of a witness; and (4) the arbitrator may admit only the parts relevant to the hearing.[30]

For cross-examination and confrontation, the following have been recommended: (1) depositions and previous testimony be admitted if a witness is unavailable; (2) hearsay be accepted when a direct witness declines to testify against a fellow employee; (3) investigation should generally not be attempted by the arbitrator; (4) where exposing the identity of a witness would damage legitimate interests of either party, the witness should be questioned by counsel in the sole presence of the arbitrator.[31]

---

[29] Marvin Hill, Jr., and Anthony V. Sinicropi, *Evidence in Arbitration* (Washington, D.C.: Bureau of National Affairs, 1980), pp. 1–108.

[30] Fleming, *Labor Arbitration Process*, p. 175.

[31] Ibid., p. 181.

Self-incrimination is prohibited in criminal trials and may also be an issue in arbitral proceedings. The arbitrator probably will not grant an absolute immunity against self-incrimination but will weigh the refusal to testify as if it were evidence. However, the arbitrator should not consider a refusal to testify as sufficient to sustain a case by itself.[32]

Arbitral Remedies

When a case is submitted to an arbitrator, usually the issues are specified and the grievant has indicated what relief is desired. The relief requested tends to vary given the type of case, but generally arbitrators will grant relief when it is found that the aggrieved party has been wrong, up to but not exceeding the relief desired.

In discipline and discharge cases, requested relief is usually for back pay for periods of suspension and discharge, restoration of employment, recision of a demotion or transfer, elimination of reprimands from personnel files, and the like. If reinstatement and/or back pay is to be granted, the arbitrator needs to determine the amount through the likely job history of the grievant, pay that he or she has earned on other jobs, and the like. Arbitrators might also reduce disciplinary measures taken if they exceed what the offense would merit, given similar situations in the grievant's organization or in other workplaces with the same settings.

More difficult cases to remedy involve such issues as subcontracting, plant closures, entitlements to overtime, assignment of work, and other economic issues. Usual remedies may require the restoration of work to the bargaining unit and payment of wages forgone by employees who would have been entitled to the work.[33]

Preparation of the Award

The award conveys the arbitrator's decision in the case, including (in most cases) a summary of the evidence presented, the reasoning behind the decision, and what action must be taken to satisfy the decision.

In preparing the award, the arbitrator must examine a number of issues. First, whether the dispute was actually arbitrable must be determined. Did the grievance allege an actual violation of the contract? Were the grievance procedure steps followed in a regular and timely manner so the grievance was submitted soon enough and the union follow-up was timely enough? If these arbitrability criteria are met, then the arbitrator proceeds with an examination of the merits.

---

[32] Ibid., p. 186.

[33] Marvin Hill, Jr., and Anthony Sinicropi, *Remedies in Arbitration* (Washington, D.C.: Bureau of National Affairs, 1981).

While the arbitrator has no statutory obligation to do so, it is important that the reason for a particular award be included to guide the parties in the future. Even though the grievance may appear trivial, the decision will govern employer and union conduct for a substantial future period, and so it is important for them to know why the issue was decided as it was.

The arbitrator must be careful to ensure that an award draws from the essence of the contract. Most contracts prohibit the arbitrator from adding to, subtracting from, or modifying the agreement. The arbitrator must show how the interpretation is within the four corners of the contract.

Occasionally, an arbitrator will find a conflict between contract language and federal labor or civil rights laws or interpretations. No clear-cut guidance exists for this situation. Some argue the arbitrator is to give primacy to a contractual interpretation,[34] while others suggest federal employment laws must supersede contract terms and influence the shape of an award where they would govern.[35]

PROCEDURAL DIFFICULTIES AND THEIR RESOLUTIONS

The prime difficulty encountered in arbitration is the same problem found in the legal system: time delays. The official AFL–CIO publication reported in 1976 that the average time from the filing of a grievance through the submission of an arbitral award was 223 days.[36] There is no reason to believe these figures have improved substantially since then, and it is not unusual to see some cases take up to two years for resolution. Table 14–1 provides the time data reported by the AFL–CIO.

The arbitral process can take more time, but the data show an average of 104 days from appointment to award. The 43-day period from the termination of the hearing to the award date is greater than the old 30-day limit previously established by the FMCS, but it may include time during which labor and management submit briefs. Thus, arbitrators may come fairly close in rendering decisions within 30 days of the receipt of all case material. One arbitrator recently noted that over about 150 recent cases, his time delay between the close of the hearing and the rendering of a decision varied from zero to 94 days,

---

[34] Bernard Meltzer, "Ruminations about Ideology, Law, and Labor Arbitration," in *The Arbitrator, the NLRB, and the Courts: Proceedings of the National Academy of Arbitrators* (Washington, D.C.: Bureau of National Affairs, 1967), p. 1.

[35] Robert Howlett, "The Arbitrator, the NLRB, and the Courts," in *The Arbitrator, the NLRB, and the Courts: Proceedings of the National Academy of Arbitrators* (Washington, D.C.: Bureau of National Affairs, 1967), p. 67.

[36] John Zalusky, "Arbitration: Updating a Vital Process," *American Federationist*, November 1976, pp. 1–8.

TABLE 14-1

Arbitration Time Delays

	Days
Grievance date to request for panel	68
Between request for panel and panel sent out	6
Panel sent out to appointment of arbitrator	45
Appointment of arbitrator to hearing date	61
Hearing date to arbitrator award	43
Total: Grievance date to award	223

Source: John Zalusky, "Arbitration: Updating a Vital Process," *American Federationist*, November 1976, p. 6.

with a mean of 30 days or less in cases in every industry except railroads. For the same cases, the time lapse between the grievance and the hearing was zero to 1,426 days, with a mean of over 100 days in all industries and a mean of over one year in steel, railroads, the federal government, and miscellaneous situations.[37]

Problems still exist with the length of time taken. "Justice delayed is justice denied" is not an empty platitude. It is important to individuals who have been disciplined to have their cases finally disposed so they can make a new employment life or return to work made whole. For the firm, a grievance involving large numbers of persons could lead to substantial back pay liabilities if long-delayed findings are adverse.

Arbitration costs also cause problems, particularly for unions. Because managements and unions usually share the cost of arbitration, a relatively poorly financed union may be reluctant to use arbitration as much as it would like. Table 14–2 gives an estimate of union costs for a typical, relatively uncomplicated arbitration case. Since the table was constructed in 1976, it is likely that the arbitrators' fees have increased substantially since then.

Expedited Arbitration

Since the early 1970s, some larger companies and unions have moved toward a scheme called *expedited arbitration*, in which time delays and costs are expected to be reduced. Rather than hearing only one case in a day, arbitrators might hear several and may submit very short written awards. Most of the cases handled under expedited arbitration are individual discipline and discharge cases or emergency cases.

Another expected advantage is that expedited arbitration will provide for the entry of new arbitrators, because relatively simple and

---

[37] Garth Mangum, "Delay in Arbitration Decisions," *Arbitration Journal*, 42 1987, p. 58.

TABLE 14–2

The Union's Cost of Traditional Arbitration for a One-Day Hearing

Prehearing:	
Lost time: Grievant and witnesses @ $10/32 hours	$ 320
Lawyer:	
Library research @ $15/4 hour	60
Interviewing witnesses @ $75/4 hours	300
Filing fee: AAA (shared equally) $100	50
Total prehearing costs	$ 730
Hearing expense:	
Arbitrator:	
Fee (shared equally) 1 hearing day	$ 200
Expenses for meals, transportation, and so on (shared equally)	100
Travel time one half day (shared equally)	100
Total arbitrator	$ 400
Transcript: $5 per page with two copies and 10-day delivery of 200 pages (shared equally)	$ 500
Lawyer: Presentation of case @ $75/hour	450
Lost time: Grievant and witnesses @ $10/32 hours	160
Hearing room: Shared equally (free under AAA)	50
Total hearing	$1160
Posthearing expense	
Arbitrator: 1½ days study time (shared equally)	$ 300
Lawyer: Preparation of posthearing brief @ $75/8 hours	600
Total posthearing	$ 900
Total cost to union	$3190

straightforward cases are generally handled by this process. Table 14–3 contains examples of expedited arbitration procedures.

Inadequate Representation

Chapter 13 noted employees in certain situations have successfully argued they were not fairly represented by their unions in the grievance procedure. In arbitration, inadequate representation can arise. Inadequate representation could be malicious, or it could occur through ineptitude. Because arbitration proceedings are viewed as final determinations by the courts, the quality of the advocacy one receives is of substantial concern.

The Supreme Court reversed an arbitration award in the discharge of an over-the-road trucker who was accused of padding expenses.[38] An adequate prehearing investigation would have disclosed that the seeming dishonesty was a result of a motel clerk charging more than the published rate and pocketing the difference. The trucker was actually blameless.

---

[38] *Hines* v. *Anchor Motor Freight, Inc.*, U.S. Supreme Court, 74-1025, 1976.

TABLE 14-3

Examples of Expedited Methods

	Steelworkers—basic steel industry	American Arbitration Association Service	AIW Local 562 Rusco, Inc.	American Postal Workers—U.S. Postal Service	Miniarbitration Columbus, Ohio
Source of arbitrators	Recent law school graduates and other sources	Special panel from AAA roster	FMCS roster	AAA, FMCS rosters	Its own "Joint Selection and Orientation Committee" from FMCS roster
Method of selecting	Preselected regional panels; administrator notifies in rotation	Appointed by AAA regional administrators	Preselected panel by rotating FMCS contracts	Appointed by AAA regional administrators	FMCS regional representative by rotation
Lawyers	No limitation, but understanding that lawyers will not be used	No limitation	No lawyers	No limitation but normally not used	No limitation
Transcript	No	No	No	No	May be used
Briefs	No	Permitted	No	No	May be used
Written description of issue	Last step grievance report	Joint submission permitted	No	Position paper	Grievance record expected
Time from request to hearing date	10 days	Approximately 3 days depending on arbitrator availability	10 days	Approximately 7 days depending on arbitrator availability	Not specified
Time of hearing to award	Bench decision or 48 hours	5 days	48 hours	Bench decision; written award, 48 hours	48 hours
Fees (plus expenses)	$100/½ day $150/day	$100 filing fee Arbitrator's normal fee	$100/½ day $150/day	$100 filing fee $100 per case	$100/½ day, 1 or 2 cases; $150/full day, 1 or 2 cases; $200/day, 3 or 4 cases

Source: John Zalusky, "Arbitration: Updating a Vital Process," *American Federationist*, November 1976, p. 4.

Within the hearing itself, the arbitrator may become aware of differences in the quality of representation. Although the arbitrator may question witnesses and probe into other matters, the umpire's impartiality in an essentially adversary hearing could be questioned as a result. Is it ethical for an arbitrator to "make a case" for an advocate who has inadequately prepared a case? This issue has not been settled. However, if it's clear to the arbitrator that the grievant's rights are not adequately represented, a later appeal could reverse the award.[39]

ARBITRATION OF DISCIPLINE CASES

A large number of cases heard by arbitrators are appeals made by employees to reconsider the evidence related to employer discipline or to reassess the severity of the punishment. Any punishment including discharge is particularly likely to go to arbitration. What principles do arbitrators apply to the evaluation of evidence and the establishment of fair punishment in industrial discipline cases?

Role of Discipline

Under the contract, employees have certain rights and obligations—as do employers. Employees have rights to their jobs as the contract reads, and employers are entitled to performance from their workers. An employer expects employees to carry out orders, regardless of the employees' interpretation of the rightness of the orders, unless they are unsafe, unhealthful, or illegal.[40] If employees believe the orders violate the contract, they are entitled to file grievances and seek relief. On the other hand, if the employees take matters into their own hands, they are guilty of insubordination and may be punished. The punishment can serve two basic purposes: (1) to motivate the individuals to avoid similar conduct in the future and (2) by example, to deter others.

Evidence

Because discipline cases are extremely important to the grievant, arbitrators require the company to present evidence showing that the grievant actually committed the offense and that the punishment is consistent with the breach of the rules. The company must also show it is not dealing with this employee in an arbitrary manner when compared to others involved in similar situations.

---

[39] See Jean T. McKelvey, "The Duty of Fair Representation: Has the Arbitrator a Responsibility?" *Arbitration Journal* 41 (1986), pp. 51–58, for one arbitrator's opinion.

[40] Dallas L. Jones, *Arbitration and Industrial Discipline* (Ann Arbor: Bureau of Industrial Relations, University of Michigan, 1961), pp. 17–18.

On the basis of this evidence, arbitrators may uphold or deny the punishment or modify it downward (but not upward) to follow the disciplinary breach more closely. Arbitrators also require the discipline to be given for just cause and not on some capricious basis.

Uses of Punishment

Punishment can be thought of in two contexts as it relates to discipline. The first sees punishment as a legitimate exercise of authority as a consequence of a breach of rules. The second sees punishment as a corrective effort to direct the employees' attention to the consequences but also to change their attitudes toward the punished behaviors.[41] Arbitrators may be concerned with these approaches, but they are perhaps more concerned with the procedural regularity of the discipline in the case at hand, in the evenness of its application across persons within the same firm, and in its fundamental fairness given societal norms.[42]

A study of arbitral decisions in discipline cases found cases divided equally in applying authoritarian or corrective discipline, with a small additional proportion using humanitarian discipline (using rules only as guidance and taking into account individual intentions). Table 14–4 shows the results. Corrective discipline is used more often for absenteeism and incompetence, while authoritarian approaches are used more often for dishonesty and illegal strike activity.[43]

Given that corrective discipline is applied in about 50 percent of reported cases, is it effective? One intensive study concluded in no case did corrective discipline turn an unsatisfactory employee into one whose performance was satisfactory. A number of reasons are suggested for this finding. First, the individual is often restored to the original work group, where behavior that resulted in the punishment is reinforced. Second, what behavior the punishment related to may not have been clearly pointed out to the grievant. And third, in some cases placing an employee in a probationary status rather than punishing him or her may be reasonable, so the contingency is on future rather than past behavior.[44]

An employee's previous work record is apparently predictive of job performance after reinstatement. Poor performance after reinstatement among a larger sample of employees was predicted by the numbers of warnings and other disciplinary action prior to being

---

[41] Ibid., pp. 2–4.

[42] Ibid., pp. 16–20.

[43] Hoyt N. Wheeler, "Punishment Theory and Industrial Discipline," *Industrial Relations*, May 1976, pp. 235–43.

TABLE 14-4

Analysis of Arbitration Decisions Relating to Discharge and Discipline by Theory of Discipline and Type of Offense, as Reported in *Labor Arbitration Reports*, May 1970 through March 1974

	Humanitarian	Corrective	Authoritarian	Total
Absenteeism, tardiness, leaving early	2	20	8	30
Dishonesty, theft, falsification of records	2	13	28	43
Incompetence, negligence, poor workmanship, violation of safety rules	1	27	9	37
Illegal strikes, strike violence, deliberate restiction of production	0	12	19	31
Intoxication, bringing intoxicants into plant	1	10	7	18
Fighting, assault, horseplay, troublemaking	3	16	15	34
Insubordination, refusal of job assignment, refusal to work overtime, also fight or altercation with supervisor	2	42	54	98
Miscellaneous rule violations	2	20	26	48
Totals	13	160	166	339
Percent	4%	47%	49%	

Source: Hoyt N. Wheeler, "Punishment Theory and Industrial Discipline,"*Industrial Relations*, May 1976, p. 239.

discharged, and discharges for absenteeism or dishonesty.[45] Among another group of reinstated employees, the evidence suggested most discharges had been for attendance problems, and the performance of reinstated employees was about average.[46]

ARBITRATION OF PAST-PRACTICE DISPUTES

Certain work practices or benefits may not be mentioned explicitly in the contract but may have been applied so consistently that there is an understanding they will continue to be applied in a similar manner. Unions may frequently negotiate clauses into contracts stating that both parties agree existing conditions will not be lowered during the present agreement.

In a variety of situations, arbitrators have ruled certain practices not mentioned in the contract are protected to the initiator, union, or

---

[45] Chalmer E. Labig, Jr., I. B. Helburn, and Robert C. Rodgers, "Discipline History, Seniority, and Reason for Discharge as Predictors of Post-Reinstatement Job Performance," *Arbitration Journal* 40 (1985), pp. 44–52.

[46] William E. Simkin, "Some Results of Reinstatement by Arbitration," *Arbitration Journal* 41 (1986), pp. 53–58.

management. If management confers a benefit but announces special circumstances each time it confers it, the employer does not establish a continuing practice. On the other hand, if management mentions a benefit as a reason for not conceding in some area during negotiations, the benefit tends to assume binding characteristics. If conditions change and management decides to drop a practice, it must do so within a reasonably short time after the change to defend itself against past-practice grievances.[47]

One arbitrator suggested eight criteria should be examined in ruling on past-practice grievances.

1. Does the practice concern a major condition of employment?
2. Was it established unilaterally?
3. Was it administered unilaterally?
4. Did either party seek to incorporate it into the body of the written agreement?
5. What is the frequency of repetition of the practice?
6. Is the practice of long standing?
7. Is it specific and detailed?
8. Do the employees rely on it?[48]

If the answers to these questions are yes or frequent, the condition will likely take on some legitimacy as a negotiated benefit.

ASSESSMENT OF ARBITRATION

Some assessments of the arbitral processes have been made throughout this chapter. This section covers the relative occurrence of types of issues in arbitration and assesses how the parties perceive the process.

The FMCS gathers data on the number of cases going to arbitration and the issues involved for panels it supplies. Table 14-5 shows the progression from 1973 through 1985. Issues taken to arbitration have declined markedly between 1981 and 1985, probably due to changes in the economic climate and also to some successes in reducing union–management conflict.

But are the parties enthusiastic about the practices? Complaints have been made about cost and time delays. And how do labor and management feel about a process in which a third party resolves their disputes?

An old joke holds, "Money doesn't buy happiness, but it's way ahead of whatever's in second place." The same may be true for

---

[47] Paul Prasow and Edward Peters, *Arbitration and Collective Bargaining: Conflict Resolution in Labor Relations* (New York: McGraw-Hill, 1970), pp. 96–121.

[48] *Jacob Ruppert* v. *Office Employees International Union Local 153*, October 19, 1960, 35 LA 505; arbitrator, Burton B. Turkus.

TABLE 14–5

Number and Percent Change in Number of Issues Reported in Applicable FMCS Closed Arbitration Award Cases for Fiscal Years 1973, 1977, 1981, and 1985; Percent Change from 1981 to 1985

Specific issues	Total number of issues				Percent change from FY 1981
	1973	1977	1981	1985	
Total	4,255	6,935	8,126	5,380	−33.8%
General issues:	1,130	1,922	1,962	1,378	−29.8%
Overtime other than pay:					
Distribution of overtime	187	183	202	112	−44.5
Compulsory overtime	17	31	23	17	−26.1
Other	—	29	49	25	−49.0
Seniority:					
Promotion and upgrading	203	253	215	156	−27.4
Layoff, bumping, and recall	264	320	361	267	−26.0
Transfer	96	96	92	61	−33.7
Other	90	102	93	73	−21.5
Union officers	27	24	41	27	−34.1
Strike and lockout	19	33	13	1	−92.3
Working conditions	48	54	57	33	−42.1
Discrimination	—	56	63	51	−19.0
Management rights	—	201	199	139	−30.1
Scheduling of work	179	137	150	105	−30.0
Work assignments	—	403	404	311	−24.0
Economic: wage rates and pay issues	581	922	930	546	−41.3%
Wage issues	—	86	107	54	−49.5
Rate of pay	—	176	176	105	−40.3
Severance pay	—	19	18	19	+5.6
Reporting, call-in, and call-back pay	86	82	72	47	−34.7
Holidays and holiday pay	119	127	129	76	−41.1
Vacations and vacation pay	113	150	142	92	−35.2
Incentive rates or standards	82	93	74	41	−44.6
Overtime pay	181	189	212	112	−47.2
Fringe benefit issues:	161	219	228	156	−31.6%
Health and welfare	51	81	86	58	−32.6
Pensions	24	25	23	20	−13.0
Other	86	113	119	78	−34.4
Discharge and disciplinary issues	1,302	2,520	3,231	2,050	−36.5%
Technical issues:	400	395	380	296	−22.1%
Job posting and bidding	—	112	108	99	−8.3
Job evaluation	400	88	75	65	−13.3
Job classification	—	195	197	132	−32.3
Scope of agreement:	186	197	231	136	−41.1%
Subcontracting	95	109	127	98	−22.8
Jurisdictional disputes	40	51	49	14	−71.4
Foreman, supervision, etc.	42	32	47	23	−51.1
Mergers, consolidations, accretion other plants	9	5	8	1	−87.5

TABLE 14–5 *(concluded)*

Specific issues	Total number of issues				Percent change from FY 1981
	1973	1977	1981	1985	
Arbitrability of grievances:	252	545	844	584	−30.8%
Procedural	143	311	434	301	−30.6
Substantive	70	115	218	146	−30.0
Procedural and substantive	10	69	82	67	−18.3
Not elsewhere classified	243	215	320	234	−26.9%

Source: U.S. Federal Mediation and Conciliation Service, *Thirty-Eighth Annual Report, Fiscal Year 1986* (Washington, D.C.: U.S. Government Printing Office, 1986), pp. 38–39; U.S. Federal Mediation and Conciliation Service, *Thirty-Fourth Annual Report, Fiscal Year 1981* (Washington, D.C.: U.S. Government Printing Office, 1981), pp. 40–41.

arbitration. It does not solve all of the problems of contract administration, but no one has devised a better substitute. A study of labor and management perceptions completed in the mid-1960s came to a number of conclusions.[49] The parties generally prefer arbitration over bargaining in unresolved disputes. While most would have left the present process untouched, some preferred the possibility of a court review. Several were concerned with a lack of adherence to rules of evidence, which makes determining how testimony is credited more difficult. Prehearing briefs could shorten hearings. Finally, as to decision making, the parties wanted an arbitrator who was willing to act as judge rather than mediator and who was willing to stay within the contract in deciding a dispute. Given the court system's reluctance to review arbitral awards, the parties desired some certainty in the conduct of the proceedings and the issues considered in rendering an award.

SUMMARY

Arbitration is a process for resolving disputes through the invitation of a neutral third party. The use of arbitration is encouraged by the courts, and the outcome of arbitral awards is generally considered nonreviewable. Supreme Court decisions in the Steelworkers' trilogy laid the groundwork for the present status of arbitration.

Arbitral hearings are quasi-judicial in nature and involve allegations of contract violations. The arbitrator hears evidence from both parties and rules on the issue in dispute.

---

[49] Dallas L. Jones and Russell A. Smith, "Management and Labor Appraisals and Criticisms of the Arbitration Process: A Report with Comments," *Michigan Law Review*, May 1964, pp. 1115–56.

A large number of arbitration proceedings are associated with individual discipline and discharge cases. Arbitration cases appear to be split about evenly in applying authoritarian or corrective standards in the use of punishment.

Arbitration has been criticized for its time delays and costs and because some decisions seem to go outside the scope of the contract or dispute. But opponents and proponents are relatively satisfied with the system.

DISCUSSION QUESTIONS

1. Given the Supreme Court and NLRB rulings, what is the present scope and finality associated with rights arbitration proceedings in the private sector?

2. What possible drawbacks do you see associated with the expansion of expedited arbitration?

3. What duty, if any, does an arbitrator owe to the parties to see that both are competently represented?

4. Give arguments for and against the greater involvement of attorneys in arbitration, as both advocates and umpires.

5. Forecast what you see as the future of labor arbitration in terms of the expansion or contraction of issues within its jurisdiction and the finality of its decisions.

CASES

About six months after the new GMFC–Local 384 contract was ratified, three grievances were sent to arbitration by the union after a failure to resolve them. The company and the union agreed that all three grievances would be heard on separate dates by the same arbitrator. Your name was on the panel the FMCS sent to the parties, and they selected you to hear the grievances. You agreed and have heard all three over the last three days. Now you have to prepare your awards.

Case 1

George Jones was a grade 8 production worker in the heavy-components assembly department. He worked with six other assemblers of the same grade, constructing cabs for power shovels. The supervisor, Ralph Barnes, was in charge of three of these heavy-assembly crews. George Jones had been with the company for about four years, but over two of these he had been laid off. Over the last six months, he had spent all of his time with his present work crew. His work record had been unremarkable. He had two unexcused absences but no problems with supervision.

On May 6, George struck a co-worker, Elliot Johnson, with his fist, rendering him unconscious. As soon as Barnes arrived on the scene and gave first aid, he asked the work crew what had happened. They had only seen Jones strike Johnson. After Johnson regained consciousness, Barnes asked him what happened. Johnson stated he and Jones had been talking when Jones suddenly turned and swung at him. Barnes then asked Jones what happened. Jones, who is the only black employee in his work group, said Johnson had been making racial slurs toward him ever since he joined the crew, and this morning he had been pushed over the brink when Johnson said, "If it weren't for affirmative action, welfare would be the only thing that would keep a shirt on your back."

From his supervisor training course, Barnes knew it was company policy to discharge anyone who struck another employee or started a fight. Thus, he sent Jones to the personnel department for termination. On the way, Jones filed a grievance with Ralph Murphy, the union steward in his area, alleging the company had violated Section 4.02 of the contract by discharging him without cause. His grievance stated the attack on Johnson was justified given his past harassment and punching him seemed to be the "only way to get him off my back."

When Murphy gave the grievance to Barnes, it was immediately denied. Barnes said, "The rule is ironclad, as far as I'm concerned. They said we supervisors didn't have any latitude on this issue."

Murphy then presented copies of the grievance to the shift IR representative, Carolyn Foster, and Neal Young, the general supervisor. In her examination of the grievance, Foster called Johnson and Cronholm, Jensen, and Albers (three other employees in the work group) to her office separately. When questioned, Johnson repeated his allegation that Jones's attack was unprovoked and adamantly denied ever making racial slurs toward him. Information from Jensen and Albert supported Johnson's denial of racial slurs, but Cronholm said he had repeatedly heard Johnson make disparaging remarks to Jones and Jones had asked him to stop. After weighing this information and considering company policy on fighting, she upheld Barnes's action.

The union continued to demand Jones's reinstatement with full back pay, and management adamantly refused.

When the case was heard, the union's grievance alleged that not only had Jones been discharged without cause (Section 4.02) but that the discharge had also been racially motivated, violating the EEO section (12.14a). In its opening argument, the company asked you to find the grievance nonarbitrable because Jones could file a charge with the EEOC under Title VII if your award upheld the discharge. The company also said the discrimination issue was not arbitrable because it had not been raised in step 3 as provided in 12.14b. You noted the arguments but reserved your ruling on arbitrability for the decision you would prepare.

Both sides presented their evidence. All of it was in substantial agreement with what Barnes and Foster had found in their investigation. Jones and Johnson held to their stories, as did Jensen, Albers, and Cronholm. The company introduced evidence to show that without exception employees had been terminated for fighting. It also provided statistics showing 12 percent of the 8 employees discharged for fighting over the past three years were black and 14 percent of the production labor force was black.

In this case, your award should contain:

1. Your ruling on the arbitrability of the grievance.
2. Your rationale in finding on the merits of the case (if arbitrable).
3. If arbitrable, the degree to which you would grant the relief Jones is asking or uphold management.

Case 2

This case has the greatest ramifications for the firm from a cost standpoint. In the past, the company has always used its own janitors for cleaning and maintenance. Due to operational requirements, most of this work is performed on the third shift. About 20 janitors are required to maintain the Central City facilities. GMFC has always had problems with absences among its janitors, but since the last contract was signed, the absence rate has increased from about 5 percent per day to 15 percent. Because of this increase, housekeeping has lagged, and GMFC officials were starting to worry about fire code violations resulting from the superficial cleaning. Management considered discharging those who were chronically absent but found on investigation that absences seemed to rotate systematically among members of the crew, as if they were planned.

As a result of management's investigation, Carolyn Foster contacted Matt Duff, Local 384's president, and asked him to enforce the contract and get the janitors' absence rate down. She told Duff the company considered the action the equivalent of a slowdown, and strong action would be taken if absence rates were not reduced. Duff protested, saying there was not concerted activity behind the absences.

When the high rate and rotating pattern persisted, the company discharged the janitors and subcontracted their work to Dependa-Kleen, a full-time janitorial service. To the company's pleasure, Dependa-Kleen was able to take over the entire operation at a lower cost than their own in-house operation had incurred prior to the absence problem.

On behalf of the janitors, Duff filed a grievance arguing the discharges violated Section 4.02. He also filed an unfair labor practice charge with the NLRB, claiming the company violated Section 8(a)(5) of the Taft-Hartley Act through its unilateral action in subcontracting the work without consulting or bargaining with the union.

The company argued it was justified in replacing the janitors because their systematic absences were a violation of the contract's no-strike or slowdown clause (Section 9.05). The company argued it was entitled to replace the participants consistent with the management rights clause, Section 4.02.

Assume the testimony at the hearing does not seriously challenge the evidence management has gathered on the increase in absences among the janitors. In this case, decide the following:

1. Would you find the grievance arbitrable given the unfair labor practice charge filed by the union?
2. Assuming you find the grievance arbitrable, frame an award and justify it.

Case 3

The maintenance electricians in the unit are assigned to repair jobs around the Central City facilities shortly after they report to work at their central shop at the beginning of a shift. Prior to ratification of the most recent contract, electricians traditionally returned to the shop for their afternoon coffee breaks. All of the electricians left their work so they would arrive at the shop to begin the break and left the shop at the end of the break to return to work.

The electrical shop supervisor, Ken Bates, issued a new policy after the new contract was approved, stating the break would commence once work stopped at the assigned location and end when work was restarted. This policy change meant some electricians would have insufficient time to return to the shop for their breaks.

The union filed a grievance alleging the company had revoked a prevailing practice that had the effect of a contract term. It also argued it had not been consulted as Article 12.03 required. The company denied the grievance, citing the language in Section 12.02.

As the arbitrator, frame an award in this dispute.

CHAPTER 15

Public-Sector Labor Relations

This chapter aims to provide information on the variety of settings within which collective bargaining is practiced in the public sector and to highlight the differences between public- and private-sector practices and within public-sector levels. The public sector consists of the myriad of separate groups of levels and jurisdictions (federal, state, municipal, and so on) among governmental units. The "customer" group affected by the outcomes in public-sector labor relations is generally much larger (for example, homeowners and apartment dwellers in a garbage collection strike) and settlement costs are much more likely to be directly passed on to the customer in the short run. Little public-sector collective bargaining took place prior to the early 1960s, as compared to the middle to late 1930s for private-sector relations.

This chapter covers the evolution of laws in the federal and state sectors, differences in coverages among jurisdictions and across occupations, union structure and organizational issues, bargaining methods and outcomes, and impasse procedures and their effectiveness.

In reading this chapter, consider the following questions:

1. How do the public and private sectors differ in their bargaining relationships, particularly concerning impasse procedures?
2. How do laws regulating labor relations in the public sector differ across both states and occupations?
3. How successful has the application of fact-finding been in the public sector?
4. How do the conduct of collective bargaining and the determinants of bargaining power differ in the public and private sectors?
5. What variables seem to have the greatest effect on bargaining outcomes?

PUBLIC–SECTOR LABOR LAW

As noted in Chapter 4, public-sector employees are not governed by the Taft-Hartley and Railway Labor acts. Federal employees are covered by a separate law, and state and local employees are covered by laws in the states in which they work, if the state has passed legislation enabling collective bargaining.

Federal Labor Relations Law

Federal employees have been involved in union activities since the 1830s. However, not until the 1880s, when Postal Service employees began to organize, did the federal government oppose unionization. Prior to passage of the Lloyd-LaFollette Act, federal employees were forbidden to communicate with Congress regarding employment conditions. Union activities increased during the 1930s, but President Roosevelt asserted that normal collective bargaining could not take place at the federal level.

After President Kennedy was elected, the federal government promulgated the first in a line of executive orders governing federal employment labor relations. A bill to allow collective bargaining for federal employees was pending in Congress when the president preempted the legislation with Executive Order 10988. The order enabled unions representing a majority of federal employees within a unit to negotiate exclusive written agreements with an agency. However, these agreements could only pertain to noneconomic and nonstaffing issues. Other labor organizations representing less than a majority but more than 10 percent of employees in a unit were entitled to consultation by the employer but could not negotiate agreements. Arbitration of grievances was allowed but was advisory to agency heads rather than binding. Most employees were entitled to organize, with the exception of managers and nonroutine personnel workers.

Civil Service Reform Act, Title VII

In January 1979, the executive orders promulgated by Presidents Kennedy, Nixon, and Ford were supplanted by the Federal Service Labor–Management Relations Statute. The act applied to employees in federal agencies except the Postal Service (covered under Taft-Hartley), the FBI, the General Accounting Office, the National Security Agency, the CIA, and agencies dealing with federal employee labor relations. Employees of the legislative and judicial branches were also excluded.

The Federal Labor Relations Authority (FLRA) was created with responsibilities similar to those of the NLRB in the private sector. The FMCS assists the agencies involved in bargaining impasses, and unresolved impasses are referred to the Federal Services Impasses Panel (FSIP).

Bargaining rights remain limited under the statute. Federal employees cannot bargain over wages and benefits, allowance to pursue political activities, classification of positions, the missions or budgets of agencies, hiring or promotion, or subcontracting. They are, however, allowed consultation rights in these areas and may negotiate on these issues if the agency allows.

Federal labor organizations cannot advocate the use of strikes, and unauthorized strikes may lead to decertification and discipline of individual members. Picketing is also unlawful if it disrupts an agency's activities.

Grievance procedures must be negotiated and must provide for binding arbitration of unresolved issues. The FLRA may review appealed arbitration awards and set them aside if they conflict with laws, rules, or regulations.

The legislation enumerates a variety of unfair labor practices. These practices are similar to those applied to the private sector, except employers and unions must not refuse the use of impasse procedures if necessary. Unions are also forbidden to call strikes, work stoppages, or slowdowns. When violations occur, the FLRA is empowered to issue cease-and-desist orders, require the renegotiation of agreements, reinstate employees with back pay, or initiate other actions necessary to redress unfair practices.[1]

State Labor Laws

Public-sector labor relations differ widely among the 50 states. Several states have no public-sector bargaining laws, a few prohibit collective bargaining in at least some nonmanagerial occupations, and most states prohibit strikes by public-sector employees. State labor laws are generally more comprehensive and were passed earlier in states in which private-sector unionization is heaviest. Unlike the private sector, some states permit collective bargaining for supervisory and managerial employees. Many states have established public employment labor relations boards or agencies to act in the same role as the NLRB in recognition and unfair labor practice situations. The availability of state public-sector bargaining laws and provisions for resolving negotiation disputes are associated with higher wages for organized employees.[2]

---

[1] Henry B. Frazier III, "Federal Employment," in *Portrait of a Process—Collective Negotiations in Public Employment,* ed. Muriel K. Gibbons, Robert B. Hersby, Jerome Lefkowitz, and Barbara Z. Tener (Fort Washington, Penn.: Labor Relations Press, 1979), pp. 421–34.

[2] Peter Feuille and John Thomas Delaney, "Collective Bargaining, Interest Arbitration, and Police Salaries," *Industrial and Labor Relations Review* 39 (1986), pp. 228–40.

JURISDICTIONS AND EMPLOYEES

While exceptions or exemptions from coverage for the private sector are relatively few under federal labor law, this is not the case in the public sector. For example, in the private sector, the law only exempts agricultural workers, domestic workers, and supervisors and managers as industrial and occupational classes covered by the act. In the public sector, differences in coverage exist by types of employees and political jurisdictions.

Sources of Employment

Some states distinguish between employees within a statutory civil service system and those outside its protection. Persons receiving jobs as the result of political appointments are usually unprotected, although the Supreme Court has limited the ability of public officials to use political party membership as a criterion for maintaining a public position.[3] In some states, civil service employees are not permitted to bargain collectively.

Levels of Government

Large differences also exist in the jurisdictions of bargaining units involved. Within states, a variety of lesser jurisdictions and semi-autonomous agencies exist. For example, a state-wide university system may be largely autonomous from a legislature in terms of its governance. Counties, cities, school boards, sewer districts, transportation authorities, and the like are all publicly governed within states, but each is responsible to a different constituency and perhaps dependent on a different source of funding.

Types of Employee Groups

Frequently, state labor laws have different provisions for employees by occupation and jurisdiction, such as teachers, police, fire fighters, state employees, and local employees. Large differences exist between states and across employee groups in terms of the collective bargaining rights and restrictions that have been legislated.

Teachers.   Teacher bargaining laws primarily apply to elementary and secondary public-school teachers. Most states with laws permitting collective bargaining for teachers also confer exclusive recognition on a majority union; impose a mutual duty on both the employer and the union to bargain; have defined impasse procedures, normally including mediation and fact-finding; and prohibit strikes. Some states allow strikes when the school district refuses to arbitrate at a bargaining impasse.

---

[3] *Elrod* v. *Burns*, U.S. Supreme Court, No. 74–1520 (1976).

Police.   Most police statutes pertain to uniformed officers employed by cities or counties. Most states permit collective bargaining for police and grant exclusive recognition to a majority union. Where bargaining is allowed, most states impose a mutual duty on both the union and the employer, but some only allow meet-and-confer privileges to the union. Most states have impasse procedures involving mediation and fact-finding, and many have arbitration statutes for dealing with impasses. Only Hawaii allows police a limited right to strike.

Fire fighters.   The International Association of Fire Fighters is one of the oldest public-sector unions and has been very successful in obtaining bargaining rights. Most states confer exclusive recognition on a majority union and require a mutual duty to bargain. Impasse procedures are generally similar to those for police, and fire fighters are forbidden to strike (except in Idaho).

State employees.   Fewer states permit bargaining for state employees than for other special occupational groups. Where permitted, bargaining is generally a mutual duty. There are fewer formal procedures for breaking impasses than there are for teachers, police, and fire fighters; and some states allow strikes if an impasse has been reached.

Local employees.   Provisions for local employees not in previously mentioned occupational classifications are largely similar to those of state employees. More states permit strikes for local employees than for other classifications.

Although most states forbid strikes, enforcing this prohibition is often difficult. A long history of public employee strikes shows that legally permissible steps to end strikes are not taken in most cases, and statutorily mandated reprisals, such as discharges, have seldom been invoked.

PUBLIC EMPLOYEE UNIONS

Public-sector unions parallel those in the private sector in terms of their constituencies because several unions representing employees in the private sector also organize in the public sector.

The public sector contains several major, exclusively public-sector employee unions. The American Federation of State, County, and Municipal Employees, AFL–CIO (AFSCME), represents state and local unit employees across occupations (see Chapter 5 for a description of its structure). The American Federation of Government Employees, AFL–CIO (AFGE), represents federal employees. Postal Service employees are represented by several national unions, such as the National Association of Letter Carriers (NALC).

Some public employees are represented by industrial-type unions (for example, AFSCME), while others are represented by craft unions.

The craft unions are less likely to be affiliated with the AFL–CIO, although some, such as the International Association of Fire Fighters (IAFF), are. The government-oriented craft unions and associations are generally older than the industrial-type unions, but they vary considerably in their original adoption of traditional trade union bargaining approaches.

A variety of public-sector bargaining representatives began as professional associations and were primarily involved in establishing standards and occupational licensing requirements and lobbying for improved funding and facilities. Others began as civil service employee associations before collective bargaining rights were granted to their members. These organizations were primarily involved in meeting and conferring with employer representatives and lobbying with legislatures. Some, like the California State Employees Association, were of sufficient size to exercise political influence through a large bloc of voters in districts where state employment was high. Associations continue to be most prevalent where laws forbid bargaining but where legislative lobbying representing numerical strength is important. Professional associations are usually organized on an occupational basis and have begun to bargain more recently than traditional unions, often as a response to organizing inroads made by unions who demanded to bargain collectively rather than to meet and confer with employers.

There are four major classifications of nonfederal public-sector labor organizations: (1) all-public-sector employee unions, (2) mixed public- and private-sector unions, (3) state and local employee associations, and (4) unions and associations representing uniformed protective services.[4] The major mixed unions are the Service Employees (SEIU), which is increasingly involved in health care, and the Teamsters. In the uniformed services, the IAFF and the Fraternal Order of Police (FOP), previously a benevolent organization, are among the largest.

As mentioned in Chapter 5, unions tend to be organized to fit the jurisdictions in which employers operate. Most national organizations bargaining at the state and local levels are organized along a federal model, such as the National Education Association. Because education laws and funding methods vary by state and most bargaining takes place at the local-school-board level, state-level services are mostly devoted to lobbying and negotiating assistance. Local districts or state organizations have fewer requirements to get approval from the national association for actions than private-sector unions do. Membership in public-sector unions has increased during the 1980s at the

---

[4] Jack Stieber, *Public-Sector Unionism* (Washington, D.C.: Brookings Institution, 1973).

same time private-sector unionization has declined. Currently, about 36 percent of public-sector employees are union members. Organizing has been more intense in the public sector, while management resistance to unions is lower.[5]

The union's organization also depends to an extent on the structure of bargaining units permitted under governing legislation. The next section explores more issues in organizing in the public sector.

BARGAINING UNITS AND ORGANIZING

Because of the variety of unions and associations involved and the differences in dates when organization took place, employers frequently bargain with several unions. Bargaining units are generally not as inclusive as those in industry but are more akin to the building trades in construction. In a given geographic area, public employees may also bargain with a variety of statutory agencies. For example, a large city may have a local government, a school board, a transit authority, a sewer district, a public utility, and so forth; and all have autonomous powers to bargain, levy taxes, and provide specific services. Separate bargaining units may exist within each of these. For example, a school board may bargain with an AFT local representing teachers, an SEIU local representing custodians, an AFSCME local representing clericals, and a Teamsters local representing bus drivers. This situation creates a possible union whipsaw of an unsophisticated management, but the costs may ultimately result in higher taxes, which bring either legislative or taxpayer referendums, or both, into play.

Given the generally broader occupational mix and relatively fewer number of people in a given occupation, public-sector unions are unlikely to seek to represent employees using an industrial model. Balancing the competing desires of various occupational groups in a collective agreement using an industrial approach is too difficult. From the employer's standpoint, the scope of the bargaining unit is likely to be limited by the extent of the taxing authority. For example, a statewide clerical bargaining unit would be appropriate for state employees but not for local government clericals, because the city may not have the revenue-producing capabilities necessary to finance wages negotiated at a state level.

---

[5] John F. Burton, Jr., and Terry Thomason, "The Extent of Collective Bargaining in the Public Sector," in *Public-Sector Bargaining*, 2nd ed., ed. Benjamin Aaron, Joyce M. Najita, and James L. Stern (Washington, D.C.: Bureau of National Affairs, 1988). pp. 1–51.

PUBLIC-SECTOR BARGAINING PROCESSES

This section examines the differences between public- and private-sector bargaining and the evolving bargaining structures found in non-federal negotiations. Management in most public-sector bargaining consists of two levels: appointed civil service officials (such as city managers and schools superintendents) and elected officials (such as mayors, city councils, and school boards). Although appointed managers may be directly responsible for negotiations, elected officials can pressure them to modify positions toward the union. Given the coverage of bargaining processes in Chapter 10, it might be reasonable to expect a need for more intraorganizational bargaining among management parties in public-sector negotiations.

Bargaining Structures

Bargaining in public employment has been much more fragmented than in the private sector. Part of this is due to legislation imposing different recognition, bargaining, impasse, and strike rules on different jurisdictions and occupations. Another reason relates to the relatively narrow governmental jurisdictions involved. For example, although teachers are a relatively homogeneous occupational group, a rather small geographic area may have several municipalities with separate school boards and separate negotiations.

On the local level a few changes are beginning to take place, particularly among teacher groups. Several National Education Association (NEA) affiliates have begun programs to increase their bargaining power with local districts or by simulating this strategy. In Michigan, local unions are expected to match a standard contract before ratification. When strikes take place, substantial financial aid to strikers is made available. Regional activities also put more pressure on school boards to settle, because replacements cannot fill all openings simultaneously. Local school boards object to this tactic because it reduces local autonomy in negotiations.

In Illinois, coordinated bargaining in 45 southern counties has apparently led to higher salary levels. In California, East San Francisco Bay teachers also moved toward coordinated bargaining. In Oregon, although work has progressed for several years, coordinated bargaining in the Portland area has been very difficult for the union to maintain.[6]

Management Organization for Bargaining

Unlike the private sector, the public sector has an ambiguous management structure. The top leadership is politically elected, while the

---

[6] *Government Employee Relations Report,* No. 725 (September 12, 1977), pp. 14–17.

ongoing management is frequently operated by career civil servants. In addition, these civil servants may belong to their own bargaining units. Evidence suggests bargaining structures become increasingly centralized over time to gain both budgetary control and to coordinate bargaining within offices where an expert bargainer exists who will have long-run responsibility for the collective bargaining agreement.[7]

Multilateral Bargaining

One major distinction exists between the public and private sectors in contract negotiations. In the public sector, the employees may strongly influence management because they are also voters, and the organizations to which they belong may be part of a political power bloc. Also, relatively large numbers of people in a defined geographic area may utilize the services provided or see their taxes affected by the outcome of the agreement. Elected public officials may have an influence on negotiations and may in turn have been endorsed by the labor organizations representing their employees. Thus, collective bargaining in the public sector may not be bilateral but rather multilateral, with public officials being approached to influence the negotiating positions of management members who are ultimately responsible to these elected officials.

Some have suggested public-sector bargaining is becoming less like private-sector labor relations. The opportunities for a sophisticated union to apply pressure along a variety of fronts move it toward a multilateral approach. Unions may exercise more political power and be more able to bring community interest or public pressure to bear in public- rather than private-sector bargaining.

Multilateral bargaining occurs when more than two groups with particular interests engage in the process simultaneously. It more likely occurs where there is internal conflict among management bargainers, where the union is politically active and involved, and where the union attempts to use a variety of impasse procedures. Activities involved in multilateral bargaining include (1) public officials taking actions influencing the negotiations outside the process, (2) union representatives discussing contract terms with management members who are not on the bargaining team, (3) community interest groups being involved, (4) city officials not implementing the agreement, and (5) mediation attempts by elected officials. With data collected from 228 fire fighter negotiations in cities natiowide, multilateral bargaining was most strongly related (in order of importance) to: (1) general conflict among city officials, (2) union political pressure tactics, (3) union impasse pressure tactics, and (4) manage-

---

[7] Milton Derber, "Management Organization for Collective Bargaining in the Public Sector," in *Public-Sector Bargaining*, 2nd ed., ed. Benjamin Aaron, Joyce M. Najita, and James L. Stern (Washington, D.C.: Bureau of National Affairs, 1988), pp. 90–123.

ment commitment to collective bargaining. The incidence of multi-lateral bargaining increased with the age of the bargaining relationship, but the comprehensiveness of state laws and the experience of the management negotiators had little impact.[8]

Some evidence is available to assess the impact of public-sector union political activity on a variety of outcomes. Unionization has had a positive impact on public-sector employees compared to those who were not unionized. Although employment decreased as wages increased, unions were able to more directly influence the electorate to vote for increased services, yielding increased employment.[9] In Texas, where a bargaining law permits local municipalities to vote to hold referenda to decide whether police and fire fighters can bargain collectively, local communities were more likely to permit bargaining where union membership was high, unions endorsed the police and fire fighter positions, and good police and fire fighter cooperation existed. Unfavorable votes were associated with active business opposition, active opposition by the present governing body or an ad hoc group, and a concurrent city council election.[10] Thus, not only are bargaining and employment outcomes affected by a multilateral approach, but the ability to bargain also may be influenced multilaterally.

Because public-sector unions appear to attempt multilateral bargaining, an assessment of its effectiveness is important. An examination of the settlement of fire fighter contracts suggests six variables were significantly related to positive union outcomes: (1) compulsory arbitration at impasse, (2) fact-finding at impasse, (3) comprehensiveness of the state's bargaining law, (4) the decision-making power of management's negotiator, (5) city council–negotiator goal incompatibility, and (6) elected official intervention at impasse. The first three most powerful variables reflect the legal environment, the next two reflect management characteristics, and the last is a multilateral bargaining component. Union pressure tactics were not significantly related to outcomes.[11]

The scope of public-sector bargaining laws reflects the relative affluence of a state.[12] The coincidence of comprehensive laws and greater ability to pay may influence bargaining outcomes toward the

[8] Thomas A. Kochan, "A Theory of Multilateral Collective Bargaining in City Government," *Industrial and Labor Relations Review*, July 1974, pp. 525–42.

[9] Lawrence M. Spizman, "Public-Sector Unions: A Study of Economic Power," *Journal of Labor Research*, Fall 1980, pp. 265–74.

[10] Darold T. Barnum and I. B. Helburn, "Influencing the Electorate: Experience with Referenda on Public Employee Bargaining," *Industrial and Labor Relations Review*, April 1982, pp. 330–42.

[11] Thomas A. Kochan and Hoyt N. Wheeler, "Municipal Collective Bargaining: A Model and Analysis of Bargaining Outcomes," *Industrial and Labor Relations Review*, October 1975, pp. 46–66.

[12] Thomas A. Kochan, "Correlations of State Public Employee Bargaining Laws," *Industrial Relations*, October 1973, pp. 322–37.

union. A comprehensive law legitimizes the union, reduces management's costs of recognition, and may legally decrease management's use of contract rejection, refusals to bargain, and other similar tactics.[13] Environmental characteristics affect not only the makeup of the bargaining teams and their interrelationships but also the power and tactics available to the parties during negotiations.

Statutory law may lag behind public opinion, because legislators enact laws after they are elected.[14] Using legislation as a lagged variable, bargaining outcomes for unions were more favorable in medium-sized municipalities (1) where only certain trades were involved, rather than a large general unit; (2) where no statutory penalty for striking existed; (3) where the union was affiliated with a public-sector national; (4) where strike activity in the state was above average; and (5) where public opinion had led to or favored a bargaining law.[15]

Bargaining Outcomes

Bargaining outcomes may have immediate effects for the employment relationship or long-run effects on the occupation as a whole. This section examines several studies of public-sector bargaining outcomes.

Public employees who bargain are often part of a monopoly. Their service is provided only by the government (for example, police protection); thus, obtaining higher bargaining outcomes should be easier because the government can more easily pass on the costs to the consumer (at least in the short run). In a study of cities with either public or private waste-management systems, the effect of unions on wages in privately managed systems was not significant; but in publicly managed systems, the effects were between 10 and 17 percent. In privately managed systems, several competing waste haulers were usually involved in the market.[16] These results seem to indicate some monopoly power available to public employers can be used to benefit wage increases.

Generally, the results of research on the effects of collective bargaining on the wages, employment, and productivity of unionized versus nonunion government employees suggests wages and benefits are higher in the unionized sector, but differences are not as great as in the private sector. Productivity results are not clear; but in the private sector, only unionized blue-collar occupations were more productive. During the 1980s, concessions were much greater in private-sector

---

13 Paul F. Gerhart, "Determinants of Bargaining in Local Government Labor Negotiations," *Industrial and Labor Relations Review*, April 1976, pp. 331–32.

14 Ibid., pp. 348–49.

15 Ibid., p. 349.

16 Linda N. Edwards and Franklin R. Edwards, "Wellington-Winter Revisited: The Case of Municipal Sanitation Collection," *Industrial and Labor Relations Review*, April 1982, pp. 307–18.

FIGURE 15–1

Union Impact on Supervisor Policy Usage

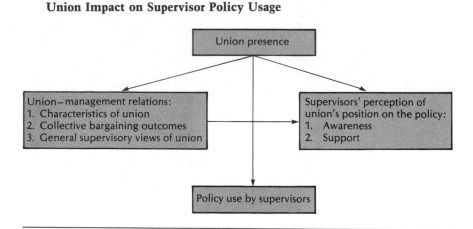

Source: Janice M. Beyer, Harrison M. Trice, and Richard E. Hunt, "The Impact of Federal-Sector Unions on Supervisors' Use of Personnel Policies," *Industrial and Labor Relations Review*, January 1980, p. 214.

contracts than in public-sector contracts, but the union wage advantage was also greater in the private sector previously.[17]

The advent of collective bargaining in the federal government has affected supervisors' use of personnel policies. Organizations may have several personnel policies that are not part of the collective agreement but may be the focus of grievances, given the manner in which supervisors implement them. Figure 15–1 suggests the supervisor is influenced by the union's presence and his perception regarding the union's position on specific policies. In a federal government study, supervisors who worked where the union was well entrenched and where it had negotiated certain policies into contracts were more aware of the unions' positions and used the policies more often.[18]

When economic effects are examined, a study of fire fighter unionization showed the union influenced total compensation, entry, and maximum salary levels. The greatest impact in the compensation area was for fringe benefits, similar to findings in the private sector. No impact was found on the length of the workweek.[19]

Teacher bargaining also has an impact on the makeup of the

---

[17] Daniel J. B. Mitchell, "Collective Bargaining and Compensation in the Public Sector," in *Public-Sector Bargaining*, 2nd ed., ed. Benjamin Aaron, Joyce M. Najita, and James L. Stern (Washington, D.C.: Bureau of National Affairs, 1988), pp. 124–59.

[18] Janice M. Beyer, Harrison M. Trice, and Richard E. Hunt, "The Impact of Federal-Sector Unions on Supervisors' Use of Personnel Policies," *Industrial and Labor Relations Review*, January 1980, pp. 212–31.

[19] Casey Ichniowski, "Economic Effects of the Fire Fighters' Union," *Industrial and Labor Relations Review*, January 1980, pp. 198–211.

compensation system. Higher levels of union activity are associated with decreased male/female and elementary/secondary pay differentials. Unionization also positively influences pay for advanced education, years of experience in general, and years of experience in the district. Measurable, job-related aspects assume a greater value for pay outcomes in situations where more union acitvity is present.[20]

IMPASSE PROCEDURES

Because strikes are generally prohibited for public-sector employees, the following outcomes can occur when an impasse is reached: management may continue the past contract, mediation may occur, the employees may go out on a legal or illegal strike or have a "sickout," fact-finding may take place, interest arbitration to resolve remaining differences may occur, or a legislative body may mandate an agreement. Fact-finding, arbitration, and strikes will be examined, with an emphasis on the first two because they don't normally occur in the private sector.

What leads to impasses in public-sector negotiations? A study of New York state police and fire fighter negotiations proposed the model shown in Figure 15-2. Environmental characteristics most strongly related to reaching an impasse included previous impasse experience, percentage of the local electorate voting Democratic in 1972 (for police), and previous starting salary (for police). Structural characteristics associated with impasses were union pressure tactics, adherence to pattern settlements (police), lack of authority for the management negotiator, internal management conflict, and pressure on union leaders (police). Interpersonal/personal factors associated with impasses included hostility, lack of management negotiator skills (fire), lack of union or management in-house negotiators, and management negotiator experience.

Negotiations involving formal impasse resolution at or beyond the fact-finding level were more likely to have had higher previous starting salaries, previous impasse experience, and be in large cities (police). Union pressure tactics were positively related, while management negotiator authority was negatively related. Finally, hostility and negotiator experience were positively related, while negotiator skill (for fire) was negatively related.[21]

---

[20] Alexander B. Holmes, "Union Activity and Teacher Salary Structure," *Industrial Relations*, Winter 1979, pp. 79–85.

[21] Thomas A. Kochan, Mordehai Mironi, Ronald G. Ehrenberg, Jean Baderschneider, and Todd Jick, *Dispute Resolution under Fact-Finding and Arbitration* (New York: American Arbitration Association, 1979), pp. 32–33.

FIGURE 15–2

Determinants of Impasses

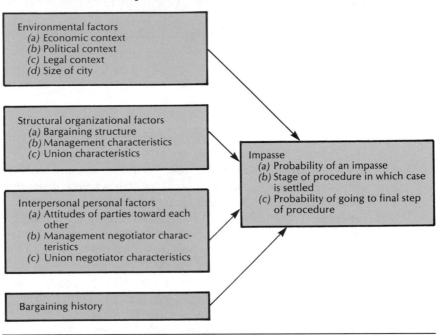

Environmental factors
   (a) Economic context
   (b) Political context
   (c) Legal context
   (d) Size of city

Structural organizational factors
   (a) Bargaining structure
   (b) Management characteristics
   (c) Union characteristics

Interpersonal personal factors
   (a) Attitudes of parties toward each other
   (b) Management negotiator characteristics
   (c) Union negotiator characteristics

Bargaining history

Impasse
   (a) Probability of an impasse
   (b) Stage of procedure in which case is settled
   (c) Probability of going to final step of procedure

Source: Thomas A. Kochan, Mordehai Mironi, Ronald G. Ehrenberg, Jean Baderschneider, and Todd Jick, *Dispute Resolution under Fact-Finding and Arbitration: An Empirical Evaluation* (New York: American Arbitration Association, 1979), p. 32.

Fact-Finding

Fact-finding began in the private sector through the establishment of fact-finding boards in the Taft-Hartley Act and the emergency board procedures of the Railway Labor Act. However, its use is presently far more prevalent in the public sector.

When an impasse exists in the private sector, the fact-finder's role is to establish a reasonable position for a settlement by objectively studying the context and issues and preparing a report of conclusions based on the setting. A primary end result sought by this process is the publication of the disputed issues and recommended settlement. In this way, public opinion may be galvanized to pressure a settlement on this factual conclusion. Fact-finding may also lead to economizing a legislature's time when it expects to impose a solution.[22]

The role of providing facts for the legislature is usually not appropriate in the public sector, because the legislators are frequently a party

---

[22] Jean T. McKelvey, "Fact-Finding in Public Employment Disputes: Promise or Illusion?" *Industrial and Labor Relations Review*, July 1969, pp. 528–30.

in the dispute (school boards, city councils, and so on). Here, the fact-finder's role may be to educate the public as to the costs of a reasonable settlement. Fact-finding may be sought by a union and a management who fear adverse public opinion if they bargain a settlement. They might reason a fact-finder would probably recommend a similar settlement to one they would negotiate, but the "facts" from a neutral seem more reasonable than a bargained settlement, which might seem collusive.[23]

Statutory Role of the Fact-Finder

Wisconsin was one of the first states to pass a comprehensive fact-finding statute. While this law was in effect, fact-finding could be initiated by either party if an impasse existed or if the other party refused to bargain. The Wisconsin Employee Relations Board (WERB) investigated the request and attempted to mediate. If the mediation failed, a neutral was appointed to examine the evidence and make recommendations for a settlement. The recommendation was sent to the parties and the WERB, which publicized it. Although the parties may have asked for fact-finding, they were under no obligation to accept the report's recommendations.[24]

Research found fact-finding cases in Wisconsin took from three months to two years from the initial request until a recommendation was issued. Fact-finders had to fit cases into their schedules, because they were usually university professors or attorneys appointed on an ad hoc basis.[25] On the other hand, in Michigan, where a strike situation led to a request for fact-finding, only about 26 days elapsed from the request to the fact-finder's report.[26] However, if dispute resolution is the criterion, the success of fact-finding is much lower than other methods once an impasse has been reached.

Fact-Finding Results

Does fact-finding accomplish what it was designed to do (that is, lead to a settlement acceptable to both parties without a work stoppage)? The answer depends on where the issue is examined and how the procedure works.

Wisconsin. A study of the early Wisconsin experience concluded the procedure was effective, because only about 11 percent of the petitions for fact-finding were not resolved. But not all cases ulti-

---

[23] Ibid., pp. 530–31.

[24] James L. Stern, "The Wisconsin Public Employee Fact-Finding Procedure," *Industrial and Labor Relations Review*, October 1966, pp. 4–5.

[25] Ibid., pp. 7–8.

[26] Russell Allen, "1967 School Disputes in Michigan," *Public Employee Organization and Bargaining* (Washington, D.C.: Bureau of National Affairs, 1968), chap. 9.

mately went to fact-finders. Of those that did, about one quarter went unresolved after a report was issued by the fact-finder. Both unions and managements were relatively positive about the procedure; however, some managements complained the fact-finder was not sufficiently aware of local problems, and some union officials decried management's ability to disregard the findings in areas where the union had little political power.[27] Since the study, arbitration has replaced fact-finding in Wisconsin.

Michigan. In school situations, fact-finding where strikes were under way was negatively viewed by the parties. Parties were not experienced enough with the procedure to present their cases adequately. Time pressures were great because strikes were already under way. Unlike Wisconsin, the state paid for the process, which reduced any cost-conscious reluctance to use it by the parties.[28]

New York. About 50 percent of the early cases referred to the Public Employee Relations Board before fact-finding was ordered were settled by mediation. Of the other half, 22 percent were mediated before a report was issued, 45 percent were settled by accepting the fact-finding report, and the other third required additional mediation or were unilaterally modified by the employer. Of 316 impasses, 9 resulted in strikes. However, remember that the statute defines an impasse as an inability to agree within 60 days of the required adoption of a budget, so the parties may still have experienced some movement in bargaining positions when an official impasse was declared.[29]

Fact-finding probably works better when the parties are unsophisticated in collective bargaining, because they may have difficulty defining a reasonable settlement. This may be reconciled with the Michigan findings, because a strike has not been called. Some labor advocates complain an employer may request the process and then reject the recommendations. Because the employer is often the legislative body that sets the rules, the union may be vulnerable if fact-finding is the only available impasse resolution procedure.

Iowa. The Iowa statute includes fact-finding, binding arbitration, and final-offer selection for all bargaining units. One major difference in Iowa's law is that the arbitrator may select from management's, the union's, or the fact-finder's recommendations as the final offer. In Iowa, the Public Employee Relations Board, rather than the parties, requests the fact-finding. Early experience suggests fact-finding reduces the number of issues taken to arbitration.[30] Parties may formulate more reasonable positions if required to use fact-finding because

---

[27] Stern, "Wisconsin Public Employee."

[28] Allen, "1967 School Disputes."

[29] McKelvey, "Fact-Finding," pp. 536, 538.

[30] Daniel G. Gallagher and Richard Pegnetter, "Impasse Resolution under the Iowa Multistep Procedure," *Industrial and Labor Relations Review*, April 1979, pp. 327–28.

fact-finders may choose one of the parties' positions. Fact-finders often act like arbitrators because they know the party may go to arbitration if it does not like the findings. About 70 percent of impasses presented to Iowa fact-finders were resolved without going to arbitration.[31]

Criteria for Fact-Finding Recommendations

In early Wisconsin experiences with fact-finding, wage comparisons were the most frequent criteria used for economic recommendations. The governmental unit's ability to pay the increase sought was also frequently considered. Some fact-finders decided what the wage settlement would have been if the union were permitted to strike. Issues of productivity and cost of living were seldom mentioned, although management and labor raised them in their presentations.[32]

Arbitration

Some laws provide mandatory arbitration of contract negotiation disputes. Where these laws exist, they apply more often to public safety divisions, primarily for the uniformed services, and are considered in lieu of granting the right to strike. With arbitration at impasse, the union is not faced with the prospect of management unilaterally continuing past terms without recourse to some other bargaining weapon. Other laws allow unions and managements to voluntarily agree to interest arbitration as a means for settling impasses in the negotiation process.

Arbitrators who handle public-sector interest cases are normally selected in the same way as those in private-sector ad hoc cases. The hearing procedure is also similar. Both sides present evidence supporting their positions, and the arbitrator determines the contract on the basis of the evidence and whatever criteria are to be used for the award.

Interest Arbitration Variants

A number of different methods are used in public-sector interest arbitrations. The typical situation is as described above. The arbitrator hears the case and determines what an appropriate settlement would be. However, some argue this approach has a chilling effect on bargaining, because the parties believe an arbitrator will split differences between them. For example, if a union wants 90 cents an hour and management is willing to give 30 cents, both may believe an arbitrator will settle on 60 cents—half-way between. It is also argued that, as the

---

[31] Daniel G. Gallagher and M. D. Chaubey, "Impasse Behavior and Tri-Offer Arbitration," *Industrial Relations*, Spring 1982, pp. 129–48.

[32] Stern, "Wisconsin Public Employee," pp. 15–17.

parties experience splitting, arbitration becomes habit forming. The parties supposedly skip negotiations and go directly to impasse, thereby availing themselves of the more effortless and less risky remedy: arbitration. This is the so-called narcotic effect. Beliefs regarding the presence of a narcotic effect have led to the implementation of several variants of interest arbitration. Early evidence suggests a narcotic effect existed because negotiations in states providing for arbitration more frequently went to impasse.[33] The current evidence regarding the repeated use of arbitration will be examined later.

Final-Offer Arbitration

In an effort to reduce the use of arbitration, final-offer arbitration has been implemented in some states. Final-offer arbitration was first proposed by Stevens as a "medicine" to cure the parties of the use of arbitration. In final-offer arbitration, each party presents its positions and the arbitrator is required to choose the positions of one party without compromise, which supposedly results in an extreme contract that the loser would do anything to avoid in the future.[34]

Some jurisdictions opt for an entire-package approach (Massachusetts and Wisconsin), while others use an issue-by-issue approach (Michigan). Selection of an entire package increases the responsibility for making a reasonable final-offer submission, because one unreasonable issue in an otherwise reasonable package may tip the scales toward the other party's offer in the arbitrator's mind. Evidence also suggests where final-offer selection is available on an issue-by-issue basis, more unresolved issues reach the arbitrator.[35]

One way interest arbitration may differ from rights arbitration is that many collective agreements and statutes permit the parties to settle after the arbitral process begins and to alter final offers. Because interest arbitration in the public sector is often conducted before a tripartite board (one labor, one management, and one neutral member), the partisans may sense which direction the neutral appears to be leaning and may settle on a concession rather than lose the issue entirely.[36]

Results of Final-Offer Laws

Final-offer procedures can be evaluated by examining whether the parties accept and comply with the awards and whether the process

[33] Hoyt N. Wheeler, "Compulsory Arbitration: A 'Narcotic Effect'?" *Industrial Relations*, February 1975, pp. 117–20.

[34] Carl M. Stevens, "Is Compulsory Arbitration Compatible with Bargaining?" *Industrial Relations*, 1966, pp. 38–50.

[35] Peter Feuille, *Final-Offer Arbitration* (Chicago: International Personnel Management Association, 1975), pp. 35–48.

[36] Ibid.

TABLE 15–1

Eugene Negotiation—Arbitration Experience (1971–1975)

Employee group	Arbitration invoked?	Items submitted to arbitrators	Outcome
1971–72 negotiations:			
Fire fighters	Yes	Entire contractual package	City first offer selected
Police patrolmen	Yes	Entire contractual package	Agreement negotiated during arbitration proceedings
AFSCME	Yes (binding fact-finding)*	Union security; all other items agreed to in negotiations	Union position (agency shop) selected
1972–73 negotiations:			
Fire fighters	Yes	Longevity pay dispute; all other items agreed to in negotiations	City alternate offer selected
Police patrolmen	No	—	Negotiated agreement
AFSCME	Yes	One-year economic package; non-economic issues agreed to in negotiations	City alternate offer selected but was moot because of three-year agreement negotiated during arbitration proceedings.
1974–75 negotiations:			
Fire fighters	No	—	Negotiated agreement
Police patrolmen	No	—	Negotiated agreement
AFSCME	No	—	Negotiated agreement

* The two sides agreed to use the fact-finding services provided free by the state and to be bound by the fact-finder's decision. Because this arbitration did not take place under the city procedure, the final-offer selection criteria did not apply in this case.

Source: Peter Feuille, *Final-Offer Arbitration* (Chicago: International Personnel Management Association, 1975), p. 17.

chills or encourages future bargaining.[37] Several studies have examined this issue and are summarized here.

Eugene, Oregon. The early experience with an entire-package, final-offer approach worked well in Eugene. No rejections of the awards occurred, fewer arbitrations were invoked in succeeding years, and the number of issues in the impasse packages decreased.[38] Table 15–1 contains the details.

Michigan. Michigan has an issue-by-issue–offer law for economic aspects and a conventional law for others. The process has had no appreciable effect on the number of cases going to arbitration in the

---

[37] Ibid., pp. 15–16.

[38] Gary Long and Peter Feuille, "Final-Offer Arbitration: 'Sudden Death' in Eugene," *Industrial and Labor Relations Review*, January 1974, pp. 186–203.

uniformed services. Deputy sheriff negotiations have tended to use the procedure slightly more often than police or fire, but this was partially attributed to a relatively newer collective bargaining relationship.[39]

Wisconsin. Wisconsin uses a package-type final-offer procedure. The Wisconsin experience does not support the idea that arbitration use declines in a package-selection environment over time.[40] Some evidence does exist, however, that its use decreases when management wins.[41] However, the total extent of arbitration use in Wisconsin on a relative basis is less than in Michigan, an issue-by-issue state.

Massachusetts. The Massachusetts law is also a package final-offer procedure. After passage of the law, arbitrations increased by almost 70 percent. Almost 40 percent of all negotiations went to impasse, but only 7 percent were ultimately decided by arbitrators. Finally, arbitrators' awards apparently closely paralleled the reports the fact-finders issued earlier during the impassee.[42]

The evidence suggests states with issue rather than package approaches have more arbitrations and more issues going before arbitrators.

What Is a *Final* Offer?

One problem is frequently encountered in final-offer arbitration: what is a *final* offer? In Wisconsin, parties are required to state their positions to the WERB when an impasse is declared. But it has been the practice there and in Michigan (where mediation by the arbitrator appears to be encouraged) to allow negotiations to narrow the differences subsequent to the arbitration request. Some see this as an advantage because the parties settle the issues. But some disputants simply see it as a no-win situation because, if they adhere to a well-thought-out final position and only the opposition expresses a willingness to move, the arbitrator may award the point to the opponent because of the apparent intransigence of the adamant party. Thus, a party may provoke an impasse to achieve what it believes it cannot get from true bargaining. Research has concluded unions gained 1 to 5 percent more in economic settlements as a result of arbitration than they would have in bargaining a settlement.[43]

---

[39] James L. Stern, Charles M. Rehmus, J. Joseph Loewenberg, Hirschel Kasper, and Barbara D. Dennis, *Final-Offer Arbitration* (Lexington, Mass.: Lexington Books, 1975), pp. 37–75.

[40] Ibid., pp. 77–115.

[41] Craig A. Olson, "Final-Offer Arbitration in Wisconsin after Five Years," *Proceedings of the Industrial Relations Research Association*, 1978, pp. 111–19.

[42] David B. Lipsky and Thomas A. Barocci, "Final-Offer Arbitration and Public-Safety Employees: The Massachusetts Experience," *Proceedings of the Industrial Relations Research Association*, 1977, pp. 65–76.

[43] Stern et al., *Final-Offer Arbitration*, pp. 77–115.

An Alternative to Final-Offer Selection

One argument levied against final-offer arbitration is that the arbitrator has knowledge of the parties' bargaining positions through public reports and their final offers. Some have argued that arbitrators should only be given information on the positions each party desires now and not evidence on previous negotiations.[44] Thus, either party runs the risk of getting less than it had already been offered in negotiations. As such, the parties may have a greater motive to settle on their own. No test has been made of this procedure in the United States, but some British experiences suggest it reduces the incidence of arbitration.

Another argument suggests in either final-offer selection or closed-offer arbitration, where the parties know this may be the consequence of an impasse, they will position their demands symmetrically around where they feel an arbitrator will rule. They are expected to use the same types of information an arbitrator would use as criteria for determining a settlement. Thus, the arbitrator's tendency to split the difference may not be related to an arbitral strategy but to a negotiation strategy.[45]

Evidence on the Narcotic Effect

A study of New York police and fire fighter impasses found that, after the impasse law was changed to allow arbitration rather than legislative action as the final step, negotiations increasingly went to impasse and were likely to proceed to the final step. However, no evidence indicated the parties were less likely to move prior to bargaining, and little evidence that the awards differed from outcomes in similar situations where bargaining was completed.[46] The study concluded arbitration seemed to chill the ability to reach a bargained settlement but not the ability to bargain.

When the New York law's effect was examined over time, a positive narcotic effect apparently existed during the early negotiation rounds but later became negative.[47] A study of negotiations following changes in the Minnesota public-sector law in 1979 suggests the narcotic effect was an "epidemic effect", with units using arbitration

---

[44] Hoyt N. Wheeler, "Closed Offer: Alternative to Final-Offer Selection," *Industrial Relations*, 1977, pp. 298–305.

[45] Henry S. Farber, "Splitting the Difference in Interest Arbitration," *Industrial and Labor Relations Review*, October 1981, pp. 70–77.

[46] Kochan et al., *Dispute Resolution*, pp. 158–59.

[47] Richard J. Butler and Ronald G. Ehrenberg, "Estimating the Narcotic Effect of Public-Sector Impasse Procedures," *Industrial and Labor Relations Review*, October 1981, pp. 3–20.

largely because other units in the same bargaining round used it. In subsequent rounds, parties appeared to avoid arbitration.[48]

The most recent evidence does not support the idea that arbitration has a narcotic effect. In fact, the opposite appears to be the case. Cross-sectional evidence finds arbitration used more widely when it becomes available but less often when it has been experienced. A longitudinal study of collective bargaining in Iowa, Indiana, and Pennsylvania supports the premise that once the novelty of arbitration has dissipated, neither negative nor positive effects occur in its use level.[49] At most it might be concluded that a more appropriate analog would be a "vaccination effect" or a "hangover effect."

Arbitration and Maturing Labor Relations

Public-sector labor legislation has almost always prohibited strikes. Because the private-sector model included them and little experience existed with other mechanisms, a great deal of experimentation has taken place. Fact-finding has decreased, both statutorily and at the individual impasse level. A variety of forms of arbitration have been implemented. Surveys suggest the usage is low and decreasing.[50] Arbitration's effectiveness or failure may also depend on prehearing processes. Where experienced negotiators are in place, mediation may be much more helpful than arbitration in fashioning an acceptable settlement.[51]

It is difficult for the parties to determine an appropriate settlement point when third-party determinations exist. Neither party knows for certain what an arbitrator will view as a correct solution. They also may have doubts as to an imposed solution's workability. The choices may also vary substantially given what constitutes a last-offer.[52]

---

[48] Paul L. Schumann, Mario F. Bognanno, and Frederic C. Champlin, "An Empirical Study of the Narcotic and Epidemic Effects of Arbitration Use," unpublished paper (Minneapolis: Industrial Relations Center, University of Minnesota, 1983); and Frederic C. Champlin and Mario F. Bognanno, "Chilling under Arbitration and Mixed Strike-Arbitration Regimes," *Journal of Labor Research* 6 (1985), pp. 375–87.

[49] James R. Chelius and Marian M. Extejt, "The Narcotic Effect of Impasse Resolution Procedures, *Industrial and Labor Relations Review* 38 (1985), pp. 629–38.

[50] Craig A. Olson, "Dispute Resolution in the Public Sector," in *Public-Sector Bargaining*, 2nd ed., ed. Benjamin Aaron, Joyce M. Najita, and James L. Stern (Washington, D.C.: Bureau of National Affairs, 1988), pp. 160–88.

[51] Paul F. Gerhart and John F. Drotning, "The Effectiveness of Public-Sector Impasse Procedures," in *Advances in Industrial and Labor Relations*, vol. 2, ed. David B. Lipsky and Joel Douglas (Greenwich, Conn.: JAI Press, 1985), pp. 143–95.

[52] For an extended analysis of bargaining and interest arbitration, see Frederic C. Champlin and Mario F. Bognanno, "A Model of Arbitration and the Incentive to Bargain," in *Advances in Industrial and Labor Relations*, vol. 3, ed. David B. Lipsky and Joel Douglas (Greenwich, Conn.: JAI Press, 1986), pp. 153–90.

Arbitral Criteria

Just as rights arbitrators apply criteria in deciding awards in grievance cases, so do arbitrators in interest cases. Some criteria are specified by law; others are specified by the arbitrators. These criteria can cause problems for both the arbitrators and the disputants.

Ability to pay is often considered. Nevada statutorily requires its assessment in arriving at an award.[53] During New York City's acute financial crisis, an arbitrator in a hospital interest arbitration mentioned ability-to-pay criteria for her low wage award.[54] The ability-to-pay issue may retard wage gains when revenues do not support wage demands. However, some have suggested that arbitrators are less concerned than are elected officials about the actual ability to pay.[55] (This is hardly surprising, because officials are generally closer to their managements than to their rank and file, who are coincidentally constituents.)

Evidence suggests managements and unions have some common and dissimilar preferences about their choice of an arbitrator. Of 69 arbitrators listed by the New Jersey Employment Relations Commission in 1980, employers and unions distinctly preferred certain arbitrators. Although management and union preferences were moderately similar and stressed the arbitrator's experience level, unions preferred arbitrators with legal backgrounds, while managements preferred economists. Both sides were influenced by the direction of the arbitrator's previous awards.[56]

The Utility of Arbitration for Unions

The public-safety unions in particular have been strong advocates of binding arbitration to resolve impasses. While arbitration does provide a method for resolving interest differences when strikes are prohibited, less information is available on the impact of the process on bargaining outcomes. Two studies found relatively minimal wage effects (0 to 5 percent) associated with arbitration.[57] However, arbitration should

---

[53] Joseph R. Grodin, "Arbitration of Public-Sector Labor Disputes," *Industrial and Labor Relations Review*, October 1974, pp. 89–102.

[54] Margery Gootnick, arbitrator, award in *League of Voluntary Hospitals and District 1199, Hospital and Health Care Employees, RWDSU*, reprinted in *Daily Labor Report*, September 16, 1976, pp. D1–D7.

[55] Raymond D. Horton, "Arbitration, Arbitrators, and the Public Interest," *Industrial and Labor Relations Review*, July 1975, pp. 497–507.

[56] David E. Bloom and C. L. Cavanagh, "An Analysis of the Selection of Arbitrators," *American Economic Review* 76 (1986), pp. 408–22.

[57] Stern et al., *Final-Offer Arbitration*, pp. 77–115; and Kochan et al., *Dispute Resolution*, pp. 158–59.

serve to raise management's offers, particularly in final-offer selection states. Management might be expected to concede toward what an arbitrator's award might be, rather than to risk the choice of a union's extreme position. And for the union's part it might take a harder line when it has a final resolution available that does not entail the risk of an illegal strike. In studying fire fighter arbitration laws, arbitration was found to be associated with higher salaries and shorter working hours the longer the law was in effect. Wage increases averaged about 11 to 22 percent higher in arbitration states.[58]

Strikes

Most states prohibit public employees to strike and have injunction and penalty provisions if strikes occur. However, the right to strike is granted to certain public employees in Alaska, Hawaii, Idaho, Minnesota, Montana, Oregon, Pennsylvania, Vermont, and Wisconsin in certain situations. Although most states forbid strikes, prohibiting them and enforcing the prohibition are two different things. The history of public employee strikes is long enough to show that legally permissible steps to end them are not taken in most cases, and statutorily mandated reprisals, such as discharges, have often not been invoked. Table 15-2 shows the relative incidence of strike activity across occupations and jurisdictions in the public sector.

Table 15-2 shows the largest number of strikes occurred at the local level, with school employees involved in more strikes than any other jurisdictional level. More days are lost by school employees from strikes, and the duration of strikes is longest for school disputes. One reason for the level and duration of school strikes is that they are often essentially costless to both employers and employees. Legislatures establish school years of certain lengths, so if a strike disrupts the first three weeks of school, the year is simply extended three weeks. The only cost to the school or the teachers is the delay in school aid receipts and wages. The incidence and duration of school strikes has been associated with state laws governing the length of the school year and the local district's willingness to tax itself for greater educational costs.[59]

Evidence regarding the incidence of strikes is mixed. For police, the evidence suggests strikes occur less often with a provision for collective bargaining and arbitration as an impasse settlement pro-

---

[58] Craig A. Olson, "The Impact of Arbitration on the Wages of Fire Fighters," *Industrial Relations*, Fall 1980, pp. 325-39.

[59] Craig A. Olson, "The Impact of Rescheduled School Days on Teacher Strikes," *Industrial and Labor Relations Review*, July 1984, pp. 515-28.

TABLE 15-2

Work Stoppages in the Public Sector, 1970–1980

Employer and year	Number	Employees involved (000)	Number of days lost (000)
Federal			
1970	3	155.8	648.3
1975	0	—	—
1980	1	.9	7.2
State			
1970	23	8.8	44.6
1975	32	66.6	300.5
1980	45	10.0	99.7
Local*			
1970	386	168.9	1,330.5
1975	446	252.0	1,903.9
1980	493	212.7	2,240.9

* Includes all stoppages in cities, countries, special districts, and school districts.

Source: "1983 Work Stoppages in Government," *Government Employee Relations Report* (Washington, D.C.: Bureau of National Affairs, 1983), p. 71:1011.

cedure.[60] On the other hand, strikes appear to be used when they are legal or not prevented as vehicles for increasing public employee bargaining power. Well-enforced penalties or threats of firing reduced public-sector strikes, while poorly enforced laws have no effect, and permissive laws increase their frequency.[61]

Generally speaking, strike activity in the public sector appears positively influenced by the rate of wage increase for private-sector employees, increases in the cost of living, and fiscal belt tightening. Unemployment in the private sector and recession periods appear related to reduced public-sector strike activity.[62]

Recent studies of teacher strikes suggest they are not used as an offensive weapon to improve outcomes more than other comparison groups but are used as defensive weapons to maintain a relative position or to reverse erosion. Data suggest that among Illinois and Iowa

[60] Casey Ichniowski, "Arbitrators and Police Bargaining: Prescriptions for the Blue Flu," *Industrial Relations*, Spring 1982, pp. 149–66; and Robert N. Horn, William J. McGuire, and Joseph Tomkiewicz, "Work Stoppages by Teachers: An Empirical Analysis," *Journal of Labor Research*, Fall 1982, pp. 487–95.

[61] Craig A. Olson, "Strikes, Strike Penalties, and Arbitration in Six States," *Industrial and Labor Relations Review* 39 (1986), pp. 539–51.

[62] William B. Nelson, Gerald W. Stone, Jr., and J. Michael Swint, "An Economic Analysis of Public-Sector Collective Bargaining and Strike Activity," *Journal of Labor Research*, Spring 1981, pp. 77–98.

teachers, strikes are only worth about $285 annually. Evidence suggests the availability of impasse resolution procedures does influence wages by about 10 percent.[63]

SUMMARY

The legal environment is a critical factor in public employee unionization because management ultimately determines the scope of bargaining rights. The mood of the electorate predicts changes in these laws in some states, but generally rights are more restrictive than in the private sector. Legislation is most conducive to bargaining in the industrialized North and East and is least conducive in rural or southern areas. Right-to-work laws for the private sector predict statutes prohibiting union activity in the public sector.

Where bargaining is permitted, the issues are much the same as in the private sector. Unionization varies, with AFSCME taking an industrial-union approach and the uniformed services generally organized on a craft basis.

Impasse resolution varies widely by jurisdiction and occupation. In the federal government, the Federal Services Impasses Panel resolves disputes. In states providing for impasse resolution by statute, arbitrators usually handle uniformed services disputes. In other areas, fact-finding, mediation, and other methods are prescribed. Strikes are forbidden in most jurisdictions.

Evidence suggests unions benefit from interest arbitration and other designated impasse procedures. Final-offer selection may reduce reliance on arbitration, but more recent evidence suggests any experience with arbitration may lessen its future usage.

DISCUSSION QUESTIONS

1. If government employees were to be given a limited right to strike, which occupations should be prohibited from striking, and under what conditions should the prohibition be enforced?

2. Because arbitrators are not responsible to the electorate, should they be allowed to make binding rulings on economic issues?

3. Civil service rules provide many public employees with a large measure of protection from arbitrary action. If so, why should public employees be allowed to organize?

4. Because fact-finding publicizes the major areas in dispute and a proposed settlement, why has it not been more successful, given the public's stake in the outcome?

---

[63] John Thomas Delaney, "Strikes, Arbitration, and Teacher Salaries: A Behavioral Analysis," *Industrial and Labor Relations Review*, April 1983, pp. 431–46.

CASE

The annual contract negotiations between the Pleasant Ridge Board of Education and the Pleasant Ridge Classroom Teachers Association (PRCTA) are due to begin one week from now on July 1. Under state law, the new contract has to be signed by September 1, or an impasse will be declared. Following an impasse, state law provides for simultaneous mediation and fact-finding. The fact-finder's report must be published no later than September 20. Under the law, the parties could arbitrate unresolved contract issues using a total-package final-offer selection approach if both agree arbitration would be binding. The state law prohibits teachers from striking, but about 10 short strikes occurred in the state last year at the time school opened.

The contract at Pleasant Ridge was not signed until November 10 last year, even though mediation and fact-finding had taken place. The PRCTA had repeatedly requested arbitration of the contract dispute, but the board refused. Although no strike occurred, two "sickouts" took place in October when teacher absence rates exceeded 90 percent and schools had to be closed. For the upcoming contract, apparently considerable sentiment exists for "hitting the bricks" if negotiations are unsatisfactory.

Presently, about 5,000 students are enrolled in the kindergarten through grade-12 programs at Pleasant Ridge. There are 250 teachers, of whom 240 are PRCTA members. Like many other established school systems, enrollment at Pleasant Ridge has been declining in recent years due to lower birthrates. Although the impact is greatest in the elementary grades (with a recent drop of about 6 percent annually), the decline in the entire system is about 3 percent annually.

The school system's operating budget is funded from two sources: state school aid based on student enrollments and local property taxes. The legislature has passed a 5 percent increase in per-student funding for the upcoming school year. Local property taxes presently provide the other 60 percent, based on a 22-mill levy against assessed market value. Fifteen mills are permanently required by state law. The other seven are supplemental and are periodically reconsidered by local voters. Five of the seven mills expire this November and will be subject to reapproval by the voters in the general election. Property values are presently appreciating by 2 percent annually.

School costs are approximately equally divided between salaries and plant, equipment, and supplies. Of the 50 percent allocated to salaries, 80 percent is paid to the instructional staff represented by the PRCTA. Nonwage costs are increasing at an annual rate of 3 percent.

The PRCTA bargaining committee has just completed its contract demands. Major areas in which it demands changes include an 8 percent salary increase, a reduction in maximum class size from 30 to 25 in the elementary grades (K–6), and the granting of tenure after the second year of teaching, instead of the fourth. Because about 2,500 students are in the K–6 program, a reduction in class sizes would have a positive impact on teacher employment. The tenure change would affect 25 second-year and 25 third-year teachers now uncovered. In case of a reduction in staff, tenured employees who are terminated are entitled to one year's pay under the contract. As part of its preparations for negotiations, the PRCTA surveyed comparable schools and found that its members' pay is about 5 percent below the market rate, that tenure is normally granted after three years, and that the median elementary class size (by contract) is 27.

As the school's governing body, the Pleasant Ridge Board of Education must ultimately approve the contract if arbitration is not used, but the school system's superintendent, personnel director, high school principal, and two elementary principals form the management bargaining team. The school board consists of five persons. Two of these are union members, and three (including these two) were endorsed by the Pleasant Ridge Central Labor Union (PRCLU) at the last election. Two others endorsed by the PRCLU lost to the other present members. At that last election, two mills of the supplementary tax were approved, but the margin was only 500 out of 10,000 votes cast.

Questions

1. What should be the initial bargaining position of the school board? What data justify this position?
2. What should the PRCTA consider a reasonable settlement to be?
3. If fact-finding takes place, what should the fact-finder use as criteria in recommending a settlement? What should the recommendation be?
4. Should the board go to arbitration if an agreement cannot be negotiated?
5. What strategies should the management and union negotiators use to win their demands?
6. If the negotiations go to arbitration as a final-offer package, what should each party's offer be for the arbitrator?

CHAPTER 16

Employee Relations in Nonunion Organizations

In reviewing the history of the labor movement and the recent evidence on the relative success of union-organizing campaigns, we can see that labor unions achieved a high-water mark in terms of the proportion of the labor force that were union members in the middle 1950s and in the numbers of workers belonging in the early 1960s. A number of imponderables make forecasts of whether these will be peaks in the history of the U.S. labor movement chancy, but the former patterns of unionization clearly do not presently exist.

This chapter explores some of the characteristics of organizations that have no substantial proportion of their employees belonging to unions. During the examination, recognize that most organizations have many employees who are not union members even though they have other employees who are. These nonunion employees often are not statutorily forbidden from collective bargaining. Few white-collar employees have unionized at the present time. The examination focuses on factors related to attempts to organize, the economic and noneconomic policies of nonunion organizations, grievance or complaint procedures in nonunion organizations, and the formation and operation of joint management–employee committees.

In reading this chapter, consider the following issues:

1. What characteristics differentiate union from nonunion organizations?
2. How do the roles of supervisors and the operation of complaint procedures differ in nonunion organizations?
3. What legal boundaries exist regarding the mechanisms for involving employees in nonunion organizations?

4. How do the operations of personnel departments differ in non-union organizations from those of unionized firms?

"UNION-FREE" ORGANIZATIONS

A "union-free" organization is entirely unorganized. Many companies in the United States fit this label, but few are extremely large. Perhaps IBM is the best example of a large organization without organized employees. Some organizations that presently have locations with bargaining units have goals to reduce or eliminate employee representation in the future.[1] These goals can be achieved as a result of decertification elections held in presently organized facilities or through closing down, selling off, or moving operations from presently organized locations to new facilities.

A study of large nonunion organizations concluded two types of firms can operate without unions. The first type is called *doctrinaire*. A doctrinaire organization explicitly desires to continue operating without unions and implements personnel policies it believes will lead employees to resist unions. Its personnel policies frequently mimic what unions have won in similar organizations through collective bargaining. The second type is called *philosophy-laden*. Such companies have no unions, but the lack of organizing is due to the employee relations climate of the organization. Management engages in personnel practices it believes are "right."[2] Evidently the policies are congruent with employee desires because union-organizing activities in these firms are practically nonexistent. These two approaches will be examined as the personnel policies of both are explored.

Union Avoidance

Employer organizations have recently become more vocal in their beliefs about the legitimacy of labor organizations. Some of their leaders have questioned whether employees want union affiliation, whether unions are the friend of the poor, or whether unions have significant political influence.[3] Management typically campaigns strongly against union representation, and partially represented companies avoid acting as neutrals in elections in nonunion plants. This approach apparently takes place without any analysis of whether the

---

[1] Audrey Freedman, *Managing Labor Relations* (New York: Conference Board, 1979), p. 5.

[2] Fred K. Foulkes, *Personnel Policies in Large Nonunion Companies* (Englewood Cliffs, N.J.: Prentice-Hall, 1980), pp. 45–57.

[3] R. Heath Larry, "Labor Power: Myth or Reality?" *MSU Business Topics*, Winter 1979, pp. 20–24.

organization would be benefited or harmed by unionization and is done simply to avoid unionization whatever the costs or benefits.[4]

Environmental Factors Associated with Union Avoidance

A variety of environmental factors appear associated with union avoidance, some of which can be influenced by employer choices. Employers generally believe locational differences in unionization can affect their ability to remain nonunion. Union penetration is highest in the Northeast and Midwest and lowest in the South and rural areas of the United States. Employers may make locational decisions to avoid highly unionized areas for two reasons. First, employers may believe employees in areas where unions have relatively little membership may be less willing to join unions. Mixed evidence exists on this point, as discussed in Chapter 6. Second, plants located in areas without unions seldom enable employees to compare the economic benefits that union and nonunion organizations provide and, as a result, may not become involved in organizing campaigns. This assumption rests on the belief employees will choose local plants as a logical comparison, not other plants in the industry.

Plant size may be viewed by employers as a factor associated with avoiding unions. The evidence on union election success covered in Chapter 6 found plants with less than 100 employees more vulnerable to unionization than larger plants. While very large plants are difficult to organize, employers may also believe the type of personnel management they would prefer to espouse is difficult to inculcate in a large plant. Thus, the trend appears to be toward siting plants in labor market areas that will support medium-sized operations and planning that the plants will generally not exceed 500 employees unless returns to scale are large. Plants also should not be smaller than 200 or so, because a union can capitalize quickly on an issue in a smaller plant.

Regardless of industry, companies founded earlier have tended to become organized, reflecting what might have been the prevailing environment for personnel practices at their founding. The periods during which the organization's predominant growth took place influence unionization. For example, organizations that were founded prior to 1950 but grew most rapidly following that date are less likely to be organized.[5]

Differences also exist between and within industries. Industries with a large proportion of white-collar workers (for example, finance) are less likely to be unionized. But within industries, some firms have

---

[4] D. Quinn Mills, "Management Performance," in *U.S. Industrial Relations, 1950–1980: A Critical Assessment*, ed. Jack Stieber, Robert B. McKersie, and D. Quinn Mills (Madison: Industrial Relations Research Association, 1981), pp. 114–16.

[5] See Arthur Stinchcombe, "Social Structure and Organizations," in *Handbook of Organizations*, ed. James G. March (Chicago: Rand McNally, 1965), pp. 142–93.

not been organized while others are essentially completely unionized. In construction, relatively new organizations remain nonunion through guaranteed employment during usual layoff periods and through the implementation of personnel policies on the organizational level. Newly incorporated, technically oriented industries also have had a relatively low level of unionization, even when they have been located in traditionally highly unionized areas.

Transient Employees and Representation

One other situation in which unionization is unlikely is with a highly unstable employee population. As noted in Chapter 6, at least 50 percent of the employees must agree that a union is necessary before representation can be gained. When turnover is extremely rapid, that level of agreement might be impossible to achieve. Unionization is also unlikely in marginal operations where advancement opportunities are extremely small, because many employees view such employment as temporary until something better comes along. Employees need to believe something is worth gaining in the employment relationship through unionization before they would be willing to expend the effort to organize.

A PHILOSOPHY–LADEN APPROACH TO EMPLOYEE RELATIONS

A model has been constructed that helps explain how the philosophy-laden approach to employee relations results in a variety of outcomes, one of which is the likely absence of a union. The model shows that environmental factors similar to those mentioned above may be involved in the location and demographics of the organization's establishments, the variety of substantive policies implemented, and company characteristics that promote the ability to achieve specific outcomes. These, in turn, lead to a particular climate or culture. The by-products of this culture are a variety of behaviors and attitudes associated with a reluctance to join unions, an avoidance of industrial conflict, and a belief that the company is a good place to work. Figure 16–1 depicts the model and its interrelationships. This model will be explored in some detail in the following sections.

Wage Policies

Large nonunion organizations generally try to lead the market in their pay levels. They try to anticipate what unions will gain at the bargaining table and provide pay increases equaling or exceeding that level, awarding them at dates before the unions gain theirs. Nonunion organizations may also implement merit pay policies in which pay in-

FIGURE 16–1

Top Management's Stated Beliefs in the Worth of the Individual, Equity, Leadership by Example, and Other Attitudes, Values, Philosophies, and Goals Concerning Employees

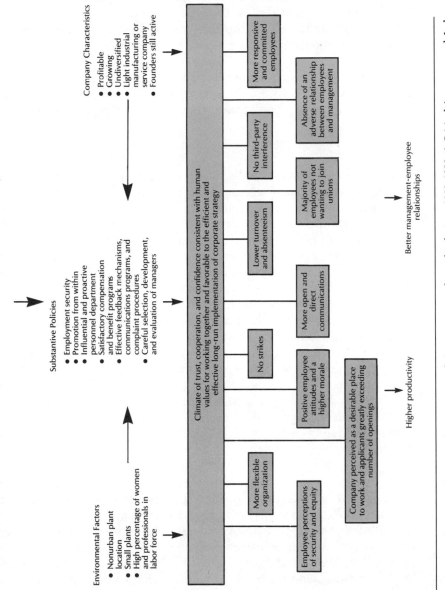

Source: Fred K. Foulkes, "Large Nonunion Employers," in *U.S. Industrial Relations, 1950–1980: A Critical Assessment*, ed. Jack Stieber, Robert B. McKersie, and D. Quinn Mills (Madison: Industrial Relations Research Association, 1981), p. 135.

creases are differentiated on the basis of performance measurements. Attention is paid to communicating pay and benefit levels and practices to employees.[6]

To accomplish these wage-level goals, an organization must compare favorably with others in its ability to pay.[7] Location in a growing industry with relatively high profits or a position as market leader in the industry should enable an organization to maintain its ability to pay.

If employee preferences are considered, as a philosophy-laden organization is expected to do, then benefit levels in nonunion organizations should closely approximate those in union organizations.

Nonwage Policies

Union organizations generally have lower turnover and higher rates of internal promotion and transfer than nonunion organizations have. If an organization sought to emulate the conditions employees desire, it would have a rationalized internal labor market with high levels of information on job opportunities available to employees.

Nonunion firms studied generally had formalized job-posting systems, with clearly communicated promotion criteria that were straightforward and emphasized both seniority and skills. Development opportunities were emphasized so that employees could develop the skills necessary to take advantage of openings likely to occur.[8]

Philosophy-laden firms generally take a career-oriented approach toward employment. Full-time nonprobationary employees are normally assumed to be likely to spend their entire careers with the organization. Thus, nonunion firms frequently require longer probationary periods or hire substantial numbers of part-time employees to provide a buffer for permanent employees during periods of fluctuating product demand.[9]

Personnel Expenditures

In unionized organizations, union representation and the negotiated contract take the place of a personnel department. Management has no real need to attend to employee desires because this is the union's responsibility, and the contract spells out how employee relations will be handled. Staffing and development needs are handled through on-the-job training, and retention of employees is gained through negotiated seniority clauses.

---

[6] Foulkes, *Personnel Policies*, pp. 158–63.

[7] Ibid., pp. 165–67.

[8] Ibid., pp. 123–45.

[9] Ibid., pp. 99–122.

Nonunion organizations have higher personnel expenditures, and a greater number of personnel workers are involved in employee relations. The organization must pay more attention to compensation because it usually tries to match or exceed what unions negotiate or to construct a particular package to attract and retain employees. Development activities are emphasized. Supervisory support for problem solving is offered through the personnel department instead of the grievance system.

EMPLOYEE "VOICE" SYSTEMS

Chapter 8 noted lower turnover in unionized situations might be related to an opportunity to voice needs for change through the grievance and negotiation processes. When these mechanisms are absent, employees desiring change may be able to achieve it only by "voting with their feet."[10]

In unionized organizations, employees can exercise their voice on immediate matters through grievance procedures and on longer-run matters through participation in negotiation committees. Those having the greatest disagreements with the organization's operations might be expected to have the most motivation to be involved in union activities at the employer level.

In nonunion organizations, the employee has no contractual entitlement to have grievances redressed or to have a voice in how the organization should be run. Some nonunion organizations, particularly those with philosophy-laden backgrounds, have constructed elaborate systems enabling employees to voice complaints and get action on them.[11]

A model system enables an employee to communicate directly with the chief executive officer of the organization, who has a department that directly investigates causes of complaints and reports its findings. The complaining employee's superiors may be a focus of the investigation, but no identification of the employee is made, and no reprisals can be taken against the group from which the complaint is made. Exhibit 16-1 is a commentary on how one of these systems works.

Several methods have been devised to reduce the possibility of employee cynicism about management's commitment to neutral grievance procedures in nonunion organizations. For example, IBM operates a system allowing employees direct anonymous access to

---

[10] A. O. Hirschman, *Exit, Voice, and Loyalty* (Cambridge, Mass.: Harvard University Press, 1970).

[11] For an overview, see R. Bernbeim, *Nonunion Complaint Systems: A Corporate Appraisal* (New York: Conference Board, 1980).

EXHIBIT 16-1

The Open-Door Policy

The Open-Door Policy is deeply ingrained in [the company's] history. This policy is a reflection of our belief in respect for the individual. It is also based on the principle that every person has a right to appeal the actions of those who are immediately over him in authority. It provides a procedure for assuring fair and individual treatment for every employee.

Should you have a problem which you believe the company can help solve, discuss it with your immediate manager or your location's personnel manager or, in the field, with the manager of your location. You will find that a frank talk with your manager is usually the easiest and most effective way to deal with the problem.

Second, if the matter is still not resolved, or is of such a nature you prefer not to discuss it with your immediate manager or location personnel manager, you should go to your local general manager, regional manager, president or general manager of your division or subsidiary, whichever is appropriate.

Third, if you feel that you have not received a satisfactory answer, you may cover the matter by mail, or personally, with the Chairman of the Board.

Source: Fred K. Foulkes, *Personnel Policies in Large Nonunion Companies* (Englewood Cliffs, N.J.: Prentice-Hall, 1980), p. 300.

---

high-level management on complaints. When complaints are received, investigations are required, and the remedial action to be taken, if any, is communicated back to the grievant. Follow-up is monitored by high-level managment.

Many firms have created an "ombudsman" position to resolve grievances. The ombudsman, while technically an employee of the firm, has certain prescribed latitudes for taking action or requiring certain decisions to be made. If a complaining employee is not satisfied with a proposed management solution, the employee can ask the ombudsman to investigate the situation.

Another innovative approach creates an employee review board to act as an impartial group to resolve outstanding grievances. At Henry Ford Hospital in Detroit, a review board of persons at the same relative organizational level as the grievant hears evidence on unresolved grievances and renders a decision binding on the hospital and the grievant.

Several large nonunion organizations also periodically conduct attitude surveys to obtain an early identification of areas that may trouble the company. These might include certain employee groups or certain employee relations policies like advancement, pay, or development opportunities. Given that attitudes may be precursors of subsequent behaviors, the diagnosis of potential problem spots allows management to conduct remedial activities to eliminate the potential areas of contention.

In some organizations, supervisors and managers are evaluated by their subordinates as well as by other performance indicators. They are expected to maintain a work environment leading to positive employee attitudes as measured by periodic surveys. When attitude surveys point out a problem, they may be required to devise action plans to eliminate difficulties.

Other Innovative Techniques

Some organizations have begun to hold mass meetings between employees and top-management officials to get a sense of possible problem areas. One new approach involves meetings between top managers and groups of lower-level employees to present current problems and gripes. This "deep-sensing" approach may give top managers a better reading on the pulse rate of employee morale, and employees in turn might expect more action on their problems.

Another approach, called *vertical staff meetings*, has been implemented by the Rocketdyne Division of Rockwell International. Here, about a dozen employees from various organization levels are picked at random to meet with the division's president at a monthly meeting. Problems disclosed by the attendees are followed up by the president's report to the participants.[12]

EMPLOYER/EMPLOYEE COMMITTEES

A number of organizations have formed various types of management–employee committees. Quality circles are one example of this type of device. But other situations involve employees in making recommendations to management regarding hiring, personnel assignments, hours, terms and conditions of employment, and other similar issues, which are the subject of collective bargaining in unionized organizations.

The Taft-Hartley Act forbids dominance of a labor organization by an employer. A critical question then becomes: Does an employer dominate a labor organization if it establishes and meets with employee committees and considers (among other things) some of these issues? The answer is not totally settled, but if an employer uses these committees as mechanisms for communication between employees

---

[12] "Vertical Staff Meetings Open Lines of Communications at Rocketdyne Plant," *World of Work Report*, 1979, pp. 27-28.

and management but not as a means to avoid being organized, it is unlikely to be considered a dominated labor organization.[13]

The communicative activities taking place in some of these committees may be similar to collecting attitude survey data from a sample of the plant population and using these data as a representation of the employees' attitudes. It also enables both groups to enrich their understanding of what each perceives as problems in the workplace and their causes.

In some situations, employers have also vested some supervisory activities in work groups. For example, General Foods established work groups in one plant that made their own work assignments, created and operated training programs, and made recommendations on staffing decisions.[14] These were found not to be employer-dominated labor organizations.[15]

DEVELOPING PRACTICES IN NONUNION EMPLOYEE RELATIONS

An increasing number of companies have explicit union-avoidance policies and tailor employee relations practices to support these goals. Several of the areas in which differences exist between companies with an explicit union-avoidance policy and those without include providing more information to employees regarding their work group's productivity; more work group discussion of quality or productivity issues; more encouragement of participative mechanisms, such as quality circles and autonomous work teams; work sharing in preference to layoffs; and the development and operation of formal complaint systems.[16] Table 16-1 shows the number of positive responses toward a variety of employee relations practices among a sample of large employers.

In addition to differences in communication and participation, a major difference between new nonunion situations and traditional unionized facilities is the organization of the workplace. In an effort to increase flexibility, employers have substantially reduced the number of job classifications in manufacturing facilities. In many situations, employees are organized into teams and the team is responsible not only for production but also for maintenance of its equipment. The team may have only one or two different jobs, which are defined on

---

[13] Raymond L. Hogler, "Employee Involvement Programs and *NLRB* v. *Scott & Fetzer Co.*: The Developing Interpretation of Section 8 (a)(2)," *Labor Law Journal*, January 1984, pp. 21–27.

[14] Richard E. Walton, "The Diffusion of New Work Structures: Explaining Why Success Didn't Take," *Organizational Dynamics*, Winter 1975, pp. 2–22.

[15] *General Foods*, 231 NLRB 1232 (1977).

[16] Audrey Freedman, *The New Look in Wage Policy and Employee Relations* (New York: Conference Board, 1985), pp. 16–20.

TABLE 16-1

Company Practices Among Nonunion Employees

	Number of Companies in which:	
Company Initiative	Managers Are Encouraged To Develop or Sustain	Practice Exists
Information-related:		
Employees are given information about competitive or economic conditions of plant or business		431
Employees track their group's quality or productivity performance		264*
Participation-related:		
Employee-participation programs (quality circles, quality-of-work-life programs)	364*	
Autonomous work teams	107*	
Employees meet in small work groups to discuss production or quality		340*
Compensation-related:		
Profit-sharing, gains-sharing, or bonus programs for non-exempt employees	191	
Employees receive productivity or other gains-sharing bonuses		121
"Payment for knowledge" compensation systems	107	
All-salaried compensation systems	173	
Miscellaneous:		
Formal complaint or grievance system	378*	
Work sharing instead of layoffs	176*	
Flex-time or other flexible work schedules	162	

* Statistically significant relationship with a company preference for union avoidance, at .05 or better.

Source: Audrey Freedman, *The New Look in Wage Policy and Employee Relations* (New York: Conference Board, 1985), p. 17.

the basis of skill level rather than the functional specialty of the jobholder.[17]

SUMMARY

The proportion of organized employees has declined markedly over the last 30 years. Part of this decline is due to changing employment patterns by occupation and industry, but some is related to improved employee relations practices by employers.

Many employers have an explicit goal of avoiding unions or ridding

---

[17] Thomas A. Kochan, Harry C. Katz, and Robert B. McKersie, *The Transformation of American Industrial Relations* (New York: Basic Books, 1986), pp. 81–108.

themselves of unions presently representing employees. Employers appear to adopt one of two approaches toward unions if they are successful in remaining union free. In the doctrinaire approach, the organization maintains employee relations systems equal to or better than what unions have negotiated in comparable organizations. In a philosophy-laden approach, the organization is not explicitly concerned about unions but provides an excellent employee relations environment that makes unions superfluous.

A variety of recently evolved systems enable managements to communicate more readily with employees and to learn sooner about issues that might make unionization attractive to employees. These early information systems can assist organizations in making an employee relations response that eliminates the issue as a source of employee frustration.

DISCUSSION QUESTIONS

1. What conditions are necessary before a union-free environment can exist in U.S. labor relations?

2. Does it make sense for an organization to establish an explicit goal to remain union free? What costs and benefits are associated with this type of goal?

3. Think about the local area in which you now reside. What characteristics appear associated with organizations that are unionized or nonunion in your local area? Would you predict present organizing patterns to continue in the future? Why or why not?

CHAPTER 17

Challenges to Collective Bargaining

It's customary to speculate about what the future holds for any area of study. Having examined the development, structure, and process of labor relations in the United States and the structure of occupations, industries, and the labor market, we can now make some projections about the directions of the labor movement.

These new directions are likely to be influenced by a number of important factors: (1) the long-run secular change in the distribution of employees across industries, with the most heavily unionized declining or growing at a below-average rate, (2) the increasingly white-collar distribution of occupations and employment coupled with their low rates of unionization, (3) the increasing proportion of the labor force made up of women and the changing age mix of the labor force, (4) the impact of significant foreign competition on several of the more basic mature industries, (5) the effect of concessions, profits, and nonunion practices on union militancy, and (6) the nature of the labor movement's leadership as unions increase merger activity and veteran leaders retire in larger numbers.

In reading this chapter, try to connect present-day practices and their deficiencies to adaptations expected in the future. Also try to apply the past history of the labor movement to predict where future changes will take place.

INDUSTRIAL CHANGE

The distribution of employees by industry since the beginning of the 20th century has seen dramatic changes, and many of these changes have influenced union membership. Early unionization was most prevalent in industries requiring highly skilled employees or where substitution for employees during strikes was difficult. The industries primarily involved were mining, contract construction, and transportation. Over time, employment in mining has declined, transportation has stabilized, and contract construction plateaued and began to decline in the early 1970s.

On the other hand, major increases in employment took place in wholesale and retail trade, finance and insurance, service industries, and state and local government jobs. These industries had low unionization in the past, because many of these employers operate relatively small establishments and the effort necessary to organize employees may not lead to high payoffs for unions. Where larger concentrations have existed and where employees have interests in long-run employment, as in government employment, unionization has been increasing at a rate faster than the employment increase. Table 17–1 displays the distribution of employment by industry between 1955 and 1987. A close examination of the table helps show why union membership rose during the 1960s while union penetration of the labor force declined. Absolute numbers of employees in manufacturing durable goods increased moderately, but the proportion of all employees in those industries declined. Table 17–2 shows the proportion of eligible employees unionized by industrial group. Many of the most heavily unionized industries have not grown significantly recently.

OCCUPATIONAL CHANGE

The pattern of employment by occupation in the United States has also changed markedly over time. Major changes in the white-collar area have included increases in professional employees and clericals. The proportion of people working in blue-collar occupations, in the aggregate, has not changed markedly over the course of this century, with most of the loss from agriculture being redistributed in the blue- and white-collar areas.

The blue-collar occupations saw an increase in the proportion of operatives through 1950. Then a long-term decline in the use of laborers and an increase in service occupations occurred. These trends for the blue-collar labor force are consistent with the peaking of labor union penetration in the early 1950s. The fall-off in the proportion of employees in lower-skilled blue-collar occupations is consistent with the decline in union penetration in the labor force.

Production and Nonproduction Workers

Marked changes have also taken place over time in the internal allocation of employees in the industrial work force, with larger proportions assigned to nonproduction jobs. Table 17–3 shows that no industry for which data were reported had a lower ratio of nonproduction to production employees in 1987 than in 1955. Industries in which the relative proportion of nonproduction workers increased the most rapidly were mining, contract construction, durable goods manufacturing, and wholesale trades. Increases were slowest for transportation and public utilities, retail trade, and service sectors.

Projections for Occupational Distributions

Department of Labor projections continue to forecast larger-than-average growth rates for occupational areas where unions have not been particularly successful or active in the past, such as professional and technical workers, clericals, and service workers. Slower-than-average growth rates are expected in such occupations as operatives and nonfarm laborers, which have been heavily unionized. Table 17–4 contains these employment projections by occupational group.

DEMOGRAPHIC CHANGES

The changing composition of the labor force as measured by population characteristics may also affect the degree to which employees become or remain organized in the future. We have recently witnessed a paradoxical period in American employment history. Beginning in 1976, employment was at or near record levels, while unemployment rates remained at or above 6 percent. One reason for this paradox was the influx of large numbers of new job-seekers, which resulted from high birthrates beginning in 1946 and continuing through the middle 1960s. Another reason was the increasingly large proportion of women who either remained working during childbearing years or decided to reenter the labor force on a permanent basis after starting a family. Labor force participation rates among women have steadily increased over the last several years without a corresponding decline in male participation. Between 1947 and 1987, participation rates for women jumped from about 32 percent to over 56 percent, while male participation declined from 87 percent to 77 percent. Overall, these changes were reflected in a 7 percent increase in the total participation rate from 59 to 66 percent.

The birthrate decline experienced in the late 1960s and 70s will mean that workers entering the labor force in the middle 1980s through at least the middle 1990s will be in relatively short supply in comparison to the past. Changes that would reduce the short-supply problems are a continuing increase in participation rates among women and a willingness of older workers to take advantage of legislation prohibiting mandatory retirement.

What might these demographic changes mean for the labor move-

TABLE 17–1

Employees on Nonagricultural Payrolls by Major Industry, 1955–1987 (000)

Year and month	Total	Total private	Goods-producing				Service-producing						Government		
			Total	Mining	Construction	Manufacturing	Total	Transportation and public utilities	Wholesale trade	Retail trade	Finance insurance and real estate	Services	Federal	State	Local
							Annual averages								
1955	50,641	43,727	20,513	792	2,839	16,882	30,128	4,141	2,926	7,610	2,298	6,240	2,187	1,168	3,558
1956	52,369	45,091	21,104	822	3,039	17,243	31,266	4,244	3,018	7,840	2,389	6,497	2,209	1,250	3,819
1957	52,853	45,239	20,964	828	2,962	17,174	31,889	4,241	3,028	7,858	2,438	6,708	2,217	1,328	4,071
1958	51,324	43,483	19,513	751	2,817	15,945	31,811	3,976	2,980	7,770	2,481	6,765	2,191	1,415	4,232
1959*	53,268	45,186	20,411	732	3,004	16,675	32,857	4,011	3,082	8,045	2,549	7,087	2,233	1,484	4,366
1960	54,189	45,836	20,434	712	2,926	16,796	33,755	4,004	3,143	8,248	2,629	7,378	2,270	1,536	4,547
1961	53,999	45,404	19,857	672	2,859	16,326	34,142	3,903	3,133	8,204	2,688	7,620	2,279	1,607	4,708
1962	55,549	46,660	20,451	650	2,948	16,853	35,098	3,906	3,198	8,368	2,754	7,982	2,340	1,668	4,881
1963	56,653	47,429	20,640	635	3,010	16,995	36,013	3,903	3,248	8,530	2,830	8,277	2,358	1,747	5,121
1964	58,283	48,686	21,005	634	3,097	17,274	37,278	3,951	3,337	8,823	2,911	8,660	2,348	1,856	5,392
1965	60,765	50,689	21,926	632	3,232	18,062	38,839	4,036	3,466	9,250	2,977	9,036	2,378	1,996	5,700
1966	63,901	53,116	23,158	627	3,317	19,214	40,743	4,158	3,597	9,648	3,058	9,498	2,564	2,141	6,080
1967	65,803	54,413	23,308	613	3,248	19,447	42,495	4,268	3,689	9,917	3,185	10,045	2,719	2,302	6,371
1968	67,897	56,058	23,737	606	3,350	19,781	44,160	4,318	3,779	10,320	3,337	10,567	2,737	2,442	6,660
1969	70,384	58,189	24,361	619	3,575	20,167	46,023	4,442	3,907	10,798	3,512	11,169	2,758	2,533	6,904
1970	70,880	58,325	23,578	623	3,588	19,367	47,302	4,515	3,993	11,047	3,645	11,548	2,731	2,664	7,158
1971	71,214	58,331	22,935	609	3,704	18,623	48,278	4,476	4,001	11,351	3,772	11,797	2,696	2,747	7,437
1972	73,675	60,341	23,668	628	3,889	19,151	50,007	4,541	4,113	11,836	3,908	12,276	2,684	2,859	7,790
1973	76,790	63,058	24,893	642	4,097	20,154	51,897	4,656	4,277	12,329	4,046	12,857	2,663	2,923	8,146
1974	78,265	64,095	24,794	697	4,020	20,077	53,471	4,725	4,433	12,554	4,148	13,441	2,724	3,039	8,407
1975	76,945	62,259	22,600	752	3,525	18,323	54,345	4,542	4,415	12,645	4,165	13,892	2,748	3,179	8,758
1976	79,382	64,511	23,352	779	3,576	18,997	56,030	4,582	4,546	13,209	4,271	14,551	2,733	3,273	8,865
1977	82,471	67,344	24,346	813	3,851	19,682	58,125	4,713	4,708	13,808	4,467	15,303	2,727	3,377	9,023
1978	86,697	71,026	25,585	851	4,229	20,505	61,113	4,923	4,969	14,573	4,724	16,252	2,753	3,474	9,446
1979	89,823	73,876	26,461	958	4,463	21,040	63,363	5,136	5,204	14,989	4,975	17,112	2,773	3,541	9,633

Year														
1980	90,406	74,166	25,658	1,027	4,346	20,285	64,748	5,146	5,275	15,035	5,160	17,890	2,866	3,610	9,765
1981	91,156	75,126	25,497	1,139	4,188	20,170	65,659	5,165	5,358	15,189	5,298	18,619	2,772	3,640	9,619
1982	89,566	73,729	23,813	1,128	3,905	18,781	65,753	5,082	5,278	15,179	5,341	19,036	2,739	3,640	9,458
1983	90,200	74,330	23,334	952	3,948	18,434	66,866	4,954	5,268	15,613	5,468	19,694	2,774	3,662	9,434
1984	94,496	78,472	24,727	966	4,383	19,378	69,769	5,159	5,555	16,545	5,689	20,797	2,807	3,734	9,482
1985	97,519	81,125	24,859	927	4,673	19,260	72,660	5,238	5,717	17,356	5,955	22,000	2,875	3,832	9,687
1986	99,610	82,900	24,681	783	4,904	18,994	74,930	5,244	5,735	17,845	6,297	23,099	2,899	3,888	9,923
1987	102,112	85,049	24,884	741	5,031	19,112	77,228	5,378	5,797	18,264	6,589	24,137	2,943	3,952	10,167

* Data include Alaska and Hawaii beginning in 1959. This inclusion resulted in an increase of 212,000 (0.4 percent) in the nonagricultural total for the March 1959 benchmark month.

NOTE: Establishment survey estimates are currently projected from March 1986 benchmark levels. When more recent benchmark data are introduced, all unadjusted data (beginning April 1986) and all seasonally adjusted data (beginning January 1983) are subject to revision.

Source: Adapted from *Employment and Earnings* (Washington, D.C.: U.S. Government Printing Office, April 1988), p. 77.

TABLE 17-2

Union Membership Proportions by Industry

50 percent and over

1. Railroads
2. Postal
3. Automobiles
4. Primary metals
5. Transportation equipment

40 to 49.9 percent

6. Communications
7. Paper
8. Stone, clay, and glass products
9. Other public utilities
10. Aircraft
11. Other transportation
12. Other transportation equipment

30 to 39.9 percent

13. Food
14. Local government
15. Fabricated metals
16. Education
17. Petroleum products
18. Mining
19. Construction
20. Tobacco products
21. Ordnance

20 to 29.9 percent

22. Rubber and plastics
23. Machinery

24. Furniture
25. Electrical equipment
26. State government
27. Chemicals
28. Apparel
29. Leather
30. Printing

10 to 19.9 percent

31. Miscellaneous services
32. Federal government
33. Lumber
34. Hospitals
35. Miscellaneous manufacturing
36. Textiles
37. Entertainment and recreation
38. Personal services
39. Forestry and fisheries
40. Welfare and religious
41. Instruments
42. Wholesale trade
43. Business and repair services
44. Medical

Less than 10 percent

45. Retail trades
46. Insurance and real estate
47. Agriculture
48. Banking and finance
49. Private household services

ment? We can only speculate, but issues related to rewards and job security are expected to increase in importance. For example, as the numbers of individuals at any given job level increase, the competition for promotions becomes more intense. If the criteria used by the organization for making employment decisions for promotions, lay-offs, and so forth are either inconsistently applied or inconsistent with the belief systems of the involved employees, we might expect some push for organizing. This could have a major impact on professional areas if opportunities for promotion into management positions decline. For example, if large numbers of engineers find themselves blocked from exiting their occupations at traditional career change points and management replaces them with more recently trained people, then unionization will be a likely reaction. Career-planning systems and careful attention to promotional criteria will be necessary in the near future to reduce employees' need to organize if firms desire to remain nonunion.

TABLE 17-3

Nonproduction Workers on Private Payrolls as Percent of Total Employment, by Industry Division: Annual Average, 1947–1984

Nonproduction workers as percent of total employment

Year	Total private	Mining	Construction	Manufacturing	Transportation and utilities	Wholesale trade	Retail trade	Finance, insurance, real estate	Services
1947	12.1	8.8	11.1	16.4		9.0	7.4	16.9	
1948	12.1	8.9	11.1	17.1		9.4	5.8	16.9	
1949	12.5	9.8	11.2	18.4		9.5	6.1	17.0	
1950	12.3	9.4	11.1	17.8		9.6	5.6	17.1	
1951	12.6	9.6	11.1	18.5		9.9	5.2	17.1	
1952	13.1	10.8	11.5	19.7		9.9	5.2	17.3	
1953	13.5	11.7	12.0	19.9		10.5	5.7	17.5	
1954	14.1	13.3	12.5	21.4		11.5	5.9	17.9	
1955	14.2	14.1	12.8	21.3		12.0	6.5	17.8	
1956	14.6	14.6	12.7	22.1		12.4	6.8	17.9	
1957	15.2	16.1	13.0	23.2		12.8	7.1	18.0	
1958	15.8	18.6	14.1	24.8		13.7	7.6	18.2	
1959	15.7	19.4	14.2	24.4		13.7	7.5	18.2	
1960	16.0	19.9	14.7	25.1		13.9	7.5	18.4	
1961	16.3	20.8	15.1	26.0		14.3	7.8	18.6	
1962	16.5	21.2	15.2	25.9		14.8	8.1	18.8	
1963	16.6	21.6	14.9	26.1		15.1	8.3	19.0	
1964	16.7	21.6	14.9	26.0	11.7	15.4	8.8	19.4	8.3
1965	16.6	21.8	14.9	25.6	11.8	15.7	8.8	19.8	8.2
1966	16.7	22.3	15.0	25.6	12.5	16.0	8.8	20.1	7.9
1967	17.0	23.5	15.6	26.4	12.9	16.4	8.9	20.4	8.0
1968	17.1	23.9	15.8	26.6	13.0	16.6	9.0	20.6	7.9
1969	17.2	23.7	15.7	26.8	13.0	16.6	8.9	20.4	8.6
1970	17.4	24.1	16.7	27.5	13.3	16.6	9.1	21.0	9.2
1971	17.5	25.3	17.1	27.3	13.5	17.1	9.3	22.1	9.7
1972	17.2	24.4	16.3	26.7	13.2	17.2	9.4	22.6	9.9
1973	17.2	24.3	16.3	26.7	13.4	17.2	9.4	22.6	9.9
1974	17.6	24.0	18.1	27.1	13.7	17.2	9.8	23.6	10.0
1975	18.1	24.1	20.3	28.8	14.3	17.6	9.9	23.8	10.2
1976	18.0	24.0	21.3	28.2	14.5	17.6	9.9	24.1	10.4
1977	18.1	24.0	21.6	28.2	15.0	17.6	9.9	24.0	10.6
1978	18.1	25.0	20.7	28.1	15.8	17.6	9.9	23.9	10.9
1979	18.3	25.0	20.1	28.4	16.3	17.8	10.1	24.0	11.2
1980	18.3	25.7	19.9	29.6	16.4	18.2	8.7	24.3	11.8
1981	18.5	28.7	19.9	30.1	17.2	18.8	9.3	24.0	11.2
1982	19.3	29.3	23.2	32.2	17.8	19.0	9.6	25.1	11.6
1983	19.3	29.2	22.8	31.9	20.3	19.5	10.1	25.5	11.4
1984*	19.3	28.5	22.5	31.1	17.7	19.4	10.6	25.5	12.1

* Preliminary.

Source: Adapted from *Employment and Earnings* (Washington, D.C.: U.S. Government Printing Office, April 1984), Table B-6.

The increasingly large proportion of women in the labor force also creates a potential opportunity for unions. The United States has a historical wage differential of about 40 percent between the pay rates of women and men with similar levels of training. Some argue this is

TABLE 17–4

Projected Job Growth, 1982–95 (000)

Industry	1982-95 New jobs	1982-95 Percent of total	1982-90 New jobs	1982-90 Percent of total	1990-95 New jobs	1990-95 Percent of total
Total new jobs	25,248	100.0	16,000	100.0	9,248	100.0
Goods-producing:	6,548	25.9	4,350	27.2	2,198	23.8
Farm	−265	−1.0	−163	−1.0	−102	−1.1
Mining	122	.5	39	.2	83	.9
Construction	2,434	9.6	1,472	9.2	962	10.4
Manufacturing	4,257	16.9	3,002	18.8	1,255	13.6
Durable	3,170	12.6	2,224	13.9	946	10.2
Nondurable	1,087	4.3	778	4.9	309	3.3
Service-producing:	18,700	74.1	11,650	72.8	7,050	76.2
Transportation, public utilities	1,094	4.3	659	4.1	435	4.7
Trade	6,009	23.8	3,819	23.9	2,190	23.7
Finance, insurance, and real estate	1,786	7.1	1,214	7.6	572	6.2
Services	8,673	34.4	5,246	32.8	3,427	37.1
Private households	−289	−1.1	−235	−1.5	−54	−.6
Government	1,427	5.7	947	5.9	480	5.2

Source: Valerie A. Personick, "The Job Outlook through 1995: Industry Output and Employment Projections," *Monthly Labor Review*, March 1984, p. 23.

due to occupational crowding by women, while others suggest it is the result of employment discrimination. Whatever the reasons, it is a potent collective bargaining issue. If employers fail to adjust wage differentials in jobs held by women that are comparable to those held by men whose pay rates are higher, then unions indicating an enthusiasm for bargaining on these issues may find occupations dominated by women easily organized.

FOREIGN COMPETITION

Foreign competition has had a major impact on employment and collective bargaining in several industries. For example, the shoe and apparel industries have undergone major retrenchments due to increased imports. Others in which major effects have been noted include steel, autos, consumer electronics, capital goods, and other manufacturing-based industries.

In response to foreign competition, the Rubber Workers and the major producers have renegotiated contracts in the rubber specialty goods indutry. Previously, these pacts had closely followed those negotiated for tire production workers, but foreign competition in footwear and other specialty items made U.S. production unprofitable at negotiated rates. During 1980 and 1981, several contracts were reopened to implement wage reductions to save jobs.

Major wage and work rule concessions were gained from unions during the economic recession of 1981–1983; concessions first occurred in industries threatened by foreign competition (autos and steel) and later in companies faced with substantial nonunion competition within their own industries (airlines, meat packing, and contract construction).

Currency differentials have had, and will continue to have, a major impact on wages and employment. For example, in 1987 and 1988, the U.S. balance of payments changed markedly as the dollar declined in comparison with foreign currencies. Manufacturing employment grew rapidly, and unemployment rates fell to their lowest levels in 15 years. However, maintaining strong exports requires a low interest rate, which makes U.S. debt less attractive to hold. Paradoxically, however, the stronger economic growth, the greater employers' need to borrow for expansion. The ability to continue strong export performance depends ultimately on productivity improvement.

CONCESSIONS, PROFITS, AND MILITANCY

The early 1980s was not the only period in U.S. economic history during which employees made wage concessions, but it was the first period since the Great Depression in which significant numbers of employees across several industries conceded economic gains. It was also the first time significant numbers of employees represented by industrial unions were required to give back past negotiated gains. The pervasiveness of the concessions is revealed in the cross section of those made by the middle of 1982, as represented by the employment situations summarized in Table 17–5.

Some of the concessions resulted from economic problems encountered by employers, but others were made because of advances in technology that radically altered the way in which products or services are produced. For example, changes in the printing industry have drastically lowered skill requirements for many occupations, enabling newly formed organizations to quickly hire and train employees to run sophisticated equipment, thus undercutting the costs of established firms. Wholesale wage concessions and the introduction of new equipment were necessary for older firms to remain competitive.

However, where employees have made concessions for employers to recapture their abilities to compete, some companies (for example, U.S. Steel) have chosen to invest the savings in other industries. In

TABLE 17–5

Selected Contract Concessions

1982 selected concession settlements *Toned boxes show where contract provisions apply.*	Company got wage/benefit freeze	Company got scheduling concessions	Company got work/rules concessions	Union got say in company decisions	Union got job security provisions	Union got future wage/benefit hikes
Kelsey-Hayes/UAW	■	■			■	
Massey-Ferguson/UAW	■	■			■	
Budd Co./UAW	■	■				
Chatham/Retail Clerks	■					
General Motors/Electricians	■	■				■
B. F. Goodrich/URW	■					
Nat'l. Auto Haulers/Teamsters	■		■			
Int'l. Harvester/UAW	■			■		
Westinghouse/Electricians			■			
Detroit Schools/multi	■					
Michigan A&P/Teamsters & Retail Clerks	■				■	
Bormans/Teamsters & Retail Clerks	■					
Nat'l. Electric Contr./Elect. Workers	■					
Hamody Bros./Food & Cmrc. Workers	■					
San Diego Symphony/Musicians	■					
Ford/UAW	■				■	
General Motors/UAW	■					
Oregon Gen'l. Contr./Carpenters	■					
Wiedeman Brewing/Teamsters	■				■	
Kroger (Mich.)/Teamsters & Retail Clerks	■					■
TWA/Airline Pilots	■		■			
Milwaukee Railroad/multi	■		■			
Union Street/Teamsters	■					
Dana Corp./UAW	■					
Trucking Mgmt./Teamsters	■		■			
Penn Dixie/Steelworkers	■					
Oscar Mayer/Food & Comm. Workers	■				■	
Pan Am/Flight Attendants	■		■			
McLouth Steel/Steelworkers	■				■	

Source: *Detroit Free Press*, May 9, 1982, p. 131.

others, high profit levels partially related to wage cutbacks and to other efficiencies have led to historic profit records (for example, autos). Perceived imbalances in compensation practices reflected in large executive bonuses could indicate future militant union action.

Finally, unions have very little bargaining power to avoid concessions in some situations. A good example is the Greyhound bus line negotiations in late 1983. While the company could capitalize in the short run on the high unemployment rate of qualified drivers to hire strike replacements, it could also make the credible threat of selling off its intercity bus operations, which could not meet investment targets the rest of the corporation felt appropriate. The labor contracts offered by a less well-financed successor might have been lower than what Greyhound was willing to offer. And, in fact, Greyhound has divested itself of its interstate bus operations.

But these concessions may have been gained at a price. Employees might be expected to demonstrate low commitment to their employers and to take advantage of future bargaining power opportunities when and if the economic situation is to their benefit. This issue bears close watching as the labor surpluses of the early 1980s turn to likely labor shortages in the early 1990s. Evidence may already support this proposition, as auto workers have been able to return to pattern agreements with the negotiation of the 1988 UAW–Chrysler agreement.

THE LABOR MOVEMENT

In the 1980s, the American Federation of Labor celebrated its 100th anniversary. This same decade, the Congress of Industrial Organizations notes its 50th. How much has the underlying philosophy of the labor movement changed since its inception? Conclusions regarding the degree of change vary broadly across observers, but the underlying philosophy and approach of organized labor probably has not. Chapter 3 noted that at the merger of the AFL and CIO, George Meany kept the faith by his statement of a set of goals for organized labor that was entirely consistent with anything Samuel Gompers would have said. The American labor movement has survived becaue it has listened to the workers it represents rather than to the general public. It has not always been as successful when it devised tactics to secure these goals, because some depend on the reaction of the public. Is the approach Meany restated in 1955 still labor's approach? The answer is probably yes.

The Leadership

Some major changes have taken place in the leadership of the labor movement over the past decade years. Lane Kirkland replaced George

Meany as president of the AFL–CIO, four Teamster presidents have been in office (as compared to four in its entire previous history), Lynn Williams (a Canadian) became the first non-U.S. president when he succeeded Lloyd McBride as president of the Steelworkers, and Owen Bieber assumed the leadership of the United Auto Workers following Douglas Fraser's retirement.

These changes have not led to wholesale shifts in union philosophy or policy. George Meany's retirement meant the United Auto Workers and the Teamsters could safely be reinvited to the fold. But not until the middle 1980s did the labor movement recognize that some fundamental changes were taking place in employee relations, employers were serious about union-avoidance strategies, and organizing new members had slipped badly. National unions are considering such alternatives as associate membership; have launched new subsidiaries, such as Local 925 (nine-to-five) of the Service Employees to organize clerical employees; and have hired college and graduate program graduates to plan and conduct organizing campaigns. Changes have occurred most rapidly in situations where unions have merged. The leadership has begun to recognize the problems and opportunities facing their unions, given the exercise of employer power, and have readjusted accordingly.

Projections from the Past

In the past, we have seen individual union leaders who have had great impacts on the course and outcomes of collective bargaining. Some who immediately come forward are Walter Reuther, John L. Lewis, Jimmy Hoffa, Philip Murray, I. W. Abel, Douglas Fraser, and Jerry Wurf. These men all had major impacts on their organizations, but none singlehandedly had a major impact on the ultimate success or failure of his organization. Regardless of the charismatic aura that John L. Lewis carried, the United Mine Workers were in a continually declining position throughout most of his presidency. And none of the unions radically changed when these men passed from leadership roles. Granted, the stewardship of Lewis' immediate successors was poor; but for the others, the underlying trends present in their organizations were not greatly altered by their replacements.

American labor may, in many ways, resemble American management. In looking at General Motors' past history, at times one person (for example, Alfred P. Sloan) held the role of chief executive officer for extended periods. Roger Smith is expected to duplicate that tenure during the 1980s. In the interim, however, top management at General Motors has turned over every three years or so because of the corporations's mandatory retirement age. Chief executives often do not reach that position until their 60s, so their tenure is short. The same holds true to some extent in many of the more mature unions. Hence, stability in philosophies and interests is ensured by the relatively short tenure of those on top.

CONCLUSION

Many factors will influence the future of collective bargaining and the shape of the labor movement. Demographics, economics, and public policy are three major factors. At the present, each of these factors is more favorable than it has been at any time during the 1980s. Unions are, in fact, beginning to increase the rate at which they win elections. Some backlash can be expected from the labor force for the relatively low bargaining power (either collectively or individually) that many employees have felt during the cutbacks and concessions associated with restructuring in the 1980s. Organized labor probably has seen the nadir of its influence in the 1980s. What will be important for the nation is that neither labor nor management leave the decade with a return to the role each played in the past. The world has changed, and labor relations as usual is incompatible with the future.

The underlying philosophy of the labor movement probably will not change radically. Some issues may become increasingly important to its members. Many may involve more of a say in how one's job is done, how the organization should be structured, and what the effect of the oganization's decisions might be for the union's *long-run* well-being. It is unlikely, however that we would come back to look at labor in 50 years and not still see its direction as being "More, more now," just as we should not expect to find management satisfied with indefinitely maintaining a particular profit level.

Case Index

Author Index

Subject Index